Computer Animation
ACM SIGGRAPH / Eurographics Symposium on Computer Animation

San Diego, California, August 3 – 4, 2007

Symposium Co-Chairs

Michael Gleicher (University of Wisconsin - Madison, USA)
Daniel Thalmann (EPFL, Switzerland)

Program Chairs

Dimitris Metaxas (Rutgers University, USA)
Jovan Popović (Massachusetts Institute of Technology, USA)

Proceedings Production Editors
Dieter Fellner (TU Braunschweig, Germany)
Stephen Spencer (The University of Washington, USA)

Co-sponsored by ACM SIGGRAPH and EUROGRAPHICS Association

The Association for Computing Machinery, Inc.
2 Penn Plaza, Suite 701
New York, New York 10121

Note to Past Authors of ACM-Published Articles
ACM intends to create a complete electronic archive of all articles and/or other material previously published by ACM. If you have written a work that was previously published by ACM in any journal or conference proceedings prior to 1978, or any SIG newsletter at any time, and you do NOT want this work to appear in the ACM Digital Library, please inform permissions@acm.org, stating the title of the work, the author(s) and where and when published.

Additional copies may be ordered prepaid from:

ACM Order Department
PO Box 11405, Church Street Station
New York, NY
10286-1405
Telephone 1-800-342-6626 (USA and Canada)
Telephone +1-212-626-0500 (all other countries)
Fax +1-212-944-1318
E-mail: acmhelp@acm.org

Eurographics Association
PO Box 16, CH-1288 Aire-la-Ville, Switzerland

Printed in the United States of America

Werner Hansmann, Werner Purgathofer, François Sillion
Series Editors

Cover design by Stefanie Behnke and Stephen Spencer

ACM ISBN 978-1-59593-624-4
ACM Order Number 428076

Eurographics ISBN 978-3-905673-44-9
AK Peters ISBN 978-1-56881-368-4

The electronic version of the proceedings is available from the Eurographics Digital Library at <http://diglib.eg.org/> and from the ACM Digital Library at <http://www.acm.org/dl/>.

Table of Contents

Table of Contents

Table of Contents

Preface

The ACM SIGGRAPH/Eurographics Symposium on Computer Animation (SCA) is the leading scientific meeting devoted exclusively to computer animation. The symposium attracts high quality papers and provides an opportunity for researchers in the area of computer animation to meet, share ideas and discuss emerging directions in the field. This year the Seventh SCA was held in San Diego, California prior to the ACM SIGGRAPH 2007 Conference.

These proceedings contain 28 papers from 81 submissions. The exceptional quality of the submitted papers made the final selection difficult. Each paper was reviewed by at least 3 members of the international program committee in a double-blind reviewing process. The acceptance decisions were made through online discussions and feedback from the entire program committee. The final program includes papers on a variety of topics, including fluids, deformable objects, behavior modeling, articulation, real time simulation, motion editing, analysis, and control.

The symposium continues to highlight promising works in progress with a poster and demo session. Our program included a special session on posters and demos which were presented and discussed in an evening reception. This program included works that were just short of the final papers program and additional posters that were selected through a separate poster-review process.

This symposium would not be possible without the continued support from ACM SIGGRAPH and Eurographics. We are especially grateful to Stephen Spencer, ACM SIGGRAPH Director for Publications, for producing this volume and James Stewart of Precision Conference Solutions for his outstanding support of SCA online review system. We also wish to thank the members of the international program committee and the external reviewers for their diligence and insightful reviews. We truly appreciate their effort and feedback in helping us choose the final program. Industrial support made it possible to organize a high-quality symposium, while maintaining reasonable registration fees. We would like to thank Adobe, Vicon, Pixar Animation Studios, Industrial Light and Magic, Autodesk, Motion Analysis Corporation, Elsevier, and Microsoft Research for their generous support.

D. Metaxas and J. Popovic
Program Chairs

M. Gleicher and D. Thalmann
Symposium Chairs

Industrial Supporters

Adobe

Autodesk

ELSEVIER

INDUSTRIAL
LIGHT & MAGIC
A LUCASFILM COMPANY

Microsoft
Research

MotionAnalysis

PIXAR
ANIMATION STUDIOS

VICON
HOUSE OF MOVES

Eurographics/ ACM SIGGRAPH Symposium on Computer Animation (2007)
D. Metaxas and J. Popovic (Editors)

Screen Space Meshes

Matthias Müller Simon Schirm Stephan Duthaler

AGEIA

Abstract

We present a simple yet powerful approach for the generation and rendering of surfaces defined by the boundary of a three-dimensional point cloud. First, a depth map plus internal and external silhouettes of the surface are generated in screen space. These are used to construct a 2D screen space triangle mesh with a new technique that is derived from Marching Squares. The resulting mesh is transformed back to 3D world space for the computation of occlusions, reflections, refraction, and other shading effects. One of the main applications for screen space meshes is the visualization of Lagrangian, particle-based fluids models. Our new method has several advantages over the full 3D Marching Cubes approach. The algorithm only generates surface where it is visible, view-dependent level of detail comes for free, and interesting visual effects are possible by filtering in screen space.

Categories and Subject Descriptors (according to ACM CCS): I.3.7 [Computer Graphics]: Three-Dimensional Graphics and Realism Animation and Virtual Reality

1. Introduction

The Marching Cubes method [LC87] is the most popular technique for generating triangle meshes along iso-surfaces of scalar fields. One important application is the reconstruction of the liquid-air interface in fluid simulations. In Eulerian fluid simulations, the liquid surface is often represented as the zero level set of the scalar level set function which is advected by the velocity field of the fluid [FF01, EMF02]. The Marching Cubes technique is then used to construct a triangle mesh along the zero level set. In Lagrangian, particle-based approaches [GM77, MCG03, PTB*03], the liquid surface is typically defined as an iso-surface of a density field which is the superposition of radially symmetric kernel functions of the individual particles [Bli82]. Again, a triangle mesh is generated using the Marching Cubes algorithm.

Although Marching Cubes is certainly the most popular and useful algorithm to generate 3D triangle meshes for iso-surfaces of scalar fields, there are some disadvantages when used for the visualization of surfaces of liquids. First, since the standard approach is camera-independent, many invisible triangles and surface details are generated. Second, the algorithm operates in three dimensions although what is sought is the front 2D surface. This surface is to be found by marching through a 3D data set.

Off-line tracking of the free surface of liquids is a well understood problem with a large body of work. However, the authors are not aware of any methods for rendering the full 3D air-liquid interface that is fast enough for the use in games. Our method closes this gap. It is significantly faster than previous methods. It does, however, only render the front most layer of the surface. This is not a limitation for opaque liquids like milk or oil and in most use cases with transparent fluids, especially in connection with fake refraction shaders, the artifacts are minimal as our examples show. The advantages of the new screen space mesh approach are

- The screen space mesh resolves parts of the surface which are close to the camera with more triangles than distant parts, yielding camera-dependent level of detail.
- Since it operates in two dimensions, a method derived from Marching Squares can be employed which is substantially faster than the 3D Marching Cubes algorithm.
- In contrast to other screen space approaches such as ray-tracing or point splatting, fast standard triangle shading hardware can be used for state-of-the-art forward shading of the surface and occlusion culling since the mesh can easily be transformed back into world space.

Symposium on Computer Animation 2007, San Diego, CA, August 03-04, 2007.
© 2007 ACM 978-1-59593-624-4/07/0008 $5.00

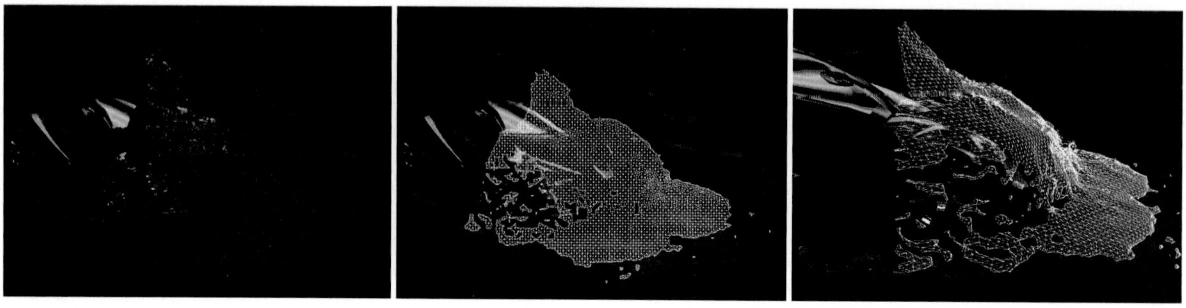

Figure 1: *Left: Final rendering. Middle: The screen space mesh. Right: Rotated view of the mesh to show its dependence on the viewing direction.*

- With a mesh defined in screen space, the smoothing of depths and silhouettes can easily be separated and controlled individually.

2. Related Work

Our approach is a screen space technique. Many rendering algorithms operate primarily in screen space. The most prominent among these is *raytracing* [Whi80]. For each pixel, a ray is cast into the scene which is then traced along reflected and refracted directions yielding view-dependent level of detail. The array of pixels could be interpreted as a high-resolution regular grid in screen space which is projected back into world space. However, in contrast to screen space meshes, ray tracing cannot directly make use of the triangle rendering pipeline of modern graphics hardware. Also, the resolution must always match the pixel resolution while the resolution of screen space meshes is adjustable to the time budget for surface rendering.

The *projected grid concept* introduced recently by Johanson *et al.* [Joh04] is more closely related to screen space meshes. It is based on earlier work on real-time ocean rendering [HNC02]. While the projected grid is designed to render unbounded water surfaces represented by height fields, screen space meshes can be used to render arbitrary three-dimensional (fluid) surfaces. Because the water surface is considered unbound in [Joh04], a projected *grid* is sufficient. No connectivity is generated in screen space and, thus, no silhouettes can be represented.

Since we present screen space meshes as a method to render the surface of point-sampled volumes, the approach is also related to point splatting methods [ZPvBG01]. The generation of the depth map is similar to a point splatting step while the rest of our algorithm deviates completely from point splatting.

3. Basic Algorithm

We expect as input a set of 3D points $\mathbf{x}_1, \ldots \mathbf{x}_N \in \mathbb{R}^3$ (in our case the locations of a set of particles simulated with Smoothed Particles Hydrodynamics), the projection matrix $\mathbf{P} \in \mathbb{R}^{4\times4}$, and a set of parameters as shown in Table 1.

The basic steps of the algorithm are:

1. Setup regular depth map
2. Find internal and external silhouettes
3. Smooth depth values
4. Generate a 2D triangle mesh using our Marching Squares related procedure
5. Smooth silhouettes
6. Transform mesh back into world space
7. Render the 3D triangle mesh

These steps are executed whenever the points change their locations or the camera moves. Steps 3. and 5. are explained in Section 4 as they are extensions to the basic method.

Parameter	Description	Range
h	screen spacing	$1-10$
r	particle size	≥ 1
n_{filter}	filter size for depth smoothing	$0-10$
n_{iters}	silhouette smoothing iterations	$0-10$
$z_{\max}$	depth connection threshold	$> r_z$

Table 1: *Summary of parameters.*

3.1. Depth Map Setup

Let W and H be the width and height of the screen in pixels. One of the input parameters of the method is the screen spacing $h \in \mathbb{R}$ which does not need to be an integer. The spacing defines a regular grid of cell size h with $N_x = \lceil \frac{W}{h} \rceil + 1$ nodes horizontally and $N_y = \lceil \frac{H}{h} \rceil + 1$ nodes vertically. The depth map $\mathbf{Z} \in \mathbb{R}^{N_x \times N_y}$ stores depth values $z_{i,j}$ at each node of the regular grid. It is generated from scratch at the beginning of each frame.

First the depth values $z_{i,j}$ are initialized with ∞. Then, the algorithm iterates through all N particles twice. In the first

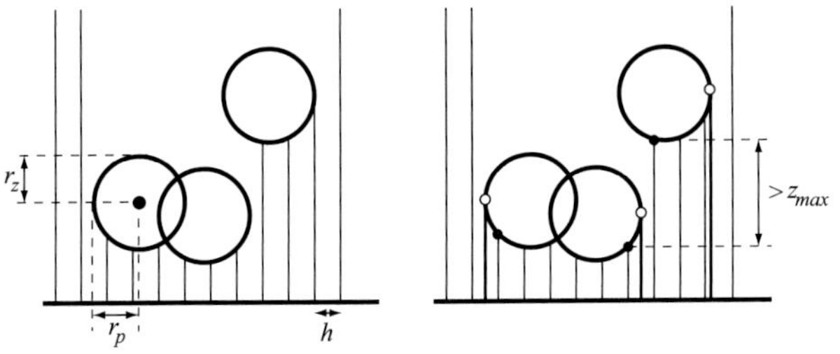

Figure 2: *Left: Side view of depth map generated by three particles. Only front most hits are considered. Large z-differences of adjacent depth values indicate inner and outer silhouettes. Right: Between adjacent nodes at most one additional node (white dot) is stored to indicate the silhouette.*

phase, the depth values are set. In the second phase, additional depth values are generated where silhouettes cut the grid (see Fig. 2). In both phases, the coordinates and radius of each particle have to be transferred from world to screen space. This is done as follows:

Let $\mathbf{x} = [x, y, z, 1]^T$ be the homogenous coordinates of the particle considered. These coordinates are transformed using the projection matrix $\mathbf{P}$ to get

$$\begin{bmatrix} x' \\ y' \\ z' \\ w \end{bmatrix} = \mathbf{P} \begin{bmatrix} x \\ y \\ z \\ 1 \end{bmatrix}. \tag{1}$$

We assume the setup of the projection matrix to be defined as in OpenGL and DirectX. In that case, perspective division (i.e. division of x', y' and z' by w) yields canonical coordinates in the range $-1 \ldots 1$ for all three coordinates. However, we perform perspective division only on x' and y' but not on the depth z' because the depth would get distorted non-linearly by this transformation. We compute the projected coordinates as

$$\begin{bmatrix} x_p \\ y_p \\ z_p \end{bmatrix} = \begin{bmatrix} W \cdot (\frac{1}{2} + \frac{1}{2}x'/w) \\ H \cdot (\frac{1}{2} + \frac{1}{2}y'/w) \\ z' \end{bmatrix}. \tag{2}$$

This way, we have $x_p \in [0 \ldots W]$, $y_p \in [0 \ldots H]$ while z_p is the non-distorted distance to the camera. Another parameter of our method is the particle size r. For the projected radii we get

$$\begin{bmatrix} r_x \\ r_y \\ r_z \end{bmatrix} = \begin{bmatrix} rW\sqrt{p_{1,1}^2 + p_{1,2}^2 + p_{1,3}^2}/w \\ rH\sqrt{p_{2,1}^2 + p_{2,2}^2 + p_{2,3}^2}/w \\ r\sqrt{p_{3,1}^2 + p_{3,2}^2 + p_{3,3}^2} \end{bmatrix}, \tag{3}$$

where the $p_{i,j}$ are the entries of the projection matrix $\mathbf{P}$. This equation only holds at the center of the screen. For a wide field of view the particles get distorted far from the center, an effect we ignore here since it only affects the shape, not the location of the particle. In OpenGL and DirectX $\sqrt{p_{3,1}^2 + p_{3,2}^2 + p_{3,3}^2} = 1$ so $r_z = r$ and z_p is the distance to the camera. We assume that the aspect ratio of the projection is chosen according to the viewport (i.e. W/H). In this case we have a single projected radius $r_p = r_x = r_y$ in the screen plane and the particles appear as circles rather than ellipses.

In the first phase, for each particle, all depth values at (i, j) with $(ih - x_p)^2 + (jh - y_p)^2 \le r_p^2$ are updated as

$$z_{i,j} \leftarrow \min\left(z_{i,j},\, z_p - r_z h_{i,j}\right), \tag{4}$$

$$\tag{5}$$

where $h_{i,j} = \sqrt{1 - \frac{(ih-x_p)^2 + (jh-y_p)^2}{r_p^2}}$. Omitting the square root in $h_{i,j}$ produces an upside down parabola instead of a spherical surface. This version is faster to compute and sufficient in most cases. The reader might want to experiment with other kernels too. At the end of the first phase, the depth map of the point cloud is coarsely sampled at the grid nodes. Similar to Marching Squares we insert additional nodes on the grid edges connecting nodes with large depth differences in order to track the silhouette in more detail as described in the next section (see also Fig. 2 right).

3.2. Silhouette Detection

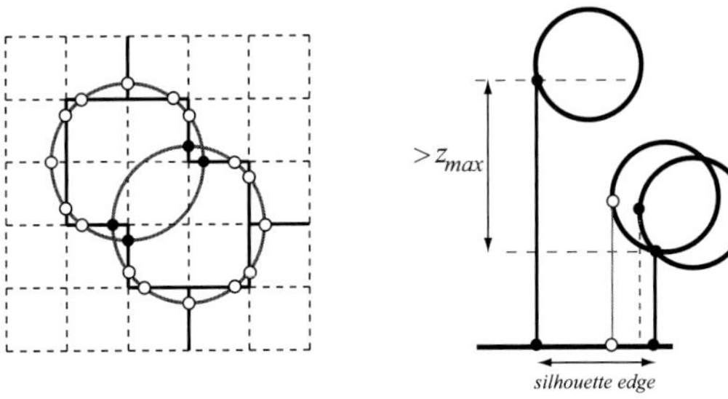

Figure 3: *Left: Top view of the grid. The depth differences at the ends of bold segments are above z_{max}, i.e. they are cut by one or more silhouettes. Right: Side view. The lower two particles generate two different cuts on the edge. Taking the cut (white point) furthest from the end with the smaller depth value (left most in this case) removes this ambiguity.*

For the detection of silhouettes, the algorithm iterates through the particles a second time. In this phase, only grid edges which connect depth values that are further apart then z_{max} are considered (see Fig. 3). We call them *silhouette edges*. The goal of the algorithm is to find one additional node (a *silhouette node*) on each silhouette edge. Each silhouette node is located between the adjacent nodes of its silhouette edge and stores the depth value of the front layer. For each particle p all cuts of the circle at position (x_p, y_p)

and radius r_p in screen space with silhouette edges are computed. Each cut is a silhouette node candidate. Its location is the location of the cut and its depth is the depth z_p of the particle. However, this point is only stored if two conditions hold:

- The depth z_p of the particle is smaller than the average depth of the silhouette edge, i.e. belongs to the front layer. This criterion can be used as an early out to avoid computing the cut point.
- The location of the cut on the silhouette edge is further from the endpoint with the smaller depth value than a potential silhouette node previously stored for this edge. In that case the new node replaces the old one (see Fig. 3 right).

3.3. Mesh Generation

The next step is to generate the vertices and triangles of the screen space mesh. Each grid node with an initialized depth value ($\neq \infty$) generates one vertex at its location with the same depth value. Each silhouette edge with only one initialized adjacent node generates one additional silhouette vertex at the location and with the depth of its silhouette node. This vertex will be on the outer silhouette. Each silhouette edge with both adjacent nodes initialized generates two vertices, both at the location of the silhouette node. One vertex associated with the end point with the smaller depth (the front vertex) gets the depth of the silhouette node. The other vertex (the back vertex) gets a depth value extrapolated from the neighborhood of endpoint with the larger depth value. These two nodes lie on an inner silhouette (see Fig. 4). In this figure linear extrapolation is used to find the depth of the back silhouette vertex which we found to be sufficient.

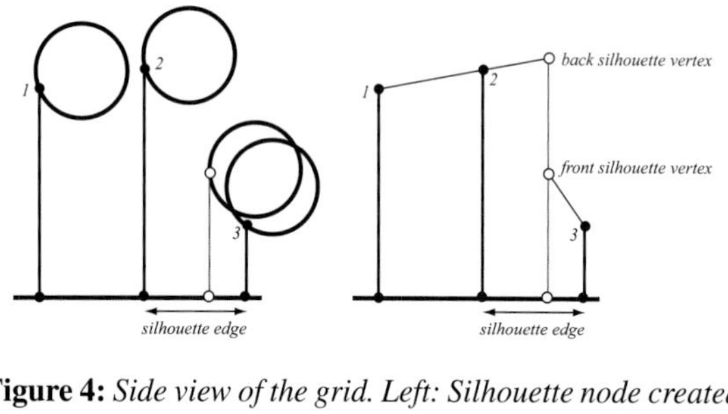

Figure 4: *Side view of the grid. Left: Silhouette node created on a silhouette edge. Right: The mesh vertices and triangles generated for this configuration. Note that two vertices with different depth values are generated for the silhouette node.*

To generate triangles, the mesh generation algorithm visits all grid cells one by one and generates triangles for them. Each of the cell's edges is either a silhouette edge or a regular edge. This leads to 16 cases as shown in Fig. 5. The number of a particular case can be computed by associating each edge with a bit and set the bit to one if the edge is cut, i.e. has a silhouette node.

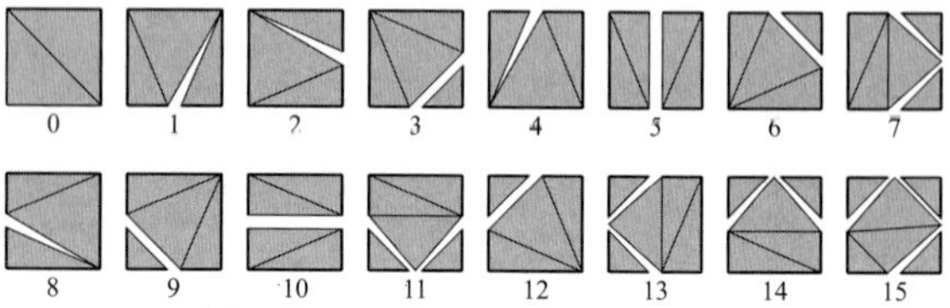

Figure 5: *All the cases for the generation of a 2D triangle mesh from cut edges.*

In Fig. 5 we have opened the cuts on each edge for illustration purposes to distinguish the silhouettes vertex associated with the left and the one associated with the right end node. From the triangles shown, only those are generated for which all three vertices exist. In the case of outer silhouettes only a subset of the triangles need to be added. Special care has to be taken for different groups of cases:

- Case 0 represents inner triangles away from silhouettes. We alternate between the configuration shown and the one which is rotated 90 degrees to get a nicer inner mesh.
- Cases $3, 5, 6, 9, 10$ and 12 are the regular situations with the silhouette entering at one edge and leaving at another. No special care has to be taken here.
- Cases $1, 2, 4$ and 8 are generated by an inner silhouette starting within the cell. The triangulation shown is not unique. To avoid flickering it is important to stick with one arbitrary choice though. The difference of the depth of the two silhouette vertices is bound by $3z_{max}$. Therefore, it is safe to connect the vertices as shown without generating arbitrarily stretched triangles.
- The remaining cases $7, 11, 13, 14$ and 15 are the pathological ones. Have a closer look at case 7. The center triangle is connected to the left two triangles. It is, thus, connected to the same layer as those. The upper right and lower right triangles each belong to different layers which can be arbitrarily far from the layer of the center triangle. Therefore a third vertex needs to be generated for the silhouette node on the right. Its depth needs to be extrapolated from the depths of the four vertices on the left. In case 15 two additional vertices are generated and connected to the layer of the lower left triangle.

3.4. Transformation to World Space and Rendering

At this stage, we have a triangle mesh with the correct connectivity and vertices in screen space, e.g. with coordinates $[x_p, y_p, z_p]^T$. In order to render this mesh and to compute reflections and refractions of the 3D environment, the vertices are projected back into world space while the connectivity is kept fixed. We, therefore, need to invert the transformation given in Eq. (1) and Eq. (2). Let $\mathbf{Q} \in \mathbb{R}^{4\times4}$ be the inverse of the projection matrix, i.e. $\mathbf{Q} = \mathbf{P}^{-1}$. With $\mathbf{Q}$, the world coordinates $[x,y,z]^T$ can be computed via the inverse projection equation

$$\begin{bmatrix} x \\ y \\ z \\ 1 \end{bmatrix} = \mathbf{Q} \begin{bmatrix} (-1+2x_p/W)w \\ (-1+2y_p/H)w \\ z_p \\ w \end{bmatrix}. \tag{6}$$

At this point, we do not have the projective divisor w. However, it can be retrieved (using the last row of the above equation) as

$$w = \frac{1 - q_{4,3}z_p}{q_{4,1}(-1+2x_p/W) + q_{4,2}(-1+2y_p/H) + q_{4,4}} \tag{7}$$

from known quantities only, before the inverse transformation is executed.

After the transformation of the mesh, we generate per-vertex normals in world space. There are several ways to compute vertex normals for a triangle mesh. We use the normalized sum of the normals of adjacent triangles weighted by the adjacent angles. Finally the triangles and normals are sent to the standard graphics pipeline.

4. Extensions

4.1. Depth Smoothing

The procedure described so far produces bumpy depth maps. Fortunately, the depth map can easily be smoothed by applying an appropriate filter. We use a separable binomial filter of user specified half-size n_{filter} (see Fig. 6), both, in i and j direction.

i-3	i-2	i-1	i	i+1	i+2	i+3
1/64	6/64	15/64	20/64	15/64	6/64	1/64

n_{Filter}

Figure 6: *Separable binomial filter with half-length $n_{filter} = 3$. The center depth value at (i,j) is replaced by the weighted sum of neighboring depth values. The weights used are shown inside the squares.*

In a first pass, the horizontal filter is applied to all values $z_{i,j} \neq \infty$ of the depth map. In a second pass the values $z_{i,j} \neq \infty$ are filtered again using the vertical version of the filter.

When applying the filter, special care has to be taken near silhouettes. When the filter is applied to a certain node, we only consider depth values within the z_{max} range from the depth of the node. However, with this procedure the boundary of the mesh can get tilted towards the camera as Fig. 7 shows. This happens because the symmetry of the filter is

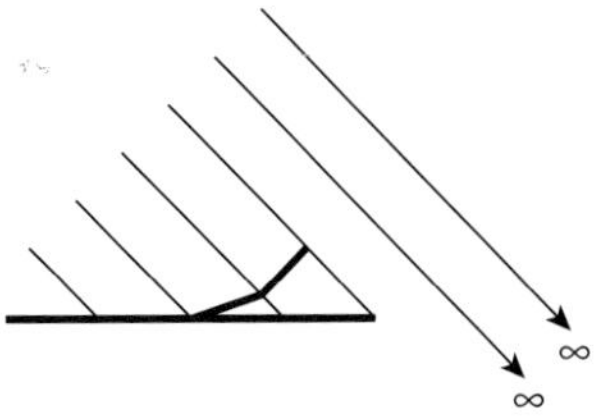

Figure 7: *If certain depth values are not considered for filtering, the mesh gets tilted towards the camera.*

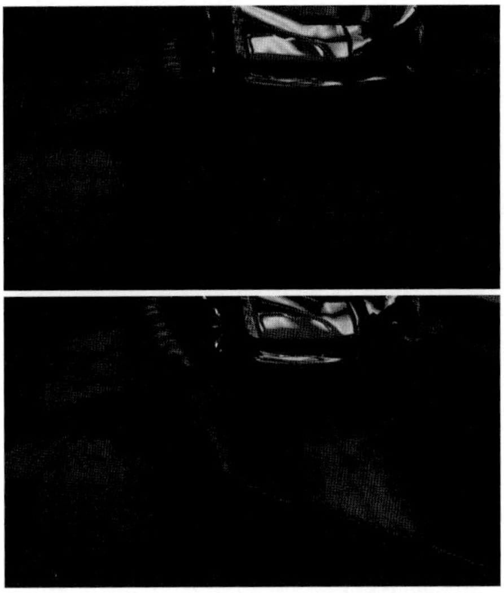

Figure 8: *Top: The standard approach produces bumpy surfaces. Bottom: A flat surface is generated by smoothing the depths in screen space.*

lost and the central value is pulled towards the values on the valid side of the filter. This problem can be solved easily. If the value at position $i+k$ is omitted, *both* position $i+k$ and position $i-k$ are ignored in the weighted sum. When the depth of a node is changed, the depths of the silhouette nodes associated with it are changed by the same amount.

4.2. Silhouette Smoothing

Smoothing of the depth values does not influence the appearance of the silhouettes of the mesh. To smooth the boundary of the mesh we smooth the screen space coordinates $[x_p, y_p]^T$ of the nodes of the mesh before the transformation to world space. We use a very simple but effective iterative scheme. In each iteration, the screen space coordinates of each vertex are replaced by the average of its own coordinates and the coordinates of all adjacent vertices. The regular internal mesh resulting from case 0 in Fig. 5 and its flipped configuration is a fix point of this smoothing procedure. Thus, it only affects the silhouettes as desired. To avoid the opening of internal silhouettes corresponding silhouette vertices are "glued" together in screen space during this process. The number of iterations n_{iters} is a user parameter. Silhouette smoothing causes shrinking of outer silhouettes. In most cases this effect is desired. In order to cover the area of a puddle the fluid particles have to have a certain size. When small groups of particles separate, the drops appear as rather large blobs. Silhouette smoothing makes the boundary of small sets of connected particles look more realistic (see Fig. 11).

5. Results

All scenes were run on a Intel dual core CPU at 2.6GHz with 2GB of RAM. In most cases the SPH simulation was the bottleneck. The car wash scene (Fig. 1) contains 16K SPH particles. It runs at 20 fps without surface generation. The frame rate drops to 19 fps for screen spacing $h = 6$ and to 18 fps for screen spacing $h = 3$ with a triangle count of 13K and 40K respectively. The dungeon scene (Fig. 11) contains 10K particles. Its frame rate drops from 23 fps to 22 for $h = 6$ with 15K triangles and to 21 fps for $h = 3$ with 60K triangles.

In both the slide scene (Fig. 9) and the wheels scene (Fig. 10) the particle count of 5K is small with respect to the number of triangles generated. Since 5K SPH particles can be simulated very efficiently – 65 fps in the slide scene – the time for the generation for the screen space mesh becomes more significant. For $h = 6$ the frame rate drops to 55 fps with 5 K triangles and to 40 fps for $h = 3$ to 40 fps with a triangle count of 20 K.

6. Conclusions and Future Work

Screen space meshes provide an efficient way to construct and visualize surfaces. We focused on the visualization of particle-based fluids. However, the approach is more general and can be applied to other related visualization problems.

The approach trades speed for certain limitations. The 3D mesh generated from the screen space mesh is only valid for the current camera position. This causes problems with shadow casting. A solution to this problem would be to generate the fluid mesh separately from the positions of the light sources. Also, only the front most surface layer is generated which does not produce visible artifacts in most scenarios as already mentioned.

Most of the algorithm steps, such as the depth map generation or the transformation of vertex positions, are well-suited to be computed on a GPU. We expect a GPU implementation to be much faster than the CPU version we have, although the CPU version already allows the generation of quite complex surfaces in real-time as our results show.

References

[Bli82] BLINN J. F.: A generalization of algebraic surface drawing. *ACM Trans. Graph. 1*, 3 (1982), 235–256.

[EMF02] ENRIGHT D., MARSCHNER S., FEDKIW R.: Animation and rendering of complex water surfaces. In *Proceedings of the 29th annual conference on Computer graphics and interactive techniques* (2002), ACM Press, pp. 736–744.

[FF01] FOSTER N., FEDKIW R.: Practical animation of liquids. In *Proceedings of the 28th annual conference on Computer graphics and interactive techniques* (2001), ACM Press, pp. 23–30.

[GM77] GINGOLD R. A., MONAGHAN J. J.: Smoothed particle hydrodynamics: theory and application to non-spherical stars. *Monthly Notices of the Royal Astronomical Society* (1977).

[HNC02] HINSINGER D., NEYRET F., CANI M.-P.: Interactive animation of ocean waves. In *Proceedings of the ACM SIGGRAPH symposium on Computer animation* (2002), ACM Press, pp. 161–166.

[Joh04] JOHANSON C.: Real-time water rendering - introducing the projected grid concept. *Master of Science Thesis (Lund University)* (2004).

[LC87] LORENSEN W. E., CLINE H. E.: Marching cubes: A high resolution 3d surface construction algorithm. In *Proceedings of the 14th annual conference on Computer graphics and interactive techniques* (1987), ACM Press, pp. 163–169.

[MCG03] MÜLLER M., CHARYPAR D., GROSS M.: Particle-based fluid simulation for interactive applications. *Proceedings of 2003 ACM SIGGRAPH Symposium on Computer Animation* (2003), 154–159.

[PTB*03] PREMOZE S., TASDIZEN T., BIGLER J., LEFOHN A., WHITAKER R. T.: Particle-based simulation of fluids. *Eurographics 22*, 3 (2003), 401–410.

[Whi80] WHITTED T.: An improved illumination model for shaded display. *Commun. ACM 23*, 6 (1980), 343–349.

[ZPvBG01] ZWICKER M., PFISTER H., VAN BAAR J., GROSS M.: Surface splatting. In *Proceedings of the 28th annual conference on Computer graphics and interactive techniques* (2001), ACM Press, pp. 371–378.

Figure 9: *Left: The original set of particles (their SPH density is color coded). Middle: Screen space mesh. Right: Final rendering.*

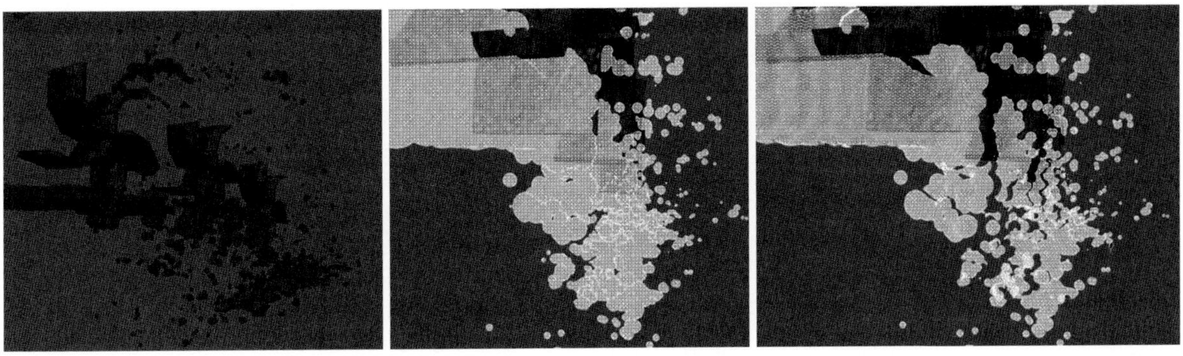

Figure 10: *Left: A scene with a complex 3D liquid boundary. Middle: The screen space mesh with internal silhouettes. Left: A rotation of the frozen mesh reveals that the internal silhouettes are disconnected in the viewing direction as desired.*

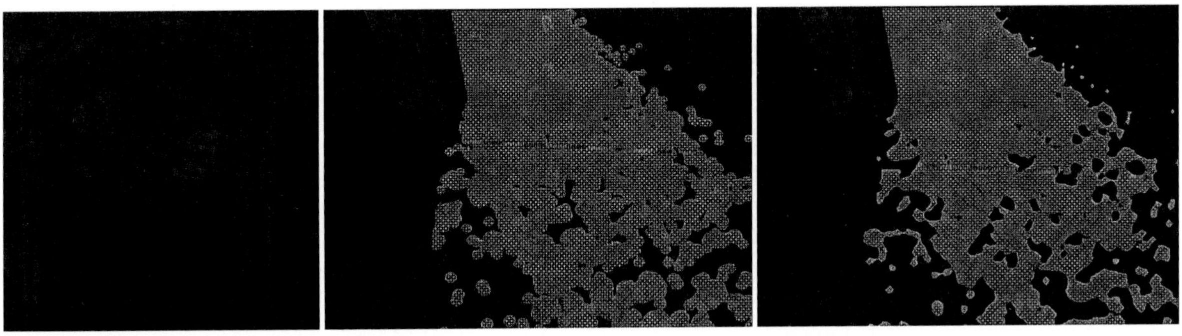

Figure 11: *Left: Flooding a corridor. Middle: Top view of the screen space mesh without silhouette smoothing. Right: Silhouette smoothing generates a surface tension effect.*

Eurographics/ ACM SIGGRAPH Symposium on Computer Animation (2007)
D. Metaxas and J. Popovic (Editors)

Legendre Fluids: A Unified Framework for Analytic Reduced Space Modeling and Rendering of Participating Media

Mohit Gupta and Srinivasa G. Narasimhan

Robotics Institute, Carnegie Mellon University

Abstract

In this paper, we present a unified framework for reduced space modeling and rendering of dynamic and non-homogenous participating media, like snow, smoke, dust and fog. The key idea is to represent the 3D spatial variation of the density, velocity and intensity fields of the media using the same analytic basis. In many situations, natural effects such as mist, outdoor smoke and dust are smooth (low frequency) phenomena, and can be compactly represented by a small number of coefficients of a Legendre polynomial basis. We derive analytic expressions for the derivative and integral operators in the Legendre coefficient space, as well as the triple product integrals of Legendre polynomials. These mathematical results allow us to solve both the Navier-Stokes equations for fluid flow and light transport equations for single scattering efficiently in the reduced Legendre space. Since our technique does not depend on volume grid resolution, we can achieve computational speedups as compared to spatial domain methods while having low memory and pre-computation requirements as compared to data-driven approaches. Also, analytic definition of derivatives and integral operators in the Legendre domain avoids the approximation errors inherent in spatial domain finite difference methods. We demonstrate many interesting visual effects resulting from particles immersed in fluids as well as volumetric scattering in non-homogenous and dynamic participating media, such as fog and mist.

Categories and Subject Descriptors (according to ACM CCS): I.3.7 [Computer Graphics]: Three-Dimensional Graphics and Realism

1. Introduction and Related Work

Participating media such as smoke, snow, dust, mist and fog exhibit a wide range of visual effects. Such media are characterized by their density, velocity and intensity fields that vary across both space and time. Accurate modeling of densities and velocities as well as rendering of intensities of these media is critical for achieving photo-realism in computer graphics. Also, many applications like games require interactive changes in lighting, view-point and the medium properties. For such applications, it is imperative to achieve these visual effects in real-time.

The first step in realizing this goal of visual realism requires modeling the time-varying density and velocity fields of participating media. The Navier-Stokes equations for incompressible fluid flow [CM90] provide a differential model for simulating the density and velocity fields. Explicit analytic solutions to Navier-Stokes equations are hard to obtain and hence, a number of works that employ numerical finite difference methods (FDM) have been proposed [FM96, FM97, Sta99, Sta01, FF01, FSJ01, NFJ02, SRF05]. Although simple to implement, such schemes require high spatial resolution to minimize the finite differencing numerical errors, placing serious demands on memory and compromising speed. Treuille et al [TMPS03] develop an approach for key-framing of fluid flows that alleviate the discretization errors. However, their approach becomes computationally prohibitive for large grid sizes. More recently, an interesting data-driven approach has been taken to simulate the velocity fields using a reduced dimensional PCA basis [TLP06]. This approach achieves considerable speed-ups and produces impressive results, but at the cost of high memory requirements and lengthy pre-computation. Furthermore, as the authors mention, it is unclear whether the approach generalizes to new fluid flows that are not represented in the pre-computation.

The second step towards the goal of creating the desired visual effects is rendering of participating media, which requires modeling the intensity fields resulting from volumetric scattering. Using the computed density field, the corresponding intensity field of the participating medium is then rendered by solving the light transport equation [Cha60]. Analogous to fluid modeling, many works that numerically solve the light transport equation based on FDMs have been proposed [KH84, Max94, Jen01, PM93, EP90, Sak90, LBC94, RT87]. As such, many of the issues related to numerical errors must be addressed here as well. While these methods

Symposium on Computer Animation 2007, San Diego, CA, August 03-04, 2007.
© 2007 ACM 978-1-59593-624-4/07/0008 $5.00

Figure 1: ***Legendre domain 3D fluid simulation and rendering:*** *In this example, we have* 3000 *snow flakes being carried by a wind field (Legendre domain fluid simulation). We add mist to the scene using Legendre domain rendering for participating media. Notice further objects appearing brighter due to the air-light effect, and distant snow-flakes becoming invisible as the mist density is increased. The clear weather Christmas image was downloaded from www.survivinggrady.com/2005_12_01_archive.html*

can produce impressive visual effects, they are too slow for interactive applications. Recent hardware-accelerated techniques [DYN02, REK*04, HL01] can significantly decrease the running times of numerical simulations, although they are specialized to particular phenomena.

In addition, note that the intensity fields depend on the illumination and viewing geometry as well as the scattering properties [NGD*06, HED05] of the participating medium. Moreover, the lighting, viewpoint and the densities of the medium may change with time. Thus, the pre-computations required are too prohibitive for data driven approaches to be applied to intensity fields. For the special case of homogeneous media, many previous analytic approaches [Max86, SRNN05, JMLH01, NN03] may be used to render the effects of scattering in real-time. However, homogeneous media are not the focus of our work.

The goal of this paper is fast modeling and rendering of dynamic and non-homogenous participating media, like smoke, dust and fog. The key idea is to represent the 3D spatial variation of the density, velocity and intensity fields using the same analytic basis. Jos Stam [Sta99] used Fourier basis to solve the diffusion and projection steps of the fluid simulation pipe-line over a domain with periodic boundary conditions. In this work, we use Legendre Polynomials [Cha60] as our basis functions. In many situations, natural effects such as mist, outdoor smoke and dust are smooth (low frequency) phenomena, and can be compactly represented by a small number of coefficients of a Legendre polynomial basis. In this work, we will focus on optically thin media where single scattering is the dominant form of light transport [SRNN05, NGD*06]. Under these conditions, the common Legendre polynomial basis for different fields allows us to analytically solve both the Navier-Stokes and light transport equations in the reduced Legendre space. It turns out that this solution requires us to analyze triple product integrals of Legendre polynomials and their sparsity [GN07], similar in spirit to the triple product wavelet integrals for relighting [NRH04].

Since all the fields are represented using Legendre polynomials, their derivatives (and integrals) can be computed analytically, thereby avoiding the numerical errors resulting from spatial finite differences approximation. Additionally, the compactness of the Legendre domain representations of natural effects makes modeling and rendering of such participating media very fast. Depending on the number of coefficients required, we achieve computational speedups of one to three orders of magnitude as compared to spatial domain techniques. At the same time, only a few coefficients must be stored in memory as compared to the full 3D volumes that must be stored for the data-driven (eg., PCA) approaches.

The main contribution of this paper is a theoretical one: a unified framework for both fluid simulation and rendering in an analytic reduced space. We believe that this is an important first step towards bridging the gap between model reduction for fluid simulation and pre-computed radiance transfer for rendering. In addition, we believe that the mathematical results derived in the paper are general enough to find use in many computer graphics applications. We demonstrate several visual effects resulting from volumetric scattering in time-varying participating media, such as shadowgrams that are cast by the medium on a background, mixing of different gaseous media and airlight effects due to depth disparities in the scene. We also show fluid simulation results illustrating snow flakes (see Figure 1) and confetti immersed in turbulent wind fields, as well as smoke density fields evolving under the influence of user-defined forces.

For the purpose of deriving the unified reduced space simulation and rendering framework, we have made several limiting assumptions such as smooth (low frequency) phenomena, no objects within the medium, single scattering, orthographic viewing and distant lighting. In Section 8, we discuss these limitations in detail, along with future research directions for extending the technique to more general settings.

2. Physical Models for Participating Media

Dynamic and non-homogenous participating media can be characterized by density, velocity and intensity fields, that vary across both space and time. Whereas Navier-Stokes equations for incompressible fluid flow model the evolution of the density and velocity fields over time, the intensity fields are rendered using light transport equations. The time evolution of the velocity field $\mathbf{u}$ is given by [CM90]:

$$\frac{\partial \mathbf{u}}{\partial t} = -(\mathbf{u}.\nabla)\mathbf{u} - \nu\nabla^2\mathbf{u} + \nabla p + \mathbf{b}, \qquad s.t. \;\; \nabla.\mathbf{u} = 0, \quad (1)$$

where, ν is the kinematic viscosity, p is the pressure field and $\mathbf{b}$ denotes the external forces (the notation used in the paper is

$\mathbf{u}$	velocity field
$u_\diamond$	$\diamond$−component of velocity field
r	density field
$\mathbf{b}$	external force field
$b_\diamond$	$\diamond$−component of force field
E^d	direct transmission intensity field
E^s	scattered intensity field
ν	kinematic viscosity
σ	extinction coefficient
β	scattering coefficient
θ	scattering angle
$\Omega(\theta)$	scattering phase function
$\omega^{\mathbf{d}}$	lighting direction
$\omega^{\mathbf{s}}$	viewing direction

Figure 2: *Notation used in our paper. $\diamond$ stands for either x, y or z.*

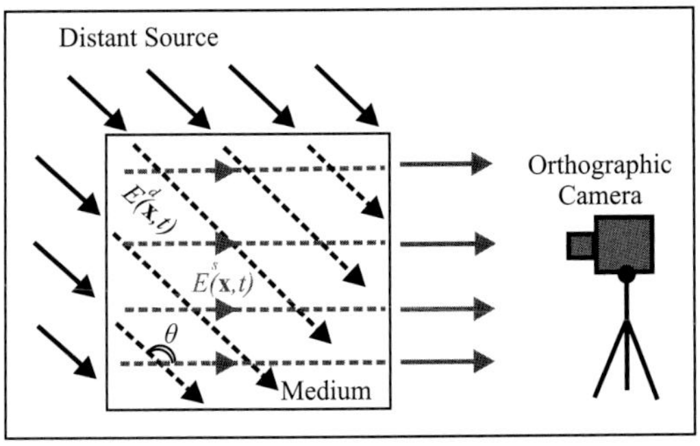

Figure 3: *The participating medium is illuminated by a distant light source and is viewed by an orthographic camera. Under the single scattering assumption, the intensity field within the medium volume can be split into two sets of light rays: the pre-scattering (direct transmission) intensity field $E^d(x,t)$ and post-scattering intensity field $E^s(x,t)$ (shown using red rays).*

given in Figure 2). Following [Sta99, CM90], Equation 1 can be written as:

$$\frac{\partial \mathbf{u}}{\partial t} = \underbrace{P}_{projection} \left(\underbrace{-(\mathbf{u}.\nabla)\mathbf{u}}_{advection} + \underbrace{\nu\nabla^2\mathbf{u}}_{diffusion} + \underbrace{\mathbf{b}}_{forces} \right) \quad (2)$$

Here, P is a linear operator which projects a vector field to its divergence free component. Equation 2 can be resolved by splitting the right hand side into four sequential steps: (i) advection, (ii) diffusion, (iii) external forces and (iv) projection [Sta99]. Similarly, the time evolution of the density field r is given by:

$$\frac{\partial r}{\partial t} = \underbrace{-(\mathbf{u}.\nabla)r}_{advection} - \underbrace{\kappa\nabla^2 r}_{diffusion} + \underbrace{-\alpha r}_{dissipation} + \underbrace{S_r}_{source}, \quad (3)$$

where, κ is the diffusion constant, α is the dissipation rate and S_r is the source term for density.

Using the density field r, we can render the intensity fields for any configuration of illumination and viewing geometry. In this work, we consider optically thin media where **single scattering** is the dominant form of light transport. Figure 3 shows an orthographic camera viewing a participating medium that is illuminated by a distant light source. Then, we can split the intensity fields into two components: the *pre-scattering* (direct transmission) intensity field $E^d(\mathbf{x},t)$, and the *post-scattering* intensity field $E^s(\mathbf{x},t)$. Mathematically, these intensity fields can be written as [Cha60]:

Orthogonality	$\int_{-1}^{1} L_i(x)L_j(x)dx = \delta_{ij}$
Derivative	$L_i'(x) = \sum_k c_{ik}L_k(x)$
Integral	$\int L_i(x)dx = \sum_k b_{ik}L_k(x)$

Figure 4: *Properties of Legendre Polynomials [Cha60].*

$$\left(\omega^d.\nabla\right)E^d = -\sigma r \cdot E^d \quad (4)$$

$$(\omega^s.\nabla)E^s = -\sigma r \cdot E^s + \beta r \cdot \Omega(\theta) \cdot E^d \quad (5)$$

Here, σ and β are the extinction and scattering coefficients respectively and $\Omega(\theta)$ is the phase function. When the camera is outside the medium, the acquired **2D image** of the medium is simply the boundary of the 3D intensity field E^s(Figure 3).

3. Compact Analytic Representation of Non-Homogenous Media

The key idea in this paper is to represent the 3D spatial variation of the density, velocity and intensity fields using the same analytic basis. We choose to use Legendre polynomials as basis functions. In many situations, natural effects such as mist, outdoor smoke and dust are smooth (low frequency) phenomena, and can be compactly represented by a small number of coefficients. Legendre polynomials are orthogonal, have global support (non-zero over the entire domain), and have analytic derivatives and integrals (Figure 4). As a result, they find wide application in mathematical physics literature in conjunction to solving differential equations [Cha60].

A function $f(x)$ can be represented as a linear combination of Legendre polynomials L_k of different orders $f(x) = \sum_k F_k L_k(x)$, where the Legendre domain coefficients $[F_k]$ can be computed analytically as:

$$F_k = \int_{-1}^{1} f(x)L_k(x)dx. \quad (6)$$

In 3D, we represent a field $f(x,y,z)$ that is smooth in x-,y- and z-directions as:

$$f(x,y,z) = \sum_{ijk} F_{ijk}L_i(z)L_j(y)L_k(x). \quad (7)$$

For notational ease, Equation 7 is written as $f(x,y,z) \Leftrightarrow [F_{ijk}]$. The Legendre representations for the various fields are given in Figure 5.

4. Analytic Operators in Legendre Space

In this section, we derive the legendre space formulations for various operators and establish that they are compact, computationally efficient, and completely analytic in nature. For ease of exposition, we illustrate the concepts with *1D* examples; analysis in *2D* and *3D* follows in an exactly similar manner.

4.1. Derivative Operator

Observe that spatial derivatives appear both in the Navier-Stokes and the light transport equations (2, 3, 4, 5) in the form of gradient and Laplacian operators. Using the property that derivative of a legendre polynomial can be expressed in terms of lower order legendre polynomials (Figure 4), we derive the

Field	Spatial $\Leftrightarrow$ Legendre
Density Field	$r \Leftrightarrow [R]$
Velocity Field	$u_{\diamond} \Leftrightarrow [U_{\diamond}]$
Divergence free Velocity Field	$\widehat{u}_{\diamond} \Leftrightarrow [\widehat{U}_{\diamond}(t)]$
External Force Field	$b_{+} \Leftrightarrow [B_{+}(t)]$
Direct Transmission Intensity Field	$E^d \Leftrightarrow [I^d]$
Scattered Intensity Field	$E^s \Leftrightarrow [I^s]$

Figure 5: *Legendre representations of various fields, where $\diamond$ stands for x,y or z. In Figures 5 and 6, sub-scripts and arguments have been dropped for brevity. For example, d and [D] should be read as $d(x,y,z,t)$ and $[D_{ijk}(t)]$ respectively.*

Operation	Operand	Result	Complexity
Derivative	$g \Leftrightarrow [G]$	$\frac{\partial}{\partial \diamond} g \Leftrightarrow D_{\diamond} \cdot [G]$	$O(K^2)$
Integral	$g \Leftrightarrow [G]$	$\int g d\diamond \Leftrightarrow \hat{I}_{\diamond} \cdot [G]$	$O(K^2)$
Product	$g \Leftrightarrow [G]$ $h \Leftrightarrow [H]$	$g \cdot h \Leftrightarrow M^G \cdot [H]$	$O(K^3)$
Truncation	$[G]$	$[G^T] = T \cdot [G]$	$O(K^2)$
Legendre to Spatial	$[G]$	g	$O(NK)$

Figure 6: *Legendre Space Operators ($\diamond$ stands for x,y or z). N is the size of the spatial grid. K is the size of legendre coefficient representation.*

derivative operator in legendre domain, which is **completely analytic**, and hence, devoid of the numerical errors resulting from the Finite Difference approximation:

$$f(x) = \sum_i F_i L_i(x) \qquad \Rightarrow f'(x) = \sum_i F_i L_i'(x) \tag{8}$$

$$\Rightarrow f'(x) = \sum_k \left(\sum_i F_i * c_{ik} \right) L_k(x) \quad \ldots \quad (Figure\ 4)$$
$$= \sum_k F'(k) L_k(x)$$

where $F'(k) = \sum_i F_i * c_{ik}$. We can write this equation in matrix form, with $[F_k']$ and $[F_i]$ as the coefficient vectors corresponding to the derivative and the original function respectively. The *derivative* operator (x-direction) in Legendre Domain is thus given by the matrix $D_x(i,k) = c_{ik}$:

$$[F_k'] = D_x * [F_i] \tag{9}$$

Derivatives in y and z and the integral operator can be defined likewise. Figure 6 lists all the legendre space operators that we derive, along with the corresponding time complexity. Given K as the size of legendre space representation $[F_i]$, the matrix-vector multiplication require $O(K^2)$ computations. Building the derivative and integral matrices is a one time operation, and takes $O(K^2)$ time.

4.2. Product Operator in Legendre Domain

The advection term in the Navier-Stokes equation (2, 3) as well as the single scattering equation for rendering (4, 5) entail multiplication of two fields to compute a third one. This motivates investigating the general problem of multiplying two functions, $h(x) = f(x).g(x)$, where both the functions and the result are represented in the Legendre Basis:

$$f(x) = \sum_j F_j L_j(x) \quad g(x) = \sum_k G_k L_k(x) \quad h(x) = \sum_i H_i L_i(x)$$

To compute the ith basis coefficient for the result, we use orthogonality of Legendre Polynomials (see Figure 4)

$$H_i = \int_{-1}^{1} L_i(x) h(x) dx = \int_{-1}^{1} L_i(x) f(x) g(x) dx$$
$$= \int_{-1}^{1} L_i(x) \left(\sum_j F_j L_j(x) \right) \left(\sum_k G_k L_k(x) \right) dx$$
$$= \sum_{jk} F_j G_k TI_{ijk}$$

where $TI_{ijk} = \int_{-1}^{1} L_i(x) L_j(x) L_k(x) dx$ is the Legendre Polynomial triple product integral, and can be pre-computed apriori. As with the derivative and integral case, we can write the above equation in matrix form as follows:

$$[H_i] = M^G * [F_j] = M^F * [G_k] \tag{10}$$

where, $M^G(i,j) = \sum_k G_k TI_{ijk}$ and $M^F(i,k) = \sum_j F_j TI_{ijk}$. Given the size of legendre representations as K, the multiplication matrix has $O(K^2)$ entries. For each entry, $O(K)$ computations are required. Thus, we need $O(K^3)$ computations to build the multiplication matrix and $O(K^2)$ time for the matrix-vector multiplication. Therefore, total time complexity of legendre space multiplication is $O(K^3)$. However, we show that the 3D tensor TI is sparse using the **Legendre Polynomials Triple Product Integrals theorem** [GN07]. Using the theorem, we show that approximately $\frac{3}{4}$ of the entries of the TI tensor are exactly zero. We exploit this sparsity to achieve computational speed-ups in the advection and the rendering stages. Indeed, the time required to construct the multiplication matrix can be reduced by a factor of 4 in $1D$ and by $4^3 = 64$ in the $3D$ case.

Lower Order Approximation: Note that multiplying two polynomials of degree K each results in a polynomial of degree $2K$. Therefore, given two functions, each with Legendre representation of size K, the Legendre representation of the product will have size $2K$. For computational savings, it is desirable to keep the size of the Legendre representation constant. To this end, we devise a simple approximation scheme using the **Chebyshev Polynomials** to truncate a given Legendre representation from $2K$ terms to K terms, while keeping the approximation error low under the L_∞ norm [GN07]. We define the **Truncation Matrix Operator T in legendre space**, such that

$$\underbrace{[F_i^T]}_{K\times 1} = \underbrace{T}_{K\times 2K} * \underbrace{[F_i]}_{2K\times 1}$$

where $[F_i]$ is the legendre representation of size $2K$, and $[F_i^T]$ is the corresponding truncated representation of size K. As with derivatives and integrals, truncation requires a matrix multiplication with a time complexity of $O(K^2)$. Building the truncation matrix T is a one time operation requiring $O(K^2)$ operations.

5. Modeling in Legendre Domain

Using the Legendre representations for fields and the operators (derivative, multiplication, truncation), we solve the Navier-Stokes equations (2, 3) in the Legendre domain. For velocity simulation, we decompose Equation 2 into the 4 sequential steps of advection, diffusion, external forces and projection [Sta99]. Now we show how each of these steps can be simulated in the Legendre domain:

5.1. Advection

In the spatial domain, the conservation form of the advection equation is given by:

$$\frac{\partial}{\partial t}u_\diamondsuit = -\nabla\cdot(\mathbf{u}u_\diamondsuit) \quad (11)$$

$$= -\left(\frac{\partial}{\partial x}u_x u_\diamondsuit + \frac{\partial}{\partial y}u_y u_\diamondsuit + \frac{\partial}{\partial z}u_z u_\diamondsuit\right) \quad (12)$$

Subscript $\diamondsuit$ denotes either x,y or z direction. This form implicitly assumes a divergence free velocity field, i.e. $\nabla\cdot\mathbf{u} = 0$.

Legendre space advection equation is then derived by substituting the legendre representations of the fields (Figure 5), along with the legendre space derivative and multiplication operators (Figure 6) in Equation 12:

$$\boxed{\frac{\partial}{\partial t}[U_\diamondsuit(t)] = -A\cdot[U_\diamondsuit(t)]} \quad (13)$$

$$\text{where } A = \underbrace{T}_{truncation} \cdot \left(\sum_\diamondsuit \underbrace{D_\diamondsuit}_{derivative} \cdot \underbrace{M^{U_\diamondsuit s}}_{multiplication}\right)$$

$\sum_\diamondsuit(\cdot)_\diamondsuit$ is short-hand for $(\cdot)_x + (\cdot)_y + (\cdot)_z$. For example, $\sum_\diamondsuit D_\diamondsuit \cdot M^{U_\diamondsuit}$ is expanded as $D_x\cdot M^{U_x} + D_y\cdot M^{U_y} + D_z\cdot M^{U_z}$. We update the legendre representations of the velocity field by computing the eigen decomposition of $A = A_E \cdot \Lambda \cdot A_E^{-1}$ [TLP06]:

$$[U_\diamondsuit(t+\triangle t)] = \left(A_E\cdot e^{\triangle t\cdot\Lambda}\cdot A_E^{-1}\right)\cdot[U_\diamondsuit(t)] \quad (14)$$

A similar approach can be used to update the density field as well. Since it uses the multiplication operator, the time complexity of Legendre advection is $O(K^3)$ (Section 4), where K is the number of coefficients. In addition to the computational speed-up, using the completely analytic Legendre domain derivative operator reduces the numerical dissipation inherent in the FDM based approximations of the derivative operator (Figure 7).

(a) Original Field (b) Legendre Advection (c) Spatial Advection

Figure 7: *Comparison between Legendre and Spatial domain advection (high intensities signify higher values of the field). Notice, that the field after advection in the spatial domain (c) has lower energy than the field resulting from analytic legendre domain advection (b). Spatial advection results in dissipation of energy due to discretization of the gradient operators. The grid size used for spatial advection was* 500^2, *while* 144 *coefficients were used for legendre advection.*

5.2. Diffusion

For the diffusion step, we solve the implicit form of diffusion equation:

$$\left(I_{N\times N} - \nu\triangle t\,\nabla^2\right)\,u_\diamondsuit(\mathbf{x},\,t+\triangle t) = u_\diamondsuit(\mathbf{x},t) \quad (15)$$

where N is the total number of simulation grid voxels. The implicit form of diffusion equation is more stable than the explicit form. However, one drawback of the implicit form is that it requires solving a large system of linear equations. Fortunately, in our case, this issue is addressed by solving the diffusion equation in the reduced legendre space. Once again, we use the legendre representation of the fields and the operators (Figures 5 and 6) to obtain the **legendre space diffusion equation:**

$$\boxed{\left(I_{K\times K} - \nu\triangle t\,D^2\right)\,[U_\diamondsuit(t+\triangle t)] = [U_\diamondsuit(t)]} \quad (16)$$

where, $D^2 = (D_x)^2 + (D_y)^2 + (D_z)^2$ is the legendre space **Laplacian** operator. Since we solve a $K\times K$ linear system, the time complexity of legendre space diffusion is $O(K^3)$. This is a considerable speed-up over solving the $(N\times N)$ system in spatial domain.

5.3. External Forces

External forces are handled by adding their legendre representation (Figure 5) to that of the velocity field:

$$\boxed{[U_\diamondsuit(t+\triangle t)] = [U_\diamondsuit(t)] + [B_\diamondsuit]\cdot\triangle t} \quad (17)$$

5.4. Projection

This step ensures that the velocity field is divergence free, which is required to satisfy mass-conservation. For the projection step, we use the implicit definition of the projection operator P:

$$\nabla^2 q = \nabla\cdot\mathbf{u} \qquad \widehat{\mathbf{u}} = P\mathbf{u} = \mathbf{u} - \nabla q \quad (18)$$

This step requires solving the following Poisson system of equation for the scalar field q: $\nabla^2 q = \nabla\cdot\mathbf{u}$. $\widehat{\mathbf{u}}$, the divergence free component of $\mathbf{u}$ ($\nabla\cdot\widehat{\mathbf{u}} = 0$), is then computed by subtracting the gradient of q from $\mathbf{u}$. The Poisson equation can be formulated as a linear system of equations by discretizing the ∇^2 operator in the spatial domain. Analogously, we can define P_L, the projection operator in the legendre space implicitly as follows:

$$\boxed{D^2\cdot[Q] = \sum_\diamondsuit D_\diamondsuit\cdot[U_\diamondsuit(t)]} \quad (19)$$

$$\boxed{[\widehat{U}_\diamondsuit(t)] = P_L\cdot[U_\diamondsuit(t)] = [U_\diamondsuit(t)] - D_\diamondsuit\cdot[Q]} \quad (20)$$

Hence, in legendre space projection step, we need to solve the linear system of equations in the unknown vector $[Q]$ (Equation 19), requiring $O(K^3)$ time. As with diffusion, this is a considerable speed-up over solving the $(N\times N)$ linear system in spatial domain. **As an additional advantage**, using the analytic definitions of the derivative operators in all the simulation steps alleviates the numerical errors resulting from spatial finite difference approximations.

5.5. Density Dissipation

For density simulation, Equation 3 is solved in the legendre space. The advection, diffusion and source terms are handled in a way similar to velocity simulation. The dissipation term is then solved in the legendre space as follows:

$$\boxed{(1+\triangle t\alpha)\cdot[R(t+\triangle t)] = [R(t)]} \tag{21}$$

Size of the Legendre representation: Figure 8 illustrates the time-evolution of 2D density and velocity fields for different sizes of Legendre representations. We start with the same low frequency density and velocity fields and apply the same forces throughout the 3 different Legendre domain simulations. We can observe that more coefficients allow for higher frequencies and vorticities as the density and velocity fields evolve. In Figures 9, 10 and 11, we also provide theoretical and empirical computational complexity of our framework as a function of the size of the Legendre representation (K). A user can use these as a guide for choosing the Legendre representation size that best addresses the demands (speed/ high frequency detail) of a particular application.

6. Rendering in Legendre Space

Rendering requires solving the light transport equations (4,5) in the Legendre domain using techniques similar to those used for the Navier-Stokes equations.

6.1. Direct Transmission intensity field

As earlier, substituting Legendre representations of various fields and Legendre operators (Figures 5 and 6) into Equation 4, we get:

$$\left(\sum_{\diamondsuit}\omega^{\mathbf{d}}_{\diamondsuit}D_{\diamondsuit}\right)\cdot[I^d] = -\sigma T\cdot M^R\cdot[I^d]$$

$$\boxed{\Rightarrow L_{\omega^{\mathbf{d}}}\cdot[I^d(t)] = \mathbf{0}} \tag{22}$$

where $L_{\omega^{\mathbf{d}}} = \left(\sum_{\diamondsuit}\omega^{\mathbf{d}}_{\diamondsuit}D_{\diamondsuit} + \sigma T\cdot M^R\right)$.

6.2. Scattered intensity field

Similarly, we can project Equation 5 into the Legendre domain:

$$\left(\sum_{\diamondsuit}\omega^{\mathbf{s}}_{\diamondsuit}D_{\diamondsuit}\right)\cdot[I^s] = -\sigma T\cdot M^R\cdot[I^s] + \beta\Omega(\theta)\cdot T\cdot M^R\cdot[I^d]$$

$$\boxed{\Rightarrow L_{\omega^{\mathbf{s}}}\cdot[I^s] = \beta\Omega(\theta)\cdot T\cdot M^R\cdot[I^d]} \tag{23}$$

where $L_{\omega^{\mathbf{s}}} = \left(\sum_{\diamondsuit}\omega^{\mathbf{s}}_{\diamondsuit}D_{\diamondsuit} + \sigma T\cdot M^R\right)$.

In the legendre space, both the light scattering equations are thus formulated as linear systems of equations in the unknowns $[I^d]$ (22) and $[I^s]$ (23). Along with the **boundary conditions**, which can be formulated as additional linear constraints, these systems can be solved in $O(K^3)$ time.

Imagine a camera observing the medium from the outside

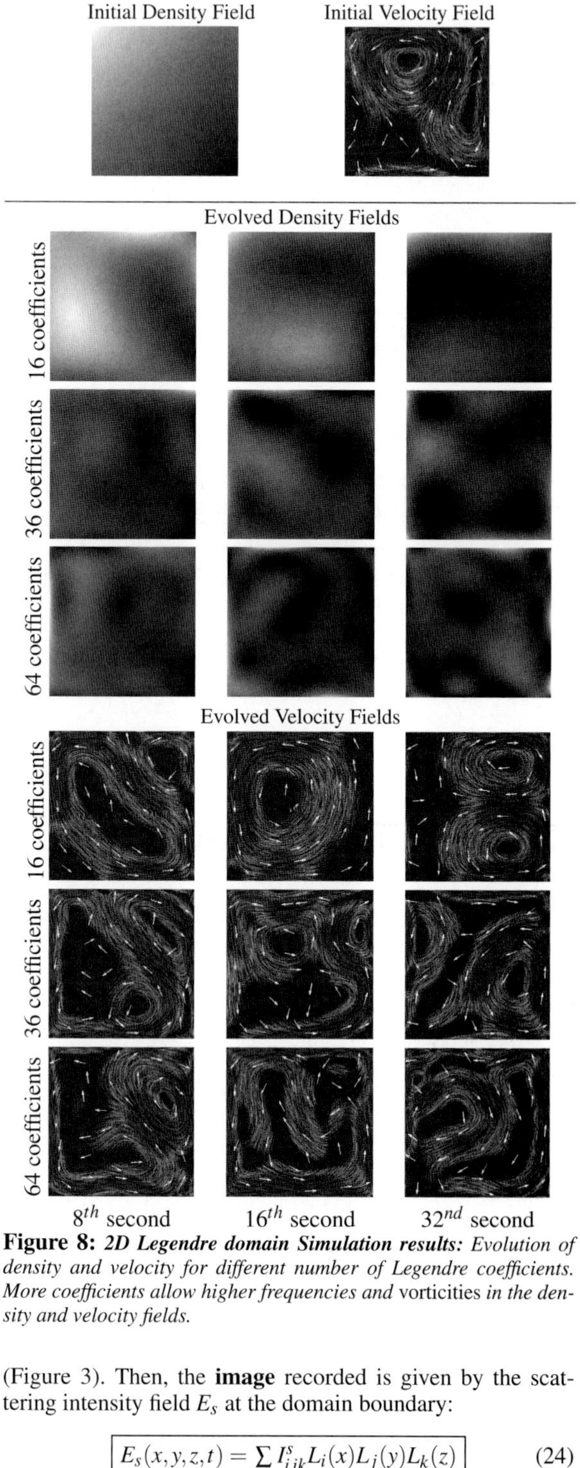

Figure 8: ***2D Legendre domain Simulation results:*** *Evolution of density and velocity for different number of Legendre coefficients. More coefficients allow higher frequencies and* vorticities *in the density and velocity fields.*

(Figure 3). Then, the **image** recorded is given by the scattering intensity field E_s at the domain boundary:

$$\boxed{E_s(x,y,z,t) = \sum_{ijk} I^s_{ijk}L_i(x)L_j(y)L_k(z)} \tag{24}$$

If the image resolution is S, then time-complexity of image computation is $O(SK)$. Note that the image computation step is output-sensitive, and can easily be parallelized. Our Legendre domain modeling and rendering framework is summarized in Figure 9.

For every time step:

• Update Velocity and Density Fields

Advection (13) and Diffusion (16) $O(K^3)$

Forces/Source (17) $O(K^2)$

Projection(19, 20) $O(K^3)$

• Update Intensity Fields

Direct Transmission(22), Scattered (23) $O(K^3)$

• Compute Image (24) $O(SK)$

Figure 9: ***Legendre domain Rendering algorithm:*** *K is the size of Legendre space representations and S is the image resolution.*

Number of Legendre Coefficients

Spatial Grid Size	16	36	64	144
200^2	500X	250X	75X	10X
300^2	1250X	625X	187X	25X
400^2	2500X	1250X	375X	50X
500^2	5000X	2500X	750X	100X

Figure 10: *Typical computational speed-ups for 2D simulation and rendering in Legendre domain as compared to the spatial domain.*

7. Results

Our results show that Legendre polynomials can express a variety of interesting density and force distributions compactly, thereby letting the user manipulate the densities, velocities and forces globally to produce the desired effects.

Particles immersed in dynamic fluid media: Figure 12 and Figure 1 show simulations of 500 pieces of confetti and 3000 snow-flakes respectively being carried by a wind field simulated using 216 Legendre coefficients each. We can notice vorticities being created in the confetti example due to the turbulent behavior of the wind field. On the other hand, the snow flakes are carried by a more gentle, *breeze-like* wind. We encourage the reader to view the animation results in the supplementary video.

Simulation of smoke and advection of scattering albedos: Figure 14 shows a vertically upwards axial impulse applied to a *vase shaped* smoke density field. Since the impulse is applied for a short duration, the density field dissolves towards the end of the simulation. For the first time, we also show advection of the optical properties of the medium (scattering albedos), in addition to the physical properties (densities and velocities), resulting in completely new colors and appearances as the medium evolves under external forces.

Single Scattering based rendering of participating media: We demonstrate the visual effects of both relighting the medium under the single scattering model, and varying the viewpoint and scattering albedos, as the medium evolves under user defined forces (supplementary video). We also show interesting effects of shadowgrams that are cast by the medium on a background plane (Figures 13 and 14).

3D Visual effects resulting from volumetric scattering in non-homogenous and dynamic participating media: In the examples of Figure 15 and Figure 1, we add non-homogenous mist to scenes with large depth variation. Notice how distant objects appear brighter due to the airlight [Kos24] effect. Reproducing such effects accurately, particularly for non-homogenous media, is critical for achieving photo-realism while rendering 3D scenes. Finally, in Figure 16, we add non-homogenous and dynamic fog to a clear day fly-through of Swiss Alps.

Number of Legendre Coefficients

Spatial Grid Size	64	125	216
20^3	100X	25X	8X
30^3	1300X	325X	105X
40^3	7500X	1875X	600X

Figure 11: *Typical computational speed-ups for 3D simulation and rendering in Legendre domain as compared to the spatial domain.*

Computational Speed-ups: Due to the compact representations of fields in the Legendre domain, we can achieve computational speed-ups of one to three orders of magnitude, depending on the number of Legendre coefficients (Figures 10 and 11). The comparison is made with our implementation of the Stable Fluids [Sta99] algorithm in the spatial domain. However, our technique places a restriction on the size of the simulation time-step; adding higher frequencies will require a progressively smaller time-step owing to stability considerations given by the CFL condition [FM97]. On the other hand, the Stable Fluids technique can support arbitrarily large time-steps. All our implementation was done in MATLAB on a 3.2GHz P-4 PC with 2 GB of RAM.

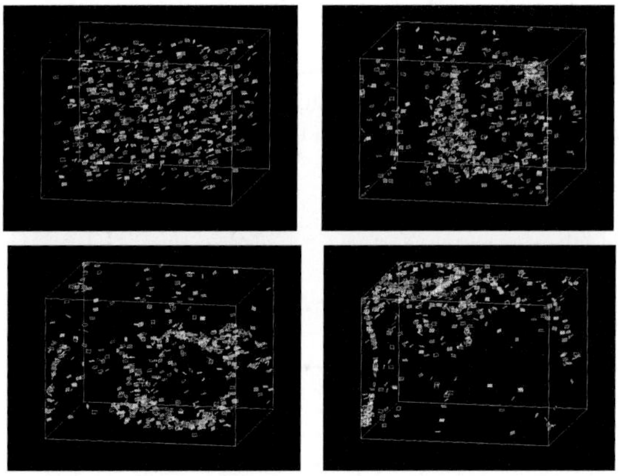

Figure 12: ***Legendre domain Simulation result:*** *500 pieces of confetti being carried by a turbulent wind field simulated using 216 Legendre coefficients.*

8. Discussion of Limitations and Future Work

Our goal in this paper is fast rendering of non-homogenous and dynamic participating media. We achieve this by representing the spatio-temporally varying intensity (rendering), as well as density and velocity (simulation) fields in a reduced analytic Legendre space. This results in a single scattering based rendering technique for smooth non-homogenous and dynamic media, a significant improvement over similar techniques which make the severely limiting assumption of homogenous medium densities [SRNN05]. We believe this is the first work that provides a unified framework for both modeling and rendering in an analytic reduced space, and hope this can help bridge the gap between model reduction in fluids and pre-computed radiance transfer in rendering. However, the speed and analytic nature of the technique come at the cost of its limited ability to handle high frequency fluid phenomena. Indeed, using only a global Legendre Polynomials basis offers limited local control and allows only for the **box-boundary conditions**, making it difficult to account for complex effects like local vorticities, turbulence and objects inside the medium. Also, being a **global sub-space method**, it offers low flexibility on the domain boundaries.

These limitations can be addressed by augmenting the global Legendre polynomials basis, which capture the majority of the energy of the fluid flow, with a local-support basis such as Haar-Wavelets or spatial voxels, thus accounting for the spatially sparse 'residual energy'. This is similar in spirit to adding local high frequency turbulence, or vorticities [FSJ01] to counter the dampening caused by the Stable Fluids semi-Lagrangian technique. Also, high frequency details in a particular dimension can be captured by keeping the full spatial representation and using Legendre expansion in the remainnig directions. Using such *hybrid bases* can provide the desired local control in addition to computational speedups, and in our opinion, forms a very promising direction for future research. Since we also make assumptions of single scattering, orthographic viewing and distant lighting, extending our system to perspective viewer and more general, nearfield lighting is another research direction worth exploring.

Acknowledgements

We would like to thank Adam Bargteil for helpful technical discussions and the anonymous reviewers for their comments and suggestions. This work was supported in parts by an NSF CAREER award #IIS-0643628, an NSF grant #CCF-0541307 and an ONR award #N00014-05-1-0188.

References

[Cha60] CHANDRASEKHAR S.: *Radiative Transfer*. Oxford Univ. Press, 1960. 1, 2, 3

[CM90] CHORIN A., MARSDEN J.: *A Mathematical Introduction to Fluid Mechanics*. Springer-Verlag. Texts in Applied Mathematics 4. Second Edition., New York, 1990. 1, 2, 3

[DYN02] DOBASHI Y., YAMAMOTO T., NISHITA T.: Interactive rendering of atmospheric scattering effects using graphics hardware. In *Graphics Hardware Workshop* (2002), pp. 99–109. 2

[EP90] EBERT D. S., PARENT R. E.: Rendering and animation of gaseous phenomena by combining fast volume and scanline a-buffer techniques. In *Proceedings of SIGGRAPH* (1990). 1

[FF01] FOSTER N., FEDKIW R.: Practical animation of liquids. In *Proceedings of SIGGRAPH* (2001), pp. 23–30. 1

[FM96] FOSTER N., METAXAS D.: Realistic animation of liquids. *Graph. Models Image Process. 58*, 5 (1996), 471–483. 1

[FM97] FOSTER N., METAXAS D.: Modeling the motion of a hot, turbulent gas. In *Proceedings of SIGGRAPH* (1997). 1, 7

[FSJ01] FEDKIW R., STAM J., JENSEN H. W.: Visual simulation of smoke. In *Proceedings of SIGGRAPH* (2001), pp. 15–22. 1, 8

[GN07] GUPTA M., NARASIMHAN S.: *Legendre polynomials Triple Product Integral and lower-degree approximation of polynomials using Chebyshev polynomials*. Tech. Rep. CMU-RI-TR-07-22, Carnegie Mellon University, May 2007. 2, 4

[HED05] HAWKINS T., EINARSSON P., DEBEVEC P.: Acquisition of time-varying participating media. *ACM Trans. Graph. 24*, 3 (2005), 812–815. 2

[HL01] HARRIS M., LASTRA A.: Real-time cloud rendering. In *Eurographics* (2001), pp. 76–84. 2

[Jen01] JENSEN H. W.: *Realistic image synthesis using photon mapping*. A. K. Peters, Ltd., Natick, MA, USA, 2001. 1

[JMLH01] JENSEN H. W., MARSCHNER S. R., LEVOY M., HANRAHAN P.: A practical model for subsurface light transport. In *Proceedings of SIGGRAPH* (2001), pp. 511–518. 2

[KH84] KAJIYA J. T., HERZEN B. P. V.: Ray tracing volume densities. *SIGGRAPH Comput. Graph. 18*, 3 (1984), 165–174. 1

[Kos24] KOSCHMIEDER H.: Theorie der horizontalen sichtweite. beitr. In *Phys. Freien Atm.* (1924), pp. 171–181. 7

[LBC94] LANGUENOU E., BOUATOUCH K., CHELLE M.: Global illumination in presence of participation media with general properties. In *Fifth Eurographics Workshop on Rendering* (1994). 1

[Max86] MAX N. L.: Atmospheric illumination and shadows. In *Proceedings of SIGGRAPH* (1986), pp. 117–124. 2

[Max94] MAX N. L.: Efficient light propagation for multiple anisotropic volume scattering. In *Fifth Eurographics Workshop on Rendering* (1994), pp. 87–104. 1

[NFJ02] NGUYEN D. Q., FEDKIW R., JENSEN H. W.: Physically based modeling and animation of fire. In *Proceedings of SIGGRAPH* (2002), pp. 721–728. 1

[NGD*06] NARASIMHAN S. G., GUPTA M., DONNER C., RAMAMOORTHI R., NAYAR S. K., JENSEN H. W.: Acquiring scattering properties of participating media by dilution. *ACM Trans. Graph. 25*, 3 (2006), 1003–1012. 2

[NN03] NARASIMHAN S. G., NAYAR S. K.: Shedding light on the weather. In *Proceedings of the IEEE Computer Society Conference on Computer Vision and Pattern Recognition* (June 2003), vol. 1, pp. 665 – 672. 2

[NRH04] NG R., RAMAMOORTHI R., HANRAHAN P.: Triple product wavelet integrals for all-frequency relighting. *ACM Trans. Graph. 23*, 3 (2004), 477–487. 2

[PM93] PATTANAIK S., MUDUR S.: Computation of global illumination in a participating medium by monte carlo simulation. *Journal of Vis. and Computer Animation 4*, 3 (1993), 133–152. 1

[REK*04] RILEY K., EBERT D., KRAUS M., TESSENDORF J., HANSEN C.: Efficient rendering of atmospheric phenomena. In *EuroGraphics Symposium on Rendering* (2004). 2

[RT87] RUSHMEIER H. E., TORRANCE K. E.: The zonal method for calculating light intensities in the presence of a participating medium. In *Proceedings of SIGGRAPH* (1987), pp. 293–302. 1

[Sak90] SAKAS G.: Fast rendering of arbitrary distributed volume densities. In *Eurographics* (1990), pp. 519–530. 1

[SRF05] SELLE A., RASMUSSEN N., FEDKIW R.: A vortex particle method for smoke, water and explosions. *ACM Trans. Graph. 24*, 3 (2005), 910–914. 1

[SRNN05] SUN B., RAMAMOORTHI R., NARASIMHAN S. G., NAYAR S. K.: A practical analytic single scattering model for real time rendering. *ACM Trans. Graph. 24*, 3 (2005). 2, 7

[Sta99] STAM J.: Stable fluids. In *Proceedings of SIGGRAPH* (1999), pp. 121–128. 1, 2, 3, 5, 7

[Sta01] STAM J.: A simple fluid solver based on the fft. *J. Graph. Tools 6*, 2 (2001), 43–52. 1

[TLP06] TREUILLE A., LEWIS A., POPOVIC Z.: Model reduction for real-time fluids. *ACM Trans. Graph. 25*, 3 (2006). 1, 5

[TMPS03] TREUILLE A., MCNAMARA A., POPOVIC Z., STAM J.: Keyframe control of smoke simulations. *ACM Trans. Graph. 22*, 3 (2003), 716–723. 1

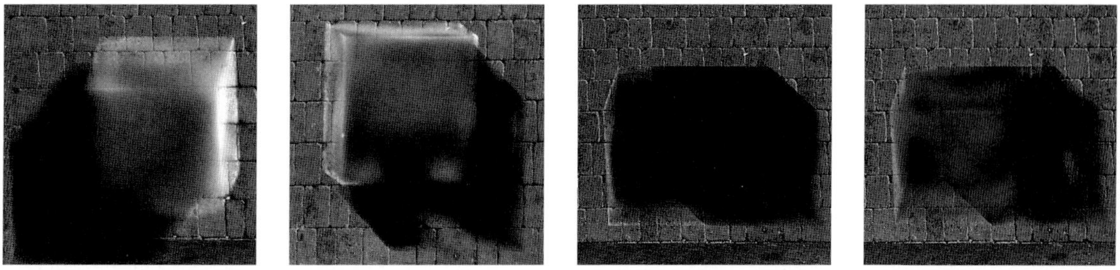

Light Source and View Point Variation Variation in Scattering Properties

Figure 13: ***3D Legendre domain Rendering:*** *Here we consider a* smoke-cube *illuminated by distant light source(s). The image is formed at an orthographic viewer observing the scene. Since the whole of our pipe-line is in the reduced Legendre domain, the user can control the view-point, lighting and scattering albedo interactively. Notice the varying shadow-gram patterns on the wall as the smoke evolves. The smoke and the shadow become darker as we decrease the albedo. Colored smoke and shadows can be created by varying the scattering properties differently across the color channels. This example required* 64 *coefficients for density and velocity, and* 216 *coefficients for intensity fields.*

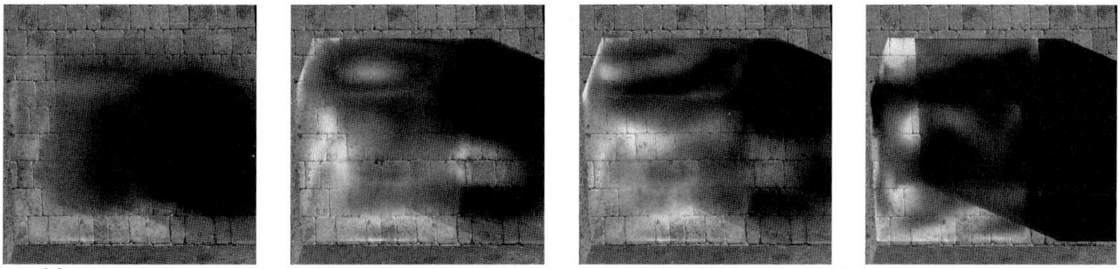

Figure 14: ***3D Legendre domain simulation and advection of optical properties:*** *3D Simulation results for a vertically upwards axial impulse applied to a* vase shaped *smoke density field.. Also, we advect the optical properties of the media (scattering albedos) along with the densities and velocities to create the effect of mixing of different media. This example required* 216 *Legendre coefficients for density and velocity fields (simulation) and* 512 *coefficients for intensity fields (rendering).*

Clear Weather Homogenous mist Non-homogenous mist Attenuation

Figure 15: ***Rendering of Non-homogenous participating media:*** *Our technique can be used to render non-homogenous media as well under the single scattering model efficiently. Here we add mist to a clear weather scene (Images courtesy Google Earth). Non-homogenous density distributions, for example the high mist density over the lake provides for more realism as compared to homogenous mist. Also, notice how distant objects appear brighter due to the air-light effect, whereas distant objects appear darker in the attenuation-only image.*

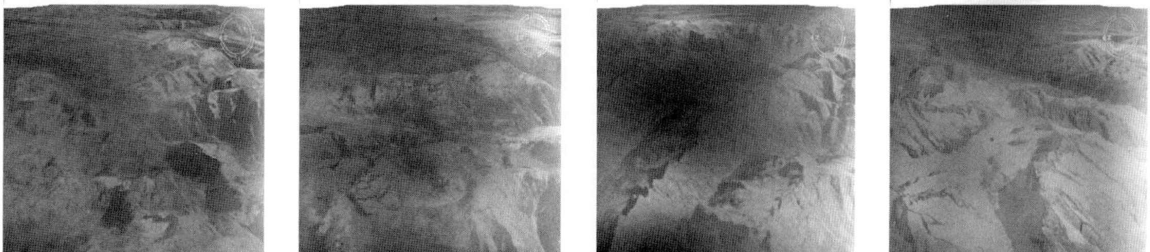

Figure 16: *Snapshots from a fly-through of Swiss Alps with Non-homogenous and dynamic fog added (Images courtesy Google Earth). Images have been tone-mapped to high-lite the non-homogeneity of the medium. Complete video is included with the supplemental material.*

Eurographics/ ACM SIGGRAPH Symposium on Computer Animation (2007)
D. Metaxas and J. Popovic (Editors)

A Simple Boiling Module

Theodore Kim[1] and Mark Carlson[2]

[1]IBM TJ Watson Research Center
[2]Walt Disney Animation Studios

Abstract

Recent efforts to visually capture the phenomena of boiling have proposed monolithic approaches that extend the basic techniques underlying existing fluid solvers. In this work, we show that if we instead treat boiling as a separate computational module to be loosely coupled to an existing solver, a very easy to implement, highly efficient algorithm can be designed that produces excellent visual results, even on coarse (64^3) grids. The algorithm is also highly SIMD-amenable, allowing the boiling computation to be farmed out to a GPU or Playstation 3 Cell processor. Our algorithm takes less than 100 lines of commented, readable C++, and can be integrated into an existing particle level set fluid solver with virtually no modifications. A serial implementation consumes between 3-5% of the overall running time, and a preliminary SIMD implementation shows that a 64^3 simulation runs at 130 FPS, making the computational cost of the module totally negligible.

Categories and Subject Descriptors (according to ACM CCS): I.3.3 [Computer Graphics]:

1. Introduction

Fluid simulation has found applications in visual effects in part because working with large amounts of real fluid can often be expensive and dangerous. In the case of a boiling fluid, these prohibitive factors are especially true. However, the physical process of boiling still creates intricate, visually desirable phenomena, so recent efforts in visual simulation have attempted to capture this phenomenon computationally.

Recent work [LSSF06, MUM*06, ZYP06, KLL*07] proposes extensions to the particle level set (PLS) method that are geared towards capturing this phenomena. We instead propose a modular approach, where the features specific to boiling are handled in a separate simulation, and then loosely coupled to an existing particle level set solver. This approach has several advantages, including simple implementation and high efficiency. In our experience, the module adds between than 3-5% to the overall running time. The algorithm is also highly SIMD-amenable, allowing the boiling computation to be farmed out to a GPU or Playstation 3 Cell processor. Since this computation would take place in parallel, the computational cost of our module would become totally negligible. In the case of a fully on-GPU level set fluid solver [CTL07], adding boiling also becomes straightforward. A working C++ implementation is available in the supplemental materials.

The modular design decouples bubble dynamics from water surface dynamics from both a visual and computational perspective. This makes it possible to tune the 'look' of the bubbles and the surface turbulence separately, and also allows the two features to be run at *different resolutions*, with

(a) With boiling module (b) Without boiling module

Figure 1: *Boiling water poured on a heating element. With the boiling module, the water jumps and pops as it hits the hot plate. A bubble automatically forms near the faucet, breaking up the (in this case) undesirable smoothness of the flow. The boiling consumed less than 5% of the running time on a 64^3 grid.*

Symposium on Computer Animation 2007, San Diego, CA, August 03-04, 2007.
© 2007 ACM 978-1-59593-624-4/07/0008 $5.00

decoupled timesteps depending on which the user deems to be the more visually relevant to their application. The module is also fluid solver agnostic, so while we use particle level set here, it could in principle be added to a Lattice Boltzmann Method [TKPR06] or Smoothed Particle Hydrodynamics [MSKG05] solver as well.

We develop a model that extends the Yanagita model of boiling [Yan92]. The Yanagita model captures the major phenomenological features of boiling using a surprisingly small number of terms. However, it notably lacks interaction with a water free boundary, and has no treatment of surface tension. The lack of surface tension results in the formation of visually disturbing 'pancake' bubbles, an artifact that must be eliminated to make the model visually viable. We propose methods for adding both of these features into the model while maintaining its overall simplicity.

2. Previous Work

Inspired by seminal works [FM96, Sta99, FF01], there has been a recent explosion in visual simulation of fluids. Many excellent works have been published, but for the sake of brevity, we will only focus on those that deal with boiling and bubble dynamics here. The interested reader is referred to the previous works sections of other recent work [KFCO06, ETK*07, LSSF06, KCC*06] for a more general overview.

Several different approaches have been applied to the problem of bubble dynamics. Roman [Rom01] stated the problem as one of a spring-mass system that handled surface tension and film elasticity. Kück et al. [KVG02] proposed a similar approach for bubble clusters, and proposed a rendering method for handling the thin film effects of conjoined bubbles. Hong and Kim [HK03] described a volume of fluid (VOF) method of handling the somewhat different case of bubbles rising in water. In a departure from the usual Eulerian methods, Müller et al. [MSKG05] proposed a particle-based method of simulating similar phenomena.

Bubbles coupled with an evolving free surface was handled by Greenwood and House [GH04] by using the particles in the particle level set method to detect when bubbles would plausibly form in the simulation. Hong and Kim [HK05] proposed a ghost fluid method [FAMO99] for handling the discontinuous pressure associated with bubble surfaces. Losasso et al. [LSSF06] extended the method to compute the ghost values on the fly for multiple fluid regions. Mihalef et al. [MUM*06] described a boiling simulation that departed from the usual particle level set in favor of a coupled level set / volume of fluid method in order to better capture surface tension effects. Zheng et al. [ZYP06] proposed a regional level set method to handle thin films, and described an unconditionally stable method of handling surface tension. Kim et al. [KLL*07] proposed a volume preserving extension.

Finally, we note that Harris et al. [HCSL02] have previously observed the SIMD-amenability of the boiling model we extend in this paper. They provide an excellent overview of the model, as well as extensive GPU implementation details.

3. The Yanagita Boiling Model

In this section, we give an overview of the Yanagita model for boiling [Yan92]. In its original form, the model is almost suitable for visual simulation, save for three significant drawbacks that we will address in the next section. The main strength of the Yanagita model is that it only needs to apply a handful of simple operators to a single heat field. No explicit tracking of pressure, phase, viscosity, or the air/water interface is performed, and yet the major visual features of boiling are captured.

We track a heat field T over a 2D regular grid. Extension to 3D is straightforward and left as an exercise to the reader. We denote the grid coordinates of T using a subscript thus: $T_{x,y}$. The current timestep t is denoted with a superscript: $T^t_{x,y}$. A single timestep of the Yanagita model involves two substeps, which we will denote $T^*_{x,y}$ and $T^{**}_{x,y}$.

First, we account for heat diffusion using the usual 5 point Laplacian:

$$T^*_{x,y} = T^t_{x,y} + \frac{\varepsilon}{4}(T^t_{x-1,y} + T^t_{x+1,y} + T^t_{x,y-1} + T^t_{x,y+1} - 4T^t_{x,y}). \tag{1}$$

The symbol ε is a diffusion constant. Next, we account for buoyancy forces in the vertical direction, which we choose to be the y direction:

$$T^{**}_{x,y} = T^*_{x,y}(1 - \frac{\gamma}{2}(\rho(T^*_{x,y+1}) - \rho(T^*_{x,y-1})). \tag{2}$$

The symbol σ is a buoyancy constant that defines the speed of the rising bubble, and ρ is a temperature-to-phase conversion function defined thus:

$$\rho(T) = \tanh(\alpha(T - T_c)). \tag{3}$$

We note that Yanagita actually refers to this quantity as 'density' but we believe it more appropriately referred to as phase since it can take on negative values. The symbol α is a smearing constant that defines how sharply to resolve the phase, and T_c is the boiling temperature of water. Finally, we must account for the latent heat released by water as it converts to steam, and the heat absorbed by steam converting back to water. Yanagita offers a somewhat unconventional treatment of this, which is perhaps best stated in two steps. First, the equation itself:

$$\begin{aligned} T^{t+1}_{x,y} = T^{**}_{x,y} &+ \eta(\text{\# neighbors converted to steam}) \\ &- \eta(\text{\# neighbors converted to water}). \end{aligned} \tag{4}$$

The symbol η is a latent heat constant. A cell converts from water to steam if its temperature crosses the boiling temperature T_c. A given cell $T_{x,y}$ converts to steam if the following is true: $(T^t_{x,y} < T_c \wedge T^{**}_{x,y} > T_c)$. Conversely, a cell converts from steam to water if the opposite is true: $(T^t_{x,y} > T_c \wedge T^{**}_{x,y} < T_c)$. Each grid cell evaluates these terms for all of its neighbors and substitutes the totals into Eqn. 4.

Since we assume that bubbles rise in the y direction, the bottom boundary is set to a fixed temperature T_{bottom} slightly less than T_c. The top boundary is set to a cooler T_{top}. For simplicity, the left and right boundaries are set to be periodic. Suitable settings for all the constants are provided in the supplemental materials.

4. An Extended Yanagita Model

There are several drawbacks to the Yanagita model that must be addressed. First, the discretization is not quite consistent, so the model is not convergent. Second, since there is no treatment of surface tension, the bubbles tend to be flat, and merge too aggressively to form 'pancake' bubbles (Figure 2). Third, the fluid is assumed to be in a box, with no treatment for an upper free boundary. We propose methods for addressing all of these drawbacks in this section.

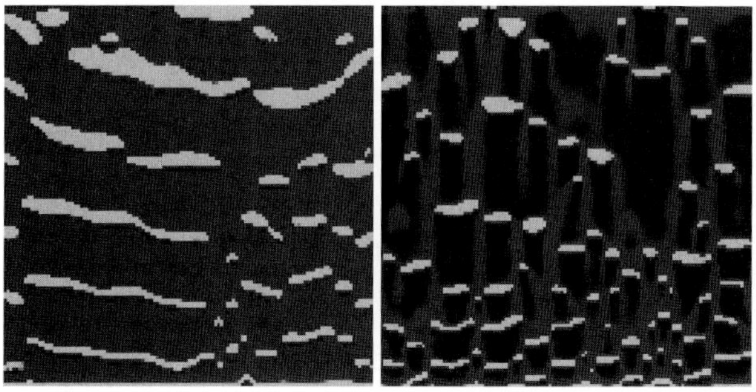

(a) Without surface tension (b) With surface tension

Figure 2: *Heat visualization of a 2D boiling simulation. Bubbles rise from the bottom towards the top.* ***Left:*** *The Yanagita model does not include surface tension, so the bubbles merge too aggressively into 'pancakes'* ***Right:*** *Our new model adds surface tension, eliminating the pancakes.*

4.1. Convergence

In its current form, the Yanagita model is not *convergent*. Usually convergence is used to describe the rate at which successive refinements to a simulation grid will approach the true solution of the underlying PDE. Yanagita did not propose an underlying PDE that corresponded to his discretization, so we adopt a looser meaning of convergence here. The Yanagita model is not convergent in the sense that doubling the resolution of the simulation does not produce a more refined version of the same simulation.

This is relevant to graphics, since users expect increased resolution to translate to refined results, not entirely different results. In order to see why the scheme is not convergent, we first posit that the model is a discretization of the following PDE:

$$\frac{\partial T}{\partial t} = \varepsilon \nabla^2 T - \gamma T \frac{\partial \rho}{\partial y} + sign\left(\frac{\partial T}{\partial t}\right) \eta \delta(T). \quad (5)$$

First, we observe that standard graphics techniques [Sta99] can be applied to stabilize the first two terms of the right hand side. Backward Euler can be applied to the diffusion term, and $\sigma T \frac{\partial \rho}{\partial y}$ is an advection term to which semi-Lagrangian techniques can be applied. Second, we observe that Yanagita's Forward Euler discretizations for both of these terms are clearly convergent, so the problem must lie in the final term.

In the last term, $\delta(T)$ is a delta function centered at T_c. This models latent heat by injecting η heat into the system when $T = T_c$. The *sign* function flips the sign of η depending on whether the latent heat of vaporization or fusion applies. While Eqn. 4 reflects the intuition behind this term, the discretization is not consistent.

In Eqn. 4, the latent heat is released directly to the cell neighbors, while from a physical standpoint, heat would be released by the current cell, and then distributed to the neighbors by diffusion. Eqn. 4 ruins the convergence of the overall scheme because in addition to modeling latent heat, it applies an infinitely fast diffusion process to the cell neighbors. A consistent discretization would instead be:

$$\begin{aligned} T^{t+1}_{x,y} = T^{**}_{x,y} &+ \eta(T^t_{x,y} < T_c \wedge T^{**}_{x,y} > T_c) \\ &- \eta(T^t_{x,y} > T_c \wedge T^{**}_{x,y} < T_c). \end{aligned} \quad (6)$$

Using this discretization, higher resolution grids display the expected behavior of producing refined versions of coarser simulations. The model is now convergent.

4.2. Surface Tension

4.2.1. Formulation

The bubbles in the Yanagita model tend to form 'pancakes', because the model does not include any treatment of surface tension. In a level set simulation, the usual method of addressing surface tension is to add forces of the form $F_{st} = -\sigma\kappa(\phi)\delta(\phi)\vec{n}$ to the velocity field of a Navier-Stokes simulation, where σ is a surface tension constant, $\kappa(\phi)$ is the local curvature of the signed distance field ϕ, $\delta(\phi)$ is a delta function that is non-zero at the interface, and $\vec{n}$ is the interface normal.

However, we do not explicitly construct a velocity field in our simulation. While such a field could easily be constructed by caching the $\gamma T \frac{\partial \rho}{\partial t}$ term, we instead propose an approach that preserves the simplicity of the Yanagita model.

We posit that by introducing an extra curvature-dependant term into Eqn. 5,

$$\frac{\partial T}{\partial t} = \varepsilon \nabla^2 T - \gamma T \frac{\partial \rho}{\partial y} + sign\left(\frac{\partial T}{\partial t}\right) \eta \delta(T) - \sigma\kappa(\rho)\delta(\rho), \quad (7)$$

we can model surface tension. The term is almost identical to the usual surface tension force, but the $\vec{n}$ term has been dropped.

Intuitively, this is equivalent to F_{st}. The physical reasoning behind surface tension is that the liquid interfaces prefer planar configurations ($\kappa = 0$). Bumps and divots in the interface, respectively the $\kappa > 0$ and $\kappa < 0$ cases, are smoothed away because they are deviations from an ideal plane. The usual F_{st} term uses the $\vec{n}$ vector to induce velocities that smooth the deviates away. Our alternate term instead smoothes these deviations away directly.

4.2.2. Computation

This formulation of surface tension introduces the need to compute the curvature of the phase field, $\kappa(\rho)$. In the level set method, curvature is usually derived directly from the signed distance field: $\kappa = \nabla \cdot \frac{\nabla\phi}{|\nabla\phi|}$. We could in principle take a similar approach, but constructing a signed distance field would again be at odds with the simplicity of our overall approach.

Instead, we use a normal differencing method [IJ85, HJ87]. Instead of computing stencils over a signed distance field, we explicitly compute surface normals and then take their differences. For each grid point p, we first compute its phase $\rho(T_p)$. For each neighbor n, we also compute its phase $\rho(T_n)$. If there is a sign flip between these phases, p is on the interface. We then compute the normals at T_p and T_n, $\vec{n}_p$ and $\vec{n}_n$. The curvature $\kappa_{p,n}$ is then computed thus:

$$\text{if}(|p-n| \leq |(\vec{n}_p + p) - (\vec{n}_p + n)|) \quad \kappa_{p,n} = \frac{|\vec{n}_p - \vec{n}_n|}{|p-n|}$$
$$\text{else}, \quad \kappa_{p,n} = -\frac{|\vec{n}_p - \vec{n}_n|}{|p-n|}.$$

The conditional detects if the two normals are pointing towards or away from each other, and assigns the sign accordingly. If we compute $\kappa_{p,n}$ over all the neighbors and take the average, then we have effectively computed the mean curvature at p. The final result is then multiplied by σ and added to Eqn. 6 to complete the integration.

4.3. Coupling to Particle Level Set

4.3.1. Surface Dynamics and Advection

The final component to our boiling simulator is a method of coupling the results of the boiling simulation to an existing particle level set (PLS) solver. While we could attempt a complex coupling, we have found a simple approach to be effective. For any cell that is on a bubble interface, and is less than 5 cells away from the level set interface, inject a force of unit magnitude in the direction of the bubble normal. If the existing PLS simulator already has a public accessor function to its signed distance field, and provides a force application function, no modifications to the simulator are necessary. In order to ensure that bubbles are eventually absorbed into the air when they reach the interface, we set $T_{x,y} = T_{top}$ in all cells where the signed distance field is greater than some small value.

This coupling qualitatively captures two visual features. Physically, when a rising bubble approaches the water/air interface, it deforms the surface outwards. When the bubble pops, it creates a void that the water rushes in to fill, creating a splash. In our simulation, a bubble initially approaches the level set interface and pushes it outwards, as expected. When the bubble passes through the interface, the bottom hemisphere injects forces that push downwards, creating a void and splash.

We would also like the bubble to move along with the flow, so we perform advection on the heat field as well. If the fluid solver already has a generic advection function, this can be accomplished by simply calling the function on T. Otherwise, a semi-Lagrangian scheme for T can easily be implemented. The full equation we are now solving becomes

$$\frac{\partial T}{\partial t} = \varepsilon\nabla^2 T - \gamma T\frac{\partial\rho}{\partial y} + sign\left(\frac{\partial T}{\partial t}\right)\eta\delta(T) - \sigma\kappa(\rho)\delta(\rho) - (\mathbf{u}\cdot\nabla)T, \tag{8}$$

where $\mathbf{u}$ is the velocity field of the fluid solver.

4.4. Fluid Solver Advection

We use BFECC [KLLR05] for the advection of the fluid velocity field. In [DL03], Dupont and Liu take special care when the velocity field is not smooth, and only use BFECC for the velocity on grid points if the velocity is smooth in *all* dimensions. Their experiments were done in 2D on a regular grid, and we found that such a harsh test in 3D on the staggered grid we use was not necessary. However, when we did nothing, the surface would tear apart too easily. We found that locally turning off BFECC on a dimension by dimension basis worked well. For example, on a cell face in the x-dimension we use BFECC if

$$|u_{i+1,j,k} - 2u_{i,j,k} + u_{i-1,j,k}| \leq$$
$$\min(|u_{i+1,j,k} - u_{i,j,k}|, |u_{i,j,k} - u_{i-1,j,k}|).$$

4.5. SIMD Parallelization

One of the strengths of this modular design is that it allows the PLS and boiling modules to execute in parallel, at different resolutions, and with decoupled timesteps. The simplicity of the boiling algorithm makes it highly SIMD-izable, allowing complementary hardware such GPUs or the Synergistic Processing Elements (SPEs) of a Playstation 3 Cell processor to execute the module concurrently with the PLS simulation.

[HCSL02] already showed that the original Yanagita

model can be ported efficiently to the GPU. Our modifications should be equally easy to port, since we have actually simplified equation 4, and the surface tension stage only requires a local grid neighborhood.

To demonstrate the ease of porting to other SIMD platforms, we instead implemented our extended Yanagita model on the SIMD units of the Cell processor. The serial version was run an Intel 3.4 Ghz Xeon, and ran at 5.35 frames per second on a 64^3 grid. We ran our Cell implementation on a IBM QS20 Cell blade, which has a total of 16 SPEs. We split the computational workload evenly between the available SPEs and measured the frames per second (FPS) as more SPEs were added. The scaling can be seen in Figure 3. We show the ideal scaling based on the FPS of one SPE for comparison. The scaling degrades as more SPEs are added because the memory bus becomes saturated, so the SPEs become starved for data.

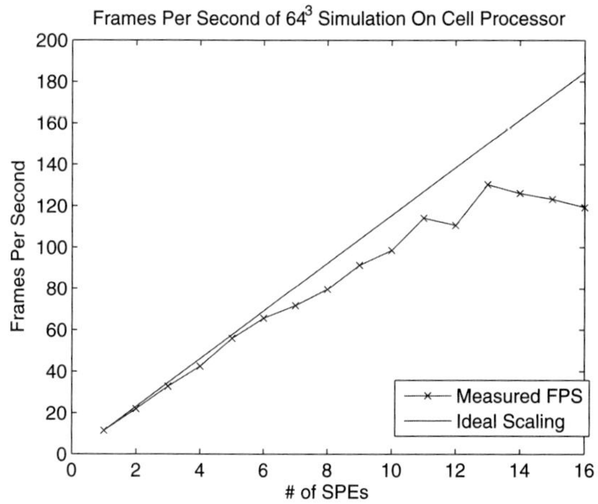

Figure 3: *Performance of a 64^3 boiling simulation on a Cell Processor. With 6 SPEs (the number in a PS3), we achieve 65.59 FPS. The performance peaks at 13 SPEs at 130.22 FPS. The scaling degrades as more SPEs are added because the memory bus becomes saturated. The CPU version runs at 5.35 FPS on a 3.4 Ghz Xeon, so the Cell offers a 24.3x speedup.*

We note that the implementation is only a prototype, and with more aggressive optimizations, even larger speedups can almost certainly be attained. Our serial implementation only consumed 3-5% of the running time to begin with, so parallel SIMD execution would make our module totally computationally negligible.

4.6. Rendering

Because of the loose coupling between the level set and boiling simulators, there is no guarantee that a bubble surface will not cause a visually disturbing interpenetration with the level set surface. However, most renderers provide a method of sidestepping this problem. The artifacts can be eliminated if a ray is not allowed to intersect a bubble surface without first passing through an odd number of level set surfaces. This information can be tracked via ray labels, a common feature of most renderers. All RenderMan compliant renderers, for example, have this feature. We used pbrt [PH04], a renderer that did not initially support ray labels, but we easily extended it to support this functionality. The light probes used in the renderings are all from Paul Debevec's High Resolution Light Probes gallery [Deb06], which he has generously made available online.

5. Results

In Figure 4 we show water boiling in a beaker, and show the viability of our coupling to PLS. The boiling module consumed less than 3% of the simulation time. In Figures 1, 5, and 6 we pour hot water onto a heating element. For comparison, we show the results of a PLS simulation without our module. As the water hits the plate, the water jumps and pops using our module, as opposed to the unconvincing smoothness of straight PLS. Additionally, a bubble forms near the faucet using our module, producing an unsteady flow that lends the results additional realism. The module consumed less than 5% of the simulation time.

Finally, to show the detail that our extended model can achieve on a relatively coarse (64^3) grid, we drop 4 hot spheres into a tank of water in Figure 7. No free surface was included in this simulation in order to draw focus to the bubbles. Note how the bubbles trail convincingly behind the spheres and continues to boil off in sheets. Without the overhead of PLS, a serial implementation runs at 2.73 frames per second; sufficient for interactive previewing of results. A full 3D SIMD implementation would almost certainly run at a real-time 30 frames per second. All the timings were performed on a 64^3 grid using a 3.4 Ghz Xeon.

6. Conclusions and Future Work

Notably, our method does not handle the case where the bubbles are advected along the free surface of the water. For this, a more sophisticated coupling to a monolithic approach [ZYP06, LSSF06, KLL*07] would be necessary. Far from the interface however, our computationally cheaper method would still be the preferred method of tracking boiling dynamics. Our module is also solver agnostic, so it should be straightforward to plug it into Lattice Boltzmann Method (LBM) or Smoothed Particle Hydrodynamics (SPH) simulations as well. However, we leave the specifics of this to future work. Finally, given the efficiency achievable with modular design for this visual feature, it begs the question of what other features can be simulated in a similar manner.

References

[CTL07] Crane K., Tariq S., Llamas I.: *GPU Gems 3*. 2007, ch. Real-time Simulation and Rendering of 3D Fluids.

[Deb06] Debevec P.: *High-Resolution Light*

Probe Image Gallery. 2006. available at http://gl.ict.usc.edu/Data/HighResProbes/.

[DL03] DUPONT T. F., LIU Y.: Back and forth error compensation and correction methods for removing errors induced by uneven gradients of the level set function. *Journal of Computational Physics* (2003), 311–324.

[ETK*07] ELCOTT S., TONG Y., KANSO E., SCHRÖDER P., DESBRUN M.: Stable, circulation-preserving, simplicial fluids. *ACM Transactions on Graphics* (2007).

[FAMO99] FEDKIW R., ASLAM T., MERRIMAN B., OSHER S.: A non-oscillatory eulerian approach to interfaces in multimaterial flows (the ghost fluid method). *Journal of Computational Physics* (1999).

[FF01] FOSTER N., FEDKIW R.: Practical animation of liquids. *Proc. of SIGGRAPH* (2001), pp. 15–22.

[FM96] FOSTER N., METAXAS D.: Realistic animation of liquids. *Proceedings Graphics Interface* (1996), 204–212.

[GH04] GREENWOOD S., HOUSE D.: Better with bubbles: Enhancing the visual realism of simulated fluids. *Proc. of ACM SIGGRAPH Symposium on Computer Animation* (2004).

[HCSL02] HARRIS M., COOMBE G., SCHEUERMANN T., LASTRA A.: Physically-based visual simulation on graphics hardware. In *Proc. 2002 SIGGRAPH / Eurographics Workshop on Graphics Hardware* (2002).

[HJ87] HOFFMAN R., JAIN A.: Segmentation and classification of range images. *IEEE Transactions on Pattern Analysis and Machine Intelligence (PAMI)* (1987).

[HK03] HONG J., KIM C.: Animation of bubbles in liquid. *Proceedings of Eurographics 2003 22*, 3 (2003).

[HK05] HONG J., KIM C.: Discontinuous fluids. *Proc. of SIGGRAPH* (2005).

[IJ85] ITTNER D., JAIN A.: 3d surface discrimination from local curvature measures. *Proceedings of Computer Vision and Pattern Recognition (CVPR)* (1985).

[KCC*06] KIM J., CHA D., CHANG B., KOO B., IHM I.: Practical animation of turbulent splashing water. In *ACM SIGGRAPH/Eurographics Symposium on Computer Animation* (2006).

[KFCO06] KLINGNER B. M., FELDMAN B. E., CHENTANEZ N., O'BRIEN J. F.: Fluid animation with dynamic meshes. In *Proceedings of ACM SIGGRAPH 2006* (Aug. 2006).

[KLL*07] KIM B., LIU Y., LLAMAS I., JIAO X., ROSSIGNAC J.: Simulation of bubbles in foam by volume control. In *Proceedings of ACM SIGGRAPH* (2007).

[KLLR05] KIM B., LIU Y., LLAMAS I., ROSSIGNAC J.: Flowfixer: Using bfecc for fluid simulation. In *Eurographics Workshop on Natural Phenomena* (2005).

[KVG02] KÜCK H., VOGELCSANG C., GREINER G.: Simulation and rendering of liquid foams. *Proceedings of Graphics Interface* (2002).

[LSSF06] LOSASSO F., SHINAR T., SELLE A., FEDKIW R.: Multiple interacting liquids. *Proc. of SIGGRAPH* (2006).

[MSKG05] MÜLLER M., SOLENTHALER B., KEISER R., GROSS M.: Particle-based fluid-fluid interaction. *Proc. of ACM SIGGRAPH Symposium on Computer Animation* (2005).

[MUM*06] MIHALEF V., UNLUSU B., METAXAS D., SUSSMAN M., HUSSAINI M.: Physics-based boiling simulation. *Proc. of ACM SIGGRAPH Symposium on Computer Animation* (2006).

[PH04] PHARR M., HUMPHREYS G.: *Physically Based Rendering: From Theory To Implementation*. Morgan Kaufmann Publishers, 2004.

[Rom01] ROMAN D.: Animation of soap bubble dynamics, cluster formation and collision. *Proceedings of Eurographics* (2001).

[Sta99] STAM J.: Stable fluids. *Proc. of SIGGRAPH* (1999), 121–128.

[TKPR06] THUEREY N., KEISER R., PAULY M., RUEDE U.: Detail-preserving fluid control. In *SCA '06: Proceedings of the 2006 ACM SIGGRAPH/Eurographics symposium on Computer animation* (2006).

[Yan92] YANAGITA T.: Phenomenology of boiling: A coupled map lattice model. *Chaos 2* (1992).

[ZYP06] ZHENG W., YONG J., PAUL J.: Simulation of bubbles. *Proc. of ACM SIGGRAPH Symposium on Computer Animation* (2006).

Figure 4: *Water boiling in a beaker. The splashing shows the viability of our coupling to particle level set.*

Figure 5: *Boiling water is poured on a hot plate. The water pops and jumps as it initially hits.* *(continues on next page)*

Figure 6: *As the box fills, the boiling breaks up the smooth water surface (see attached video)*

Figure 7: *Four spheres dropped into water. This* 64^3 *simulation runs at 5.35 FPS (CPU) and 130 FPS (Cell).*

Eurographics/ ACM SIGGRAPH Symposium on Computer Animation (2007)
D. Metaxas and J. Popovic (Editors)

Flipping with Physics: Motion Editing for Acrobatics

Anna Majkowska and Petros Faloutsos

University of California, Los Angeles

Abstract

Complex acrobatic stunts, such as double or triple flips, can be performed only by highly skilled athletes. On the other hand, simpler tricks, such as single-flip jumps, are relatively easy to master. We present a method for creating complex, multi-flip ballistic motions from simple, single-flip jumps. Our approach also allows an animator to interact with the system by introducing modifications to a ballistic phase of a motion. Our method automatically adjusts motion trajectories, to assure physical validity of the motion after the modifications. The presented technique is efficient and produces physically valid results without resorting to computationally expensive optimization. To validate our approach we present the results of a study of user sensitivity to errors in angular momentum and take-off angle. The study shows that small changes of these parameters introduced by our method are not perceptible to a viewer.

Categories and Subject Descriptors (according to ACM CCS): I.3.7 [Computing Methodologies]: Computer GraphicsThree-Dimensional Graphics and Realism: Animation

1. Introduction

In 1905 Francis Gouleau of France achieved the first double backward somersault from a stand [V-F59]. Many modern acrobats have tried to repeat this feat and failed. On the other hand, a single backward somersault from a stand can be performed by even a beginning gymnast. In this paper we propose a technique that can recreate Gouleau's performance in a fraction of a second using a motion capture recording of a single backward flip (see Fig 4a). Our algorithm takes as an input a simple ballistic motion, such as a single somersault, and creates a more complex animation, such as a multiple somersault, by rotating and repeating fragments of motion, while maintaining physically-valid momentum profiles.

Our algorithm automatically applies simple motion editing operations to create superhuman motions or acrobatic stunts that would be difficult to record in a motion capture studio. Because it does not employ computationally expensive algorithms, our work can produce complex acrobatic motions in milliseconds after a pre-processing step of a few seconds. Therefore, our technique can be used to create multiple animated characters performing acrobatic motions in real-time. At the same time, by exploiting characteristics of ballistic motions, the proposed technique creates animations that satisfy the laws of linear and angular momentum conservation. Our algorithm can be applied to a variety of ballistic motions but is especially useful in motions with a significant amount of rotation during the flight phase, such as acrobatic flips and twists, skiing and snowboarding tricks, or martial arts moves.

Reusing motion capture data allows us to preserve the unique style of a performer more easily than with other methods, such as physical simulation or optimization techniques. While new optimization methods, for example the one proposed by Liu et al [LHP05] based on joint preferences, go a long way towards explaining biological aspects of motion style, there are still elements of style that cannot be easily characterized and are best captured by data-driven techniques. For example, acrobatic coach and human motion researcher Hartley D. Price compliments Russian athletes on their skills: "Russians were not content to merely perform the skill. They went one step farther and added a breathtaking flavor to the performance, leaving no doubt where the complete understanding was." [V-F59]. While highly skilled athletes can add certain flavors to their performance, beginners often make small errors which also make their motion unique and difficult to create with generative methods.

The challenge of reusing motion capture data lies in the fact that complex, multi-flip jumps differ considerably from

Symposium on Computer Animation 2007, San Diego, CA, August 03-04, 2007.
© 2007 ACM 978-1-59593-624-4/07/0008 $5.00

their simple, single-flip counterparts. While the take-off and landing poses do not change significantly with a varying number of flips (see Section 5.3), in the multi-flip motions the rotation is faster and the flight phase longer. This results in the need for a more rapid build-up of momentum in the take-off phase and its quicker release during landing. To account for these differences, our technique adjusts motion timing and modifies flight trajectories. The trajectory modifications can introduce small changes in the take-off angle, while numerical approximations during the retiming step can cause small errors in angular momentum computations. However, we found that these changes are not perceptible in the motions generated with our method. To validate this result, we conducted a user study. We knew from previous research that most humans have difficulties noticing even significant discrepancies in angular momentum when observing motions of simple objects [ODGK03]. We were curious to find out if these results could be extended to human motion as well. Our results show that motions with small changes in angular momentum (both smooth and abrupt) as well as changes in take-off angle were not perceived as less correct than the original motions. In fact, surprisingly, sometimes they were perceived as more correct. The detailed results of our study are presented in Section 7.

In this paper we present the following contributions:

- an efficient technique for creating complex acrobatic motions with multiple flips from simple jumps, while obeying momentum conservation laws,
- a method for estimating mass distribution from motion capture data, which increases the accuracy of momentum computation,
- results of a study on human perception which measures sensitivity to errors in angular momentum and take-off angle.

2. Related Work

The generation of physically valid acrobatic motions has been a subject of intensive study. Control mechanisms have been successfully applied to create a wide range of of acrobatic motions. These include: somersaults [HWBO95, LvdPF00], high dives [WH00], kip stunts [FvdPT01, LvdPF00] as well as ski and snowboard tricks [ZvdP05]. While control algorithms create physically valid (though sometimes robotic-looking) motions, creation of controllers is still a difficult and time-consuming process.

Optimization techniques with physics constraints have become a prominent method for generating realistic highly dynamic motions [WK88, LGC94, PA00, LP02, FP03, SHP04]. The complexity and running time of the optimization methods have been significantly reduced in recent works: [LP02, FP03, SHP04]. However, even with these improvements, generating motions with optimization techniques typically takes a few minutes, which limits their applicability in real-time and interactive applications. Many works apply spacetime optimization to the problem of editing ballistic motions [WK88, SHP04, RGBC96, SP05, ALP06, MPS06]. These techniques allow animators to synthesize new, physically valid motions while preserving realism and style of motion. While many of these techniques could be applied to the problem of creating complex acrobatic motions, this paper shows that for such motions time-consuming optimization techniques are not necessary. High-effort ballistic motions can be synthesized and edited extremely efficiently using only basic motion editing operations.

The results of our perceptual study contribute to the area of human perception of motion. Reitsma and Pollard [RP03] studied human sensitivity to changes in vertical and horizontal acceleration and modifications of gravity. Safanova and Hodgins [SH05] observed that motion interpolation can cause large fluctuations in angular momentum which are often unnoticed if the resulting changes in angular velocities are small. O'Sullivan et al. [ODGK03] studied perception of angular distortions and velocity changes in post-collision trajectories for simple objects such as spheres, blocks and T-shapes. We contribute to this body of knowledge by measuring human sensitivity to distortions in angular momentum and take-off angle in human acrobatic motions.

Our method for estimating mass distribution is similar to the approach proposed in [BSP02]. In their work, Bhat and colleagues apply optimization to estimate motion and physical parameters of a rigid body in free flight from video, given the body's mass distribution as an input. In contrast, our technique uses 3D motion data to estimate not only motion parameters, but the mass distribution as well.

3. Overview

Our algorithm works in two stages: a pre-processing stage, which needs to be executed only once when a new motion is added to the system, and a run-time jump generation stage (see Figure 1). In the pre-processing stage, we first find a ballistic phase in the input motion. Next, taking advantage of linear momentum conservation, we estimate our character's mass distribution and inertia tensors for each body part. Finally, given the masses and the inertias, we compute the linear and angular momentum in each motion frame.

In the run-time jump generation stage (see Figure 2), we first employ a search algorithm to identify fragments of motion that can be rotated and joined together to create a more complex performance. Next, we retime the resulting motion to maintain continuity of momentum curves. As a last step, our algorithm repositions the character so its center of mass follows physically correct trajectories. We also provide functionality for user motion editing: an animator can, for example, change the position of the legs from tucked to straight, to create a more difficult jump. When legs are straightened, their distance from the center of mass increases and the jump rotation must slow down. Our algorithm can automatically adjust the edited motion to assure physical correctness. Similarly, different jumps can be joined together during the flight and adjusted to ensure correct momentum profiles. We de-

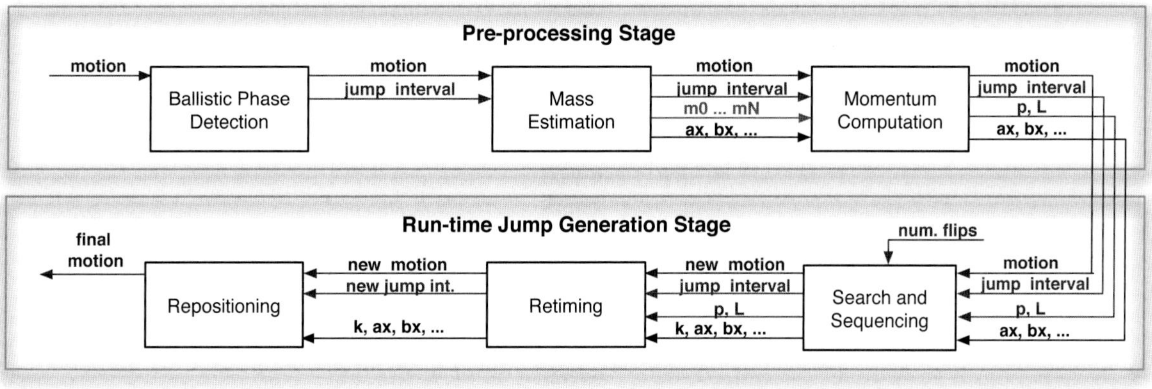

Figure 1: *Schematic diagram of our method's pre-processing stage (top) and the run-time jump generation stage (bottom).*

scribe the preprocessing steps of our algorithm in Section 4 and the run-time jump generation stage in Section 5.

4. Pre-processing Stage

In the pre-processing stage, our algorithm computes motion parameters such as mass distribution, linear and angular momentums, and jump duration (see Figure 1). These parameters need to be computed only once for each motion and can then be used multiple times in the run-time jump generation stage to create various ballistic motions.

4.1. Ballistic Phase Detection

In this step of our algorithm we determine where ballistic phases occur in the input motion. This information is first used to estimate the character's masses, then to run the search algorithm, and finally to create a new motion and retime it correctly. Our jump phase detection algorithm is based on the constraint method proposed by [LP02]. That is, we recognize that during the take-off and landing phases the character's feet or hands remain planted on the ground for a certain amount of time. We don't know the exact position of the ground in our motions (there can be multi-level environments). However, we can assume that intervals where at least one end effector is not moving significantly are good candidates for border frames of the ballistic motion.

Sometimes during the ballistic phase, one of the limbs can remain in the same place for significant time. Therefore, we add an additional condition, based on the pattern of linear momentum build-up and release. Typically, during take-off, linear momentum slightly drops and then suddenly increases. Similarly, during landing, there is first a sudden drop in momentum and then a slight increase. We used the momentum change conditions (first down, then up) together with the constraint method to find the longest ballistic interval in each motion. With this technique we managed to correctly find jump phases in all of our motion clips. Because in this step we do not yet know the character's estimated mass distribution, we use an average mass distribution of a human body (obtained from [DG67]) to compute the linear momentum. In our results this approximation did not affect the accuracy of the output.

4.2. Estimating Mass Distribution

Applying momentum conservation laws to motion capture data is a key element of our approach. The knowledge of a character's mass distribution, though typically not provided with motion capture data, is necessary for the computation of linear and angular momentums. Since we are working with motions with long ballistic phases, we have the advantage of being able to compute the mass distribution from the input motion alone. During a flight phase, the character's center of mass (COM) over time follows a line in the x and z dimensions and a parabola in the y (vertical) dimension due to gravity. Using this property we compute the masses of the body parts which minimize the distance between the character's COM calculated from the motion data and the correct COM trajectory, which is a line in x, z dimensions and a parabola in y.

To achieve this we formulate a simple linear least-squares optimization problem:

$$\min_{\substack{m_1,\ldots,m_n \\ a_x,b_x,a_z,b_z \\ a_y,b_y,c_y}} \left\| \left(\sum_{i=1}^{n} \frac{m_i}{M} pos_i(t) \right) - COM(t) \right\|^2 \quad \text{for } t = 0 \ldots T$$

with additional conditions that the sum of the masses is constant: $\sum_{i=1}^{n} m_i = M$ and that $m_i \geq 0$. In the above equation T is the duration of the flight phase, $pos_i(t)$ is the position of i-th body part at time t obtained from the motion data and $COM(t) = [a_x t + b_x, a_y t^2 + b_y t + c_y, a_z t + b_z]^T$ is the correct COM trajectory. Note that in our optimization we search both for mass distribution and the COM trajectory parameters a_x, b_x, a_y, b_y, c_y, a_z, b_z. We do not use the real-world gravity coefficient in our model because in motion capture data the character's joint lengths are often scaled compared to the real-world values. Using the results of our optimization we can compute the scaling factor as: $s = 2a_y/g$, where g is the gravity coefficient.

The $3(T+1)$ equations constructed from the above formula don't always have a unique solution. To minimize the number of optimized variables, we assume perfect symmetry between right and left limbs. Even with this modification, we found that the optimization still commonly produced solutions unrealistic for human body mass distribution. Although our optimization algorithm allowed us to specify a reasonable mass distribution $m_1^0, \ldots, m_n^0$ (obtained from [DG67]) as a starting point, the results of the optimization still suffered from overfitting. Overfitting occurred because the optimization algorithm attempted to "explain" inherent errors in the motion data. This caused large shifts in mass distribution, which resulted in only small improvements in the optimization results. To alleviate this problem, we added another equation to our problem formulation, which made the optimization algorithm favor solutions close to the initial distribution:

$$\min_{m_i} W \left\| m_i - m_i^0 \right\|^2 \quad \text{for} \quad i = 0 \ldots n$$

where W is a small constant. This formulation removes the overfitting problem as only large improvements in the optimization can sway the results significantly from the initial solution. Given the mass distribution and the skeleton proportions (obtained from mocap), we compute inertia tensors by approximating each body part with an ellipsoid of a constant density, as proposed in [LHP05]. We obtain typical densities of body parts from [DG67].

In our method we take advantage of the regular shape of COM trajectories during the flight phase due to the linear momentum conservation. We also tried to utilize the angular momentum conservation property to increase the number of constraints in the optimization problem. Unfortunately, computed derivatives contained too much noise, due to numerical errors in our motion data, to be useful in our optimization.

Our technique of mass estimation is useful for momentum computations as it reduces the deviation of linear momentum during the flight phase from the physically correct pattern. In our computations the reduction was 30% compared to the momentum values computed with the initial mass distribution. It is difficult to evaluate how well our method estimates the real-world mass distribution of a performer, since we do not know the actual masses of our performer's body parts (hence the need for estimation). However, a video recording of the motion capture session showed that the performer of our motions was tall. Tall males typically exhibit lower weight of limbs and higher weight of the trunk as the percentage of total weight, compared to a person of an average height [CM69]. The results of our optimization showed the same pattern in the estimated masses compared to the average mass distribution.

4.3. Momentum Computation

Given the mass distribution, computing the momentum is straightforward. The linear momentum $\mathbf{p}$ at time t can be computed as:

$$\mathbf{p}(t) = \sum_{i=1}^{N} m_i \mathbf{v}_i(t),$$

where m_i is the mass of i-th body part and $\mathbf{v}_i(t)$ is its velocity at time t. Angular momentum $\mathbf{L}$ for a system of rigid bodies can be computed as follows:

$$\mathbf{L}(t) = \sum_{i=1}^{N} \mathbf{R}_i(t)\mathbf{I}_i\mathbf{R}_i(t)^T + m_i(pos_i(t) - COM(t)) \times \mathbf{v}_i(t),$$

where $\mathbf{R}_i(t)$ is the rotation matrix for i-th body part in world coordinates, $pos_i(t)$ and $\mathbf{I}_i$ are the i-th body position and inertia matrix respectively, and $COM(t)$ is the character's center of mass at time t.

5. Run-Time Jump Generation Stage

In the run-time jump generation stage, our algorithm creates a complex multi-flip motion from an easier, single-flip jump using basic motion editing operations (see Figures 1 and 2). These operations and their impact on momentum are described in Section 5.1. The jump generation stage starts with a search, which finds and glues together fragments of motion to produce a longer sequence (Section 5.2). Next, the resulting motion is retimed to assure continuity of angular and linear momentums during take-off, flight, and landing phases (Section 5.3). Finally, the motion frames are repositioned to maintain correct COM trajectories in the ballistic phase (Section 5.4). Additionally, we provide functionality for user motion editing: an animator can modify character's poses during flight, and our algorithm then automatically adjusts the new motion to assure conservation of linear and angular momentums (Section 5.5).

5.1. Editing Operations and Their Impact on Momentum

In our algorithm, we employ three basic motion editing operations: repositioning, rotation and retiming by interpolation. In this section we analyze their impact on linear and angular momentums. We also show how these operations are used in our method to maintain the momentum conservation property during flight and assure continuity of momentum during take-off and landing.

Repositioning of the center of mass. Changes in the COM trajectory do not affect the character's angular momentum, which is computed with respect to the character's COM. We use this property in the last step of the run-time jump generation stage, when adjusting the COM trajectory to the longer flight phase.

Rotation around the angular momentum vector. Rotating a fragment of a ballistic motion around the axis defined by a

Figure 2: *Outline of the run-time jump generation stage of our algorithm. a) Input motion. b) First, the search algorithm finds a self-looping sequence B; root positions are ignored. c) Next, the sequence B is rotated around the angular momentum vector and repeated to obtain a double-flip. d) The resulting sequence is retimed to assure continuity of linear momentum during take-off and landing. e) In the final step, the character's COM is repositioned to follow correct trajectories under gravity.*

character's center of mass and the angular momentum vector will not affect the angular momentum within this motion fragment. Intuitively, angular momentum is a vector that remains constant in the given reference frame during the jump duration. If we rotate our reference frame around the axis defined by that vector and the COM, then all points on that axis will remain unchanged. More formally, angular momentum of a system around its COM can be defined as

$$\mathbf{L} = \sum_i m_i(\mathbf{r}_i \times \mathbf{v}_i) = \sum_i m_i(|\mathbf{r}_i||\mathbf{v}_i|\sin\theta_i\,\hat{\mathbf{n}}),$$

where m_i is the mass of a particle, $\mathbf{r}_i$ is the distance from the COM, $\mathbf{v}_i$ is the particle's velocity w.r.t. the COM, θ_i is the angle between $\mathbf{r}_i$ and $\mathbf{v}_i$, and $\hat{\mathbf{n}}$ is a unit vector perpendicular to $\mathbf{r}_i$ and $\mathbf{v}_i$. If we rotate the reference frame by some angle ϕ around the axis defined by the center of mass and the angular momentum vector the new angular momentum will be:

$$\begin{aligned}\mathbf{L}^{new} &= \sum_i m_i(|\mathbf{r}_i||\mathbf{v}_i|\sin\theta_i R(\phi)\hat{\mathbf{n}}) = R(\phi)\sum_i m_i(\mathbf{r}_i \times \mathbf{v}_i)\\ &= R(\phi)\cdot\mathbf{L} = \mathbf{L},\end{aligned}$$

because the axis of rotation is parallel to $\mathbf{L}$. We use this property in the sequencing step to increase the number of flips, while conserving angular momentum.

Motion retiming. Uniform retiming scales the linear and angular momentum linearly. A motion fragment with linear momentum $\mathbf{p}$ and angular momentum $\mathbf{L}$ retimed by a factor of n has momentums equal to $n\mathbf{p}$ and $n\mathbf{L}$. This is due to scaling of velocities during retiming:

$$\mathbf{v}_i^{new} = \frac{\mathrm{d}(r_i(nt))}{\mathrm{d}t} = \frac{\mathrm{d}(r_i(nt))}{\mathrm{d}(nt)}\frac{\mathrm{d}(nt)}{\mathrm{d}t} = n\mathbf{v}_i.$$

While this is true in the continuous case, applying this rule to motion capture data, where derivatives are computed numerically, causes errors. However, for $\frac{1}{2} \leq n \leq 2$, these errors in our motions are within 20% range and according to our study (Section 7) are not perceptible in the resulting motion. We use retiming to assure continuity of linear momentum during take-off and landing and to adjust momentums to motion changes made by an animator.

5.2. Search and Sequencing

The search algorithm attempts to find a fragment of ballistic motion, which can be repeated in the new sequence after rotation around the axis defined by the angular momentum vector $\mathbf{L}$ and the character's COM. In other words, it finds a sequence of frames $\mathbf{F_B} = f_m, f_{m+1}, \dots f_n$ and an angle ϕ, such that

$$R(f_m, \mathbf{L}, \phi) \approx f_n.$$

That is, frame f_m after rotation by ϕ around $\mathbf{L}$ is similar to f_n (we describe the similarity measure in Appendix A). We call the jump fragment $\mathbf{F_B}$ with this property a *self-looping sequence*. $\mathbf{F_B}$ is then progressively rotated and repeated multiple times to create a longer jump with more flips. For example, in Figure 2c the self-looping motion is repeated four times to create a double flip.

In other words, we use the initial motion sequence:

$$\mathbf{F} = [\mathbf{F_S},\ \mathbf{F_B},\ \mathbf{F_E}],$$

where $\mathbf{F_S} = f_1, \dots, f_{m-1}$ and $\mathbf{F_E} = f_{n+1}, \dots, f_{end}$, to create a new, longer sequence with more flips:

$$\mathbf{F}^{new} = [\mathbf{F_S},\ \mathbf{F_B},\ \mathbf{R_B}(\phi),\ \mathbf{R_B}(2\phi),\ \dots,\ \mathbf{R_B}(r\phi)],$$

where $\mathbf{R_B}(\phi)$ is the sequence $\mathbf{F_B}$ with all frames rotated by ϕ around $\mathbf{L}$. The parameter r denotes the number of repetitions of $\mathbf{F_B}$ in $\mathbf{F}^{new}$ and depends on the number of flips we want to obtain in the new motion. For example, in Figure 2 we construct a double flip, which involves the root rotation of 4π around $\mathbf{L}$. The rotation around $\mathbf{L}$ in $\mathbf{F_R}$ is $\phi \approx \frac{3\pi}{4}$ and rotations in $\mathbf{F_S}$ and $\mathbf{F_E}$ are close to $\frac{\pi}{2}$. Therefore we need to repeat the self-looping sequence four times. We compute r as $r = \lceil (2\pi \cdot \text{num\_flips} - \phi_S - \phi_E)/\phi \rceil$, where ϕ_S and ϕ_E are amounts of rotation around $\mathbf{L}$ in $\mathbf{F_S}$ and $\mathbf{F_E}$ respectively. Note that since we are rotating the self-looping sequence around its angular momentum vector, the angular momentum in $[\mathbf{F_B}, \mathbf{R_B}(\phi), \ldots, \mathbf{R_B}(r\phi)]$ will remain approximately constant when computed with respect to the COM.

The newly created sequence $\mathbf{F}^{new}$ contains a take-off phase and multiple rotations. Next, we perform a second search, to add the landing phase to $\mathbf{F}^{new}$. We find two frames $f \in [\mathbf{R_B}((r-1)\phi), \mathbf{R_B}(r\phi)]$ and $g \in \mathbf{F_E}$, such that $f \approx g$. The resulting sequence $\mathbf{F}^*$ will consist of $\mathbf{F_S}$, $[\mathbf{F_B}, \mathbf{R_B}(\phi), \ldots, \mathbf{R_B}(r\phi)]$ truncated to end at frame f, and $\mathbf{F_E}$, truncated to start at frame g. As a last step, to eliminate small discontinuities in transitions between motion fragments, we smooth joint angles by slerping over small windows of frames.

If the ballistic motion does not contain self-looping sequences (there are no similar frames f_m and f_n), our algorithm can still be applied. The transition between any two chosen frames of ballistic motion can be created by an animator or automatically by smoothing. Although during the transition the angular momentum will not be constant, we can adjust it by applying non-uniform motion retiming as described in Section 5.5. The same algorithm can be easily modified to join two different motions during the jump phase. As long as the two motions have the same angular momentum direction, the magnitudes can be adjusted by retiming.

5.3. Retiming

In the search step we constructed a complex motion with multiple rotations and a longer ballistic phase compared to the original motion. Differences in the flight phase duration and COM trajectories affect the momentum build-up during take-off and its release during landing. One of challenges here is to adapt the take-off and landing phases to reflect the changes in the flight phase and to assure continuity of linear and angular momentums.

For low-effort jumps, changes in momentum build-up are associated with significant changes in take-off poses. For example, a character might bend the knees more to achieve a longer or higher jump. Surprisingly perhaps, the same is not true for the high-effort ballistic motions, such as acrobatic flips or long jumps, where the athletes are operating close to the limit of their physical abilities. Research suggests that the approach speed is the main factor affecting the performance in high-effort motions, while take-off poses vary little with changing performance levels. Bridgett and Linthorne [BL06] evaluate long jumps performed by professional athletes with maximum effort and conclude that

Joint	Single flip (deg) a	Double flip (deg) b	Ang. vel. (deg/sec) ω	Time (sec) $\lvert a-b \rvert/\omega$
ankle	125	125	821	0.00
knee	174	168	278	0.02
hip	175	202	715	0.02
trunk	78	99	931	0.02
shoulder	154	153	157	0.01

Table 1: *Comparison of take-off poses for a single and double backflip. Differences between the joint angles in the two take-offs are negligible; with given angular velocities, it takes less than a duration of one frame to transition between them. Data adapted from [KY03] and [KY04].*

variations in run up speed account for 96% of the variation in jump distance. Seyfarth, Blickhan and van Leeuwen [SBvL00] report that the optimal jumping technique defined by leg angles is not affected by changes in approach speed or muscle design. In acrobatic motion research, King and Yeadon [KY03, KY04] present data on joint angles during take-off for a single and double backflip from a round-off (see Table 1). Differences in joint angles are negligible: it would take less than 0.02 second to transition between these two take-offs, due to high angular velocities of body parts.

While there is less scientific data on the landing phase, our conversations with gymnastic coaches [Bel, Nel] reveal that a perfectly executed double flip will have a very similar landing to a correctly carried out single flip, but will be performed faster.

Since in high-effort motions take-off and landing do not vary significantly with performance level, we can achieve natural-looking motions and eliminate momentum discontinuities by simply retiming motion fragments so that they are performed faster. We retime the take-off, flight and landing phases by the same factor k. Retiming will scale the angular momentum by a factor of k in all phases of motion. During flight, linear momentum will be adjusted by repositioning of the character's COM, but retiming also increases linear momentum k times during take-off and landing, and reduces the duration of the ballistic phase by a factor of k. In Appendix B we show that there exists a single scaling factor k^* which assures the continuity of the linear momentum curve. In practice however, small discontinuities in linear momentum are not perceptible to the human eye. Therefore we can adjust k to obtain different jump heights and rotation speeds. In our results we typically chose $k \approx 0.7k^*$, as we found higher jumps with slower rotations to be more aesthetically pleasing.

5.4. Repositioning

In this step we adjust the character's center of mass in each flight frame of the newly constructed motion, so that it follows physically valid trajectories. Computing the COM position along x and z axes is simple, given values a_x, b_x, a_z and b_z computed in the mass estimation step (Section 4.2) and retiming factor k chosen in the retiming step (Section 5.3):

$$\begin{aligned} COM_x^{new}(t) &= k \cdot a_x t + b_x \\ COM_z^{new}(t) &= k \cdot a_z t + b_z \\ t &= 0 \ldots T^{new}, \end{aligned}$$

where T^{new} is the duration of the ballistic phase in the new motion.We also offset the COM trajectory after the jump to maintain the continuity of motion:

$$\begin{aligned} \text{offset}_x &= COM_x^{new}(T^{new}) - COM_x(T) \\ \text{offset}_z &= COM_z^{new}(T^{new}) - COM_z(T). \end{aligned}$$

In the case of the y (vertical) axis, we need to modify the parabolic trajectory by scaling the initial velocity b_y at $t = 0$:

$$COM_y^{new}(t) = a_y t^2 + k \cdot b_y t + c_y \quad \text{for} \quad t = 0 \ldots T^{new}.$$

The change in initial velocity causes a (typically small) change in the take-off angle. However, our study indicates (Section 7) that such small changes are not perceptible.

Using the above formulas, we can also make non-trivial modifications to the character's trajectory by modifying c_y and adjusting the scaling factor k (see Appendix B). For example in Figure 4c we changed the height from which the character takes off. In the original motion the take-off and landing were at the same level.

5.5. User Modifications

Our method allows an animator to modify a motion during the flight phase, for example by changing the leg position from tucked straight. When legs are straightened, their distance from the center of mass increases, which causes an increase in the overall body inertia. Since the momentum must remain constant, the jump rotation must slow down. Our algorithm can automatically adjust the edited motion to assure the conservation of angular momentum. As long as the modifications do not introduce significant changes in the direction of the angular momentum vector $\mathbf{L}$, changes in the magnitude of $\mathbf{L}$ can be eliminated by first retiming the motion and then repositioning the character's COM during the flight phase.

Since momentum in the modified motion changes over time, the retiming factor must change as well. We create a new, retimed frame sequence by computing which frame should be displayed next, given the number of the previous frame in the retimed sequence:

$$\text{next\_frame} = \text{last\_frame} + \frac{1}{ratio(\text{last\_frame})},$$

where $ratio(f) = |\mathbf{L}_{modif}(f)|/|\mathbf{L}(f)|$ is a ratio between the angular momentum magnitude $|\mathbf{L}_{modif}|$ in the modified motion and the angular momentum magnitude $|\mathbf{L}|$ in the original motion at a frame f. For in-between frames, we linearly interpolate the joint angles and compute the angular momentums from the interpolated values. While retiming does not eliminate all angular momentum errors, it reduces them significantly (see Figure 3). Before the retiming, angular momentum error was over 50% and could be detected by most viewers (see Table 2). Our method reduces the error to 20% or less, so that according to our study it is no longer perceptible.

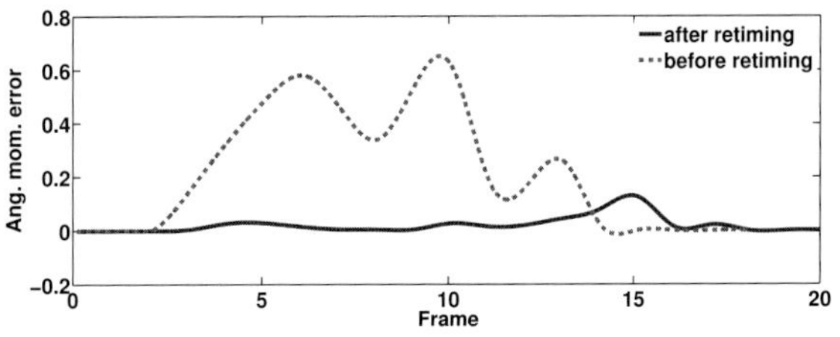

Figure 3: *Errors in the angular momentum in a motion modified by an animator before and after retiming relative to the original motion. Retiming causes significant reduction in the relative error.*

6. Results

We applied our technique to a variety of acrobatic motions from the CMU motion capture database [cmu] and commercial databases. Figure 4a presents a double backward somersault from a stand generated with our technique and the comparison with the original single-flip motion. The generated motion exhibits faster rotation and more rapid take-off and landing compared to the original jump, to accommodate changes in momentum due to the longer ballistic phase. Figure 4b shows the results of a user's editing operations. A tucked forward flip is modified by an animator to become a straight-leg jump. Our system retimes and repositions the motion to adapt to inertia changes. This causes the flight phase to be longer with slower rotation and greater jump height compared to the original motion. Take-off and landing phases are also modified due to the change in length of the flight phase. Figure 4c presents the results of joining together two acrobatic motions, an aerial cartwheel and a forward flip, to create a new stunt. The motions are retimed so that the angular momentums during the flight phase are equal in both of them. This example also shows the capability of our technique to easily change the height from which the character takes off.

Running time. The pre-processing stage of our algorithm took about 3 seconds. The run-time jump generation stage for a two-flip jump took 3.69 ms, a three-flip jump 4.60 ms and a four-flip jump 5.09 ms.

7. Experimental Evaluation

We studied human sensitivity to errors in angular momentum and take-off angle, to find out how the approximations introduced by our method affect viewers' perception of the generated motions.

a)
b)
c)
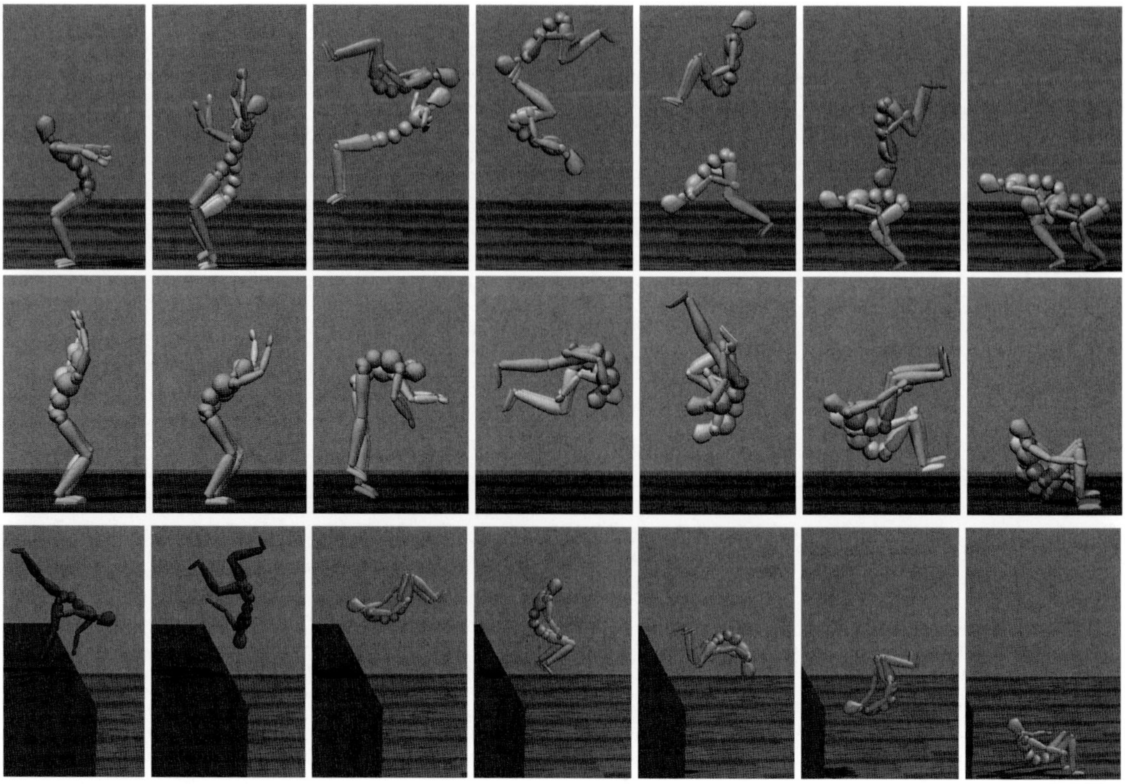

Figure 4: *a) A double backward somersault from a stand generated with our technique (in turquoise) compared with the original single-flip motion (in yellow). b) The results of a user's editing operation compared with the original motion. c) The results of joining together an aerial cartwheel (in red) and a forward flip (in turquoise).*

Participants. The study involved 19 student volunteers (3 women and 15 men) ranging in age from 20 to 25 years (3 participants did not specify their age). None of the volunteers had significant experience in computer animation or gymnastics.

Stimuli. Animations of single-flip forward and backward somersaults were created as a stimuli. All animations were rendered in the same style with the same camera configuration and the same take-off position. Original motion capture clips were used as base motions. Errors in angular momentum were created by the motion retiming during the flight phase. We tested both abrupt changes - sudden introduction of retiming in the middle of the flight phase, and smooth changes in angular momentum - retiming factor growing linearly and achieving maximum value just before landing. Both abrupt and smooth errors ranged from -50% to 50% of the original angular momentum magnitude. The errors didn't change the direction of the angular momentum vector. Errors in take-off angle were introduced by modifying the linear velocity in the flight phase along the direction of the jump and ranged from 0 to 40%.

Procedure. Participants were told that they were about to see a sequence of motions, some of which were physically correct and some of which were not. They were not informed how many of the motions contained errors or what kind of errors were introduced, but they were shown examples of correct motions to give them a reference point. Participants were instructed to mark each of the test motions either as correct or incorrect. The test motions were arranged randomly within each error group and then interleaved to reduce the learning effect. Each motion was shown twice.

Results. Similar to findings reported by [ODGK03] for simple objects, our subjects were not sensitive to even significant changes in angular momentum during ballistic motion. For example, for both smooth and abrupt changes, a 25% increase in angular momentum was imperceptible and as likely to be classified physically valid as the original motion. Surprisingly, motions with smooth decreases in momentum often scored higher than the original motions. This might be caused by humans overestimating the effect of air friction on the motion.

Likewise, our subjects proved not to be sensitive to errors in the take-off angle. A 30% change was perceived as physically valid as often as the original motion. Perhaps even

Ang. mom. modif.	Error level 0%	17 %	25%	37%	50%
smooth incr.	72 (.00)	71 (.05)	72 (.00)		41 (.81)
smooth decr.	72 (.00)	79 (-.22)	78 (-.18)	78 (-.18)	62 (.27)
abrupt incr.	72 (.00)	76 (-.13)	78 (-.18)	48 (.63)	44 (.75)
abrupt decr.	72 (.00)	83 (-.38)	68 (.11)	33 (1.0)	22 (1.4)
Take-off ang. modif.	**Error level 0%**	**10 %**	**20%**	**30%**	**40%**
incr.	63 (.00)	81 (-.53)	50 (.34)	63 (.00)	18 (1.3)

Table 2: *Results of our study: mean ratings (in percent) and sensitivity levels (in parenthesis). Sensitivity less or equal to zero means that participants could not detect errors.*

more surprising is the fact that the higher error didn't necessarily cause increased sensitivity: a 10% change scored significantly higher than the original motion and a 30% change was viewed as correct more often than a 20% change. This shows that most humans have relatively little experience with high-effort ballistic motions and find it difficult to estimate their correctness. The results of the study are summarized in Table 2.

8. Conclusions and Future Work

Our method for creating complex ballistic motions from simpler jumps is efficient because it uses only basic editing operations. Our approach works especially well with high-effort motions, which do not exhibit significant changes in take-off and landing poses with varying levels of effort. For low-energy jumps, it would be interesting to explore the possibilities of using our technique jointly with optimization methods, such as the ones proposed in [SP05] or [LP02], in order to adapt take-off and landing poses to different jump lengths. Another possible extension to this work would be a method which allows an animator to introduce changes to in-flight motion which significantly alter the direction of the angular momentum vector. The property of angular momentum conservation could then be restored by rotating the character appropriately.

Acknowledgments

The work in this paper was partially supported by NSF under contract CCF-0429983. We would like to thank coaches Ron Bell and Marshall Nelson for their assistance in this project and Brian Allen, Sung-Hee Lee, Shawn Singh, Andrew Sorensen and Victor Zordan for their helpful comments and discussion. We would also like to thank Intel Corp., Microsoft Corp., ATI Corp. and AGEIA Corp. for their support through equipment and software grants.

Appendix A: Similarity Measure

In our search algorithm we use a comparison function which computes the distance between two poses while ignoring their positions in space and global rotations around **L**. Our comparison method is similar to previous approaches [LCR*02, KGP02, AF02, ZMCF05]. However, in contrast to the above methods, we first rotate the skeleton around the momentum vector before the comparison to minimize differences in body orientation between compared frames. In other words, given two frames f_1 and f_2, we first compute rotation angle ϕ around **L**, by projecting the angle between root orientations in f_1 and f_2 on a plane perpendicular to **L**. Next, we rotate f_2 by ϕ to remove the differences in global orientations around **L**. Finally, we compute the distance between the two frames as a weighted sum of differences between global orientations, joint angles and angular velocities.

Similarly to [ZMCF05], we assign higher weights to joints close to the trunk, as differences in limb positions can be easily smoothed by blending. We used the same set of weights ($w_{root} = 2$, $w_{trunk} = w_{thigh} = 0.7$, $w_{knee} = 0.5$, $w_{shoulder} = 0.3$, $w_{elbow} = 0.1$) for all of our motions.

Appendix B: Computing Scaling Factor k^*

The retiming process affects the linear momentum in two directions: it increases the momentum during take-off and landing, and also decreases the necessary momentum build-up by reducing the flight duration. Therefore, the take-off velocity is scaled: $\mathbf{v}_0^* = k^*\mathbf{v}_0$, and the duration of the flight is shortened: $T^* = T/k^*$, where $\mathbf{v}_0$ is the take-off velocity along the y axis in the original motion and T is the duration of the flight phase before retiming. Given the parabola equation: $y^*(t) = -\frac{1}{2}gt^2 + \mathbf{v}_0^* t + y_{start}$ and the end condition: $y^*(T^*) = y_{end}$ we solve for the factor k^* which assures the continuity of the linear momentum curve:

$$k^* = \sqrt{\frac{\frac{1}{2}gT}{\mathbf{v}_0 - \frac{\Delta y}{T}}},$$

where g is the gravity coefficient, and $\Delta y = y_{end} - y_{start}$ is the difference in COM heights between take-off and landing.

References

[AF02] ARIKAN O., FORSYTH D. A.: Interactive motion generation from examples. In *SIGGRAPH '02: Proceedings of the 29th annual conference on Computer graphics and interactive techniques* (2002).

[ALP06] ABE Y., LIU C. K., POPOVIĆ Z.: Momentum-based parameterization of dynamic character motion. *Graph. Models 68*, 2 (2006), 194–211.

[Bel] BELL R.:. Personal communication. Gymnastic coach and competition judge, Olympic gymnast.

[BL06] BRIDGETT L., LINTHORNE N.: Changes in long jump take-off technique with increasing run-up speed. *Journal of Sports Sciences 24*, 8 (2006), 889–897.

[BSP02] BHAT K. S., SEITZ S. M., POPOVIC J.: Computing the physical parameters of rigid-body motion from video. In *ECCV (1)* (2002), pp. 551–565.

[CM69] CLAUSER C. E., MCCONVILLE J. T.: *Weight, Volume, and Center of Mass of Segments of the Human Body*. National Technical Information Service, 1969.

[cmu] CMU graphics lab motion capture database. http://mocap.cs.cmu.edu/.

[DG67] DEMPSTER W. T., GAUGHRAN G. R. L.: Properties of body segments based on size and weight. *American Journal of Anatomy 120*, 1 (1967), 33–54.

[FP03] FANG A. C., POLLARD N. S.: Efficient synthesis of physically valid human motion. In *SIGGRAPH '03: ACM SIGGRAPH 2003 Papers* (2003), pp. 417–426.

[FvdPT01] FALOUTSOS P., VAN DE PANNE M., TERZOPOULOS D.: The virtual stuntman: dynamic characters with a repertoire of autonomous motor skills. *Computers and Graphics 25*, 6 (2001), 933–953.

[HWBO95] HODGINS J. K., WOOTEN W. L., BROGAN D. C., O'BRIEN J. F.: Animating human athletics. In *In Proceedings of SIGGRAPH 95* (August 1995), pp. 71 – 78.

[KGP02] KOVAR L., GLEICHER M., PIGHIN F.: Motion graphs. In *SIGGRAPH '02: Proceedings of the 29th annual conference on Computer graphics and interactive techniques* (2002), pp. 473–482.

[KY03] KING M. A., YEADON M. R.: Coping with perturbations to a layout somersault in tumbling. *Journal of Biomechanics 36*, 7 (2003), 921–927.

[KY04] KING M. A., YEADON M. R.: Maximising somersault rotation in tumbling. *Journal of Biomechanics 37*, 4 (2004), 471–477.

[LCR*02] LEE J., CHAI J., REITSMA P. S. A., HODGINS J. K., POLLARD N. S.: Interactive control of avatars animated with human motion data. In *SIGGRAPH '02: Proceedings of the 29th annual conference on Computer graphics and interactive techniques* (2002), pp. 491–500.

[LGC94] LIU Z., GORTLER S. J., COHEN M. F.: Hierarchical spacetime control. In *SIGGRAPH '94: Proceedings of the 21st annual conference on Computer graphics and interactive techniques* (1994), pp. 35–42.

[LHP05] LIU C. K., HERTZMANN A., POPOVIĆ Z.: Learning physics-based motion style with nonlinear inverse optimization. In *SIGGRAPH '05: ACM SIGGRAPH 2005 Papers* (2005), pp. 1071–1081.

[LP02] LIU C. K., POPOVIĆ Z.: Synthesis of complex dynamic character motion from simple animations. In *SIGGRAPH '02: Proceedings of the 29th annual conference on Computer graphics and interactive techniques* (2002), pp. 408–416.

[LvdPF00] LASZLO J., VAN DE PANNE M., FIUME E.: Interactive control for physically-based animation. In *SIGGRAPH '00: Proceedings of the 27th annual conference on Computer graphics and interactive techniques* (2000), pp. 201–208.

[MPS06] MCCANN J., POLLARD N. S., SRINIVASA S.: Physics-based motion retiming. In *SCA '06: Proceedings of the 2006 ACM SIGGRAPH/Eurographics symposium on Computer animation* (2006), pp. 205–214.

[Nel] NELSON M.:. Personal communication. Gymnastic coach, former gymnast (three-time NCAA champion).

[ODGK03] O'SULLIVAN C., DINGLIANA J., GIANG T., KAISER M. K.: Evaluating the visual fidelity of physically based animations. In *SIGGRAPH '03: ACM SIGGRAPH 2003 Papers* (2003), pp. 527–536.

[PA00] PANDY M. G., ANDERSON F. C.: Dynamic simulation of human movement using large-scale models of the body. In *Proc. IEEE Intl. Conference on Robotics and Automation* (2000), pp. 676–681.

[RGBC96] ROSE C., GUENTER B., BODENHEIMER B., COHEN M. F.: Efficient generation of motion transitions using spacetime constraints. In *SIGGRAPH '96: Proceedings of the 23rd annual conference on Computer graphics and interactive techniques* (1996), pp. 147–154.

[RP03] REITSMA P. S. A., POLLARD N. S.: Perceptual metrics for character animation: sensitivity to errors in ballistic motion. In *SIGGRAPH '03: ACM SIGGRAPH 2003 Papers* (2003), pp. 537–542.

[SBvL00] SEYFARTH A., BLICKHAN R., VAN LEEUWEN J. L.: Optimum take-off techniques and muscle design for long jump. *J. Exp. Biol 203* (2000), 741–750.

[SH05] SAFONOVA A., HODGINS J. K.: Analyzing the physical correctness of interpolated human motion. In *SCA '05: Proceedings of the 2005 ACM SIGGRAPH/Eurographics symposium on Computer animation* (2005), pp. 171–180.

[SHP04] SAFONOVA A., HODGINS J. K., POLLARD N. S.: Synthesizing physically realistic human motion in low-dimensional, behavior-specific spaces. In *SIGGRAPH '04: ACM SIGGRAPH 2004 Papers* (2004), pp. 514–521.

[SP05] SULEJMANPASIĆ A., POPOVIĆ J.: Adaptation of performed ballistic motion. *ACM Transactions on Graphics 24*, 1 (2005), 165–179.

[V-F59] V-FIVE ASSOCIATION OF AMERICA: *Gymnastics and tumbling, prepared by Hartley D. Price [and others] for the V-Five Association of America.* Annapolis : United States Naval Institute, 1959.

[WH00] WOOTEN W. L., HODGINS J. K.: Simulating leaping, tumbling, landing, and balancing humans. In *ICRA* (2000), pp. 656–662.

[WK88] WITKIN A., KASS M.: Spacetime constraints. In *SIGGRAPH '88: Proceedings of the 15th annual conference on Computer graphics and interactive techniques* (1988), pp. 159–168.

[ZMCF05] ZORDAN V. B., MAJKOWSKA A., CHIU B., FAST M.: Dynamic response for motion capture animation. In *SIGGRAPH '05: ACM SIGGRAPH 2005 Papers* (2005), pp. 697–701.

[ZvdP05] ZHAO P., VAN DE PANNE M.: User interfaces for interactive control of physics-based 3d characters. In *I3D '05: Proceedings of the 2005 symposium on Interactive 3D graphics and games* (2005), pp. 87–94.

Eurographics/ ACM SIGGRAPH Symposium on Computer Animation (2007)
D. Metaxas and J. Popovic (Editors)

Guided Time Warping for Motion Editing

Eugene Hsu   Marco da Silva   Jovan Popović

Computer Science and Artificial Intelligence Laboratory
Massachusetts Institute of Technology

Abstract

Time warping allows users to modify timing without affecting poses. It has many applications in animation systems for motion editing, such as refining motions to meet new timing constraints or modifying the acting of animated characters. However, time warping typically requires many manual adjustments to achieve the desired results. We present a technique which simplifies this process by allowing time warps to be guided by a provided reference motion. Given few timing constraints, it computes a warp that both satisfies these constraints and maximizes local timing similarities to the reference. The algorithm is fast enough to incorporate into standard animation workflows. We apply the technique to two common tasks: preserving the natural timing of motions under new time constraints and modifying the timing of motions for stylistic effects.

Categories and Subject Descriptors (according to ACM CCS): I.3.7 [Computer Graphics]: Three-Dimensional Graphics and Realism

1. Introduction

A motion that at first appears perfect, whether it is keyframed, captured, or synthesized, will often require further adjustment when it is combined with other elements in a scene. Modern animation systems provide a number of tools that transform motions to meet new requirements. The *time warp* is one such tool that allows users to adjust the timing of animated characters without affecting their poses. Its importance follows from the fact that poses often must remain fixed in later stages of the animation pipeline, since they provide the interface through which artists collaborate. Any significant spatial changes to a character often necessitate equally significant changes to the environment, lighting, or camera placement. Timing is one of the few aspects that can be changed without significantly disrupting workflow.

Typical time warps, however, require significant manual intervention. After describing high-level synchronization or duration requirements using keytimes, current animation tools also require users to adjust a curve to achieve the desired effect. These manual steps are further complicated by the fact that changes to timing, unlike changes to poses, inherently cannot provide instant visual feedback. Manual time warping typically requires alternating between tuning the time-warp curve and reviewing the results. This process is laborious even for the most talented animator.

Our guided time warping algorithm aims to simplify this task. As with traditional techniques, users begin by specifying rough timing constraints using keytimes. Instead of tedious manual refinement, users can select a reference motion that exhibits the desired timing properties. The algorithm then computes a time-warp curve that satisfies the constraints and mimics the timing properties of the reference.

Internally, our technique solves a discrete optimization that balances the goals of preserving the original motion and mimicking the timing of the provided reference. The constraints of the optimization emphasize content preservation to ensure that the results do not circumvent the intent of the user. The objective function uses a local measure of timing similarity that guides the solution towards the reference without requiring registered motions.

We demonstrate the applicability of guided time warping to several common timing tasks. It is often necessary, for instance, to adjust the duration of a motion to meet time constraints, synchronize it with other scene elements, or match external signals. Existing animation systems only offer spline-based time warps which generally require significant tuning to achieve natural results. Here, guided time warping can use the motion as its own reference to preserve its natural timing properties without needing additional adjustments. This is illustrated in Figure 1.

Symposium on Computer Animation 2007, San Diego, CA, August 03-04, 2007.
© 2007 ACM 978-1-59593-624-4/07/0008 $5.00

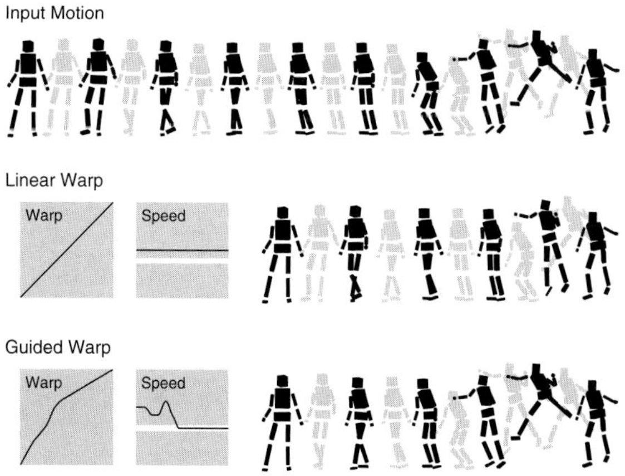

Figure 1: *Time warps are often applied to modify the durations of motions.* TOP: *In the provided input motion, a character turns, pauses, and jumps.* MIDDLE: *To shorten this motion, spline-based warping techniques perform a linear warp that speeds up all parts of the motion equally. This yields an implausibly quick jump.* BOTTOM: *Our technique guides the warp towards a more natural result without requiring additional constraints.*

Careful adjustments of timing can also be used to affect critical qualities of animation. Animators routinely use time warps to change factors such as anticipation, weight, emotion, and style. Such tasks require a great deal of skill and patience. Guided time warping can be used to propagate carefully tuned timing modifications to other portions of an animation. For instance, an animator can edit a single gait cycle and use our technique to replicate its timing modifications to an entire set of walking motions.

We present our technique as a new motion editing tool that addresses one of the most important aspects of animation: timing. The application of time warps can achieve surprisingly flexible edits without disrupting carefully tuned spatial relationships. Guided time warping can help animators achieve these results more easily and has the potential to augment existing motion synthesis techniques.

2. Related Work

The usefulness of the time warp operation is underscored by its almost universal appearance in professional animation tools such as Autodesk Maya, 3D Studio Max, and Avid SOFTIMAGE|XSI. In addition, time warping can be found in many video editing and compositing tools including Adobe After Effects and Apple Final Cut Pro. Within these tools, time warps are used routinely to create remarkable results. However, the methods available in these products are basic variants of the spline-based technique proposed by Witkin and Popović [WP95] and thus require a significant amount of skill and patience.

In the research community, the importance of timing in animation has long been appreciated. Lasseter's seminal work describes how even the slightest timing differences can greatly affect the perception of action and intention [Las87]. More recently, a number of interactive techniques have been proposed to address the timing problem. Performance-driven animation techniques allow the user to act out animations using various interfaces (e.g., [DYP03, TBvdP04]). Terra and Metoyer present a technique that is targeted specifically towards time warping [TM04].

Acting out a motion is a more intuitive way to achieve proper timing, but it still requires time and skill. McCann and colleagues [MPS06] describe a technique to compute physically accurate time warps. Our technique aims for greater generality by relying on data. By doing so, it can capture qualities of animation that may be difficult or impossible to describe using notions of physical consistency or optimality. Furthermore, many animations draw their appeal from their stylized interpretations of realism, which can not be described using physical techniques.

Motion data has been used successfully for many problems in computer animation. Nonparametric methods assemble short segments of motion data to generate results that match user specifications, such as desired paths on the ground or scripts of actions to perform [KGP02, LCR*02, AF02, AFO03]. Of particular relevance to our work are methods that detect repeatable actions [GVdG00] or record timing variations for a particular action [SSSE00]. The timing problem is only partially addressed by these techniques because they leave the original timing intact at all but a predetermined set of jump points.

Parametric methods employ different models of time. Blending and morphing methods (e.g., [BW95, RCB98]) extrapolate timing using linear combinations of time warps. Their flexibility is limited by the availability of multiple registered examples of particular actions. Statistical parameterizations add flexibility, but generally involve complex model estimation procedures for carefully constructed examples [HPP05] or large data sets [BH00, LWS02]. By focusing exclusively on timing, guided time warping avoids the need for explicit registration and computationally expensive learning procedures.

We drew motivation for our work from the speech domain, which has employed time warps to compress speech signals for the purpose of rapid review (e.g., [CWS98]). Such techniques perform nonlinear time warps to preserve comprehensibility, showing that far higher playback rates can be achieved than with linear warps. Unfortunately, they would be difficult to apply directly to our task because of their reliance on specific knowledge about speech understanding. The current understanding of motion in computer graphics does not provide the same guidelines.

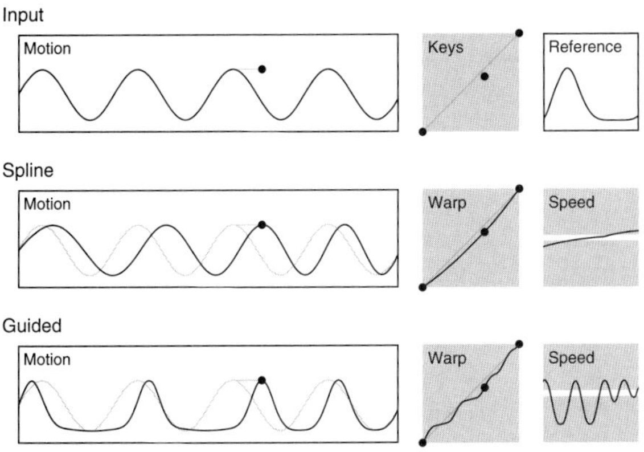

Figure 2: TOP: *A user provides an input motion, a set of keytimes, and a reference motion.* MIDDLE: *A spline-based technique computes a smooth warp that satisfies the constraints but ignores the reference motion.* BOTTOM: *Guided time warping satisfies the constraints and approximates the timing properties of the reference motion. A spline-based technique would require significant manual refinement to achieve the same results.*

3. Method

The guided time warping problem can be stated as follows. A user provides an *input motion*, *keytimes*, and a *reference motion*. Our technique aims to compute a time warp that interpolates the keytimes, yielding an *output motion* that is similar to both the input and the reference, as shown in Figure 2. These two conflicting goals are reconciled by using different definitions of similarity.

For similarity to the input motion, we enforce constraints on the time warp to ensure that it preserves the content of the input motion independently of temporal transformations. This is vital to ensure that our technique does not undermine the intent of the animator. Our constraint formulation is inspired by dynamic time warping. We realize these constraints in a discrete formulation (§3.1).

For similarity to the reference, we define an objective that evaluates the *local* similarity of a candidate output motion to the reference. The input and reference motions will often contain different sequences of actions, precluding the use of standard correspondence techniques. Instead, we pursue local *timing* similarities, in contrast to the global *content* similarities achieved by dynamic time warping. A key intuition in our work is the application of a local score function that captures the timing properties of the reference motion (§3.2).

The objective function, subject to the previously mentioned constraints, is minimized by mapping the problem to a constrained path search. This yields an efficient dynamic programming solution (§3.3). Simple postprocessing operations are then applied to achieve the desired results (§3.4).

3.1. Constraints

Time warps can only reproduce poses from the input motion, but their general application can still yield results that look vastly different. An animator may desire such effects, but producing them automatically without explicit instructions to do so can lead to unexpected and undesirable results. For instance, a general time warp could be used to lengthen a walk motion by repeating gait cycles. In earlier prototyping, this may be acceptable. But when environments are considered, such a change could mean the difference between approaching an obstacle and walking straight through it. Our technique realizes these concerns by enforcing constraints that ensure that the content of the input is preserved.

We borrow our constraint formulation from dynamic time warping [RJ93]. This algorithm is commonly used in computer animation to find global correspondences between motions (e.g., [RCB98]), but it can also be viewed as a time-invariant similarity measure. The latter perspective offers a convenient and proven way to define preservation of input content: the result of the any time warp must be *identical* to the input motion under the allowed transformations. Since time warps do not change poses, this can be performed by simply enforcing the constraints of dynamic time warping within our optimization.

In the context of our problem, the constraints of dynamic time warping can be stated as follows. It requires *complete* time warps, in that they subjectively contain the entirety of the input motion. In other words, large blocks of motion should not be deleted, although it is acceptable to speed through them quickly. It also requires *monotonic* time warps, in that they do not loop or reverse time.

We enforce these constraints in a discrete time compression, which we define as follows. Given a sequence of input frames $\{\mathbf{x}_1, \ldots, \mathbf{x}_n\}$, any time warp can be specified by a subsequence of its frame indices. The identity time warp is defined by the complete subsequence $\{1, \ldots, n\}$. Any subsequence of the identity time warp yields a monotonic time warp, as its indices must be strictly increasing. Any monotonic time warp is also complete if it includes 1 and n, and satisfies the property that no two adjacent elements differ by more than some integer s. The latter constraint forces the speed of the output to not exceed s times the original speed; this prevents the time warp from skipping large blocks of frames. These concepts are illustrated in Figure 3.

Time compressions are only one of many possible time warps. However, we can reduce other desired warps to compression by suitable transformations. Time modifications and expansions are reformulated as compressions by upsampling the input. Backward time warps can be converted to forward time warps by reversing the input. Finally, time warps with multiple keytimes can be split into subproblems of one of the aforementioned cases. As such, we will limit our subsequent discussion to the case of compression.

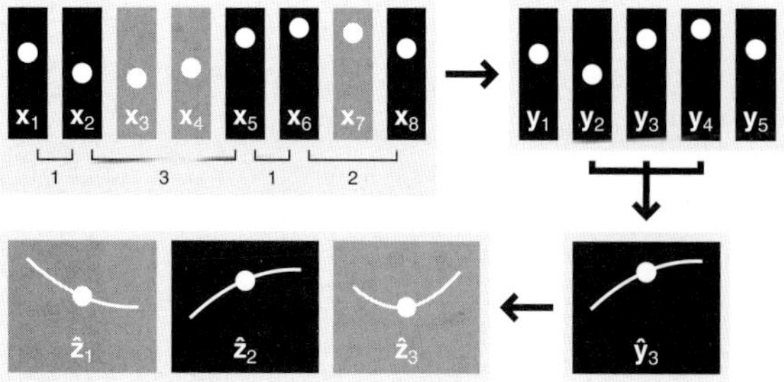

Figure 3: *An input motion is compressed by selecting a subsequence of its frames. Our constraints require that the first and last frames are retained and that no gap between selected frames exceeds a certain amount. The resulting output is scored by computing local velocity and acceleration estimates and comparing them to equivalently computed values in the provided reference.*

3.2. Objective

We aim to compute the quality of a candidate time warp with respect to a provided reference motion. As mentioned before, finding a global correspondence between the input motion and the reference motion is generally neither possible nor desirable.

Our technique uses a measure of local similarity to the reference motion. It stems from the following intuition: a pose is an indication of activity, and that activity is likely to be executed with a certain timing. For example, a sitting pose changes more slowly than a jumping pose. The input motion may already exhibit such canonical timings, but time warps induce changes to the velocity and acceleration of each pose. Certain poses, such as ones from walking, exhibit natural variations in velocity and acceleration. Other poses, such as ones from jumping, exhibit nearly constant acceleration. At a minimum, our objective should capture these variations.

Our solution uses a local score function that computes whether the velocities and accelerations induced by the time warp resemble those that appear in the reference motion. In the context of discrete compression, this can be more formally defined as follows. Suppose a candidate time warp yields an output of $\{\mathbf{y}_1, \ldots, \mathbf{y}_m\}$. Using finite differences, we compute feature vectors for each frame that encode pose, velocity, and acceleration. The local score of a frame is then defined as its distance to the nearest equivalently computed feature vector from the reference motion. The value of the objective function is defined as a sum of local scores:

$$\sum_{i=2}^{m-1} f(\mathbf{y}_{i-1}, \mathbf{y}_i, \mathbf{y}_{i+1}) . \quad (1)$$

To compute meaningful velocities and accelerations, we must first choose a proper representation of poses. We follow the approach of Arikan and Forsyth [AF02] and compute feature vectors for joint *positions* in the torso coordinate system of the character. This transformation allows frames to be represented independently of global position and orientation, thus increasing the generality of the local timing models.

The function $f(\mathbf{y}_{i-1}, \mathbf{y}_i, \mathbf{y}_{i+1})$ is evaluated as follows. We use the adjacent frames to compute finite-difference approximations of $\dot{\mathbf{y}}_i$ and $\ddot{\mathbf{y}}_i$. These terms are assembled into a feature vector $\hat{\mathbf{y}}_i = [\mathbf{y}_i, \dot{\mathbf{y}}_i, \ddot{\mathbf{y}}_i]$. We perform a k-nearest-neighbor query on equivalently computed feature vectors for the reference $\hat{\mathbf{z}}_j$. The value of f is then defined as the average Euclidean distance between the feature vector and its nearest neighbors:

$$f(\mathbf{y}_{i-1}, \mathbf{y}_i, \mathbf{y}_{i+1}) = \frac{1}{k} \sum_{\hat{\mathbf{z}}_j \in N_i} \left\| \hat{\mathbf{y}}_i - \hat{\mathbf{z}}_j \right\| . \quad (2)$$

Here, N_i is the set of k-nearest-neigbhors to $\hat{\mathbf{y}}_i$. For the typical case of smaller reference motions, this can be performed with a linear search. For larger reference motions, we use an approximate nearest-neighbor data structure [AMN*98].

One concern that arises here is that of temporal aliasing. Our technique shares this issue with the dynamic time warping algorithm, as it also employs a discrete signal representation. However, we must take greater precautions, as aliasing artifacts can be exacerbated by the application of finite-difference estimators. We initially experimented with multiscale representations of the input motion to account for variable sampling, but found in the end that prefiltering with a uniform low-pass filter was sufficient.

Our decision to avoid higher-order derivatives was motivated by the need to balance the flexibility and generality of the local timing model. Higher-order derivatives would more accurately reflect the local properties of a given reference frame, but they would also be more sensitive to slight differences and provide less meaningful feature vectors. Ultimately, our choice was made by a combination of intuition and experimentation.

Before arriving at the current solution, we first tried a purely kinematic approach that attempted to preserve velocities and accelerations of the input motion. We found that this strategy works fairly well when the goal is to match the timing of the input motion as much as possible. However, it can not be applied to more interesting cases in which the input and reference differ.

We also considered a number of parametric statistical models for the conditional probabilities of velocity and acceleration given a certain pose. We found that, in practical use, the small sizes of the provided reference motions made it difficult to produce reliable estimates without overfitting. While various forms of priors and dimensionality reduction could be applied, we opted for the nearest-neighbor approach because of its relative simplicity and successful application towards a number of difficult modeling problems in graphics (e.g., [FTP03]) and other domains.

3.3. Optimization

Given the constraints and objective function described in the previous sections, we can define a globally optimal optimization procedure by transforming the problem into a constrained shortest path search. Note that, as with dynamic time warping, we define global optimality with respect to a discrete formulation.

We construct vertices that correspond to *pairs* of input frames that may occur together in the warped output. This allows us to represent the local terms of the objective function as edge weights. Formally, we denote each vertex by an ordered pair of frames $(\mathbf{x}_i, \mathbf{x}_j)$, where $i < j$ and $j - i \leq s$. We define directed edges connecting vertices $(\mathbf{x}_i, \mathbf{x}_j)$ to $(\mathbf{x}_j, \mathbf{x}_k)$ with weight $f(\mathbf{x}_i, \mathbf{x}_j, \mathbf{x}_k)$. This yields a directed acyclic graph with ns vertices and ns^2 edges.

Any path from $(\mathbf{x}_1, \mathbf{x}_i)$ to $(\mathbf{x}_j, \mathbf{x}_n)$ yields a time warp that satisfies the desired constraints, and the total weight of such a path is precisely the value of our objective. For example, suppose the input consists of frames $\{\mathbf{x}_1, \ldots, \mathbf{x}_8\}$. Then a time warp $\{1, 2, 5, 6, 8\}$ corresponds to the path $(\mathbf{x}_1, \mathbf{x}_2) \rightarrow (\mathbf{x}_2, \mathbf{x}_5) \rightarrow (\mathbf{x}_5, \mathbf{x}_6) \rightarrow (\mathbf{x}_6, \mathbf{x}_8)$. The edge weights sum to the value of the objective: $f(\mathbf{x}_1, \mathbf{x}_2, \mathbf{x}_5) + f(\mathbf{x}_2, \mathbf{x}_5, \mathbf{x}_6) + f(\mathbf{x}_5, \mathbf{x}_6, \mathbf{x}_8)$. This example is shown in Figure 3.

A simple shortest path search will yield the optimal time warp of the input if no other constraints are given. Since the graph is directed and acyclic, such a search is linear in the size of the input motion: $O(ns^2)$. However, in most cases, we wish to find the optimal time warp given a target duration m (although we show one example in our results in which this is not the case). This condition can be satisified by constraining the number of edges in the shortest path search [Sai68]. Specifically, we want the shortest path from $(\mathbf{x}_1, \mathbf{x}_i)$ to $(\mathbf{x}_j, \mathbf{x}_n)$ with precisely $(m-2)$ edges.

The algorithm exploits the fact that the shortest path with p edges must contain a shortest path of $(p-1)$ edges. This is formalized by the following recurrence:

$$c_1(\mathbf{x}_i, \mathbf{x}_j) = 0, \quad (3)$$

$$c_p(\mathbf{x}_j, \mathbf{x}_k) = \min_i c_{p-1}(\mathbf{x}_i, \mathbf{x}_j) + f(\mathbf{x}_i, \mathbf{x}_j, \mathbf{x}_k), \quad (4)$$

where $c_p(\mathbf{x}_i, \mathbf{x}_j)$ is the cost of the shortest p-edge path to vertex $(\mathbf{x}_i, \mathbf{x}_j)$. The minimization proceeds by dynamic programming: first compute all 1-edge shortest paths, extend those paths to yield 2-edge shortest paths, and so on. The optimal warp can be recovered by backtracking from the vertex that minimizes $c_{m-2}(\mathbf{x}_j, \mathbf{x}_n)$.

Equivalently, this optimization can be viewed as a *standard* shortest path search on a directed acyclic graph with vertices $\{(\mathbf{x}_i, \mathbf{x}_j)\} \times \{1, \ldots, m-2\}$ and directed edges $(\mathbf{x}_i, \mathbf{x}_j, p) \rightarrow (\mathbf{x}_j, \mathbf{x}_k, p+1)$. Here, the $\times$ operator denotes the Cartesian set product. From this perspective, the time complexity of $O(mns^2)$ directly follows. Note that this is asymptotically identical to dynamic time warping.

So far, we have only described the case when the the first and last frames of the output are required to match the first and last frames of the input, respectively. Intermediate constraints may arise when more than two keytimes are specified. These can be enforced by requiring the path to pass through specific vertices $(\mathbf{x}_i, \mathbf{x}_j)$ at specific points p during the optimization procedure, which essentially restarts the optimization with a modified initialization.

This latter observation can be exploited to achieve a significant, although heuristic, speed improvement to our technique: we first solve a warp on a subsampled version of the input motion (say, at 5 Hz instead of 30 Hz). The low-resolution solution can then be used to set intermediate keytimes for a full-resolution search. In practice, we found that this optimization could significantly improve runtimes with minimal degradation of quality.

3.4. Postprocessing

Our technique produces a discrete approximation to the optimal time warp. A direct playback of the selected frames will often yield jumpy results. We resolve this issue by applying a moving average filter to the warp, which is then used to resample the joint angles of the input motion using quaternion slerp interpolation.

Time warps, regardless of how they are generated, can modify the frequency content of the input. For instance, compressions of time can cause a barely perceivable sway to become a nervous jitter. Conversely, expansions of time can yield overly smoothed results. Such results are sometimes desirable, but they can be distracting in many applications.

A simple solution to the compression issue is to apply a uniform smoothing to the output motion, but doing so also dampens important details such as environmental contacts. Such contacts should ideally be identified and incorporated into a smoothing process. Unfortunately, this is problematic for motion-capture data, as robust contact detection is difficult and prone to error.

We instead chose to extend the simple solution by applying a local averaging operation to each frame using a window size equal to the amount of compression. This approach exploits the observation that undesirable high-frequency details are only introduced during higher compressions and adapts the amount of smoothing accordingly. While it can still cause certain details to be lost, we found that it produces good results in practice.

The expansion issue is more difficult to resolve, as restoring high frequencies involves hallucinating information absent from the original motion. Existing techniques could be applied to restore detail and texture (e.g., [PB02]). We chose to present our results without additional modification because we did not find such artifacts to be very distracting.

4. Results

We demonstrate the application of our technique to editing longer input motions rather than interpolating closely spaced keytimes. This emulates the typical use of keyframing tools for time warping: animators first set keytimes to meet duration or synchronization requirements and then add intermediate keytimes to achieve the desired results. In these cases, guided time warping can be used to create a detailed time warp without further user intervention. We envision this to be the primary use of our technique.

All of our evaluations are performed on motion capture data downsampled to 30 Hz. We believe our technique to be equally applicable towards high-quality keyframe animation, but we unfortunately did not have access to such data sets. Given the difficulty of presenting our results in figure form, we instead refer to specific examples shown in our accompanying video as V1–V8.

Our first set of results (V1–V5) emphasize how our technique can change the durations of input motions while preserving their own natural timing properties. We also show results (V6–V8) in which we modify the timing properies for different stylistic effects.

4.1. Preservation

Time warping is commonly applied to modify the duration of motions while preserving the natural timing properties of input motion as much as possible. As described previously, our technique can be applied to this task by providing the input motion as its own reference. In our video, we compare our preservation results to those achieved by linear warping. Since duration changes are only specified with two keytimes, this emulates the behavior of spline-based solutions such as motion warping [WP95] when given the same task.

Our first evaluations (V1–V3) test a simple base case for our technique: silence removal. This commonly used approach for audio can be applied to motions by detecting periods of inactivity. However, a naive implementation of such a technique would be difficult to tune, as it is rare that motions are perfectly static. In contrast, our technique smoothly speeds through low-activity periods in the motion.

These evaluations highlight another desirable aspect of our technique: it manages to preserve the timing of ballistic activities (jumping and falling) without any prior knowledge of torques, constraints, or gravity. Instead, our objective function realizes that accelerations during such motions are practically constant and thus penalizes any temporal deviations. In fact, when presented with the task of shortening a more challenging motion with only walking and jumping (V4), the walking portions are sped up extensively while the jumping portions are preserved with framewise accuracy. In contrast, a linear scaling of the time axis yields slightly slower locomotion, but implausible jumps. These results are mirrored for expansions of the time axis (V5).

4.2. Modification

Sometimes time warps are used for the express purpose of deviating from natural timing. To apply our technique for such tasks, the user simply has to provide a reference motion with the desired timing properties. Note that our present formulation requires the reference motion to have the same skeleton as the input.

Our first modification evaluation (V6) shows a limited form of style modification to a weak boxing sequence. By providing an aggressive sequence of punches as a reference, our method warps the original input to provide the desired effect while maintaining its duration. Hsu and colleagues [HPP05] present a similar evaluation which relies on the availability of matched pairs of motions. Guided time warping has no such requirement: the provided input and reference motions can have a different sequence of punches. Although their technique can modify poses as well, there are benefits to restricting modifications to the time axis, as evidenced by our application of the computed time warp to video footage taken during the capture session. This is shown in Figure 4 and in our accompanying video.

While it may be possible to provide canned reference motions, it is often the case that the only motion available is the one to be modified. In these situations, animators typically must resort to manual warping. Our technique can applied to simplify this task. We captured a standard locomotion sequence and adjusted a small segment of it to look more like a limp (V7). This was a slow process, and repeating it for the rest of the motion would have been very tedious. Instead, we used guided time warping to propagate the timing properties of the modified segment to the remainder of the clip. One important note about this result is the somewhat unnatural upper body movement in both the reference and the output. This is an unfortunate artifact of any time warping algorithm, since poses in a true limp differ from those in a normal walk. In spite of this, we chose to include this example because it highlights the ability of our technique to work with very short reference motions.

McCann and colleagues [MPS06] demonstrated a physical approach to solve a similar task to the previous example using a modification of gravity. While this may appear to be simpler than our technique, it requires estimating physical parameters which are often unavailable for animated characters. Furthermore, it is often desirable to have motions that defy physical laws. We demonstrate one such application by automatically emphasizing jumps using slow motion (V8). For this example, we performed a manual time warp to a brief portion of the input motion and used it as a reference. The result shows the remainder of the jumps emphasized in a similar fashion, despite the fact that the jumps in the input differ significantly from those in the reference. For this evaluation, we did not care how long the output was, so we ran an unconstrained version of our shortest path search (§3.2).

Trial	n	m	r	s	Objective	Optimization	Heuristic
V1	493	280	493	8	1.3 s	2.7 s	0.17 s
V2	316	180	316	10	1.7 s	1.4 s	0.11 s
V3	378	180	378	8	1.9 s	1.4 s	0.14 s
V4	486	320	486	8	1.0 s	2.6 s	0.20 s
V5	401	150	101	4	0.3 s	0.7 s	0.06 s
V6	601	301	301	8	1.3 s	3.8 s	0.23 s
V7	573	143	45	8	0.9 s	1.8 s	0.14 s
V8	1524	590	91	8	2.5 s	0.1 s	—

Table 1: *Parameters and running times for our evaluations, measured on a 2.4 GHz Pentium 4 PC. The fast optimization time for V8 is due to its unconstrained optimization.*

4.3. Performance

Details of our evaluations are given in Table 1. We used $k = 3$ nearest neighbors for our local score function. The values n, m, and r are frame counts for the input, output, and reference motions, respectively. The value s is the frame skip limit, as defined in §3.1. These frame counts are given *after* reduction to compression. The time expansion for V5, for instance, was implemented by first upsampling a 101-frame input to 401 frames and then compressing it using the original 101-frame input as the reference. A similar tactic was employed for V6, V7, and V8, as they required both compressions and expansions of the time axis.

We provide separate timings for the objective evaluation (§3.2) and optimization (§3.3) components of our technique. The former was implemented in C++ using publicly available software [AMN*98], and the latter was implemented in MATLAB. The cited timings use our full optimization procedure. We also applied the heuristic from §3.3 by downsampling our motions by a factor of eight. This yields much faster optimization times with little effect on quality. However, it does not change objective evaluation times because it eventually performs a pruned search at full resolution.

5. Conclusion

Time warping is a fundamental motion editing operation that can be used for a variety of applications. However, time warps must be carefully constructed to ensure that the desired results are achieved. Guided time warping provides a simple alternative to tedious manual specification that can fit into existing animation workflows.

One limitation of our technique, as presented, is that it can sometimes be uncompromisingly automatic. After keytimes and a reference motion are provided, an animator has little control over the shape of the resulting warp curve. More keytimes could be specified, but it may also be desirable to add smoothness and tangent constraints. These would be difficult to encode into guided time warping due to its local objective. A possible solution might employ motion interpolation methods (e.g., [KG03]): by blending between guided warps and spline warps of the same motion, a user effectively has continuous control over the influence of the reference.

Figure 4: *Guided time warping is not only useful for warping animated sequences, but other types of signals as well. We used the output of our technique to warp video sequences taken during our motion capture session. Here, a weak boxing sequence is made to look more aggressive.*

Our results show the preservation of plausible jumps, but it is important to emphasize that our technique does not explicitly maintain physical consistency. When this is a priority, other techniques should be applied [MPS06]. A benefit using a data model is its capability to handle non-physical animations. Our focus on animated characters suggests the use of our technique for cartoons and special effects. However, a broader view of non-physical animation encompasses things such as camera movement, motion graphics, video footage, and so on. In future work, we hope to expand upon possible applications of our technique in these areas.

Ultimately, all time warps are limited by the fact that they can not create or modify actual postures. No amount of temporal adjustment can convert a slow walk into a fast sprint, let alone convert a poorly constructed motion into a good one. As such, we view our technique as complementary to motion synthesis methods in two regards. From an application perspective, guided time warping is intended for use in later stages of the animation pipeline, when full resynthesis is often impractical. From a technical perspective, our technique can add new capabilities to existing synthesis techniques by providing a more flexible representation of timing.

Acknowledgements

We thank the members of the MIT CSAIL Computer Graphics Group for valuable advice and assistance. This work was supported in part by the Singapore-MIT GAMBIT Game Lab and software donations from Autodesk.

References

[AF02] ARIKAN O., FORSYTH D. A.: Interactive motion generation from examples. *ACM Transactions on Graphics 21*, 3 (July 2002), 483–490.

[AFO03] ARIKAN O., FORSYTH D. A., O'BRIEN J. F.: Motion synthesis from annotations. *ACM Transactions on Graphics 22*, 3 (July 2003), 402–408.

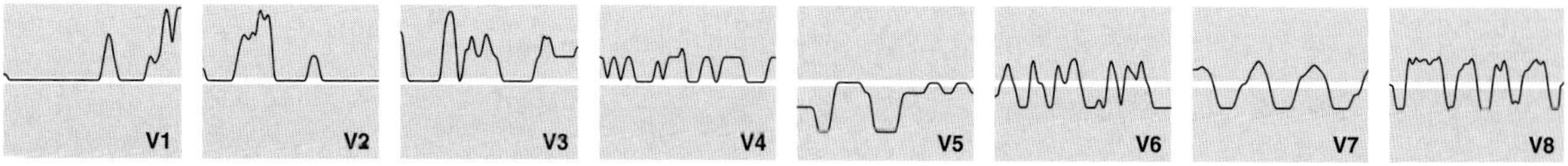

Figure 5: *Derivatives of time warps for our video evaluations, shown on logarithmic scales. The center lines in each plot correspond to unit time, and the limits correspond to tenfold slow-motion and fast-forward.*

[AMN*98] ARYA S., MOUNT D. M., NETANYAHU N. S., SILVERMAN R., WU A. Y.: An optimal algorithm for approximate nearest neighbor searching fixed dimensions. *Journal of the ACM 45*, 6 (1998), 891–923.

[BH00] BRAND M., HERTZMANN A.: Style machines. In *Proceedings of ACM SIGGRAPH 2000* (July 2000), Annual Conference Series, ACM SIGGRAPH, pp. 183–192.

[BW95] BRUDERLIN A., WILLIAMS L.: Motion signal processing. In *Computer Graphics (Proceedings of SIGGRAPH 95)* (Aug. 1995), Annual Conference Series, ACM SIGGRAPH, pp. 97–104.

[CWS98] COVELL M., WITHGOTT M., SLANEY M.: Mach1: Nonuniform time-scale modification of speech. In *Proceedings of 1998 IEEE International Conference on Acoustics, Speech, and Signal Processing* (1998), pp. 328–338.

[DYP03] DONTCHEVA M., YNGVE G., POPOVIĆ Z.: Layered acting for character animation. *ACM Transactions on Graphics 22*, 3 (July 2003), 409–416.

[FTP03] FREEMAN W. T., TENENBAUM J. B., PASZTOR E.: Learning style translation for the lines of a drawing. *ACM Transactions on Graphics 22*, 1 (Jan. 2003), 33–46.

[GVdG00] GOMES J., VELHO L., DA SILVA F. W., GOLDENSTEIN S. K.: Motion processing using variable harmonic components. In *Computer Animation 2000* (May 2000), pp. 62–70.

[HPP05] HSU E., PULLI K., POPOVIĆ J.: Style translation for human motion. *ACM Transactions on Graphics 24*, 3 (Aug. 2005), 1082–1089.

[KG03] KOVAR L., GLEICHER M.: Flexible automatic motion blending with registration curves. In *Symposium on Computer Animation (SCA)* (Aug. 2003), ACM Press, pp. 214–224.

[KGP02] KOVAR L., GLEICHER M., PIGHIN F.: Motion graphs. *ACM Transactions on Graphics 21*, 3 (July 2002), 473–482.

[Las87] LASSETER J.: Principles of traditional animation applied to 3d computer animation. In *Computer Graphics (Proceedings of SIGGRAPH 87)* (July 1987), vol. 21, pp. 35–44.

[LCR*02] LEE J., CHAI J., REITSMA P. S. A., HODGINS J. K., POLLARD N. S.: Interactive control of avatars animated with human motion data. *ACM Transactions on Graphics 21*, 3 (July 2002), 491–500.

[LWS02] LI Y., WANG T., SHUM H.-Y.: Motion texture: A two-level statistical model for character motion synthesis. *ACM Transactions on Graphics 21*, 3 (July 2002), 465–472.

[MPS06] MCCANN J., POLLARD N. S., SRINIVASA S.: Physics-based motion retiming. In *2006 ACM SIGGRAPH / Eurographics Symposium on Computer Animation* (Sept. 2006), pp. 205–214.

[PB02] PULLEN K., BREGLER C.: Motion capture assisted animation: Texturing and synthesis. *ACM Transactions on Graphics 21*, 3 (July 2002), 501–508.

[RCB98] ROSE C., COHEN M. F., BODENHEIMER B.: Verbs and adverbs: Multidimensional motion interpolation. *IEEE Computer Graphics and Applications 18*, 5 (1998), 32–40.

[RJ93] RABINER L. R., JUANG B.-H.: *Fundamentals of Speech Recognition.* Prentice Hall, Englewood Cliffs, New Jersey, 1993.

[Sai68] SAIGAL R.: A constrained shortest route problem. *Operations Research 16*, 1 (Jan.–Feb. 1968), 205–209.

[SSSE00] SCHÖDL A., SZELISKI R., SALESIN D. H., ESSA I.: Video textures. In *Proceedings of ACM SIGGRAPH 2000* (July 2000), Annual Conference Series, pp. 489–498.

[TBvdP04] THORNE M., BURKE D., VAN DE PANNE M.: Motion doodles: an interface for sketching character motion. *ACM Transactions on Graphics 23*, 3 (Aug. 2004), 424–431.

[TM04] TERRA S. C. L., METOYER R. A.: Performance timing for keyframe animation. In *2004 ACM SIGGRAPH / Eurographics Symposium on Computer Animation* (July 2004), pp. 253–258.

[WP95] WITKIN A., POPOVIĆ Z.: Motion warping. In *Computer Graphics (Proceedings of SIGGRAPH 95)* (Aug. 1995), Annual Conference Series, ACM SIGGRAPH, pp. 105–108.

Eurographics/ ACM SIGGRAPH Symposium on Computer Animation (2007)
D. Metaxas and J. Popovic (Editors)

Dynamic, Expressive Speech Animation From a Single Mesh

Kevin Wampler †1, Daichi Sasaki ‡2, Li Zhang §3, and Zoran Popović ¶1

[1]Univeristy of Washington [2]Sony [3]Columbia University

Abstract

In this work we present a method for human face animation which allows us to generate animations for a novel person given just a single mesh of their face. These animations can be of arbitrary text and may include emotional expressions. We build a multilinear model from data which encapsulates the variation in dynamic face motions over changes in identity, expression, and over different texts. We then describe a synthesis method consisting of a phoneme planning and a blending stage which uses this model as a base and attempts to preserve both face shape and dynamics given a novel text and an emotion at each point in time.

Categories and Subject Descriptors (according to ACM CCS): I.3.7 [Computer Graphics]: Animation

1. Introduction

Of all the visual forms which computer graphics seeks to emulate, the human face is one of the most challenging. From birth we are continuously exposed to faces, and come to be extremely adept at recognizing even slight flaws in the form or motion of a synthesized reproduction. This difficulty, combined with the tremendous usefulness of synthetic human face animations in a variety of applications, has yielded a large and varied body of research resulting in a parametrized, physics-based, video-based and motion-capture driven speech animations.

Although current techniques are able to generate highly realistic face surface meshes and rendering, facial animation, and in particular that of speech, remains a challenge. Speech animation is challenging primarily due to its complex non-linear nature: speech can be viewed as an optimal control problem where we find the shortest and most compact deformations of the face and oral cavity which could produce the desired sound sequence. As a result, the production of the same sound (phoneme) often requires completely different facial motion depending on a number of preceding and subsequent phonemes. This motion is often very fast and is often modulated by the emotional expression of speech. Recent speech models tailored for one specific person can look good, especially with a large corpus of subject-specific data. The problem gets significantly more complex when we generate a speech animation of an arbitrary person's mesh, because data captured for a specific face only partly transfers to a different face. This is primarily because different facial structures have different optimal facial motions even for the same desired phoneme sequences. Ultimately, we would like to generate a speech animation of any phoneme-segmented text, in any given emotional expression, performed by a given facial mesh. Such a method would be extremely useful for numerous applications in digital entertainment where a demand for rapid synthesis of human speech appears endless. Despite this usefulness, we are not aware of any fully automatic methods which attempt to model the variation in face dynamics without requiring video data for the face to be modeled.

This paper takes a modest step towards solving this general problem. We take a data-driven approach to leverage realistic animation nuances observed in real faces. One primary difficulty with data-driven methods is the effort required in the data collection process. Even in cases where little human intervention is needed, a large amount of video is required to successfully reanimate a person speaking. This problem is particularly bad in the case of capturing 3D data, because the video must be captured in a specialized setup, and hand

† e-mail: wampler@cs.washington.edu
‡ e-mail: Daichi.Sasaki@jp.sony.com
§ e-mail: lizhang@cs.columbia.edu
¶ e-mail: zoran@cs.washington.edu

Symposium on Computer Animation 2007, San Diego, CA, August 03-04, 2007.
© 2007 ACM 978-1-59593-624-4/07/0008 $5.00

tweaking/analysis of the resulting data is often needed. In some cases the person to be synthesized may also be unavailable or expensive to capture.

We present an animation synthesis method which models the full variation in facial shape and dynamics over both identity and emotional expression. We can furthermore create such an animation from a single static mesh of a person's face. The synthesized animations can contain arbitrary text and changes in emotional expression.

Although our model is created from captured data sequences, we collect the data only once and assemble it into a compact multilinear model. This model gives us a representation of the space of speech motions in which both the identity and expression of the speaker can be independently varied. Once this model is created, we can synthesize 3D speech snippets of people which are not in the original data by providing only a static mesh of a target person. These animation snippets are used in an anime (motion snippet) planning process followed by a blending operation to produce a continuous speech animation.

We describe a visual speech synthesis algorithm which functions well on our model. This is made particularly challenging by the limited amount of per-person data that we are able to collect. Fortunately, by carefully mimicking both the form and dynamics of the speech samples generated by the multilinear model we are able to successfully synthesize realistic animations.

Contributions. To the best of the author's knowledge ours is the first fully automatic method to address the variation in facial dynamics without requiring per-person video data. We model this variation over the full space of identity and emotional expression and can fit the model to a single mesh of a person's face. The initial data collection required to build our model limits the amount of underlying per-person data we can gather, so we describe a novel expressive speech synthesis algorithm which gives comparable results to current 3D face animation systems, but which requires significantly less per-person captured data in the underlying model.

2. Related work

A great array of research in modeling and animating human faces has been done over a span of several decades. The general approaches with which this problem can be approached can roughly be grouped into four categories: hand-parameterized, physical, statistical, and data-driven. The earliest methods, including Parks's pioneering work [Par82] and the Facial Action Coding System (FACS) [EF78] fell into the first of these categories. In an effort to achieve greater realism, others have sought to model or approximate action of muscles in the human face [Wat87, KP05], even including such aspects as physically based skin-tissue deformation [LTW95, SSRMF06].

Some of the most successful approaches, particularly in automatic speech motion synthesis, have employed data of facial poses or motion as a major component. This has the advantage of potentially circumventing difficult questions about the musculature and physical properties of the face by interpolating or extrapolating from data which is known to be correct. One major challenge which this (and other) visual speech synthesis methods is to reproduce the effect of *coarticulation* – that the same phoneme may be pronounced in different ways depending on its context. Coarticulation has been modeled with many methods, including weighted viseme influence falloffs [EGP02], splines [MKPG05], learning polynomial approximations of viseme pairs or triplets [KB06], hidden Markov models [Bra99], and dynamic programming methods [BCS97, CTFP05].

Some of these visual speech synthesis methods operate by replaying pieces of the data directly while other learn a more compact generative model from an input database. Video rewrite [BCS97] generates novel 2D video given a speech sequence by breaking the input video into triphones and reordering their frames in a way which attempts to minimize discontinuities. Trainable Videorealistic Speech Animation [EGP02] presents a more flexible method which learns a multidimensional morphable model (MMM) [JP98] that allows low-artifact interpolation between a set of key images extracted from video data. Each viseme is modeled as a multidimensional gaussian of MMM parameters and a smooth trajectory is synthesized through these gaussians given a novel phoneme sequence. High quality results are obtained by learning the mean and covariance of the gaussians the video data. While both of these techniques operate only on 2D video, they could probably be modified to operate in 3D as well, although it is less clear how well they would incorporate emotions. 2D approaches, however, do have the advantage that they are naturally photorealistic and capture details of the teeth and tongue.

In a recent approach to 3D speech animation which supports emotions, Expressive Speech-Driven Facial Animation [CTFP05] utilizes a database of 3D video of face marker positions captured during speech. This data is represented as an *anime graph*. An *anime* here means the mouth shape during the pronunciation of a phoneme, and differs from a viseme in that it includes the full temporal motion of the mouth while a viseme is just a single static mouth shape. Given a novel speech sequence, this graph is searched for a sequence of animes which match the phonemes in the text and which includes to as great a degree as possible continuous sequences of animes from the data. In the case of a tie audio features and face shape continuity are used to select the animes.

One problem with such data based approaches is the time and effort required to capture the initial data. This presents a significant problem in creating animations of different people, because the data must be recaptured for each person that one wishes to animate. This in particularly problematic when generating 3D animations, as it is extremely unlikely that such data already exists, meaning that the person must be often be hired to participate in a capture session. In addition accurate capture of 3D facial motion generally requires specialized equipment and some amount of manual labor. Our method eases this data collection burden by working well with approximately 1 minute of data per person and emotion (as opposed to 10 minutes for most other data-driven methods). Furthermore, this data collection only needs to be done once, after which new animations can be synthesized from a single mesh.

Though it is not particularly well explored, there exist a few other techniques for automatic synthesizing animations from a static input mesh. In Voice Puppetry [Bra99] a mouth motion is synthesized according to voice input, and the shape of the mouth is then applied to an image. In Reanimating Faces in Images and Video [BBVP03] a similar approach is taken, but a 3D mesh is first fit to an image and the image is animated via this mesh. Although they show some impressive reanimations, the focus is on the fitting step and the automatically generated animations do not exhibit realistic dynamics. This method also does not handle speech and expressions simultaneously. Another approach is described by Müller et. al. [MKPG05]. They calculate face motions for input text by filling an interpolating spline to the phonemes and then using this spline to drive a set of face deformations found by ICA. The shape of the visemes are personalized to an input mesh, but all animations would share the same dynamics. The method also does not handle speech with expressions directly, though expressions may be added by an animator in a way which does not account for individualized differences.

Two interesting alternatives for generating speech animation are performance-based animation [Wil90,xCXH03] and face shape transfer [CB05,CE05]. A good survey of face transfer methods is given in "Facial Motion Retargeting" [PL06]. In performance-based animation, vision techniques are used to track the facial motion of a person from a video. These facial motions are then applied to a model in order to animate it. Often this is combined with face transfer methods which allow the face being animated to have a different geometry from the one driving the animation. Often such techniques rely on a sparse set of correspondences between the captured and synthesized models to be created and perform scattered data interpolation to transfer each frame of the capture video.

In both synthetic and performance based facial animation, it is often desirable to be able to independently modify the identity and expression of the synthesized video after its initial capture. One fruitful approach to this problem is to use a *multilinear* model. Multilinear models have been shown to be effect in providing decoupled parameterizations facial images [VT02], textures [VT04], and a variety of other applications. Multilinear models have also been used for face transfer in performance-based animation [VBPP05]. They employ a model built from static 3D face scans in several different identities, emotions and visemes. Using model based tracking the multilinear parameters of the model are estimated from a video. These parameters can then be altered to change the identity or emotion of the speaker. Although performance-driven animation can produce very realistic animations, a video must be captured to drive each animation which one desires to create. In some circumstances this is an acceptable tradeoff, but it precludes these techniques from being used in cases where the animation must be automatically synthesized.

Our work demonstrates a multilinear model learned from a set of 3D face motion capture. In contrast to current data-driven methods which account for personalized dynamics, we can create an animation for a new person without requiring any data other than out model and a single mesh of their face, and in particular do not require any video to be captured of them. In contrast to existing methods of animating from a single new face mesh [BBVP03,MKPG05] we capture individual variations in both the deformations and dynamics of a face and naturally handle emotions. Our speech synthesis algorithm also performs well with less per-person initial data than required by existing methods.

3. Data collection

As our model is data-driven, we must first collect a set of data to use with it. This process is both human and computer time intensive, but fortunately only needs to be done once. We use a face capture system developed by Zhang et al. [ZSCS04] to collect high-resolution shape and texture in real time. We also record voice with a video camera for speech sequences. A monitor is placed in front of the subject instructing when to say each sentence.

Our data set consists of 60 face mesh sequences from 15 individuals (Figure 1) in each of the four emotions of neutral, angry, disgusted, and happy. Each sequence contains a series of eight sentences taking in total 50-seconds to speak (including silence). The sentences in joint contain all the English monophones, although some appear only once and we capture only a small fraction of the naturally occurring triphones. We use speech recognition software [Cam] to segment the sentences into individual phonemes. As this process is not entirely accurate we manually correct the timings of some phonemes, particularly those which are both quick and visually distinct such as /b/, /m/, and /p/

The reconstructed mesh sequences run at 20 frames-per-second (fps). Each mesh has roughly 23K vertices with a single color associated with each vertex. By fitting a template mesh to the range scans, we further ensure that all of the generated meshes are in full correspondence. The meshes are also rigidly aligned so that the vertices on the forehead and nose are as close as possible (in the least squares sense) to those of a template mesh. We also manually correct the

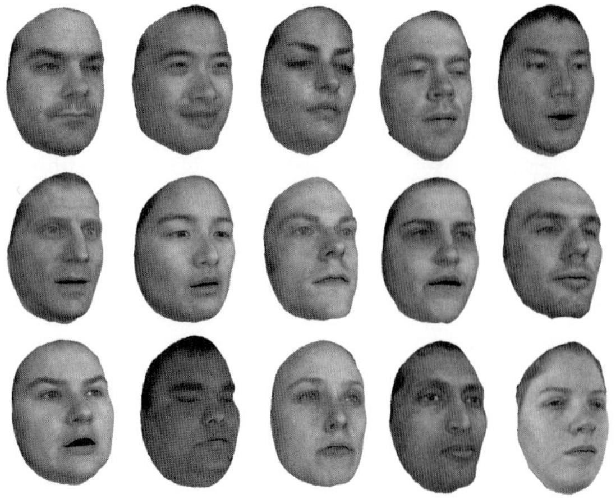

Figure 1: *The 15 identities in our model. In order to test our method on novel meshes, we build a reduced model which omits the identity to be synthesized.*

meshes to ensure that the lips fully close during the /b/, /m/, and /p/ phonemes.

4. Multilinear model

The underlying model for our method is based on the common observation that when dealing with 3D meshes the space of shapes formed by a human face can be well modeled with linear blends of a collection of basis faces. For example a linear combination of the vertex positions of a face mesh with a neutral expression and a mesh with a happy expression generally yields a realistic mesh exhibiting an expression somewhere between happy and neutral. Similarly, a linear model can be used to model the variation in the shape of the face between different people with the same expression.

While a linear model works well for constructing face meshes from a single parameter space, such as identity or expression, we wish to be able to describe the identity and expression of a face entirely independently. Thus instead of matrix-based approach which constructs a face as a linear combination of basis faces we employ a multilinear tensor-based approach.

Tensors are a natural generalization of scalars, vectors, and matrices to transformations of arbitrary order, and can be represented by n-dimensional arrays. Whereas scalars can be used to represent all linear transformations from $\mathbb{R}$ to $\mathbb{R}$, vectors from $\mathbb{R}^a$ to $\mathbb{R}$ (by using the dot product), and matrices from $\mathbb{R}^a$ to $\mathbb{R}^b$, a general tensor can represent any transformation from $\mathbb{R}^a \times \mathbb{R}^b \times \cdots \times \mathbb{R}^m$ to $\mathbb{R}^x \times \mathbb{R}^y \times \cdots \times \mathbb{R}^n$ such that the transformation is linear between any pair of the vector spaces with the others held fixed. Such a tensor is called a rank $a \times \cdots \times m \times x \times \cdots \times n$ tensor, and can be represented by a multidimensional array with these dimensions. A tensor thus allows us to represent a transformation from multiple parameter spaces (such as identity and expression) into the vertex positions of a mesh while cleanly maintaining the separability of the input parameters.

In addition to modeling the variation in facial geometry over identity and expression the model must be well suited to the synthesis of speech animations. This requires that given a sequence of phonemes, we are able to associate a mesh or sequence of meshes describing the shape of the face (primarily the shape of the mouth) over each of the phonemes. Often this is modeled with a single mesh per phoneme describing the shape (termed a *viseme*) that the mouth should form in its pronunciation.

In order to correctly reconstruct the motion of a face as well as its shape, we instead explicitly store the full motion of a face throughout the duration of a phoneme's duration. In addition, if a phoneme occurs multiple times in the data, we explicitly store the motions for each of these so that we may model the variation in the way that a phoneme may be formed. We will borrow the terminology of [CTFP05] and refer to such a small clip of motion as an *anime*. Our core model is thus conceptually a collection of mappings $\mathcal{V}_j : e \times i \rightarrow m \times t$ (where e is the space of expressions, i is the space of identities, t is time, m is the set of vertex positions for the resulting mesh, and j is the index of the anime in our data). In practice however, we internally store this as a single tensor $\mathcal{V} : e \times i \rightarrow m \times t$ which concatenates all the animes and then simply store a list of the time intervals at which each anime occurred.

This tensor can be assembled almost directly from the captured range scans. For each expression and identity we associate a single coordinate of the corresponding dimensions in $\mathcal{V}$. Each sequence of range scans then gives a $t \times m$ subtensor. Because our multilinear model requires that all the instances of an anime be temporally aligned, we resample each sequence so that the length of each anime is the maximum of its lengths in all of the sequences.

The representation of $\mathcal{V}$ as created from the data is extremely large ($\sim 40GB$) and contains many redundancies in the parameters. In order to alleviate both of these problems we use a tensor approximation algorithm to create a reduced version of this tensor. This algorithm is conceptually similar to a higher-order analogue of matrix singular value decomposition [Lat97]. To actually perform this compression we use an out-of-core tensor approximation algorithm similar to that of Wang et. al. [WWS*05], but modified to place more weight on accurately approximating facial features such as the lips and regions around the eyes.

4.1. Identity from mesh

One particularly useful application of our model involves the synthesis of animations of a person who is not in the origi-

input: $targetMesh, \mathcal{T}, w_a, \ldots, w_m$
while not converged
  $currentMesh = \mathcal{T} \times_a w_a \cdots \times_m w_m$
  rigid align $targetMesh$ with $currentMesh$
  for $i = a$ to m
    $M = \mathcal{T} \times_a w_a \cdots \times_{i-1} w_{i-1} \times_{i+1} w_{i+1} \cdots \times_m w_m$
    $w_i = argmin_v \{|targetmesh - Mv|\}\ st. \forall j : v_j \geq 0$
  end
end

Figure 2: *Pesudocode for fitting the parameters of a multilinear model to an example output mesh.*

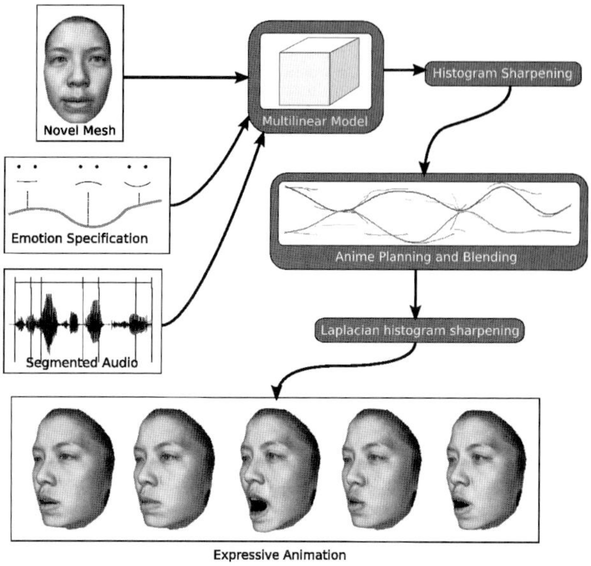

Figure 3: *An illustration of the steps in our synthesis algorithm. We take as input a single mesh, a specification of emotional expression at each point in time, and an audio clip which has been segmented into phonemes. Our multilinear model generates animes which are then blended into a smooth animation. We also employ a pair of sharpening stages.*

nal data. This entails finding the vector in the identity space of out model that gives rise to meshes best resembling the new person. We have addressed this problem for the case in which a single mesh of the person is known by employing an iterative fitting algorithm similar to that described in [VBPP05].

To fit our model to a target mesh, m, we find the vectors in the parameter space of the model which best reproduce the given mesh. This is achieved through an iterative scheme which optimizes each dimension in our model in turn. Starting at an arbitrary point in the space of out model, we generate a face mesh and determine the rotation and translation needed to place it in as close a correspondence to the m as possible. Then, for each dimension i we take a tensor representing a static version of our model and collapse it into a matrix by mode-multiplying it by the current parameter guesses, w_j, for all dimensions j other than i and the dimension corresponding to vertex positions. This yields a system of linear equations which we wish to solve in a least squared sense to get a new estimate for the w_i. We note, however, that non-convex combinations of basis meshes (ie. negative numbers in w_i) can yield unrealistic results. We therefore find w_i by solving the quadratic programming problem of linear least squares with non-negativity constraints. We repeat this for each parameter dimension and then iterate the whole process until convergence. A pseudocode version of this algorithm is shown in figure 2. If, for example, the expression of m is known, it is an easy matter to fix the values of these parameters and only optimize within a subset of the parameters, which may potentially speed up or improve the fit.

5. Animation Synthesis

To synthesize an animation we require a description of the identity, $I(t)$, and emotional expression, $E(t)$, of a person at each point in time in the animation as well as a sequence of phonemes describing what the synthesized speaker is to say. $I(t)$ will of course generally be constant, and we construct $E(t)$ by interpolating between keyframes. The sequence of timed phoneme intervals can be extracted from an audio using standard speech recognition software.

Once $I(t)$, $E(t)$, and a phoneme sequence have been supplied by the user, the animation synthesis algorithm proceeds in two main phases. First, since there may be multiple animes in the model for any given phoneme in the input sequence, we associate a specific anime with each phoneme. These are chosen in a manner which takes into account coarticulation effects and which yields a sequence in which each anime blends relatively well into its neighbors. If we concatenate the animation clips for these animes together directly the resulting animation exhibits very distracting discontinuities, so we instead use a blending phase which combines them into a smooth result. We also take measures to counteract over-smoothing which may occur in this process. An illustration of the synthesis steps can be seen in figure 3.

Throughout the following descriptions it is notationally convenient to ignore the multilinear interpolation in the model and simply refer directly to the sequence of meshes that constitute animes. In reality however, these meshes must be generated from the multilinear model. To generate a mesh which will be associated with time t in the synthesized animation, we must collapse the tensor $\mathcal{V}_i$ corresponding to the ith anime in the data by the model parameters at t. Formally, we calculate the mesh as $\mathcal{V}_i \times_2 1_f \times_3 I(t) \times_4 E(t)$ where 1_f is a vector which has all zeros except for a one at the frame of the anime that is to be extracted (we can omit this term if meshes for the entire anime are desired). For values of f which are not integers we use cubic interpolation.

5.1. Anime selection

In a sequence of phonemes that is to be synthesized, it is common that many of the phonemes will occur multiple times in $\mathcal{V}$. That is, there may be several different animes which correspond to a given phoneme. We treat each of these as a potential face motion that may correspond to the phoneme. This redundancy give us a notion of the impact that coarticulation or other factors may have on the pronunciation of a phoneme, but also provides the possibility of making unrealistic choices in this pronunciation. We describe a graph-based dynamic programming algorithm which chooses a consistent and plausible set of animes for a phoneme sequence.

Because our amount of per-person data is so small, we are very limited in the methods which we may use to reproduce coarticulation effects. Existing techniques, such as learning coarticulation models for pairs or triplets of phonemes [DLN05], attempting to string together long sequences of phonemes [CTFP05], or accurately learning accurate per-phoneme influences [EGP02] cannot be reliably applied. For this reason, we use a method which does not explicitly assume anything other than that a single anime exists for each phoneme and which takes direct advantage of the options afforded by any redundancies.

Given a sequence of phonemes we wish to associate a specific anime with each in a way which best captures coarticulation effects and overall smoothness. Let p_i be the ith phoneme in the input sequence and $v_{i,1}, v_{i,2}, \ldots, v_{i,n}$ be the animes corresponding to the appearances of p_i in the data (as obtained from each $\mathcal{V}_i$ by using the identity and expression functions). For each pair of adjacent phonemes, p_i, p_{i+1} there are many possible pairings of corresponding animes, $v_{i,j}, v_{i+1,k}$, and we associate a weight, $d(v_{i,j}, v_{i+1,k})$ which attempts to approximate the visual error of the pairing.

After experimenting with several options, we have settled on a definition of $d(v_{i,j}, v_{i+1,k})$ which performs a computation over the entire extent of the animes by considering the overlap error: $d_2(v_{(i,j)+1}, v_{i+1,j}) + d_2(v_{i,j}, v_{(i+1,j)-1})$ where d_2 measures the similarity between two animes. That is, we attempt to minimize the difference between the viseme chosen to come after $v_{i,j}$ in the output animation and what actually came after $v_{i,j}$ in the data (and similarly for $v_{i+1,j}$).

We have achieved the best results by defining $d_2(v_a, v_b)$ as the sum of an instantaneous error function, f over the entire duration of the two animes, $d_2(v_a, v_b) = \int f(v_a(t), v_b(t))\, dt$. We then define f as a weighted sum of derivatives: $f = w_p||v_a(t) - v_b(t)|| + w_v||\frac{dv_a}{dt}(t) - \frac{dv_b}{dt}(t)|| + w_a||\frac{d^2v_a}{dt^2}(t) - \frac{d^2v_b}{dt^2}(t)||$. Intuitively this is reasonable, as it simply indicates that coarticulation effects are determined not only by the instantaneous shape of the mouth, but also by the speed at which it is moving as well as its acceleration (which is related to the muscle forces being exerted). We use weights $w_p = 1$, $w_v = 0$, and $w_a = 35$, which were found such that a synthesized sequence was as close as possible to a known ground truth animation. These weights were at or near the optimum for all the identities and emotions in our data. Higher weights on the position term tend to lead to sequences with a distracting non-smooth appearance and higher weights on the acceleration term lead to sequences which are overly smooth.

Once the cost of each possible anime pairing for the phonemes in the input sequence has been found, it is straightforward to find a sequence of animes with minimum cost. We represent the animes in a graph, with one node for each possible anime and a weighted edge for the cost of choosing each adjacent pair of animes. The minimum cost sequence of visemes is then the lowest weight path from any node in the first column to any node in the last column, and can be found using a standard shortest-path algorithm (Figure 4).

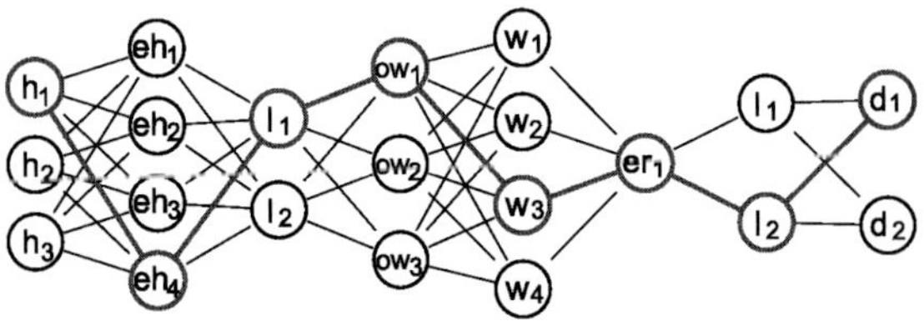

Figure 4: *An example anime graph for the phrase "hello world". One possible lowest-weight path is highlighted in red. The chosen path helps ensure that the anime snippets can be blended into a realistic result.*

5.2. Anime blending

Once an anime has been associated with each phoneme, the resulting animation clips must be combined into a single animation. If the clips were sufficiently coherent this could probably be accomplished with relatively simple cross-fading techniques. Unfortunately owing to the limited number of animes in our input data these techniques yield animations with highly distracting unrealistic mouth movements. We instead consider more intricate blending techniques.

We use a blending method which chooses a trajectory which strikes a tradeoff between matching the shape of the faces in the animes and their *accelerations*. The motivation behind incorporating accelerations is similar to that behind gradient domain blending [LZPW03]. Accelerations are invariant to changes in position and velocity and produce a much smoother blend. Acceleration based blending also captures

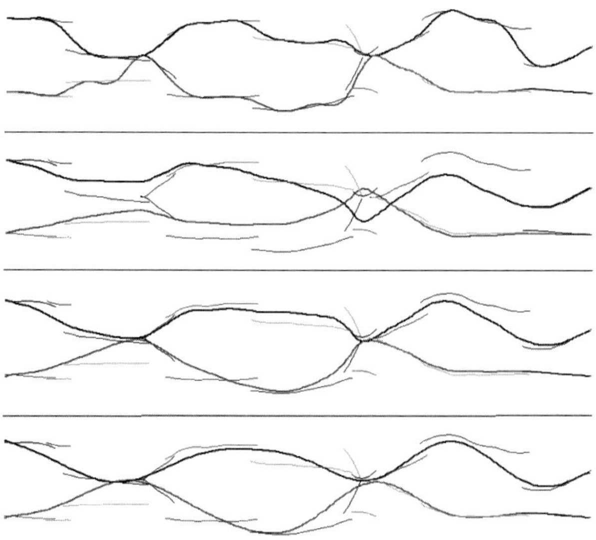

Figure 5: *Plots of the upper and lower lip positions over time for four different blending methods. From top to bottom, position blending, acceleration blending, combined position and acceleration blending, and combined blending with smoothness as used in our synthesis algorithm. This thin lines are the input animes and the thick lines the blended result.*

sudden changes in the face, which are correlated with distinctive speech features.

We find that, in general, position based blending produces animations which preserve the shape of the face well, but have distracting dynamic artifacts that appear as a sort of 'jittering' at transitions between animes. Acceleration based blending produces results with more realistic dynamics, but creates artifacts in the shape of the face (Figure 5). We achieve realistic dynamics while still preserving the correct shape of the face by performing a blend which optimizes a weighted average of the positions and accelerations in the clips. Although not necessarily discernible from these plots, this method still exhibits some distracting jitter, though much less so that position-based blending. We therefore also optimize the blended sequence with respect to a smoothing term (fig.5,bottom).

Formally, we assign weights to the importance of position, acceleration, and smoothness as 1, w_a, and w_s respectively. We then generate a final animation through a sparse linear least squares optimization. Let $f_1,\ldots,f_n$ be the frames in the output animation, and for a frame f_i let $d_i, d_j, \ldots$ be the frames in the data from the viseme clips overlapping f_i. We create three linear constraints on f_i: $f_i = d_j$, $w_a(f_{i+1} - 2f_i + f_{i-1}) = w_a(d_{j+1} - 2d_j + dj - 1)$, and the fourth order smoothness constraint [EGP02], $w_s(-f_{i-3} + 6f_{i-2} - 15f_{i-1} + 20f_i - 15f_{i+1} + 6f_{i+2} - f_{i+3}) = 0$. We have found that the weights $w_a = 20$ and $w_s = 200$ provide good results over all of the wide range of faces we have tested.

Although we found a blending method combining position and acceleration to be most effective at generating pleasing results, there are a few critical cases where it fails. These are times when the mouth needs to attain a specific closed or partially closed shape, such as the lips being closed on a /b/, /p/, or /m/ or with the bottom lip touching the upper teeth on a /f/ or /v/. For these 'critical phonemes' we increase the weight on the position term by $12(lip_i + 1)^{-1}$ where lip_i is the distance between the upper and lower lips at frame i and 12 is a scaling factor related to the dimensions of a face in our model (approximately the average value of lip_i in our data). A more rigorous method would attempt to learn the position term weighting function on a per-phoneme basis in a manner similar to [EGP02], but we have found that this simple method works well in practice.

5.3. Sharpness preservation

The animations synthesized with the heretofore described methods have relatively realistic shape and motion, but exhibit a noticeable amount of spatial and temporal blurring. This blurring is a result of both the multilinear interpolation in our core model, and of the anime blending in our synthesis method. In order to preserve the sharpness of the original data and of the input mesh, we employ a multilinear sharpening method and a pair of post processing steps.

We use a very simple method to preserve spatial sharpness. When we fit an input mesh, m_{rest}, into the identity parameter space of our model, the result, v_{rest} has a shape which is close to that of the input mesh, but in which small-scale features such as creases and wrinkles are blurred out. We can, however, compute a spatial sharpening operator to retrieve the identity mesh by computing $ss(v) = v + (m_{rest} - v_{rest})$. This operator is applied to each frame in the animation as a post-processing step and has the effect of re-introducing the spatial mesh features lost in our model. Because out synthesized meshes have their large-scale characteristics very close to those of the input mesh, no undesirable visual artifacts are introduced by this simplistic method.

In contrast to the spatial blurring, the temporal blurring is a product of both the multilinear interpolation in our model and of the anime blending process. We tackle each of these sources independently by enforcing statistics from the data sequences upon both the synthesized animes and the final synthesized sequence respectively using a histogram matching technique related to that described for texture synthesis in [MZD05].

To counteract blurring from the multilinear interpolation in each anime model, $\mathcal{V}_i$, we construct a histogram of the values of each principal components of the meshes in each of the 15×4 sequences. As was noted in [MZD05], histograms are most naturally interpolated by the interpolation of the inverse cumulative distribution functions (ICDFs), so we compute an ICDF for each of these sequence histograms. These ICDFs are then assembled into a tensor which has a similar structure to V_i, but instead of representing a mapping $e \times i \rightarrow m \times t$, represents a mapping $e \times i \rightarrow m \times ICDF$. Given an anime and identity and emotion vectors, we can compute a target ICDF for each principal component by multilinear interpolation. We then perform histogram matching on the components of the mesh to force their values to match those predicted by the interpolated ICDF.

The blurring resulting from the anime blending is treated in a similar manner, but applied as a postprocessing step to the entire animation. For each sequence in the compressed model, we build a laplacian pyramid and compute a histogram ICDF tensor for the each principal components at each of these pyramid level. Given a synthesized animation, we apply histogram mapping to its laplacian pyramid to match its frequency distribution to that interpolated from the data. Since the identity or expression parameters may not remain constant throughout an animation, we interpolate the target ICDFs and histogram match independently for each frame. As this method can produce artifacts in animation for which the frequency statistics are far from the data, we only apply it to animations over four seconds in length.

Since we apply histogram matching to each of the principal components independently, subtle but extremely distracting 'swimming' artifacts can be introduced into the animation. At the cost of a some amount of precision in the sharpening, we force the components to cohere by only considering direct amplifications of the face deformations in the non-sharpened animation. For the face at each frame, $v_{i,1}$, let its sharpened version be $v_{i,2}$. Instead of using this mesh in the sharpened sequence, we use a mesh of the form $v_{rest} + x(v_{i,1} - v_{rest})$ where the optimal value of x is found by linear least-squares to yield a result best matching $v_{1,2}$.

6. Results

We have demonstrated a method for representing the space of facial dynamics over variations in identity, expression, and phoneme. Combined with a synthesis method designed to work well with small amounts of facial data we can generate expressive speech animations for a new person by fitting the model to a static mash of their face. Figure 6 shows two frames from a synthetic animation consisting of happy and disgusted expressions while figure 7 shows a result of synthesis from our Japanese model.

We base our synthesis on a set of 3D facial motion capture sequences. Each sequence contains eight sentences containing all the phonemes of the English language. We captured these sentences for each of 15 different people in four different emotions. We are also in the process of creating a similar model for Japanese using professional actors. Our current

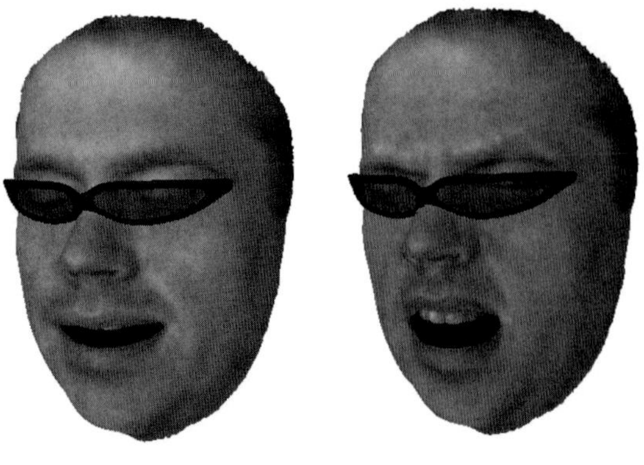

Figure 6: *Two frames from an animation synthesized by our method for a novel mesh. This illustrates the result of applying happy and disgusted expression parameters.*

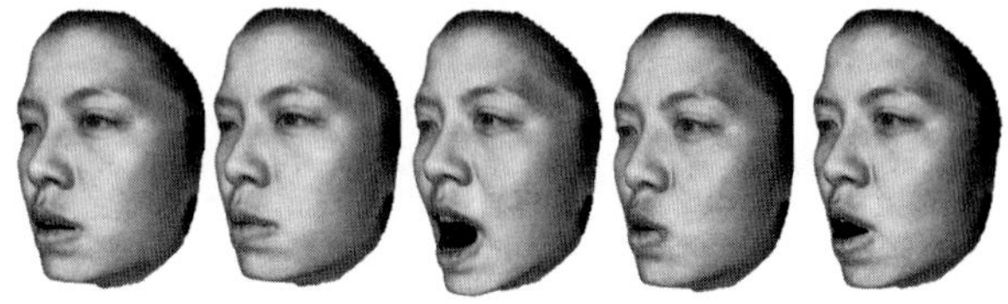

Figure 7: *A sampling of frames from an animation produced by our system using our Japanese model. A transition from normal to exaggerated speech occurs between frames two and three.*

Japanese model contains only two identities in the neutral and exaggerated expressions. Because of the small size of the identity space, it can only animate some of our 3D test meshes without significant artifacts. We are currently working on expanding both the number of identities and emotions in this model.

We have experimented with evaluating the necessity of various parts of our synthesis method. Most notable are the problems encountered if we omit the use of our multilinear model and simply transfer vertex displacements from an animation synthesized from an identity in our data. We find that in this case we often get incorrect fittings of the model to the input mesh, resulting in artifacts such as lips that are to puckered or which self-intersect. Even when these artifacts are not exhibited, the animation can display noticeably incorrect dynamics. We also observe serious artifacts without anime planning or with using a blending function which only considers position and smoothness. Omitting the histogram sharpening does not seriously degrade the animation, but the results do appear somewhat less animated.

Our method produces animations with individualized shape and dynamics while automatically handling speech and emotional expression simultaneously. Our results are not, however, as realistic as the best image-based speech synthesis methods. We believe that this is largely due to the lack of correct tongue motion and unrealistic rendering in our animations. We do note, however, that we can animate expressive speech for a new person without requiring any video of the person, as is needed by many of the most successful image based techniques. We are not yet able to match the realism achievable through performance-driven animation. This is not surprising, as performance-driven animation can capture many subtle content-related cues that are not possible to automatically reproduce without reliable natural language parsing. There are some situations, however, in which performance-based animation is not applicable, such as rendering animations for automatically generated text, and in any case there is an overhead in capturing the video to drive the performance.

7. Conclusions and future work

We have described fully automatic a method for synthesizing facial animations from a single static mesh which is the first to account for variations in facial dynamics over identity and emotional expression. This makes the generation of realistic animations for a new person a simple task which does not involve any specialized video capture equipment. Our framework relies on a collection of 3D facial motion capture, and organizes this data into a multilinear model capturing the space of facial dynamics over each phoneme. We then use a synthesis algorithm consisting of anime planning, blending, and sharpening stages which works with this model. Our method produces reasonable results and is general enough to be applied to other languages.

Although we are pleased with the results of this method and feel they are comparable to existing methods requiring a significant amount of data for each person to be synthesized, achieving fully realistic expressive 3D face animation remains a difficult problem with many questions that have yet to be answered. Despite our sharpening stages, our results still exhibit some degree of over-smoothing, and can occasionally contain small but noticeable errors in face dynamics. In addition, we have found that using facial motion capture of local computer science students was perhaps not the best way to capture vibrant emotional expressions. We have addressed this in our Japanese model by hiring professional actors. The data collection process required by our method is also time and labor intensive, although it only has to be done once.

We have also solicited the advice of some highly experienced lip-readers on how to best improve our method. They note that the lack of a tongue strongly detracts from the believability of our results. They also note that the lack of full-facial cues for the meaning of words, such as meaningful shakes of the head and realistic eye movements make even our captured data very difficult to lip-read. We performed a small pilot study with expert lip-readers who compared data-captured speech with speech animation from our model. Primarily due to the lack of eyes and tongue, no lip readers were able to read the captured data playback nor the animations even when provided the context for the spoken sentences. They have also suggested that capturing the speech-related motion of the throat would be useful.

In addition to addressing these concerns there are several other things which we hope to achieve in the future. Our method requires complete capture of all the combinations of each of the parameters which we wish to be able to vary in the animations. This is feasible for just identity and expression, but becomes problematic if we wish to include other things as well, such as speed, energy, or age. In general it would be desirable to be able to suffice with only a small sparse sampling of the full space of all parameter combinations. The techniques of [VBPP05] may be of some help here, but it remains an open question how to accurately infer faces from a very sparse sampling such as would be available for a model with many dimensions. We would also like to include better rendering and integrate the face animation into a full head and neck model. Although we have not focused on capturing eye or head motion in this work, doing this accurately will be necessary for fully realistic animation. Finally, it would be useful to be able to create 3D animations from a single photograph, perhaps using methods similar existing mesh-from-photograph techniques [BV99].

References

[BBVP03] BLANZ V., BASSO C., VETTER T., POGGIO T.: Reanimating faces in images and video. In *EUROGRAPHICS 2003 (EUROGRAPHICS-03) : the European Association for Computer Graphics, 24th Annual Conference* (Granada, Spain, 2003), Brunet P., Fellner D. W., (Eds.), vol. 22 of *Computer Graphics Forum*, The Eurographics Association, Blackwell, pp. 641–650.

[BCS97] BREGLER C., COVELL M., SLANEY M.: Video rewrite: driving visual speech with audio. In *SIGGRAPH '97: Proceedings of the 24th annual conference on Computer graphics and interactive techniques* (New York, NY, USA, 1997), ACM Press/Addison-Wesley Publishing Co., pp. 353–360.

[Bra99] BRAND M.: Voice puppetry. In *SIGGRAPH '99: Proceedings of the 26th annual conference on Computer graphics and interactive techniques* (New York, NY, USA, 1999), ACM Press/Addison-Wesley Publishing Co., pp. 21–28.

[BV99] BLANZ V., VETTER T.: A morphable model for the synthesis of 3d faces. In *SIGGRAPH '99: Proceedings of the 26th annual conference on Computer graphics and interactive techniques* (New York, NY, USA, 1999), ACM Press/Addison-Wesley Publishing Co., pp. 187–194.

[Cam] CAMBRIDGE UNIVERSITY ENGINEERING DEPARTMENT: Hidden markov model toolkit. http://htk.eng.cam.ac.uk/.

[CB05] CHUANG E., BREGLER C.: Mood swings: expressive speech animation. *ACM Trans. Graph. 24*, 2 (2005), 331–347.

[CE05] CHANG Y.-J., EZZAT T.: Transferable videorealistic speech animation. In *SCA '05: Proceedings of the 2005 ACM SIGGRAPH/Eurographics symposium on Computer animation* (New York, NY, USA, 2005), ACM Press, pp. 143–151.

[CTFP05] CAO Y., TIEN W. C., FALOUTSOS P., PIGHIN F.: Expressive speech-driven facial animation. *ACM Trans. Graph. 24*, 4 (2005), 1283–1302.

[DLN05] DENG Z., LEWIS J., NEUMANN U.: Synthesizing speech animation by learning compact speech co-articulation models. In *Computer Graphics International* (2005), pp. 19–25.

[EF78] EKMAN P., FRIESEN W.: The facial action coding system: A technique for the measurement of facial movement, 1978.

[EGP02] EZZAT T., GEIGER G., POGGIO T.: Trainable videorealistic speech animation. In *SIGGRAPH '02: Proceedings of the 29th annual conference on Computer graphics and interactive techniques* (New York, NY, USA, 2002), ACM Press, pp. 388–398.

[JP98] JONES M. J., POGGIO T.: Multidimensional morphable models: A framework for representing and matching object classes. *Int. J. Comput. Vision 29*, 2 (1998), 107–131.

[KB06] KIM T.-Y., BULUT M.: Expressive facial animation synthesis by learning speech coarticulation and expression spaces. *IEEE Transactions on Visualization and Computer Graphics 12*, 6 (2006), 1523–1534. Member-Zhigang Deng and Member-Ulrich Neumann and Member-J. P. Lewis and Senior Member-Shrikanth Narayanan.

[KP05] KING M.-S. A., PARENT M.-R. E.: Creating speech-synchronized animation. *IEEE Transactions on Visualization and Computer Graphics 11*, 3 (2005), 341–352.

[Lat97] LATHAUWER L. D.: *Signal Processing based on Multilinear Algebra*. PhD thesis, Faculteit der Toegepaste Wetenschappen. Katholieke Universiteit Leuven, 1997.

[LTW95] LEE Y., TERZOPOULOS D., WALTERS K.: Realistic modeling for facial animation. In *SIGGRAPH '95: Proceedings of the 22nd annual conference on Computer graphics and interactive techniques* (New York, NY, USA, 1995), ACM Press, pp. 55–62.

[LZPW03] LEVIN A., ZOMET A., PELEG S., WEISS Y.: Seamless image stitching in the gradient domain, 2003.

[MKPG05] MUELLER P., KALBERER G. A., PROESMANS M., GOOL L. V.: Realistic speech animation based on observed 3d face dynamics. *IEE Proc. Vision, Image and Signal Processing 152* (August 2005), 491–500.

[MZD05] MATUSIK W., ZWICKER M., DURAND F.: Texture design using a simplicial complex of morphable textures. In *SIGGRAPH '05: ACM SIGGRAPH 2005 Papers* (New York, NY, USA, 2005), ACM Press, pp. 787–794.

[Par82] PARKE F. I.: Parameterized models for facial animation. *j-IEEE-CGA 2*, 9 (nov 1982), 61–64, 66–68.

[PL06] PIGHIN F., LEWIS J. P.: Facial motion retargeting. In *SIGGRAPH '06: ACM SIGGRAPH 2006 Courses* (New York, NY, USA, 2006), ACM Press, p. 2.

[SSRMF06] SIFAKIS E., SELLE A., ROBINSON-MOSHER A., FEDKIW R.: Simulating speech with a physics-based facial muscle model. In *SCA '06: Proceedings of the 2006 ACM SIGGRAPH/Eurographics symposium on Computer animation* (Aire-la-Ville, Switzerland, Switzerland, 2006), Eurographics Association, pp. 261–270.

[VBPP05] VLASIC D., BRAND M., PFISTER H., POPOVIĆ J. P.: Face transfer with multilinear models. *ACM Trans. Graph. 24*, 3 (2005), 426–433.

[VT02] VASILESCU M. A. O., TERZOPOULOS D.: Multilinear analysis of image ensembles: Tensorfaces. In *ECCV '02: Proceedings of the 7th European Conference on Computer Vision-Part I* (London, UK, 2002), Springer-Verlag, pp. 447–460.

[VT04] VASILESCU M. A. O., TERZOPOULOS D.: Tensortextures: multilinear image-based rendering. In *SIGGRAPH '04: ACM SIGGRAPH 2004 Papers* (New York, NY, USA, 2004), ACM Press, pp. 336–342.

[Wat87] WATERS K.: A muscle model for animation three-dimensional facial expression. In *SIGGRAPH '87: Proceedings of the 14th annual conference on Computer graphics and interactive techniques* (New York, NY, USA, 1987), ACM Press, pp. 17–24.

[Wil90] WILLIAMS L.: Performance-driven facial animation. In *SIGGRAPH '90: Proceedings of the 17th annual conference on Computer graphics and interactive techniques* (New York, NY, USA, 1990), ACM Press, pp. 235–242.

[WWS*05] WANG H., WU Q., SHI L., YU Y., AHUJA N.: Out-of-core tensor approximation of multi-dimensional matrices of visual data. *ACM Trans. Graph. 24*, 3 (2005), 527–535.

[xCXH03] XIANG CHAI J., XIAO J., HODGINS J.: Vision-based control of 3d facial animation. In *SCA '03: Proceedings of the 2003 ACM SIGGRAPH/Eurographics symposium on Computer animation* (Aire-la-Ville, Switzerland, Switzerland, 2003), Eurographics Association, pp. 193–206.

[ZSCS04] ZHANG L., SNAVELY N., CURLESS B., SEITZ S. M.: Spacetime faces: high resolution capture for modeling and animation. *ACM Trans. Graph. 23*, 3 (2004), 548–558.

Eurographics/ ACM SIGGRAPH Symposium on Computer Animation (2007)
D. Metaxas and J. Popovic (Editors)

CoRdE: Cosserat Rod Elements for the Dynamic Simulation of One-Dimensional Elastic Objects

J. Spillmann M. Teschner

Computer Graphics, University of Freiburg, Germany

Abstract

Simulating one-dimensional elastic objects such as threads, ropes or hair strands is a difficult problem, especially if material torsion is considered. In this paper, we present CoRdE*(french 'rope'), a novel deformation model for the dynamic interactive simulation of elastic rods with torsion. We derive continuous energies for a dynamically deforming rod based on the Cosserat theory of elastic rods. We then discretize the rod and compute energies per element by employing finite element methods. Thus, the global dynamic behavior is independent of the discretization. The dynamic evolution of the rod is obtained by numerical integration of the resulting Lagrange equations of motion. We further show how this system of equations can be decoupled and efficiently solved.*
Since the centerline of the rod is explicitly represented, the deformation model allows for accurate contact and self-contact handling. Thus, we can reproduce many important looping phenomena. Further, a broad variety of different materials can be simulated at interactive rates. Experiments underline the physical plausibility of our deformation model.

Categories and Subject Descriptors (according to ACM CCS): I.3.7 [Computer Graphics]: Three-Dimensional Graphics and Realism: Animation

Keywords: Physically-based modeling, Lagrangian dynamics, Elastic rods, Cosserat theory

1. Introduction

Physically-based modeling of elastic objects has always been an active research area in computer graphics. In the past, approaches have been proposed to model one-, two- and three-dimensional elastic objects. Elastic objects whose configuration space is one-dimensional play an important role in many research fields, e. g. in engineering or microbiology. In computer animation, one-dimensional objects represent threads, ropes or hair strands. These objects are consistently denoted as *elastic rods*, independent of their actual material properties.

Despite the fact that the configuration space of a rod has only one dimension, its mathematical representation is difficult. This comes from the observation that an elastic rod can not only bend or stretch, but also twist around its centerline. Thus, the configuration of a deformed rod can not be described in terms of the position of its centerline alone. Instead, the orientation of each cross-section introduces an additional degree of freedom. Since the positions and orientations are mechanically coupled, a rod is an intrinsically constrained system. In the late 19th century, the Cosserat brothers introduced a theory for elastic rods. Nowadays, this approach has become a fundamental part of nonlinear elasticity theory.

In computer graphics, many approaches have been presented that model elastic rods with unoriented mass-spring chains without torsion [BLM04]. However, many important nonlinear effects such as bifurcation or out-of-plane buckling (see Fig. 1) arise solely due to the presence of torsional torques. Recently, approaches have been proposed that employ the Cosserat theory of elastic rods to handle the dynamics of hair strands or catheters in virtual surgery [BAC*06,Pai02]. These approaches result in boundary value problems that can be solved by employing shooting methods. They are, however, less suitable for handling contacts and self-contacts. Still, many effects such as looping phenomena require a robust handling of self-contacts, as illustrated in Fig. 1.

Our contribution. We propose CoRdE, a physically-based deformation model for one-dimensional elastic objects with torsion that is inspired by the Cosserat theory of elastic rods. Our deformation model can be used to simulate a broad variety of materials, ranging from flexible structures such as threads, ropes or hair strands to stiff objects with intrinsic bending and torsion such as springs or wires. We formulate the continuous kinetic, potential and dissipation energy for the elastic rod based on quaternion algebra. To simulate the rod dynamics, we discretize the rod into elements. From the continuous energies, we derive discrete energies by employing finite element methods. As a consequence, the global behavior of the rod is independent of the discretization. The equations of motion are obtained by taking variations of the Lagrangian. We then show how to

Symposium on Computer Animation 2007, San Diego, CA, August 03-04, 2007.
© 2007 ACM 978-1-59593-624-4/07/0008 $5.00

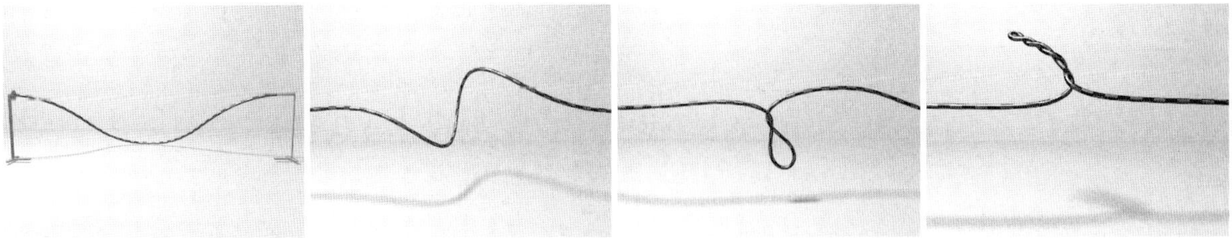

Figure 1: *Dynamic looping phenomenon of a rod under torsional strain: A rod is spanned between two anchors, and its ends are clamped. A torque transducer on the left varies the end-to-end rotation of the rod. We observe a bifurcation sequence that results in a looping with an increasing number of self-contacts. This behavior can not be reproduced by approaches that do not consider material torsion.*

decouple the resulting system of equations in order to solve it directly. In addition, we model the internal friction such that the rigid body motion of the rod is not affected.

In contrast to existing approaches that simulate the rod by solving a boundary value problem, e. g. [BAC*06, Pai02], we can handle complex collision and self-collision configurations. Thus, our deformation model enables the dynamic simulation of knots and looping phenomena. Moreover, the approach is elegant and simple to implement, and since it is linear in the number of nodes, ropes and threads can be animated at interactive rates.

Organization. After discussing the previous work, we give in Section 3 a short introduction of the Cosserat model for elastic rods that is essential for an understanding of our approach. Further, we derive expressions for the continuous potential, kinetic and dissipation energy of the deforming rod. In order to numerically simulate the rod, it is necessary to discretize it into elements, as discussed in Section 4. The potential, kinetic and dissipation energy of each element is then expressed in terms of the continuous energies. This section results in the discrete equations of motion for the rod. These equations could be solved by employing iterative numerical methods. However, this can not be done at interactive rates. Thus, we discuss in Section 5 how to decouple the system of equations such that it can be solved directly. This will include some important simplifications of the problem that result in an elegant and fast method. In Section 6, we evaluate our deformation model with respect to physical plausibility and applicability.

2. Related work

The Cosserat theory of elastic rods is well-investigated in the field of nonlinear elasticity. A comprehensive discussion of the topic is given in the book of Antman [Ant95]. Amongst others, Cosserat rods are used in robotics, micro-electronic mechanical systems [CLW06], and in computational biology to model the mechanics of DNA molecules [MM96].

In physics, most approaches deal with the analysis of elastic rod equilibria, assuming that the rods are unshearable and inextensible. The definition of a position and an orientation of the start and end point of the rod results in a boundary value problem (BVP). The analysis and numerical solution of the corresponding system of ordinary differential equations is discussed in, e. g., [Keh97]. The analysis of the dynamics of inextensible rods is considered in, e. g., [Dic94]. Our approach is inspired by finite element methods based on the Cosserat theory, notably by the works of Simo et al. [Sim85] and Cao et al. [CLW06]. In contrast to these works, we gain efficiency and simplicity by decoupling the resulting system of equations.

Physically-based simulation and animation of deformable objects is an important research area in computer graphics. A good overview on the topic is given in [NMK*05]. Physically-based animation of solids is also discussed in [MG04]. There exist two different classes of approaches to simulate and animate elastic rods, namely by considering the rod as a chain of linear objects, or by considering the rod as a curve in space. E. g. Chang et al. [CJY02] proposed an approach that is focused on hair interactions, where the hair strand is modeled from clusters linked by bending springs. Brown et al. [BLM04] published an approach to simulate knotting of ropes, including a robust collision handling scheme. They model the rope from a chain of masses and springs. However, in contrast to our deformation model, neither of these models is able to handle torsional torques. A deformable model that handles torsional torques has been presented by Wang et al. [WBD*05]. Similar to [BLM04], they model a thread from a chain of springs. In addition, they link the segments by torsional springs. In contrast to their work, we employ an energy-based approach to compute the restoration forces. Recently, Hadap [Had06] describes a methodology based on differential algebraic equations to simulate chain of rigid bodies that includes torsional stiffness dynamics. In turn, this approach is computationally expensive and thus less suitable for interactive applications.

Pioneering work in modeling elastic rods from curves has been done by Terzopoulos [TPBF87] by proposing the energy formulation of the curve in space subject to geometric deformation. Later, Qin and Terzopoulos [QT96] proposed a physically-based deformation model of a NURBS curve. They derive continuous kinetic and deformation energies, and evolve the curve by employing Lagrangian mechanics. A finite element analysis enables the simulation of the curve at interactive rates. Similar in spirit is the approach of Remion et al. [RNG00]. They employ successions of spline segments to model knitted cloth. In contrast to [QT96], they consider the control points as the degrees of freedom of the continuous object. The use of splines was also suggested by Lenoir et al. and by Phillips et al. [LMGC02, PLK02] in order to model threads. These approaches can also handle complex collision configuration. However, they have in common that material torsion can not be represented. In contrast, our deformable model handles both bending and torsion of rods in contact.

The Cosserat theory for elastic rods has first been introduced to the community by Pai in 2002 [Pai02]. He models the statics of thin deformable structures such as catheters or sutures. He assumes the rod to be unshearable and inextensible. The configuration of the rod is obtained by solving the resulting BVP. This approach provides an efficient and physically correct way to animate continuous elastic rods. However, the model does not handle dynamics. Furthermore, self-contact and interactions require numerically sensitive shooting techniques to solve the differential equations.

Recently, Bertails et al. [BAC*06] proposed an important extension of Pai's work. Their approach is a combination of a discrete and a continuous model. They simulate hair strands as chains of helical segments. Similar to the classical Cosserat rod model, they define appropriate start and end conditions. The dynamics of the super-helices are obtained by feeding the Lagrangian equation of motion with the appropriate energy terms. The configuration of the hair strand is reconstructed from the generalized coordinates that conform to twist and curvature of the segments. This deformable model is by far the most advanced way to represent elastic rods. However, it has some important restrictions: Since the segments have an intrinsic curvature, the simulation of n-point contacts [vdHNGT03] or knots requires a large number of segments. As their approach has complexity $\mathcal{O}(N^2)$ with N the number of segments, such self-collision configurations can hardly be simulated at interactive rates. In contrast, our scheme is linear in the number of elements, and designed to handle complex contact configurations such as knots. Further, we replace the viscous dissipation energy of [BAC*06] by a term that additionally considers internal friction without affecting the rigid body motion of the rod.

The approaches that are most closely related to ours are the works of Grégoire et al. [GS06] and Loock et al. [LS01]. They proposed to model a cable from joined elements where each element has a position and an orientation, the latter expressed in terms of quaternions. Then they derive constraint energies and associated forces. The goal is to find static equilibria states of cables in virtual assembly simulation. We augment their work by considering the dynamics of rods, which provides unique challenges. Further, we employ finite element methods to derive discrete energies while they simulate the rod as a simple mass-spring system.

3. Cosserat theory of elastic rods

In this section, we give a brief introduction of the Cosserat theory of elastic rods. For a more comprehensive discussion of the topic, we refer to the book of Antman [Ant95].

3.1. Representation of rods

A rod can be thought of as a long and thin deformable body. We assume that its length is significantly larger than its radius, and thus we do not explicitly represent its volume. Instead, we characterize the continuous configuration of the rod by the *centerline* $\mathbf{r}(\sigma) = (r_x(\sigma), r_y(\sigma), r_z(\sigma))^\mathsf{T}$. Here, $\mathbf{r}(\sigma) : [0,1] \longrightarrow \mathbb{R}^3$ assigns a position in space to each line parameter value $\sigma \in [0,1]$.

With this concept alone, we can not express the torsion of the rod. Thus, we think in each mass point of the rod a right-handed orthonormal basis $\mathbf{d}_1(\sigma), \mathbf{d}_2(\sigma), \mathbf{d}_3(\sigma)$. The $\mathbf{d}_i$ are called *directors*. $\mathbf{d}_3(\sigma)$ is defined to be tangential to the centerline, thus $\mathbf{d}_3$ is parallel to $\mathbf{r}'$:

$$\frac{\mathbf{r}'}{\|\mathbf{r}'\|} - \mathbf{d}_3 = 0 \qquad (1)$$

This important constraint realizes the mechanical coupling between the centerline and its orientation. Later, it will turn out that this constraint is not implicitly fulfilled but has to be explicitly enforced. Fig. 2 illustrates the representation of the rod. Notice that the prime $y'(\sigma,t)$ always denotes the spatial derivative $\frac{\partial y}{\partial \sigma}$, while the dot $\dot{y}(\sigma,t)$ denotes the temporal derivative $\frac{\partial y}{\partial t}$.

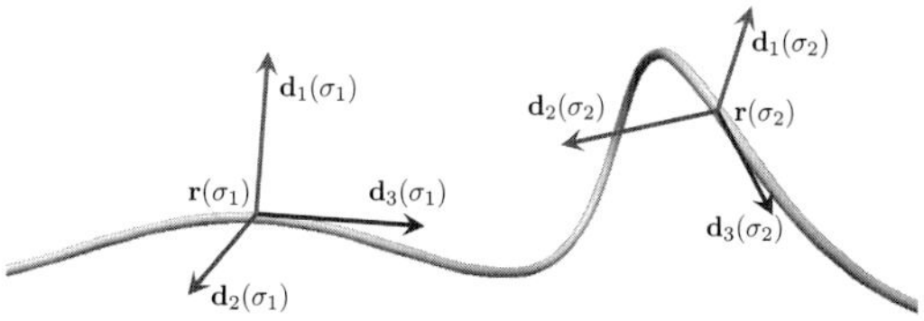

Figure 2: *The configuration of the rod is defined by its centerline* $\mathbf{r}(\sigma)$. *Further, the orientation of each mass point of the rod is represented by an orthonormal basis, called the directors.* $\mathbf{d}_3(\sigma)$ *is constrained to be parallel to* $\mathbf{r}'(\sigma)$

The length of the spatial derivative $\|\mathbf{r}'(\sigma)\|$ indicates the stretch of the centerline $\mathbf{r}$ at σ. Without loss of generality, we assume the length of the rod to be 1. As a consequence, $\|\mathbf{r}'\| = 1$ if the rod is unstretched. Some variants of the Cosserat rod model [MM96, BAC*06] consider the rod to be inextensible, which does, however, lead to stiff equations.

The spatial derivatives $\mathbf{d}_k'$ of the directors indicate the spatial rate of change in bending and torsion. From differential geometry, it is known that there exists a vector $\mathbf{u}$ with

$$\mathbf{d}_k' = \mathbf{u} \times \mathbf{d}_k, \qquad k = 1,2,3 \qquad (2)$$

$\mathbf{u}$ is called the *Darboux vector*. The Darboux vector is an important quantity in the Cosserat theory since the strain rates for the bending and torsion can be expressed as

$$u_k = \mathbf{u} \cdot \mathbf{d}_k, \qquad k = 1,2,3 \qquad (3)$$

The values u_1 and u_2 measure the strain in the two bending directions while u_3 measures the torsional strain. Later, we derive the expression for the potential energy from these strain rates.

The temporal derivative $\dot{\mathbf{r}}(\sigma)$ of the centerline indicates the translational velocity of the mass point at σ. The angular velocity ω is related to the temporal derivatives of the directors by

$$\dot{\mathbf{d}}_k = \omega \times \mathbf{d}_k, \qquad k = 1,2,3 \qquad (4)$$

The components $\omega_k = \omega \cdot \mathbf{d}_k$ measure the angular velocity of the cross section rotating around director $\mathbf{d}_k$.

3.2. Representation of rotation

In order to relate the directors $\mathbf{d}_i$ to the reference frame, we have to choose a representation of rotation, i. e. a representation for the group of orthogonal rotations SO(3). In the literature, both Euler angles, and quaternions (also known as Euler parameters) have been proposed.

The Euler angles use the minimum number of parameters to represent the rotation, but they suffer from singularities such as the gimbal lock. Having this in mind, we use quaternions to represent the rotation. A quaternion can be thought of as a quadruple $\mathbf{q} = (q_1, q_2, q_3, q_4)^\mathsf{T}$ with $q_i \in \mathbb{R}$. Only unit quaternions represent pure rotations, thus the q_i are not independent but coupled by the constraint $\|\mathbf{q}\| = 1$. The directors $\mathbf{d}_i$ in terms of the quaternion $\mathbf{q}$ are given by:

$$\mathbf{d}_1 = \begin{pmatrix} q_1^2 - q_2^2 - q_3^2 + q_4^2 \\ 2(q_1q_2 + q_3q_4) \\ 2(q_1q_3 - q_2q_4) \end{pmatrix}, \mathbf{d}_2 = \begin{pmatrix} 2(q_1q_2 - q_3q_4) \\ -q_1^2 + q_2^2 - q_3^2 + q_4^2 \\ 2(q_2q_3 + q_1q_4) \end{pmatrix}$$

$$\mathbf{d}_3 = \begin{pmatrix} 2(q_1q_3 + q_2q_4) \\ 2(q_2q_3 - q_1q_4) \\ -q_1^2 - q_2^2 + q_3^2 + q_4^2 \end{pmatrix} \tag{5}$$

The strain rates u_k in the local frame are obtained as

$$u_k = \frac{2}{\|\mathbf{q}\|^2} \mathbf{B}_k \mathbf{q} \cdot \mathbf{q}' \tag{6}$$

where $\mathbf{B}_k \in \mathbb{R}^{4\times 4}$ is a constant skew-symmetric matrix. For the angular velocity components ω_k in the local frame, a similar relation is stated as

$$\omega_k = \frac{2}{\|\mathbf{q}\|^2} \mathbf{B}_k \mathbf{q} \cdot \dot{\mathbf{q}} \tag{7}$$

The angular velocity components ω_k^0 with respect to the reference frame are

$$\omega_k^0 = \frac{2}{\|\mathbf{q}\|^2} \mathbf{B}_k^0 \mathbf{q} \cdot \dot{\mathbf{q}} \tag{8}$$

where $\mathbf{B}_k^0 \in \mathbb{R}^{4\times 4}$ is a constant skew-symmetric matrix. ω^0 is required to derive the angular dissipation energy. The derivation of (6) and (7) and the expressions for $\mathbf{B}_k$ and $\mathbf{B}_k^0$ are given in the Appendix.

3.3. Energy formulation

Based upon the strain-displacement and angular velocity relations (6), (7) and (8), we derive the continuous kinetic, potential and dissipation energy of the deformed rod.

3.3.1. Potential energy

The potential energy consists of two parts, namely the energy V_s of the stretch deformation, and the energy V_b of the bending and torsional deformation. The stretch energy V_s is given as

$$V_s = \frac{1}{2} \int_0^1 K_s (\|\mathbf{r}'\| - 1)^2 d\sigma \tag{9}$$

where shear is neglected. K_s is the stretching stiffness constant that is computed from a stretching Young's modulus E_s with $K_s = E_s \pi r^2$. The bending energy V_b follows from the strain rates (6)

$$V_b = \frac{1}{2} \int_0^1 \sum_{k=1}^{3} K_{kk} \left(\frac{2}{\|\mathbf{q}\|^2} \mathbf{B}_k \mathbf{q} \cdot \mathbf{q}' - \hat{u}_k\right)^2 d\sigma \tag{10}$$

The $\hat{u}_k$ conform to the intrinsic bending and torsion of the rod and $\mathbf{K} = (K_{kk}) \in \mathbb{R}^{3\times 3}$ is the stiffness tensor. Since we assume that the rod has a uniform cross section, we can neglect the off-diagonal terms in $\mathbf{K}$. From textbooks on mechanics we get

$$K_{11} = K_{22} = E\frac{\pi r^2}{4}, \quad K_{33} = G\frac{\pi r^2}{2} \tag{11}$$

with E denoting the Young's modulus governing the bending resistance, G denoting the shear modulus governing the torsional resistance, and r denoting the radius of the rod's cross section.

For ideal rods, the stretching Young's modulus E_s is equal to the bending Young's modulus E. However, in order to get an additional degree of freedom, it is useful to define two independent constants E and E_s. This is motivated by the observation that e. g. nylon ropes do not have a uniform cross section, but are composed of several strands. As a consequence, the observed bending resistance is much lower than the theoretical bending resistance computed from the Young's modulus.

Together, we obtain the potential energy V as $V = V_s + V_b$. The values for r, E, E_s and G depend on the simulated material (see Appendix).

3.3.2. Kinetic energy

The kinetic energy of the rod consists of two parts, namely the translational energy T_t of the centerline $\mathbf{r}$, and the rotational energy T_r of the rod cross section. The translational energy is

$$T_t = \frac{1}{2} \int_0^1 \rho \pi r^2 \dot{\mathbf{r}} \cdot \dot{\mathbf{r}} d\sigma \tag{12}$$

where ρ is the density per unit length, and r is the radius of the rod. The rotational energy follows from the expressions for the angular velocities (7)

$$T_r = \frac{1}{2} \int_0^1 \sum_{k=1}^{3} I_{kk} \left(\frac{2}{\|\mathbf{q}\|^2} \mathbf{B}_k \mathbf{q} \cdot \dot{\mathbf{q}}\right)^2 d\sigma \tag{13}$$

where $\mathbf{I} = (I_{kk}) \in \mathbb{R}^{3\times 3}$ is the inertia tensor that is approximated as

$$I_{11} = I_{22} = \rho\frac{\pi r^2}{4}, \quad I_{33} = \rho\frac{\pi r^2}{2} \tag{14}$$

As before, the off-diagonal terms in $\mathbf{I}$ can be neglected. The total kinetic energy T is then $T = T_t + T_r$. The numerical values for ρ and r are given in the Appendix.

3.3.3. Dissipation energy

The dissipation energy captures internal friction and visco-elastic effects. A heuristic model for visco-elastic effects has been proposed in [BAC*06]. To model internal friction, we propose an approach that is inspired by the pioneering work of Baraff and Witkin [BW98] on constrained cloth simulation.

The internal friction damps relative velocity in the rod. The relative translational velocity can be computed as the spatial derivative of the temporal derivative of the centerline **r** acting in the tangential direction $\mathbf{r}'$. The translational dissipation energy D_t is

$$D_t = \frac{1}{2}\int_0^1 \gamma_t \mathbf{v}^{(rel)} \cdot \mathbf{v}^{(rel)} d\sigma \tag{15}$$

where γ_t is the translational internal friction coefficient. $\mathbf{v}^{(rel)} = \frac{1}{\|\mathbf{r}'\|^2}\mathbf{r}'(\dot{\mathbf{r}}' \cdot \mathbf{r}')$ is the projected relative translational velocity of the mass points.

The relative angular velocity is obtained from the spatial derivative of the angular velocity ω_0. It is important to compute the angular velocity in the reference frame in order to consider all quantities in the same basis. The rotational dissipation energy D_r is then

$$D_r = \frac{1}{2}\int_0^1 \gamma_r \omega_0' \cdot \omega_0' d\sigma \tag{16}$$

where γ_r is the rotational internal friction coefficient. ω_0 can be obtained from (8). The total dissipation energy $D = D_t + D_r$ is the sum of the translational and rotational dissipation energy.

3.4. Lagrangian equation of motion

The dynamic equilibrium configuration of an elastic rod is characterized as a critical point of the Lagrangian $L = T - V + D$ subject to the holonomic constraints

$$\mathbf{C}_p \equiv \frac{\mathbf{r}'}{\|\mathbf{r}'\|} - \mathbf{d}_3 = 0 \tag{17}$$

$$C_q \equiv \|\mathbf{q}\|^2 - 1 = 0 \tag{18}$$

The vector-valued constraint (17) states that the third director conforms to the spatial derivative of the centerline **r**. This constraint couples the orientations and the positions of the rod. The scalar constraint (18) states that the quaternion has unit length and thus represents a proper rotation.

By employing calculus of variations and by introducing Lagrangian multipliers $\lambda \in \mathbb{R}^3$ and $\mu \in \mathbb{R}$ for the constraints, we obtain the Lagrangian equation of motion for an elastic rod:

$$\frac{d}{dt}\frac{\partial T}{\partial \dot{g}_i} - \frac{\partial T}{\partial g_i} + \frac{\partial V}{\partial g_i} + \frac{\partial D}{\partial \dot{g}_i} + \lambda \cdot \frac{\partial \mathbf{C}_p}{\partial g_i} + \mu\frac{\partial C_q}{\partial g_i} = \int_0^1 \mathbf{F}_e d\sigma \tag{19}$$

Here, the $g_i \in \{r_x, r_y, r_z, q_1, q_2, q_3, q_4\}$ are the coordinates, and $\mathbf{F}_e$ are external forces and torques. Details can be found in the book of Goldstein [Gol81].

4. Discrete energy formulation

In this section, we discretize the rod into elements. We then derive expressions for the potential and kinetic energy per element by employing finite element methods. This discretization allows for an efficient numerical solution of the equations of motion (19).

4.1. Discretization of the rod

We represent the centerline $\mathbf{r}(\sigma)$ of the rod as a chain of N nodes $\mathbf{r}_i \in \mathbb{R}^3, i \in [1, N]$. The centerline elements $\mathbf{r}_{i+1} - \mathbf{r}_i$ may differ in size. The orientations of the centerline elements are represented by quaternions $\mathbf{q}_j, j \in [1, N-1]$, as illustrated in Fig. 3. A similar representation has been proposed by Grégoire and Schömer in [GS06]. In contrast to pure geometric approaches such as [LMGC02], this representation allows to model material torsion.

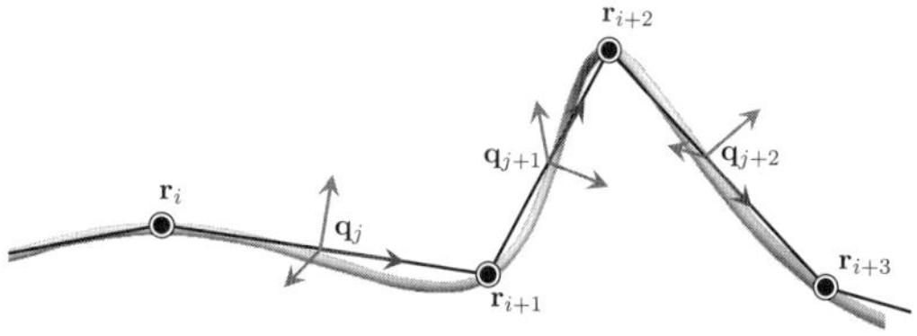

Figure 3: *The centerline of the rod is discretized into nodes $\mathbf{r}_i$. The orientation of the centerline element $\mathbf{r}_{i+1} - \mathbf{r}_i$ is represented by a quaternion $\mathbf{q}_j$ that is attached to the centerline element at its midpoint.*

The discrete spatial derivative $\mathbf{r}_i'$ of the centerline is obtained as $\mathbf{r}_i' = \frac{\mathbf{r}_{i+1} - \mathbf{r}_i}{\|\mathbf{r}_{i+1} - \mathbf{r}_i\|}$. By assuming a high stretch stiffness, we approximate $\mathbf{r}_i'$ as

$$\mathbf{r}_i' \approx \frac{1}{l_i}(\mathbf{r}_{i+1} - \mathbf{r}_i) \tag{20}$$

where $l_i = \|\mathbf{r}_{i+1}^0 - \mathbf{r}_i^0\|$ is the resting length of the centerline element i. Here, the $\mathbf{r}_i^0$ are the initial positions of the mass points.

To derive an expression for the discrete spatial derivative $\mathbf{q}_j'$ of the orientation, we consider that the quaternion $\mathbf{q}_j$ represents the orientation of the centerline element $\mathbf{r}_{i+1} - \mathbf{r}_i$. Thus, an orientation element j starts at the midpoint of centerline element i and ends at the midpoint of centerline element $i+1$. For $\mathbf{q}_j'$, we thus approximate

$$\mathbf{q}_j' \approx \frac{1}{l_j}(\mathbf{q}_{j+1} - \mathbf{q}_j) \tag{21}$$

where $l_j = \frac{1}{2}(\|\mathbf{r}_{i+2}^0 - \mathbf{r}_{i+1}^0\| + \|\mathbf{r}_{i+1}^0 - \mathbf{r}_i^0\|)$ is the resting length of the orientation element j.

4.2. Discrete energies

In this section, we derive the formulations of the potential, kinetic and dissipation energy for the discrete Cosserat rod. We compute the energies per centerline and orientation element by integrating the energies over the length of the respective element. The total energy of the rod could then be obtained by summing up the individual energies. However, this will not be necessary since we solve the Lagrangian equation of motion per node.

In our discrete setting, the displacements are only given at the nodes. Therefore, we interpolate the displacements within the elements. For simplicity, we employ constant shape functions $\bar{\mathbf{r}}(\xi)$ and $\bar{\mathbf{q}}(\xi)$, i. e.

$$\bar{\mathbf{r}}_i(\xi) = \bar{\mathbf{r}}_i = \frac{1}{2}(\mathbf{r}_i + \mathbf{r}_{i+1}) \tag{22}$$

and

$$\bar{\mathbf{q}}_j(\xi) = \bar{\mathbf{q}}_j = \frac{1}{2}(\mathbf{q}_j + \mathbf{q}_{j+1}) \tag{23}$$

These shape functions result in particularly simple expressions when integrated over the element length. Experiments indicate that higher-order shape functions do barely increase the visual plausibility, but require significantly more computations.

4.2.1. Discrete potential energy

To derive the expression for the stretch energy, we integrate over the length l_i of the centerline segment i. Assuming that the spatial derivative $\mathbf{r}_i'$ stays constant per element, the stretch energy per element i follows from (9) as

$$\begin{aligned} V_s[i] &= \frac{1}{2}\int_0^{l_i} K_s(\|\mathbf{r}_i'\| - 1)^2 d\xi \\ &= \frac{1}{2} l_i K_s(\frac{1}{l_i}\sqrt{(\mathbf{r}_{i+1} - \mathbf{r}_i)\cdot(\mathbf{r}_{i+1} - \mathbf{r}_i)} - 1)^2 \end{aligned} \tag{24}$$

To derive the expression for the bending energy, we integrate over the length l_j of the orientation element j. We further assume that the spatial derivative $\mathbf{q}_j'$ stays constant. Thus

$$V_b[j] = \frac{1}{2}\int_0^{l_j}\sum_{k=1}^{3} K_{kk}(\underbrace{\frac{2}{\|\bar{\mathbf{q}}_j\|^2}}_{\approx 2}\mathbf{B}_k\bar{\mathbf{q}}_j\cdot\mathbf{q}_j' - \hat{u}_k)^2 d\xi \tag{25}$$

$$= \frac{l_j}{2}\sum_{k=1}^{3} K_{kk}(\mathbf{B}_k(\mathbf{q}_j + \mathbf{q}_{j+1})\cdot\frac{1}{l_j}(\mathbf{q}_{j+1} - \mathbf{q}_j) - \hat{u}_k)^2$$

where we made the simplifying assumption that the quaternions have unit length, which is justified since the unit-constraint (18) is explicitly enforced.

4.2.2. Discrete kinetic energy

Similar to the previous section, we consider the kinetic translational energy per centerline element, and the kinetic rotational energy per orientation element. By plugging (22) into (12) and integrating over the centerline element i, we get

$$\begin{aligned} T_t[i] &= \frac{1}{2}\int_0^{l_i} \rho\pi r^2 \dot{\bar{\mathbf{r}}}_i\cdot\dot{\bar{\mathbf{r}}}_i d\xi \\ &= \frac{1}{8}\rho\pi r^2 l_i(\dot{\mathbf{r}}_{i+1} + \dot{\mathbf{r}}_i)\cdot(\dot{\mathbf{r}}_{i+1} + \dot{\mathbf{r}}_i) \end{aligned} \tag{26}$$

For the rotational kinetic energy, we integrate over the orientation element j. The resulting energy expression is

$$T_r[j] = \frac{1}{2}\int_0^{l_j}\sum_{k=1}^{3} I_{kk}(\underbrace{\frac{2}{\|\bar{\mathbf{q}}_j\|^2}}_{\approx 2}\mathbf{B}_k\bar{\mathbf{q}}_j\cdot\dot{\bar{\mathbf{q}}}_j)^2 d\xi$$

$$= \frac{l_j}{8}\sum_{k=1}^{3} I_{kk}(\mathbf{B}_k(\mathbf{q}_j + \mathbf{q}_{j+1})\cdot(\dot{\mathbf{q}}_j + \dot{\mathbf{q}}_{j+1}))^2 \tag{27}$$

4.2.3. Discrete dissipation energy

To obtain the dissipation energy expression, we proceed as in the previous sections. Again, the translational dissipation energy is obtained by integrating over the centerline elements, and the rotational dissipation energy is obtained by integrating over the orientation elements. For the translational dissipation energy D_t we get

$$\begin{aligned} D_t[i] &= \frac{1}{2}\int_0^{l_i} \gamma_t \mathbf{v}_i^{(rel)}\cdot\mathbf{v}_i^{(rel)} d\xi \\ &= \frac{l_i}{2}\gamma_t\mathbf{v}_i^{(rel)}\cdot\mathbf{v}_i^{(rel)} \end{aligned} \tag{28}$$

with the projected relative translational velocity $\mathbf{v}_i^{(rel)}$ as

$$\begin{aligned} \mathbf{v}_i^{(rel)} &= \underbrace{\frac{1}{\|\mathbf{r}_i'\|^2}}_{\approx 1}\mathbf{r}_i'(\dot{\mathbf{r}}_i'\cdot\mathbf{r}_i') \\ &= \frac{1}{l_i^3}(\mathbf{r}_{i+1} - \mathbf{r}_i)\Big((\dot{\mathbf{r}}_{i+1} - \dot{\mathbf{r}}_i)\cdot(\mathbf{r}_{i+1} - \mathbf{r}_i)\Big) \end{aligned} \tag{29}$$

where we made the simplifying assumption that $\|\mathbf{r}_i'\| \approx 1$, which is valid for rods with a large stretching stiffness. The rotational dissipation energy D_r is obtained as

$$\begin{aligned} D_r[j] &= \frac{1}{2}\int_0^{l_j}\gamma_r\sum_{k=1}^{3}(\frac{1}{l_j}2\mathbf{B}_k^0\mathbf{q}_{j+1}\dot{\mathbf{q}}_{j+1} - \frac{1}{l_j}2\mathbf{B}_k^0\mathbf{q}_j\dot{\mathbf{q}}_j)^2 d\xi \\ &= \frac{2}{l_j}\gamma_r\sum_{k=1}^{3}(\mathbf{B}_k^0\mathbf{q}_{j+1}\dot{\mathbf{q}}_{j+1} - \mathbf{B}_k^0\mathbf{q}_j\dot{\mathbf{q}}_j)^2 \end{aligned} \tag{30}$$

where we assume $\|\mathbf{q}_j\| \approx 1$ for all j. Notice that here we do not interpolate the displacements within the orientation element but compute the relative rotational velocity between the two orientation nodes. It is important to take the relative velocities with respect to the reference frame.

5. Numerical solution

In the last section, we have divided the rod into elements. For each element, we have derived the potential, kinetic and dissipation energy. We now show how we can solve the Lagrangian equation of motion by employing those energy terms. We further propose an efficient implementation of the necessary constraints such that the system of equations is decoupled.

5.1. Assembly of the equations of motion

The Lagrangian equation of motion (19) characterizes the dynamic equilibrium of the rod. By substituting the continuous energies in (19) with the per-element energies derived in the previous section, we arrive at the discrete Lagrangian equation of motion that characterizes the dynamic equilibrium per element. The necessary symbolic differentiation is performed by employing the computer algebra software Maple. This results in a system of equations of the form

$$\mathbf{M}\ddot{\mathbf{g}} + \mathbf{f}(\dot{\mathbf{g}},\mathbf{g}) = (\mathbf{F}_e\ \tau_e)^{\mathsf{T}} \tag{31}$$

The matrix $\mathbf{M}(\dot{\mathbf{g}},\mathbf{g})$ contains nonlinear terms in $\dot{\mathbf{g}} = \{\dot{\mathbf{r}},\dot{\mathbf{q}}\}$ and $\mathbf{g} = \{\mathbf{r},\mathbf{q}\}$. Further, $\mathbf{f}(\dot{\mathbf{g}},\mathbf{g})$ conforms to a nonlinear stiffness function that is obtained by symbolically differentiating the potential and dissipation energy with respect to the coordinates. Evaluating this function results in internal forces and torques. $\mathbf{F}_e$ and τ_e are the external forces and torques that act on the rod.

The system of equations can be solved by employing iterative methods, e. g. with a conjugate gradient method. However, the numerical solution is expensive and can hardly be done at interactive rates for larger rods. In the next two sections, we propose two simplifications of the problem that result in a decoupled system of equations that can be solved directly.

5.2. Implementation of the constraints

The coupling between the orientation of the rod and its centerline is realized by the constraint (17). To implement the constraints in (19), we have introduced Lagrangian multipliers.

At this point, we underline that a Cosserat rod is an intrinsically constrained system. In computer graphics, many approaches have been presented on maintaining constraints in dynamic systems. An application of Lagrangian multipliers to articulated rigid bodies has e. g. been proposed by Baraff [Bar96]. Earlier, Witkin et al. [WFB87] have proposed to express geometric constraints by energy functions, an approach that is also known as *penalty method*. They formulated a constraint as an energy function $E(\mathbf{x}) : \mathbb{R}^n \to \mathbb{R}$ with $E(\mathbf{x}) = 0$ if the constraint is satisfied. Differentiating this energy function with respect to $\mathbf{x}$ yields constraint forces $\mathbf{F}$ that accelerate the system towards the desired configuration.

The advantage of the penalty method is its efficiency: The constraints do not appear as additional equations in the Lagrangian equation of motion, but they act as additional forces on the system. The disadvantage is the loss of physical accuracy: Since the constraint forces act during a time period h on the system, they violate the principle of virtual power [Gol81]. However, since our goal is to obtain a simulation that behaves in a physical plausible way, we decided to employ energy constraints. We thus express the parallel constraint (17) by an energy function

$$E_p = \frac{1}{2}\int_0^1 \kappa\left(\frac{\mathbf{r}'}{\|\mathbf{r}'\|} - \mathbf{d}_3\right)\cdot\left(\frac{\mathbf{r}'}{\|\mathbf{r}'\|} - \mathbf{d}_3\right)d\sigma \qquad (32)$$

where κ is a spring constant. In our discrete model, the direction of the centerline element $\mathbf{r}_{i+1} - \mathbf{r}_i$ has to conform to the third director of the basis representing the orientation of this element. Thus, the discrete constraint energy per centerline element reads as

$$\begin{aligned} E_p[i] &= \frac{1}{2}\int_0^{l_i} \kappa\Big(\frac{\mathbf{r}_i'}{\|\mathbf{r}_i'\|} - \mathbf{d}_3(\mathbf{q}_i)\Big)\cdot\Big(\frac{\mathbf{r}_i'}{\|\mathbf{r}_i'\|} - \mathbf{d}_3(\mathbf{q}_i)\Big)d\xi \qquad (33) \\ &= \frac{l_i}{2}\kappa\Big(\frac{\mathbf{r}_{i+1}-\mathbf{r}_i}{\|\mathbf{r}_{i+1}-\mathbf{r}_i\|} - \mathbf{d}_3(\mathbf{q}_i)\Big)\cdot\Big(\frac{\mathbf{r}_{i+1}-\mathbf{r}_i}{\|\mathbf{r}_{i+1}-\mathbf{r}_i\|} - \mathbf{d}_3(\mathbf{q}_i)\Big) \end{aligned}$$

What have we gained with this constraint transformation? The constraint energy $E_p[i]$ can now be treated as an additional potential energy term in the Lagrangian equation of motion of the rod. By symbolic differentiation, we obtain an additional internal force term acting on the mass points and an additional internal torque term acting on the quaternions. In fact, these forces and torques are responsible for many rod phenomena such as buckling and looping. The numerical values of κ depend on the simulated material (see Appendix).

To enforce the quaternion unit length constraint (18), we employ an even simpler method that is sometimes referred as coordinate projection [ESF98]: In each iteration of the numerical simulation, we explicitly renormalize the quaternions $\hat{\mathbf{q}}$, i. e. $\mathbf{q}_i \leftarrow \frac{\hat{\mathbf{q}}_i}{\|\hat{\mathbf{q}}_i\|}$. Although this technique does not guarantee energy conservation, it does not harm the visual quality of the simulation.

5.3. Decoupling of the state equations

By expressing the constraint (17) by an energy function, we have reduced the number of equations in (31). The accelerations $\ddot{\mathbf{q}}$ and $\ddot{\mathbf{r}}$ are obtained by inverting the mass matrix $\mathbf{M}$. This is accomplished by considering the structure of $\mathbf{M}$. Since the positions and orientations are exclusively coupled by the constraint energy, $\mathbf{M}$ has a block-diagonal form

$$\mathbf{M} = \begin{pmatrix} \mathbf{M}_r & \mathbf{0} \\ \mathbf{0} & \mathbf{M}_q \end{pmatrix} \qquad (34)$$

where $\mathbf{M}_r$ is the mass matrix governing the state equations of the mass points $\mathbf{r}_i$, and $\mathbf{M}_q$ is the mass matrix of the quaternions $\mathbf{q}_j$.

Since we assume that the mass is lumped in the mass points $\mathbf{r}_i$, the mass matrix $\mathbf{M}_r$ is diagonal. The equations of motion for the mass points are obtained as

$$\begin{aligned} \dot{\mathbf{v}}_i &= \frac{\mathbf{F}_i}{m_i} \\ \dot{\mathbf{r}}_i &= \mathbf{v}_i \end{aligned} \qquad (35)$$

where $\mathbf{F}_i$ is the sum of internal and external forces acting on the mass point, $\mathbf{v}_i$ its velocity, and m_i its mass.

The mass matrix $\mathbf{M}_q$ governing the evolution of the quaternions is not diagonal. However, it is possible to express the equations of motion not by the quaternions and their time derivatives, but to use the angular velocities ω_j together with the quaternions $\mathbf{q}_j$ as state variables [SM06]. This results in a diagonalized system of equations for the quaternions,

$$\begin{aligned} \dot{\omega}_j &= \mathbf{I}^{-1}(\tau_j - \omega_j \times \mathbf{I}\omega_j) \\ \dot{\mathbf{q}}_j &= \tfrac{1}{2}\mathbf{Q}_j\begin{pmatrix} 0 \\ \omega_j \end{pmatrix} \end{aligned} \qquad (36)$$

Here, τ_j is the sum of internal and external torques that act on the quaternion, $\mathbf{I}$ is the inertia tensor, and $\mathbf{Q}_j$ is the quaternion matrix of $\mathbf{q}_j$. The quaternion matrix allows to write a quaternion multiplication as a matrix-vector product,

(35) and (36) define an initial value problem (IVP), where the initial configuration of the rod is user-defined. The IVP is solved by numerical integration, as discussed in the subsequent section.

5.4. Numerical solution of the initial value problem

We summarize the simulation process. The stiffness function $\mathbf{f}(\dot{\mathbf{r}}, \mathbf{r}, \dot{\mathbf{q}}, \mathbf{q})$ that governs the computation of the internal forces and torques is obtained by differentiating the potential and constraint energy with respect to the coordinates $\mathbf{r}$ and

$\mathbf{q}$, and by differentiating the dissipation energy with respect to the time derivatives $\dot{\mathbf{r}}$ and $\dot{\mathbf{q}}$. This symbolic differentiation is done as a preprocessing step.

Subsequent positions $\mathbf{r}^{t+h}$ and orientations $\mathbf{q}^{t+h}$ are obtained by time integration of the state equations (35) and (36). The internal forces and torques are obtained from evaluating $\mathbf{f}(\dot{\mathbf{r}}^t, \mathbf{r}^t, \dot{\mathbf{q}}^t, \mathbf{q}^t)$ in the current configuration of the rod. External forces include gravity, contact forces, and user interactions. External torques are neglected. We denote the resulting sum of internal and external forces in the current configuration as $\mathbf{F}^t$ and the resulting internal torques as τ^t.

To evolve the mass points, we numerically integrate the state equations (35) by employing a semi-implicit Euler scheme:

$$\mathbf{v}_i^{t+h} = \mathbf{v}_i^t + \frac{h}{m_i}\mathbf{F}^t \qquad (37)$$

$$\mathbf{r}_i^{t+h} = \mathbf{r}_i^t + h\mathbf{v}_i^{t+h} \qquad (38)$$

This scheme provides sufficient conditional stability at minor computational overhead.

The evolution of the orientations is slightly more involved. The torques $\tau^t \in \mathbb{R}^4$ resulting from evaluating $\mathbf{f}$ are dual to the quaternions. However, to evolve the angular velocities ω, we need to transform the τ^t into Euclidean torques $\tilde{\tau}^t \in \mathbb{R}^3$. This transformation is accomplished by a multiplication with the transposed quaternion matrix,

$$\begin{pmatrix} 0 \\ \tilde{\tau}_j \end{pmatrix} = \frac{1}{2}\mathbf{Q}_j^{\mathrm{T}}\tau_j \qquad (39)$$

For details on quaternion transformations we refer to Schwab and Meijaard [SM06]. The numerical integration of the rotational state equations (36) is also realized with the semi-implicit Euler scheme,

$$\omega_j^{t+h} = \mathbf{I}^{-1}(\tilde{\tau}_j^t - \omega_j^t \times (\mathbf{I}\omega_j^t))h + \omega_j^t \qquad (40)$$

$$\hat{\mathbf{q}}_j^{t+h} = \frac{1}{2}\mathbf{Q}_j^t \begin{pmatrix} 0 \\ \omega_j^{t+h} \end{pmatrix} h + \mathbf{q}_j^t \qquad (41)$$

$$\mathbf{q}_j^{t+h} = \frac{\hat{\mathbf{q}}_j^{t+h}}{\|\hat{\mathbf{q}}_j^{t+h}\|} \qquad (42)$$

where the last step explicitly normalizes the quaternions.

6. Results

The purpose of the experiments is to illustrate the physical plausibility of our deformation model. Further, we show that the approach is well-suited for interactive applications.

To enable contact and self-contact configurations, we have implemented a standard deformable model collision handling scheme [TKH*05]. To detect collisions, we employ axis-aligned bounding box hierarchies, and to compute the repulsion forces, we employ an adaptation of the constraint-based response scheme from [SBT07]. All experiments have been staged on an Intel Xeon PC, 3.8GHz. The offline rendering is accomplished with a raytracer, the real-time rendering with OpenGL. For rendering, the rods are skinned with a tubical, B-spline interpolated surface mesh.

# Elements	Force comp. [ms]	Integration [ms]
50	0.051	0.018
100	0.096	0.035
1000	0.91	0.33

Table 1: *Timings for the force computation and integration of discretized rods. The timings indicate that the method is linear in the number of elements.*

6.1. Discrete rods

The purpose of these experiments is to show that the dynamic global behavior of real rods can be reproduced. The material parameters are summarized in Tab. 2 in the Appendix.

In a first experiment, we study the global deformation of clamped rods that occur when the end-to-end rotation is varied. These experiments are inspired by recent research in the field of nonlinear mechanics [vdHNGT03]. The experimental setup is shown in Fig. 1 on the left. A torque transducer exerts a continued torsional rotation on the rod, while the right end of the rod stays clamped. The rod forms a looping with an increasing number of self-contacts. The number of self-contacts is obviously limited by the number of elements of the rod. The radius and the location of the loop are influenced by the ratio of bending and torsion stiffness [vdHNGT03]. The time step of the simulation is $h = 0.1$ms. The rod is discretized into 100 elements. To validate our deformation model, we performed the same experiment with a real rope. Fig. 4 illustrates the looping sequence of the rope under torsional strain. Although the material parameters of the real rope differ in magnitude, its global deformation is comparable to the simulated virtual rope.

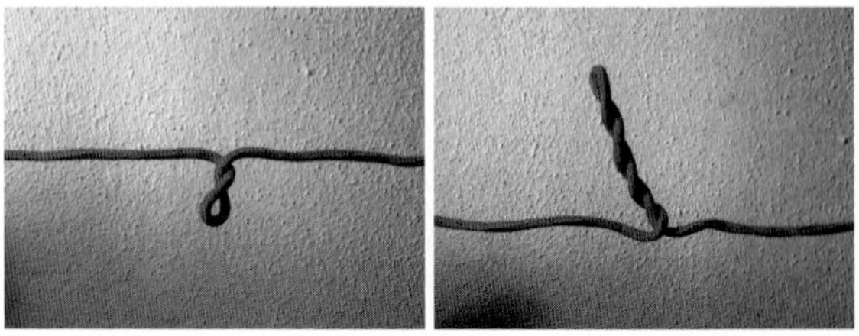

Figure 4: *To validate our deformation model, we performed the varied end-to-end rotation experiment with a real rope. The global deformation is comparable to the simulated virtual rope in Fig. 1.*

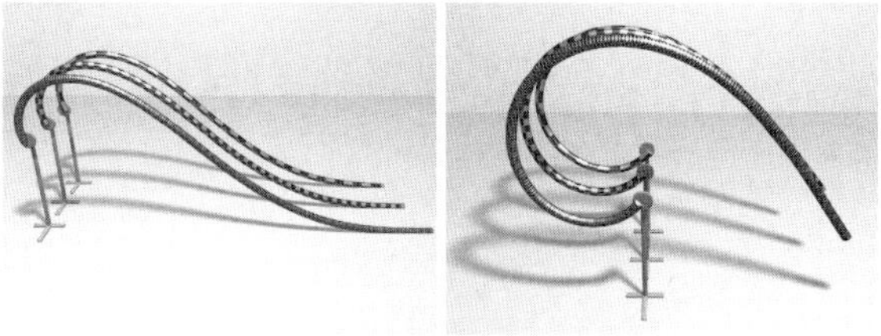

Figure 5: *Coiling up three clamped rods. The rods are discretized into 1000, 100 and 50 elements, illustrating that the global deformation is independent of the discretization.*

In a second experiment, we clamp the left ends of three rods to torque transducers. The transducers exert a continued rotation on the rods, thus coiling up the rods (see Fig. 5). The front rod is discretized into 1000 elements, the middle rod is discretized into 100 elements and the back rod is discretized into 50 elements. The time step is $h = 0.1$ms. The figures illustrate that the global deformation of the rods is independent of the discretization. Further, this experiment illustrates that our deformation model is linear in the number of elements. Timings are summarized in Tab. 1.

6.2. Pre-shaped stiff objects

Due to the robustness of our deformation model, a broad variety of different materials can be simulated. We can simulate highly flexible structures such as ropes as well as stiff objects such as bars. By defining an intrinsic bending and torsion, it is also possible to simulate pre-shaped objects such as springs. In these experiments, we model stiff wire-like objects whose material parameters are summarized in Tab. 2 in the Appendix. Each rod is discretized into 50 elements. The stiff equations require a small time step $h = 0.05$ms. Fig. 6 illustrates the dynamic simulations.

Figure 6: *Dynamic simulation of stiff objects. Left: Stacking of rods. Right: Objects with intrinsic bending and torsion.*

6.3. Virtual interactive ropes and threads

Since our approach is linear in the number of elements, elastic rods can be simulated at interactive rates. Further, internal friction minimizes oscillations and makes the material look more realistic.

To illustrate that our deformation model can be used in interactive applications, we run a simulation of a thread consisting of 100 elements. Its material parameters are summarized in Tab. 2 in the Appendix. While one end of the thread is clamped, the user can freely interact with the centerline (Fig. 7). In this experiment, the user ties a knot into the thread. The time step is $h = 2$ms, and the configuration is rendered after 20 simulation steps. The simulation runs at 26 frames per second. As indicated in Fig. 7 on the bottom right, it is also possible to interact with an intrinsically coiled thread.

7. Conclusion and future work

We have presented CoRDE, a physically-based deformation model to simulate one-dimensional elastic objects. The deformation model is inspired by the Cosserat theory of elastic rods. We have discretized the rod into elements. For each element, we have derived the Lagrange equations

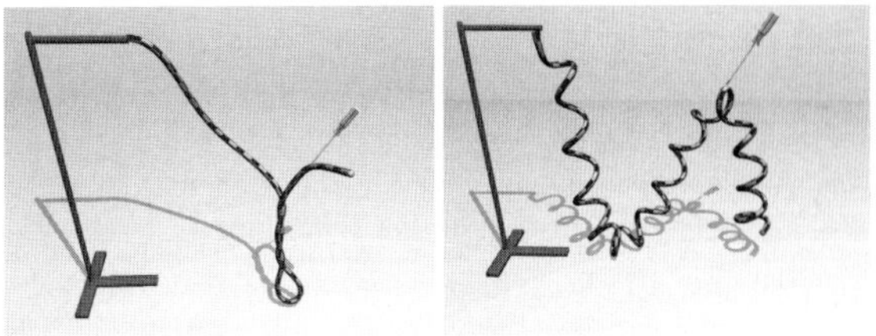

Figure 7: *Interactive simulation of threads. The user can freely interact with the thread. Oscillations are minimized by modeling internal friction.*

of motion by employing finite element methods. By numerically integrating these equations, the rod is evolved in time. In contrast to previous mass-spring approaches, the rod behavior is independent of the underlying discretization, and the finite element approach enables physically plausible simulation. In contrast to previous boundary value approaches [Pai02, BAC*06], the nodal approach allows for accurate and efficient collision and self-collision handling.

By employing our deformation model, a broad variety of different materials can be plausibly simulated and animated. This is partially enabled by modeling internal friction such that the rigid body motion of the rod is not affected. Since our method is linear in the number of nodes, the approach is particularly interesting for interactive applications. Moreover, the approach is elegant and simple to implement.

However, this deformation model is just a starting point for future research. In order to improve the physical accuracy of the method, a constraint handling that considers the principle of virtual power would be favorable. Since the constraint couples positions and orientations, this is a challenging problem. Further, virtual suturing requires that the thread can be tied to tight knots, which requires a solid collision handling. Currently, we are investigating into improved collision detection and response methods. Since the elements may differ in size, the rod can be adaptively refined in regions where precise collision handling is necessary.

References

[Ant95] ANTMAN S. S.: *Nonlinear Problems of Elasticity*. Springer Verlag, 1995.

[BAC*06] BERTAILS F., AUDOLY B., CANI M.-P., QUERLEUX B., LEROY F., LÉVÊQUE J.-L.: Super-helices for predicting the dynamics of natural hair. In *ACM Transactions on Graphics (Proc. SIGGRAPH)* (2006), pp. 1180–1187.

[Bar96] BARAFF D.: Linear-time dynamics using lagrange multipliers. *Computer Graphics (Proc. SIGGRAPH)* (1996), 137–146.

[BLM04] BROWN J., LATOMBE J.-C., MONTGOMERY K.: Real-time knot tying simulation. *The Visual Computer 20*, 2–3 (2004), 165–179.

[BW98] BARAFF D., WITKIN A.: Large steps in cloth simulation. In *Proc. SIGGRAPH* (1998), pp. 43–54.

[CJY02] CHANG J. T., JIN J., YU Y.: A practical model for hair mutual interactions. In *Proc. ACM SIGGRAPH/Eurographics symposium on Computer animation* (2002), pp. 73–80.

[CLW06] CAO D. Q., LIU D., WANG C. H.-T.: Three dimensional nonlinear dynamics of slender structures: Cosserat rod element approach. *International Journal of Solids and Structures 43*, 3–4 (2006), 760–783.

[Dic94] DICHMANN D. J.: *Hamiltonian Dynamics of a Spatial Elastica and the Stability of Solitary Waves*. PhD thesis, 1994. University of Maryland.

[ESF98] EICH-SOELLNER E., FÜHRER C.: *Numerical methods in multibody dynamics*. European Consortium for Mathematics in Industry. B. G. Teubner, Stuttgart, 1998.

[Gol81] GOLDSTEIN H.: *Classical Mechanics*, 2 ed. Addison-Wesley, 1981.

[GS06] GRÉGOIRE M., SCHÖMER E.: Interactive simulation of one-dimensional flexible parts. In *Proc. ACM Symposium on Solid and physical modeling* (2006), pp. 95–103.

[Had06] HADAP S.: Oriented strands: dynamics of stiff multi-body system. In *Proc. ACM SIGGRAPH/Eurographics symposium on Computer animation* (2006), pp. 91–100.

[Keh97] KEHRBAUM S.: *Hamiltonian Formulations of the Equilibrium Conditions Governing Elastic Rods: Qualitative Analysis and Effective Properties.* PhD thesis, 1997. University of Maryland.

[LMGC02] LENOIR J., MESEURE P., GRISONI L., CHAILLOU C.: Surgical thread simulation. *Modelling & Simulation for Computer-aided Medicine and Surgery* (2002), 102–107.

[LS01] LOOCK A., SCHÖMER E.: A virtual environment for interactive assembly simulation: From rigid bodies to deformable cables. In *Proc. 5th World Multiconference on Systemics, Cybernetics and Informatics* (2001), vol. 3, pp. 325–332.

[MG04] MÜLLER M., GROSS M.: Interactive virtual materials. In *Proc. Graphics interface* (2004), pp. 239–246.

[MM96] MANNING R. S., MADDOCKS J. H.: A continuum rod model of sequence-dependent dna structure. *J. Chem. Phys. 105* (1996), 5626–5646.

[NMK*05] NEALAN A., MÜLLER M., KEISER R., BOXERMANN E., CARLSON M.: Physically Based Deformable Models in Computer Graphics. In *Eurographics-STAR* (2005), pp. 71–94.

[Pai02] PAI D.: Strands: Interactive simulation of thin solids using cosserat models. *Computer Graphics Forum (Eurographics) 21*, 3 (2002), 347–352.

[PLK02] PHILLIPS J., LADD A., KAVRAKI L. E.: Simulated knot tying. In *Proc. IEEE International Conference on Robotics & Automation* (2002), pp. 841–846.

[QT96] QIN H., TERZOPOULOS D.: D-NURBS: A Physics-Based Framework for Geometric Design. *IEEE Transactions on Visualization and Computer Graphics 2*, 1 (1996), 85–96.

[RNG00] REMION Y., NOURRIT J.-M., GILLARD D.: A dynamic animation engine for generic spline objects. *Journal of Visualization and Computer Animation 11*, 1 (2000), 17–26.

[SBT07] SPILLMANN J., BECKER M., TESCHNER M.: Non-iterative computation of contact forces for deformable objects. *Journal of WSCG 15*, 1-3 (2007), 33–40.

[Sim85] SIMO J. C.: A finite strain beam formulation. the three-dimensional dynamic problem. part I. *Computer Methods in Applied Mechanics and Engineering 49* (1985), 55–70.

[SM06] SCHWAB A. L., MEIJAARD J. P.: How to draw euler angles and utilize euler parameters. In *Proc. IDETC/CIE 2006, ASME 2006 International Design Engineering Technical Conferences & Computers and Information in Engineering Conference* (2006).

[TKH*05] TESCHNER M., KIMMERLE S., HEIDELBERGER B., ZACHMANN G., RAGHUPATHI L., FUHRMANN A., CANI M.-P., FAURE F., MAGNENAT-THALMANN N., STRASSER W., VOLINO P.: Collision Detection for Deformable Objects. *Computer Graphics Forum 24*, 1 (2005), 61–81.

[TPBF87] TERZOPOULOS D., PLATT J., BARR A., FLEISCHER K.: Elastically deformable models. *Computer Graphics (Proc. SIGGRAPH) 21*, 4 (1987), 205–214.

[vdHNGT03] VAN DER HEIJDEN G., NEUKIRCH S., GOSS V., THOMPSON J.: Instability and self-contact phenomena in the writhing of clamped rods. *International Journal of Mechanical Sciences 45*, 1 (2003), 161–196.

[WBD*05] WANG F., BURDET E., DHANIK A., POSTON T., TEO C.: Dynamic thread for real-time knot-tying. In *Proc. First Joint Eurohaptics Conference and Symposium on Haptic Interfaces for Virtual Environment and Teleoperator Systems* (2005), pp. 507–508.

[WFB87] WITKIN A., FLEISCHER K., BARR A.: Energy constraints on parameterized models. *Computer Graphics 21*, 4 (1987), 225–232.

Appendix A: Derivation of strain rates in terms of quaternions

In this section, we derive the expression (6) that relates the strain rates u_k to the quaternions $\mathbf{q}$. The derivation of the relation between the angular velocity ω and the quaternions $\mathbf{q}$ is similar. The construction is a summary from the corresponding issue in the thesis of Dichmann [Dic94]. For further details, we refer the reader to the cited document.

We know that there exists the Darboux vector $\mathbf{u}$ that is related to the directors $\mathbf{d}_k$ by

$$\mathbf{d}'_k = \mathbf{u} \times \mathbf{d}_k, \qquad k = 1,2,3 \tag{43}$$

where the components u_k of $\mathbf{u}$ are directly proportional to the strain rates. Since the $\mathbf{d}_k$ define an orthonormal basis, we write $\mathbf{u} = u_1\mathbf{d}_1 + u_2\mathbf{d}_2 + u_3\mathbf{d}_3$. For $\mathbf{d}'_3$, we then obtain for example

$$\begin{aligned} \mathbf{d}'_3 &= (u_1\mathbf{d}_1 + u_2\mathbf{d}_2 + u_3\mathbf{d}_3) \times \mathbf{d}_3 \\ &= u_1\mathbf{d}_1 \times \mathbf{d}_3 + u_2\mathbf{d}_2 \times \mathbf{d}_3 + u_3\mathbf{d}_3 \times \mathbf{d}_3 \\ &= -u_1\mathbf{d}_2 + u_2\mathbf{d}_1 \end{aligned} \tag{44}$$

where we used the identities $\mathbf{d}_3 = \mathbf{d}_1 \times \mathbf{d}_2$ and $\mathbf{d}_k \times \mathbf{d}_k = 0, k = 1,2,3$. Multiplying (44) by $-\mathbf{d}_2$ yields

$$-\mathbf{d}_2 \cdot \mathbf{d}'_3 = u_1\mathbf{d}_2 \cdot \mathbf{d}_2 - u_2\mathbf{d}_1 \cdot \mathbf{d}_2 = u_1 \tag{45}$$

For u_2 and u_3, we similarly obtain $u_2 = -\mathbf{d}_3 \cdot \mathbf{d}'_1$ and $u_3 = -\mathbf{d}_1 \cdot \mathbf{d}'_2$.

The relation between the directors $\mathbf{d}_k$ and the quaternion $\mathbf{q}$ is given in (5). To compute $\mathbf{d}'_k$, we note that $\mathbf{d}'_k$ is a function of $\mathbf{q}$ and $\mathbf{q}$ is a function of the curve parameter σ:

$$\mathbf{d}'_k = \mathbf{d}'_k(\mathbf{q}(\sigma)) = \frac{\partial \mathbf{d}_k(\mathbf{q}(\sigma))}{\partial \sigma} = \frac{\partial \mathbf{d}_k}{\partial \mathbf{q}} \frac{\partial \mathbf{q}}{\partial \sigma} = \mathbf{J}_k \mathbf{q}' \tag{46}$$

where we employed the chain rule of partial differentiation. $\mathbf{J}_k$ is the Jacobi matrix $\mathbf{J}_k = \frac{\partial \mathbf{d}_k}{\partial \mathbf{q}}$ that is obtained by symbolic differentiation. For u_1, we now write

$$u_1 = -\mathbf{d}_2 \cdot \mathbf{J}_3 \mathbf{q}' = -\mathbf{J}_3^{\mathsf{T}} \mathbf{d}_2 \cdot \mathbf{q}' \tag{47}$$

which results from applying basic linear algebra identities. Similar expressions are obtained for u_2 and u_3. To bring (47) to the desired form (6), we symbolically evaluate the product $\mathbf{J}_3^{\mathsf{T}}\mathbf{d}_2$ to obtain

$$\mathbf{J}_3^{\mathsf{T}}\mathbf{d}_2 = \frac{2}{\|\mathbf{q}\|^2} \begin{pmatrix} q_4 & q_3 & -q_2 & -q_1 \end{pmatrix}^{\mathsf{T}} = \frac{2}{\|\mathbf{q}\|^2} \mathbf{B}_1 \mathbf{q} \tag{48}$$

with the skew-symmetric matrix $\mathbf{B}_1$

$$\mathbf{B}_1 = \begin{pmatrix} 0 & 0 & 0 & 1 \\ 0 & 0 & 1 & 0 \\ 0 & -1 & 0 & 0 \\ -1 & 0 & 0 & 0 \end{pmatrix}$$

The strain rate u_1 can then be obtained by combining (47) and (48). The matrices $\mathbf{B}_2$ and $\mathbf{B}_3$ are obtained in a similar manner as

$$\mathbf{B}_2 = \begin{pmatrix} 0 & 0 & -1 & 0 \\ 0 & 0 & 0 & 1 \\ 1 & 0 & 0 & 0 \\ 0 & -1 & 0 & 0 \end{pmatrix}, \quad \mathbf{B}_3 = \begin{pmatrix} 0 & 1 & 0 & 0 \\ -1 & 0 & 0 & 0 \\ 0 & 0 & 0 & 1 \\ 0 & 0 & -1 & 0 \end{pmatrix}$$

The skew-symmetric matrices $\mathbf{B}_k$ and the resulting vectors $\mathbf{B}_k\mathbf{q}$ have several important properties that are discussed in [Dic94]. A similar analysis [Dic94] can be done to obtain the angular velocities ω_k^0 with respect to the reference frame, resulting in matrices $\mathbf{B}_k^0$:

$$\mathbf{B}_1^0 = \begin{pmatrix} 0 & 0 & 0 & 1 \\ 0 & 0 & -1 & 0 \\ 0 & 1 & 0 & 0 \\ -1 & 0 & 0 & 0 \end{pmatrix}, \quad \mathbf{B}_2^0 = \begin{pmatrix} 0 & 0 & 1 & 0 \\ 0 & 0 & 0 & 1 \\ -1 & 0 & 0 & 0 \\ 0 & -1 & 0 & 0 \end{pmatrix}$$

and

$$\mathbf{B}_3^0 = \begin{pmatrix} 0 & -1 & 0 & 0 \\ 1 & 0 & 0 & 0 \\ 0 & 0 & 0 & 1 \\ 0 & 0 & -1 & 0 \end{pmatrix}$$

Appendix B: Material parameters

	Ropes	Wires	Threads
Length [m]	10	0.1	1
Radius r [m]	0.01	0.001	0.001
Density ρ [kg m^{-3}]	1300	7860	1300
Young modulus E [MPa]	0.5	200	10^{-5}
Shearing modulus G [MPa]	0.5	100	10^{-5}
Stretch modulus E_s [MPa]	20	100	0.02
Spring const. κ [10^3 kg m s^{-2}]	100	300	0.1
γ_t [10^{-6} kg m^3 s^{-1}]	10	0.05	1
γ_r [10^{-6} kg m^3 s^{-1}]	1	0.01	0.1

Table 2: *Material parameters for the objects simulated in the experiments. The parameter values have been determined by visually comparing the behavior of the simulated objects to their real counterparts.*

Eurographics/ ACM SIGGRAPH Symposium on Computer Animation (2007)
D. Metaxas and J. Popovic (Editors)

Arbitrary Cutting of Deformable Tetrahedralized Objects

Eftychios Sifakis† Stanford University Intel Corporation
Kevin G. Der † Stanford University
Ronald Fedkiw† Stanford University Industrial Light+Magic

Abstract

We propose a flexible geometric algorithm for placing arbitrary cracks and incisions on tetrahedralized deformable objects. Although techniques based on remeshing can also accommodate arbitrary fracture patterns, this flexibility comes at the risk of creating sliver elements leading to models that are inappropriate for subsequent simulation. Furthermore, interactive applications such as virtual surgery simulation require both a relatively low resolution mesh for efficient simulation of elastic deformation and highly detailed surface geometry to facilitate accurate manipulation and cut placement. Thus, we embed a high resolution material boundary mesh into a coarser tetrahedral mesh using our cutting algorithm as a meshing tool, obtaining meshes that can be efficiently simulated while preserving surface detail. Our algorithm is similar to the virtual node algorithm in that we avoid sliver elements and their associated stringent timestep restrictions, but it is significantly more general allowing for the arbitrary cutting of existing cuts, sub-tetrahedron resolution (e.g. we cut a single tetrahedron into over a thousand pieces), progressive introduction of cuts while the object is deforming, and moreover the ability to accurately cut the high resolution embedded mesh.

Categories and Subject Descriptors (according to ACM CCS): I.3.5 [Computer Graphics]: Physically based modeling I.3.7 [Computer Graphics]: Animation

1. Introduction

Methods for modeling and animating cracks and incisions on rigid or deformable solids have received significant attention in computer graphics, some dating back to the early days of deformable models [TF88a, TF88b]. One class of applications dealt with modeling the phenomena of material failure and fracture (see e.g. [OH99, OBH02]) while other methods focused on incisions that are explicitly placed on a deformable model, for example in the context of a surgical manipulation in a virtual simulation environment.

Virtual surgery in particular has spawned a very active thread of research due to the high visibility and impact of such applications as well as the unique algorithmic requirements it entails. Interactivity in a virtual surgery application mandates the use of a relatively coarse simulation mesh to obtain high frame rates. At the same time, a substantially higher resolution is required on the surface geometry to prevent distorting features that are essential in planning incisions and manipulating the flesh. These requirements place severe limitations on the design of a cutting algorithm. For example, methods that decompose tetrahedra into subelements in order to cut the mesh (e.g. [BMG99, BGTG03]) create many more tetrahedra (essentially making a fine resolution mesh near the cuts) and create ill-conditioned tetrahedra that impose severe time step restrictions (see e.g. [MK00, BG00]) making the simulation impractical even on the low resolution base mesh. Thus, some authors have avoided element decomposition resorting instead to other techniques such as deleting any element touched by the blade [FDA02], or restricting cutting to mesh element boundaries [NvdS00]. Whereas the second option can produce a jagged surface, subsequent snapping of nodes can smooth the cut surface [NvdS01,SHS01]. Of course, this also tends to produce sliver elements, and some authors have proposed the use of meshing algorithms such as edge collapse to remove degenerate tetrahedra [GO01, SHGS06].

Although first proposed in the context of fracture, the virtual node algorithm [MBF04] alleviates many of the aforementioned difficulties. By duplicating elements to obtain new degrees of freedom necessary for modeling the topological change, it preserves the conditioning of the initial mesh while creating a minimal number of new elements. Thus one obtains the goal of a low number of well-conditioned elements. A limitation of the virtual node algorithm is that if the mesh were completely fractured, the smallest possible units would be individual nodes surrounded by their incident material. A tetrahedron can be cut at most once along

† email: {sifakis|kder|fedkiw}@cs.stanford.edu

Symposium on Computer Animation 2007, San Diego, CA, August 03-04, 2007.
© 2007 ACM 978-1-59593-624-4/07/0008 $5.00

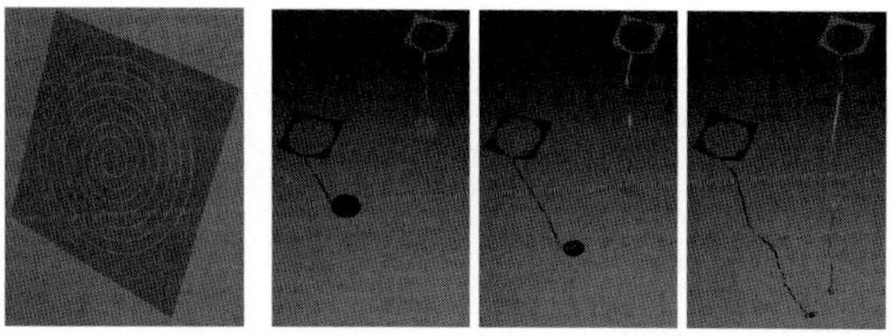

Figure 1: *A spiral cut applied to a piece of cloth leads to the unwinding of a long ribbon. The uncut triangulated surface consists of 128 triangles, while the final embedding mesh contains 587 triangles.*

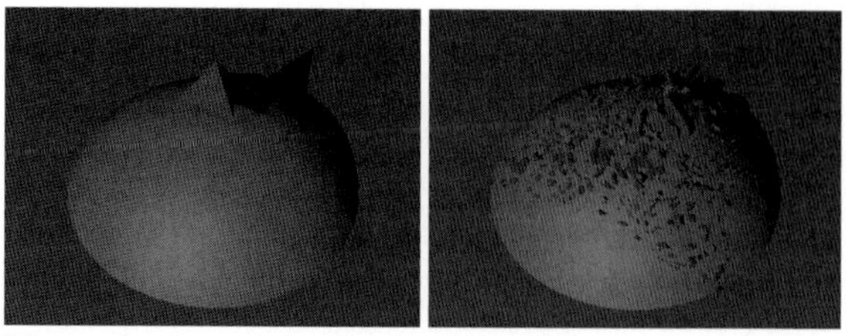

Figure 2: *Our algorithm is used to slice a single tetrahedron into over a thousand pieces placing no restriction on the placement or number of cuts. These pieces are not constrained to lie on nodes or faces, and most of them are completely within the tetrahedron. Many are even too small to visualize. However since they are embedded in a tetrahedron equivalent to the original one, they are efficient to simulate.*

each edge and can only be fractured into four pieces. Thus, the resolution of the simulation mesh effectively limits the resolution of the cutting surface. For a virtual surgery application, where a coarser mesh and precise cuts are required, such restrictions could be detrimental. For example, even a simple V-shaped cut would typically have to be heavily distorted so that the cutting surface only "turns" along element boundaries. More elaborate cuts, such as T-shaped incisions, would incur even more serious distortion or could even lead to spurious material connections. For fracture on the other hand, where finer meshes are typically used and jagged cracks are acceptable, these restrictions are not as severe. An improved version of the virtual node algorithm was proposed in [TSSB*05] for embedding a high resolution tetrahedral muscle geometry into a coarser resolution tetrahedral simulation mesh. They diagrammatically showed that the virtual node concept could be extended to split a tetrahedron into as many pieces as required to embed arbitrary geometry, and used the high resolution tetrahedral muscle geometry mesh to prescribe the connectivity of the coarse embedding mesh. An important limitation of their method, however, is the requirement for a full tetrahedralization of the embedded geometry (rather than a description of its boundary surface), rendering it inapplicable to virtual surgery applications which define a cutting surface without any predetermined notion of volumetric connectivity.

[SOG06] proposed a meshless method for simulating a finite element constitutive model similar to the fracture work in [PKA*05] (see also [WSG05]). However, they stress that the crack itself is better modeled with explicit triangulated geometry rather than with the meshless method. This decoupling of the cutting surface from the simulation geometry (i.e. an explicit triangulated cutting surface combined with a meshless discretization of the simulation geometry) is similar in spirit to the fracture work of [MTG04, MBF04] both of which embedded a triangulated surface into a background simulation mesh. Stressing that this explicit triangulation of the cutting surface permits geometric operations such as subdivision and self-intersection resolution, we devise a novel algorithm that allows for a direct implementation of the conceptual diagram from [TSSB*05] without requiring any predetermined notion of volumetric connectivity (as they do). Thus, our algorithm can also be used as an embedded meshing tool which, using only the boundary surface of an input object, will embed it in an arbitrary simulation mesh duplicating the degrees of freedom of the embedding mesh as needed to resolve the topology and connectivity of the original embedded object. This feature is demonstrated in figure 10 where a high-resolution triangulated surface of a face is used to carve an embedded flesh volume out of a coarser embedding mesh. In this example, embedding tetrahedra touching both the upper and the lower lip are automatically duplicated to allow opening of the mouth. Finally, such embedded models may be further cut if desired, as shown in figure 10.

Our main contribution is a cutting algorithm that yields efficient simulation models while imposing no restriction on the geometry of the cuts. In this aspect it combines the favorable traits of other methods in the literature while alleviating most of their limitations. For example, it provides the versatility of remeshing-based or point-based methods in accommodating arbitrary cuts, while maintaining the simplicity and efficiency of an underlying tetrahedral representation (unlike point-based methods) and preventing stringent timestep restrictions due to ill-conditioned sliver elements (unlike methods based on remeshing). Similar to the virtual node algorithm it creates new degrees of freedom to reflect the topological changes incurred by the cuts while preserving the good conditioning of the initial mesh, but avoids the restrictions on the geometry of the cutting surface imposed by the formulation of [MBF04]. When used as an embedded meshing tool, it provides the freedom to embed an arbitrary high resolution geometry in a coarser simulation mesh in the fashion of [TSSB*05] but only requires a surface representation of the embedded geometry as contrasted to the full volumetric representation required by their approach. Finally, our method supports incremental introduction of cuts as well as cutting an object while it deforms.

2. Previous Work

[NTB*91,HTK98,MMA99,SWB01] broke connections between elements under high stress, [NF99] addressed blast waves, [MG04, MTG04] considered fracture along element

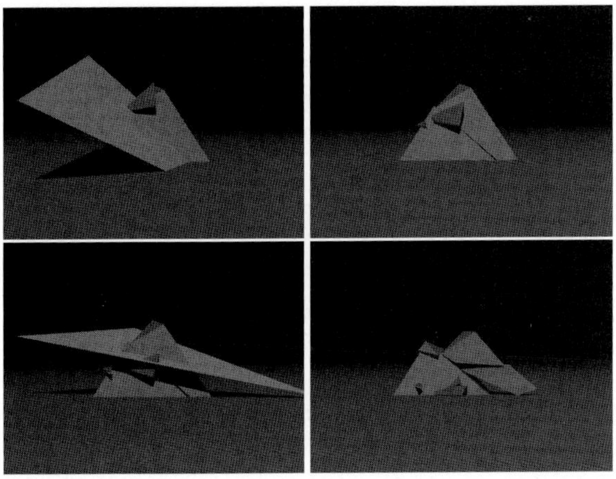

Figure 3: *A single tetrahedron is progressively cut (including through previous cuts) as the fragments are simulated. Each cut consists of a single triangle depicted in gold.*

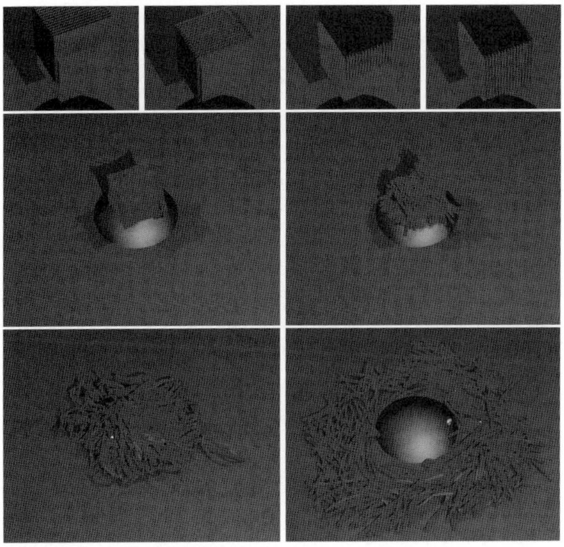

Figure 4: *32 intersecting planes slice a 320 element tetrahedral mesh into 289 sticks. 8K embedding tetrahedra are created after the cutting operation.*

boundaries in an FFD framework, [OH99, YOH00, OBH02] handled fracture events using continuous remeshing, and [MMDJ01] treated fragments as rigid bodies in between collisions. The virtual node algorithm has also been used for melting and burning solids [LIGF06]. [GSH*05, GLB*06] treated the fracture of thin shells, and [BHTF06] addressed the fracture of rigid materials. Modeling of cuts has also been addressed in the context of virtual surgery, especially on facial models [KGC*96, PRZ92, KGPG96] where the cut surface is the result of an explicit surgical manipulation, rather than a physical Rankine condition for fracture.

3. Cutting Algorithm

In our approach there are two simulation primitives, a background tetrahedral simulation mesh and a triangulated cutting surface. When embedding a high resolution material surface mesh into the background tetrahedral mesh, the high resolution surface is considered part of the cutting surface and in fact our cutting algorithm is used to generate this embedded geometry (see Figure 10). Virtual surgery applications progressively add triangles to the cutting surface along the blade's swept front, while fracture applications add triangles based on stress criteria.

3.1. The Cutting Surface

Triangles in the cutting surface may be initially intersecting, e.g. T-cuts are common to many surgical procedures. Leveraging our explicit description of the cutting surface, we resolve self-intersections through subdivision of the cutting triangles. One approach is to compute intersections among all triangles in the cutting surface and then to retriangulate into an intersection-free surface, but we have found that using a polygonal subdivision is more robust and efficient. In particular, one could triangulate our polygonal elements, but subsequent cuts that yield intersections would force further subdivision of these triangles unnecessarily creating more triangles and possibly poorly conditioned triangles. Given a soup of cutting triangles, the polygonal subdivision is unique and can be updated incrementally preserving uniqueness whereas the triangulation is not unique, based on heuristics, and may be found suboptimal when further cutting triangles are added. This means that one would be forced to undo previous triangulations in order to avoid degeneracies and poor conditioning due to newly introduced cuts, hindering the incremental nature of the algorithm.

Our approach is to resolve the cutting triangles into an intersection-free, nonmanifold *polygon mesh*. Each cutting triangle is subdivided into a number of polygons, whose edges are line segments that result from the pairwise intersection of this cutting triangle with all other cutting triangles. When adding new cuts incrementally, these new triangles are resolved with the existing polygons obviating the need to re-examine all past cuts. We will of course eventually triangulate these polygons for collisions and visualization, but the potentially resulting sliver elements are not used by our cutting algorithm and thus do not impact its conditioning.

We compute the polygonization of any triangle in the triangle soup as follows. A node of the polygon mesh is defined in one of three possible ways: a vertex of a triangle in the soup, an intersection between a triangle edge and a face at a point interior to the face, or an intersection of three triangles that occurs at a point interior to all three (see Figure 6). Each triangle is then subdivided into polygons by connecting incident nodes with segments. We place segments between any two incident nodes that are also on a given second triangle. That is, if node 1 and node 2 are both incident on triangle 1 and triangle 2, then a segment is added between

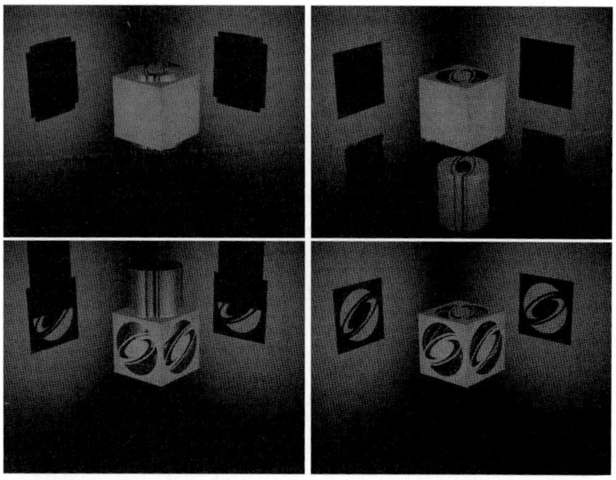

Figure 5: *A cookie cutter surface is used to cut away pieces of a 625 element tetrahedral mesh. Alternating between rotating and cutting allows the pattern to appear on all sides.*

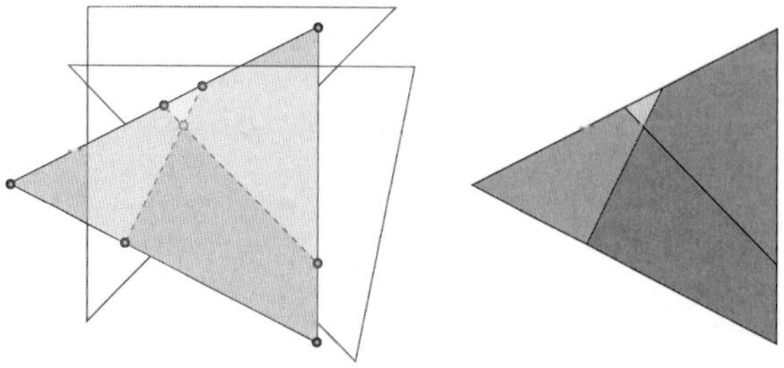

Figure 6: *Left: A triangle (colored blue) in the triangle soup intersects with other triangles. Nodes in the polygon mesh can be vertices of a triangle (shown in purple), intersections of triangle edges with triangle interiors (red), or intersections of three triangles (yellow). Right: We construct segments between nodes to tessellate the triangle into polygons that are intersection-free with all other cutting triangles.*

them. We also add segments between any two nodes that lie on the same edge of a triangle from the soup. This definition results in overlapping segments when multiple nodes are collinear, and thus we only construct the minimal set of non-overlapping segments. Finally, the triangle is projected into two spatial dimensions where a boundary tracking algorithm is used to identify each closed polygon (see Figure 6).

3.2. Clipping to the Simulation Mesh

Besides resolving the cutting surface into non-intersecting polygons rather than triangles, a second key to our approach is to further subdivide the cutting surface in a manner that removes intersections with the faces of the tetrahedral simulation mesh. This allows for a tetrahedron-centric approach to the algorithm facilitating subsequent topological processing. This also preserves the incremental nature of the algorithm, since adding a new cut only affects the intersected tetrahedra. Thus, most importantly, we treat both cutting triangles and tetrahedron faces as elements of a large triangle soup and we resolve *all* of these triangles simultaneously into an intersection-free polygon mesh. As mentioned in the previous subsection, incrementally added cutting triangles are resolved with the the existing polygon mesh where our notion of a polygon mesh now includes polygons on tetrahedron faces as well.

In practice, our tetrahedron-centric algorithm is carried out as follows. First, a tetrahedron intersected by a cutting triangle is assigned a copy of that triangle for independent processing, where the triangle is projected into the tetrahedron's barycentric space. When polygonizing that triangle copy, we do so using a pool of segments collected only from the faces of this tetrahedron and any other cutting triangles that intersect this tetrahedron. The resulting polygons can be independently generated per tetrahedron. Since the faces of the tetrahedron are also in the triangle soup, no polygon segment crosses a tetrahedron boundary, allowing us to trivially prune away polygons that are not on or within the tetrahedron. Note that neighboring tetrahedra that share a face will find the exact same polygons on that common face. See Figure 7, which illustrates a two-dimensional version of our algorithm, where a cutting segment spans three triangles from the background mesh. Since each triangle owns a copy of this cutting segment stored in barycentric coordinates, subsequent deformation of the mesh leads to three non-coincident copies of this cutting segment that only agree at element boundaries.

3.3. Per-Tetrahedron Subdivision

After each tetrahedron has generated its subset of the polygon mesh, we determine the volumetric connected components of material within each tetrahedron. Each connected component is a polyhedron that we compute using boundary tracking on the polygons in the tetrahedron. Then each connected component is embedded in a duplicate copy of the original tetrahedron. Unlike the virtual node algorithm, con-

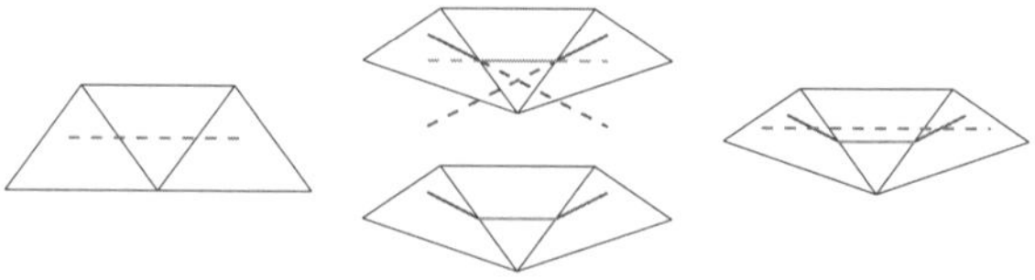

Figure 7: *Clipping the cutting elements in a two-dimensional version of our algorithm. A cutting segment spans three embedding triangles (left). Each triangle receives a copy of the segment. When the embedding deforms, the copies only remain coincident at element boundaries and are clipped to their respective embedding elements (middle). A second cut applied after deformation may intersect the first cut in multiple locations, which is easily resolved with our element-centric approach (right).*

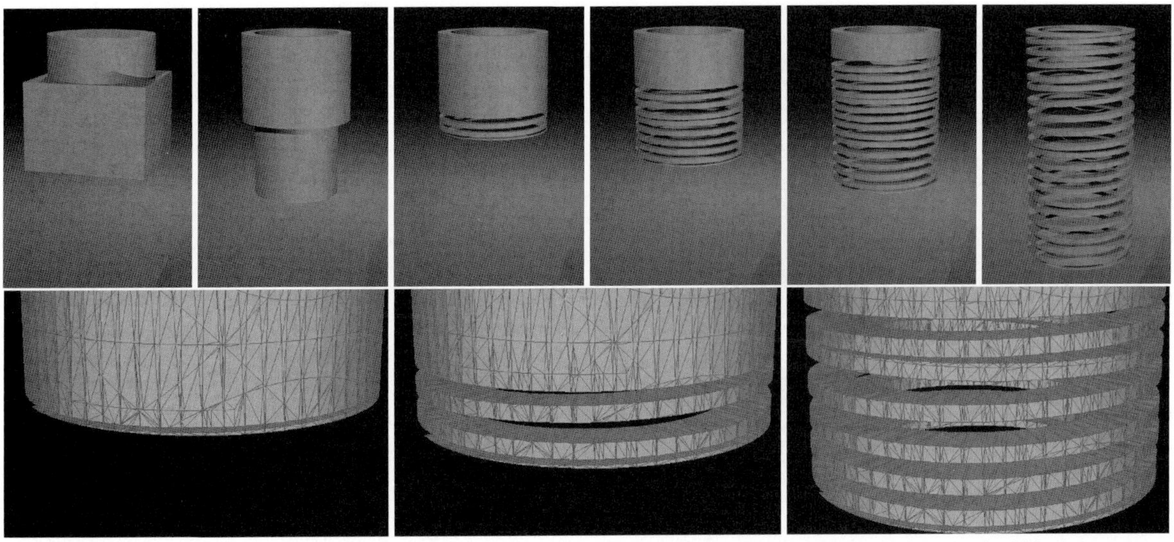

Figure 8: *Top: Using two cylindrical surfaces and a helical surface, we progressively carve a slinky out of a 320 element tetrahedral mesh, which expands and oscillates as it is cut. Bottom: A wireframe rendering reveals the automatic re-triangulation of the material surface as the cutting surface is spiraling up the deforming cylinder. The embedding mesh of the fully cut slinky contains 4713 tetrahedra.*

nected components may be completely interior to a tetrahedron and need not be incident on a node or a face (see Figure 2). When constructing the polygon mesh, tetrahedra that are only partially filled with material require special consideration. They are handled by constructing only the subset of the polygon mesh that is on or within actual material. This is straightforward since the material boundary is already a subset of the previously generated polygon mesh.

3.4. Determining Material Connectivity

Once each tetrahedron has been partitioned into its connected components, we identify pairs of connected components across adjacent tetrahedra as materially contiguous. We do so by examining each pair of tetrahedra that share a common face. Each tetrahedron has been duplicated into identical copies, each containing a single connected component of material embedded within it. The goal is to determine if a copy of tetrahedron A contains material contiguous to material in some copy of tetrahedron B, which we do by individually examining each possible pair of tetrahedron copies. We denote the copies as contiguous if their shared face contains a common polygon (see Figure 9). Finally, we collapse nodes on common faces of materially contiguous tetrahedra to obtain the final simulation mesh.

4. Examples

After cutting, we triangulate the resulting material surface for collisions, self-collisions, and rendering. We determine the material surface simply by keeping only the polygons incident on exactly one tetrahedron, removing those from the material's interior. The boundary polygons that remain are subsequently triangulated. We employ the hybrid framework of [SSIF07] to simulate the embedded material geometry, allowing us to use an arbitrary finite element constitutive model while resolving object collisions and self-collisions on a *soft constrained* copy (see [SSIF07]) of the material surface.

Figure 1 shows a two-dimensional version of our algorithm used to make a spiral-shaped cut into a suspended piece of cloth. Figure 3 illustrates that we can progressively cut a single tetrahedron into multiple pieces as it deforms. Figure 2 shows a single tetrahedron cut into over a thousand pieces by fifty cutting triangles, many of which only partially intersect the tetrahedron rather than slicing completely through it. Figure 4 shows 32 intersecting planes cutting a cube into 289 sticks. In addition, our cutting algorithm can be used to sculpt objects with high surface detail embedded

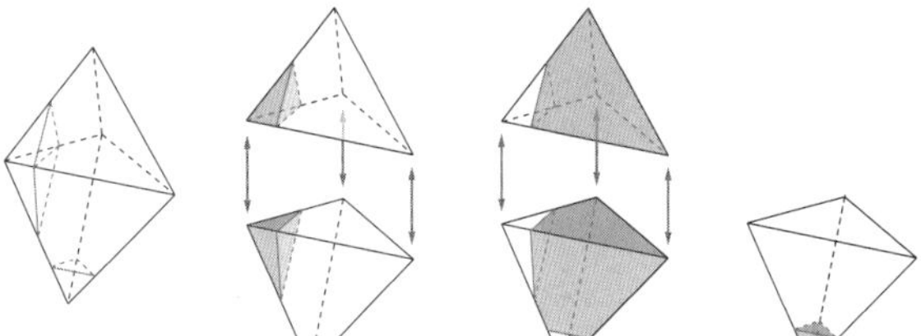

Figure 9: *A polygon mesh resulting from two cuts (left). Each connected component in a tetrahedron is embedded in a duplicate tetrahedron identical to the original. Two pairs of tetrahedra copies are found to be materially contiguous (two middle figures), while one copy of the lower tetrahedron remains materially disjoint (right).*

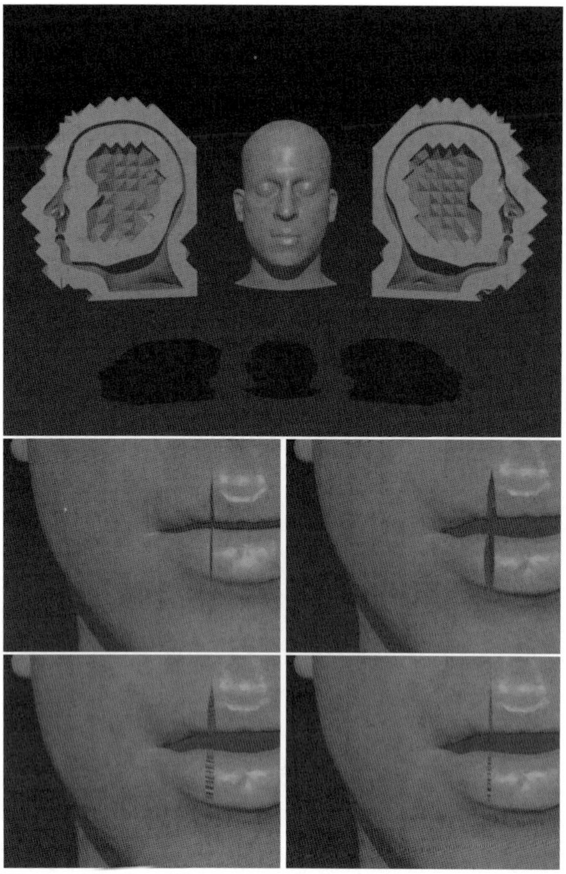

Figure 10: *Top: Using a triangulated skin surface as the cutting geometry, we carve an embedded flesh volume out of a BCC simulation mesh. Middle: An additional incision across the lips is made on the embedded mesh (left). The cut is simulated by pushing the flesh outwards from inside the mouth (right). Bottom: Applying springs across the cut closes the incision.*

within coarse simulation geometry. In Figure 5, we apply a cookie-cutter normal to each face of a cube. In Figure 8, we progressively sculpt a slinky out of a block. Figure 10 (top) shows our algorithm used as a meshing tool to embed a 250k triangle scan of the human face into an 850k tetrahedral simulation mesh. The resulting face model itself can then be further cut, as shown in Figure 10 (middle).

5. Discussion and Limitations

Despite the versatility of our cutting algorithm, a number of notable limitations exist. Our formulation assumes that cuts are introduced in the form of triangulated surfaces. Although this accommodates processes such as material fracture or explicit cutting (e.g. surgical incisions) by discretizing the cracks or incisions into a triangulated surface, there may be certain cases (e.g. elaborate scalpel models, embeddeding of geometries represented by spline or subdivision surfaces) where this additional triangulation is inconvenient. We note however that, with adequate refinement, a triangulated surface can represent any cut and even an increased triangle count on the cutting surface will not have a negative impact on the complexity or conditioning of the embedding simulation mesh.

Embedding the high resolution material surface in a coarser simulation mesh prevents CFL restrictions associated with small or sliver elements. Nevertheless, our framework may still create small or ill-conditioned triangles on the material surface which can still have a negative effect on collision handling. This is less of a problem for object collisions and more important for self-collisions, highlighting the need for robust collision handling schemes. Finally, although our algorithm can process any arbitrary cutting surface, a cut that partially intersects a tetrahedron without separating it into disconnected fragments will not allow the material to separate within that embedding tetrahedron. However, subsequent cuts can extend this cut into one that fully slices through the tetrahedron. Such partial cuts are geometrically resolved by our algorithm even if the embedding constraint does not allow separation of the material surface on either side of the cut. A subelement elasticity model (such as the soft binding formulation of [SSIF07]) could enable separation of these two surfaces, if desired.

6. Conclusion

We proposed a new cutting algorithm that allows for arbitrary cutting of tetrahedral meshes including those that possess a higher-resolution embedded material surface. We illustrated the efficacy of our algorithm on a number of examples ranging from cutting a single tetrahedron into over a thousand pieces to modeling and cutting a high-resolution face model embedded in a BCC simulation mesh.

Appendix A: Implementation Notes

In section 3 we defined our geometrical algorithm without descending into the implementation details of each geometric operation. This appendix provides specific details on the data structures and code organization in our implementation.

Our principle data structures are:

Per-tetrahedron Triangle List. Each embedding tetrahedron stores all triangles that border the material contained inside it. Prior to any cuts, each tetrahedron's triangle list contains just its four faces. After subsequent cutting, the triangles list will also contain triangles of the cutting surface. Barycentric coordinates of the triangle vertices with respect to the tetrahedron are also stored.

Per-tetrahedron Polygon Mesh. Each tetrahedron stores the polygonized boundary of its embedded material.

Intersection Registry. As mentioned in section 3.1 the points referenced by our algorithm are either vertices of the polygon soup, intersections of an edge and a triangle, or intersections of three triangles. In fact, we represent all such points as the intersection of three triangles using the following process. If a segment *pq* is common to triangles *pqr* and *pqs*, then the intersection between *pq* and a different triangle *xyz* is encoded as the intersection of the three triangles *pqr*, *pqs* and *xyz*. If *pqr* is the only triangle incident on *pq*, we introduce a virtual triangle *pq*ø (where ø denotes an unspecified auxiliary point) such that the same point is encoded as the intersection of *pqr*, *pq*ø, and *xyz*. Similarly, a vertex *p* of the triangle soup is represented as the common point of three triangles *pqr*, *pst*, and *puv*. If no such three triangles exist, e.g. if *p* only appears on *pqr*, the point may be described as the intersection of *pqr*, *pq*ø, and *pr*ø, where the last two virtual triangles have been introduced accordingly. The intersection registry stores which triangles intersect at each polygon point (which may be more than three) and determines whether the intersection of three given triangles has already been registered (possibly as the intersection of three different triangles). Additionally, we store the barycentric coordinates of each intersection point with respect to each of the triangles defining the intersection. Note that virtual triangles pose no problem as the barycentric weight of the virtual vertex will be identically zero.

An uncut tetrahedralized volume is initialized with the triangle list containing the faces of each tetrahedron, the polygon mesh containing the same faces as the polygonal (triangular) boundaries of each uncut tetrahedron, and the intersection registry containing all the vertices of the uncut volume as the intersection of all embedding faces incident on each of them.

Each new cutting triangle T_{new} added to the triangle soup is processed according to the following steps.

Intersection with embedding volume. T_{new} is assigned a unique index. We compute the set of embedding tetrahedra that intersect T_{new} (in world space as the embedding volume may have deformed) and create a copy T^k_{new} for each of them assigning each copy a unique index. Each T^k_{new} is appended to the triangle list for its corresponding tetrahedron, converted to barycentric coordinates with respect to it, and keeps a record of the unique index of its parent T_{new}.

Computation of new intersections. Each new triangle T^k_{new} is intersected against all possible pairs of old triangles in the list of its respective tetrahedron. If the intersection already exists, the intersection registry is updated to include T^k_{new} as a triangle incident on this intersection. Otherwise, a new intersection is registered and a unique index is assigned.

Update of old polygons. Any old polygon edge in the polygon mesh for a tetrahedron intersected by T_{new} that contains a newly introduced intersection point is bisected into two collinear edges, and the polygon mesh is updated accordingly. Additionally, any newly created segments on the plane of an existing polygon are tested for intersection against that polygon. If they are found to be intersecting, the old polygons are split to include the new segment.

Creation of new polygons. Each triangle T^k_{new} is clipped to the material contained in the embedding tetrahedron to yield a new polygon, which is added to the polygon mesh.

Computation of connected components. The polygon mesh for each tetrahedron is used to compute the new connected components of material, as in section 3.3. Each component is defined as a polyhedral volume and the tetrahedron is split into as many copies as distinct material fragments.

Topology update based on connectivity. The process of section 3.4 is used to rebuild the topology of the embedding volume. All of our data structures are updated to reflect the topological changes.

This process may be iterated for each new triangle added to the cutting surface. In practice, we have generalized the previous steps to accommodate the introduction of any number of new cutting triangles at once.

Acknowledgments

Research supported in part by an ONR YIP award and a PECASE award (ONR N00014-01-1-0620), a Packard Foundation Fellowship, ONR N0014-06-1-0393, ONR N00014-05-1-0479 for a computing cluster, ONR N00014-02-1-0720, ONR N00014-06-1-0505, ARO DAAD19-03-1-0331, NSF CCF-0541148, NSF ITR-0205671, NSF IIS-0326388, NSF ACI-0323866 and NIH U54-GM072970. Special thanks to Joseph Teran, Court Cutting and Aaron Oliker for invaluable feedback on developing this algorithm in the context of a surgical simulator.

References

[BG00] BIELSER D., GROSS M.: Interactive simulation of surgical cuts. In *Pacific Graph.* (2000), pp. 116–125.

[BGTG03] BIELSER D., GLARDON P., TESCHNER M., GROSS M.: A state machine for real-time cutting of tetrahedral meshes. In *Pacific Graph.* (2003), pp. 377–386.

[BHTF06] BAO Z., HONG J., TERAN J., FEDKIW R.: Fracturing rigid materials. *IEEE Trans. Viz. Comput. Graph.* (2006). (in press).

[BMG99] BIELSER D., MAIWALD V. A., GROSS M. H.: Interactive cuts through 3-dimensional soft tissue. In *Eurographics* (1999).

[FDA02] FOREST C., DELINGETTE H., AYACHE N.: Removing tetrahedra from a manifold mesh. In *Comput. Anim.* (2002), pp. 225–229.

[GLB*06] GUO X., LI X., BAO Y., GU X., QIN H.: Meshless thin-shell simulation based on global conformal parameterization. *IEEE Trans. on Vis. and Comput. Graph. 12*, 3 (2006), 375–385.

[GO01] GANOVELLI F., O'SULLIVAN C.: Animating cuts with on-the-fly re-meshing. In *Eurographics 2001, Short Presentations Programme* (2001).

[GSH*05] GINGOLD Y., SECORD A., HAN J., GRINSPUN E., ZORIN D.: A discrete model for inelastic deformations of thin shells. In *Poster, Eurographics/ACM SIGGRAPH Symp. on Comput. Anima.* (2005).

[HTK98] HIROTA K., TANOUE Y., KANEKO T.: Generation of crack patterns with a physical model. *The Vis. Comput. 14* (1998), 126–187.

[KGC*96] KOCH R. M., GROSS M. H., CARLS F. R., VON BUREN D. F., FANKHAUSER G., PARISH Y. I. H.: Simulating facial surgery using finite element models. *Comput. Graph. 30*, Annual Conf. Series (1996), 421–428.

[KGPG96] KEEVE E., GIROD S., PFEIFLE P., GIROD B.: Anatomy-based facial tissue modeling using the finite element method. In *Proc. of Visualization* (1996), pp. 21–28.

[LIGF06] LOSASSO F., IRVING G., GUENDELMAN E., FEDKIW R.: Melting and burning solids into liquids and gases. *IEEE Trans. on Vis. and Comput. Graph. 12*, 3 (2006), 343–352.

[MBF04] MOLINO N., BAO Z., FEDKIW R.: A virtual node algorithm for changing mesh topology during simulation. *ACM Trans. Graph. (SIGGRAPH Proc.) 23* (2004), 385–392.

[MG04] MÜLLER M., GROSS M.: Interactive virtual materials. In *Graph. Interface* (May 2004), pp. 239–246.

[MK00] MOR A., KANADE T.: Modifying soft tissue models: progressive cutting with minimal new element creation. In *MICCAI* (2000), pp. 598–607.

[MMA99] MAZARAK O., MARTINS C., AMANATIDES J.: Animating exploding objects. In *Proc. of Graph. Interface 1999* (1999), pp. 211–218.

[MMDJ01] MÜLLER M., MCMILLAN L., DORSEY J., JAGNOW R.: Real-time simulation of deformation and fracture of stiff materials. In *Comput. Anim. and Sim. '01* (2001), Proc. Eurographics Wrkshp., Eurographics Assoc., pp. 99–111.

[MTG04] MÜLLER M., TESCHNER M., GROSS M.: Physically-based simulation of objects represented by surface meshes. In *Proc. Comput. Graph. Int.* (June 2004), pp. 156–165.

[NF99] NEFF M., FIUME E.: A visual model for blast waves and fracture. In *Proc. of Graph. Interface 1999* (1999), pp. 193–202.

[NTB*91] NORTON A., TURK G., BACON B., GERTH J., SWEENEY P.: Animation of fracture by physical modeling. *Vis. Comput. 7*, 4 (1991), 210–219.

[NvdS00] NIENHUYS H.-W., VAN DER STAPPEN A. F.: Combining finite element deformation with cutting for surgery simulations. In *Eurographics 2000, Short Presentations Programme* (2000).

[NvdS01] NIENHUYS H.-W., VAN DER STAPPEN A. F.: *Supporting cuts and finite element deformation in interactive surgery simulation.* Tech. rep., Utrecht University, Institute for Information and Computing Sciences, 2001.

[OBH02] O'BRIEN J., BARGTEIL A., HODGINS J.: Graphical modeling of ductile fracture. *ACM Trans. Graph. (SIGGRAPH Proc.) 21* (2002), 291–294.

[OH99] O'BRIEN J., HODGINS J.: Graphical modeling and animation of brittle fracture. In *Proc. of SIGGRAPH 1999* (1999), pp. 137–146.

[PKA*05] PAULY M., KEISER R., ADAMS B., DUTRÉ P., GROSS M., GUIBAS L.: Meshless animation of fracturing solids. *ACM Trans. Graph. (SIGGRAPH Proc.) 24*, 3 (2005), 957–964.

[PRZ92] PIEPER S., ROSEN J., ZELTZER D.: Interactive graphics for plastic surgery: A task-level analysis and implementation. In *Proc. of Symp. on Int. 3D Graph.* (1992), ACM Press, pp. 127–134.

[SHGS06] STEINEMANN D., HARDERS M., GROSS M., SZEKELY G.: Hybrid cutting of deformable solids. In *Proc. of the IEEE Virtual Reality Conference* (2006), pp. 35–42.

[SHS01] SERBY D., HARDERS M., SZÉKELY G.: A new approach to cutting into finite element models. In *MICCAI* (2001), pp. 425–433.

[SOG06] STEINEMANN D., OTADUY M. A., GROSS M.: Fast arbitrary splitting of deforming objects. In *Proc. of the ACM SIGGRAPH/Eurographics Symp. on Comput. Anim.* (2006), pp. 63–72.

[SSIF07] SIFAKIS E., SHINAR T., IRVING G., FEDKIW R.: Hybrid simulation of deformable solids. In *Proc. of ACM SIGGRAPH/Eurographics Symp. on Comput. Anim. (in press)* (2007).

[SWB01] SMITH J., WITKIN A., BARAFF D.: Fast and controllable simulation of the shattering of brittle objects. In *Comput. Graph. Forum*, Duke D., Scopigno R., (Eds.), vol. 20(2). Blackwell Publishing, 2001, pp. 81–91.

[TF88a] TERZOPOULOS D., FLEISCHER K.: Deformable models. *The Vis. Comput. 4*, 6 (1988), 306–331.

[TF88b] TERZOPOULOS D., FLEISCHER K.: Modeling inelastic deformation: viscoelasticity, plasticity, fracture. *Comput. Graph. (SIGGRAPH Proc.)* (1988), 269–278.

[TSSB*05] TERAN J., SIFAKIS E., SALINAS-BLEMKER S., NG-THOW-HING V., LAU C., FEDKIW R.: Creating and simulating skeletal muscle from the visible human data set. *IEEE Trans. on Vis. and Comput. Graph. 11*, 3 (2005), 317–328.

[WSG05] WICKE M., STEINEMANN D., GROSS M.: Efficient animation of point-sampled thin shells. In *Proc. of Eurographics* (2005), vol. 24.

[YOH00] YNGVE G. D., O'BRIEN J. F., HODGINS J. K.: Animating explosions. In *Proc. of ACM SIGGRAPH 2000* (2000), pp. 29–36.

Eurographics/ ACM SIGGRAPH Symposium on Computer Animation (2007)
D. Metaxas and J. Popovic (Editors)

Hybrid Simulation of Deformable Solids

Eftychios Sifakis† Stanford University Intel Corporation

Tamar Shinar† Stanford University

Geoffrey Irving† Stanford University Pixar Animation Studios

Ronald Fedkiw† Stanford University Industrial Light+Magic

Abstract

Although mesh-based methods are efficient for simulating simple hyperelasticity, maintaining and adapting a mesh-based representation is less appealing in more complex scenarios, e.g. collision, plasticity and fracture. Thus, meshless or point-based methods have enjoyed recent popularity due to their added flexibility in dealing with these situations. Our approach begins with an initial mesh that is either conforming (as generated by one's favorite meshing algorithm) or non-conforming (e.g. a BCC background lattice). We then propose a framework for embedding arbitrary sample points into this initial mesh allowing for the straightforward handling of collisions, plasticity and fracture without the need for complex remeshing. A straightforward consequence of this new framework is the ability to naturally handle T-junctions alleviating the requirement for a manifold initial mesh. The arbitrarily added embedded points are endowed with full simulation capability allowing them to collide, interact with each other, and interact with the parent geometry in the fashion of a particle-centric simulation system. We demonstrate how this formulation facilitates tasks such as arbitrary refinement or resampling for collision processing, the handling of multiple and possibly conflicting constraints (e.g. when cloth is nonphysically pinched between two objects), the straightforward treatment of fracture, and sub-element resolution of elasticity and plasticity.

Categories and Subject Descriptors (according to ACM CCS): I.3.5 [Computer Graphics]: Physically based modeling I.3.7 [Computer Graphics]: Animation

1. Introduction

Simulation of deformable models was pioneered in computer graphics by [TPBF87, TF88a, TF88b]. It has influenced research in cloth animation [BW98], muscle and face simulation [TSSB*05, SNF05], flesh deformation [CGC*02b], virtual surgery [SHGS06] and fracture [OH99].

Mesh-based methods require the generation of an initial simulation mesh, which can be conforming (e.g. [MBTF03, ACSYD05]), or non-conforming when used in conjunction with an embedded simulation technique (e.g. [CGC*02a, CGC*02b, MBF04, MG04, MTG04]) in which case a simple cube or BCC background mesh can be used. Generation of a conforming simulation mesh is typically nontrivial and is best suited to applications that require no changes to the initial mesh. However, if the mesh needs to be adapted on the fly, e.g. for fracture [OH99], remeshing can be prohibitively expensive and can introduce poor quality elements. [MBF04] proposed a partial solution that uses embedded simulation technology to fracture tessellated objects without continuous remeshing, allowing elements to be modeled as partially full of material. Limitations, including the restriction that edges cannot be fractured twice, prevent this method from being completely general. Collision processing can often require more surface resolution than is present in the initial simulation mesh. While some have considered adaptive frameworks [DDCB01, GKS02, CGC*02b], it is wasteful to refine the full volumetric mesh in the vicinity of the boundaries solely for collisions. Although not as efficient as mesh-based methods for the simulation of elastic deformation, point-based methods provide added flexibility making them attractive for applications involving fracture, virtual surgery, resampling for collision handling, etc., see e.g. [MKN*04, PKA*05, SOG06, WSG05, MHTG05].

Starting with either a conforming or non-conforming mesh, we propose a method for embedding an arbitrary point in this mesh. We call this a *hard binding*. To derive the relationships between physical quantities of the embedded point and the mesh, we start by considering a hypothetical refinement of the mesh that resolves the embedded point. We compute internal finite element forces for these hypothetical subelements and illustrate how to redistribute these forces to the parent mesh. The mass of the embedded particle is redistributed to the parent mesh as well. This redistribution is

† email: {sifakis|shinar|irving|fedkiw}@graphics.stanford.edu

Symposium on Computer Animation 2007, San Diego, CA, August 03-04, 2007.
© 2007 ACM 978-1-59593-624-4/07/0008 $5.00

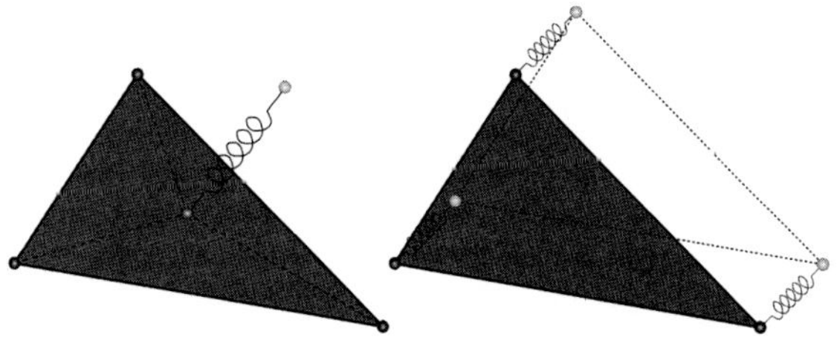

Figure 1: *Parent particles (blue), hard bound target locations (red) and soft bound particles (yellow). Soft bound duplication of a hard bound target location (left), and three soft bound duplications of parent particles (right).*

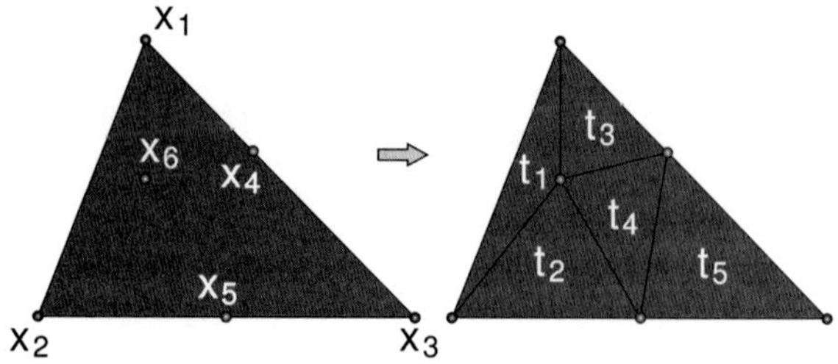

Figure 2: *Resolution of hard bound particles (depicted in red) via refinement of the parent element.*

shown to be independent of the chosen refinement. Notably, this approach results in automatic and natural handling of T-junctions, as masses and forces of T-junction nodes can be redistributed to the parent mesh. This specific handling of T-junctions is similar to that in [LC06]. We then generalize this approach to arbitrary embeddings. Hard bound particles have their mass and any forces or impulses applied to them redistributed to the parents in a natural fashion while maintaining the notion of an *effective mass* so that they can fully participate in various numerical algorithms.

A hard binding constrains an embedded particle to its barycentrically determined location (a similar heuristic was given in [GBT06]). Thus, hard bound particles are not particles at all (i.e. they do not possess any degrees of freedom), but merely target locations that live on the parent mesh. In order to transition to a fully particle-centric simulation framework, we create the notion of a *soft binding*. A soft binding is an abstract connection between a real particle with full degrees of freedom and a hard binding target location enabling full two-way interaction. Soft bound particles are free to interact with each other and the parent mesh constituting a fully particle-centric framework. Soft bindings can be created between any particle and any target location even duplicating the original degrees of freedom in the mesh itself (see figure 1). The soft binding mechanism is responsible for the two-way interaction between the particle-based system and the mesh-based framework. Although one could implement this connection using simple springs, we have designed a more sophisticated soft binding interface which is notably fully implicit allowing one to stiffen the two-way interaction to the point where the soft bound particle always lies on its target location up to numerical precision, without stability issues or additional time step restrictions.

Our work shares the motivation of [GBT06] to incorporate particle constraints in the simulation of deformable objects, and the function of their geometric constraints is conceptually analogous to our hard bindings. However, their approach works by introducing external forces dependent on the integration method used whereas our hard bindings are enforced through the conjugate operations of force distribution and velocity interpolation. That is, instead of forcing our constrained degrees of freedom toward their target locations, we directly project them out of the equations of motion. This allows seamless incorporation of such constraints into any time integration scheme, including globally coupled implicit schemes. Another major difference is that our framework allows optional drift of particles away from their target locations through soft bindings.

Novel contributions of our work include the tight integration of hard binding constraints and unconditionally stable binding spring forces into the semi-implicit Newmark time integration scheme, lag-free duplication of degrees of freedom through soft bindings by force transfer from parent particles, and integration of rigid/deformable coupling into the Newmark scheme and conjugate gradient solver. We present these contributions as part of a broad hybrid simulation framework building on simple, physically motivated principles. We demonstrate the features of this framework with examples that include dynamically adapting the surface sampling density for collisions, duplicating parent mesh particles to resolve conflicting constraints caused by the non-physical pinching of cloth, the facilitation of fracture and cutting algorithms, and an extension of our framework to two-way interactions with rigid bodies.

2. Hard Bindings

The simulation mesh is subject to internal forces, from for example finite elements, as well as external forces from gravity, friction, collisions, etc., and we want these forces to act on the hard bound particles as well. We motivate our approach for propagating forces to the parent mesh by considering a refinement that resolves all the hard bound particles. Figure 2 shows three hard bound particles along with an associated refinement. Although this refinement is not unique, it turns out that the propagation of physical properties from the hard bound particles to the parent mesh is independent of the tessellation used and can be performed without explicitly refining the parent element. Internal forces are defined on the subelements in standard fashion, but must be remapped to the parent particles since the hard bound particles are not free to move independently.

Conservative forces can be defined in terms of the gradient $\mathbf{f} = -\partial\Psi(\mathbf{x})/\partial\mathbf{x}$ of the potential energy $\Psi(\mathbf{x})$. The potential energy of the parent triangle is $\Psi = \sum \Psi_i$, where Ψ_i

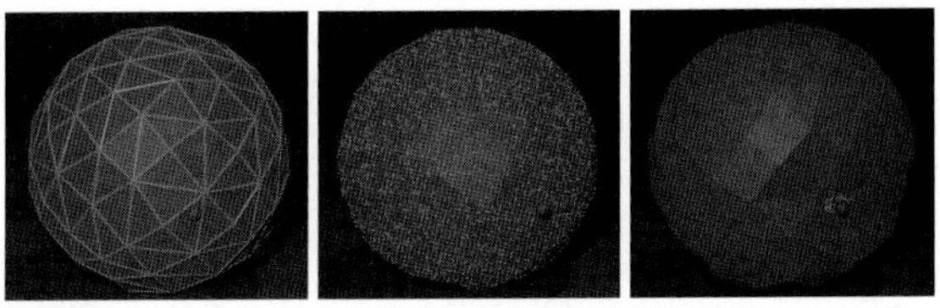

Figure 3: *(Left) A coarse deformable ball is penetrated by a kinematic sphere. (Center) Sprinkling hard bound particles on the surface of the sphere allows one to resolve the collisions without requiring refinement of the tetrahedral simulation mesh. (Right) Hard bound particles can be dynamically added and removed based on proximity to collision objects.*

is the potential energy of subtriangle t_i. Each Ψ_i is naturally defined in terms of the positions of the vertices of triangle t_i rather than the positions of the parent particles, although the former are fully determined by the latter through the binding constraint. Let $\mathbf{x}_i$ denote the positions of the vertices of triangle t_i, e.g. $\mathbf{x}_2$ is composed of the positions of particles $\{x_2, x_5, x_6\}$ in figure 2. The parent triangle vertices $\{x_1, x_2, x_3\}$ are represented by $\mathbf{x}$. Using this notation, the three forces on the parent particles are

$$\mathbf{f} = -\sum_i \frac{\partial \Psi_i}{\partial \mathbf{x}} = -\sum_i \left(\frac{\partial \mathbf{x}_i}{\partial \mathbf{x}}\right)^T \frac{\partial \Psi_i}{\partial \mathbf{x}_i} = \sum_i \left(\frac{\partial \mathbf{x}_i}{\partial \mathbf{x}}\right)^T \mathbf{f}_i \quad (1)$$

where $\mathbf{f}_i = -\partial\Psi_i/\partial\mathbf{x}_i$ are the three vertex forces computed on each subtriangle t_i. The Jacobian $\partial\mathbf{x}_i/\partial\mathbf{x}$ is constant for each triangle t_i and contains the barycentric coordinates of $\mathbf{x}_i$ with respect to the vertices $\mathbf{x}$ of the parent triangle. Equation (1) can be extended to the computation of elastic force differentials for implicit or quasistatic time integration via

$$\delta\mathbf{f}|_{\delta\mathbf{x}} = \sum_i \left(\frac{\partial \mathbf{x}_i}{\partial \mathbf{x}}\right)^T \delta\mathbf{f}_i|_{\delta\mathbf{x}_i} \quad (2)$$

Equation (2) is obtained by taking the directional derivative of (1), assuming that the Jacobian $\partial\mathbf{x}_i/\partial\mathbf{x}$ is constant (i.e. the binding constraint is linear), which is always the case for the barycentric embeddings used here. Nonlinear binding constraints would result in additional terms in equation (2).

From equations (1) and (2) we can write the net force and force differential on a single parent particle as

$$f_k = \sum_{t_i} \sum_{x_j \in t_i} w_k^j f_j^i \quad \text{and} \quad \delta f_k|_{\delta\mathbf{x}} = \sum_{t_i} \sum_{x_j \in t_i} w_k^j \left.\delta f_j^i\right|_{\delta\mathbf{x}_i} \quad (3)$$

where w_k^j is the barycentric weight of particle j with respect to particle k of the parent triangle and f_j^i is the force on particle j from subtriangle t_i. In practice we implement equation (3) by accumulating all forces on both parent and hard bound particles from all their incident elements and subsequently redistributing the force on each hard bound particle to its parents weighted by its barycentric weights. Note that the final force distribution does not depend on the tessellation used but only on the barycentric weights of the hard bound particles.

We use equation (3) for velocity dependent damping forces as well noting that it preserves the symmetry and definiteness of the linear damping forces allowing for our semi-implicit time integration framework. We consider the linear damping model $\bar{\mathbf{f}} = \bar{\mathbf{G}}\bar{\mathbf{v}}$ where $\bar{\mathbf{G}}$ is symmetric negative definite, and the force $\bar{\mathbf{f}}$ and velocity $\bar{\mathbf{v}}$ refer to *all* particles, including hard bound particles. The velocities of this extended set of particles are expressed in terms of the velocities of the parent particles, $\bar{\mathbf{v}} = \mathbf{W}\mathbf{v}$. Using this notation, equation (1) reduces to $\mathbf{f} = \mathbf{W}^T\bar{\mathbf{f}} = \mathbf{W}^T\bar{\mathbf{G}}\mathbf{W}\mathbf{v} = \mathbf{G}\mathbf{v}$ where $\mathbf{G} = \mathbf{W}^T\bar{\mathbf{G}}\mathbf{W}$ preserves both symmetry and negative definiteness of the original damping matrix $\bar{\mathbf{G}}$. A similar derivation shows that the distribution scheme for force differentials given in equation (3) preserves symmetry and negative definiteness of the elastic stiffness matrix, which is an important property for schemes that use an implicit or quasistatic treatment of elastic forces as well.

After forces have been computed and redistributed to the parent particles, accelerations are computed via $\mathbf{a} = \mathbf{M}^{-1}\mathbf{f}$ where $\mathbf{M}$ is diagonal in a typical lumped mass formulation. We store the lumped masses of the parent particles in a vector $\mathbf{m}$, which is the diagonal of $\mathbf{M}$. In analogy to our force derivation, we write the mass vector as the gradient of total momentum with respect to velocity, i.e. $\mathbf{m} = \partial P/\partial\mathbf{v}$. Let $\bar{\mathbf{m}}$ be the masses of all particles. As is typical, one could compute the initial mass of hard bound particles by refining the parent mesh as in figure 2 and assigning one third the mass of each triangle to its vertices, although any scheme for assigning mass (including uniform mass) is allowed. The total momentum is then given as $P = \bar{\mathbf{m}}^T\bar{\mathbf{v}}$, thus $\mathbf{m} = \frac{\partial}{\partial\mathbf{v}}P = \frac{\partial}{\partial\mathbf{v}}\left(\bar{\mathbf{m}}^T\bar{\mathbf{v}}\right) = \frac{\partial}{\partial\mathbf{v}}\left(\bar{\mathbf{m}}^T\mathbf{W}\mathbf{v}\right) = \mathbf{W}^T\bar{\mathbf{m}}$ indicating that masses of hard bound particles should be redistributed to the parents based on the barycentric weights, i.e. the same as for force redistribution. More generally in a non-lumped mass formulation, the mass matrix is given by the Hessian of the kinetic energy as $\mathbf{M} = \mathbf{W}^T\bar{\mathbf{M}}\mathbf{W}$ (see [Sif07]).

Although hard bound particles have no mass or momentum, an *effective mass* is useful for many numerical algorithms. We define the effective mass as the ratio of an applied force to the resultant acceleration of the hard bound particle, i.e. $f_e = m_e a_e$. Denoting the binding weights by w_i, the applied force is distributed to the parent particles via $f_i = w_i f_e$ and the acceleration of the bound particle is $a_e = \sum w_i a_i$. Combining these equations gives

$$\frac{f_e}{m_e} = a_e = \sum w_i a_i = \sum w_i \frac{f_i}{m_i} = f_e \sum \frac{w_i^2}{m_i} \Rightarrow \frac{1}{m_e} = \sum \frac{w_i^2}{m_i} \quad (4)$$

The effective mass is used in the determination of stability restrictions for forces defined on the hard bound particle, e.g. if a hard bound particle is connected to a spring, the effective mass would be used to compute the harmonic mass.

One often needs to apply impulses to hard bound particles, e.g. for collisions. An impulse j_e applied to a hard bound particle is the result of a force f_e acting on the parti-

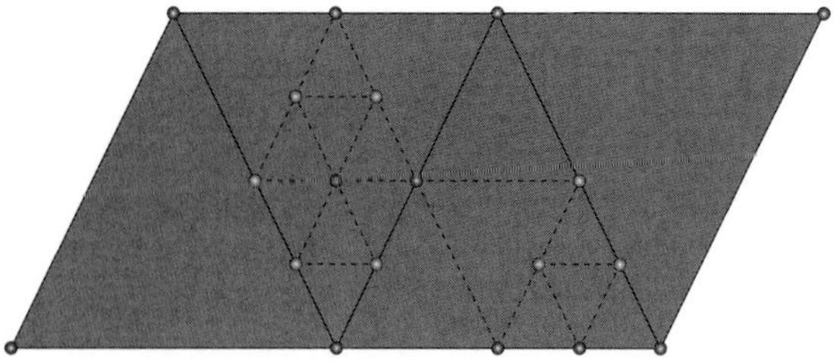

Figure 4: *Two levels of non-graded red refinement leading to T-junctions (red). The T-junctions do not have a complete one-ring of triangles. Our framework treats the T-junction nodes as hard bound particles (red) embedded in the parent mesh (blue).*

cle for an infinitesimal interval Δt, i.e. $j_e = f_e \Delta t$, and from equation (3) we obtain $j_i = w_i j_e$. Furthermore, changes in velocity are governed by $\Delta v_i = j_i/m_i = w_i(m_e/m_i)\Delta v_e$, and displacements follow $\Delta x_i = w_i(m_e/m_i)\Delta x_e$ assuming that $\Delta x_e = \Delta t v_e$.

Figure 3 illustrates the utility of hard bindings in processing collisions. A typical approach to collision processing (due to its simplicity) is to collide the points (possibly only the surface points) of a deformable object with implicitly represented collision geometry, and we collide each tetrahedral mesh node from the sphere's surface with the ground and the kinematically controlled red sphere. Although ground collisions are sufficiently resolved, the kinematically controlled red sphere passes directly through the deformable object, missing any potential collisions with surface particles. Although one might adaptively refine tetrahedra near the colliding red sphere, this increases the total tetrahedra that need to be simulated and the smaller edge lengths lead to a stiffer time step restriction. Our hard binding framework allows us to simply sprinkle particles on the surface of the sphere at a higher density than the tetrahedral mesh for the sake of collisions. This can be done statically or even adaptively based on proximity to collision objects (similar in spirit to [GD04]).

2.1. T-junctions

Figure 4 depicts four coarse triangles undergoing up to two levels of non-graded red refinement leading to a number of T-junctions. Structured adaptive meshing schemes such as [MBTF03] resolve these T-junctions via a combination of red and green refinement. This produces both more elements increasing computational cost as well as lower quality green elements which adversely affect the time step restriction. Additional savings may be realized by exploiting the regularity of adaptive red-only refinements where all elements in the mesh are identical up to rotation and scaling requiring only the storage of a scale factor per element to encode the rest state. For every T-junction, we compute its parents by recursively tracking the endpoints of refined segments. This leads to the barycentric embedding of hard bound particles

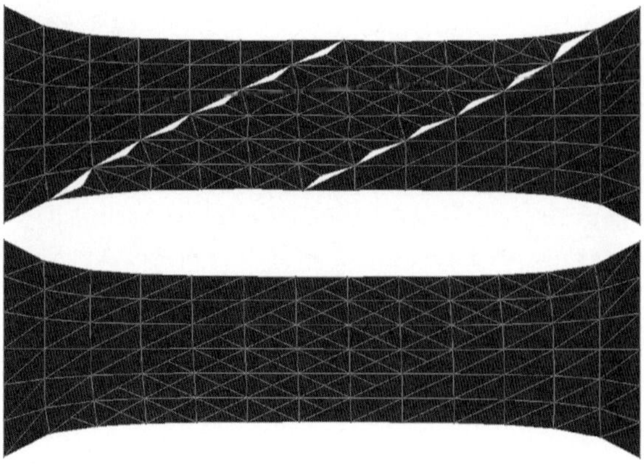

Figure 5: *An elastic sheet meshed with T-junctions is quasistatically stretched without bindings (top) and using hard bindings (bottom).*

on segments or triangles in two spatial dimensions, and on segments, triangles or tetrahedra in three spatial dimensions. Figure 5 illustrates that the straightforward simulation of a T-junction mesh leads to gaps in the mesh (top), while treating T-junction particles as hard bound particles properly constrains them to their incident edges (bottom). We note that T-junctions have also been treated using hierarchical bases (see e.g. [GKS02]).

2.2. Arbitrary embeddings

Although our framework is described in the context of a parent simulation mesh outfitted with a number of embedded particles that will be extended into a fully particle-centric simulation framework (in section 3), here we give an example to illustrate that our framework is more general than this. That is, we switch from the notion of a parent simulation mesh with an embedded set of particles to a parent point cloud simulation system with an embedded mesh. In the context of free-form deformations, one might use a nearest neighbor approach to compute a mesh-free discretization of internal forces on the point cloud, and subsequently move the embedded mesh kinematically. Of course, this can lead to potentially severe distortions of the embedded mesh, especially since the point cloud sampling of deformation is very different from that perceived by the embedded mesh. This can be alleviated by computing the internal forces on the embedded mesh itself, as we do in the elastic ribbon shown in figure 6, and then mapping the resultant forces to the point cloud. Using these forces, we still time integrate the point cloud particles and kinematically enslave the embedded mesh, but the deformation of space is now sampled more adequately for the purpose of simulating the embedded mesh. Note that the kinematic motion of the ribbon is dictated by the k closest parent particles of the point cloud.

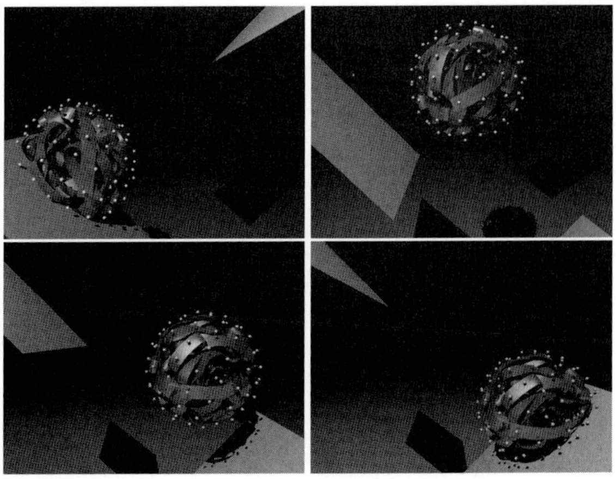

Figure 6: *A ribbon is kinematically embedded in a point cloud. Instead of using a standard mesh-free discretization of the point cloud, we endow the ribbon with a constitutive model which is used to compute elastic forces that are subsequently mapped to the point cloud. The first approach penalizes point cloud deformation and has no direct knowledge of deformation artifacts within the ribbon, while our approach directly penalizes distortions in the ribbon (2.3 sec/frame).*

3. Soft Bindings

The hard bound particle framework is limited because the hard bound particles are kinematically constrained to the parent mesh rather than possessing real degrees of freedom. Thus, specialized algorithms would be required for collision processing, etc. We overcome these issues by introducing the notion of a *soft binding* which couples a new, fully simulation capable particle with an existing parent particle or hard bound particle target location as illustrated in figure 1. We can then ignore hard bound particles for the purpose of collisions and apply collision processing uniformly to parent particles and soft bound particles.

Under no external influence such as collisions or soft bound particle intrinsic forces, soft bound particles should follow their target positions. This is achieved by applying the force that leads to a matching acceleration between the soft bound particle and its target, i.e. the soft bound particles *inherit* elasticity and similar forces from the parent mesh. If the acceleration of a hard bound particle is $a_e = \sum w_i a_i = \sum w_i (f_i/m_i)$, the force that is applied to the soft bound particle to match this acceleration is $f_s = m_s \sum w_i (f_i/m_i)$ where m_s is the mass of the soft bound particle. Note that we only use this process to remap elastic forces, since applying it to damping forces would compromise the symmetry of the damping matrix in our implicit time integration scheme.

The mass of each soft bound particle is set to the *effective mass* of its target (which is just the mass for parent particles). This duplication of mass does not change the effective total mass of the object as measured by applied forces, because our mapping of forces from the parent mesh to the soft

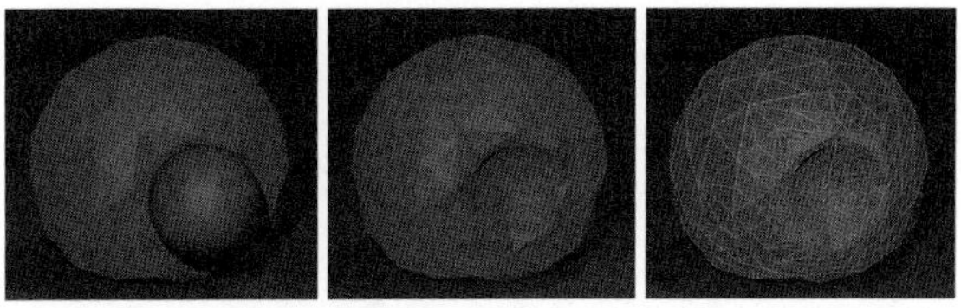

Figure 7: *(Left) A coarse deformable ball collides with a kinematic sphere. (Middle) Soft bindings enable subtetrahedron elasticity in response to the collision. (Right) The dynamically refined surface mesh.*

bound particles properly accelerates those particles. However, a mass assignment stemming from a consistent physical principle would be desirable.

The coupling strategy between soft bound particles and their targets depends on whether short term or long term drift is desired. Therefore we give separate algorithms for short term and long term drift below.

3.1. Synchronized coupling

The most straightforward way to transfer information from the target particle to the soft bound particle is by directly copying the target state. At first glance, this appears to nullify the desired properties of soft bound particles effectively reducing them to hard bound particles. However, in contrast with hard bound particles which are kept consistent with their target state at all times, soft bound particles are synchronized to their target state at specific points of the time integration loop allowing drift between two subsequent synchronizations. Apart from collision processing, additional forces may also be used to cause drift in soft bound particles, e.g. a soft bound copy of the surface of a volumetric object could be endowed with shell elastic forces. We subsequently propagate any drift from their target locations back to their parents, prior to the next synchronization of soft bindings with their target state.

To propagate drift from a soft bound particle to its target, we compute the discrepancy in position $\Delta x = x - x_e$ and velocity $\Delta v = v - v_e$, where x_e and v_e are the position and velocity of the (possibly hard bound) target particle. If the target particle is part of the parent mesh these increments are directly applied to its position and velocity, while if it is hard bound we use the formulas in section 2 to propagate these increments to the hard bound particle's parent particles. This method for projecting soft bound particles onto their target locations could also be used as a more physically based post-simulation correction to the T-junction nodes in [DMG05].

3.2. Coupling through binding springs

The synchronized coupling scheme only allows for short term drift of the soft bound particles limiting their added simulation capabilities. If long term drift is desired, we instead employ a spring-like force between the soft bound par-

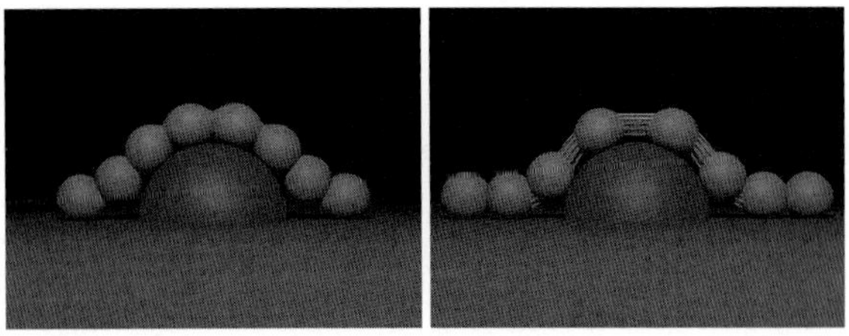

Figure 8: *(Left) Several spheres stitched together using stiff implicit binding springs. (Right) Lowering the binding spring stiffness leads to drift. The binding springs are depicted as orange cylinders (30 sec/frame).*

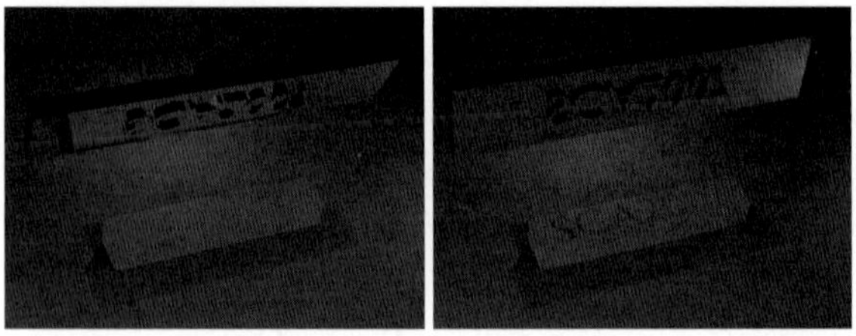

Figure 9: *Allowing the hard bound target positions to drift, one can model subtetrahedron plasticity resulting from collisions of soft bound particles (3 sec/frame).*

ticle and its respective target particle (similar in spirit to a PD controller). This *binding spring* force is

$$f^b = -f_e^b = -k(x-x_e) - b(v-v_e). \quad (5)$$

Note that the binding spring has zero rest length and thus linearizing about the rest state results in a multidirectional (as opposed to the typical directional) damping term. We will capitalize on this fact in our time integration scheme. Binding springs more readily allow for full simulation capabilities in the soft bound particles. One no longer needs to propagate information from the soft bound particles to the parents or to synchronize the soft bound particles, but rather the soft bound particles and parents are now implicitly coupled in a two-way fashion via these binding springs. We emphasize that the important properties of soft bindings depend on the combination of binding springs with force mapping, and would not be achieved through springs alone. Note that a limitation of our approach is that damping forces are not mapped from parents to soft bound particles (to preserve symmetry). Even in the absence of collisions, this leads to drift that has to be corrected via the binding springs.

In figure 7 a coarse tetrahedralized volume has its surface mesh adaptively and dynamically refined based on proximity to collision geometry, and the soft bound particles present at every vertex of the surface mesh provide for subtetrahedron deformation.

3.3. Time integration

Our time integration scheme is a variant of the semi-implicit modified Newmark integration scheme of [ITF04]. The deformable object is evolved from time t^n to t^{n+1} as follows:

1. $\tilde{\mathbf{v}}^{n+\frac{1}{2}} = \mathbf{v}^n + \frac{\Delta t}{2}\mathbf{a}(t^{n+\frac{1}{2}}, \mathbf{x}^n, \tilde{\mathbf{v}}^{n+\frac{1}{2}})$
2. $\tilde{\mathbf{x}}^{n+1} = \mathbf{x}^n + \Delta t \tilde{\mathbf{v}}^{n+\frac{1}{2}}$
3. Process collisions $(\tilde{\mathbf{x}}^{n+1}, \mathbf{v}_n) \rightarrow (\mathbf{x}^{n+1}, \tilde{\mathbf{v}}_n)$

4*. $\mathbf{v}^{n+1} = \tilde{\mathbf{v}}^n + \frac{\Delta t}{2}\left(\mathbf{a}(t^{n+\frac{1}{2}}, \mathbf{x}^{n+\frac{1}{2}}, \tilde{\mathbf{v}}^n) + \mathbf{a}(t^{n+\frac{1}{2}}, \mathbf{x}^{n+\frac{1}{2}}, \mathbf{v}^{n+1})\right)$

where $\mathbf{x}^{n+1/2} = (\mathbf{x}^n + \mathbf{x}^{n+1})/2$. Our scheme deviates from that of [ITF04] in that the trapezoidal velocity update in step 4^* uses $\mathbf{x}^{n+1/2}$. This substitution retains second order accuracy and allows for fully implicit integration of our binding spring forces. Under the common assumption that the velocity dependent forces are linear, we can rewrite step 4^* as

4. $\mathbf{v}^{n+\frac{1}{2}} = \tilde{\mathbf{v}}^n + \frac{\Delta t}{2}\mathbf{a}\left(t^{n+\frac{1}{2}}, \mathbf{x}^{n+\frac{1}{2}}, \mathbf{v}^{n+\frac{1}{2}}\right)$
5. $\mathbf{v}^{n+1} = 2\mathbf{v}^{n+\frac{1}{2}} - \tilde{\mathbf{v}}^n$

The version of trapezoidal rule in step 4^* can suffer from poor numerical conditioning when the two acceleration terms are rather large but of opposite sign, whereas steps 4 and 5 use a completely robust backward Euler update followed by extrapolation. That is, in the limit of a large time step the first acceleration term in step 4^* pushes a positive coefficient c of an eigenvector toward $-\infty$ while the second acceleration term brings that value back from $-\infty$ to $-c$, possibly failing due to loss of precision. However, in the same large time step limit, step 4 damps c to 0 and step 5 robustly extrapolates c through 0 to $-c$.

The time step restriction imposed by a single binding spring is $\Delta t < (b + \sqrt{b^2 + 4\mu k})/k$ where μ is the reduced mass. As is typical, this drives the time step to zero as the spring constant is increased, and thus we propose a fully implicit treatment of the binding springs leveraging the fact that our binding springs are fully linear in both position and velocity (which is not the case for nonzero rest length springs).

Equation (5) can be written in matrix form as $\mathbf{f}^b = -\mathbf{K}\mathbf{x} - \mathbf{B}\mathbf{v}$, where the stiffness and damping matrices $\mathbf{K}$ and $\mathbf{B}$ are symmetric positive semi-definite. We apply our time integration scheme to this force, with the modification that in step 1 we use the half time step position $\tilde{\mathbf{x}}^{n+1/2}$, making this step fully implicit:

$$\tilde{\mathbf{v}}^{n+\frac{1}{2}} = \mathbf{v}^n + \frac{\Delta t}{2}\mathbf{a}^b(t^{n+\frac{1}{2}}, \tilde{\mathbf{x}}^{n+\frac{1}{2}}, \tilde{\mathbf{v}}^{n+\frac{1}{2}}) \quad (6)$$

$$= \mathbf{v}^n + \frac{\Delta t}{2}\left(-\mathbf{M}^{-1}\mathbf{K}\tilde{\mathbf{x}}^{n+\frac{1}{2}} - \mathbf{M}^{-1}\mathbf{B}\tilde{\mathbf{v}}^{n+\frac{1}{2}}\right). \quad (7)$$

Substituting $\tilde{\mathbf{x}}^{n+1/2} = \frac{1}{2}(\mathbf{x}^n + \tilde{\mathbf{x}}^{n+1}) = \mathbf{x}^n + \frac{\Delta t}{2}\tilde{\mathbf{v}}^{n+1/2}$, where the last equality comes from step 2, gives

$$\left(\mathbf{I} + \frac{\Delta t}{2}\mathbf{M}^{-1}\mathbf{B} + \frac{\Delta t^2}{4}\mathbf{M}^{-1}\mathbf{K}\right)\tilde{\mathbf{v}}^{n+\frac{1}{2}} = \mathbf{v}^n - \frac{\Delta t}{2}\mathbf{M}^{-1}\mathbf{K}\mathbf{x}^n \quad (8)$$

which is a true backward Euler step implicit in both position and velocity with no time step restriction. We emphasize that equation (6) only replaces step 1 in our time integration loop,

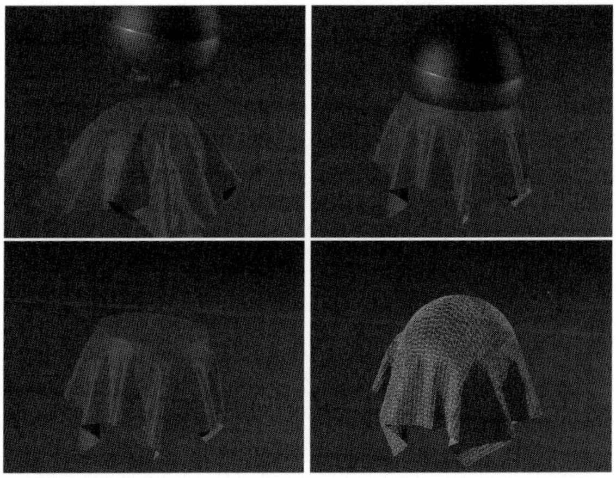

Figure 10: *Cloth pinched between two spheres. Conflicting constraints are resolved by allowing drift of duplicate surfaces using soft bindings (2.8 min/frame, 150×150 mesh).*

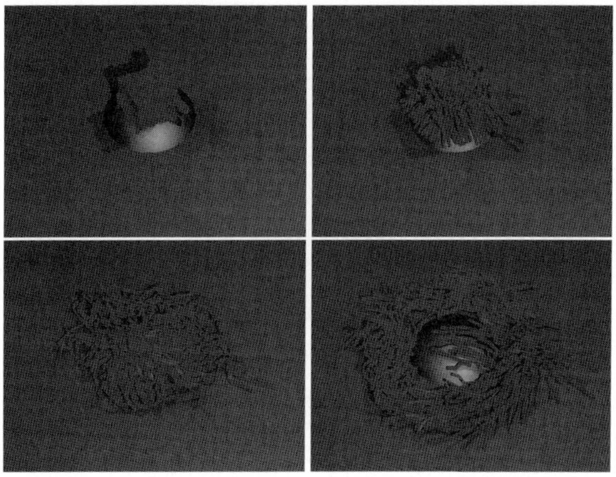

Figure 11: *A coarse 320 tetrahedra cube mesh is cut into 289 sticks. Object collisions and self-collisions are resolved by the soft bound embedded surface.*

and step 4 still requires the use of $\mathbf{x}^{n+1/2}$. Our modifications to [ITF04] are crucial for unconditional stability, e.g. using $\mathbf{x}^{n+1}$ instead of $\mathbf{x}^{n+1/2}$ in step 4 leads to a time step restriction of $\Delta t < (b + \sqrt{b^2 + 8\mu k})/2k$. We stress that this implicit treatment of elastic forces is only used on the binding springs and that all other elastic forces are treated explicitly in order to more accurately resolve dynamic motion.

4. Examples

We used critical damping for the soft binding springs in our examples. The stiffness parameters were set experimentally. Figure 8 shows eight deformable spheres stitched together using implicit binding springs as described in section 3.2. On the left the binding springs are made sufficiently stiff to retain coincidence of the connecting points without incurring additional time step restrictions. The binding springs are visible on the right where their stiffness is reduced. In figure 9 we begin with a coarse deformable block. We then create a duplicate copy of the top surface, which is refined and hard bound to the block. Next, we use binding springs to attach a soft bound duplicate of this refined surface for collision with a stamp. When collisions stretch these binding springs to a length beyond a prescribed threshold the hard bound target particles are moved in material space (and a new barycentric embedding is computed) to bring the length back down to this threshold, analogous to typical plastic yield. We are careful not to move any hard bound target particle outside the material.

Using a variant of the virtual node algorithm [MBF04], we cut a coarse cube mesh consisting of 320 tetrahedra into 289 sticks as shown in figure 11. Each stick is composed of a number of tetrahedra that are only partially filled with material and the polygonization of the material surface is augmented with soft bindings to resolve self-collisions and object collisions. See [SDF07] which is enabled by our new hybrid simulation framework.

Figure 10 shows cloth pinched between two kinematically controlled spheres producing contradictory collision constraints (see [BWK03]). For each particle in the cloth mesh that is pinched between the two spheres, we create two duplicate soft bound particles which each collide with only one of the two spheres. Collisions with the sphere pull these soft bound particles away from their hard bound target locations on the cloth surface resulting in binding spring forces that pull the cloth mesh in both directions equilibrating in a steady state. In the absence of any other forces, the soft bound particles would slide along the sphere in an attempt to minimize the length of the underlying binding springs. However, we map the mesh-based constitutive model forces of the cloth to the soft bound particles making them behave in a fashion similar to their hard bound counterparts, i.e. resisting stretching. Figure 10 (lower right) is a visualization of the effect of mapping the constitutive model forces from the hard bound target locations to their soft bound counterparts. That is, it is similar to creating a mesh which connects all the drifted soft bound particles to each other and to the parent mesh as depicted schematically by the orange wireframe. In fact, one could envision this as simulating three distinct meshes: the parent mesh given by the cloth itself, the orange wireframe mesh, and a second wireframe mesh which agrees with the bottom half of the orange wireframe but is concave up elsewhere resolving collisions with the top sphere. However, we do not need to construct these duplicate meshes, and instead automatically inherit these properties from the parent simulation mesh.

Figure 12 depicts the dynamic simulation of a muscle-driven facial model for speech articulation from [SNF05]. The surface geometry is embedded in a non-graded adaptive red-only BCC mesh with 135K tetrahedral elements (an 85%

reduction from the mesh size in [SSRMF06]. Hard bindings are used to simulate the resulting T-junctions, while soft bound particles are used to model the high resolution surface and also used for collisions, self-collisions and boundary conditions. Since the simulation mesh does not conform to the geometry of the cranium and jawbone, we use soft bound particles on the high-resolution surface to enforce bone attachments as well. A higher stiffness was used to attach the embedded free skin surface to its hard bound counterpart, and a lower stiffness was used for the connections between soft-bound bone attachments and their hard bound targets.

5. Extensions to Rigid Body Coupling

Various authors have considered the two-way coupling of rigid and deformable bodies using a variety of schemes, see e.g. [BW97, OZH00, JV03, LF04]. We present preliminary results showing that our hybrid framework can be applied to these types of problems as well.

We consider the rigid body frame (x_c, q), twist (v_c, ω) and inertia tensor $I(q) = R(q)I_0R(q)^T$, where I_0 is a diagonal inertia tensor and $R(q)$ is the rotation matrix associated with the current orientation. To facilitate our hybrid formulation, we define a *rigid body particle* with the same state as a rigid body. A rigid body hard binding is defined by embedding a particle onto a fixed object space location r_0. Consequently, the kinematic state of the bound particle is given as $x_e = x_c + r(q)$ and $v_e = v_c + \omega \times r(q)$ where $r(q) = R(q)r_0$ is the world space displacement of the embedded particle from the center of mass of the rigid body. We can write $v_e = W(q)(v_c, \omega)$ with the aid of the interpolation matrix $W(q) = (\mathbb{I} \;\; r(q)^{*T})$ where $\mathbb{I}$ is the 3×3 identity matrix and $r(q)^*$ is the cross product matrix. Although x_e cannot be written in similar form, a linearized

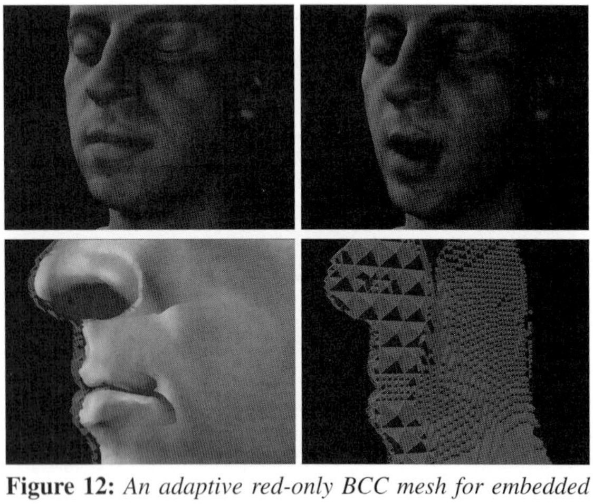

Figure 12: *An adaptive red-only BCC mesh for embedded simulation of a muscle-driven face model. Hard bindings are used for T-junctions, and soft bindings are used for collisions and boundary conditions (18 min/frame).*

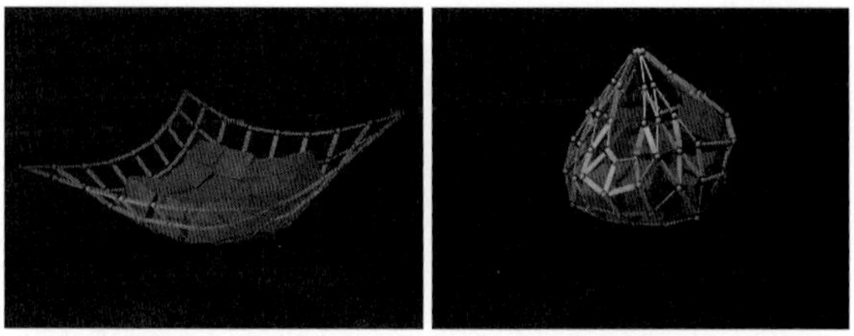

Figure 13: *A net is constructed using binding springs to create simple point joints between hard bound particles on different rigid bodies.*

change in the frame of the rigid body particle admits a similar mapping, i.e. $\Delta x_e = W(q)(\Delta x_c, \Delta q)$, where Δx_c is the displacement of the center of mass and Δq is the vector whose cross product matrix is the linearized rotation satisfying $R(q(t+\Delta t)) = R(q(t)) + \Delta q^* + O(\Delta t^2)$.

Applying a force f_e to the hard bound particle results in a wrench $(f_c, \tau) = W(q)^T f_e$ where $f_c = f_e$ is applied to the center of mass and $\tau = r(q) \times f_e$ is the torque. Next consider a velocity-dependent damping force $f_e = G_e v_e$ on a hard bound particle, which results in $(f_c, \tau) = W(q)^T G_e W(q)(v_c, \omega) = G(v_c, \omega)$ where $G = W(q)^T G_e W(q)$ maps twists to wrenches directly and retains the symmetry and definiteness of the damping matrix G_e. Similarly elastic wrench differentials are given by $(\Delta f_c, \Delta\tau) = W(q)^T K_e W(q)(\Delta x_c, \Delta q) = K(\Delta x_c, \Delta q)$ where $K = W(q)^T K_e W(q)$ is the stiffness matrix expressed in terms of the rigid body particle and $K_e = \partial f_e / \partial x_e$ is the stiffness matrix expressed in terms of the hard bound particle. We use these results to treat rigid body particles in the same fashion as other parent particles in our time integration scheme. Note that the definition of the global damping matrix $\mathbf{G} = \mathbf{W}^T \bar{\mathbf{G}} \mathbf{W}$ and global stiffness matrix $\mathbf{K} = \mathbf{W}^T \bar{\mathbf{K}} \mathbf{W}$ trivially extends to the case of rigid body bindings, by incorporating the interpolation matrix $W(q)$ into the global matrix $\mathbf{W}$ used in these equations. Finally, the global mass matrix $\mathbf{M}$ is augmented with the diagonal entry $\mathrm{diag}(m\mathbb{I}, I)$ for each rigid body particle.

We preliminarily couple our hybrid simulation of rigid body particles to a state-of-the-art rigid body simulation scheme as follows:

1. Copy the state of the rigid bodies to the rigid body particles
2. Compute $\tilde{\mathbf{v}}^{n+\frac{1}{2}}$ as in section 3.3
3. Compute $\tilde{\mathbf{x}}^{n+1}$ using $\tilde{\mathbf{x}}_{\mathbf{c}}^{n+1} = \mathbf{x}_{\mathbf{c}}^n + \Delta t \tilde{\mathbf{v}}_{\mathbf{c}}^{n+\frac{1}{2}}$ and $\tilde{\mathbf{q}}^{n+1} = \mathbf{q}(\Delta t \omega^{n+\frac{1}{2}})\mathbf{q}^n$
4. Process collisions for deformable objects only
5. Compute $\mathbf{v}^{n+1}$ using steps 4 and 5 from section 3.3
6. Copy *momentum only* from the rigid body particles to the rigid bodies
7. Separately, time integrate and collide the rigid bodies

This last step evolves the rigid bodies forward in time using a standard scheme as in [GBF03], and the two-way cou-

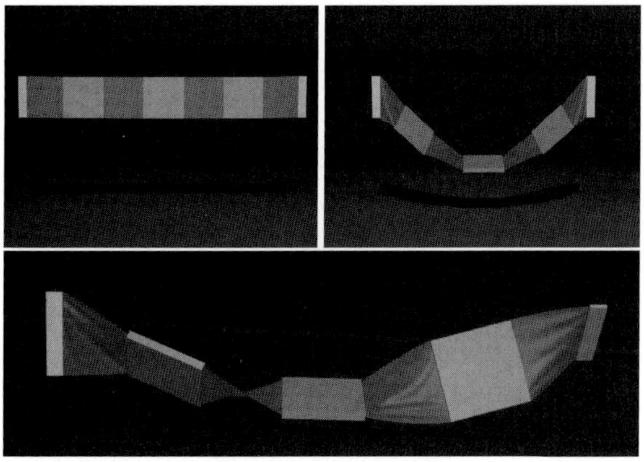

Figure 14: *Coupled simulation of rigid plates and cloth sheets, where cloth particles have been hard bound to the rigid plates. Each of the three rigid plates as well as the two constrained rigid bodies depicted in orange are represented by single rigid body particles.*

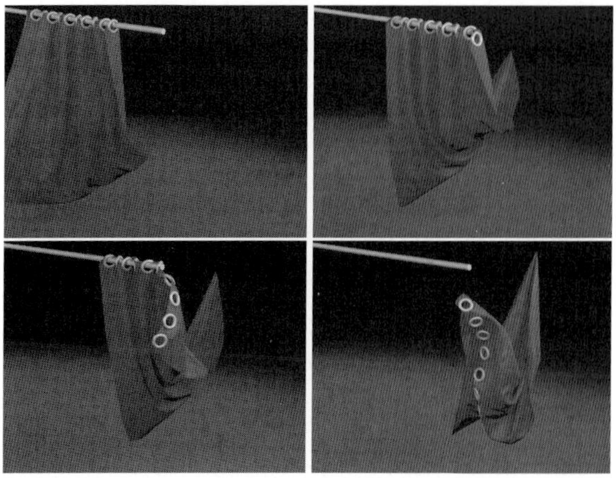

Figure 15: *Simulation of a cloth curtain with a number of particles hard bound on rigid rings that are used to suspend the cloth from a curtain rod. Each of the ten rings is modeled with a single rigid body particle.*

pling is integrated into the standard rigid body solver using steps 1 through 6 where only the effects of momentum are preserved. Although it may be possible to extend the rigid body particles to include more advanced contact, collision, friction, stacking and complex articulation, it is not yet clear how this could be done and we defer it to future work. Figure 13 shows the use of implicitly integrated binding springs to enforce a simple point joint articulation between rigid body hard bound particles. Figures 14 and 15 illustrate two-way coupling between cloth and rigid bodies.

6. Conclusion

We proposed a novel method for augmenting a mesh-based approach to deformable solids simulation with point-based simulation technology. Current limitations include the exclusion of damping terms in the mapping of forces from parents to soft bound particles. Even in the absence of collisions, this leads to drift that has to be corrected via the binding springs. Furthermore, soft bound particles are assigned mass in addition to the mass carried by their parents. Force mapping partially compensates for this by duplicating momentum along with mass on the soft bound particles. Nevertheless, when binding springs are used instead of synchronized coupling, collision handling may be adversely affected by the different amounts of mass assigned to the soft bound surface and its hard bound counterpart. Finally our coupling of deformable and rigid bodies is preliminary and requires separate handling of rigid and deformable body collisions, limiting the applicability of this scheme for scenarios involving complex contact, stacking, friction and articulation.

Acknowledgments

Research supported in part by an ONR YIP award and a PECASE award (ONR N00014-01-1-0620), a Packard Foundation Fellowship, ONR N0014-06-1-0393, ONR N00014-05-1-0479 for a computing cluster, ONR N00014-02-1-0720, ONR N00014-06-1-0505, ARO DAAD19-03-1-0331, NSF CCF-0541148, NSF ITR-0205671, NSF IIS-0326388, NSF ACI-0323866 and NIH U54-GM072970. Special thanks to Rachel Weinstein and Ranjitha Kumar for their help in simulation and rendering.

References

[ACSYD05] ALLIEZ P., COHEN-STEINER D., YVINEC M., DESBRUN M.: Variational tetrahedral meshing. *ACM Trans. Graph. (SIGGRAPH Proc.) 24*, 3 (2005), 617–625.

[BW97] BARAFF D., WITKIN A.: *Partitioned Dynamics*. Tech. rep., Carnegie Mellon University, 1997.

[BW98] BARAFF D., WITKIN A.: Large steps in cloth simulation. In *Proc. SIGGRAPH 98* (1998), pp. 43–54.

[BWK03] BARAFF D., WITKIN A., KASS M.: Untangling cloth. *ACM Trans. Graph. (SIGGRAPH Proc.) 22* (2003), 862–870.

[CGC*02a] CAPELL S., GREEN S., CURLESS B., DUCHAMP T., POPOVIĆ Z.: Interactive skeleton-driven dynamic deformations. *ACM Trans. Graph. (SIGGRAPH Proc.) 21* (2002), 586–593.

[CGC*02b] CAPELL S., GREEN S., CURLESS B., DUCHAMP T., POPOVIĆ Z.: A multiresolution framework for dynamic deformations. In *ACM SIGGRAPH Symp. on Comput. Anim.* (2002), ACM Press, pp. 41–48.

[DDCB01] DEBUNNE G., DESBRUN M., CANI M., BARR A.: Dynamic real-time deformations using space & time adaptive sampling. In *Proc. SIGGRAPH 2001* (2001), vol. 20, pp. 31–36.

[DMG05] DEQUIDT J., MARCHAL D., GRISONI L.: Time-critical animation of deformable solids: Collision detection and deformable objects. *Computer Animation and Virtual Worlds 16*, 3-4 (2005), 177–187.

[GBF03] GUENDELMAN E., BRIDSON R., FEDKIW R.: Nonconvex rigid bodies with stacking. *ACM Trans. Graph. (SIGGRAPH Proc.) 22*, 3 (2003), 871–878.

[GBT06] GISSLER M., BECKER M., TESCHNER M.: Local constraint methods for deformable objects. In *Proc. of the 3rd Workshop in VR Interactions and Physical Simulation (VRIPHYS)* (2006), pp. 1–8.

[GD04] GUY S., DEBUNNE G.: *Monte-Carlo collision detection*. Tech. Rep. RR-5136, INRIA, March 2004.

[GKS02] GRINSPUN E., KRYSL P., SCHRÖDER P.: CHARMS: A simple framework for adaptive simulation. *ACM Trans. Graph. (SIGGRAPH Proc.) 21* (2002), 281–290.

[ITF04] IRVING G., TERAN J., FEDKIW R.: Invertible finite elements for robust simulation of large deformation. In *Proc. of the ACM SIGGRAPH/Eurographics Symp. on Comput. Anim.* (2004), pp. 131–140.

[JV03] JANSSON J., VERGEEST J.: Combining deformable and rigid body mechanics simulation. *The Vis. Comput. J.* (2003).

[LC06] LOUBÈRE R., CARAMANA E. J.: The force/work differencing of exceptional points in the discrete, compatible formulation of lagrangian hydrodynamics. *J. Comput. Phys. 216* (2006), 1–18.

[LF04] LENOIR J., FONTENEAU S.: Mixing deformable and rigid-body mechanics simulation. In *Comput. Graph. Int.* (june 16-19 2004), pp. 327–334.

[MBF04] MOLINO N., BAO Z., FEDKIW R.: A virtual node algorithm for changing mesh topology during simulation. *ACM Trans. Graph. (SIGGRAPH Proc.) 23* (2004), 385–392.

[MBTF03] MOLINO N., BRIDSON R., TERAN J., FEDKIW R.: A crystalline, red green strategy for meshing highly deformable objects with tetrahedra. In *12th Int. Meshing Roundtable* (2003), pp. 103–114.

[MG04] MÜLLER M., GROSS M.: Interactive virtual materials. In *Graph. Interface* (May 2004), pp. 239–246.

[MHTG05] MÜLLER M., HEIDELBERGER B., TESCHNER M., GROSS M.: Meshless deformations based on shape matching. *ACM Trans. Graph. (SIGGRAPH Proc.)* (2005), 471–478.

[MKN*04] MÜLLER M., KEISER R., NEALEN A., PAULY M., GROSS M., ALEXA M.: Point based animation of elastic, plastic and melting objects. In *Proc. of the 2004 ACM SIGGRAPH/Eurographics Symp. on Comput. Anim.* (2004), pp. 141–151.

[MTG04] MÜLLER M., TESCHNER M., GROSS M.: Physically-based simulation of objects represented by surface meshes. In *Proc. Comput. Graph. Int.* (June 2004), pp. 156–165.

[OH99] O'BRIEN J., HODGINS J.: Graphical modeling and animation of brittle fracture. In *Proc. of SIGGRAPH 1999* (1999), pp. 137–146.

[OZH00] O'BRIEN J. F., ZORDAN V. B., HODGINS J. K.: Combining active and passive simulations for secondary motion. *IEEE Comput. Graph. Appl. 20* (2000).

[PKA*05] PAULY M., KEISER R., ADAMS B., DUTRÉ P., GROSS M., GUIBAS L.: Meshless animation of fracturing solids. *ACM Trans. Graph. (SIGGRAPH Proc.) 24*, 3 (2005), 957–964.

[SDF07] SIFAKIS E., DER K., FEDKIW R.: Arbitrary cutting of deformable tetrahedralized objects. In *Proc. of ACM SIGGRAPH/Eurographics Symp. on Comput. Anim. (in press)* (2007).

[SHGS06] STEINEMANN D., HARDERS M., GROSS M., SZEKELY G.: Hybrid cutting of deformable solids. In *Proc. of the IEEE Virtual Reality Conference* (2006), pp. 35–42.

[Sif07] SIFAKIS E.: *Algorithmic aspects of the simulation and control of computer generated human anatomy models*. PhD thesis, Stanford University, June 2007.

[SNF05] SIFAKIS E., NEVEROV I., FEDKIW R.: Automatic determination of facial muscle activations from sparse motion capture marker data. *ACM Trans. Graph. (SIGGRAPH Proc.)* (2005).

[SOG06] STEINEMANN D., OTADUY M. A., GROSS M.: Fast arbitrary splitting of deforming objects. In *Proc. of the ACM SIGGRAPH/Eurographics Symp. on Comput. Anim.* (2006), pp. 63–72.

[SSRMF06] SIFAKIS E., SELLE A., ROBINSON-MOSHER A., FEDKIW R.: Simulating speech with a physics-based facial muscle model. *ACM SIGGRAPH/Eurographics Symp. on Comput. Anim.* (2006), 261–270.

[TF88a] TERZOPOULOS D., FLEISCHER K.: Deformable models. *The Vis. Comput. 4*, 6 (1988), 306–331.

[TF88b] TERZOPOULOS D., FLEISCHER K.: Modeling inelastic deformation: viscoelasticity, plasticity, fracture. *Comput. Graph. (SIGGRAPH Proc.)* (1988), 269–278.

[TPBF87] TERZOPOULOS D., PLATT J., BARR A., FLEISCHER K.: Elastically deformable models. *Comput. Graph. (Proc. SIGGRAPH 87) 21*, 4 (1987), 205–214.

[TSSB*05] TERAN J., SIFAKIS E., SALINAS-BLEMKER S., NG-THOW-HING V., LAU C., FEDKIW R.: Creating and simulating skeletal muscle from the visible human data set. *IEEE Trans. on Vis. and Comput. Graph. 11*, 3 (2005), 317–328.

[WSG05] WICKE M., STEINEMANN D., GROSS M.: Efficient animation of point-sampled thin shells. In *Proc. of Eurographics* (2005), vol. 24.

Eurographics/ ACM SIGGRAPH Symposium on Computer Animation (2007)
D. Metaxas and J. Popovic (Editors)

Cubic Shells

Akash Garg
Columbia University, USA

Eitan Grinspun
Columbia University, USA

Max Wardetzky
Freie Universität Berlin, Germany

Denis Zorin
New York University, USA

Abstract

Hinge-based bending models are widely used in the physically-based animation of cloth, thin plates and shells. We propose a hinge-based model that is simpler to implement, more efficient to compute, and offers a greater number of effective material parameters than existing models. Our formulation builds on two mathematical observations: (a) the bending energy of curved flexible surfaces can be expressed as a cubic polynomial *if the surface does not stretch; (b) a general class of anisotropic materials—those that are* orthotropic*—is captured by appropriate choice of a single stiffness per hinge. Our contribution impacts a general range of surface animation applications, from isotropic cloth and thin plates to orthotropic fracturing thin shells.*

1. Introduction

Many animation applications require simple and efficient simulation of a general class of elastic surfaces. This class includes objects that are (a) flat (plates) or curved (shells) in their undeformed state, (b) flexible or nearly rigid and (c) isotropic or anisotropic in their response to bending. In mesh-based simulation, *hinge-based* methods are preferred for their simplicity and economy of computation. Considering every two triangles meeting at an edge to be a bending hinge, such methods require that some function of the dihedral angle is subject to a restoring force. Empirically, hinge-based models are known to work well for isotropic materials, and for geometric models of anisotropy based on Euler's curvature formula [BW98, VMT06]. For a survey of bending models used in animation, see [TW06].

Contributions. We present what we believe is the simplest and most efficient hinge-based bending model to encompass the spectrums (a), (b), and (c), at the cost of restricting our attention to *quasi-inextensible* surfaces, *i.e.*, surfaces that prefer to bend much more than to stretch. Our model is based on a mathematical analysis of the hinge-based approach resulting in two main insights:

First, we introduce a hinge-based bending model that preserves a key property of the smooth setting: the bending energy of a thin shell is *cubic* under isometric deformations. To understand the consequences of this statement, consider that bending energy is in general a highly nonlinear functional of the surface position; therefore, the implementation of implicit solvers for thin shells involves relatively complex derivation and costly computation of the nonlinear bending force Jacobian. However, under the assumption of quasi-isometry, we show that implementation can be reduced to a one-time precomputation of an approximate Jacobian matrix, and implicit time stepping routines can use an inexact Newton method for significant performance gains. Shells simulated with this method conserve both linear and angular momenta.

Second, we treat anisotropy, where mechanical response depends on the direction of applied strain. We present a bending model for *orthotropic* materials, exposing an important physical parameter—the *shear modulus*—which affects the *drapability* of a fabric [SM02]. Perhaps due to their small stencil, hinge-based models in computer animation have thus far eluded the incorporation of orthotropic response.

Our work builds on a foundation laid out by Bergou *et al.* [BWH*06], who demonstrated that in the special case of isotropic thin *plates* undergoing isometric deformations, the bending energy is quadratic, and correspondingly the forces are linear, in mesh positions; see also Volino and Magnenat-Thalmann [VMT06] for a linear bending force. In contrast, we consider inextensible thin *shells*, whose bending energy is cubic, with correspondingly quadratic forces.

Overview. By first considering *isotropic* bending, we expose the cubic nature of bending energies in the smooth (§2.1) as well as discrete settings (§2.2), establishing the *cubic hinge* (§3) as our discrete building block. Next, we introduce *orthotropy* (§4) and show that it is captured by a scalar hinge stiffness (§4.1). Finally, we describe the efficient implementation of orthotropic cubic shells (§5–§6), and discuss a battery of experiments demonstrating the efficiency and efficacy of our model (§7–§8).

Symposium on Computer Animation 2007, San Diego, CA, August 03-04, 2007.
© 2007 ACM 978-1-59593-624-4/07/0008 $5.00

2. Isotropic bending

2.1. Smooth setting

Consider a surface deformed away from its natural (*undeformed*) shape. To this deformation we associate the isotropic bending energy

$$E_{\mathrm{b}}(\mathbf{x}) = \frac{1}{2}\int_S (H-\overline{H})^2 \mathrm{d}A\,. \qquad (1)$$

This is the integral, over the undeformed surface, of the squared change in mean curvature. Here $\mathbf{x}$ is the position of the deformed surface, and H is the mean curvature function of the deformed surface. A bar (*e.g.*, $\overline{H}$) denotes the corresponding quantity evaluated on the undeformed surface. Whereas we consider arbitrary undeformed shapes, the special case of flat undeformed shapes ($\overline{H}=0$) was explored by Bergou *et al.* [BWH*06].

Although not immediately apparent from (1), $E_{\mathrm{b}}(\mathbf{x})$ is actually a *cubic polynomial* in $\mathbf{x}$ under *isometric deformations*, *i.e.*, if the surface is allowed to bend but not to stretch. To see this, rewrite (1) as

$$E_{\mathrm{b}}(\mathbf{x}) = \frac{1}{2}\int_S \left(\langle \mathbf{H},\mathbf{H}\rangle - 2\langle \mathbf{H},\overline{H}\hat{\mathbf{n}}\rangle + \overline{H}^2\right)\mathrm{d}A\,. \qquad (2)$$

Here $\langle\cdot,\cdot\rangle$ denotes the standard inner product in 3-space, and $\mathbf{H}=H\hat{\mathbf{n}}$ stands for the mean curvature *normal*, a vector parallel to the surface's unit normal, $\hat{\mathbf{n}}$. Bergou *et al.* observed that the mean curvature vector can be expressed as $\mathbf{H}=\Delta\mathbf{x}$, *i.e.*, the surface's intrinsic Laplacian applied to the position of the surface. For isometric deformations of the surface, two facts follow: (F1) Since Δ is intrinsic, $\mathbf{H}$ is *linear in surface position*, thus $\langle\mathbf{H},\mathbf{H}\rangle$ is quadratic in $\mathbf{x}$ [BWH*06]. (F2) The surface normal is quadratic[†] in $\mathbf{x}$; therefore, $\langle\mathbf{H},\overline{H}\hat{\mathbf{n}}\rangle$ is cubic. It follows that $E_{\mathrm{b}}(\mathbf{x})$ is a cubic polynomial in $\mathbf{x}$, because $\langle\mathbf{H},\overline{H}\hat{\mathbf{n}}\rangle$ is cubic, $\langle\mathbf{H},\mathbf{H}\rangle$ is quadratic, and $\overline{H}^2$ does not depend on $\mathbf{x}$. While Bergou *et al.* discussed (F1) for thin plates ($\overline{H}=0$), (F2) is unique to shells ($\overline{H}\neq 0$) and presents our central technical challenge.

The *cubic shells* idea is to develop a discrete analogue of this picture.

2.2. Discrete setting

Consider a triangle mesh whose shape before deformation is given by the vector of vertex positions $\bar{\mathbf{x}}$. When the mesh is deformed to position $\mathbf{x}$, the usual hinge-based bending energy [BW98, BMF03, GHDS03, BWH*06, TW06] is given

† To see that $\hat{\mathbf{n}}$ is quadratic, write $\hat{\mathbf{n}} = \frac{\partial\mathbf{x}}{\partial u}\times\frac{\partial\mathbf{x}}{\partial v}$, and observe that orthonormality of tangent vectors, $\frac{\partial\mathbf{x}}{\partial u}$ and $\frac{\partial\mathbf{x}}{\partial v}$, is preserved under isometric deformations.

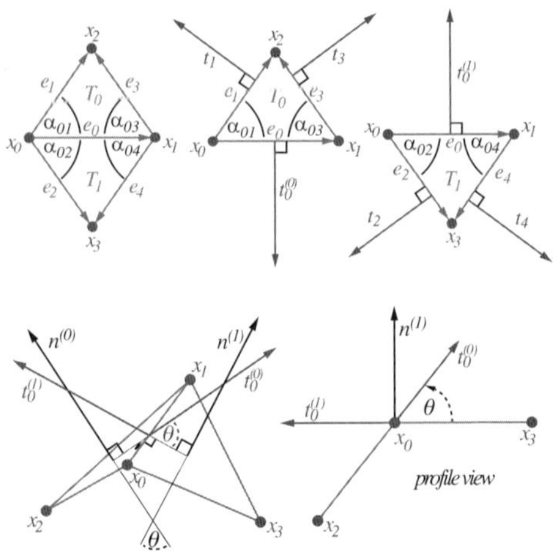

Figure 1: Top-left: *Hinge stencil for an interior edge.* Top-middle and -right: *Perpendicular vectors used in the computation.* Bottom: *Hinge in 3-space with corresponding labels.*

by[‡]

$$E_{\mathrm{b}}(\mathbf{x}) = \frac{1}{2}\sum_i \frac{3|\bar{\mathbf{e}}_i|^2}{\bar{A}_i}\left(2\sin\frac{\theta_i-\bar{\theta}_i}{2}\right)^2\,. \qquad (3)$$

Here the sum is taken over all interior edges, $\bar{A}_i$ denotes the combined area of the two triangles incident to edge $\bar{\mathbf{e}}_i$, and θ_i denotes the dihedral angle at edge i.

Our goal is to establish an important, and previously overlooked, property of (3): under isometric deformations, it is a cubic polynomial in $\mathbf{x}$. This observation will expose a much more efficient implementation than is directly evident from (3); for details on this implementation, refer directly to §5.

The discrete energy (3) can be written as a sum over contributions from every hinge (indexed by i). Using the identity $2\sin^2 u = 1-\cos 2u$, with $u=(\theta-\bar{\theta})/2$, we arrive at an expression of energy associated to the ith hinge:

$$E_{\mathrm{b}}(\mathbf{x})_i = \frac{3|\bar{\mathbf{e}}_i|^2}{\bar{A}_i}(1-\cos(\theta_i-\bar{\theta}_i))\,. \qquad (4)$$

In the following section, we prove that for isometric deformations this hinge energy is cubic in $\mathbf{x}$.

3. The cubic hinge

Our derivation uses the geometric construction in Figure 1, which defines *local indices* of the triangles, $\{T_0,T_1\}$, edge vectors, $\{\mathbf{e}_0,\ldots,\mathbf{e}_4\}$, and vertex positions, $\{\mathbf{x}_0,\ldots,\mathbf{x}_3\}$, associated to a hinge. Note the construction of *perpendiculars* $\mathbf{t}_i$: each edge vector $\mathbf{e}_i$ is rotated 90 degrees, on the

‡ For planar rest state ($\bar{\theta}=0$) we have $\lim_{\theta\to 0} 2\sin\theta/2 = \lim_{\theta\to 0} 2\tan\theta/2 = \theta$, so that models that use $2\sin\theta/2$, $2\tan\theta/2$, or θ coincide in the limit of an appropriate refinement sequence.

plane of the triangle, to point outwards (thus $|\mathbf{t}_i| = |\mathbf{e}_i|$ and $\langle \mathbf{t}_i, \mathbf{e}_i \rangle = 0$). Since $\mathbf{e}_0$ is associated to two triangles, we construct two perpendiculars, $\mathbf{t}_0^{(0)}$ and $\mathbf{t}_0^{(1)}$, on the planes of triangles T_0 and T_1 respectively.

Expressing the perpendiculars $\mathbf{t}_0^{(0)}$ (resp. $\mathbf{t}_0^{(1)}$) in the edge basis $\{\mathbf{e}_1, \mathbf{e}_3\}$ (resp. $\{\mathbf{e}_2, \mathbf{e}_4\}$) we obtain

$$\mathbf{t}_0^{(0)} = -\cot\alpha_{03}\mathbf{e}_1 - \cot\alpha_{01}\mathbf{e}_3 \,, \quad (5)$$

$$\mathbf{t}_0^{(1)} = -\cot\alpha_{04}\mathbf{e}_2 - \cot\alpha_{02}\mathbf{e}_4 \,. \quad (6)$$

Under isometric deformation, interior angles remain constant, therefore $\mathbf{t}_0^{(0)}$ and $\mathbf{t}_0^{(1)}$ are *linear expressions* in the position of the mesh. Furthermore, the geometry of Fig. 1-bottom reveals that§

$$\cos\theta = \frac{-\langle \mathbf{t}_0^{(0)}, \mathbf{t}_0^{(1)} \rangle}{|\mathbf{e}_0|^2}, \quad \text{and} \quad \sin\theta = -\frac{\beta[\mathbf{e}_0, \mathbf{e}_1, \mathbf{e}_2]}{|\mathbf{e}_0|^2},$$

where $[\mathbf{e}_i, \mathbf{e}_j, \mathbf{e}_k]$ is the scalar triple product $(\mathbf{e}_i \times \mathbf{e}_j) \cdot \mathbf{e}_k$, and $\beta = \frac{1}{|\mathbf{e}_0|}(\cot\alpha_{01} + \cot\alpha_{03})(\cot\alpha_{02} + \cot\alpha_{04})$.

Expanding (4) by the identity $\cos(\theta - \bar{\theta}) = \cos\theta\cos\bar{\theta} + \sin\theta\sin\bar{\theta}$, substituting the above expressions for $\cos\theta$ and $\sin\theta$, and simplifying the resulting expression by using the isometry assumption ($|\bar{\mathbf{e}}_i| = |\mathbf{e}_i|$) we find that (4) equals

$$\underbrace{\frac{3}{\bar{A}_0}\left(|\bar{\mathbf{e}}_0|^2 + \langle \mathbf{t}_0^{(0)}, \mathbf{t}_0^{(1)} \rangle \cos\bar{\theta}\right)}_{\text{thin plate component}} + \underbrace{\frac{3\bar{\beta}}{\bar{A}_0}[\mathbf{e}_0, \mathbf{e}_1, \mathbf{e}_2]\sin\bar{\theta}}_{\text{cubic term}} \,. \quad (7)$$

Under isometry, the energy associated to an individual hinge is a cubic polynomial in $\mathbf{x}$. Just as in the smooth picture, the discrete $E_b(\mathbf{x})$ is cubic. Note that for the special case $\bar{\theta} = 0$, we recover the quadratic bending thin *plate* energy of [BWH*06] simply by substituting (5) and (6) into (7).

4. Orthotropy

We now generalize our bending model to *orthotropic* materials—an important class of anisotropic materials whose elastic properties depend on the direction along which they are measured [VK01]. A fully general linear elasticity model for deformable surfaces has six parameters (not counting the choice of anisotropy axes) some of which are hard to interpret intuitively. We focus on a more restricted *orthotropic* elasticity model whose four parameters have more intuitive meaning and appear to be useful for material behavior control in animation. Most common man-made materials are orthotropic, for example, cloth, plastic reinforced by fibers, sheet metal, and paper. Non-orthotropic thin materials are less common (*e.g.*, thin sheets obtained by cutting a 3D orthotropic material at an angle, or composite materials). For cloth, orthotropic approximation naturally matches most of the parameters of the Kawabata cloth evaluation system [Kaw80], a commonly used system for characterizing cloth properties, as explained below.

We are primarily interested in how these material parameters affect *bending*, rather than in-plane deformations. From the four parameters of orthotropic materials, one parameter can be eliminated if we assume that bending the surface along material directions does not have any effect on bending on the other direction (this corresponds to having zero Poisson ratio in the isotropic case). For simplicity we will assume that this is the case, and briefly discuss the role of the Poisson ratio at the end of this section.

The most obvious of the remaining three parameters are two Young's moduli, Y^0 and Y^1, which determine bending stiffness along two material directions. The third parameter is the *shear modulus*, G^{01}, which, for in-plane deformations, determines the resistance to shear. In the case of bending, the shear modulus allows for additional directional variability of bending stiffness. Specifically, bending stiffness at an angle α with respect to the material axis 0, is given by (up to a scale factor):

$$Y^0\cos^4\alpha + Y^1\sin^4\alpha + 2G^{01}\sin^2\alpha\cos^2\alpha \,. \quad (8)$$

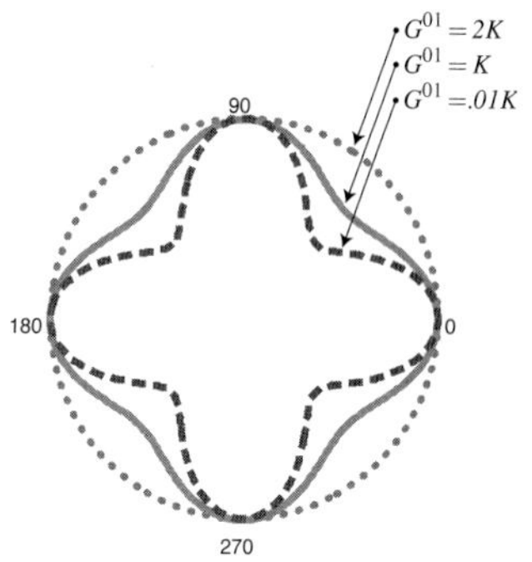

Consider the adjacent plot of *directional stiffness* as a function of α, for three materials all sharing $Y^0 = Y^1$, but with shear moduli $0.1K$, K, and $2K$. Note that for low shear, typical for cloth, the maximal to minimal bending stiffness ratio is 2. As shown in Figure 4, this has a significant effect on drapability, and *cannot* be achieved by a simple model using just two parameters. Similarly, the shear modulus affects resistance of cloth to *twisting*, even if $Y^0 = Y^1$, as twisting may lead to diagonal bending.

Directional stiffness is particularly important in the case of *quasi-inextensible* flat sheets. Such sheets have small Gaussian curvature (the product of the two principal curvatures), which implies that strong bending can be present only in a single direction.

In contrast to directional stiffness, forces arising from the interaction of *multiple* bending directions (*e.g.*, due to the Poisson ratio in the isotropic case) appear to be qualitatively less important. In fact, one can show that for directional stiffness this interaction results in effective increase in the shear

§ The expression for $\sin\theta$ was derived from

$$\sin\theta = \frac{\langle \mathbf{t}_0^{(0)}, \mathbf{n}^{(1)} \rangle}{|\mathbf{e}_0|^2} = -\frac{[\mathbf{t}_0^{(0)}, \mathbf{t}_0^{(1)}, \mathbf{e}_0]}{|\mathbf{e}_0|^3} = -\frac{\beta[\mathbf{e}_0, \mathbf{e}_1, \mathbf{e}_2]}{|\mathbf{e}_0|^2},$$

where $\mathbf{n}^{(1)} = (|\mathbf{e}_0|/|\mathbf{e}_4 \times \mathbf{e}_2|)\mathbf{e}_4 \times \mathbf{e}_2$ is a scaled triangle normal. The last step is obtained by using (5) and (6) to replace $\mathbf{t}_0^{(0)}$ and $\mathbf{t}_0^{(1)}$, followed by observing that $\mathbf{e}_4 = \mathbf{e}_2 - \mathbf{e}_0$ and $\mathbf{e}_3 = \mathbf{e}_1 - \mathbf{e}_0$.

modulus. One can prove that in the simple case of bending of a plate with fixed boundaries the bending forces (unlike stretching) are independent of the Poisson ratio.

The Kawabata system characterizes cloth by its resistance to bending along warp and along weft directions, and by tensile, shearing and compressive stiffnesses measured as functions of deformation. In the orthotropic elasticity model, stiffnesses are assumed to be independent of the deformation, which appears to be a good approximation for qualitative modeling. Furthermore, plasticity effects are ignored, and the compressive and tensile stiffnesses are assumed to be equal. As pointed out in [BD94], linear elasticity provides a good approximation for Kawabata measurements for small deformations, although it ignores some of the subtler initial-resistance effects.

Given Kawabata measurements of a fabric, Y^1 and Y^0 can be inferred from directional bending stiffnesses and tensile measurements, and G^{01} from shear measurements. Alternatively, Y^1, Y^0, G^{01}, and the material axes may be directly controlled by an artist, adjusting parameters based on the notion that Y^1 and Y^0 determine resistance to bending along the two orthogonal material directions and G^{01} determines the resistance of the material to draping over an object.

Given the material parameters, and applying a standard formulation of Hooke's law for orthotropic materials, we can express the bending energy density of a deformed surface as a function of bending strain ε, using one additional material parameter $Y^{01} = \nu_{01}Y^1 = \nu_{10}Y^0$, where ν_{10} and ν_{01} are Poisson ratios (which always satisfy $\nu^{01}/Y^0 = \nu^{10}/Y^1$). The energy density is

$$c\left(Y^0\varepsilon_{00}^2 + Y^1\varepsilon_{11}^2 + 2Y^{01}\varepsilon_{00}\varepsilon_{11}\right) + 2hG^{01}\varepsilon_{01}^2\,, \qquad (9)$$

where $c = hY^0Y^1/(Y^0Y^1 - Y^{01}Y^{01})$, $h = \tau^3/12$, and τ is the sheet thickness. The bending strain is the shape operator [dC92] for surface, which for a quadratic bending energy reduces to the matrix of second partial derivatives. For the special case of isotropic materials, $Y^0 = Y^1 = 2(1+\nu)G^{01} = Y^{01}/\nu$.

In the following section, we show that orthotropic effects can be captured by weighting each hinge stiffness by a scalar factor, $\bar{\lambda}_i$. For convenience of implementation, the results of this derivation are summarized in §5.1.

4.1. Derivation of hinge stencil orthotropy

In §2.2 we discussed a simple model of discrete bending energy for isotropic shells. We based this model on summing the contributions of squared mean curvatures over interior edges. While discrete mean curvatures suffice to cover the isotropic case, we must use a discretization of the full shape operator in the anisotropic case. Indeed, smooth anisotropic energy density (9) requires expressing the discrete shape operator as a symmetric 2×2 matrix in the material frame—as the entries of this matrix measure bending and shearing stiffness in principal material directions. A hinge-based discrete shape operator $\mathbf{S}$ has been successfully applied in geometric modeling [HP04]. Here we augment the geometric modeling view by two aspects: (a) we express $\mathbf{S}$ in a material frame as opposed to its original expression in a principal curvature frame, and (b) we show how $\mathbf{S}$ leads to a scalar stiffness-correcting factor per edge covering the discrete orthotropic case.

Let us briefly recall the geometric view based on discrete principal curvatures taken in [HP04]. It is well-known from the smooth case [dC92] that $\mathbf{S}$ corresponds to a quadratic form whose (orthogonal) eigenvectors correspond to the two principal curvature directions, and its eigenvalues correspond to the principal curvatures, κ_0 and κ_1. Recall also that mean curvature is given as $H = \kappa_0 + \kappa_1$. In the discrete *edge-based* view, [HP04] defines the two principal curvature directions as (1) the direction along the edge and (2) the direction perpendicular to the edge—with no curvature ($\kappa_0 = 0$) along the edge and normal curvature ($\kappa_1 = \kappa$) perpendicular to the edge. Consequently, $H = \kappa$, and in the edge-based principal curvature frame, the discrete shape operator takes the form

$$\mathbf{S} = \begin{pmatrix} 0 & 0 \\ 0 & \kappa \end{pmatrix} = H\begin{pmatrix} 0 & 0 \\ 0 & 1 \end{pmatrix}.$$

We note that this hinge-based shape operator is mesh dependent (in particular, principal directions are tied to edge directions). However, if the edge directions are distributed evenly, on the average the true shape operator is well approximated.

In order to express $\mathbf{S}$ in the material frame, we treat the mesh area associated with each hinge stencil as a *homogeneous* piece of material, *i.e.*, we assume that the material parameters cY^0, cY^1, cY^{01}, hG^{01}, and the material axes are *constant* over hinge stencils. Denoting by γ_0 the angle between edge $\mathbf{e}_i$ and the first material axis, $\hat{\mathbf{y}}_a$, and using the fact that the shape operator transforms like a quadratic form, we obtain that $\mathbf{S}$ takes the form

$$\mathbf{S}_i = H_i\begin{pmatrix} \sin^2\gamma_0 & -\sin\gamma_0\cos\gamma_0 \\ -\sin\gamma_0\cos\gamma_0 & \cos^2\gamma_0 \end{pmatrix},$$

when expressed in the material frame of the edge i. Finally, using the smooth energy density (9) and setting $\varepsilon = \mathbf{S}$, it follows from basic trigonometric identities that the discrete orthotropic density can be written as

$$\underbrace{\left((cY^0)\sin^4\gamma_0 + (cY^1)\cos^4\gamma_0 + \frac{1}{2}\left(cY^{01} + hG^{01}\right)\sin^2(2\gamma_0)\right)}_{\bar{\lambda}_i}\cdot H_i^2\,,$$

providing a way to adjust hinge weights to effect orthotropic response.

This completes the requisite derivations for orthotropic cubic shells. In the following, we discuss the implementation of our model (§5–§6) and demonstrate the generality of the model with various simulation examples (§7).

5. Implementing cubic shells

In this section we describe the computation of forces and force Jacobians for the cubic shells energy, (7). Consider a mesh with n vertices and coordinate vectors $\mathbf{x}^x, \mathbf{x}^y, \mathbf{x}^z \in \mathbb{R}^n$. *Hinge-centric* computations are expressed in terms of the hinge's *local indices* (Fig. 1) for triangles, $\{T_0, T_1\}$, edge vectors, $\{\mathbf{e}_0, \ldots, \mathbf{e}_4\}$, and vertex positions, $\{\mathbf{x}_0, \ldots, \mathbf{x}_3\}$.

Precomputation. Recall that quantities that depend only on the undeformed positions are decorated with a bar, *e.g.*, $\bar{\mathbf{x}}$. Compute barred quantities once, before the simulation.

One-time matrix assembly. Assemble the global $n \times n$ matrix, $\overline{\mathbf{Q}}$, by iterating over hinge stencils. In the usual style of *stiffness matrix assembly* [ZT89], $\overline{\mathbf{Q}}$ accumulates contributions from each *local* 4×4 matrix, $\overline{\mathbf{Q}}_i$:

$$\overline{\mathbf{Q}}_i = \left(\frac{3\bar{\lambda}_i \cos \bar{\theta}_i}{\bar{A}_i} \right) \bar{K}_i^T \bar{K}_i \, ,$$

where $\bar{\lambda}_i$ is the stiffness of the hinge, $\bar{A}_i$ is the combined area of the two hinge triangles, and $\bar{\theta}_i$ is the undeformed hinge angle. In local indices, $\cos \bar{\theta} = -\langle \bar{\mathbf{t}}_0^{(0)}, \bar{\mathbf{t}}_0^{(1)} \rangle / |\bar{\mathbf{e}}_0|^2$, and $\bar{K} = (\bar{c}_{03} + \bar{c}_{04}, \bar{c}_{01} + \bar{c}_{02}, -\bar{c}_{01} - \bar{c}_{03}, -\bar{c}_{02} - \bar{c}_{04}) \in \mathbb{R}^4$, where $\bar{c}_{jk} = \cot \angle \bar{\mathbf{e}}_j, \bar{\mathbf{e}}_k$.

Force computation. Compute forces by adding thin plate and nonflat contributions. Compute thin plate contributions globally as the matrix-vector products $\mathbf{f}^x = \overline{\mathbf{Q}}\mathbf{x}^x$, $\mathbf{f}^y = \overline{\mathbf{Q}}\mathbf{x}^y$, $\mathbf{f}^z = \overline{\mathbf{Q}}\mathbf{x}^z$. Compute nonflat contributions by accumulating local hinge contributions

$$\mathbf{f}_0 = -\mathbf{f}_1 - \mathbf{f}_2 - \mathbf{f}_3 \, , \qquad \mathbf{f}_1 = \bar{k}(\mathbf{e}_1 \times \mathbf{e}_2) \, ,$$
$$\mathbf{f}_2 = \bar{k}(\mathbf{e}_2 \times \mathbf{e}_0) \, , \qquad \mathbf{f}_3 = \bar{k}(\mathbf{e}_0 \times \mathbf{e}_1) \, ,$$

where $\bar{k} = 3\bar{\lambda}_i(\bar{c}_{01} - \bar{c}_{03})(\bar{c}_{04} - \bar{c}_{02})[\bar{\mathbf{e}}_0, \bar{\mathbf{e}}_1, \bar{\mathbf{e}}_2]/(\bar{A}_0 |\bar{\mathbf{e}}_0|^3)$.

Force Jacobian computation. The exact force Jacobian ($\mathbb{R}^{3n} \times \mathbb{R}^{3n}$) is obtained by adding the thin plate and the nonflat contributions. The thin plate contributions are given by $\partial \mathbf{f}^x / \partial \mathbf{x}^x = \partial \mathbf{f}^y / \partial \mathbf{x}^y = \partial \mathbf{f}^z / \partial \mathbf{x}^z = \overline{\mathbf{Q}}$. For best performance (without sacrifice of accuracy), the nonflat contribution is omitted (as explained in §6); for completeness of exposition the nonflat contribution is detailed in the Appendix A.

5.1. Orthotropic hinge

The simple expressions above are all that is required to implement a cubic hinge-based bending force, given a stiffness value $\bar{\lambda}_i$ per hinge. For homogeneous isotropic materials, $\bar{\lambda}_i = \bar{\lambda}$ does not vary over the mesh, and the above derivation suffices; if a general class of orthotropic materials is desired, then $\bar{\lambda}_i$ should be computed by the formula derived in (§4.1); recall $\bar{\lambda}_i =$

$$(cY^0) \sin^4 \gamma_0 + (cY^1) \cos^4 \gamma_0 + \frac{1}{2} \left(cY^{01} + hG^{01} \right) \sin^2(2\gamma_0) \, ,$$

where γ_0 is the angle between the hinge edge and the first material axis, $\hat{\mathbf{y}}_0$, and Y^0, Y^1, Y^{01}, and G^{01} are the material parameters described above. The above expression is all that is needed to implement orthotropic bending for cubic shells, and indeed for any existing hinge-based model.

In our implementation, the (spatially-varying) direction of $\hat{\mathbf{y}}_0$ is encoded by a coordinate function over a given parameterization of the surface. In particular, we use the color values of a texture map to encode the direction of the material axis.

6. Efficient simulation of thin shells

The separability of the force Jacobian of cubic shells into a constant and linear term opens several interesting possibilities for efficient time integration of thin shell dynamics. Among common discrete time-stepping schemes [Hau04, HLW06, BW98], implicit schemes are popular in animation due to their stability. Implicit schemes advance time by solving a (typically nonlinear) system of equations. The system is usually solved by repeated Newton iterations (although *semi-implicit* methods complete a single Newton iteration) [PTVF92]. Each Newton iteration requires an evaluation of the force, $-\nabla E$, as well as the force Jacobian.

The fixed points of Newton's method remain unaltered when the nonlinear system Jacobian is replaced by any invertible matrix. An inexact Newton's method [Mor99] uses this fact in replacing a costly Jacobian with an inexpensive approximant. Hauth [Hau04] used an approximation of the in-plane stretching force Jacobian, and an inexact Newton framework, to accelerate cloth simulations; our work is similar, but we approximate the bending Jacobian. Wardetzky *et al.* [WBH*] also used an inexact Newton solve, in a mesh smoothing application; in contrast to that application, we treat the dynamics of shells having nonflat undeformed configurations.

Experiment. We consider the application of the inexact Newton's method with approximations to the bending force Jacobian. To provide a standard and easily-reproducible point of reference, we consider the Euler method, fully-implicit on stretching and bending elastic forces, without any additional damping forces.

In our experiments we pair two possible bending forces with three possible force Jacobians. For the two forces we consider the *nonlinear hinge* (NH)—the force resulting from treating bending energy fully nonlinearly (*i.e.*, by dropping the isometry assumption)—and the *cubic shells force* (CS) arising from our cubic energy as discussed in the previous section. For the three force Jacobians we consider the *nonlinear hinge Jacobian* (NH), the *entire* cubic shells Jacobian (CS), and the *constant part* (CC) of the cubic shells Jacobian. A particular choice of (inexact) Newton is denoted by a 2-tuple, *e.g.*, (CS,CC) denotes the use of the cubic shell bending forces paired with an approximate constant Jacobian; (NH,NH) denotes the usual fully-implicit implementation of the nonlinear hinge.

As a baseline, we run (NH,NH) at the maximum stable step

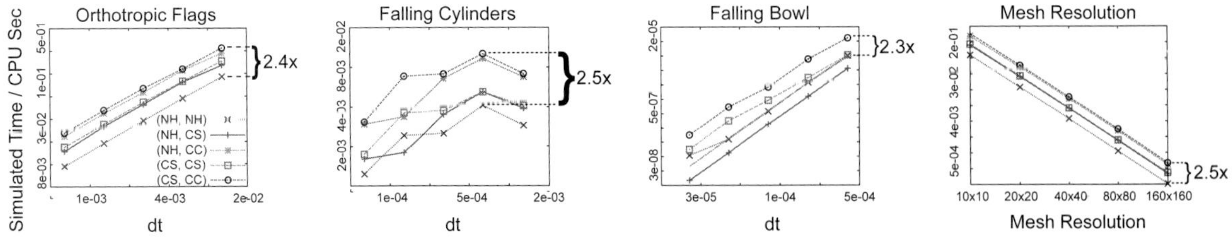

Figure 2: (Left:*) Performance measured in completed simulation time per CPU second (y-axes) as a function of discrete time step (x-axes). Higher values mean better performance. In an inexact Newton framework, Cubic Shells dominate performance for all tested scenarios, including (left-to-right) Orthotropic Flags (Fig. 5), Falling Cylinders (Fig. 3), and Falling Bowl (Fig. 7).* Right: *Performance as a function of mesh resolution (from* 10×10 *to* 160×160 *regular grids), demonstrating that the benefits of cubic shells are not resolution-dependent. Timing numbers include timestepping and collision detection/response.*

size, and four smaller step sizes; these step sizes are reused in runs of (NH, CS), (NH, CC), (CS, CS), (CS, CC). We measure performance of these runs for various problem scenarios (see §7 and video).

We record the performance of each method, measured as the ratio *completed simulation time per CPU second, i.e.*, higher values mean better performance (see Figure 2–left). The cubic shells with an approximate *constant* Jacobian, (CS,CC), dominates all methods for all problem scenarios. Note that the performance gains observed for (CS, CC) are independent of mesh resolution (see Figure 2–right).

7. Visual impact of orthotropic parameters

Orthotropic parameters provide additional artistic control over the dynamics of wrinkles and folds. Consider for example a flag tailored by cutting a rectangular pattern from an orthotropic textile. The orientation of warp and weft relative to the flag's pattern, as well as the values of Young's and shear moduli, have considerable visual impact on the resulting dynamics (see Fig. 5 and accompanying video).

The orthotropic shear modulus plays an important role in the *drapability* of a fabric [SM02]; the shear modulus is *not* captured by geometric models that employ Euler's formula, such as [BW98, VMT06], or elliptic interpolation, such as [CK03]. A high shear modulus tends to align folds and wrinkles to the material axes; a lower shear modulus allows the fabric to fold along other directions, and therefore to obtain a closer fit to the body. The first two frames of Fig. 4 compare a high and low shear modulus, respectively, illustrating the intuitive notion of drapability. When a high shear modulus is desired (leftmost frame), the Young's modulus is a poor substitute—it is unable to capture stiff extrusion of the poncho around the shoulders without introducing extraneous stiffness elsewhere.

Furthermore, orthotropy has a strong effect on the interaction between a material and its environment. We simulate the fall and bounce of four elastic cylinders, each with a different orientation for its principal material axis. The resulting animation (Fig. 3 and accompanying video) reveals the extreme variations in deformation and overall trajectory that arise purely from changing the orthotropic parameters.

Orthotropy indirectly enriches any other technologies implemented in the simulator, such as viscoelasticity or fracture [TF88]. For example, the anisotropic bending resulting from collisions produces distinctive fracture patterns both for plates (Fig. 6) and shells (Fig. 7). For a summary of the fracture algorithm refer to Appendix B.

8. Discussion

Limitations. The cubic hinge does not overcome those limitations that are shared by all hinge-based approaches. In particular, the simplicity of hinge-based models comes at the cost of limited convergence behavior and meshing-dependence [GGRZ06].

Implicit to the cubic hinge is the assumption that the surface deforms isometrically, *i.e.*, without stretching. A natural question, then, is how much stretching is permissible in practice, and what are the failure modes of the model under excessive stretching? To explore these questions, we re-simulate the falling cylinder and falling bowl using progressively lower stretching resistance. Both examples remain well-behaved so long as the stretching stiffness is two orders of magnitude greater than the bending stiffness; during the simulation, the meshes stretch by as much as 15%.

If we reduce stretching stiffness even further, then for the thin *shell* examples we observe a slow, noticeable stretching of the surface, in particular, in an expanding (not oscillatory) mode. This is perhaps not surprising, since a cubic energy is not bounded from below; under normal (quasi-isometric) circumstances, the stretching resistance prevents this infinite well from being exploited.

We repeat the above experiment with the billowing flag. Since the flag has a flat undeformed configuration, the cubic energy term vanishes, leaving a quadratic energy bounded from below. We observe that the flag simulation is well-behaved even when strong wind induces stretching of 300%.

Conserved momenta. In all circumstances (even when parasitic stretching is observed due to a broken isometry assumption), the simulated model conserves linear and angular momenta. To see this, note that the quadratic forces arising from the cubic energy are *not* approximated (only their Jacobian is); since the cubic energy is invariant under rigid body transformations of the deformed (and also the undeformed) configuration, forces induced by this energy do not apply a global acceleration or torque.

Due to its simplicity, efficiency, and generality, we expect cubic shells to be of practical relevance in computer animation.

Acknowledgments We thank David Harmon for providing robust collision detection and response code. We thank David Eberle and the anonymous reviewers for their feedback. This work was supported in part by the DFG Research Center MATHEON in Berlin, the NSF (MSPA-IIS-05-28402, CSR-CNS-06-14770, CCR-0093390, CAREER-CCF-06-43268), Autodesk, Elsevier, mental images, NVIDIA, and an IBM Faculty Parternship award.

References

[BD94] BREEN D., DONALD H.: House, and Michael J. Wozny. Predicting the drape of woven cloth using interacting particles. *Proceedings of SIGGRAPH '94* (1994), 365–372.

[BMF03] BRIDSON R., MARINO S., FEDKIW R.: Simulation of clothing with folds and wrinkles. *SCA* (2003), 28–36.

[BW98] BARAFF D., WITKIN A.: Large steps in cloth simulation. In *SIGGRAPH* (1998), ACM Press, pp. 43–54.

[BWH*06] BERGOU M., WARDETZKY M., HARMON D., ZORIN D., GRINSPUN E.: A quadratic bending model for inextensible surfaces. In *SGP* (2006), pp. 227–230.

[CK03] CHOI K.-J., KO H.-S.: Extending the immediate buckling model to triangular meshes for simulating complex clothes. In *Eurographics 2003 Short Presentations* (2003), pp. 187–191.

[dC92] DO CARMO M.: *Riemannian Geometry*. Mathematics: Theory and Applications. Birkhäuser, 1992.

[GGRZ06] GRINSPUN E., GINGOLD Y., REISMAN J., ZORIN D.: Computing discrete shape operators on general meshes. *Comput. Graph. Forum 25*, 3 (2006).

[GHDS03] GRINSPUN E., HIRANI A. N., DESBRUN M., SCHRÖDER P.: Discrete shells. *SCA* (2003), 62–67.

[GSH*04] GINGOLD Y., SECORD A., HAN J. Y., GRINSPUN E., ZORIN D.: *A Discrete Model for Inelastic Deformation of Thin Shells*. Tech. rep., Aug 2004.

[Hau04] HAUTH M.: *Visual Simulation of Deformable Models*. PhD thesis, University of Tübingen, 2004.

[HLW06] HAIRER E., LUBICH C., WANNER G.: *Geometric Numerical Integration: Structure-Preserving Algorithms for Ordinary Differential Equations*. Springer, 2006.

[HP04] HILDEBRANDT K., POLTHIER K.: Anisotropic filtering of non-linear surface features. *CGF 23*, 3 (2004), 391–400.

[Kaw80] KAWABATA S.: *The Standardization and Analysis of Hand Evaluation*. The Hand Evaluation and Standardization Committee, The Textile Machinery Society of Japan, 1980.

[MBF04] MOLINO N., BAO Z., FEDKIW R.: A virtual node algorithm for changing mesh topology during simulation. In *SIGGRAPH* (2004), pp. 385–392.

[Mor99] MORINI B.: Convergence behaviour of inexact newton methods. *Math. of Comp. 68*, 228 (1999), 1605–1613.

[OH99] O'BRIEN J. F., HODGINS J. K.: Graphical modeling and animation of brittle fracture. In *SIGGRAPH* (1999), pp. 137–146.

[PTVF92] PRESS W. H., TEUKOLSKY S. A., VETTERLING W. T., FLANNERY B. P.: *Numerical Recipes in C: The Art of Scientific Computing*. Cam. Univ. Press, 1992.

[SM02] SIDABRAITE V., MASTEIKAITE V.: A preliminary study for evaluation of skirt asymmetric drape. *International Journal of Clothing Science and Technology 14*, 5 (2002), 286–298.

[TF88] TERZOPOULOS D., FLEISCHER K.: Modeling inelastic deformation: Viscoelasticity, plasticity, fracture. In *SIGGRAPH* (1988), pp. 269–278.

[TW06] THOMASZEWSKI B., WACKER M.: Bending Models for Thin Flexible Objects. In *WSCG Short Comm.* (2006).

[VK01] VENTSEL E., KRAUTHAMMER T.: *Thin Plates and Shells*. CRC Press, 2001.

[VMT06] VOLINO P., MAGNENAT-THALMANN N.: Simple linear bending stiffness in particle systems. In *SCA* (2006), pp. 101–106.

[WBH*] WARDETZKY M., BERGOU M., HARMON D., ZORIN D., GRINSPUN E.: Discrete Quadratic Bending Energies. To appear in CAGD, 2007.

[ZT89] ZIENKIEWICZ O. C., TAYLOR R. L.: *The finite element method*. McGraw Hill, 1989.

Appendix A: Neglected term in force Jacobian

As discussed in §6, we advocate the use of an inexact Newton's method, using only the constant portion of the force Jacobian given in §5. Indeed, for optimal performance (and no loss of accuracy) one should omit calculation of the linear component arising from the nonflat undeformed configuration. However, for completeness of presentation, we include the expression for this linear component below.

With respect to the local position vector $(\mathbf{x}_0, \mathbf{x}_1, \mathbf{x}_2, \mathbf{x}_3) \in \mathbb{R}^{12}$, and the corresponding local force vector $\mathbf{f} = (\mathbf{f}_0, \mathbf{f}_1, \mathbf{f}_2, \mathbf{f}_3) \in \mathbb{R}^{12}$, the local force Jacobian $(\mathbb{R}^{12} \times \mathbb{R}^{12})$ is given by

$$\bar{k} \begin{pmatrix} 0 & (\mathbf{e}_1 - \mathbf{e}_2)^* & (\mathbf{e}_2 - \mathbf{e}_0)^* & (\mathbf{e}_0 - \mathbf{e}_1)^* \\ -(\mathbf{e}_1 - \mathbf{e}_2)^* & 0 & -\mathbf{e}_2^* & \mathbf{e}_1^* \\ -(\mathbf{e}_2 - \mathbf{e}_0)^* & \mathbf{e}_2^* & 0 & -\mathbf{e}_0^* \\ -(\mathbf{e}_0 - \mathbf{e}_1)^* & -\mathbf{e}_1^* & \mathbf{e}_0^* & 0 \end{pmatrix},$$

where each entry represents a 3×3 skew-symmetric subblock; the asterisk applied to a vector, $\mathbf{v}^*$, produces the matrix

$$\mathbf{v}^* = \begin{pmatrix} 0 & -\mathbf{v}_z & \mathbf{v}_y \\ \mathbf{v}_z & 0 & -\mathbf{v}_x \\ -\mathbf{v}_y & \mathbf{v}_x & 0 \end{pmatrix},$$

corresponding to the cross product operation $\mathbf{v} \times (\cdot)$. The local force Jacobian is assembled into the global $\mathbb{R}^{3n} \times \mathbb{R}^{3n}$ Jacobian in the usual manner. While it is most easily expressed by a skew-symmetric matrix of skew-symmetric subblocks, note that Hess $G(\mathbf{e}_0)$ is indeed symmetric.

Appendix B: Implementing fracture

The material fractures when internal strain exceeds a threshold. For simplicity we only consider fracture along existing mesh edges; however, this limitation can be easily removed, see *e.g.*, [OH99, MBF04, GSH*04]. A hinge edge, $\mathbf{e}_i$, fractures if the bending strain, $\frac{|\mathbf{e}_i|}{\bar{A}_i}(\theta_i - \bar{\theta}_i)$, exceeds a material-dependent threshold.

Fracture may be viewed as the transition when an interior edge becomes a boundary edge. A mesh edge has one of three states: INTERIOR→FRACTURED-INTERIOR→BOUNDARY, where the arrows indicate allowable state transitions. An INTERIOR edge becomes FRACTURED-INTERIOR if the strain threshold is exceeded; a FRACTURED-INTERIOR edge becomes BOUNDARY only as a consequence of explicit changes to mesh connectivity, as explained below.

A BOUNDARY vertex is a vertex incident on a FRACTURED-INTERIOR or BOUNDARY edge. A FRACTURED-INTERIOR edge, e_i, may be in one of three configurations, distinguished by the number of incident BOUNDARY vertices:

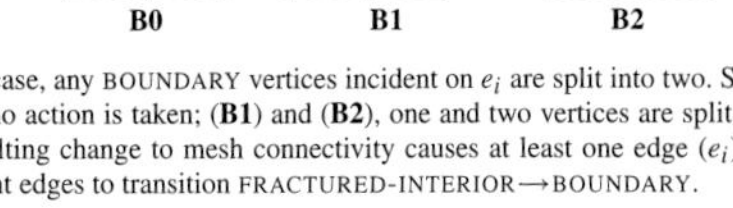

B0 **B1** **B2**

In each case, any BOUNDARY vertices incident on e_i are split into two. Specifically, in case: (**B0**), no action is taken; (**B1**) and (**B2**), one and two vertices are split, respectively, and the resulting change to mesh connectivity causes at least one edge (e_i) but possibly other incident edges to transition FRACTURED-INTERIOR→BOUNDARY.

Figure 3: *Thin-shell simulation of falling orthotropic cylinders. Material axes vary from left-to-right: isotropic, vertical, horizontal, diagonal. Left Image: stress formed on the cylinders upon impact. Right Image: the effects of anisotropy after impact. Note the extreme flatenning of the cylinder with axis aligned vertically and the high bounce of the cylinder with axis aligned horizontally.*

$Y^0 = Y^1 = 0.01, G^{01} = 100$ | $Y^0 = Y^1 = 0.01, G^{01} = 0$ | $Y = 0.2$ | $Y = 0.35$ | $Y = 0.5$

Figure 4: *Shear vs. no bending shear: a high bending shear modulus tends to align folds and wrinkles to the material axes (leftmost); a lower shear modulus allows the fabric to fold along other directions, and therefore to obtain a closer fit to the body (second frame). Shearing effects cannot be reproduced by simply tuning Young moduli (3 unsuccessful attempts shown on the right).*

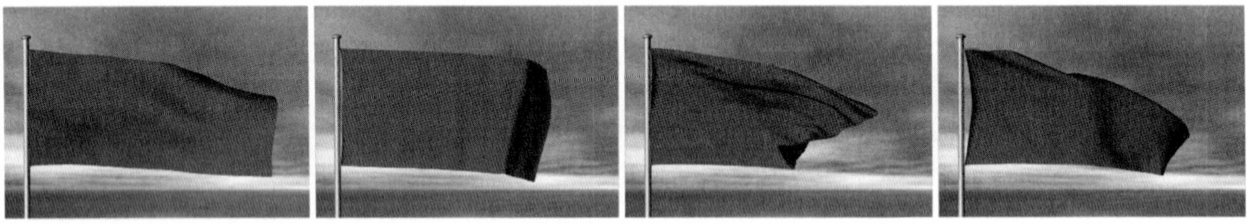

Figure 5: *Varying material axes at no additional cost. From left-to-right: isotropic, vertical, horizontal and diagonal.*

Figure 6: *Thin plates: adjustable directions of fracture patterns. Left-to-right: isotropic, vertical, horizontal and diagonal.*

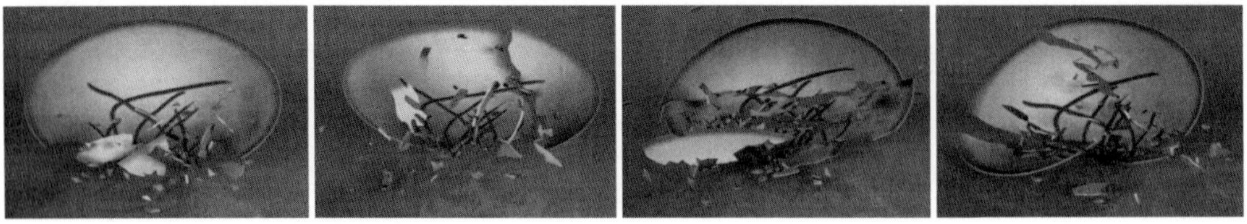

Figure 7: *Thin shells: adjustable directions of fracture patterns. Left-to-right: isotropic, vertical, horizontal and diagonal.*

Eurographics/ ACM SIGGRAPH Symposium on Computer Animation (2007)
D. Metaxas and J. Popovic (Editors)

Controlling Individual Agents in High-Density Crowd Simulation

N. Pelechano, J.M. Allbeck and N.I. Badler

University of Pennsylvania, USA

Abstract

Simulating the motion of realistic, large, dense crowds of autonomous agents is still a challenge for the computer graphics community. Typical approaches either resemble particle simulations (where agents lack orientation controls) or are conservative in the range of human motion possible (agents lack psychological state and aren't allowed to 'push' each other). Our HiDAC system (for High-Density Autonomous Crowds) focuses on the problem of simulating the local motion and global wayfinding behaviors of crowds moving in a natural manner within dynamically changing virtual environments. By applying a combination of psychological and geometrical rules with a social and physical forces model, HiDAC exhibits a wide variety of emergent behaviors from agent line formation to pushing behavior and its consequences; relative to the current situation, personalities of the individuals and perceived social density.

CR Categories: I.3.7 [Computer Graphics]: Three-Dimensional Graphics and Realism—Animation; I.6.8 [Simulation and Modeling]: Types of Simulation—Animation

1 Introduction

Animating motion for large crowds has been an important goal in the computer graphics, movie and video games communities. There has been a considerable effort on locomotion, path planning, navigation in large virtual environments, and realistic behavior simulation using cognitive models.

We classify crowd agent motions by three main approaches: *social forces* models, *rule based* models and *cellular automata* models. Although much effort has gone into improving the behavioral realism of each of these approaches, none of the current models can realistically animate *high-density* crowds. Social forces models tend to create simulations that look more like particle animation than human movement. Cellular automata models limit agent spatial movements and tend to expose the underlying checkerboard of cells when crowd density is high. Finally, rule based models either don't consider collision detection and repulsion at all or adopt very conservative approaches through the use of waiting rules, which work fine for low densities in everyday life simulation, but lack realism for high-density or panic situations.

Figure 1 shows a taxonomy for crowd simulation and compares our model (HiDAC: High-Density Autonomous Crowds) with the main models in the literature along the dimensions of animation realism and crowd density.

HiDAC addresses the problem of simulating high-density crowds of autonomous agents moving in a natural manner in dynamically changing virtual environments. Our solution to the problem of realistically simulating local motion under different situations and agent personalities uses psychological, physiological and geometrical rules combined with physical forces. Since applying the same

Symposium on Computer Animation 2007, San Diego, CA, August 03-04, 2007.
© 2007 ACM 978-1-59593-624-4/07/0008 $5.00

rules to all agents leads to homogeneous behavior, agents are given different psychological (e.g., impatience, panic, personality attributes) and physiological (e.g., locomotion, energy level) traits that trigger individual heterogeneous behaviors. Each agent is also endowed with perception and reacts to static and dynamic objects and other agents within the nearby space.

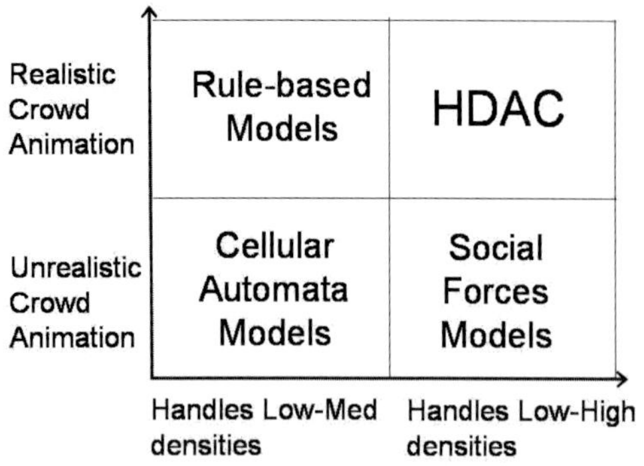

Figure 1: *Current models framework and our approach for low-level motion (HiDAC).*

Realistic movement may be defined as the emergence of crowd behaviors consistent with real observed crowds, and appropriate individual collision avoidance and collision response. We achieve such realism through contextual application of physical and geometric algorithms. Over longer distances tangential forces gently steer agents around obstacles, while over shorter distances collision response is applied to avoid overlapping. Pushing behavior between agents arises from varying the long/short personal space threshold of each individual. Agents in a hurry will not respect others' personal space and will appear to push their way through the crowd. In contrast, more 'polite' agents will respect lines and wait for others to move first.

Each agent has an influence disk (region) in front of them that triggers waiting behavior. Relaxed agents temporarily stop when another agent moves into their path, while impatient agents do not respond to this feedback and tend to 'push'. Our model stops impatient agents from appearing to 'vibrate' as they try to force their way through dense crowds: we add temporal stopping states to prevent the agent from trying to move during a short interval of time although it can still be pushed by others.

Our agents' behavior is determined by a high-level algorithm (including: navigation in complex virtual environments, learning, communicating and decision-making) [PB06], [POS05] and low-level motion controllers. Here we focus on a new approach for high-density crowds and so we will not explain in depth the algorithm for setting attractor points that drives high-level navigational behaviors.

The reminder of this paper begins with a review of related work. We then present an architectural overview of HiDAC. Section 4 describes the methods by which we combine a forces model with a set of psychological, physiological and geometrical rules to achieve realistic crowd movement. Finally, we present results and conclusions.

2 Related Work

Many crowd simulation methods derive from Helbing's empirical Social Forces model [HFV00] which applies repulsion and tangential forces to simulate interactions between people and obstacles, realistic 'pushing' behaviors and variable flow rates. The main disadvantage of this approach is that agents appear to 'shake' or 'vibrate' unnaturally in high-density crowds. There has been much work done using particle simulation approaches for low-density crowds. Particle systems and dynamics have been used for modeling the motion of groups with significant physics [BH97]. Individualism has been used to extend the social forces model [BMO*03]. Some recent work has focused on extending Helbing's model [HBJ*05], [LKF05] but has resulted in equations that are not applicable in real-time simulations. Crowd simulation systems have been described based on continuum dynamics instead of agent rules and run at interactive rates [TCP06].

Rule-based models [Rey87], [Rey99] achieve more realistic human movement for low and medium density crowds, but cannot handle contact between individuals and therefore fail to simulate 'pushing' behavior. These models usually adopt a conservative approach by avoiding contact and, when densities are high, applying 'wait' rules to enforce ordered crowd behavior without the need to calculate collision detection and response. Cognitive models have been used in combination with rule-based models to achieve more realistic behaviors for pedestrian simulation [ST05]. Different behavioral rules can be applied to the crowd, group or individuals to achieve more believable overall crowd behavior [OCV*02], [SBC*06], [TMK99].

Cellular-automata models [Che04], [KNN03], [TLC*01] are fast and simple to implement, but do not allow for contact between agents. Floor space is discretized and individuals can only move when the adjacent cell is free. Higher-level behaviors can be incorporated by pre-computing paths towards high-level goals and storing them within the grid [LMM03].

In order to navigate a complex environment, we need to have some high-level representation of the environment. Among the most popular techniques for crowd navigation are: cell and portal graphs [LCC06], [PB06], [PLT05], potential fields [Che04], and roadmaps [BLA02], [KSL*96], [SKG05]. Information can be embedded in the high-level representation of the virtual environment to achieve real-time crowd simulation [FBT99], [PB06], [TD00].

In multi-agent systems, each agent needs to sense the environment to perceive changes and react to them [TT94]. Perception is often simulated by casting a set of rays and finding their intersection with obstacles around the object [BNT94], [PHL05], [ST05]. Massive SW has also developed a crowd simulation system with vision-based behavior [MS05].

3 Architecture Overview

HiDAC is a multi-agent system without a centralized controller. Each agent has its own behavior based on personality variables that represent physiological and psychological factors observed in real people. Agent behaviors are computed at two levels:

- High-level behavior: navigation, learning, communication between agents, and decision-making. [PB06]
- Low-level motion: perception and a set of reactive behaviors for collision avoidance, detection and response in order to move within a bounded space.

Figure 2 shows the interaction between the two levels. The High-Level module receives information about bottlenecks and door changes that have been perceived by the agent and makes decisions based on that information and its current knowledge of the environment. Once the high-level decides the next room to walk to, it sends the next attractor point to the Low-Level module to carry out the required motion to reach it. When the Low-Level module reaches the attractor, it queries the High-Level module for the next attractor in its path towards the destination.

The Motion sub-module queries the Perception sub-module about positions and angles of obstacles, crowd density ahead of the agent, and velocity of dynamic obstacles. Based on information perceived and the internal state of the agent (current behavior, panic, impatience, etc.), the Motion sub-module calculates the velocity and next position of the agent, and sends a message to the Locomotion sub-module to execute the correct feet movements.

Both high-level and low-level agent behavior are affected by psychological and physiological attributes. The high-level is affected by changes in psychological state (panic or impatience), thus altering the decision-making process. Agent memory and orientation abilities are also affected by psychological states.

The low level is also affected by changes in the agent's psychological state which trigger modification of its speed, fall probability, pushing thresholds, etc. The psychological model needs to have as input information about environment events detected by the agent's perception system and information obtained through communication. This information is combined with the agent's current emotional state, possibly modifying it, to provide updated input to both low and high-level modules.

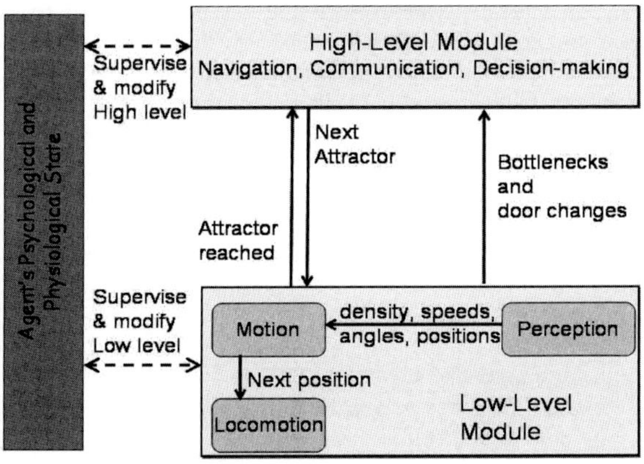

Figure 2: *Architecture Overview.*

4 Local Motion Approach

Local agent motion is based on a combination of geometrical information and psychological rules with a forces model to enable a wide variety of behaviors resembling those of real people. HiDAC uses psychological attributes (panic, impatience) and geometrical rules (distance, areas of influence, relative angles) to eliminate unrealistic artifacts and to allow new behaviors:

- Preventing agents from appearing to vibrate
- Creating natural bi-directional flow rates
- Queuing and other organized behavior
- Pushing through a crowd
- Agents falling and becoming obstacles
- Propagating panic
- Exhibiting impatience
- Reacting in real time to changes in the environment

4.1 The HiDAC Model

HiDAC is a parameterized social forces model that depends on psychological and geometrical rules. Its High-Level module determines which attractor point (waypoint or portal) an agent walks to within a room. [PB06]. Collision avoidance, detection and response are performed only with the people in the same room, and with static elements of that room (walls and obstacles). When people are crossing portals, care must be taken to avoid intersection between agents leaving and agents entering. HiDAC keeps track of the people currently crossing a portal, so that when an agent is near a door, collision detection is performed against agents in the room and agents crossing the doorway.

Collision detection and response must be performed with those agents that are overlapping the agent from any direction. In contrast, collision avoidance is only performed against individuals that appear in the desired direction of movement, and therefore are relevant to an agent's future position.

The movement of agent i ($\mathbf{F}_i^{To}$) depends on the desired attractor ($\mathbf{F}_i^{At}$), while avoiding walls w ($\mathbf{F}_{wi}^{Wa}$), obstacles k ($\mathbf{F}_{ki}^{Ob}$) and other agents j ($\mathbf{F}_{ji}^{Ot}$) and trying to keep its previous direction of movement to avoid abrupt changes in its trajectory ($\mathbf{F}_i^{To}[n-1]$). All these forces are summed together with different weights w_i that are the result of psychological and/or geometrical rules, and determine the importance of each force on the final desired direction of movement:

$$\mathbf{F}_i^{To}[n] = \mathbf{F}_i^{To}[n-1] + \mathbf{F}_i^{At}[n]w_i^{At} + \sum_w \mathbf{F}_{wi}^{Wa}[n]w_i^{Wa} + \\ + \sum_k \mathbf{F}_{ki}^{Ob}[n]w_i^{Ob} + \sum_{j(\neq i)} \mathbf{F}_{ji}^{Ot}[n]w_i^{Ot} \quad (1)$$

The force vector is therefore:

$$\mathbf{f}_i^{To} = \frac{\mathbf{F}_i^{To}}{\left|\mathbf{F}_i^{To}\right|} \quad (2)$$

And finally the new desired position $\mathbf{p}_i[n+1]$ for agent i is calculated as:

$$\mathbf{p}_i[n+1]=\mathbf{p}_i[n]+\alpha_i[n]v_i[n]\left((1-\beta_i[n])\mathbf{f}_i^{To}[n]+\beta_i[n]\mathbf{F}_i^{Fa}[n]\right)T+\mathbf{r}_i[n] \quad (3)$$

where:

- $v_i[n]$ is the magnitude of the velocity in the simulation step n. The velocity at each time step is calculated as:

$$v_i[n]=\begin{cases} v_i[n]=v_i[n-1]+aT & \text{if } v_i[n]<v_i^{MAX} \\ v_i^{MAX} & \text{otherwise}\end{cases}$$

  where a is a constant that represents the acceleration of the agent when it starts walking until it reaches v_i^{MAX} .
- v_i^{MAX} is the agent's maximum walking velocity. It can be set to depend on agent capability (normal, handicapped) and modified dynamically if the agent enters panic mode or is injured.
- $\mathbf{r}_i$ is the result of the repulsion forces that affect the agent when it overlaps with a wall, obstacle or another agent; these will be introduced in section 4.1.2.
- α represents whether the agent will move in this step in its desired direction of movement or instead be pushed by a repulsion force.

$$\alpha_i=\begin{cases} 0 & \text{if } |\mathbf{r}_i|>0 \vee StoppingRule \vee WaitingRule \\ 1 & \text{otherwise}\end{cases}$$

  The *StoppingRule* and *WaitingRule* are used to avoid shaking behavior and to allow for line formation, respectively. These rules will be explained in sections 4.1.3 and 4.1.4.
- β_i is used to give priority to avoiding fallen agents on the floor:

$$\beta_i=\begin{cases} 0.5 & \text{if distance to fallen agent} < 2m \\ 0 & \text{otherwise}\end{cases}$$

- $\mathbf{F}_i^{Fa}$ is the avoidance force to avoid fallen agents and will be explained in detail in section 4.1.6.
- T is the increment in time between simulation steps.

4.1.1 Avoidance Forces

Autonomous agents need to perceive the environment to avoid static and dynamic obstacles while walking to a attractor. HiDAC provides efficient perception through a cell and portal graph. Each cell corresponds to a room, and contains information about all the static objects within it. As the agents traverse the environment, the lists of dynamic objects within each room are rapidly updated; thus an agent can obtain obstacle data by querying the cell.

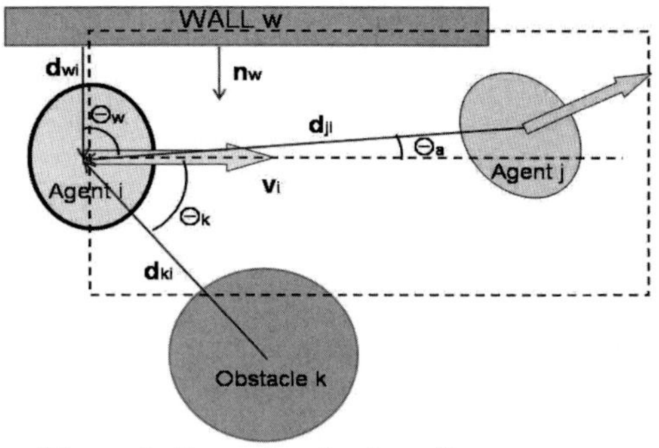

Figure 3: *Perception for the yellow agent.*

For each obstacle, wall and agent we need to calculate its distance to agent i and, if it is close enough, then we calculate the angle between agent i's desired direction and the line joining the center of agent i and the obstacle. This information is used to determine whether it falls within the rectangle of influence (Figure 3). The distance and the angle provide enough information to establish how relevant that obstacle is to the trajectory. As they navigate the environment, agents also update their perceived density of the crowd ahead which will be necessary to their decision-making process.

Wall and Obstacle Avoidance:

Avoidance forces are calculated only for relevant obstacles, walls and agents: those falling within the rectangle of influence.

The avoidance force for obstacle k is:

$$\mathbf{F}_{ki}^{Ob}=\frac{(\mathbf{d}_{ki}\times\mathbf{v}_i)\times\mathbf{d}_{ki}}{|(\mathbf{d}_{ki}\times\mathbf{v}_i)\times\mathbf{d}_{ki}|} \quad (4)$$

The avoidance force for wall w is:

$$\mathbf{F}_{wi}^{Wa}=\frac{(\mathbf{n}_w\times\mathbf{v}_i)\times\mathbf{n}_w}{|(\mathbf{n}_w\times\mathbf{v}_i)\times\mathbf{n}_w|} \quad (5)$$

Other Agent Avoidance: Overtaking and bi-directional flow:

To exhibit realistic counterflows and overtaking behaviors, we include rules that modify some parameters of the forces model. This approach allows us to simulate human behavior by setting parameters related to real human movement. The parameters that affect the tangential forces for obstacle avoidance are:

- Distance to obstacles
- Direction of other agents relative to agent i's desired velocity vector ($\mathbf{v}_i$).
- Density of the crowd

If an agent appears in the rectangle of influence, then tangential forces (described below) will be applied in order to slightly modify the direction of movement and make a curve in the trajectory to avoid collision.

The angle between two agents' velocity vectors determines whether their movements are confluent or opposed. This angle is also used to simulate human decision-making of how to react to an imminent collision. For example, if we are walking on the left side of a corridor, and another person walks towards us on our right, none of us would change direction, but if we are both walking in the middle of the corridor, the majority of people have a tendency to move towards their right side. Therefore, when the velocity vectors are almost collinear, the tangential forces will point to the right.

Suppose an agent i detects agent j and agent l as possible obstacles (Figure 4). We calculate the distance vector towards agent i for each of them ($\mathbf{d}_{ji}$ and $\mathbf{d}_{li}$). Agent j is farther away than l, but since it is moving against agent i, the perception algorithm establishes this obstacle as having higher priority. We select an agent to be avoided if it falls within the influence rectangle, unless that agent is walking in the opposite direction and with distance smaller than D_i-1.5, where D_i is the length of the rectangle.

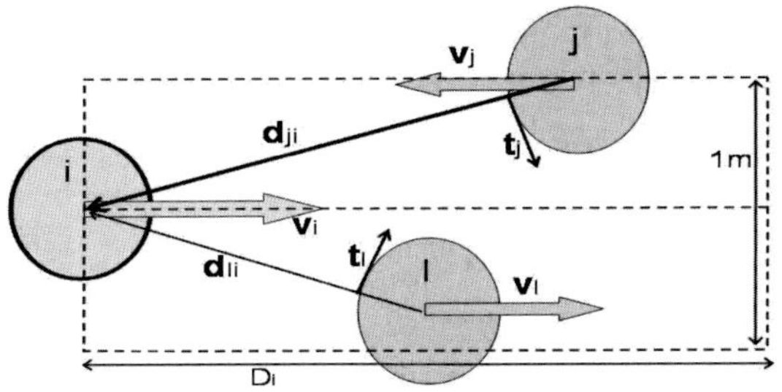

Figure 4: *Collision Avoidance rectangle of influence.*

The tangential force ($\mathbf{t}_j$) that will steer agent *i* to avoid *j* is:

$$\mathbf{t}_j = \frac{(\mathbf{d}_{ji} \times \mathbf{v}_i) \times \mathbf{d}_{ji}}{\left| (\mathbf{d}_{ji} \times \mathbf{v}_i) \times \mathbf{d}_{ji} \right|} \quad (6)$$

Next, the normalized tangential vector is multiplied by two scalar weights to obtain the final avoidance force

$$\mathbf{F}_{ji}^{Ot} = \mathbf{t}_j w_i^d w_i^o \quad (7)$$

where w_i^d is the weight due to the distance between agents, and increases as the distance between the two agents becomes smaller and thus the agent *i* trajectory will change more abruptly as the distance to agent *j* decreases:

$$w_i^d = (d_{ji} - D_i)^2 \quad (8)$$

and w_i^o is the weight due to the difference in orientation of the velocity vectors. It distinguishes whether the perceived agent is moving in the same direction as agent *i* or against it, and thus the magnitude will be higher to avoid counter flow.

$$w_i^o = \begin{cases} 1.2 & if(\mathbf{v}_i \cdot \mathbf{v}_j) > 0 \\ 2.4 & otherwise \end{cases} \quad (9)$$

The last parameter to consider is the crowd density, which each agent perceives at any given time. If the crowd is very dispersed, then people look for avoidance from far away and keep their preference for the right hand side of the space (D_i=3m); but when the crowd is very dense, then the right preference is not so obvious and several bi-directional flows can emerge (D_i=1.5m). Modifying the length of the collision avoidance rectangle and reducing the angle for right preference based on perceived density achieves this behavior.

Figure 5 shows different bi-directional flow-rate formation for low and high densities. Figure 5b shows the result if the length of viewing rectangle and right preference parameters are not affected by density. The emergent behavior shows an unrealistic "triangle" of people moving in opposite directions, and awhile later in the simulation, two perfectly formed groups of people appear to move in opposite directions, which is less common in real high-density crowds.

HiDAC produces an interesting emergent counterflow behavior for high-density crowds (Figure 5c): the formation of lanes of people moving in the same direction intermingled among lanes moving in the opposite direction. This is a behavior that is often observed in real crowds, and it emerges here even though it is not explicitly implemented.

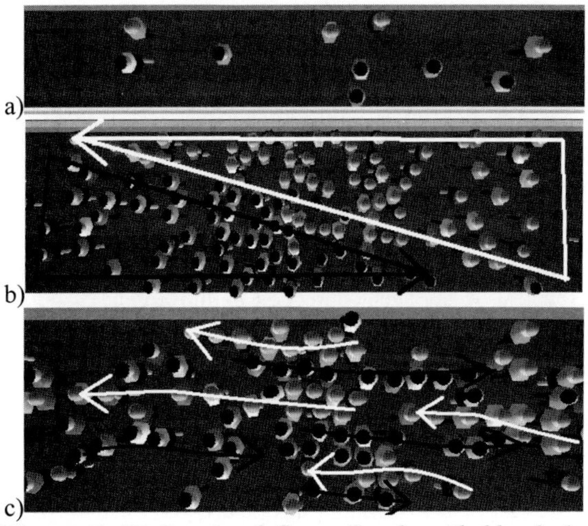

Figure 5: *Bi-directional flows. People with blonde hair walk towards the left, while dark-haired people walk towards the right. (a) low-density flows, (b) high-density without altering the viewing rectangle and right preference, (c) high-density with HiDAC.*

4.1.2 Repulsion Forces

When an agent's position overlaps with any static or dynamic obstacle, wall or agent then a collision response force applies. The repulsion force $\mathbf{r}_i$ from equation (3) is calculated as:

$$\mathbf{r}_i[n] = \sum_w \mathbf{F}_{wi}^{R\_Wa}[n] + \sum_k \mathbf{F}_{ki}^{R\_Ob}[n] + \lambda \sum_{j(\neq i)} \mathbf{F}_{ji}^{R\_Ot}[n] \quad (10)$$

where $\mathbf{F}_{wi}^{R\_Wa}$ is the repulsion force from wall *w*, $\mathbf{F}_{ki}^{R\_Ob}$ is the repulsion force from obstacle *k* and $\mathbf{F}_{ji}^{R\_Ot}$ is the repulsion force from another agent *j*:

$$\mathbf{F}_{wi}^{R\_Wa}[n] = \frac{\mathbf{n}_w (r_i + \varepsilon_i - d_{wi}[n])}{d_{wi}[n]} \quad (11)$$

$$\mathbf{F}_{ki}^{R\_Ob}[n] = \frac{(\mathbf{p}_i[n] - \mathbf{p}_k[n])(r_i + \varepsilon_i + r_k - d_{ki}[n])}{d_{ki}[n]} \quad (12)$$

$$\mathbf{F}_{ji}^{R\_Ot}[n] = \frac{(\mathbf{p}_i[n] - \mathbf{p}_j[n])(r_i + \varepsilon_i + r_j - d_{ji}[n])}{d_{ji}[n]} \quad (13)$$

where p_i is the position of agent *i*, p_j is the position of agent *j* and p_k is the position of obstacle *k*. Radii r_k, r_i, and r_j belong to obstacle *k* and agents *i* and *j*, respectively. Similarly, d_{ji} and d_{ki} are the distances between the centers of agent *i* and *j*, and the centers of agent *i* and obstacle *k*; d_{wi} is the shortest distance from the center of agent *i* to the wall *w*.

λ in equation 10 is used to set priorities between agents (that can be pushed) and walls or obstacles (that cannot be pushed). If there is repulsion from walls or obstacles, then λ is set to 0.3 to give preference to avoiding intersection with walls or obstacles over agents that can be pushed away.

Finally ε_i and ε_j are small personal space thresholds that the agents have and are used for the purpose of assigning different pushing abilities based on personality (discussed in section 4.1.5).

4.1.3. Solution to "shaking" problem in high-densities

When an agent encounters a bottleneck in a high-density crowd, applying a basic forces model leads to an unnatural behavior where agents appear to vibrate continuously. This behavior must be avoided (We have verified that this phenomenon is not based on our physics simulation implementation or its stepsize). In HiDAC we incorporate "stopping rules." These rules are applied based on the personality of the agent, direction of movement of other agents, and current situation (panic vs. normal).

When repulsion forces from other agents appear against the agent's desired direction of movement, and the agent is not in panic state, then the *stopping rule* applies:

$$\text{If}\left(\left(\mathbf{v}_j \cdot \mathbf{F}_i^{R\_Ot}[n]\right) < 0\right) \wedge \left(\neg panic\right) \text{then}$$

$$StoppingRule = TRUE$$

In order to avoid deadlocks, a timer is set to a random value within a small range, and when the timer reaches 0, the agent will set *StoppingRule=FALSE,* so that in the next simulation step the agent will try to move again

When *StoppingRule* is *true*, the parameter α_i in equation (3) is set to 0, which implies that the agent will only change position if it is pushed by other agents; otherwise it will inhibit the intention to move for several simulation steps. This effect drastically reduces the shaking behavior observed in the social force model without increasing the computational time of the algorithm.

Only forces directed backward are relevant (Figure 6).

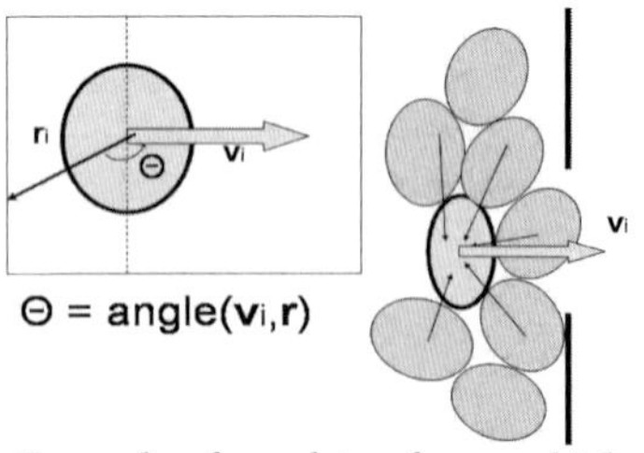

Figure 6: *Example of repulsion forces which are necessary to apply braking forces.*

If the forces appear to be towards our desired movement, we cannot decrease their intensity by not moving forward and therefore no reaction is necessary.

This method succeeds in reducing shaking behavior, while still allowing body contact and thus pushing behavior. Since stopping rules do not apply when the agent is being pushed forwards, this achieves the desired emergent result of people appearing to be pushed through doorways when there is a high-density crowd behind them.

4.1.4. Organized behavior - queuing

In a "normal" (non-panic) situation, people will respect lines and wait for others to walk first. Such organized behavior emerges by adding influence disks ahead of each agent that drive the temporal waiting behavior; they work similar to the *stopping rules*. Figure 7 shows the area that triggers waiting behaviors in a non-panicked agent *i* in a high-density crowd when another agent *j*, walking in the same direction, falls within the disk: agent *i* sets *WaitingRule=TRUE* and a timer starts. Agent *i* moves again when its area of influence does not satisfy the conditions for waiting, or when the timer reaches the value 0 to avoid deadlocks. The radius of the influence disk depends on personality (different people tend to respect different distances) and type of behavior desired: e.g., panicking agents will not respect these distances.

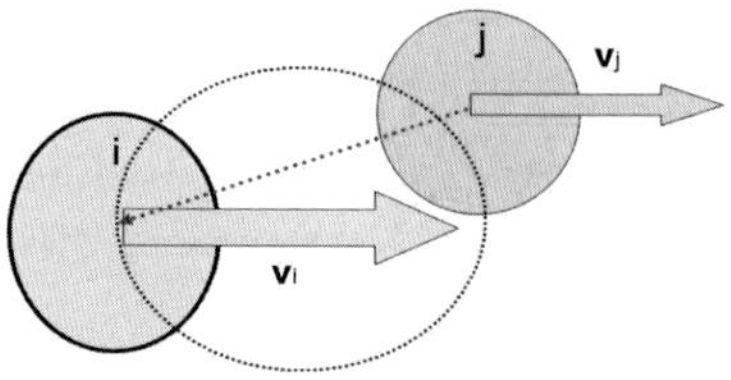

Figure 7: *Area of influence for waiting behaviors.*

For simulations of "normal" situations (e.g., individuals leaving a cinema after a movie) all the agents exhibit waiting behavior when there is no available space ahead of them. The emergent behavior observed corresponds to queuing. Since agents use tangential forces to move within a crowd while avoiding others, the strength of those tangential forces will lead to narrow or wide queues, as can be observed in Figure 8. The user can specify those tangential forces to be minimum, medium or maximum.

Figure 8: *Examples of wide and thin queues emerging when animating a "normal" scenario.*

4.1.5. Pushing behavior

Pushing behavior emerges because HiDAC can handle not only collision avoidance but also collision detection and response. Agents have different behaviors that can be triggered at any time. During an organized situation, individuals wait for space available before moving, but when in panic, they try to move until they collide with other individuals who impede forward progress. By combining both behaviors simultaneously for a heterogeneous crowd, we observe an emergent behavior where some individuals that do not respect personal space will get very close to other agents and push them away in order to open a path through a dense crowd. The effect of being pushed away is achieved by applying collision response forces and different personal space thresholds (ε_i and ε_j from the repulsion equations 11, 12 and 13).

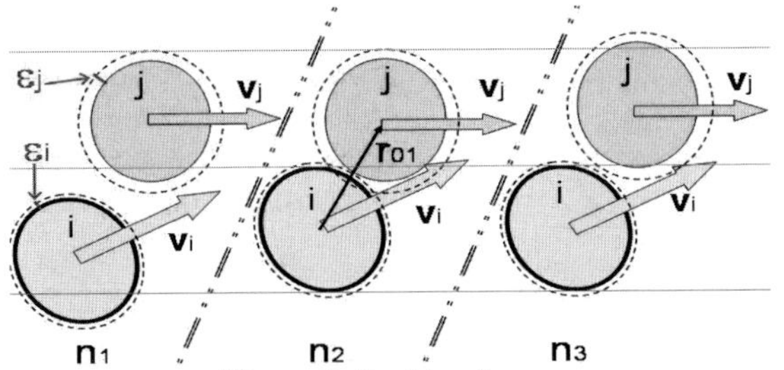

Figure 9: *Pushing forces.*

An agent suffers a repulsion force from another agent when its personal space is overlapped. Figure 9 shows a sequence of simulation steps, where a smaller personal space threshold ε_i allows agent *i* to get closer to agent *j* who has a larger personal space threshold ε_j. Thus agent *i* can push away agent *j* while agent *i* is not being pushed and can continue with its desired trajectory.

Figure 10 shows an example where the top left room has been filled with panicked people (represented by red-heads) who will tend to push others away, while the other three rooms contain individuals following more organized behaviors. After a few seconds of simulation, the red-headed people have managed to almost empty their room by pushing others away in the corridor in order to reach the exit faster. Individuals in the other rooms are calmly waiting for their turn to get through the door.

4.1.6. Falling and becoming obstacles

A benefit to a physical social force model is that one might use it to gauge potential injury arising from high-density situations. When the majority of pushing forces affecting one individual are approximately in the same direction, the agent will receive a sum of forces with magnitude high enough to make it lose equilibrium. At this moment the person may fall and become an obstacle for the rest of the crowd.

Figure 10: *Red-headed people exhibit panic behavior and push others to open their way through the crowd.*

Fallen agents represent a different type of obstacle because, unlike walls and columns, a body on the floor is an obstacle that should be avoided, but if necessary (or unavoidable) can be stepped over. In HiDAC, fallen individuals become a rectangular obstacle (a bounding box covering the torso and head, but not the legs since other individuals can easily step over that part of the agent). When other agents approach this new obstacle, weak tangential forces are applied in order to walk around the fallen agent ($\mathbf{F}_i^{Fa}$ in equation 3), but repulsive forces are not applied. Therefore, when the crowd is extremely dense and the pushing forces from behind are strong, the result is that agents may walk over the body on the floor, as has been observed in actual extreme situations. Figure 11 shows an example of this behavior (where the crowd density is artificially low for visibility).

Figure 11: *Agents avoiding a fallen agent.*

4.1.7 Panic Propagation

HiDAC can simulate an emergency evacuation. When an alarm goes off some agents will start in the panic mode. While in panic they tend to move faster, push, and exhibit agitated behavior. All these behaviors depend on the agent personality and levels of panic. As the agents start running, they may provoke panic in other agents whose behavior will be modified in turn. To propagate panic, we use either communication between agents (managed by the High-Level behavior module), or perception to detect relevant changes in low-level behaviors, such as increasing crowd densities and number of people pushing or both.

4.1.8 Avoiding bottlenecks and interactive changes in the environment

When dealing with high-density crowds in buildings, bottlenecks can appear in the portals. HiDAC incorporates a high-level decision process that will allow impatient agents to react to this situation by finding an alternative path. As the low-level algorithm detects the bottleneck, it sends that information to the high-level which will try to find an alternative route based on what the agent can perceive from its current position (doors, obstacles) and the knowledge that the agent has about the internal connectivity of the building. If an alternative path is available, the high-level chooses a new portal as the goal and sets an attractor point to change the direction of movement.

Figure 12 shows a bottleneck and how impatient individuals (represented by the blonde people) have sought and walked toward an alternative door.

Figure 12: *Impatient people avoiding bottlenecks.*

When a change occurs in the environment (e.g., a door is blocked by fire) agents perceive and react to it. For an access change, the High-Level module needs to make a new wayfinding decision. The agent detects this change in real time and sets its destination to the new attractor set by the High-Level.

Figure 13 shows a sequence where dynamic wayfinding is forced by opening and closing doors, and agents must search for alternative paths. All low-level behaviors are still active during these activities.

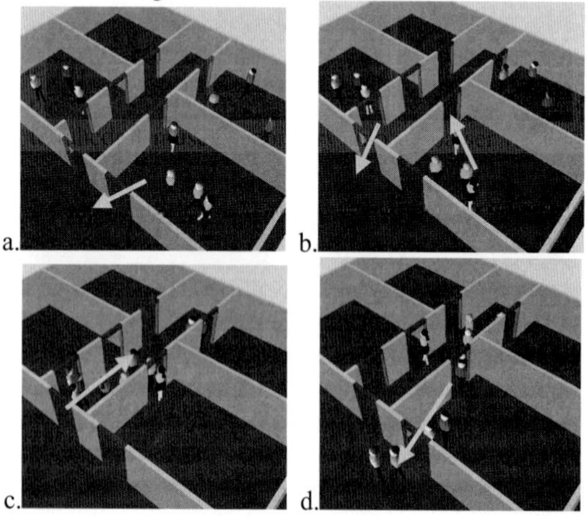

Figure 13: *Interaction with dynamic changes in the environment. Agents react to doors being closed and opened during the simulation.*

These examples show the interaction between High-Level and Low-Level modules to achieve realistic simulations with dynamic changes in the environment geometry.

Figure 14 shows the 2D and 3D view of a high density crowd. On the 2D view we can observe the red rectangle of influence for one of the agents (affects agent avoidance forces), the agents that affect the perceived density (with red points in the center of each agent), the avoidance forces with obstacles and walls in cyan, the avoidance forces with other agents in dark blue, and the stopping rules represented by circles of the same color as the agent waiting. The vector in the same color as the agent indicates the velocity direction.

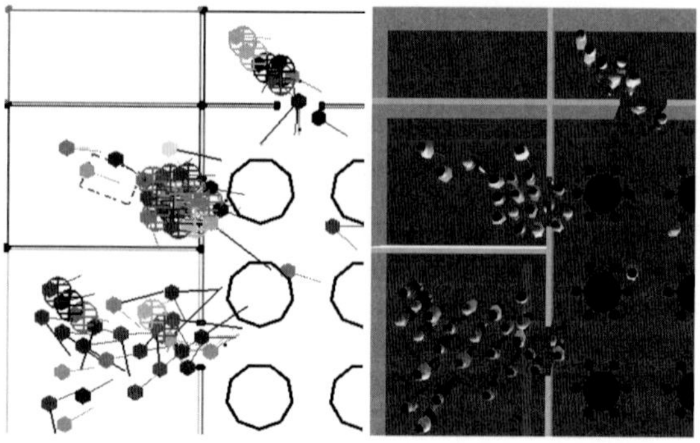

Figure 14: *2D and 3D view of a high density crowd.*

5 Results

We have presented a number of simulations that show HiDAC's visual output, and described methods for achieving many goals that enable realistic simulation of high-density crowds:

Goal	Method
Fast perception of environment	Influence rectangles, distances, angles and directions of movement are used to prioritize obstacles.
Eliminate shaking behavior	Apply stopping rules to forces model.
Natural bi-directional flow	Variable length influence rectangles and different 'right' preferences.
Queuing behavior	Influence discs triggering waiting behavior based on agent direction.
Pushing behavior	Collision response based on variable 'personal space thresholds'.
Falling agents becoming new obstacles	Apply tangential forces for obstacle avoidance but not repulsion forces.
Panic propagation	Modify agent behavior based on personality and perception of other agents' level of panic.
Crowd impatience	Dynamically modifying route selection based on environmental changes.

We have run simulation tests on a 2.99 GHz Intel Xeon with 2GB of RAM measuring frame rates both for simulation only and for simulation and 3D rendering. When doing only simulation, HiDAC can handle up to 1800 agents with a frame rate of 25Hz. Simulation and 3D rendering using an NVIDIA Quadro FX 3400/4400 graphics system can achieve 25 frames/second (not using GPU rendering) for up to 600 simple 3D virtual human figures ("crayon figures") each with about 100 vertices. For the frame rate tests, we used a large complex environment with 85 rooms and 53,448 vertices overall.

6 Conclusions

HiDAC can be tuned to simulate different types of crowds, ranging from extreme panic situations (fire evacuation) to high-density crowds under calm conditions (leaving a cinema after a movie). Also we allow for heterogeneous crowds where a number of different behaviors can be exhibited simultaneously.

Unlike cellular automata and rule-based models, HiDAC can realistically simulate an individual trying to force its way through a crowd by pushing others, and unlike social forces models, our agents can exhibit more respectful behavior when desired and make decisions in terms of letting others walk first and queuing when necessary. These emergent behaviors are driven by the combination of psychological and physiological rules together with a social forces model. "Impatience" has been integrated in order to avoid the sheep-like behavior that many crowd simulation models exhibit.

We have shown novel extensions to social forces models by adding stopping rules and influence region controls that mitigate agent vibration while not increasing computational time. Our system uses the best features of both rule-based and social forces systems, while eliminating their disadvantages. The implementation allows real-time simulations for hundreds of individualized agents.

The social force model extensions also mitigate combinatorial problems associated with the possible geometric arrangements of large numbers of agents. Rather than analyze all possible spatial configurations or force agents into discrete cells, HiDAC uses general behaviors based on surrounding social forces and crowd density perception to limit influences and consequences to a small number of nearby agents.

We have expanded on our previously reported work that included higher level concepts such as leadership, agent communication, levels of environmental knowledge, and way finding, by greatly improving lower level agent interactions, such as reduced vibrations, natural bi-directional flows, queuing behavior, pushing, falling, panic propagation, impatience, and real time reactions to changes in the environment, thereby increasing the heterogeneity of the crowd.

While HiDAC's combination of a social forces model, rule-based model, and unique extensions enable a variety of behaviors, achieving these behaviors for different scenarios (e.g. a typical mall scene versus a building evacuation) requires a user to set a few low level parameters. Though these parameters are limited in number and would not be overwhelming to a user, they currently would require the user to understand some of the lower level methodologies of HiDAC in order to achieve the desired behaviors. We are currently working on mapping these parameters to agent properties that would enable a user to create a crowd simulation based on the properties of individuals in the crowd instead of lower level parameters. In addition to expanding this personality model, we are also working to add in agent actions other than locomotion. Working toward an integrated model of crowd behavior given an individual's personality, changing physiological state, and personal goals and values is imminently feasible [POS05]. Because the model already uses some psychological, physiological, and social factors, the simulation can use this dynamic information to further select and animate specific agent task actions with the environment and interactions with other agents.

6 Acknowledgements

This research was partially supported by the National Science Foundation grant IIS-0200983, Office of Naval Research Virtual Technologies and Environments grant N0001 4-04-1-0259, Army Research Office grant N61339-05-C-0081, and a Fulbright scholarship. We also thank Autodesk and Cal3D for their software and Jeff Wajcs and everyone in HMS for their assistance. Special thanks to Joan Pelechano for his rigorous review of our physics equations.

References

[BLA02] BAYAZIT, O.B., LIEN, J.-M. and AMATO, N.M., Roadmap-based flocking for complex environments. in *Proceedings of Pacific Conference on Computer Graphics and Applications*, (2002), 104-113.

[BNT94] BOULIC, R., NOSER, H. and THALMANN, D., Automatic derivation of curved human walking trajectories from synthetic vision. in *Proceedings of Computer Animation*, (1994), IEEE Computer Society Press, 93-103.

[BMO*03] BRAUN, A., MUSSE, S.R., OLIVEIRA, L.P.L. and BODMANN, B.E.J., Modeling Individual Behaviors in Crowd Simulation. in *Proceedings of Computer Animation and Social Agents*, (2003), 143-148.

[BH97] BROGAN, D. and HODGINS, J. Group Behaviors for Systems with Significant Dynamics. *Autonomous Robots*, *4*, 1997. 137-153.

[Che04] CHENNEY, S., Flow Tiles. in *ACM SIGGRAPH/ Eurographics Proceedings of Symposium on Computer Animation*, (2004), 233-242.

[FBT99] FARENC, N., BOULIC, R. and THALMANN, D., An informed environment dedicated to the simulation of virtual humans in urban context. in *Proceedings of Eurographics*, (1999), 309-318.

[HBJ*05] HELBING, BUZNA, JOHANSSON and WERNER Self-Organized Pedestrian Crowd Dynamics. *Transportation Science*, *39* (1), 2005. 1-24.

[HFV00] HELBING, D., FARKAS, I. and VICSEK, T. Simulating dynamical features of escape panic. *Nature*, *407*, 2000. 487-490.

[KSL*96] KAVRAKI, L., SVESTKA, P., LATOMBE, J. and OVERMARS, M. Probabilistic roadmaps for path planning in high-dimensional configuration spaces. *IEEE Transaction on Robotics and Automation*, *12* (4), 1996. 566-580.

[KNN03] KIRCHNER, A., NAMAZI, A., NISHINARI, K. and SCHADSCHNEIDER, A., Role of Conflicts in the Floor Field Cellular Automaton Model for Pedestrian Dynamics. in *2nd International Conference on Pedestrians and Evacuation Dynamics*, (2003), 51-62.

[LKF05] LAKOBA, KAUP and FINKELSTEIN Modification of the Helbing-Molnar-Farkas-Vicsek Social Force Model for Pedestrian Evolution. *Simulation*, *81* (5), 2005. 339-352.

[LCC06] LERNER, A., CHRYSANTHOU, Y. and COHEN-OR, D., Efficient cells-and-portals partitioning. in *Computer Animation & Virtual Worlds*, (2006), Wiley, 21-40.

[LMM03] LOSCOS, C., MARCHAL, D. and MEYER, A. Intuitive crowd behaviour in dense urban environments using local laws. *IEEE Theory and Practice of Computer Graphics*, 2003. 122.

[MS05] MASSIVE_SOFTWARE_INC. 3D animation system for crowd-related visual effects, http://www.massivesoftware.com, 2005.

[OCV*02] O'SULLIVAN, C., CASSELL, J., VILHJALMSSON, H., DOBBYN, S., PETERS, C., LEESON, W., GIANG, T. and DINGLIANA, J., Crowd and Group Simulation with Levels of Detail for Geometry, Motion and Behavior. in *Third Irish Workshop on Computer Graphics*, (2002).

[PHL05] PAN, X., HAN, C.S. and LAW, K.H., A Multi-agent Based Simulation Framework for the Study of Human and Social Behavior in Egress Analysis. in *The International Conference on Computing in Civil Engineering*, (Cancun, 2005).

[PB06] PELECHANO, N. and BADLER, N. Modeling Crowd and Trained Leader Behavior during Building Evacuation. *IEEE Computer Graphics and Applications*, *26* (6), 2006. 80-86.

[POS05] PELECHANO, N., O'BRIEN, K., SILVERMAN, B. and BADLER, N., Crowd Simulation Incorporating Agent Psychological Models, Roles and Communication. in *First International Workshop on Crowd Simulation. (V-CROWDS '05)*, (2005).

[PLT05] PETTRE, J., LAUMOND, J.-P. and THALMANN, D., A Navigation Graph for real-time crowd animation on multilayered and uneven terrain. in *First International Workshop on Crowd Simulation*, (2005), 81-90.

[Rey87] REYNOLDS, C., Flocks, herds, and schools: A distributed behavior model. in *Proceedings of ACM SIGGRAPH*, (1987), 25-34.

[Rey99] REYNOLDS, C., Steering behaviors for autonomous characters. in *Game Developers Conference*, (1999), 763-782.

[ST05] SHAO, W. and TERZOPOULOS, D., Autonomous pedestrians. in *Proceedings of ACM SIGGRAPH / Eurographics Symposium on Computer Animation*, (2005), 19-28.

[SBC*06] SILVERMAN, B., BHARATHY, G., CORNWELL, J. and O'BRIEN, K. Human Behavior Models for Agents in Simulators and Games: Part II - Gamebots for a Foreign Culture. *Presence*, *15* (2), 2006. 163-185.

[SKG05] SUNG, M., KOVAR, L. and GLEICHER, M., Fast and accurate goal-directed motion synthesis for crowds. in *Symposium on Computer Animation*, (2005), 291-300.

[TLC*01] TECCHIA, F., LOSCOS, C., CONROY, R. and CHRYSANTHOU, Y., Agent behavior simulator (ABS): A platform for urban behavior development. in *Proceedings of ACM/EG Games Technology Conference*, (2001).

[TMK99] THALMANN, D., MUSSE, S.R. and KALLMANN, M., Virtual Humans' Behavior: Individuals, Groups, and Crowds. in *Proceedings of Digital Media Futures*, (1999), 13-15.

[TD00] THOMAS, G. and DONIKIAN, S., Virtual Humans Animation in Informed Urban Environments. in *Proceedings of Computer Animation*, (2000), 112.

[TCP06] TREUILLE, A., COOPER, S. and POPIVIC, Z., Continuum Crowds. in *ACM Transactions on Graphics (SIGGRAPH 2006)*, (2006), 1160-1168.

[TT94] TU, X. and TERZOPOULOS, D., Artificial Fishes: Physics, Locomotion, Perception, Behavior. in *Proceedings of ACM SIGGRAPH*, (1994), 43-50.

Eurographics/ ACM SIGGRAPH Symposium on Computer Animation (2007)
D. Metaxas and J. Popovic (Editors)

Group Behavior from Video: A Data-Driven Approach to Crowd Simulation

Kang Hoon Lee, Myung Geol Choi, Qyoun Hong and Jehee Lee

Seoul National University†

Abstract

Crowd simulation techniques have frequently been used to animate a large group of virtual humans in computer graphics applications. We present a data-driven method of simulating a crowd of virtual humans that exhibit behaviors imitating real human crowds. To do so, we record the motion of a human crowd from an aerial view using a camcorder, extract the two-dimensional moving trajectories of each individual in the crowd, and then learn an agent model from observed trajectories. The agent model decides each agent's actions based on features of the environment and the motion of nearby agents in the crowd. Once the agent model is learned, we can simulate a virtual crowd that behaves similarly to the real crowd in the video. The versatility and flexibility of our approach is demonstrated through examples in which various characteristics of group behaviors are captured and reproduced in simulated crowds.

Categories and Subject Descriptors (according to ACM CCS): I.3.7 [Three-Dimensional Graphics and Realism]: Animation

1. Introduction

The group behavior of human crowds in the real world varies significantly depending on time, place, the level of stress, the age of people, and many other social and psychological factors. These variations in group behavior are often characterized by observable features such as interpersonal space, the fluidity of formation, the level of energy, the uniformity of distribution, the style of interpersonal interactions, and so on.

The most popular approach to crowd simulation is based on agent models. Each individual agent perceives nearby environments and other agents, and decides its actions based on a set of simple rules with a few tunable parameters. A big advantage of agent-based models is that the integration of individual rule-based actions exhibits collective group behavior of enormous complexity and subtlety. The downside to this approach is that the crowd behavior is affected indirectly and unintuitively by tuning parameters and changing rules. This makes it difficult to produce a desired style of group behavior using agent-based models.

† e-mail: {zoi,mingle,mani83,jehee}@mrl.snu.ac.kr

We present a data-driven method of simulating a crowd of virtual humans that exhibit behavior imitating real human crowds. Our simulation method is also agent-based, but the behavior patterns of each individual agent are learned (rather than hard-coded) from a video clip that recorded a crowd of people from an aerial view. From the video, we would like to understand what each person perceived and how he/she acted in the perceived situation at every time instance. To do so, we track the two-dimensional moving trajectories of people and extract the context of the motion using vision-based tracking techniques. As a result of visual tracking, we acquire a large collection of state-action pairs, from which our virtual human learns which actions to take for any given situation.

Learning group behavior from videos is a challenging problem because the motion of each individual is influenced by many factors that are not captured in the video. We assume that each person in the video has separate mechanisms for deciding his/her high-level behavior and low-level motion. The low-level motion is assumed to be controlled based only on features of the environment and the motion of nearby individuals in the crowd. In this work, we focus on learning an agent model that controls the low-level motion of each agent

Symposium on Computer Animation 2007, San Diego, CA, August 03-04, 2007.
© 2007 ACM 978-1-59593-624-4/07/0008 $5.00

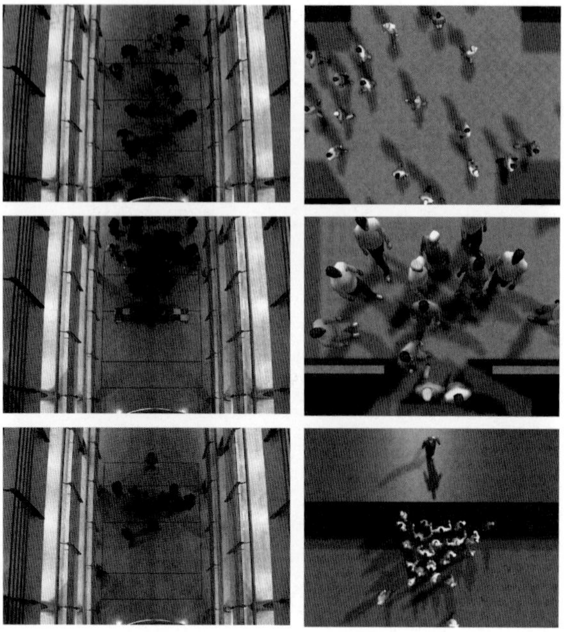

Figure 1: *Group behavior models are learned from crowd videos.*

in the crowd. Our learning algorithm is based on a locally weighted linear regression [AMS97], which is further elaborated to cope with complex group behaviors in a variety of environments.

Although multiple object tracking has been extensively studied in computer vision, automatic tracking of densely populated pedestrians is still challenging in practice. Instead, our system offers a semi-automated tracker and a keyframe-based interactive interface to users for allowing user intervention. Most of vision-based tracking algorithms track targets forward in time starting from their initial locations. This approach often suffers from the "hijacking" problem, that is, a tracker missing its own target and being attracted by another target. Our user interface system allows the user to refine the (possibly flawed) tracking result by inserting keyframes incrementally in a top-down manner.

We demonstrate the power of our approach through examples, in which subtle characteristics of captured group behaviors are reproduced, and through comparison with Reynolds' flocking algorithm. Our data-driven behavior model can be learned to imitate the rule-based flocking algorithm. We also demonstrate that captured insect behaviors can be adapted for simulating human crowds.

2. Related Work

Crowd simulation and group behavior control have gained significant interests in computer graphics, robotics, and urban planning. Since the rule-based agent model was introduced in the seminal work of Reynolds [Rey87], many variants of agent models have been explored in research community and employed in commercial products such as Massive [Mas06]. A number of researchers addressed the problem of creating a "smarter" agent that can decide its actions based on social, psychological, cognitive reasoning [MT97, POSB05, FTT99, MH04, ST05], and have pathfinding capability facilitated by global path planning methods [LC03, BLA03, LD04, PdHCM*06, GKM*01, KO04, SKG05]. Some researchers focused on an alternative approach that makes the environment "smarter" by embedding a repertoire of control modules into environment objects so that an agent can be provided with control strategies appropriate to its location and situation in the environment [SGC04, ACT05, LCL06]. We adopt this approach to allow the user to construct high-level group behavior scenarios flexibly by arranging a set of learned behavior models in the environment.

Crowd modeling has also been studied in the urban planning and fluid dynamics communities. Helbing and his colleagues [HMFB01] suggested a social force model of individual pedestrian dynamics. Kirchner and Schadschneider [KS02] simulated the evacuation process of a human crowd in a panic situation using cellular automata. Hughes [Hug03] formulated the behavior of a human crowd as a flowing continuum. Treuille et al. [TCP06] further elaborated Hughes' continuum crowd model and suggested a numerical method for simulating and visualizing crowd flow. Chenney [Che04] explored a way of designing stationary flow fields by tiling small rectangular regions of velocity fileds.

The computer vision community has developed a number of algorithms to track multiple moving objects in a video. To name only a few of them, Comaniciu et al. [CRM03] presented a kernel-based object tracking method that represents targets by feature histograms and tracks the targets using gradient-based optimization. Zhao and Nevatia [ZN04] addressed tracking multiple humans and inferring their coarse three-dimensional postures from a prior locomotion model. Khan et al. [KBD05] proposed a MCMC-based multi-target tracker that addressed a variable number of interacting targets. Egerstedt et al. [EBD*05] applied this MCMC-based tracker to trace the moving trajectories of ants and built a model that informs what the ants were doing in the video.

Reproducing observed movement patterns in a simulated environment has been explored in computer animation, roboics, and pedestrian research. Lai et al. [LCF05] presented a data-driven method of creating and dynamically updating group formations from a set of formation patterns. Brogan and Johnson [BJ03] and Fajen et al. [FWTK] showed that human walking data can be used to improve the quality of planned paths by adapting their steering models to the observed data. In pedestrian research community, several researchers addressed the problem of reconstructing crowd phenomena from video by tuning the parameters of their microscopic pedestrian models [Sti00, Tek02]. We share the basic motivation with these approaches. The main advantage of our approach is the ability to imitate a wide range of group behavior patterns and styles by using a regression-based learning method.

3. Video Capture and Processing

Human crowds are ubiquitous. Interesting crowd behaviors can be found in any downtown streets and buildings. We installed a camcorder above the crowds as high up as possible to observe them from an aerial view with minimal parallax effects, as long as each individual in the crowds is recognizable in the video. This setup makes the tracking procedure less painful because of minimal overlap of people. We also recorded crowd videos in a controlled environment. In recorded videos, about 40 volunteers displayed a variety of group behavior scenarios as instructed. The scenarios include pedestrians crossing and streaming through a variety of environment features, lining up in front of a ticket booth, watching a performance at streets, wandering around, chatting in small groups, just standing idly, and so on.

The crowd video includes a lot of information. From the video, we need to identify environment features (such as walls and obstacles), track two-dimensional trajectories of individuals, and understand their high-level behaviors. At a preprocessing phase, per-pixel median filtering is applied to the video for background subtraction. Then, the user annotates environment features manually on a video frame. Since our videos do not include any dynamically moving objects other than people, the manual annotation is not a burden.

Tracking individual trajectories from the video is a notoriously difficult problem. Inspired by the keyframe-based tracking interface of Agarwala et al. [AHSS04], we built a simple keyframe-based user interface system that allows the user to track multiple targets in the video semi-automatically. Our system employs a kernel-based tracking algorithm proposed by Comaniciu et al. [CRM03] for tracking targets. This algorithm works well in a short term duration, but often fails for an extended duration of tracking. In order to achieve better reliability, our system requires the user to specify both initial and final locations of each individual in the video. Then, the tracker is used to trace the target trajectory forward in time from the initial location and also trace backward in time from the final location. The forward trajectory and the backward trajectory are linearly blended to produce a more reliable trajectory. If this trajectory is unsatisfactory, the user may browse video frames and specify the location of the target at an intermediate video frame. The bi-directional tracking is then applied to two separate (initial-to-intermediate and intermediate-to-final) time intervals. In this way, the user can refine the trajectory adaptively until a satisfactory result is obtained. Additionally, Gaussian filtering is applied to resultant trajectories in order to smooth out noisy oscillations.

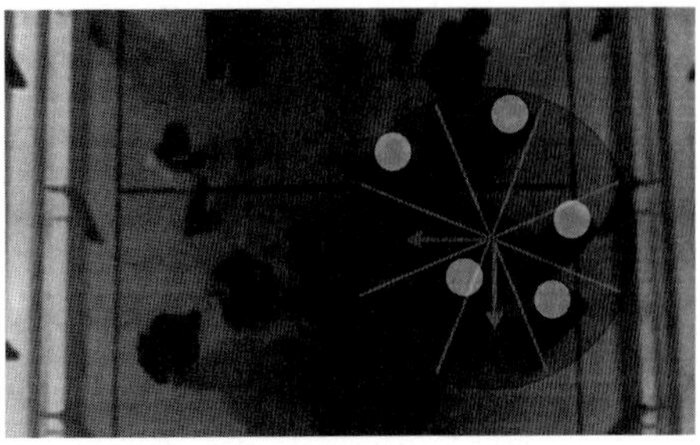

Figure 2: *The neighborhood formation is encoded with respect to the local coordinate system shown in red and blue arrows. The subjects were instructed to pretend that they are walking along corridors.*

Understanding high-level behaviors of individuals is even more challenging. At a ticket booth, for instance, some people would wait in line while some others would pass by or wander around. Although we have not yet found a general method of classifying different high-level behaviors automatically from the video, we found that a set of simple rules can be applied to identify specific behaviors effectively. For example, the moving speed and relative distance between nearby agents can be used to differentiate individuals waiting in line, passing by, and just wandering around. In our experiments, we manually annotated individual trajectories with the type of high-level behaviors facilitated by these heuristic rules.

4. State-Action Trajectories

Our crowd simulation system creates a number of agents that decide actions based on their limited perception capability. The behavior model of each agent is learned from state-action samples $\{(\mathbf{s}_i, \mathbf{a}_i)\}$ obtained from crowd videos. The state $\mathbf{s} \in \mathbb{R}^N$ of each agent reflects the motion of nearby agents, its own motion, and environment features. The action $\mathbf{a} \in \mathbb{R}^2$ of each agent is simply a two-dimensional vector that corresponds to the instantaneous speed and moving direction of the agent. To learn behaviors effectively, it is very important to have a low-dimensional state space, in which various aspects of group behaviors are compactly characterized. We selected four features to model the agent's state vector:

- **Self speed:** The instantaneous speed of the agent is computed as the distance between the current position of the agent and its position at the previous time instance divided by the time interval.
- **Neighborhood formation:** The motion of the agent is greatly influenced by the formation of nearby agents in the crowd. Closer agents would have stronger influence on the

behavior model and agents farther than a user-provided threshold distance r have no influence. The threshold distance r depends on the density of the crowd. To effectively represent this information by a fixed and relatively low dimensional vector, we divide the space around the agent into a set of eight radial regions (see Figure 2). Within each radial region, the distance to the nearest agent is a determining factor. The feature value for each radial region is

$$f = \begin{cases} (r-d)^2/r^2, & \text{if } d < r \\ 0, & \text{otherwise} \end{cases} \quad (1)$$

where d is the distance to the nearest agent in the radial region. In order to reflect the temporal change of the neighborhood formation, the state vector includes feature values from two successive (the current and the previous) frames. Thus, the neighborhood formation takes 16 entries in the state vector.

- **Pivot:** Behaviors, such as passing through gates and waiting in line, would take place with respect to the relevant objects. We assume that each behavior we intend to model can have at most one pivot object. In that case, the state vector includes the position and orientation of the agent with respect to the pivot object and its neighborhood formation is also represented with respect to the coordinate system attached to the pivot object.
- **Intended moving direction:** Each individual in a human crowd behaves with intention, which is an important factor of understanding individual behaviors. The intention is often implicit and may not be captured in crowd videos. We approximately estimate the intended moving direction of a pedestrian by averaging the moving directions in a window of past and future frames. The window size was ten frames (one second) in our experiments. This estimation is rough, but still useful for high-level control of pedestrians.

Each feature is empirically weighed according to its relative influence on the group behaviors (see Table 1). When the crowd is dense, we weighs the neighborhood formation over the other features in order to avoid collisions between agents. The intended moving direction is the most important feature for locomotion.

The observed states are represented by 21-dimensional vectors. We use a principle component analysis (PCA) to reparameterize the state space in a low-dimensional (8 to 12 dimensional in our experiments) space for efficient learning of behavior models.

5. Group Behavior Model

We model the group behavior in the video with a two-level hierarchical structure consisting of high-level behavior models and low-level action models (see Figure 3 left). The behavior model consists of a set of low-level action models and decides the transitioning between them to reproduce globally plausible group behavior patterns in crowd videos. Each low-level model describes a primitive action that can be represented by a simple learning model.

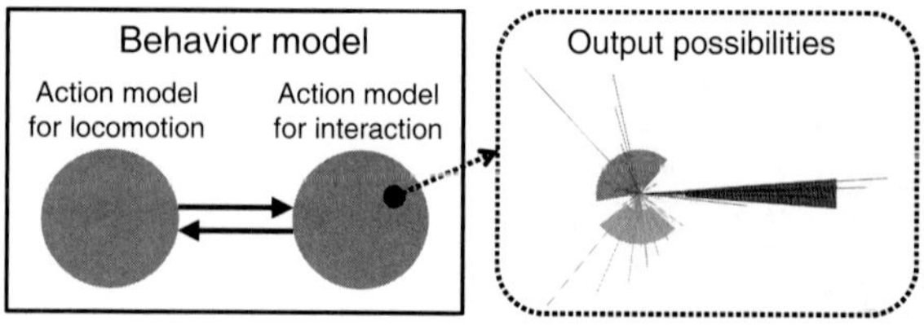

Figure 3: *Overview of our group behavior model. (Left) A high-level behavior model consists of low-level action models, depicted as the gray circles. At runtime, the behavior model decides the transitioning between low-level action models. (Right) For steering each agent, the corresponding active low-level model sorts output possibilities (shown as radial lines) into groups and selects a plausible output statistically. The translucent radial windows show the range of allowable perturbations.*

The state-action trajectories acquired from the processed video are segmented and classified into groups according to the annotated behavior patterns, and each group is used to learn a corresponding action model. The action model can be considered as a function that takes the state of an agent as input and produces a desired action of the agent at the next time instance. Given novel state s observed in simulation, our action model has to decide an action with respect to the training data. There are many approaches addressing this problem. For example, we can simply choose the nearest sample from the training set and select its associated action as output. This approach is simple and efficient, but the disadvantage is that the mapping between inputs and outputs are discontinuous. So, drastically different output actions can be produced for similar input states.

An alternative approach is to select nearby samples and combine them to produce an output. To do so, we employ a locally weighted linear regression method [AMS97], which requires that the model be *Markovian*. In other words, the agent's decision as to how to act should depend only on the current state. This condition is not satisfied in our group behavior learning problem. In crowd videos, each individual used to make different decisions at the same perceived state. We address this problem by clustering output possibilities and selecting a plausible output probabilistically (see Figure 3 right). We focus on the construction of action models in this section and discuss high-level behavior models in Section 6.1.

5.1. Neighborhood Search and Clustering

The basic idea of locally weighted regression is to search a small set of state-action samples that are similar to the current query state and estimate a linear regression model from the neighboring samples to determine an appropriate output action for the query state. The neighborhood search is the most computation-demanding component of locally weighted learning. In order to locate k-nearest neighbors efficiently, we store training data in a kd-tree and search k-nearest neighbors approximately within a small error bound using ANN library [MA06].

The neighboring samples thus obtained may represent a non-Markovian behavior that can produce more than one output possibility. In order to identify multiple output possibilities, we use k-means clustering algorithm, which sorts the neighboring samples into clusters at run time (see Figure 3 right). Each cluster includes samples with similar output actions. The number of clusters to be sorted out depends on the diversity of behaviors displayed in the video. The probability of selecting a cluster is inversely proportional to the mean deviations from the cluster selected at the previous time step. More specifically, the probability p_i of selecting the i-th cluster of mean $\mathbf{m}_i$ is

$$p_i = \frac{1/\|\mathbf{m}_i - \mathbf{m}_{prev}\|}{\sum_{j=1}^{K} 1/\|\mathbf{m}_j - \mathbf{m}_{prev}\|} \tag{2}$$

where $\mathbf{m}_{prev}$ is the mean vector of the previously selected cluster and K is the number of clusters.

5.2. Locally Weighted Linear Regression

Given samples $\{(\mathbf{s}_i, \mathbf{a}_i)\}_{i=1}^{k}$ where $\mathbf{s}_i$ is a vector-valued input state and $\mathbf{a}_i = (x_i, y_i)$ is a two-dimensional output, we first consider a regression model that produces the x-coordinates of output vectors. A regression model for y-coordinates can be built similarly. A linear fitting model can be described as a matrix equation $S\beta = \mathbf{x}$, where S is a matrix whose i-th row is $\mathbf{s}_i^T$, $\mathbf{x}$ is a vector whose i-th element is x_i, and β is a vector of the model parameters. Locally weighted linear regression estimates the model parameters

$$\beta = (S^T WS)^{-1} S^T W\mathbf{x}, \tag{3}$$

where W is a diagonal weight matrix with $W_{ii} = \exp\big(-\frac{1}{2\sigma}(\mathbf{s}-\mathbf{s}_i)^T(\mathbf{s}-\mathbf{s}_i)\big)$. This regression weighs near samples more than farther samples. Bandwidth σ determines how weights fall off with distance from $\mathbf{s}$.

5.3. Attraction

The strategy of reacting similarly at similar situations may fail if the situation encountered by an agent is significantly different from any state-action samples in the training data. In that case, the nearest samples are not really similar and a linear regression model would produce extremely extrapolated outputs. To avoid excessive extrapolations, we make a small perturbation to the output of locally weighted linear regression. The range of perturbation is limited by a constant multiple of standard deviations from the mean direction and distance (see Figure 3). Within the range, a perturbation is decided in such a way that the moving direction is steered toward the nearest sample configuration. To do so, we regularly sample output possibilities in the perturbation region and select the one that minimizes the distance to the nearest sample in the training data. Attraction to the nearest sample keeps the local formation of agents not to drift away from sample formations observed from the video.

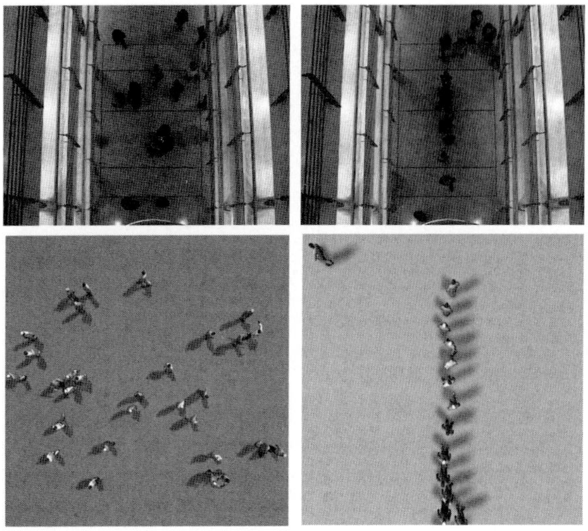

Figure 4: *Various interaction patterns in group behavior. (Top) We captured our subjects chatting in small groups and waiting in line. (Bottom) The learned action models produced the extended formations of corresponding styles.*

6. Crowd Simulation

6.1. High-Level Behavior

To make our agents not only react immediately with respect to perceived situations but also decide their high-level behaviors actively, we provide them with a high-level decision model composed of a set of learned low-level action models. In our system, this scheme is implemented as a finite state machine, in which each action model corresponds to a state. To reproduce global behavior patterns observed in training video, we encode the transition conditions between action models and control parameters such as the average duration of staying in each action model. These control parameters are measured from crowd video.

A typical example of high-level behavior is observed in a form of repeated transition between locomotion and group interaction. An agent moves around, joins a small group of agents for interaction, and leaves the group, repeatedly (see

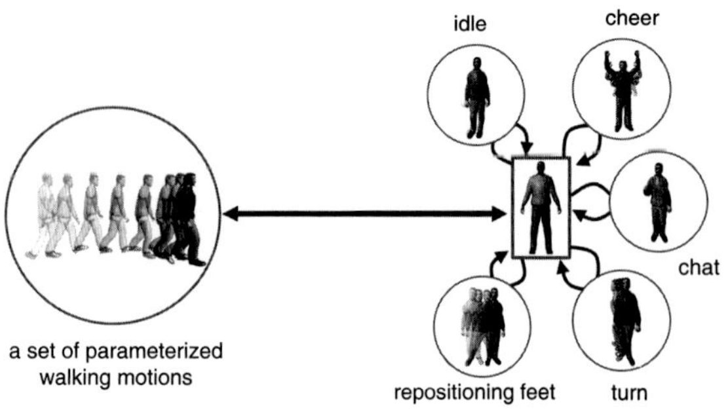

Figure 5: *A transition graph for full-body motion synthesis.*

Figure 4). These groups can be formed and disappeared dynamically. From the video, we measure the average size of agent groups, the average duration of staying, and the average interpersonal distance in groups. A new group is formed when more than two agents meet within the average interpersonal distance. If an agent approaches a group within its average interpersonal distance, the agent may be accepted to join the group probabilistically not to make the group too large beyond the average group size. Some action models enforce spatial constraints for transitioning. For example, the group of agents forms a line in front of a ticket booth. This group allows new members to join only at the end of the line and only the member at the front of the line can leave the group.

In order to simulate crowds in complex virtual environments, each agent need to adapt to their surroundings such as narrow gates, corridors and crosswalks. Our system allows the user to create the layout of an environment and annotate the environment what behavior models are appropriate in which part of the environment. Each agent in the crowd chooses its behavior model according to the annotation.

6.2. Full-body Motion Synthesis

For visually appealing and realistic crowd behaviors, we synthesize the full-body motion of human-like characters along the two-dimensional point trajectories of simulated agents. Since detailed full-body motions are not captured from the video, the context of motions along the trajectories are partly inferred from the trajectories and partly obtained from manual annotations.

We employ data-driven motion synthesis methods that utilize motion capture data. Two groups of motion data, locomotion and in-place motion, were collected to synthesize full-body animation of individual agents. In order to build locomotion library, our motion capture subject walked in various speeds and turning angles. The in-place motion library includes chatting, standing idly, cheering, turning, and repositioning feet.

The locomotion of a full-body character is parameterized by speeds and turning angles, and can be synthesized to walk along a two-dimensional trajectory. For parameterizing and blending example motions, we use an on-line motion blending method suggested by Park et al. [PSKS04]. This technique allows us to blend motion segments precisely at the granularity of frames. The in-place motions and the parameterized walking motions are integrated into a transition graph so that transitions between them can be made immediately (see Figure 5).

Synthesizing full-body motions along a given trajectory requires a lookahead search to determine which connecting transition to choose among many transition possibilities. When the computational cost is a major concern, a short period of lookahead time (0.66 seconds in our experiments) is used to decide transitions and the root node (the pelvis) of each articulated character is simply made to follow its target trajectory while allowing its feet to slide on the ground. In order to maximize the animation quality, each character searches a longer period of time to make a better decision of transitioning and prevents feet from sliding by using hierarchical displacement mapping [LS99].

7. Experimental Results

We recorded a variety of group behavior scenarios of about an hour in a rectangular region of 10m x 10m (see Table 1). In the videos, about forty volunteers walked in a variety of environment setups including corridors, corners and crossroads (Locomotion), passed through narrow gates (Passing gates), stopped and watched a street performance (Stage), waited in line (Line), chatted in small groups (Chat), and walked in various styles (Commuter, Stroller, Tourist). For each video, we tracked individual trajectories and annotated walls and pivots (such as the gate and the stage) if necessary. It took about thirty minutes to postprocess two hundred frames. In each individual frame, about twenty people are traced. The coordinate system was decided appropriately depending on the presence of pivots and the type of behaviors. For each query at runtime, we found one hundred of the nearest samples from training data and sorted them into three groups. The bandwidth of the kernel used in locally weighted linear regression was adaptively adjusted to the distance to the fifth nearest sample.

Styles. We acquired a collection of videos that recorded human crowds exhibiting different behavioral patterns, including the styles of busy commuters, relaxed strollers, and wandering tourists. Our behavior model captured these stylistic variations and reproduced them successfully in simulated crowds (see Figure 6).

Simulated crowds. To access the performance, we used our data-driven method to imitate Reynolds' rule-based algorithms. We collected a set of 4617 state-action samples from a simulated crowd controlled by Reynolds' leader-follower

Figure 6: *The snapshots of crowd simulation reveal subtleties in group behaviors. (Top left) Various collision avoidance strategies are implicitly encoded in our data-driven behavior model and reproduced in the simulation. (Top right) Three characters meet at the gate. A similar situation observed in the video is reproduced so that the character at the middle gives way to the other two and waited until they pass through the gate. (Bottom) The stylistic variations in group behavior are reproduced in the simulated crowds. The agents in the left figure tend to keep pace with nearby agents whereas the agents in the right try to pass the others at variable speed.*

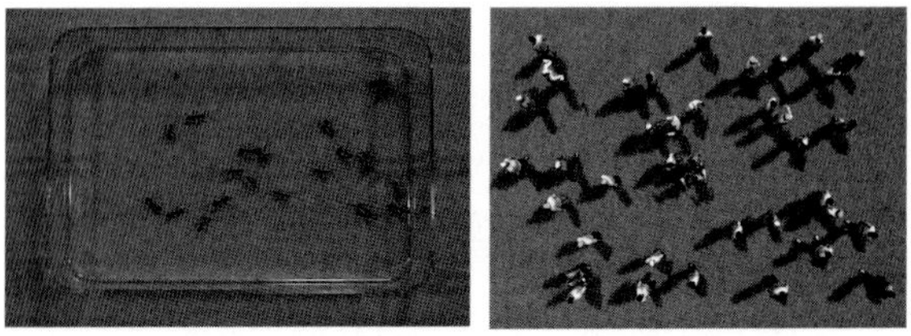

Figure 7: *The locomotion and interaction behavior models are learned from the ants video on the left and these behavior models are used to simulate virtual human crowds on the right. The ants video used courtesy of BioTracking project at Georgia Institute of Technology.*

model. Our behavior model learned from simulated training data similarly reproduced the characteristics of the rule-based behavior.

Ants. The group behaviors of animals and insects can also be applied to humans, thus creating a virtual human crowd that exhibit their behaviors. In the ants video, twenty ants are roaming around, approaching other ants, and interacting with each other by antennal contact. We learned an agent model from the ants video and applied this model to simulate a virtual human crowd (see Figure 7). To do so, we classified observed ant states into either locomotion or interaction automatically using simple rules; A group of ants staying within a threshold distance for more than one second are considered to be interacting with each other. All the other behaviors are classified as locomotion. The size and the velocity of ant trajectories were scaled appropriately in order to compensate for the scale difference between humans and ants.

Evacuation. Our approach is useful in simulating an evacuation scenario, in which a realistic group behavior plays an important role. In Figure 8, 80 agents are initially scattered in the five rooms, which are connected to the corridors leading to the building exit. Appropriate behavior models were annotated on the environment layout in such a way that the agents can leave the room and rush to the exit for evacuation. Similar to real emergency situations, bottlenecks were formed at narrow gates and junctions in simulation.

Small town performance. We built a small virtual town populated by 300 residents (see Figure 9). In a public square in the town, break dancers show their performance. The resident people are wandering around on the streets, chatting, gathering to watch the performance, and cheering. Generating 1000 frames of crowd simulation took about 5 minutes with 3D rendering disabled.

8. Discussion

The primary advantage of our approach is its capability of reproducing realistic human group behaviors in simulated environments. In our experiments, we observed the complexity and subtle details of simulated behavioral patterns that cannot easily be accomplished by using rule-based agent models. Our approach is especially useful for applications that need to simulate a large repertoire of realistic interactions among human characters.

The memory and computation costs of our regression-based learning algorithm increase with the amount of training data. The memory cost is not generally a problem, because it increases linearly with the size of training data. The computation cost is more serious, because the controller performs a neighborhood search for regression at run time. The computational cost was mitigated by maintaining data in *k*d-trees, which facilitate efficient spatial query processing.

We have visually compared the original videos and simulated crowds to see if human group behaviors are successfully captured and reproduced in the simulated environment. Though this visual comparison is an effective way of evaluating the quality and similarity of group behaviors in a subjective point of view, we also need a quantitative method of evaluating and characterizing group behaviors. The statistical measures, such as the average interpersonal space,

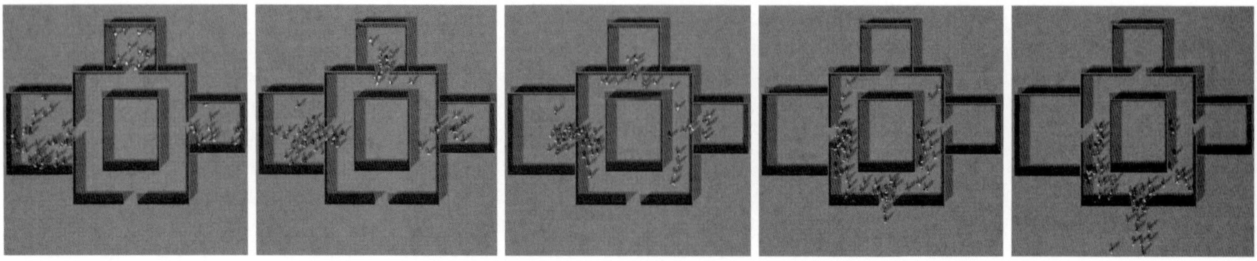

Figure 8: *Evacuation*

Figure 9: *Break dancer performance in the small town. The bottom right image is the layout of the town annotated by embedded behavior models. The characters in the blue region is directed to move to the gates and the characters in the pink region is provided with the "Passing gate" behavior model. The green, light green, purple annotations correspond to "chat", "ants", and "stage" behavior models, respectively. Building geometry models used courtesy of Pascal Mueller and Simon Haegler, copyright ETH Zurich.*

Behavior Models	# of video frames	# of (s,a) samples	Coordinate system	Neighborhood radius	Feature weights			
					Speed	Formation	Pivot	Direction
Locomotion	3000	2204	local	1.5 to 2 (m)	1	100	0	1
Passing gate	400	1216	pivot	1 (m)	1	100	10	0
Chat	1200	1041	pivot	1 (m)	1	100	0	0
Line	1200	927	pivot	1 (m)	1	10	10	0
Stage	600	640	pivot	1 (m)	1	100	1	0
Ants	3277	(interaction) 936	pivot	3 (cm)	1	100	0	0
		(locomotion) 1244	local	3 (cm)	1	10	0	100
Reynolds	10000	4617	local	2 (m)	1	1	500	0
Commuter	700	963	local	1 (m)	1	1	0	1
Stroller	700	1277	local	1 (m)	100	1	0	100
Tourist	1500	1226	local	1 (m)	1	50	0	1

Table 1: *Experimental data. The videos are sampled at the rate of 10 frames per second. The state of each individual is represented with respect to either a local, moving coordinate system or a fixed coordinate system. The radius of a perceived neighborhood was determined based on the density of the crowd. The feature weights for self speed, neighborhood formation, pivot, and intended moving direction are provided.*

the density and uniformity of distribution, the regularity of formation, and the temporal and spatial coherence of group interactions, might be used to quantify the characteristics of group behaviors.

The flexibility of crowd simulation could be increased by parameterizing group behaviors learned from video. A promising scenario is to install multiple camcorders at fixed locations for an extended period of time and collect video clips that record crowd behaviors at a variety of time, seasons, weather conditions, and spatial locations. These collection would allow us to build a parameterized behavior model that can be adapt for environment factors.

Acknowledgements

We would like to thank the Georgia Tech BORG laboratory for allowing us to experiment with the ants video and the trajectory data from the BioTracking project. We are also very grateful to Pascal Mueller and Simon Haegler for granting us to use their urban model. This research work was partly supported by the IITA under the ITRC support program.

References

[ACT05] Abaci T., Cíger J., Thalmann D.: Planning with smart objects. In *WSCG (Short Papers)* (2005), pp. 25–28. 2

[AHSS04] Agarwala A., Hertzmann A., Salesin D. H., Seitz S. M.: Keyframe-based tracking for rotoscoping and animation. *ACM Transactions on Graphics (SIGGRAPH 2004) 23*, 3 (2004), 584–591. 3

[AMS97] Atkeson C. G., Moore A. W., Schaal S.: Locally weighted learning. *Artificial Intelligence Review 11*, 1-5 (1997), 11–73. 2, 4

[BJ03] Brogan D., Johnson N.: Realistic human walking paths. In *CASA '03: Proceedings of the 16th International Conference on Computer Animation and Social Agents* (2003), pp. 94–101. 2

[BLA03] Bayazit O. B., Lien J.-M., Amato N. M.: Better group behaviors in complex environments using global roadmaps. In *ICAL 2003: Proceedings of the eighth international conference on Artificial life* (2003), pp. 362–370. 2

[Che04] Chenney S.: Flow tiles. In *SCA '04: Proceedings of the 2004 ACM SIGGRAPH/Eurographics Symposium on Computer Animation* (2004), pp. 233–242. 2

[CRM03] Commanciu D., Ramesh V., Meer P.: Kernel-based object tracking. *IEEE Transactions on Pattern Analysis and Maching Intelligence 25*, 5 (2003), 564–577. 2, 3

[EBD*05] Egerstedt M., Balch T., Dellaert F., Delmotte F., Khan Z.: What are the ants doing? vision-based tracking and reconstruction of control programs. In *Proceedings of IEEE International Conference on Robotics and Automation (ICRA)* (2005). 2

[FTT99] Funge J., Tu X., Terzopoulos D.: Cognitive modeling: knowledge, reasoning and planning for intelligent characters. In *SIGGRAPH '99: Proceedings of the 26th annual conference on Computer graphics and interactive techniques* (1999), pp. 29–38. 2

[FWTK] Fajen B. R., Warren W. H., Temizer S., Kaelbling L. P.: A dynamical model of visually-guided steering, obstacle avoidance, and route selection. *International Journal of Computer Vision.* 2

[GKM*01] Goldenstein S., Karavelas M., Metaxas D., Guibas L., Aaron E., Goswami

A.: Scalable behaviors for crowd simulation. *Computer & Graphics 25*, 6 (2001), 983–998. 2

[HMFB01] HELBING D., MOLNAR P., FARKAS I. J., BOLAY K.: Self-organizing pedestrian movement. *Environment and Planning B: Planning and Design 28* (2001), 361–383. 2

[Hug03] HUGHES R. L.: The flow of human crowds. *Annual Review of Fluid Mechanics 35* (2003), 169–182. 2

[KBD05] KHAN Z., BALCH T., DELLAERT F.: Mcmc-based particle filtering for tracking a variable number of interacting targets. *IEEE Transactions on Pattern Analysis and Machine Intelligence 27*, 11 (2005), 1805–1918. 2

[KO04] KAMPHUIS A., OVERMARS M. H.: Finding paths for coherent groups using clearance. In *SCA '04: Proceedings of the 2004 ACM SIGGRAPH/Eurographics Symposium on Computer Animation* (2004), pp. 233–242. 2

[KS02] KIRCHNER A., SCHADSCHNEIDER A.: Simulation of evacuation processes using a bionics-inspired cellular automaton model for pedestrian dynamics. *Physica A: Statistical Mechanics and its Applications 312(1–2)* (2002), 260–276. 2

[LC03] LI T.-Y., CHOU H.-C.: Motion planning for a crowd of robots. In *ICRA '03: Proceedings of IEEE international conference on Robotics and Automation* (2003), pp. 4215–4221. 2

[LCF05] LAI Y.-C., CHENNEY S., FAN S.: Group motion graphs. In *SCA '05: Proceedings of the 2005 ACM SIGGRAPH/Eurographics Symposium on Computer Animation* (2005), pp. 281–290. 2

[LCL06] LEE K. H., CHOI M. G., LEE J.: Motion patches: building blocks for virtual environments annotated with motion data. *ACM Transactions on Graphics (SIGGRAPH 2006) 25*, 3 (2006), 898–906. 2

[LD04] LAMARCHE F., DONIKIAN S.: Crowd of virtual humans: A new approach for real time navigation in complex and structured environments. *Computer Graphics Forum (Eurographics 2004) 23*, 3 (2004), 509–518. 2

[LS99] LEE J., SHIN S. Y.: A hierarchical approach to interactive motion editing for human-like figures. In *SIGGRAPH '99: Proceedings of the 26th annual conference on Computer graphics and interactive techniques* (1999), pp. 39–48. 6

[MA06] MOUNT D., ARYA S.: Ann: Library for approximate nearest neighbor searching, http://www.cs.sunysb.edu/ algorith/implement/ann/distrib/index1.html, 2006. 5

[Mas06] MASSIVE SOFTWARE: http://www.massivesoftware.com/, 2006. 2

[MH04] METOYER R. A., HODGINS J. K.: Reactive pedestrian path following from examples. *The Visual Computer 20*, 10 (2004), 635–649. 2

[MT97] MUSSE S. R., THALMANN D.: A model of human crowd behavior: Group inter-relationship and collision detection analysis. In *Computer Animation and Simulation '97* (1997), pp. 39–51. 2

[PdHCM*06] PETTRE J., DE HERAS CIECHOMSKI P., MAIM J., YERSIN B., LAUMOND J.-P., THALMANN D.: Real-time navigating crowds: scalable simulation and rendering. *Computer Animation and Virtual Worlds 17*, 3–4 (2006), 445–455. 2

[POSB05] PELECHANO N., O'BRIEN K., SILVERMAN B., BADLER N.: Crowd simulation incorporating agent psychological models, roles and communication. In *V-CROWDS '05: Proceedings of the First International Workshop on Crowd Simulation* (2005), pp. 24–25. 2

[PSKS04] PARK S. I., SHIN H. J., KIM T., SHIN S. Y.: On-line motion blending for real-time locomotion generation. *Computer Animation and Virtual Worlds 15*, 3 (2004), 125–138. 6

[Rey87] REYNOLDS C. W.: Flocks, herds and schools: A distributed behavioral model. In *SIGGRAPH '87: Proceedings of the 14th annual conference on Computer graphics and interactive techniques* (1987), pp. 25–34. 2

[SGC04] SUNG M., GLEICHER M., CHENNEY S.: Scalable behaviors for crowd simulation. *Computer Graphics Forum (Eurographics 2004) 23*, 3 (2004), 519–528. 2

[SKG05] SUNG M., KOVAR L., GLEICHER M.: Fast and accurate goal-directed motion synthesis for crowds. In *SCA '05: Proceedings of the 2005 ACM SIGGRAPH/Eurographics Symposium on Computer Animation* (2005), pp. 291–300. 2

[ST05] SHAO W., TERZOPOULOS D.: Autonomous pedestrians. In *SCA '05: Proceedings of the 2005 ACM SIGGRAPH/Eurographics symposium on Computer animation* (2005), pp. 19–28. 2

[Sti00] STILL G. K.: *Crowd Dynamics*. PhD thesis, University of Warwik, 2000. 3

[TCP06] TREUILLE A., COOPER S., POPOVIC Z.: Continuum crowds. *ACM Trans. Graph. 25*, 3 (2006), 1160–1168. 2

[Tek02] TEKNOMO K.: *Microscopic Pedestrian Flow Characteristics: Development of an Image Processing Data Collection and Simulation Model*. PhD thesis, Tohoku University, 2002. 3

[ZN04] ZHAO T., NEVATIA R.: Tracking multiple humans in crowded environment. *IEEE Computer Society Conference on Computer Vision and Pattern Recognition 2* (2004), 406–413. 2

Eurographics/ ACM SIGGRAPH Symposium on Computer Animation (2007)
D. Metaxas and J. Popovic (Editors)

A Decision Network Framework for the Behavioral Animation of Virtual Humans

Qinxin Yu[1,3] and Demetri Terzopoulos[2,3]

[1]Artificialife Inc., Montreal, QC, Canada
[2]University of California, Los Angeles, CA, USA
[3]University of Toronto, Toronto, ON, Canada

Abstract

We introduce a framework for advanced behavioral animation in virtual humans, which addresses the challenging open problem of simulating social interactions between pedestrians in urban settings. Based on hierarchical decision networks, our novel framework combines probability, decision, and graph theories for complex behavior modeling and intelligent action selection subject to manifold internal and external factors in the presence of uncertain knowledge. It yields autonomous characters that can make nontrivial interpretations and arrive at rational decisions dependent on multiple considerations. We demonstrate our framework in behavioral animation scenarios involving interacting autonomous pedestrians, including an elaborate emergency response animation.

1. Introduction

Creating autonomous characters with humanlike behaviors is a serious challenge. Our goal is to develop advanced behavioral systems for virtual humans. In particular, we address the level of decision-making that enables the characters to interact appropriately with their perceived environment, especially with other virtual humans. We focus on action selection; i.e., on simulating how humans decide what to do at any given time. To this end, we introduce a *decision network framework* for specifying and activating human behaviors that is easy to define and modify, scalable, and ostensibly emulates how people make decisions.

Uncertainty and complexity are characteristics of human behavior that make it especially difficult to simulate. Uncertainty has largely been ignored in prior behavior models, particularly uncertainty resulting from the natural limitations of perception, especially perception of the intentions of other people. Furthermore, no systematic approach has been proposed to deal with complexity. Our decision network framework addresses both issues. Decision networks are a generalization of Bayesian networks [Pea88], also known as probabilistic graphical models, which combine probability theory and graph theory to capture uncertain knowledge in a natural and efficient manner. An attractive feature of the decision network is that it is a powerful tool for modeling decision making under uncertainty. It provides an elegant and rigorous mathematical formalism for modeling complicated relationships among random variables and an intuitive visualization of these relationships as a graphical structure, thus facilitating comprehension and debugging. Furthermore, the modularity of a decision network facilitates the intuitive reduction of a complex behavior into manageable components.

Our work should not be misconstrued as yet another effort on so-called "crowd simulation." Our objectives differ. In particular, we are *not* interested in modeling multitudes of rather simple characters. Instead, we seek to develop complex autonomous individuals that, in addition to motor and perceptual components, include broad behavioral repertoires that are much more challenging to model. Our self-animating pedestrians can independently assess the interrelationships among all the relevant factors to make rational decisions in the presence of uncertainty. Hence, they are suitable for animating the detailed behavioral interactions of small social groups.

2. Related Work

Human modeling is a broad, multifaceted subject in computer graphics. The goal of our work is autonomous virtual humans that behave intelligently in complex, synthetic worlds [ST05]. To that end, we focus on human behavioral modeling. Since the introduction of behavioral animation by Reynolds [Rey87], researchers have pursued the ethological approach to modeling animal behaviors, where the autonomous character takes actions based on its inter-

Symposium on Computer Animation 2007, San Diego, CA, August 03-04, 2007.
© 2007 ACM 978-1-59593-624-4/07/0008 $5.00

nal state and its perceptual interpretation of external stimuli [TT94, BDI*02]. Human behavior, by far the most complex of animal behaviors, is the subject of multiple disciplines, including ethology, psychology, sociology, and anthropology. Our work addresses the human character's autonomy and interaction in its virtual environment, aside from natural verbal communication and dialog, nor do we consider the cognitive level of decision making, which concerns what a character knows, how that knowledge is acquired, and how it can be used to reason and plan actions [FTT99].

In the area of human behavioral animation, Musse and Thalmann [MT97] simulated crowd behavior using a rule-based system. Badler et al. [BAZB02] proposed a Parameterized Action Representation (PAR), which includes specifications for low-level animation concepts, and descriptions of primitive or complex actions, with action selection based on the conditions specified in the PAR structure.

Closer to our approach, Ball and Breese [BB00] encoded emotions and personality using Bayesian networks. Unlike our work, however, their emphasis was on conversational agents with speech recognition and generation. Kshirsagar and Thalmann [Ksh02] also used a Bayesian network to model personality and mood in a chat application, as did Egges et al. [EZKT03] to model mood in their conversational agent. The work closest to ours is that by Hy et al. [HABL04] who simulated simple behaviors for a first-person shooter game character by using a Bayesian network to specify finite-state-machine-like behavior selection, and to learn by imitating a human player. Unlike us, they did not simulate human interactions.

Although prior animation work and existing computer game titles have used finite state machines, fuzzy logic, neural nets, scripting, smart environments, and Bayesian networks, to our knowledge, ours is the first effort in computer graphics to develop and demonstrate a unified framework for behavioral animation based on *decision networks*. The decision network (or "influence diagram"), which was introduced by Howard and Matheson [HM81] in the area of decision analysis, combines probability theory and utility theory to provide a simple visual representation of a decision problem. Decision networks extend Bayesian networks by adding actions and utilities.

Compared with other common decision-making mechanisms such as fuzzy logic [Zad88] and neural networks [Bis95], or rule-based architectures [LNR87], decision networks offer the advantage of providing an intuitive yet rigorous way to identify and display the essential elements of the problem, including objectives, uncertainties, interpretations, and decisions, and how they influence each other, as well as the clear attribution of outcomes to the inputs that generated them. We assert that decision networks are significantly better able to simulate social interactions among autonomous pedestrians.

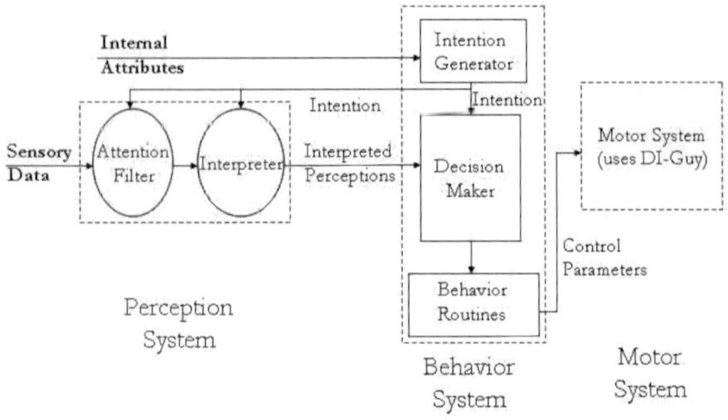

Figure 1: *Autonomous Virtual Pedestrian Model.*

3. Virtual Human Model

To evaluate our framework, we have implemented a virtual human model based on the software that was described in [ST05], including the environment model of the original Pennsylvania Train Station in New York City. Fig. 1 illustrates the architecture of our virtual pedestrian. Like real pedestrians, the synthetic humans sense their virtual environment, interpret the sensory stimuli, make decisions based on their perceptual interpretations, and act in accordance with their decisions. The important contribution of our human model is the behavior submodel, in which we exploit decision networks to simulate complex interactions between multiple pedestrians and to model the effect of different personalities on their decisions.

Each character acts autonomously within the virtual environment. To understand the structure of our system, let us consider an arbitrary character, say Jane. At any given time, Jane's intention generator assesses her current intention based on internal attributes and memory. Jane observes her surroundings to determine what objects are within her 180-degree field of view. The perceptual data Jane can gather by querying the environment model includes the position, speed, and orientation of objects in the environment, including other characters as well as their gaze directions.

Jane's attention mechanism guides her gaze depending on which objects are of interest given her current intention, or if an object attracts attention by making a sudden movement [EY97]. When Jane attends to a character she recognizes, or to a character with which she may be interested in interacting, or when there is a potential collision with some character, she draws inferences about the character using the interpreter in her perception system and decides how to interact with them. This decision making process is accomplished within our novel behavioral framework.

In particular, Jane is equipped with the new behavioral models that we develop in the next section. She also possesses a set of behavior routines that enable her to carry out primitive actions, such as walking to certain locations. Once an action selection decision is made, the relevant behavior routines are invoked to carry out the necessary actions. At a lower level, her motor system is responsible for carrying out the actual primitive movements such as walking and running. Her geometric body model and its primitive movements are provided by Boston Dynamics Inc.'s DI-Guy API.

Jane must remember the sequence of tasks she wants to perform. For this purpose, we implement a stack based memory in her behavior system, as was done in [ST05], enabling her to maintain persistence in her behaviors, while also adapting to the changing environment by storing new interim goals that attract her attention.

We have designed behavior routines to couple the decisions made at the behavioral level to the low-level DI-Guy motor system. Unfortunately, DI-Guy characters suffer limitations not just in their appearance but also in their motor skills, which restricts the possible motions that may be used in actions triggered by our decision network framework. For one character to interpret the behavior of another, it must make observations. Currently there are only a limited set of cues upon which our virtual humans can base their observations, since their facial expressions and gestures are highly constrained. The available cues include change in direction, change in speed, gaze direction [Pet05], and body orientation. Change in speed is an especially unreliable visual cue as DI-Guy characters cannot change their speed quickly.

4. Behavioral Modeling Using Decision Networks

Our new behavioral modeling approach employs decision networks as its core methodology. We have applied our decision network framework to the design of interaction models between virtual humans, guided by our commonsense knowledge of how real humans behave in similar circumstances. After motivating our framework in the next section, we present in subsequent sections four specific behavior models implemented within the framework—emergency response behavior, acquaintance behavior, partnering behavior, and collision avoidance behavior.

4.1. Decision Network Framework

A complex human behavior usually requires a sequence of assessments and decisions to be made. To model the behavior, the various contributing factors as well as their interrelationships must be identified, specified, and quantified. A decision network encodes events, represented by nodal variables, and causal relationships between them, represented by directed edges. This facilitates behavioral modeling as it is natural to think of behaviors as causal relations between events. A decision network computes rational decisions based on what the agent *wants* and what it *believes*, whereas a purely logical agent would not be able to handle uncertainty combined with conflicting goals [RN03].

We take advantage of the features of decision networks that address the key issues identified in Section 1. The uncertainties associated with various variables of interest are represented by the probability distributions encoded in the decision network. The decision network's powerful inferencing capability enables the explanation of observations made about the world, as well as predictions based on the evidence. The use of decision networks provides a convenient way to control how the character makes decisions. Adjusting the conditional probabilities and the utility functions will influence how the decision gets made. Another way to exert control is to adjust internal parameters, which will be monitored at simulation time by the network in order to make inferences and assessments.

In our application, not every decision need take all sensory and internal factors into consideration. To avoid the potential intractability of large decision networks, we build the behavioral model as a hierarchical set of relatively small decision networks. The hierarchical structure helps to ensure a manageable number of variables in each individual network and reusability of the functionality of component networks. At the lower level, a separate, smaller decision network structure is implemented for each decision item, while at higher level(s) the decision network structure at each node represents how a decision is made based on results from its children nodes. Decision network behavior models are also readily extensible, as we will demonstrate in Section 4.2.4.

Fortunately, there is no need to reinvent the wheel when applying decision networks. We use Netica (www.norsys.com), which is a commercial-quality implementation of Bayesian and decision networks along with a convenient GUI. It uses the junction tree algorithm to evaluate the networks and draw inferences. †

Applying our decision network framework, we have developed a set of networks that implement each of the four behavior models. Each network is responsible for drawing an inference or making a sub-decision that contributes to the final behavior. They are invoked only when there is a need to make the corresponding inference or decision.

4.2. Emergency Response Behavior

Our highest-level and most elaborate new behavior model is the emergency response behavior, which simulates how people might respond to an emergency situation in a public space like the train station. This behavior will serve as a concrete example to explain in detail how the decision networks are constructed, how the network parameters are adjusted and, subsequently, how we can obtain various possible decisions automatically from them and even extend them.

4.2.1. Network Construction

Our framework facilitates the application of commonsense knowledge. Regardless of the methodology that one uses to

† The role played by Netica, and DI-Guy for that matter, in our work is no different than the role played by, say, Matlab and Maya in many CG research projects. Netica serves simply as a software tool.

design a behavior model, it is natural for the designer to think in terms of what factors cause what effects, eventually leading to a decision underlying action selection. For human character animation, it often suffices to consider the various factors that contribute to making the appropriate decision in some real-life scenario. Since decision networks represent causal relationships, one can start the construction process by considering the root cause. Once we have determined the variables representing the factors we would like to consider and have understood the causal relationships among them, we effectively have designed the network topology. It then remains to complete the network by filling in the associated probability or utility values. Given sufficient data, it is possible in principle to train decision networks automatically. In modeling human behaviors, however, we often lack the necessary data to do so. Hence, we rely on intuition and common sense to tune the network parameters.

In particular, we approach the task of modeling how people respond to an emergency situation by considering their possible reactions when encountering such a situation. When someone collapses in a public place, for example, some people may approach to investigate, while others may prefer to avoid the situation and carry on with what they were doing. Of the people who do decide to approach the scene, the more concerned among them will run over, while the less concerned will walk. These will be the three possible intitial reactions from which our virtual pedestrian character can select.

Next, we consider the factors that affect this action selection decision. Three main factors come to mind: how serious the character thinks the situation is, how much the character wants to help others, and how courageous the character is. A timid character may shy away from an emergency situation in order to avoid confronting a potentially unpleasant scene at close range. Having identified these three factors, we simply use a random variable to represent each factor, and create a *chance node* (circle) for each variable, as shown in Fig. 2. The action selection decision is represented with a *decision node* (square). We also need to add a *utility node* (diamond) to indicate the character's preferences over the three input factors on the decision.

To complete the network, we must define the *prior probabilities* for the three chance nodes (upper table). The seriousness of the situation must be assessed, so its value should be set based on the interpretation result. To keep the network structure modular and hierarchical, the interpretation result can be obtained from a separate network. The prior probabilities for the Help and Courage nodes are set directly based on the character's internal factors and personality, which are represented on a continuous scale from 0.0 to 1.0. The *utility table* entries (lower table) are set based on our intuition about the character's preference over the three possible actions given the state of the input factors. For example, for a strong, helpful character, when the situation is considered serious, the character is most likely to run over and investigate, less likely to walk over and check out the situation, and least likely to ignore it. The corresponding utility values are

P(Serious)		P(Help)		P(Courage)	
yes	no	yes	no	s	w
sr	1.0-sr	he	1.0-he	n	1.0-n

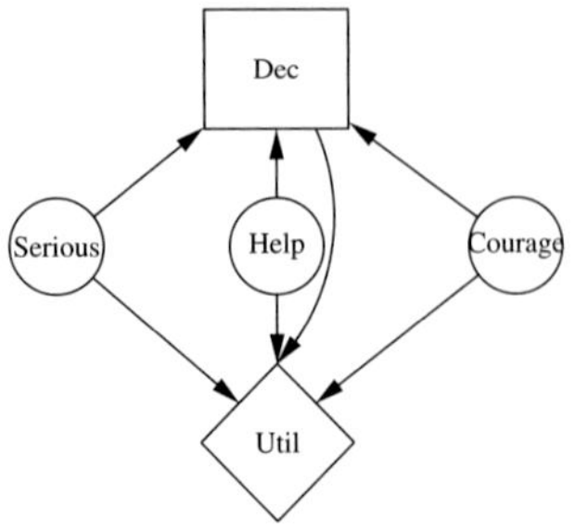

Serious=*yes*				Serious=*no*			
Help	Courage	Dec	Util	Help	Courage	Dec	Util
yes	s	ig	-10	yes	s	ig	-5
yes	s	run	8	yes	s	run	5
yes	s	obs	6	yes	s	obs	3
yes	w	ig	-8	yes	w	ig	3
yes	w	run	6	yes	w	run	2
yes	w	obs	7	yes	w	obs	4
no	s	ig	1	no	s	ig	5
no	s	run	3	no	s	run	1
no	s	obs	5	no	s	obs	2
no	w	ig	3	no	w	ig	6
no	w	run	1	no	w	run	0
no	w	obs	2	no	w	obs	2

Figure 2: *Network to determine how to respond to the emergency. Variable values s: strong, w: weak, ig: ignore, run: run over to check, obs: walk over to check.*

P(Serious)	
yes	no
0.5	0.5

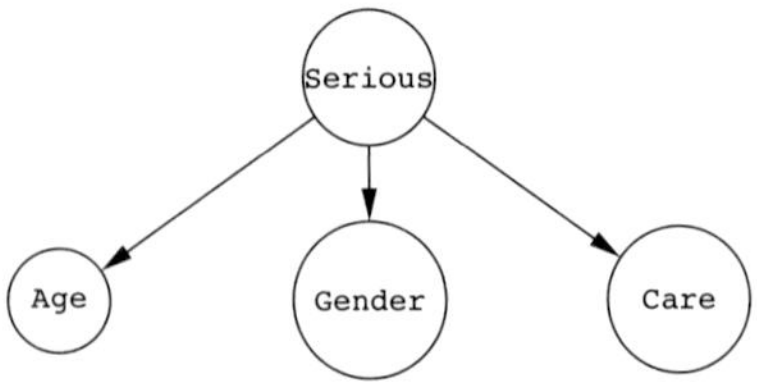

	P(Age)			P(Gender)		P(Care)	
Serious	y	p	o	male	female	yes	no
yes	0.3	0.2	0.5	0.3	0.7	0.9	0.1
no	0.3	0.5	0.2	0.7	0.3	0.1	0.9

Figure 3: *Network to assess the seriousness of the situation. Variable values: y: young, p: prime age, o: old.*

accordingly set for this input combination, with the highest utility assigned to the run action, since the network evaluation will choose the action with the highest utility value.

The Serious node represents the character's interpretation of the emergency scene that it is observing. This interpretation process is captured by a separate network (Fig. 3). Similar to the construction of the network of Fig. 2, we create a chance node for each of the cues people look for when encountering such a scenario in real life, and which are also observable in our characters given their limited DI-Guy motor system. In our current implementation, we selected the

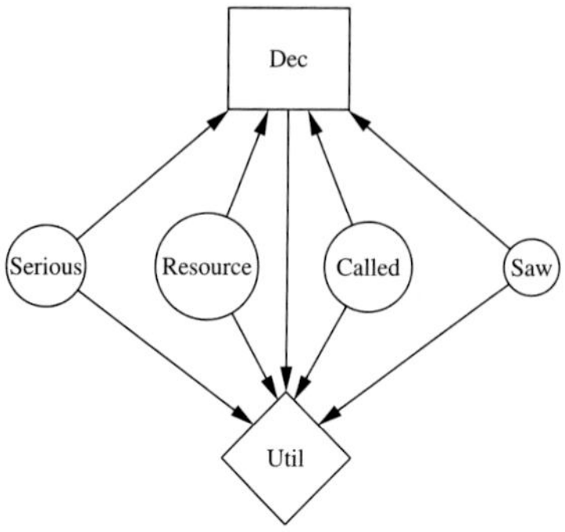

Figure 4: *Network to decide if should go fetch a police officer.*

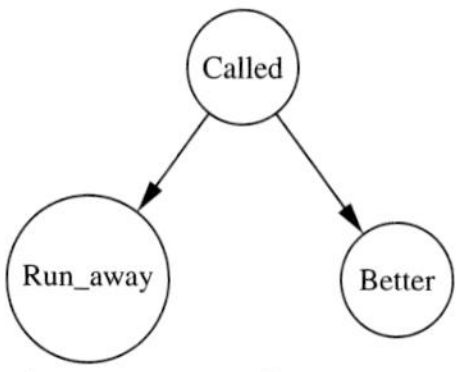

Figure 5: *Network to assess if someone else is calling the police.*

age and gender of the patient, and how caring the character is about others. The conditional probabilities are set based on the seriousness judgment and the chances that the corresponding cues will be observed.

The aforementioned procedure constructs the networks needed to decide the initial reaction to an emergency situation. Among the characters who have chosen to investigate, some may decide to seek assistance using the decision network shown in Fig. 4. This decision depends on how serious the character regards the situation and how resourceful the character is in finding help, including whether or not the character has noticed a law enforcement officer earlier and can estimate the officer's current location, and the character's assessment of whether someone else is already seeking assistance. This assessment is made by observing whether another character is running away from the emergency scene and if it seems likely that the character can summon help more quickly (Fig. 5).

Some characters may choose to leave the scene after being present for some time and unable to do much to help, a decision process implemented by the network of Fig. 6. The contributing factors include how impatient the character is, if the character is in a hurry, the time that it has been idling at the scene, if someone is already summoning help, and how altruistic the character is.

Thus, we have constructed all the networks that our virtual characters use to decide how to respond to emergency situations. The probability and utility parameters are set based on the designer's intuitions, but they may need to be fine-tuned to truly reflect how the designer wants the characters to make decisions. The next section describes the tuning process.

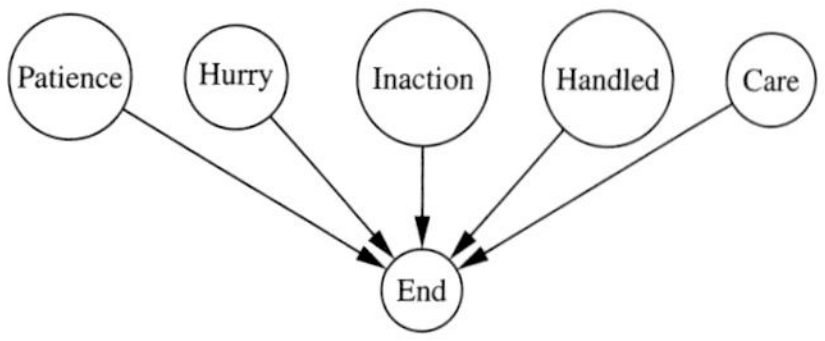

Figure 6: *Network for deciding to end the emergency response behavior.*

4.2.2. Adjustment of Network Parameters

Each network can be tested separately to ensure that its parameter settings allow it to make reasonable decisions in accordance with the designer's intentions. Netica provides a GUI for defining and evaluating the networks. Therefore, once the networks have been constructed, one can easily fine tune the parameters through the GUI by testing various values and assessing the corresponding network evaluation results in order to make the necessary adjustments.

Since our framework makes it easy to trace how a conclusion is drawn, when we see an undesirable result, we can quickly identify the cause and fix it. For example, consider the network of Fig. 3. Suppose that we initially assigned $P(\text{Care} = \mathit{yes} \,|\, \text{Serious} = \mathit{yes}) = 0.6$ and $P(\text{Care} = \mathit{yes} \,|\, \text{Serious} = \mathit{no}) = 0.4$. Trying the input combination of a male patient in his prime and a fully caring character, the situation is interpreted to be not serious. This is undesirable, since we want the caring character to consider the case serious even when the patient is a male in his prime. This evaluation result indicates that we have not given enough influence to the Care variable and need to increase the probability of its value being *yes* when the situation is serious, and similarly increase the probability of its value being *no* when the situation is not serious. Setting $P(\text{Care} = \mathit{yes} \,|\, \text{Serious} = \mathit{yes}) = 0.9$ and $P(\text{Care} = \mathit{yes} \,|\, \text{Serious} = \mathit{no}) = 0.1$ yields desirable results.

In our experience, the probabilities need not be set precisely for the decision process to work well; a range of parameter values will usually work. Fine tuning the parameters in this way is a quick and intuitive process. Given the same network structure, by modifying various conditional probability and utility parameter settings, the behavior designer can create a variety of characters that will decide to take quite different actions when faced with the same internal and external factors, even "irrational characters" if that is what the designer wants.

4.2.3. Network Capabilities

Our decision network framework includes theoretically sound inference algorithms. They make interpretations based on the evidence collected, including uncertain evidence. Once the networks have been constructed, corresponding decisions based on various input combinations are automatically generated. Regardless of the number of influencing factors and how many possible states each factor can take, for every possible combination the network is able to draw a corresponding conclusion by executing the inference algorithm.

Input factors include observations made about the character's external environment and the character's own internal factors and personality traits. Differences in these factors lead to different decisions. There can be many possible input factor combinations, but the same networks can automatically accommodate them. In the network of Fig. 2, all the input factors are binary. When we know for certain which state they are in, they are entered as *hard evidence*. However, most of the time, these factors are not strictly in one state or another. For example, the assessment of seriousness that comes from the network of Fig. 3 is represented with probability values to indicate different degrees of seriousness. In the real world, people can vary in their willingness to help others and their level of courage. In our network, these assessments can be represented on a continuous scale from 0.0 to 1.0, rather than as binary variables, and entered as the prior probability for their corresponding nodes. Different degrees of various personality traits may lead to different decisions. The network is capable of drawing inferences and making decisions incorporating these uncertainties and various other parameter inputs.

4.2.4. Network Extension

Since our framework supports a modular representation, it is easy to make extensions. When we need to add a new factor to be considered in a decision process, all we need do is add a node for it in the corresponding network and add the associated links to indicate its relationship with existing nodes. We must also add the associated conditional probabilities for the new node and make the necessary adjustments to nodes affected by the node addition.

For example, suppose we want to consider the effect of emotion on the emergency response behavior. A depressed character that is feeling low may lose interest in other things, including helping others. This would involve adding to the network of Fig. 2 a new chance node, Depress, which represents the state of depression, and links from it to the utility and decision nodes, since it is also an input factor for the decision process. Under the assumption that when the character is not depressed, it should act the same as before the inclusion of this new emotional factor, then the utility values when Depress = *no* should remain the same, and we need only update the utility values when Depress = *yes*. Given this extended network, with the same seriousness assessment and the same helpfulness and courage for the character, it will decide to ignore the incident instead of walk over to the scene.

The hierarchical structure of our networks keeps the scale of addition and modification to associated probability and utility settings manageable. For example, suppose that we want to model multiple emotional factors. We can reduce the number of entries that must be added to the utility table by building a subnetwork, where the overall effect from the emotional components is assessed first, and then only add that effect to the utility table. Hence, extension can be easily accomplished within our framework as the changes needed are isolated to the concerned network(s), with the addition of the corresponding nodes and links.

4.3. Acquaintance Behavior

Interpretation becomes more important in interactions between pedestrians. For example, when two pedestrians who know each other meet on the street, how they react to one another depends not only on their own intentions, but also on their interpretation of what the other pedestrian will do. We have developed an acquaintance behavior model to simulate this interaction. When two characters meet, they will choose among talking to each other, acknowledging one another without stopping to chat, or ignoring one another. For the acquaintance model, two pedestrians will not talk with each other unless both are willing to talk; hence, a reasonably accurate interpretation is needed.

Character A's interpretation of character B's intention is divided into an assessment of whether or not B is just starting to do something with A (showing an intention to talk, or to greet), or was already in the process of doing something with A, as they exhibit different cues. When B is just starting to do something with A, it would most likely be looking at A; if it wants to talk with A, it would most likely start to walk towards A and slow down. The absence of these cues is evidence that B intends to ignore A. When B is in the process of carrying out its intended action with A—for example, trying to talk with A—it may already be in the course of walking towards A, hence need not change direction at the moment. The prerequisite is that the previous interpretation already indicated that B had the intention of doing a certain action with A.

The difficulty in making such an interpretation is further complicated by the fact that B may intend to do something with A, but is temporarily interrupted by the need to avoid collision. Hence, an assessment is required first of whether or not B is in collision avoidance mode. Such an assessment is made based on change in direction, change in speed, whether B is facing some obstacles, and determination of whether B is just starting to avoid collision or is in the middle of collision avoidance. B talking with a third party will also prevent it from talking with A. Figs. 7, 8, and 9 show the networks for interpreting B's action at the moment, whether it be meeting with others, avoiding collision, or just walking.

Once this observation is made, further decisions are made based on its result. If the interpreted action for B is talking with another character, no further action is taken (in future work, we may implement the possibility of A joining the conversation). If B is in the middle of avoiding a collision, the previous interpretation for B was maintained. In the absence of any special action detection, A will continue to assess B's intention (Fig. 10). In addition, A evaluates its own intended action based on how friendly it is with B, if it is in a hurry, and how much it desires to greet or talk to B.

The decision network which determines the action to be taken is depicted in Fig. 11. The distance factor is added since the character may be uncertain about the interpretation and, hence, may take several time steps to decide. In the meantime, it is not committing to any action. However, as the two characters approach each other to within a certain threshold, a decision must be made based on information available at the time. The distance factor here indicates if such a threshold has been met. The utility function is a balance among the internal desire and the interpreted intention of the other party. The decision can take on the value of talk, greet, or ignore the other party, or uncertain, which means further observation is necessary.

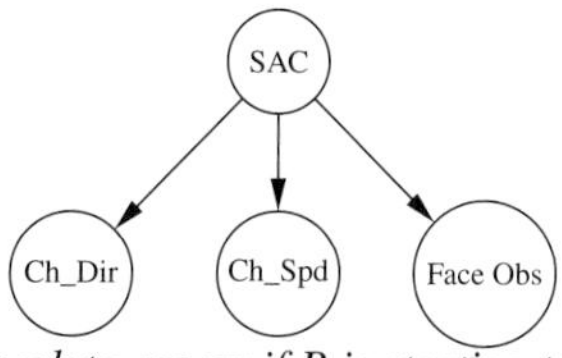

Figure 7: *Network to assess if B is starting to avoid a collision.*

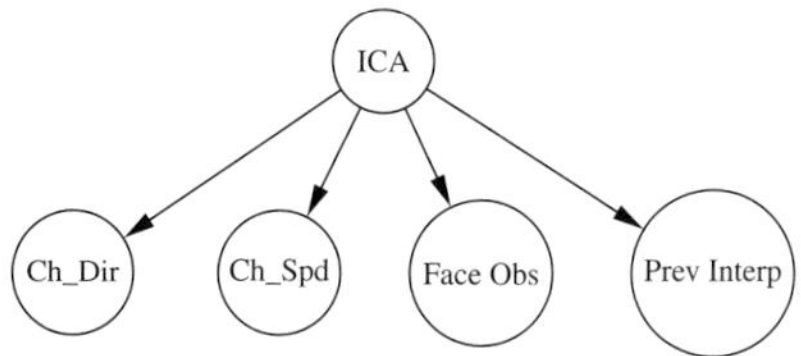

Figure 8: *Network to assess if B is already in collision avoidance.*

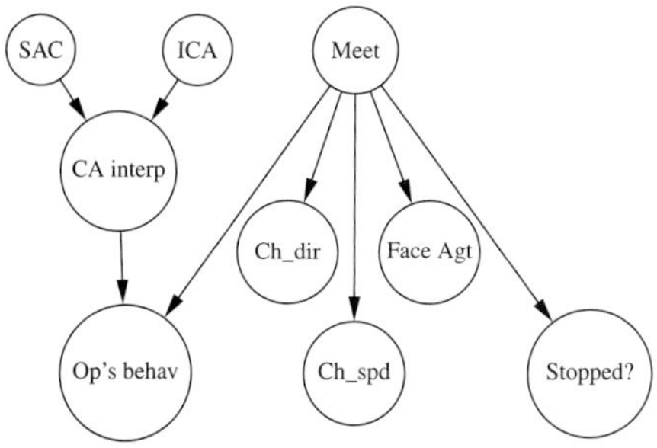

Figure 9: *Network to interpret B's behavior.*

4.4. Partnering Behavior

It is quite natural for friends meeting unexpectedly to form partnerships if circumstances permit. We have developed a partnering model to simulate such behavior. There are several possible scenarios. When one character sees another friend character ahead, it needs to decide whether to catch up and try to partner with that character; then the other character must decide whether to accept the advance. When two characters meet on the street, they may have a chat and then decide if they want to partner. In the first case, the initiating character A must first decide if it wants to catch up and form

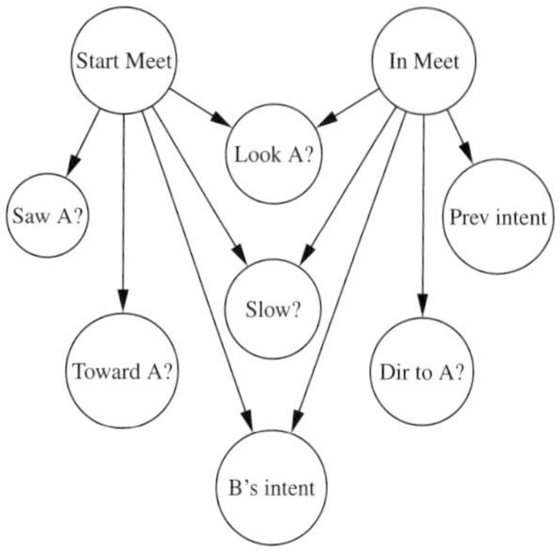

Figure 10: *Network to interpret character B's intended action with A.*

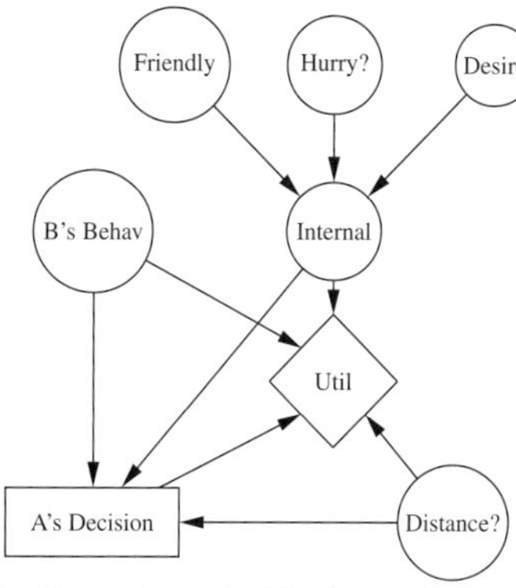

Figure 11: *Network to decide the action to be taken by A with B.*

a partnership with character B in view. This decision must take into consideration A's intention, personality, if A feels its goal matches that of B, and its perception of B's intention. Fig. 12 shows the decision network for deciding whether or not to form a partnership with the potential partner.

Once A decides to form a partnership with B in view, it will try to catch up and express its partnership request. B must then decide whether to accept this request. As shown in Fig. 13, how friendly B feels about A, if B is social, and B's desire all affect the decision. In addition, how persistent B is in pursuing its own intention and how long A has persisted in making the advance also play a role in B's reaction.

As B makes up its mind, A is observing B and tries to assess if B has accepted its advance (Fig. 14). Not all observed data have equal reliability. For example, when trying to interpret B's response to character A's request to partner, B looking at A and stopping are much stronger indications than B turning to face A. When B accepts A's request, B may or may not choose to face A directly. To accommodate this difference in reliability of the observed data, some adjustments are made in the network; hence, the additional reliability chance node (Fig. 14).

If B accepts A's request, the two characters will form a pair and proceed. Should B refuse the request, A must then

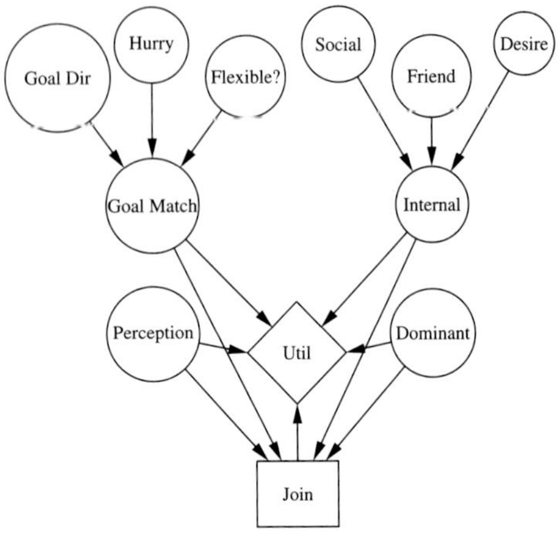

Figure 12: *Network to decide whether to form a partnership.*

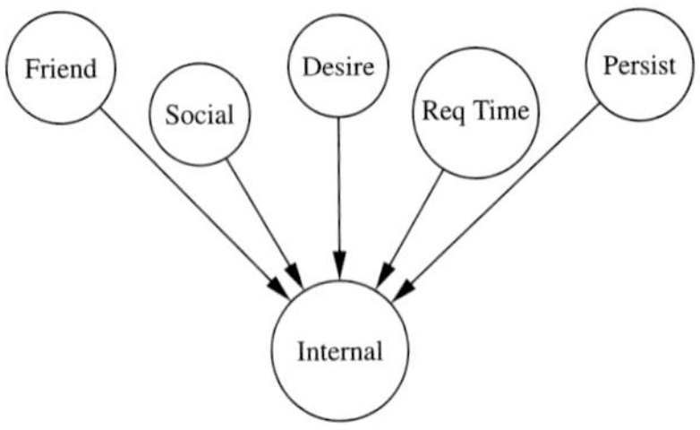

Figure 13: *Network to assess whether to accept a partnering request.*

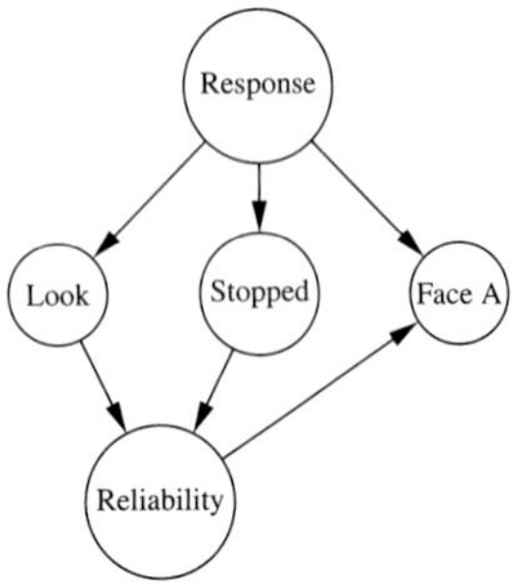

Figure 14: *Network to interpret B's response to A's pair-up request.*

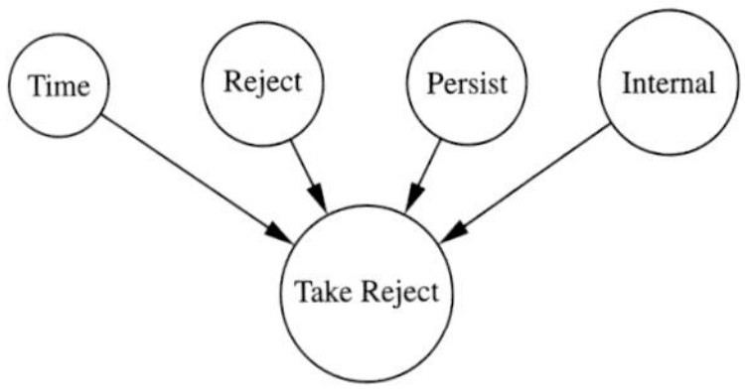

Figure 15: *Network to assess how to take rejection.*

decide how it will react to the rejection; i.e., give up or continue its persuasion effort (Fig. 15). This cycle of A making a request, B deciding whether to accept it, A's interpretation of B's response, and decision about what to do next continues until either B is persuaded to accept the partnership offer or A gives up. Once a partnership is formed, negotiation continues between the partners to maintain the partnership and handle unexpected events, such as collision threats, and making decisions together as a team.

4.5. Collision Avoidance Behavior

Our framework is also applicable to low-level collision avoidance behavior modeling. Much behavioral animation research has focused on collision avoidance. Our framework incorporates the interpretation of the opposing character's avoidance intention, which is absent in earlier models. Our model implements a local object avoidance strategy rather than global path finding.

The character first tries to avoid any static obstacles. The avoidance strategy includes the options of steering to the left, steering to the right, or stopping when in imminent danger of collision. As for dynamic obstacles, a collision possibility value is computed for each obstacle and the one with the highest value assumes priority for avoidance. The optimal avoidance strategy can be one of the following: no avoidance, speed up, slow down, stop, steer towards left, steer towards right, steer towards left with speed change, steer towards right with speed change, stop while steering towards left, and stop while steering towards right. Due to the limitations of the motor system, where a speed change command has a delayed effect, currently we do not use the speed change options, but have left them in place in case a better motor system becomes available. The utility values are weights associated with the avoidance strategy options, which are determined by our observations of how real humans balance avoidance choices under different circumstances.

The details of our collison avoidance decision networks are presented elsewhere [Yu07].

5. Animation Results

We have equipped our virtual humans with the aforementioned behavior models which take advantage of our decision network framework's ability to handle uncertainty and behavioral complexity. As described above, the collision avoidance model anticipates the opposing character's avoidance strategy and makes a decision accordingly. In addition to simulating the interpretations that a character draws about its environment and about its potential partner's intentions, the acquaintance, partnership, and emergency response models also take into account the effect that personality and internal factors have on decision making. Decisions are made based on observations and the analysis of objects that fall within the character's focus of attention. Our accompanying animations demonstrate the effectiveness of our decision network framework.

Our most complex animation is the "emergency response" animation illustrated in Fig. 16. A young female commuter

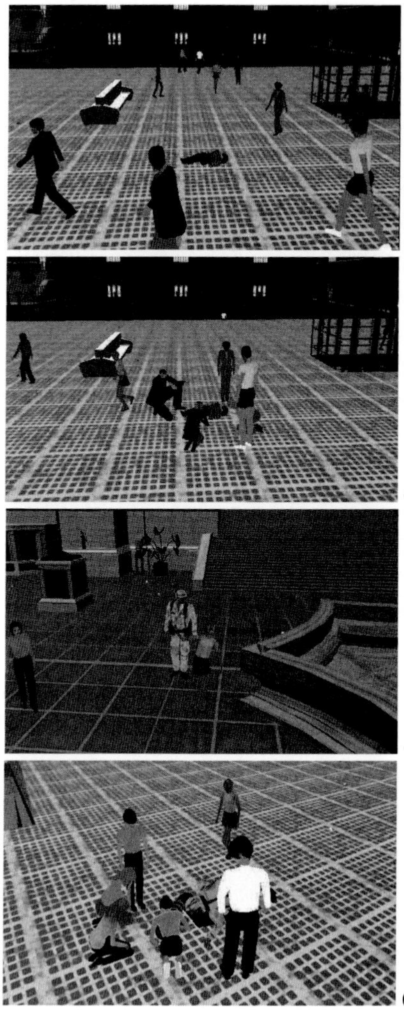

Figure 16: *Still frames from the emergency response animation. (a) Female fainted on floor in concourse. (b) Commuters gather around to attend to patient; a woman runs for help. (c) Woman finds a security officer in the main waiting room. (d) The officer attends to the patient.*

feels ill, staggers, and then faints to the floor of the concourse area in the virtual Penn Station. Some commuters around her turn their heads to look, but keep on walking. Others walk over to see what happened. The most concerned run over to investigate. After observing the patient's situation, a female commuter recalls seeing a security officer in the main waiting room of the station and, hoping that he is still there, decides to run over to ask for help. While she is gone, some of the commuters attending to the patient decide to leave as they determine that they cannot do much more given that someone has already gone to summon assistance, while some new passers-by approach to investigate the scene. The security officer who was summoned eventually reaches the scene, examines the patient and decides to radio paramedics for further assistance.

Shorter simulations demonstrate the functionality of the partnering behavior model, differing only by internal factor and personality settings. One animation shows pedestrian A eventually giving up on the decision to partner with B, after repeatedly being shunned by B. A second animation shows a pedestrian A who notices a friend B walking ahead, catches up, and tries to partner with B. Because of an earlier quarrel with A, B initially refuses A's advance, but reconsiders upon A's insistence.

Our framework is efficient. The network with the largest utility table takes from 1 to 2 msec to build and compile in Netica and usually less than 1 msec to evaluate. The emergency response network takes about 1 msec to compile and 1 msec to evaluate. At run time, the behavior models are event triggered—i.e., whenever the circumstances trigger certain behaviors, the corresponding networks are evaluated to make the necessary decisions, but they are invoked only on a need-to-use basis. Collision detection takes place every few time steps, but the collision avoidance networks are invoked only when a potential collision is detected. These networks are invoked the most frequently. Each character independently makes its own decisions based on what it can observe of its environment and its personal internal factors. Although different execution times are needed to arrive at different decisions, this does not adversely affect the parallel simulation of different characters. On an Intel Xeon 3.2GHz PC with 1GB RAM, the behavior system for a single pedestrian usually takes under 1 millisecond to execute.

6. Conclusion

We have introduced a decision network framework for advanced behavioral animation in virtual humans. To our knowledge, ours is the first virtual human behavior modeling system and architecture that is based on decision networks, and the first use of decision networks in computer graphics. Our decision network framework offers several advantages. It has the ability to handle uncertainties, which are largely ignored in previous behavior models. Having the characters act based on the often imprecise interpretation of their surroundings rather than on exact information gained through querying the world database results in more realistic simulations that more faithfully approximate how real people behave. This also facilitates the simulation of interactions between characters.

Because decision networks offer a formal yet easy to understand representation of the world and the behavior system, our framework makes it easier to translate the character designer's commonsense knowledge into code that governs the characters' decisions. It facilitates parameter fine-tuning and debugging, and makes it easy to identify what factors contribute to the final decision. Modifications take only minutes to complete, as the structure is so clear, compact, and modular. Given the same network topology, we can have characters reasoning and acting quite differently by specifying different probability and utility settings. Decision networks also make the behavioral model flexible and able to respond sensibly to a wide range of changes in the character's internal and external environment. Our results demonstrate the effectiveness of our framework. Its hierarchical structure keeps computational complexity at bay, and its clarity provides insights into behavioral mechanisms while facilitating the design, implementation, and debugging of behaviors. The network construction and parameter adjustment took less than a day of effort for each of our behavior models.

Although our decision network framework is general and largely independent of the underlying motor system, the specific behavior models we have built rely on the limited cues that our virtual humans can observe about one another to arrive at interpretations. As better motion APIs become available that provide a richer variety of human-like visual cues, more varied and accurate interpretations will be possible and the quality of the behavior model will improve.

Decision networks are not suitable for handling domains with co-related decision factors [Jen01], as the large computational requirements for such domains would make it intractable to handle complex problems. Given its acyclic nature, the decision network is also not appropriate for modeling behaviors that involve cyclic causal chains or recursive plans. One way to resolve this is to use dynamic decision networks which handle time series of decision problems by regarding causation as a temporal phenomenon.

In future work, we plan to expand our interaction models to simulate more sophisticated coordination and cooperation behaviors among multiple characters. We would also like to develop an intuitive user interface to facilitate the graphical construction of behavior models, enabling the user to input parameters that specify personality traits and internal factors on the fly; these values will be entered as evidence to the behavior models so that the simulation will immediately reflect the changes.

Acknowledgements

We would like to thank Wei Shao for kindly providing his software system for use in our research. We also thank Hanieh Bastani, Sam Hasinoff, and Mike Daum for their voice acting for the animation audio tracks, which are dramatizations of what the characters might say were they able to speak.

References

[BAZB02] BADLER N. I., ALLBECK J. M., ZHAO L., BYUN M.: Representing and parameterizing agent behaviors. In *Computer Animation* (2002), pp. 133–143.

[BB00] BALL G., BREESE J.: Emotion and personality in a conversational character. In *Embodied Conversational Agents* (2000), MIT Press, Cambridge, MA, pp. 189–219.

[BDI*02] BLUMBERG B., DOWNIE M., IVANOV Y., BERLIN M., JOHNSON M. P., TOMLINSON B.: Integrated learning for interactive synthetic characters. In *Proc. ACM SIGGRAPH 02* (San Antonio, TX, 2002), pp. 417–426.

[Bis95] BISHOP C. M.: *Neural Networks for Pattern Recognition*. Oxford University Press, Oxford, UK, 1995.

[EY97] EGETH H. E., YANTIS S.: Visual attention: Control, representation, and time course. *Annu. Rev. Psychology 4* (1997), 269–297.

[EZKT03] EGGES A., ZHANG X., KSHIRSAGAR S., THALMANN N. M.: Emotional communication with virtual humans. In *Multimedia Modelling* (Taiwan, 2003).

[FTT99] FUNGE J., TU X., TERZOPOULOS D.: Cognitive modeling: Knowledge, reasoning and planning for intelligent characters. In *Proc. ACM SIGGRAPH 99* (Los Angeles, CA, 1999), pp. 29–38.

[HABL04] HY R. L., ARRIGONI A., BESSIÈRE P., LEBELTEL O.: Teaching bayesian behaviours to video game characters. *Robotics and Autonomous Systems 47*, 3 (2004), 177–185.

[HM81] HOWARD R., MATHESON J.: Influence diagrams. *In Howard, R. and Matheson, J., editors, Readings on the Principles and Applications of Decision Analysis II* (1981), 721–762.

[Jen01] JENSEN F. V.: Bayesian networks and decision graphs. In *Bayesian networks and decision graphs*. Springer, 2001.

[Ksh02] KSHIRSAGAR S.: A multilayer personality model. In *Proceedings of the 2nd interna-tional symposium on Smart graphics* (2002), pp. 107–115.

[LNR87] LAIRD J. E., NEWELL A., ROSENBLOOM P. S.: Soar: An architecture for general intelligence. *Artif. Intell. 33*, 1 (1987), 1–64.

[MT97] MUSSE S. R., THALMANN D.: A model of human crowd behavior: Group inter-relationship and collision detection analysis. In *Computer Animation and Simulation '97, Proc. EG Workshop* (Budapest, 1997), Springer-Verlag, pp. 39–52.

[Pea88] PEARL J.: *Probabilistic Reasoning in Intelligent Systems: Networks of Plausible Inference*. Morgan Kaufman, San Mateo, CA, 1988.

[Pet05] PETERS C.: Foundations for an agent theory of mind model for conversation initiation in virtual environments. In *Proceedings of the AISB '05 symposium on Virtual Social Agents: Mind-Minding Agents* (Hatfield, England, 2005).

[Rey87] REYNOLDS C.: Flocks, herds, and schools: A distributed behavioral model. *Proceedings of ACM Computer Graphics 21*, 4 (Jul 1987), 25–33.

[RN03] RUSSELL S., NORVIG P.: *Artificial Intelligence - A Modern Approach*. Prentice Hall, Englewood Cliffs, NJ, 2003.

[ST05] SHAO W., TERZOPOULOS D.: Autonomous pedestrians. In *Proc. SIGGRAPH/EG Symposium on Computer Animation (SCA'05)* (Los Angeles, CA, July 2005), pp. 19–28.

[TT94] TU X., TERZOPOULOS D.: Artificial fishes: Physics, locomotion, perception, behavior. *Computer Graphics (Proc. SIGGRAPH'94)* (1994), 43–50.

[Yu07] YU Q.: *A Decision Network Framework for the Behavioral Animation of Virtual Humans*. PhD thesis, Department of Computer Science, University of Toronto, Toronto, ON, Canada, January 2007.

[Zad88] ZADEH L. A.: Fuzzy logic. *Computer 21*, 4 (April 1988), 83–93.

Eurographics/ ACM SIGGRAPH Symposium on Computer Animation (2007)
D. Metaxas and J. Popovic (Editors)

Kinodynamic skinning using volume-preserving deformations

Alexis Angelidis[†] and Karan Singh[‡]

Department of Computer Science
University of Toronto

Abstract

We present a new approach to character skinning where divergence-free vector fields induced by skeletal motion, describe the velocity of skin deformation. The joint transformations for a pose relative to a rest pose create a bend deformation field, resulting in pose-dependent or kinematic skin deformations, varying smoothly across joints. The bend deformation parameters are interactively controlled to capture the varying deformability of bone and other anatomic tissue within an overall fold-over free and volume-preserving skin deformation. Subsequently, we represent the dynamics of skeletal motion, tissue elasticity, muscular tension and the environment as forces that are mapped to vortices at tissue interfaces. A simplified Biot-Savart law in the context of elastic deformation recovers a divergence-free velocity field from the vorticity. Finally, we apply a new stable technique to efficiently integrate points along their deformation trajectories. Adding these dynamic forces over a window of time prior to a given pose provides a continuum of user controllable kinodynamic skinning. A comprehensive implementation using a typical animator workflow in Maya *shows our approach to be effective for complex character skinning.*

Categories and Subject Descriptors (according to ACM CCS): I.3.3 [Computer Graphics]: Character Skinning

1. Introduction

Character modeling and setup is a tedious process. Digital character geometry in a rest or bind pose is first created from artist sketches and maquettes. This geometry specifies both the external appearance of the character skin and implicitly embodies an underlying anatomy. The subsequent challenging problem of constructing a mapping from articulations of an underlying skeletal hierarchy to a deformation of the skin geometry is referred to as *character skinning* (see Figures 1,2). Skin deformations need to be generally smooth, intersection-free and computationally efficient. Furthermore, they need to capture variations in surface shape resulting from the dynamic shape and material properties of the implicit underlying anatomy. Bulging, creasing, sagging and dynamic secondary motion are examples of the visual impact underlying anatomy has on the surface of skin [CHP89]. A skinned character rigged for animation is ready to come to life in able hands. The skill of the animator, however, is transmitted through the character rig and can be completely destroyed by unconvincing skin deformations.

A popular technique in deformable object simulation is to separate the overall deformation into rigid and deformable components [PCLS05]. Such approaches are well-suited to character skins where the non-rigid deformation of the skin is small relative to the overall articulation of the character. Perhaps a more animator appropriate separation is based on differentials of character pose (see Figure 1). We refer to skin deformations that are purely a function of the skeletal pose as *kinematic* skinning. Deformations resulting from higher order time derivatives of skeletal pose and other dynamic forces are referred to as *dynamic* skinning. Kinematic skinning mostly comprises the articulated rigid body transformation of anatomy. We do, however, include pose dependent deformations such as bone protrusion, skin creasing around joints and the volume-preserving bulging resulting from active and passive contraction of tense muscle. Dynamic skinning captures the elastic tissue deformations generated by the character's skeletal motion and other environmental forces. In commercial practice, skinning is almost always kinematic since true dynamic skinning requires a temporal simulation to determine the skin shape and this impairs

[†] e-mail: silex@pixar.com
[‡] e-mail: karan@dgp.toronto.edu

Symposium on Computer Animation 2007, San Diego, CA, August 03-04, 2007.
© 2007 ACM 978-1-59593-624-4/07/0008 $5.00

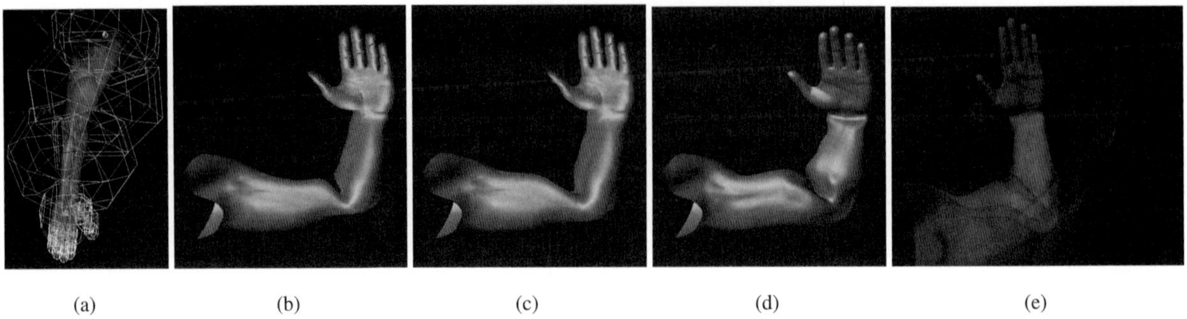

Figure 1: *Kinodynamic skinning: The undeformed skin setup in the bind pose (a), is kinematically skinned traditionally (b), with volume-preservation (c), and bone, tissue, and contracted muscle (d) and with elastic muscle dynamics (in flesh tone)(e).*

an animator's interactive control over the character [LCF00]. As a result dynamic skinning effects are usually added as needed post-hoc.

Motivation: A number of traditional deformation principles [TJ81] are applicable to character skinning. To a first approximation the skin behaves like an articulated rigid body. Particularly in the region around joints, however, it is visually important that the deformation is smooth and foldover-free (see Figure 1b). Clothing, fur and muscle dynamics are often modeled as physical simulations, for which self-intersection free skin geometry is a desirable property. Volume-controllable skin is also desirable since anatomic tissue and cavities, while largely volume-preserving are indeed selectively compressible. The skin should locally capture the deformation behavior of underlying bone, soft tissue (see Figure 1c) or contracting muscle (see Figure 1d). Finally, much of a character's visual appeal lies in the dynamic secondary motion of elastic anatomic tissue induced by skeletal motion and other external forces (see Figure 1e). We also observe that most dynamic skin deformations are localized in time around forces induced by skeletal motion due to strong elastic restorative forces and damping. This temporally local property of dynamic skinning makes it both possible and desirable to incorporate the effects of dynamic skinning in an animator interactive setting.

Approach: We first choose a deformation framework that addresses our character skinning goals. Divergence-free vector fields that define the deformation trajectory of points in space are foldover-free and volume-preserving [ACWK04], [vFTS06]. We thus use this fundamental property to specify all elements of skin deformation. The smooth, foldover-free, articulated rigid body like behavior is clearly the most signicant aspect of skinning. We address this in the context of traditional linear-blend skinning by developing a closed form solution to the integration of deformation trajectories. Bending around joints induces a divergence-free deformation velocity as shown by [vFTS06]. We show how this deformation can be decomposed into our closed form skinning solution overlaid with a numerically integrated volume-preserving term. The bend deformation can be decomposed into the cross product of the gradient of two scalar fields [vFTS06]. We show how user control over the coefficients [Kot91] of this decomposition allows the local modeling of bone and soft tissue behavior, while preserving an overall divergence-free field. We then model anatomic tissue and muscle dynamics using a sampling of vorticity under the skin. The velocity field of these vortices is divergence-free by construction [ACWK04] and captures the animator desired effects of musculoskeletal dynamics. The overall system is interactive and homogenous in its approach to skin deformation and allows us to perform *kinodynamic* skinning, where dynamic effects resulting over a user defined window of time prior to the present can be incorporated into our kinematic skinning workflow in real-time (see Figure 4).

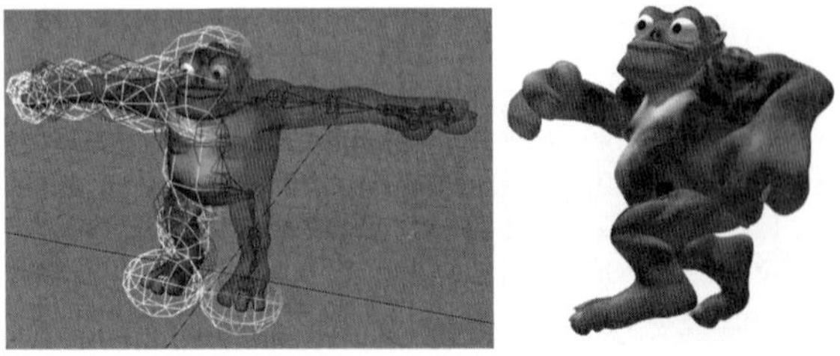

Figure 2: *A large implicit anatomy between skin and skeleton here makes skinning challenging. The troll is shown overlaid with ellipsoidal primitives capturing anatomic tissue in the bind pose and the subsequent skinned result.*

Contributions: The chief contribution of this paper is a character skinning system that is fold-over free and volume-preserving, captures anatomic tissue properties and interactively captures both kinematic and dynamic skinning with a traditional character rigging workflow. In the construction of this system we first describe a new analytic solution to fold-over free linear blend skinning. We also adapt the Clebsch decomposition of the bend deformation of [vFTS06] to account for the varying rigidity of bone and other anatomic tissue under the skin. We further describe a novel approach to dynamic volume-preserving object deformation based on vortex samples. We propose an efficient and stable integration of these vector fields that describe skin deformations discretized over pose-space, time or both in a kinodynamic setting. The techniques presented here are implemented as a *Maya* plug-in and seamlessly integrate into a typical character rigging process.

2. Related Work

Approaches to character skinning and more generally object deformation can be broadly classified as geometric or physically based. In the context of skinning many approaches further incorporate anatomic elements of varying sophistication.

Animators continue to prefer interactivity, precision and temporal independence of keyframing for expressive character animation and by extension prefer purely geometric approaches to character skinning [LCF00]. Geometric skinning approaches typically define the deformation at vertices of skin geometry as a weighted blend of skeletal joint transformations [MG03]. Vertex weights are determined by proximity to skeletal segments by default for a given rest or bind pose. This approach produces smooth deformation, but the results appear closer to a flexed pipe than to deforming tissue [LCF00]. Indirect skinning approaches improve provide richer behaviour and control [CHP89] [MT97] [SK00] [HYC*05]. Here skeletal articulations control spatial deformers, such as a free-form deformation lattice [SP86], which in turn deform the skin. The spatial deformers typically have a much lower resolution than skin geometry, making it easier to hand craft their skeletal mapping. Within the geometric domain, example based approaches have recently gained in popularity [LCF00] [SCFRC01] [ACP02] [KJP02] [WP02] [MG03]. Here the surface skin is sculpted in various poses, and deformation is defined as sparse data interpolation [LCF00] [ACP02] or by fitting to parameters of a simple deformation model [MG03]. Geometric approaches by themselves are efficient and provide direct animator control, but do not easily capture nuances of anatomic deformation [Sin95]. This has been highlighted by a large body of anatomy based skinning [SPCM97] [WG97] [AHS03] which wrap a skin around a given anatomic structure. Most notably, *outside-in* skinning [PCLS05] fits anatomy to a given skin geometry that subsequently augments traditional geometric skinning effectively. None of these approaches, unfortunately, specifically address geometric self-intersections or volume-preservation of the skin in a theoretically robust fashion. Such properties, however, have been successfully developed in the context of geometric modeling [ACWK04] [vFTS06] and we do indeed generalize the bend deformation presented in [vFTS06] to handle part of the skinning process.

Physically based simulation for object deformation is a rich area of ongoing research. Damped spring-mass systems [LTW95] [MHTG05] [LCA05], the finite element method (FEM) [CGC*02] [CBC*05] [TSIF05] and modal analysis [JP02] are among the popular approaches to capture the physics of deformable objects. We contribute a new interactive technique based on dynamic vortex samples to this body of research. Our approach is best suited to volume-preserving deformations of objects with layers of varying deformability. Our dynamic vortex samples can easily be created automatically or by a user arbitrarily in space and like [MHTG05] do not require explicit topological connectivity to each other.

In the context of skinning, a volumetric FEM mesh is used within a dynamic simulation to tie the surface skin to skeletal motion [CGC*02] or precomputed with modal analysis and added to kinematic skinning as a deformation texture [JP02]. Despite the availability of these approaches, physically based skinning has not been popular in commercial animation, due to a lack of efficiency and instant animator feedback during skeletal keyframing. We address this problem by proposing the idea of kinodynamic skinning where our dynamic skin deformations are accumulated over a discretization of pose-space and a finite window of time at interactive rates (see Figure 4). Our approach to dynamics has the advantages of a skin topology independent setup and inherent volume-preservation in an efficient and stable framework.

Finally, we note that the anatomic properties captured in this paper are coarse and intended for animator use, unlike research targeted at accurately modeling human musculoskeletal architecture [TSB*05].

3. Kinodynamic skinning

We begin by formally defining the problem of kinodynamic skinning (depicted visually in Figure 4). We represent a skeletal pose S, as the 4x4 parent relative transform matrices $< R_1, R_2, .., R_n >$ of a hierarchy of n joints. We also denote the world space joint transform for limb i in pose S by L_i. Hierarchically, $L_i = L_{pr(i)} R_i$, where $pr(i)$ is the parent of i (see Figure 3). The skin geometry resulting from the kinematic skinning of S is denoted by G_S. Kinematic skin deformation is strictly a function of skeletal pose and hence G_S is unique. The undeformed geometric skin G is associated with a special pose called the rest or bind pose B. The bind pose joint transforms for limb i are denoted as R_{Bi} and L_{Bi}. Kinematic skinning is the function that deforms G to G_S, based on the pose-space transformation from B to S (see Figure 4).

In traditional geometric skinning [LCF00] the position of deformed points is a function of this pose transformation. In our approach the pose transformation instead defines a *pose-space* velocity for the deformation of points in space. The pose transformation thus needs to be discretized to integrate the deformation of points in pose-space. Now consider some

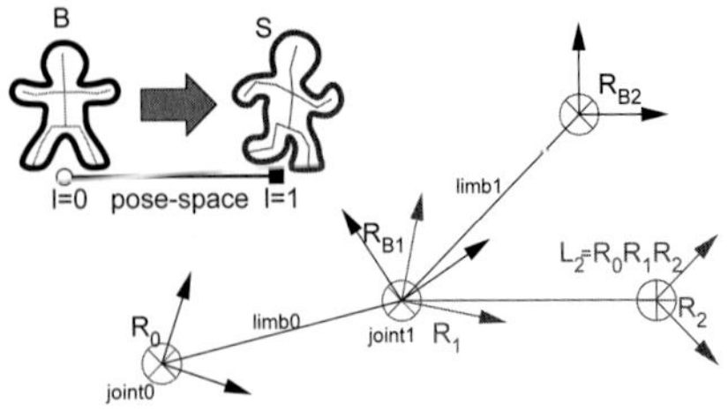

Figure 3: *Local R_i and world L_i joint transforms*

pose on the animation timeline S_t, t units of time prior to pose S. A similar temporal discretization would be necessary to solve for dynamic deformations from S_t to S. Given a time window of t units, kinodynamic skinning solves for skin deformation in pose-space from B to S_t and from S_t to S over time (see Figure 4). A window of size zero is kinematic skinning and increasing the window size incorporates more dynamism, with small window sizes ensuring a realtime response. Dynamic simulations over a small prior window of time can only be applied successfully in scenarios such as character skinning where the elastic restorative forces and damping are strong and the resulting dynamic deformations are transient. Note that the results over a finite window are not the same as running the entire simulation but that the results are close for short lived dynamic deformations.

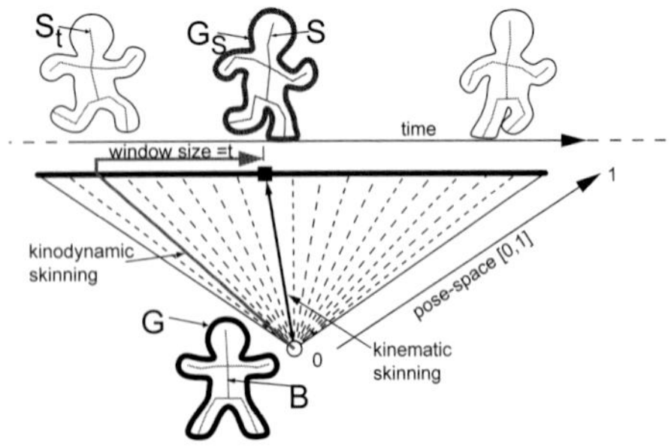

Figure 4: *Kinodynamic skinning*

4. Kinematic skinning details

In traditional linear blend skinning [LCF00], undeformed skin proximal to a limb i can be rigidly transformed from the bind pose B to a pose S by the transform $T_i = L_i L_{Bi}{}^{-1}$. Smooth transitions across joints are achieved by weight averaging these transforms, using a partition of unity weight vector $< w_1, w_2, .., w_n >$ defined for each skin point p. p is thus deformed to p_S in pose S as:

$$p_S = \sum_{i=1}^{n} w_i T_i p \tag{1}$$

Equation 1, however, produces two undesirable effects around joints: the *collapsing elbow* and the *candy-wrapper* effect [MG03] (see Figure 7a). In both cases one typically observes self-intersecting geometry and an extreme loss of volume for large joint rotations. Although hand-crafted skin examples in extreme poses [LCF00] [SCFRC01] can alleviate the problem, they do not explicitly avoid self-intersecting configurations.

4.1. Fold-over free skinning

The Jacobian J_f of a spatial deformation function f represents the directional gradients of deformation and its determinant captures conditions for foldover-free ($Det(J_f) > 0$) and volume-preserving ($Det(J_f) = 1$) skinning in the neighborhood of a point. A divergence-free deformation velocity field is thus volume-preserving [ACWK04], [vFTS06].

Consider the continuous motion in pose-space from the bind to current pose. Equation 1 differentiated over a pose parameterization $l \in [0,1]$ from the bind pose B to current pose S gives us:

$$\dot{p}_S = \sum_{i=1}^{n} w_i \dot{T}_i p \tag{2}$$

$\dot{T}_i$ is the sum of the world space velocities $\dot{L}_j$ induced by every joint j in the hierarchy from the root to i (denoted by the ancestor set $an(i)$). Formally:

$$\dot{T}_i = \sum_{j \in an(i)} \dot{L}_j (L_{Bj}{}^{-1}) \tag{3}$$

The world space velocity $\dot{L}_k$ induced by any limb k is simply its locally induced velocity $\dot{R}_k$, transformed to world space or $\dot{L}_k = L_{pr(k)} \dot{R}_k$.

Integrating this trajectory of p in Equation 2 can be done in discrete steps of $\mathrm{d}l$, defined over a pose parameterization $l \in [0,1]$ from the bind pose B to current pose S:

$$p(l + \mathrm{d}l) = p(l) + \mathrm{d}l\ \dot{p}(l) \tag{4}$$

The accuracy can be improved naively with more steps or with adaptive steps using a Runge-Kutta method [vFTS06].

Alternately, we can write Equation 2 in pose-space as:

$$p(l + \mathrm{d}l) = \sum_{i=1}^{n} w_i\ T_i(l) p(l) \tag{5}$$

where $T_i(l) = L_i(l + \mathrm{d}l) L_i(l)^{-1}$ is a fractional transformation of limb i in pose-space corresponding to a step of length dl at a pose S, and $L_i(l) = \prod_{j \in an(i)} (R_j R_j^{-1})^l R_j$ defines a continuum of world space joint transforms. This hierarchical accumulation of the delta transformations can be computed numerically as shown by [Ale02] or more robustly using the closed form we derive in Appendix B. The step size provides a trade-off between speed and accuracy with a step of length 1 being equivalent to traditional smooth skinning Equation 1. We find in practice that a fixed number of 4-8 steps of Equation 5 produces foldover-free deformations at interactive rates (see Figure 5). The matrices $T_i(l)$, being independent of skin points, can be pre-computed once for the skeletal hierarchy at each discretized pose-space step. Equation 5, however, does not provide any control over the volume of the deforming skin.

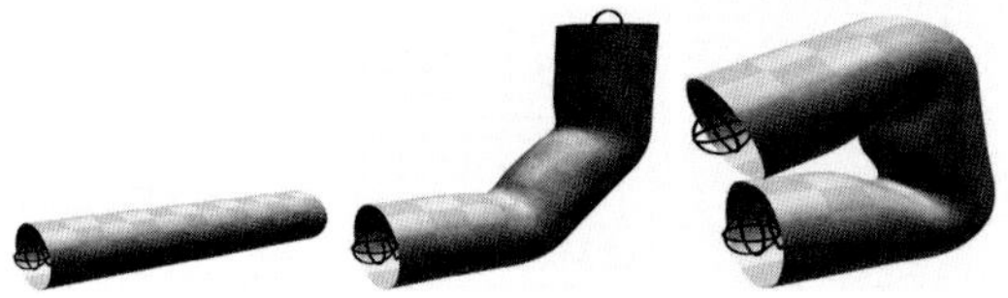

Figure 5: *Solving Equation 5 guarantees fold-over free deformations.*

4.2. Volume-preserving skinning

Let us now focus on the local rotational velocity $\dot{R}_k$ of joint k. Rotation is an inviscid motion and its velocity field can be decomposed into a pair of scalar fields (ϕ_k, ψ_k) (given in Appendix A) using a Clebsch decomposition [Kot91]. The cross product of the gradient of these fields produces a divergence free volume-preserving deformation field as shown by [vFTS06]. We substitute this decomposition into a combination of Equation 2 and Equation 3 to obtain Equation 6. First we replace T_i in Equation 2 by Equation 3. We then denote $p_j = L_B j^{-1} \cdot p$ as the point defined local to limb j. We write $\dot{L}_j$ as $L_{pr(j)} \dot{R}_j$ and replace the rotational velocity $\dot{R}_j$ by its Clebsch decomposition. Finally we split weight w_i (a scalar field) among ϕ and ψ using α_i and β_i such that $\alpha_i + \beta_i = 1$. Denoting the gradient operator as ∇ we get:

$$\begin{aligned} \dot{p} &= \sum_{i=1}^{n} \sum_{j \in an(i)} L_{pr(j)} (\nabla w_i^{\alpha_i} \phi_j) \times (\nabla w_i^{\beta_i} \psi_j) p_j \\ &= \sum_{i=1}^{n} \left(w_i \dot{T}_i p + \sum_{j \in an(i)} \nabla w_i \times (\alpha_i \phi_j \nabla \psi_j - \beta_i \psi_j \nabla \phi_j) \right) \end{aligned} \quad (6)$$

Note that the first term is exactly Equation 2 and can be solved using the analytic solution in Appendix B. The second term makes the field solenoidal, and can be solved numerically. Thus:

$$\begin{aligned} p(l + \mathrm{d}l) &= \sum_{i=1}^{n} w_i \, T_i(l) p(l) + \\ \mathrm{d}l & \sum_{j \in an(i)} \nabla w_i \times (\alpha_i \phi_j \nabla \psi_j - \beta_i \psi_j \nabla \phi_j) \end{aligned} \quad (7)$$

The solenoidal volume-preserving term for joint i is controlled using α_i and β_i and can range from Equation 5 ($\alpha_i = \beta_i = 0$) to more or less deformation along the axes shown in Figure 6. Under extreme joint articulations (see Figure 7b) precise volume-preservation can result in undesirable artifacts. These artifacts can be alleviated by modulating α_i and β_i, which give the animator control over the change in volume upon deformation (see Figure 7c).

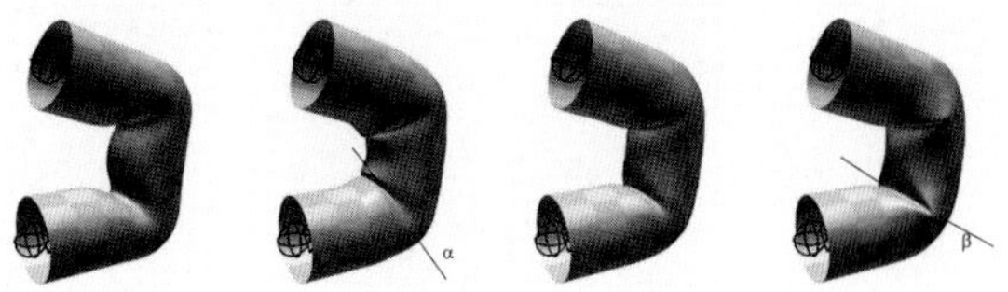

(a) $\alpha = \beta = 0$ (b) $\alpha = \frac{1}{4}, \beta = \frac{3}{4}$ (c) $\alpha = \beta = \frac{1}{2}$ (d) $\alpha = \frac{3}{4}, \beta = \frac{1}{4}$

Figure 6: *Volume is preserved when $\alpha + \beta = 1$, with control over the directional incompressibility shown in (b),(c),(d).*

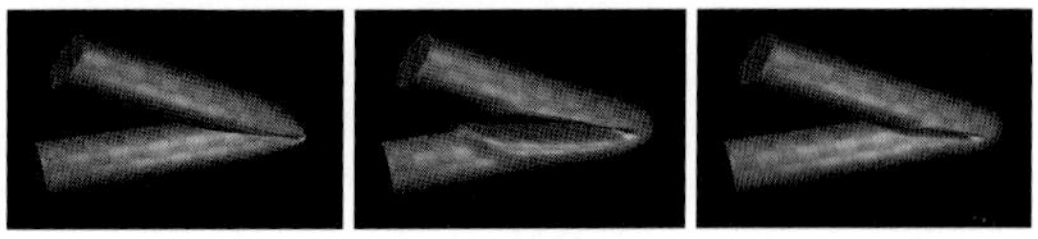

(a) (b) (c)

Figure 7: *Skinning behavior under extreme joint articulation: (a) linear blend, (b) volume-preserving $\alpha = \beta = 0.5$ and (c) volume-controlled $\alpha = 0.1, \beta = 0.3$.*

4.3. Deformable tissue weights

The skin weights, w_i, associated with limb i define both the locality of the skin surface affected by the limb, and a simplified model of the anatomy under the skin. Users interactively paint weights on the control vertices of the skin geometry or specify these weights using implicit falloff functions (see Figure 2). Weight gradients ∇w_i, for user painted weights are computed from a scalar field defined as an offset volume around the surface i.e. the weight value at a point is the weight at the closest point on the skin surface attenuated by it's distance from the surface. In this paper user painted weights and implicit function primitives are used to define *bone weights* that cause regions to move rigidly with limbs, and *soft tissue* weights that capture varying rigidity.

Soft Tissue: is modeled by interactively placing an ellipsoidal primitive around a region of skin (see Figure 2a). To compute the tissue weight μ at a point p we first transform p

Figure 8: *Bone and soft tissue deformation at a joint.*

to a local point by the transform that maps the ellipsoid to a canonical sphere at the origin. We then apply a common radial falloff function $f(d)$ based on the distance d of the local point from the origin. f is monotonic, C^1, numerically close to C^2, almost antisymmetric about $1/2$, and uses the squared distance. For example we use:

$$\mu(p) = f(d) = (d^2-1)^2, \text{if } d < 1 \text{ and } 0 \text{ otherwise.} \quad (8)$$

Bone: We define the bone weight χ at a point to be 1 for points inside the bone and 0 for points outside. In practice we ignore the large discontinuous gradient of χ at the bone surface and practically use a sharp distance falloff to 0 outside the bone.

In Equation 7, we now set $w_i = \chi_i + \mu_i$ and ∇w_i is simply $\nabla \mu_i$. We note here that χ_i and μ_i are defined in the local space of limb i and could be a sum of many implicit primitive functions.

The results of tissue variation can be seen in Figures 1 and 8. Note that by using arbitrarily shaped implicit function primitives [PCLS05], we can also model differently shaped underlying anatomic structures.

Having modeled the contributions of passive anatomic elements of kinematic skinning, we turn our attention to dynamic skinning effects.

5. Dynamic Skinning

We propose a new approach to modeling the dynamics of incompressible anatomic material: vortex deformers. Intuitively, a user creates shapes that capture a desired deformable surface (see Figure 9). We automatically create vortex samples that capture vorticity at points on these shapes. This vorticity is then dynamically updated by musculoskeletal motion and other environment forces. From these vortex samples we are able to recover a deformation velocity field which is divergence-free by construction and fits seamlessly with the velocity fields thus far that represent the kinematic skin of the character.

5.1. Vortex deformers

The motion of a 3D deformable material can be described by the motion of its velocity field v as discussed thus far or its vorticity field w. The velocity and vorticity at a point p can be converted into each other through a pair of mutually inverse relations, the *curl* ($\nabla\times$) and the *Biot-Savart law*:

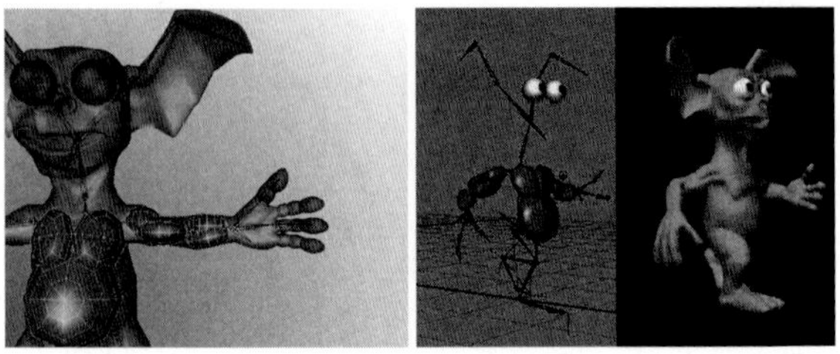

Figure 9: *The muscle shapes are placed in the skeleton's hierarchy. Deformed proxy muscles are not required but are useful in visualizing the dynamics of the character.*

$$\begin{aligned} w(p) &= (\nabla \times v)(p) \\ v(p) &= \iiint_{x\in\mathbb{R}^3} \frac{w(x)\times(p-x)}{4\pi\|p-x\|^3}\,\mathrm{d}x \end{aligned} \quad (9)$$

The Biot-Savart law gives the simplest inverse of $\nabla\times$. Others are obtained by adding a curl-free field to the velocity. A difference between the above equations is that the computation of $w(p)$ requires v at a point, while the computation of $v(p)$ requires w in $\mathbb{R}^3$. The integrand of the Biot-Savart law has a geometric interpretation: the velocity induced by one vorticity vector $w(x)$ is that of a rotation whose magnitude decreases away from its center x according to the radial function $\frac{1}{4\pi\|d\|^3}$. Given that the sum of rotational velocity fields is an incompressible velocity field [ACWK04], the velocity defined by the Biot-Savart law clearly preserves volume. Our deformable elastic material model is composed of two main parts: a motion equation for the vorticity, and an approximated Biot-Savart law to recover the velocity.

Let us first develop the latter. Consider a material M_0 of density ρ_0 embedded in a medium of density ρ_1 (see Figure 10a). The motion of M_0 can be defined at the interface between the two media only (see justification in Appendix C). If we consider an element of volume V intersecting the interface on an area h, with normal n pointing outwards from M_0 as shown in Figure 10a, then the variation over time of the vorticity $W = \iiint_{x\in V} w \,\mathrm{d}V$ carried by the element of volume V is defined as

$$\frac{\mathrm{d}W}{\mathrm{d}t} = 2h\frac{\rho_1-\rho_0}{\rho_1+\rho_0} n\times(F-a) \quad (10)$$

where a is the acceleration and F is the sum of the forces. Since we are interested in materials much heavier than air (the medium in which M_0 is embedded), we typically set $\rho_1 = 0$.

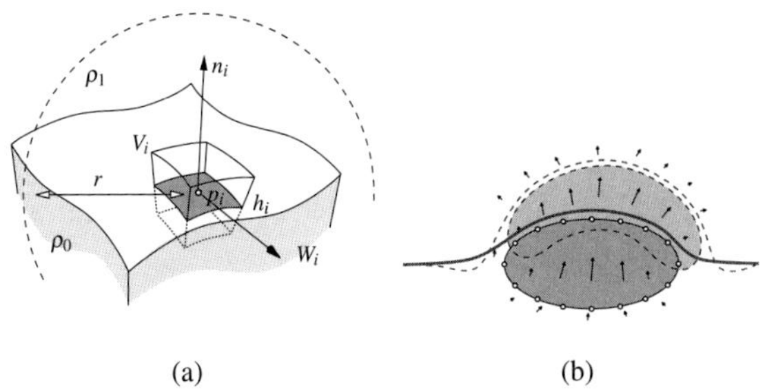

Figure 10: *Vortex deformers: (a) a single vortex sample defined by $\{p_i, n_i, a_i, h_i, W_i, u_i\}$ and (b) a deformation (in red) defined by a velocity field induced by* fixed samples *on the surface of an undeformed shape (in gray).*

5.2. Vorticity induced velocity field

We now define the animated velocity field that describes the deformation. To animate a deformable object, we discretize the continuum's variables at elements of the object's surface: a set of positions p_i placed on the initial undeformed surface have an area h_i, normal n_i, surface vorticity W_i and acceleration a_i (see Figure 10). To define the velocity field induced by the elements of surface, we approximate the Biot-Savart law in Equation 9 by replacing the falloff function $\frac{1}{4\pi d^3}$ with the finite extent falloff function f used in Equation 8, so that:

$$\boxed{\dot{p} = \sum_i f((\|p - p_i\|/r)^2)\, W_i \times (p - p_i)} \qquad (11)$$

In the context of muscle modeling a finite falloff function f is good for two reasons. First, the distance between the muscle vortices and the skin over them is typically small and second, unlike vortices in fluids we do not want a muscle vortex to influence distant skin points that likely belong to another part of the body. An exception to this is when body parts collide and then the colliding skin points are close to the muscle vortices. The default falloff distance r is thus a multiple of the distance between a muscle vortex and the proximal skin surface above it but is ultimately under animator control. The positions p_i are held fixed in the object's local frame (see Figure 10b). Thus only W_i is numerically animated, with Equation 10. To simulate multiple objects, the total velocity v_{total} is obtained by summing all the velocity fields or by combining the velocities in a more controlled manner (see Section 5.4). The new position p_t of a point p after δt seconds is defined with a forward integration $p_t = p + \delta t v_{total}(p)$ similar to the pose-space Equation 4.

5.3. Forces

We now model the necessary forces that would update the vorticity in Equation 10. The assumptions for our deformable framework are elasticity and incompressibility. The latter is captured implicitly by our vortex samples. To animate compressible material or very large scale deformations, it would be necessary to both assign new positions to the existing vortex samples p_i and to resample the vortices on the deformable interface for an adequate discretization. For elastic objects or those with small scale deformations we can afford the approximation of keeping the sampling and locations p_i of vortices constant in the local frame of the objects. Thus, unlike other forces, a restorative elastic force is required in our approach.

Stable Elasticity: The various assumptions and approximations of our model (see Appendix C) make it difficult to express the elastic force, which is not necessarily curl-free, in a similar way to the forces F of Equation 10. However, since we know the object is at rest when all vorticity $W_i = 0$, we define a linear force that pulls W_i towards 0, as opposed to a force that would pull deformed pointd p'_i towards their rest state p_i [MHTG05]. The elastic force F_e is
$F_e(p_i) = -k_s W_i$,

where k_s is the stiffness of the material. As this force is applied to W_i, we need to represent the *vortical velocity* with a vector u_i. The force F_e defines the new vortical velocity u'_i and surface vorticity W'_i at the next time step:

$$\boxed{u'_i = u_i + \delta t(F_e - k_d u_i)} \qquad (12)$$

$$\boxed{W'_i = W_i + \delta t \|u'_i\| \frac{W_i}{\|W_i\|}} \qquad (13)$$

Where $k_d u_i$ is a classic damping term. Note that this scheme preserves the direction of W_i, and of the various schemes we have tried it is the most stable.

Shear Strain: The magnitude of elastic force is based on the material's strain. Let us denote the displacement gradient tensor by $J = I + \delta t \nabla v(p)$. The strain tensor $\varepsilon = J^{\mathrm{T}} \cdot J - I$ is central to modeling accurately elastic forces [NMK*05], and measures two kinds of strain: *shear strain* and *compression strain.* Since our equations model an incompressible velocity field, there is no strain due to compression. The shear strain is the change in angle of previously orthogonal directions, and for a pair of unit orthogonal vectors τ_0 and τ_1 it is measured as the dot product $(J\tau_0) \cdot (J\tau_1)$. Since we consider isotropic materials, we do not privilege any direction. By integrating all possible pairs of unit orthogonal directions over a sphere, the shear strain is:

$$\boxed{S_i = \frac{2\pi}{30}\Big((\varepsilon_{00} - \varepsilon_{11})^2 + (\varepsilon_{11} - \varepsilon_{22})^2 + (\varepsilon_{22} - \varepsilon_{00})^2 + 6\,(\varepsilon_{01}^2 + \varepsilon_{12}^2 + \varepsilon_{20}^2)\Big)} \qquad (14)$$

where ε_{ij} are elements of the strain tensor ε. This strain, evaluated at each location p_i is multiplied to the elastic force F_e. Shear strain computation requires W_i, making the complexity of computing strain for n surface elements $O(n^2)$. Enabling shear strain thus diminishes interactivity and is also not visually significant in many cases and thus can typically be disabled.

Plasticity: While muscles are elastic they are active elements that when internally contracted in a state of equilibrium can be conceived as having been plastically deformed. We can define this material state with rest state vorticity vectors W_i other than 0. Clearly specifying such vectors would be an impossible user task. The user instead specifies a desired a plastic shape (by displacing the vortices of the original shape) and we compute the appropriate W_i as follows. Since Equation 11 expresses the velocity V as a function of W_j and can be written in the form $V(p_{i\in[1,n]}) = \sum_j M_{i,j} \cdot W_j$, we structure the equations as a linear system:

$$\begin{pmatrix} V(p_1) \\ \vdots \\ V(p_n) \end{pmatrix} = \begin{pmatrix} M_{1,1} & \cdots & M_{1,n} \\ \vdots & \ddots & \vdots \\ M_{n,1} & \cdots & M_{n,n} \end{pmatrix} \begin{pmatrix} W_1 \\ \vdots \\ W_n \end{pmatrix} \tag{15}$$

where $V(p_i)$ is the desired displacements of p_i. The M matrix may be singular since the user is likely to specify a target shape with a different volume from the initial one. We therefore use the Moore-Penrose pseudo-inverse, which provides the least square solution for the W_i.

Gravity: and other curl-free environment forces can be easily added to our system $F_g(p_i) = g$. Note the strong persistant environment forces can cause the kinodynamic simulation over a small window of time to differ signicantly from the true dynamic simulation.

Squash-and-Stretch: is a desirable property for character animation [TJ81]. In our approach squash-and-stretch can be achieved conveniently by defining a force F_{ss} that pushes or pulls the deformable shape along an axis n_{ss}, with respect to a center $\tilde{c}$ (see Figure 11a,b):
$F_{ss}(p_i) = ((p_i - \tilde{c}) \cdot n_{ss})\, k_{ss}\, n_{ss}$.
A negative k_{ss} squashes the object, while a positive k_{ss} stretches the object.

Life: In reality active muscles produce joint motion. Animators, however, directly specify joint motion that muscles and skin follow passively. The *life* force causes muscles to deform as though they were actively causing the joint motion that has been authored by the animator. We show how adding the acceleration as an external force F_l makes the material actively deform:
$F_l(p_i) = k_l a_i$
Note that for $k_l = 1$, the acceleration component disappears completely and thus the overall dynamics can be *smoothly switched off*. As k_l is increased, the object becomes more of an actor.

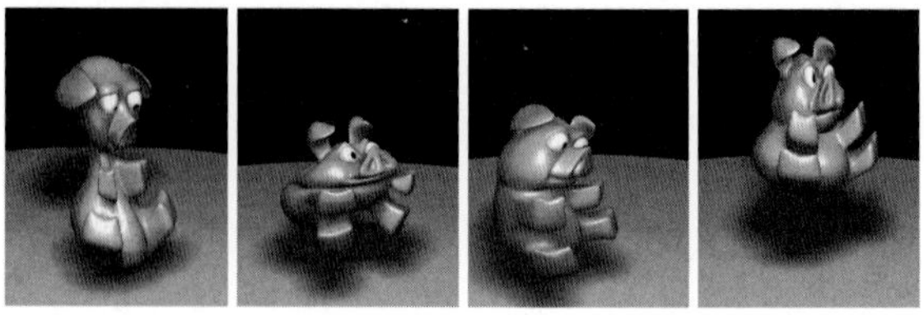

(a) (b) (c) (d)
Figure 11: *Animating squash-stretch (a)(b), and life (c)(d).*

5.4. Dynamic skinning workflow

The dynamic skinning workflow builds upon the traditional kinematic approach we presented in Section 4. The user places local muscle shapes under the skin and binds them to the skeletal structure, as is typical [PCLS05]. We automatically create vortex samples on the surface of muscle shapes (say at every control vertex) and their positions p_i are kept constant in a local skeletal frame. While they play no part in the actual skin deformation we find it useful to define proxy muscle shapes to interactively visualize how the muscle shape would deform. If we denote by V_j the velocity induced by the jth muscle, a straightforward way to compute the new position of vortex point on the proxy muscle $p'_k = p_k + \delta t \sum_j V_j(q_k)$. In general vortex deformers define a dynamic 3D deformation velcity field that is added to the kinematically controlled velocity field in Equation 4 (parameterized over time instead of pose-space). The user can specify per muscle weights on a skin surface in a fashion identical to the deformable tissue weights in Section 4.3. If a skin vertex q_k, has a per muscle weight $m_{j,k}$ then deformation over δt is:

$$\mathrm{q}'_k = \mathrm{q}_k + \delta t \sum_j m_{j,k}\, \mathrm{V}_j(\mathrm{q}_k) \tag{16}$$

We now put the kinematic and dynamic skinning back together as outlined in Figure 4.

6. Kinodynamic skinning algorithm

Given a pose S and time window t, the skin is first kinematically deformed to the pose S_t, t units of time prior to the present ($S_t = S$ if no animation has been specified on the timeline). This skinning solution is a combination of a fold-over free deformation computed in closed form and a volume-preserving deformation velocity term computed numerically. A dynamic simulation is then run from pose S_t to S over time t. The kinematic deformation trajectories over time are simply added to those defined by the vortex dynamics. We integrate the trajectories using a simple explicit Euler solver. Since we work in a vorticity space, we can bound the values without affecting the visual quality, making our method stable for arbitrary long time steps. A step in this simulation is as follows:

1. Each vortex sample i $\{p_i, n_i, a_i, h_i, W_i, u_i\}$ (see Figure 10a) is initialized. p_i and n_i rigidly track the skeletal pose and the areas h_i of each sample is kept constant. W_i, a_i and u_i are initialized to 0.
2. Given the current skeletal pose compute the current position p_i, normal n_i and acceleration a_i in world coordinates for all vortex samples i.
3. Compute the external forces F_i (gravity, squash-and-stretch and life as described in Section 5.3. Using the external forces F_i and the acceleration a_i, update W_i with Equation 10.
4. Compute the elastic force $F_e(p_i)$, and its effect by updating u_i and to W_i, using Equation 12. Use the shear if enabled.
5. Add the velocity defined in Equation 16 to the pose-space kinematic skinning velocity defined in Equation 4 (as the skeleton transforms from s_t to S).
6. Numerically update the skin vertex positions and proxy muscles if desired, given the overall skin deformation velocity field.

7. Implementation and results

Our deformation approach has been implemented as a 3D deformer plug-in in *Maya* and can be procedurally combined with other deformers like lattices [SP86] or sculpt objects [PCLS05] for the general modeling and deformation of incompressible, elastic objects. As is standard practice in object skinning or deformation, a user can selectively associate skin points to joints or muscles in Maya. The advantages are improved efficiency and more precise association of anatomy to skin that when using simple falloff function shapes. The disadvantages are that forced association if not performed carefully can destroy the volume controlled and globally foldover-free surface deformations we set out to capture.

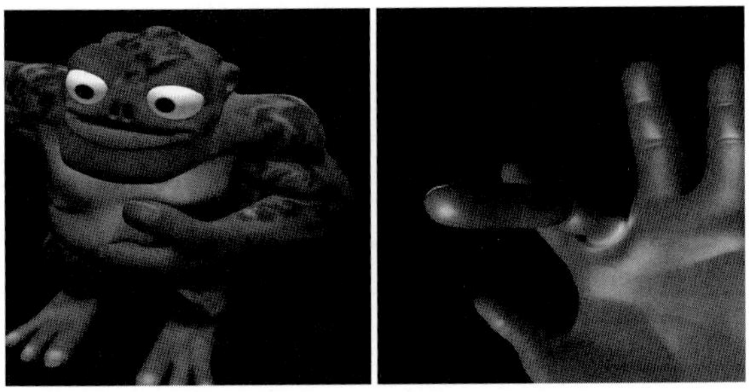

(a) (b)

Figure 12: *Extreme articulations: (a) Global fold-over free skinning shown as the hand pushes into the belly of the troll, (b) Metacarpophalangeal joint flexion.*

Animator control: Our formulation builds upon typical linear blend skinning (see Equation 1). Equation 5 discretizes the rotation of a joint i in Equation 1 into small steps, recomputing w_i for skin points at each step. This results in globally foldover-free skinning as seen in Figure 12a, where points on the trollŠs belly acquire a non-zero weight with respect to arm joints as the arm moves into the belly. Since the weights w_i are recomputed they need to be defined in 3D space. We accomplish this using ellipsoidal and arbitrary star shaped [PCLS05] falloff functions and user painted surface weights that falloff with distance from the surface. We provide two different falloff functions that capture bone or soft tissue behavior.

Volume-preservation is further built upon the foldover-free skinning of Equation 5 using a Clebsch decomposition (see Appendix A or [vFTS06]) of the rotation around a joint i (see Equation 7). The user can control the amount of volume conservation in two orthogonal directions using weights α_i and β_i. These weights scale ϕ_i and ψ_i by ${w_i}^{\alpha_i}$ and ${w_i}^{\beta_i}$ prior to computing their gradients and subsequent cross product, so that the final vector field remains divergence-free. While volume-preservation ($\alpha_i + \beta_i = 1$) is desirable it can be excessive in extreme articulation (see Figure 7b) and users can modulate it by reducing α_i and β_i for large rotations (see Figure 7c and Figure 12b). Indeed anatomic structures and cavities have some compressibility and animators can qualitatively control this in our approach. Further control over where the volume goes comes from the fact that only soft tissue functions (bones have a zero weight gradient) participate in the volume preservation term of Equation 7.

User control over dynamics is simpler. The user simply positions muscle primitives under the skin (see Figure 9) similar to many anatomic skinning approaches and specifies any external forces as described in section 5.3. The radius of influence r in Equation 11 allows a user to control the locality of muscle deformation. The dynamic window and physical muscle attributes of density ρ, stiffness k_s and damping k_d are also under interactive animator control. The quality of the motion can be adjusted and visualized at a high frame rate by displaying the deformed muscles (see Figure 9b).

Efficiency: The refresh rates of our technique within Maya (including Maya's display and dependency graph evaluation overhead) on models (see Figure 9) of around 8000 vertices are around:
30 fps for Maya smooth skinning (linear blend skinning).
5 fps for the Clebsch decomposition based kinematic skinning.
12 fps for the vortex deformer based dynamics with 12 muscles.
4 fps for the complete kinodynamic solution.

Theoretically the complexity scales linearly with both the number of vertices and the number of muscle vortices (without modeling material shear). In practice, for the complete kinodynamic solution we observe 4, 9, 24 and 42 fps for 8000, 4000, 2000 and 1000 vertices and 12 muscles, measured on a Pentium®4–2.40GHz–512 Mb RAM.

Refresh rates of the vortex dynamics examples within our standalone program are much better, > 90 fps, showing the promise of better performance if these techniques are implemented directly within a commercial animation system.

8. Conclusion

We have presented a number of concepts in this paper. Firstly we find the idea of kinodynamic skinning to be worthwhile in the context of transient dynamic deformations and may be applicable to other combinations of geometric and physically based simulations. Our kinematic skinning approach is effective and the closed form fold-over free term which has by far the largest deformation magnitude (see Appendix B), makes the overall approach very stable. We also extend the bend deformation of [vFTS06] to add a volume-preserving term to the kinematic skin (see Appendix A). Finally we show vortex deformers to be a compelling technique for modeling the dynamics of elastic incompressible materials. Most importantly, all these techniques work well together within a typical interactive character skinning framework (see Figure 13).

Popular example based skinning approaches that use scattered data interpolation can be thought of as having an example set of bind poses with corresponding skin geometry [LCF00] [WP02], [MG03]. We note here that our kinematic skinning is constructed from a single bind pose. Using multiple example skins to be combined in a volume-preserving fashion is subject to future work.

Our dynamics approach makes a number of approximations and assumptions tailored to expressive character animation and is thus not suited to applications where the precise modeling of anatomic tissue is required [TSB*05]. The acceleration and velocity of vortex samples are strictly controlled by the skeletal frame they are bound to and not induced in terms of vorticity w. Our muscle model for is thus a mixture of the vorticity and velocity equation of motion. Although our muscles primitives preserve volume, the skin surface is an approximation to the muscles. Finally, in our current implementation the dynamic interaction between two muscles from different parts of a character falls off continuously with the distance between them. In reality these muscles only interact if and when these body parts make contact. We acknowledge these limitations of our model as subject to future work.

Our emphasis at present has been an advance in the quality and control of kinodynamic skin deformation. Although we do not compete with linear blend skinning on efficiency for games and highly interactive applications, for high-end animation authoring the rates are adequately interactive. Furthermore, the use of low-res skin geometry and proxy muscles is common in commercial animation when character complexity hinders animator interactivity.

Despite some of these shortcomings our approach makes a number of contributions to the current state of the art of character skinning.

Figure 13: *A stomach muscle adds dynamism to Master Pai.*

Appendix A: Clebsch Decomposition of a Rotation

Let us look at the velocity of a rotation at a point p around an axis n (see Figure 14):

$$v(p) = \theta\, n \times (p - c) + t\, n \qquad (17)$$

Let $q = p - c$. Vectors $a = n \times q \times n$, $b = n \times q$ and n form a right-handed orthonormal basis . Since a rotation is a solenoidal or divergence-free flow, it can be decomposed in two irrotational or curl-free vector fields $\nabla\phi$ and $\nabla\psi$ orthogonal to v [Rut89]:

$$v = \nabla\phi \times \nabla\psi \quad \text{where} \begin{cases} \nabla\phi &= \theta n - t\frac{b}{(b\cdot b)} \\ \nabla\psi &= a \end{cases} \qquad (18)$$

The vectors of the field $\nabla\psi$ are contained in planes perpendicular to n. The integration of $\nabla\phi$ and $\nabla\psi$ gives:

$$\begin{array}{rcl} \phi &=& \theta\, q \cdot n - t \arctan(q\cdot a,\, q \cdot b) \\ \psi &=& \frac{1}{2}(b \cdot b) \end{array}, \qquad (19)$$

The pair (ϕ, ψ) is the Clebsch decomposition of the rotation.

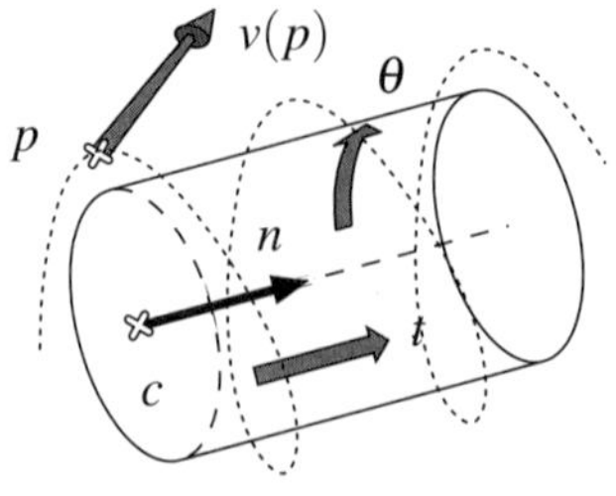

Figure 14: *Variables defining the velocity field of a rotation. Any point on the line (c,n) may be used instead of c. Note that n does not have to correspond to the axis of a joint.*

Appendix B: Fraction of a Matrix

We denote with a non-rational exponent the fraction of a matrix: M^l. If our method is implemented in an animation package, this can be done by using the package's matrix parameterization if available, or with $M^l = \exp(l \log M)$ in the more general case, where:

$$\log(M) = -\sum_{k=1}^{\infty} \frac{(\mathrm{I}-M)^k}{k} \qquad \exp(N) = \sum_{k=0}^{\infty} \frac{N^k}{k!} \tag{20}$$

There is a stable way to evaluate these series numerically [Ale02], and in the case where M is the matrix of a twist, there is a closed-form which we provide here. First, the matrix M of the twist must be expressed in terms of (t, θ, n, c). Let us write M in terms of a 3×3 submatrix R and a point h:

$$M = \begin{pmatrix} & R & & h \\ 0 & 0 & 0 & 1 \end{pmatrix} \tag{21}$$

If $R = \mathrm{I}$, then M is a translation, and:

$$\begin{array}{rclcrcl} t & = & \|h\| & \quad & n & = & h/t \\ \theta & = & 0 & & c & = & 0 \end{array} \tag{22}$$

Otherwise, n is the eigenvector associated to eigenvalue 1 of the matrix R, $t = h \cdot n$, c is found by solving $(R - \mathrm{I}) \cdot c = t\, n - h$, and given any unit vector u orthogonal to n, $\theta = \arctan(u \cdot (M \cdot u), (n \times u) \cdot (M \cdot u))$. This decomposition of M provides the closed-form of $\log M$:

$$\log M = \begin{pmatrix} 0 & -w_z & w_y & m_x \\ w_z & 0 & -w_x & m_y \\ -w_y & w_x & 0 & m_z \\ 0 & 0 & 0 & 0 \end{pmatrix} \tag{23}$$

where $w = \theta\, n$ and $m = c \times w + t\, n$

And the closed-form for $\exp N$ is:

$$\exp N = \mathrm{I} + N + \frac{1-\cos\theta}{\theta^2} N^2 + \frac{\theta - \sin\theta}{\theta^3} N^3 \tag{24}$$

Note that for a translation, $\lim_{\theta \to 0} \exp N = \mathrm{I} + N$.

Appendix C: Discontinuity Model

Let us consider the equations that describes the motion of the velocity field of an inviscid incompressible fluid:

$$\left\{ \begin{array}{rcl} \frac{\mathrm{d}v}{\mathrm{d}t} & = & -\frac{1}{\rho} \nabla p + F \\ \nabla \cdot v & = & 0 \end{array} \right. \tag{25}$$

where p is the pressure, ρ is the density and F is the sum of the external forces per unit mass. Let us multiplying the first equation by ρ, apply to it the curl operator $\nabla \times$, and assume that the external forces is a curl-free field $\nabla \times F = 0$. We obtain the equation of the motion of w:

$$\frac{\mathrm{d}w}{\mathrm{d}t} = \frac{\nabla \rho}{\rho} \times (F - a) + w \cdot \nabla v \tag{26}$$

The last term means that w is carried by material lines that stretch with the fluid. Since we focus on elastic material close to their equilibrium state, we assume that $w \cdot \nabla v = 0$. To define ρ, we assume the density ρ_0 and ρ_1 of the two continua constant, thus the function ρ is discontinuous at the continua interface. Let us define the signed distance to the interface as negative in the material M_0 and positive in M_1, and use the Heaviside step function H:

$$\rho(d) = \rho_1 H(d) + \rho_0 H(-d) \tag{27}$$

$$\text{where} \quad H(d) = \left\{ \begin{array}{ll} 0 & \text{if } d < 0 \\ \frac{1}{2} & \text{if } d = 0 \\ 1 & \text{otherwise} \end{array} \right.$$

Dealing with the discontinuity is cumbersome. Fortunately, the analytical integration of Equation 26 in a small volume V makes the function H disappear:

$$\iiint_V \frac{\mathrm{d}w}{\mathrm{d}t}\, \mathrm{d}V = \left\{ \begin{array}{l} 0 \text{ if } V \text{ does not intersects the interface} \\ 2h \frac{\rho_1 - \rho_0}{\rho_1 + \rho_0} n \times (F - a) \text{ otherwise} \end{array} \right.$$

Finally, using Reynolds' transport theorem for incompressible materials, $\iiint_V \frac{\mathrm{d}w}{\mathrm{d}t}\, \mathrm{d}V = \frac{\mathrm{d}}{\mathrm{d}t} \iiint_V w\, \mathrm{d}V$ [Rut89]. Thus the above describes the variation of vorticity for elements of volume near the interface.

References

[ACP02] Allen B., Curless B., Popović Z.: Articulated body deformation from range scan data. *ACM Trans. Graph. 21*, 3 (2002), 612–619.

[ACWK04] Angelidis A., Cani M.-P., Wyvill G., King S.: Swirling-Sweepers: Constant-Volume Modeling. In *Pacific Graphics 2004* (Oct 2004), pp. 10–15.

[AHS03] Albrecht I., Haber J., Seidel H.-P.: Construction and animation of anatomically based human hand models. In *SCA '03: Proceedings of the 2003 ACM SIGGRAPH/Eurographics Symposium on Computer animation* (Aire-la-Ville, Switzerland, Switzerland, 2003), Eurographics Association, pp. 98–109.

[Ale02] Alexa M.: Linear Combination of Transformations. *ACM Trans. Graph. 21*, 3 (Jul 2002), 380–387.

[CBC*05] Capell S., Burkhart M., Curless B., Duchamp T., Popović Z.: Physically Based Rigging for Deformable Characters. In *SCA'05: Proc. of the 2005 Symposium on Computer Animation* (Jul 2005), pp. 301–310.

[CGC*02] Capell S., Green S., Curless B., Duchamp T., Popović Z.: Interactive Skeleton-Driven Dynamic Deformations. *ACM Trans. Graph. 21*, 3 (Jul 2002), 586–593.

[CHP89] Chadwick J. E., Haumann D. R., Parent R. E.: Layered construction for deformable animated characters. In *SIGGRAPH '89: Proceedings of the 16th annual conference on Computer graphics and interactive techniques* (New York, NY, USA, 1989), ACM Press, pp. 243–252.

[HYC*05] Hyun D., Yoon S., Chang J., Seong J., Kim M., Juttler B.: Sweep-based Human Deformation. In *Pacific Graphics* (Oct 2005), pp. 542–550.

[JP02] JAMES D. L., PAI D. K.: DyRT: Dynamic Response Textures for Real Time Deformation Simulation with Graphics Hardware. *ACM Trans. Graph. 21*, 3 (Jul 2002), 582–585.

[KJP02] KRY P. G., JAMES D. L., PAI D. K.: Eigenskin: real time large deformation character skinning in hardware. In *SCA '02: Proceedings of the 2002 ACM SIGGRAPH/Eurographics symposium on Computer animation* (New York, NY, USA, 2002), ACM Press, pp. 153–159.

[Kot91] KOTIUGA P.: Clebsch potentials and the visualization of three-dimensional solenoidal vector fields. *IEEE Transactions on Magnetics 27(5)* (Sep 1991), 3986–3989.

[LCA05] LARBOULETTE C., CANI M.-P., ARNALDI B.: Dynamic skinning: adding real-time dynamic effects to an existing character animation. In *SCCG '05: Proceedings of the 21st spring conference on Computer graphics* (New York, NY, USA, 2005), ACM Press, pp. 87–93.

[LCF00] LEWIS J., CORDNER M., FONG N.: Pose Space Deformation: A Unified Approach to Shape Interpolation and Skeleton-Driven Deformation. In *ACM Trans. Graph. (Proc of SIGGRAPH'99)* (Jul 2000), pp. 165–172.

[LTW95] LEE Y., TERZOPOULOS D., WALTERS K.: Realistic modeling for facial animation. In *SIGGRAPH '95: Proceedings of the 22nd annual conference on Computer graphics and interactive techniques* (New York, NY, USA, 1995), ACM Press, pp. 55–62.

[MG03] MOHR A., GLEICHER M.: Building Efficient, Accurate Character Skins from Examples. *ACM Trans. Graph. 22*, 3 (Jul 2003), 562–568.

[MHTG05] MULLER M., HEIDELBERGER B., TESCHNER M., GROSS M.: Meshless deformations based on shape matching. In *SIGGRAPH '05: ACM SIGGRAPH 2005 Papers* (New York, NY, USA, 2005), ACM Press, pp. 471–478.

[MT97] MOCCOZET L., THALMANN N. M.: Dirichlet free-form deformations and their application to hand simulation. In *CA '97: Proceedings of the Computer Animation* (Washington, DC, USA, 1997), IEEE Computer Society, p. 93.

[NMK*05] NEALEN A., MALLER M., KEISER R., BOXERMAN E., CARLSON M.: Physically based deformable models in computer graphics. In *Eurographics 2005 State of the Art Report* (Sep 2005).

[PCLS05] PRATSCHER M., COLEMAN P., LASZLO J., SINGH K.: Outside-In Anatomy Based Character Rigging. In *SCA'05: Proc. of the 2005 Symposium on Computer Animation* (Jul 2005), pp. 329–338.

[Rut89] RUTHERFORD A.: *Vectors, Tensors, and the Basic Equations of Fluid Mechanics.* Dover Publications, Inc, 1989.

[SCFRC01] SLOAN P.-P. J., CHARLES F. ROSE I., COHEN M. F.: Shape by example. In *SI3D '01: Proceedings of the 2001 symposium on Interactive 3D graphics* (New York, NY, USA, 2001), ACM Press, pp. 135–143.

[Sin95] SINGH K.: *Realistic Human Figure Synthesis and Animation for VR Applications.* PhD thesis, The Ohio State University, 1995.

[SK00] SINGH K., KOKKEVIS E.: Skinning Characters using Surface-Oriented Free-Form Deformations. In *Graphics Interface* (2000), pp. 35–42.

[SP86] SEDERBERG T., PARRY S.: Free-Form Deformation of Solid Geometric Models. In *ACM Trans. Graph. (Proc of SIGGRAPH'86)* (Aug 1986), pp. 151–160.

[SPCM97] SCHEEPERS F., PARENT R. E., CARLSON W. E., MAY S. F.: Anatomy-Based Modeling of the Human Musculature. In *ACM Trans. Graph. (Proc of SIGGRAPH'97)* (Aug 1997), pp. 163–172.

[TJ81] THOMAS F., JOHNSTON O.: *The illusion of life.* Hyperion, 1981.

[TSB*05] TERAN J., SIFAKIS E., BLEMKER S. S., NG-THOW-HING V., LAU C., FEDKIW R.: Creating and simulating skeletal muscle from the visible human data set. *IEEE Transactions on Visualization and Computer Graphics 11*, 3 (2005), 317–328.

[TSIF05] TERAN J., SIFAKIS E., IRVING G., FEDKIW R.: Robust Quasistatic Finite Elements and Flesh Simulation. In *SCA'05: Proc. of the 2005 Symposium on Computer Animation* (Jul 2005), pp. 181–190.

[vFTS06] VON FUNCK W., THEISEL H., SEIDEL H.-P.: Vector field based shape deformations. *ACM Trans. Graph. 25*, 3 (2006), 1118–1125.

[WG97] WILHELMS J., GELDER A. V.: Anatomically Based Modeling. In *ACM Trans. Graph. (Proc of SIGGRAPH'97)* (Aug 1997), pp. 173–180.

[WP02] WANG X. C., PHILLIPS C.: Multi-weight enveloping: least-squares approximation techniques for skin animation. In *SCA '02: Proceedings of the 2002 ACM SIGGRAPH/Eurographics symposium on Computer animation* (New York, NY, USA, 2002), ACM Press, pp. 129–138.

Eurographics/ ACM SIGGRAPH Symposium on Computer Animation (2007)
D. Metaxas and J. Popovic (Editors)

Deformation Styles for Spline-based Skeletal Animation

Sven Forstmann and Jun Ohya [1] Artus Krohn-Grimberghe[2] Ryan McDougall[3]

[1]GITS Faculty, Waseda University, Tokyo, Japan
[2]Karlsruhe University, Karlsruhe, Germany
[3]3D Incorporated, Yokohama, Japan

Abstract

We present a novel skinned skeletal animation system based on spline-aligned deformations for providing high quality and fully designable deformations in real-time. Our ambition is to allow artists the easy creation of abstract, pose-dependent deformation behaviors that might directly be assigned to a large variety of target objects simultaneously. To achieve this goal, we introduce the usage of deformation styles and demonstrate their applicability by our animation system. We therefore enhance spline-skinned skeletal animation with two sweep-based free-form-deformation (FFD) variants. The two FFD variants are pose-dependent, driven by three textures and three curves, which can be designed by the artist. As the three textures are similar to height-maps, their creation is very intuitive. Once designed, the deformation styles can be directly applied to any number of targets for imitating material behaviors of cloth, metal or even muscles. Our GPU based implementation shows promising results for real-time usage, as about 30 Million vertices per second can be animated. The basic spline-skinning even reaches more than twice the speed and gets close to the performance of skeletal subspace deformation (SSD). Furthermore, our method can easily be combined along with other existing deformation techniques as pose space deformation or SSD.

Categories and Subject Descriptors (according to ACM CCS): I.3.5 [Computer Graphics]: Computational Geometry and Object ModelingHierarchy and geometric transformations I.3.5 [Computer Graphics]: Computational Geometry and Object ModelingSplines I.3.7 [Computer Graphics]: Three-Dimensional Graphics and RealismAnimation

1. Introduction

Character animation is one of the major components in most digital productions, including cinematic productions as well as interactive applications as video games. To cover the required deformation issue, many approaches have been suggested over time, ranging from free-form-deformation (FFD) based techniques over skeletal methods to advanced algorithms, which also take a mesh's topology, physical constraints and even authentic data from laser-scans into account. In the recent years, especially one method has widely found acceptance to cover skeletal animation: the so-called linear blend or matrix skinning, also known as skeletal subspace deformation (SSD). It is the most popular method among all authoring tools and interactive applications. The key of SSD's success easy to explain: it is simple and well-balanced—in terms of quality, speed and implementation complexity.

However, it is far from perfect, since its deformations expose the well-known candy-wrapper effect for twisting operations and collapsing geometry while bending. This issue is very annoying for artists and has inspired many researchers to come up with new solutions and alternative methods. Unfortunately, most inventions have not found their way into practical usage—and the reason is easy to explain: Often, methods are either very complex, so it is hard to accomplish their implementation in a reasonable time, or their computation is simply too demanding. Especially in real-time applications as for example video games, fast evaluations are mandatory. However, also in offline rendering systems, as for cinematic productions, time is an important and non-negligible factor.

We are therefore concerned with a practical solution that provides high quality deformations, easy handling, a fast and stable evaluation, hardware accelerator compliance, an easy

Symposium on Computer Animation 2007, San Diego, CA, August 03-04, 2007.
© 2007 ACM 978-1-59593-624-4/07/0008 $5.00

implementation and compliance to existing skeletal animation methods.

A further and maybe even more important issue for an animation system's success is the degree of freedom to adjust a deformation. Here, especially pose-space-deformation (PSD) has made an important contribution to allow artists the design for each pose of an animation individually. However, PSD has a significant restriction: If an artist has enhanced a certain pose—for example by modeling a joints muscle- or cloth-like behavior—it is not possible to reuse this particular behavior for any other joint. Our main goal is therefore to create a system allowing the abstract and reusable design of a joints deformation behavior. This property allows one deformation behavior to be applied immediately to a large number of various targets, reducing an artist's work considerably.

2. Concept and Design

For creating the animation system, we carefully took our design goals into account. As for the foundation of our skinned skeletal animation system, we decided to use spline-aligned deformation [SF98]. It naturally provides high-quality bend and twist deformations without exposing unwanted artifacts like SSD. Another advantage is their fast and stable evaluation—an important property for our desired implementation on the GPU. As for the spline function, we use a special polynomial based spline with variable exponent that is dependent on only three control-points for highest performance.

In order to achieve reusable pose dependent designs, our central aim, we introduce the usage of deformation styles. The idea is to allow the abstract design of a deformation behavior, without requiring any knowledge about the underlying geometry it is applied to. This is one step forward beyond PSD, since PSD always has to be aware of the geometry it is applied to. To solve this problem efficiently, we decided to utilize two sweep-based FFD variants, which are attached to each joint.

The first of our two methods is based on a high-resolution, radial FFD grid, which is wrapped around the spline. It allows the creation of high resolution concentric deformation effects such as for metal, cloth or even muscle bulges. It is driven by three scale textures, which are weighted blended, depending on the spline's pose. The three textures are utilized for frontal, lateral and radial scaling. Our second FFD variant is a rectangular scale envelope that is supposed to allow a simple definition of more general scalings. The artist therefore draws three outlining curves for the frontal, lateral and radial direction. Goals of the second variant include the design of folds to prevent self-intersections near the elbow or the modeling of major lateral bulges for soft-bodies.

3. Contributions

Our skinned skeletal animation system can list the following four contributions:

Reusable deformation-styles: The presented system allows the abstract design of pose-dependent deformation behaviors for the imitation of complex material deformations. Once designed, a style can immediately be applied to an arbitrary number of joints simultaneously. This saves time for the artist during the modeling phase, and may further save memory during run-time, as each style needs to be stored only once.

Fast computation: We achieved a very efficient GPU based implementation of the spline-based skinned skeletal animation system, which outperforms the GPU based implementation described in [FO06] by factor three for the basic spline skinning without deformation-styles. Our algorithm's speed without deformation-styles further gets close to the performance of SSD, which is often referred to as the fastest skinned skeletal animation system. For the case of deformation styles being included, our system still shows a very competitive speed, as the vertex deformation rate remains high at 30 Million vertices per second on our testing system.

Simplicity: Our algorithm is based on simple mathematics and does not contain complex data structures or the requirement of comprehensive mathematical libraries. We assume the implementation to be feasible in a reasonable time without complications. Furthermore, the designed deformation styles cover the complete pose-space of a joint and hence avoid the usage of radial basic functions for the interpolation between certain poses.

Memory usage: In contrast to the GPU-based spline-aligned skeletal animation system [FO06], where each vertex and each normal of the animated mesh were required to be stored three times (once for each spline), our novel algorithm requires them to be stored only once.

4. Related Work

Over time, many methods have appeared to achieve the animation of characters, where the most important methods can be divided into FFD [SP86], SSD [MTLT88], shape blending and spline aligned deformations [SF98]. They form the foundation for many subsequent research approaches and reappeared in countless variants and combinations since their initial invention. In order to increase the deformation quality and realism for skeletal animations, various methods have been suggested.

Methods that directly improve upon SSD are [KZ05] and [KCOZ06]. They change the interpolation domain from matrices to quaternions or even dual quaternions. This successfully avoids effects as collapsing geometry by preserving a high computational speed.

A different and more flexible approach is to use spline

aligned deformations and apply them in a skinned way to character animation. Two methods to achieve this are [FO06] and [YSZ06]. As for [YSZ06], the focus lies especially on the modeling case, as their implementation is a plugin for the commercial software Maya, while [FO06] focusses on the application in real-time systems by extensive usage of the GPU. A related approach in this context is also [CSM05], where curve skeletons are introduced and discussed in general.

A method advancing on FFD is sweep-based FFD [YK06]. It provides the ability to efficiently model radial deformations by allowing the user to edit cross-sections along spline-curves. In the presented system, we utilize two variants of sweep-based FFDs to apply our deformation styles to the geometry. A further sweep-based algorithm is [HYC*05]. The authors use sweep-based deformation to create skinned skeletal animation. To a certain degree, this allows the creation of customized deformations, as the user can model muscles, which are taken into account during the deformation.

To provide more realistic deformations, advanced methods such as [BMGK06], [MG04], [CGC*02] and [PJS06] have been invented. They allow the adjustment of the material stiffness, which directly affects the deformation. Other methods, such as [ZHS*05] construct an inner graph to preserve the mesh's inner volume while deforming.

A method allowing the reuse of deformations is [SP04], where the animation of one mesh may drive the deformation of a another, similar mesh. Different from ours, their method is targeted on reusing the complete deformation, while our method is especially focused on reusing a deformation's behavior.

Example based methods allow the pose-dependent modification of animations. They have been introduced by pose-space-deformation (PSD) [LCF00] and advanced by [TRN06] and [SCFRC01]. PSD basically allows the artist to individualize particular poses, where intermediate poses are calculated by interpolation. In our case, pose-dependent deformations can also be modeled by the artist, but in a different way. Instead of directly modifying a certain vertex in a certain pose, our method targets at a more abstract design, covering all poses at once.

Different from the former approaches are cloth simulations to provide realistic deformations and surface details. A comprehensive overview can be found in [MTV05]. Related to cloth and somehow similar to our method, also [VMT99], [JJT05] and [LC04] allow the design of surface details for the animation. However, different from our design, all three methods apply surface details in direction to the surface normal instead of using FFD, and dependent on the local mesh deformation instead of utilizing the skeleton's pose. A method different from PSD to apply surface details based on the pose, is [DJW*06], where wrinkles are generated procedurally to create cloth-like behaviors.

5. Splines

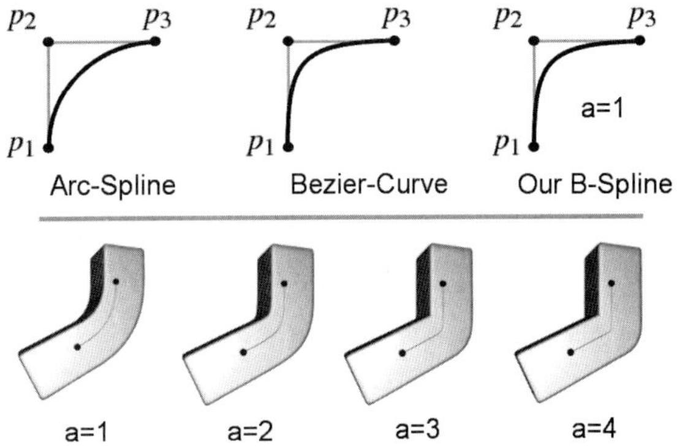

Figure 1: *Spline functions: In the upper row, we compare our short-listed spline functions. The lower row shows the ability of our spline to adjust the stiffness by parameter a.*

In order to achieve spline-aligned deformation, we first have to find a suitable spline-function. For making a decision, we short-listed the trigonometric Arc-spline and the polynomial Bézier-spline. Both can be evaluated very fast, which is important for our GPU-based implementation. In order to provide highest performance, we have further decided to limit the number of control points to three. However, both functions do not naturally allow a modification of the curve stiffness without adding further control points. In our approach, the second control point basically represents a joint's rotation center, and hence, additional control points will complicate the computation. Since we want to keep a simple and easy handling, we remained using three control points $p_{1,2,3}$ and modified the basic Bézier spline function f_b to create a new spline function f_m, providing an additional parameter a for a continuous variable adjustment of the spline's stiffness (Fig.1):

$$\Delta_{12} = p_2 - p_1$$
$$\Delta_{23} = p_3 - p_2$$

$$\forall x \in \mathbb{R} \mid x \in [0,1]$$
$$\forall a \in \mathbb{R} \mid a \geq 2$$

Conventional Bezier curve:

$$f_b(x) = p_1 \cdot (1-x)^2 + p_2 \cdot (2 \cdot x \cdot (1-x)) + p_3 \cdot x^2$$
$$f_b'(x) = p_1 \cdot 2 \cdot (x-1) + p_2 \cdot (2-4x) + p_3 \cdot 2 \cdot x$$

Our modified Bezier curve:

$$f_m(x) = p_1 + \Delta_{12} \cdot (1-(1-x)^a) + \Delta_{23} \cdot x^a$$
$$f_m'(x) = \Delta_{12} \cdot a \cdot (1-x)^{a-1} + \Delta_{23} \cdot a \cdot x^{a-1}$$

5.1. Spline Aligned Deformation

In order to apply our spline as a geometric deformation, it is necessary to construct a complete coordinate-system around

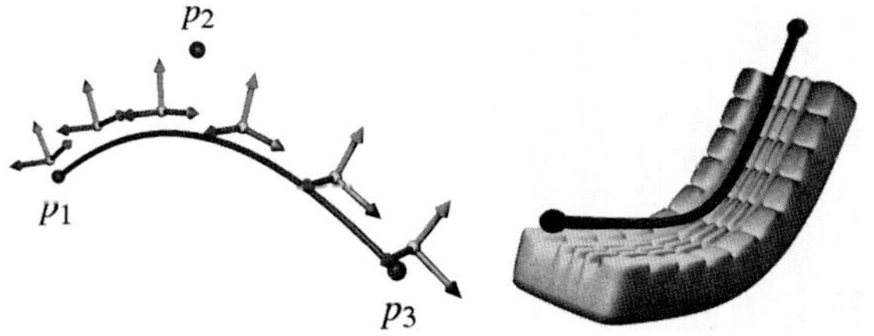

Figure 2: *The spline coordinate system: The left side shows the spline function in violet together with the spline's coordinate system. The spline's tangent is indicated in blue, the normal in red, the binormal in green and the origin of each coordinate system in yellow. On the right-hand side, we can see an example deformation.*

it, the so-called Frenet-frame, as shown in Fig.2. We can compute a complete orthonormal basis b for each position of the spline, consisting of origin b_O, normal b_N, tangent b_T and binormal b_B as follows:

$$\begin{aligned} b_T(x) &= f'_m(x) \\ b_N &= \Delta_{12} \times \Delta_{23} \\ b_B(x) &= b_N \times b_T(x) \\ b_O(x) &= f_m(x) \end{aligned}$$

$$B = [b_N \mid b_B \mid b_T \mid b_O]$$

$$B = \begin{bmatrix} b_N.x & b_B.x & b_T.x & b_O.x \\ b_N.y & b_B.y & b_T.y & b_O.y \\ b_N.z & b_B.z & b_T.z & b_O.z \\ 0 & 0 & 0 & 1 \end{bmatrix}$$

The origin of the coordinate frame is simply the spline function f_m itself. Then, the tangent is equal to the spline's derivative f'_m, the normal can be pre-calculated as it is perpendicular to the three control points $p_{1,2,3}$ and finally the binormal can be computed as cross-product of the normal and the tangent vector. We can further create the 4x4 transformation matrix B by arranging our four computed vectors as column vectors.

5.2. Spline Binding

Prior to the deformation, we have to map all vertices of our target mesh perpendicular to a definite position x on the spline. We achieve this by utilizing a binary search algorithm, starting at $x = 0.5$ as it is shown in Fig. 3. In order to determine the search direction for x at each step, we can utilize the perpendicular constraint based on the scalar product $\langle \cdot \mid \cdot \rangle$, the vertex v and the plane defined by b_T and b_O as follows:

$$\langle b_T(x) \mid v - b_O(x) \rangle = \begin{cases} < 0, & \text{v lies in front of the plane} \\ = 0, & \text{v lies in the plane (solved)} \\ > 0, & \text{v lies behind the plane} \end{cases}$$

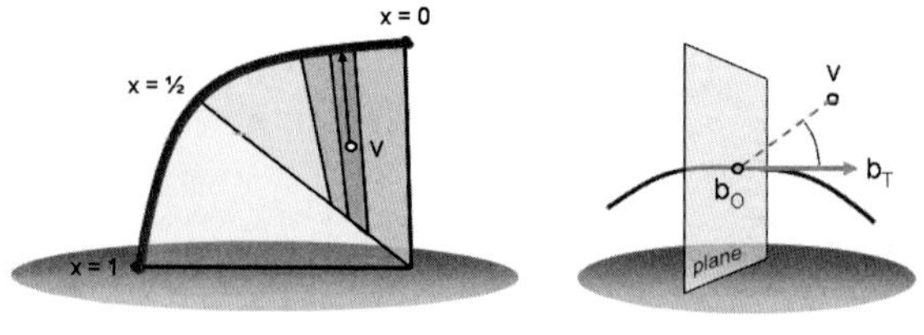

Figure 3: *The binding process: The left side shows the perpendicular mapping of vertex v to the spline by using binary search. The right side shows a way to determine the search direction in each step.*

For further computations, we introduce the spline-basis representation v' of v according to the spline's matrix B:

$$v' = B^{-1} \cdot v$$

6. Deformation Styles

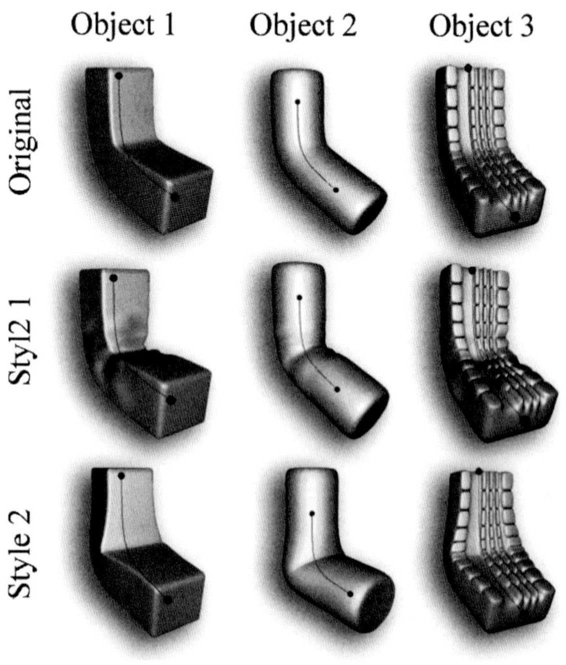

Figure 4: *Deformation Styles: We applied two different deformation styles equally to three objects. Style 1 shows the radial, texture based approach while Style 2 is an example for the rectangular, curve-based method.*

In order to allow a more flexible adjustment of the spline-aligned deformation, we are introducing the use of deformation styles. They allow the pose-dependent modeling of a joint's deformation which can be used to create material behaviors of metal, cloth or muscles. Each style is created from the combination of two pose-dependent FFD variants, where each variant has its own advantages that cannot be replaced by the other. The first method applies a radial scale envelope (Fig.4, Style 1) while the second method is using a rectangular scale envelope (Fig. 4, Style 2).

6.1. Radial Scale Envelope

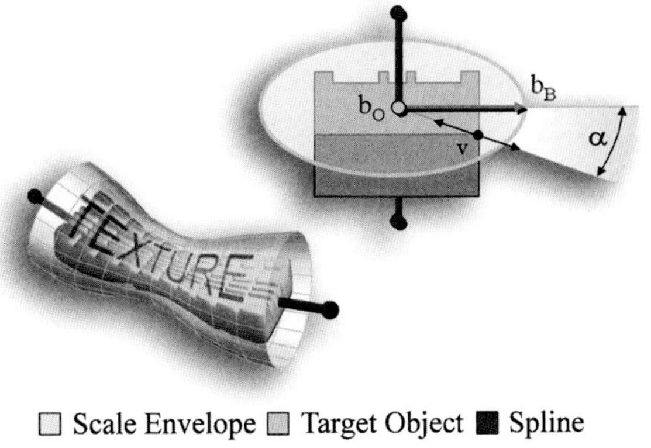

Figure 5: *Radial Scale Envelope: The lower left side shows an example envelope while the upper right side shows the concentric scaling of v in relation to the spline.*

The Radial Scale Envelope is shown in Fig.4 as Style 1 and designed to allow high resolution skin deformation effects such as folds and wrinkles, for example. The algorithm basically applies the deformation by concentrically scaling a vertex v of the target object in relation to the spline origin b_O, as it is shown in Fig.5. The scaling is determined by a radial scale function S_{rs}, which depends on the two-dimensional position (x,α) on the envelopes surface and the pose of the joint. The pose is defined by the joint's twist γ and the joint's bend-angle β, where β is based on the two vectors Δ_{12} and Δ_{23}. The angle α denotes the angle between the vertex v and the spline's binormal b_B in relation to the spline's origin b_O. We define our deformation function D_{rad} to evaluate the deformed vertex as follows.

$$\forall \alpha, \beta \in [0, \pi]$$
$$\forall \gamma \geq 0$$

$$D_{rad}(v') = v' \cdot S_{rs}(x, \alpha, \beta, \gamma)$$

Since the scaling needs to be applied in spline space, we are using v' instead of v. This simplifies our calculation, as the origin in spline-space is b_O and the multiplication of v' by any scalar is equal to scaling v' in relation to b_O.

6.2. Radial Scale Function and Textures

The scale function S_{rs} is the heart of the radial deformation and computes the scaling based on three scale textures, shown in Fig.6, upper row. The first texture T_f is used for frontal scaling, the second for lateral (T_l) and the third for

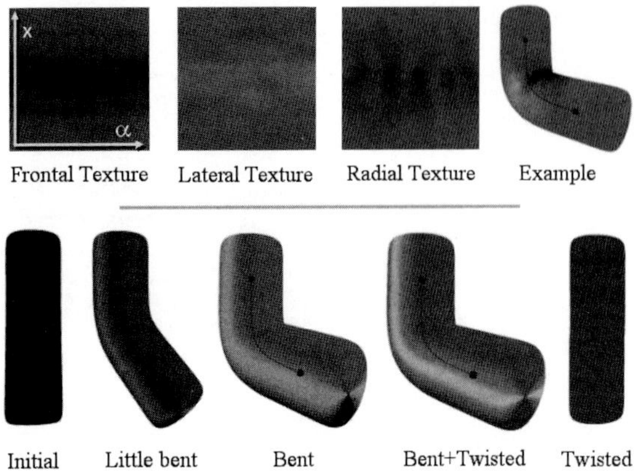

Figure 6: *Scale Textures: The upper row shows the three scale textures that were used to create Style 1 in Fig.4 and an example object where the textures are applied. The lower row shows the pose-dependent weight calculation to apply the three textures, where red corresponds to the weight of the frontal scale texture, green to the lateral and blue to the radial.*

radial (T_r). The weight distribution for the three textures can be seen in Fig.6, lower row. The weight for the frontal texture w_f represented by red, for the lateral w_l by green and for the radial w_r by blue. In order to compute the scale factor for a certain vertex v, we sample all three textures at the texture-coordinate $(x,\alpha/\pi)$, evaluate the three pose-dependent weights $w_{f,l,r}$ and compute the scaling result S_{rs} as follows.

$$\forall w_f, w_l, w_r \in [0, 1]$$
$$\forall w_{sum}, t_f, t_l, t_r, T_f, T_l, T_r \geq 0$$

$$w_f = \max(-\cos(\alpha), 0) \cdot \beta$$
$$w_l = |\sin(\alpha)| \cdot \beta$$
$$w_r = \gamma$$
$$w_{sum} = w_f + w_l + w_r$$

$$t_f = w_f \cdot T_f(x, \alpha/\pi)$$
$$t_l = w_l \cdot T_l(x, \alpha/\pi)$$
$$t_r = w_r \cdot T_r(x, \alpha/\pi)$$

$$S_{rs} = (t_f + t_l + t_r)/\max(1, w_{sum}) + \max(1 - w_{sum}, 0)$$

The idea of this formula is basically to compute the weight for the frontal and the lateral texture based on the angle α and the radial weight based on the twist angle γ. In our formula, w_{sum} represents the sum of all weights, and $t_{f,l,r}$ the weighted texture samples. In order to preserve unity scaling for identity textures at any pose, our formula meets the following condition:

$$\forall x, \alpha \mid T_{f,l,r}(x, \alpha/\pi) = 1 : S_{rs}(x, \alpha, \beta, \gamma) = 1, \forall \beta, \gamma$$

6.3. Rectangular Scale Envelope

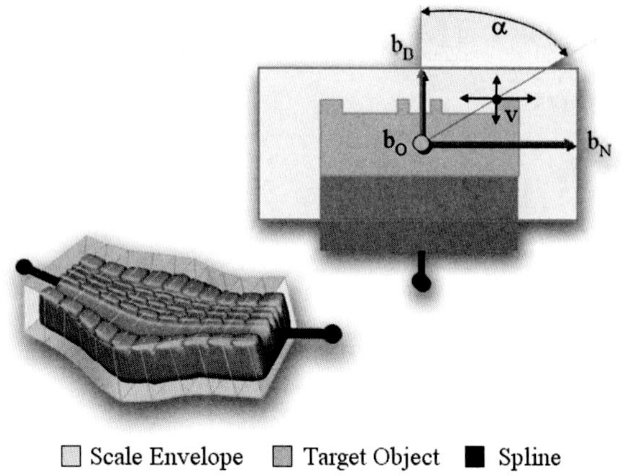

Figure 7: *Rectangular Scale Envelope: The left side shows the application to an example object while the right side shows the scaling of v corresponding to b_B and b_N*

The rectangular scale envelope is shown in Fig.4 as Style 2 and thought to allow the design of the deformations contour. The algorithm basically applies scaling of a vertex v in the two directions b_B and b_N independently, as shown in Fig.7. This is very different from the former radial method that applies a concentric scaling. The purpose of the rectangular approach is the modeling of major frontal folds or lateral effects such as creating bulges. In order to design the deformation, the artist has the freedom to create three functions, which drive the scaling in the frontal, lateral and radial direction.

The scaling is driven by two scaling functions $S_{f,l}$, whereas S_f applies frontal scaling in direction of b_B and S_l the lateral in direction b_N. More specifically, we can write the deformation function D_{rect} as follows:

$$D_{rect}(v') = \begin{bmatrix} v'_x \cdot S_l(x, \beta, \gamma) \\ v'_y \cdot S_f(x, \alpha, \beta, \gamma) \\ v'_z \\ 1 \end{bmatrix}$$

The rectangular scaling is also calculated in spline space, and we therefore use v' instead of v. The spline-space representation v' of v is very handy, as the x-axis in spline space is along b_N and the y-axis along b_B. This allows an easy application of the two scaling functions S_f (frontal) and S_l (lateral). As before, the angle α defines the angle between v and b_B in relation to b_O. The two angles β and γ define the spline's pose.

6.4. Rectangular Scale Functions

For designing the rectangular scale envelope, the artist can define three curves $C_{f,l,r}$, which directly affect the contour of the deformed object in frontal (C_f), lateral (C_l) and radial

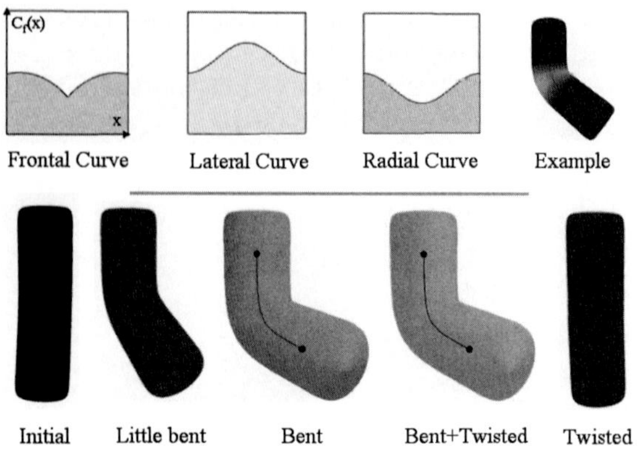

Figure 8: *Rectangular Scaling: The upper row shows the three scale functions that were used to create Style 2 in Fig.4. In the example object on the right, we can see the scale factors while bending. Green represents the lateral and red for the frontal scaling. The lower row shows the pose-dependent weights. Red corresponds to the weight of the frontal scale function, green to the lateral and blue to the radial.*

(C_r) direction. Fig.8, uppper row, shows the three curves that have been used to create Style 2 in Fig.4. The three curves are basically applied to the two scaling functions $S_{f,l}$ as the textures $T_{f,l,r}$ have been applied to S_{rs} before. The only difference is, that we have to separately treat frontal and lateral scaling. We can further simplify the calculation of the lateral weight w'_l as it is not depending on α anymore and write the formula for S_f and S_l as follows.

$$\forall C_f, C_l, C_r, c_f, c_l, c_r, w'_l, w_{sum1}, w_{sum2} \geq 0$$

$$w'_l = \beta$$
$$w_{sum1} = w_f + w_r$$
$$w_{sum2} = w'_l + w_r$$

$$c_f = w_f \cdot C_f(x)$$
$$c_l = w'_l \cdot C_l(x)$$
$$c_r = w_r \cdot C_r(x)$$

$$S_f = (c_f + c_r)/\max(1, w_{sum1}) + \max(1 - w_{sum1}, 0)$$
$$S_l = (c_l + c_r)/\max(1, w_{sum2}) + \max(1 - w_{sum2}, 0)$$

To get an idea of the pose-dependent weights that are used to define the importance of each curve C, we include a couple of example poses in Fig.8, lower row. They demonstrate the weights by color indication. For the computation of S_f and S_l, we introduce three new variables in addition to the previous formula of S_{rs}. The first is w'_l, our new lateral weight, the second w_{sum1} to store the frontal weight and the third w_{sum2} to store the radial weight. As for the radial scaling function S_{rs}, our frontal and lateral scaling functions S_f and S_l also have to preserve unity scaling ($S_{f,l} = 1$) for identity curves ($C_{f,l,r} = 1$).

7. Deformation Styles and Spline Skinning

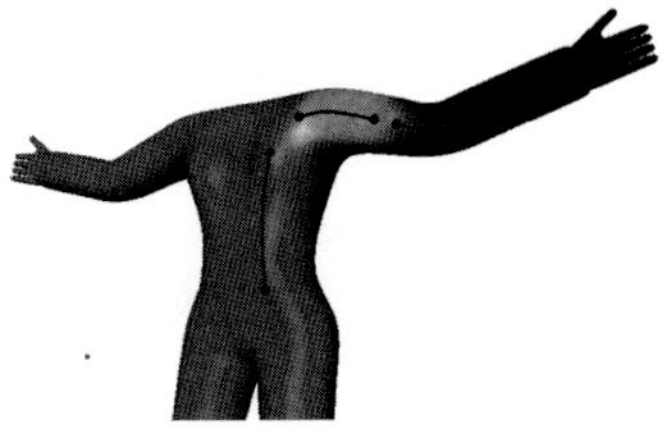

Figure 9: *Spline skinning: The colors indicate the weight for each spline. Red is related to the body spline, green to the shoulder and blue to the elbow.*

To compute our final deformed vertex v_f for n influencing splines B_i, we can simply associate our prior deformations D_{rect} and D_{rad} as follows:

$$v_f = \sum_{i=1}^{n} w_i \cdot B_i \cdot D_{rect}(D_{rad}({B'}_i^{-1} \cdot v))$$

For the formula, we use two different spline bases. The basis of the actual pose is defined by B, while B' defines the basis while binding. We successively apply our radial deformation first, then our rectangular scaling and the spline deformation last, before using the skinning weights w_i for computing the final result. In transition areas where two or more splines meet, styles are blended automatically depending on the skinning weights. For the basic case, in which only spline skinning is used, we get the well-known formula of SSD by pre-computing B''_i:

$$B''_i = B_i \cdot {B'}_i^{-1}$$

$$v_f = \sum_{i=1}^{n} w_i \cdot B''_i \cdot v$$

The skinning weights are defined by the artist, who can paint them onto the surface as in Fig.9. This is already a common technique in most professional modeling tools such as Maya or 3DS Max. To preserve a correct scaling, all weights w_i must sum up to one.

8. Implementation Details

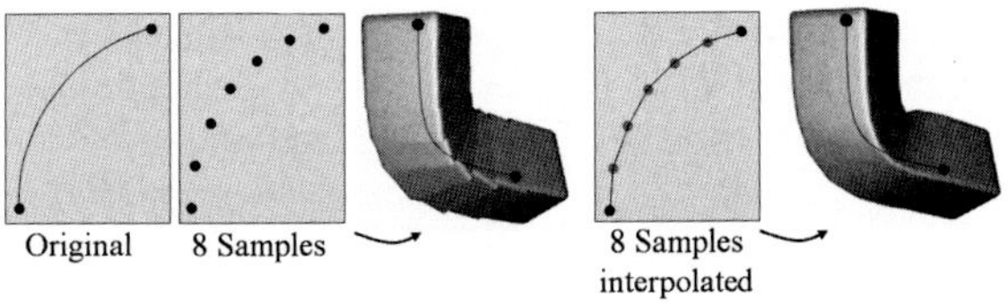

Figure 10: *Spline discretization: Pre-computing all splines is one of the key improvements in our implementation to increase the speed.*

In order to achieve an efficient GPU-based implementation, we had to introduce several optimizations and restrictions to our algorithm. Our first optimization is to separate the spline computation from the per-vertex deformation. In our initial implementation, we were required to evaluate three spline bases per vertex, which was quite demanding. Therefore, we outsourced the computation of the spline basis B to a preprocessing step. There we sample the spline at a fixed number of positions and store the result into three float textures. We require three textures since we need to store the complete basis B consisting of 12 variables at each position, which is equal to three RGBA pixels.

Now, for deforming one vertex, it is sufficient to only sample the pre-computed textures at the splines position x, which is much faster. Here we also profit from the graphic cards texture-filtering feature, as we can directly receive the linearly interpolated spline basis. Without this feature, our spline will show aliasing effects as in Fig.10.

To further improve the speed, we limited the number of influencing spline curves per vertex to three and only apply one deformation style to the most relevant spline. This is sufficient for most cases, as the joint centers of different joints are usually distant enough to prevent errors. As for the deformation, we deform each triangle's vertices and surface normals—but we do not include binormals and tangent vectors. Another issue is the computation accuracy. As recent graphic cards show a weakness to 32-Bit floating point texture filtering, we decided to use 16-Bit textures, which still provides enough accuracy for satisfying results. The filtering of 32-Bit textures is often too slow or even unsupported.

9. Limitations

Even though our method has many advantages in the design of high quality deformations, there are also certain limitations. This first is volume preservation. Since our method is completely dependent on the artist's design, it is up to the artist to design a deformation that seems to preserve the volume or one that models a hollow material and not preserves it. Our second issue is related to PSD. Unlike PSD, where each vertex of a target mesh can freely be modeled pose-dependently, our deformation styles can only affect vertices that are close to the joint they are attached to. Their movement is further defined by the constraints of sweep based FFD. Our last issue regards self intersections. The proposed method does not compute or automatically prevent them—however, the artist may create deformation styles that give the impression of an intersection-free deformation.

10. Results

The first results of our approach can already be seen in Fig.4, where two styles are applied to three objects. Since the objects are very different, we can successfully demonstrate the geometry independence of our method. More appealingly, Fig.11 can demonstrate the effectiveness of our algorithm. We applied a metal-like behavior to a cuboid and created snapshots from various poses.

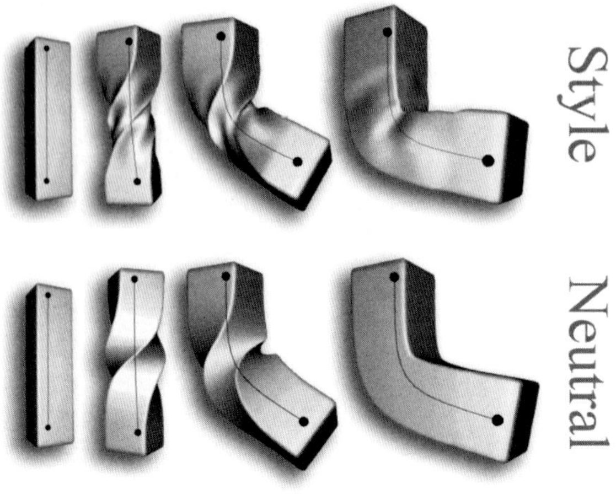

Figure 11: *Metal: This figure shows the animation of designed metal, which smoothly deforms as the pose changes.*

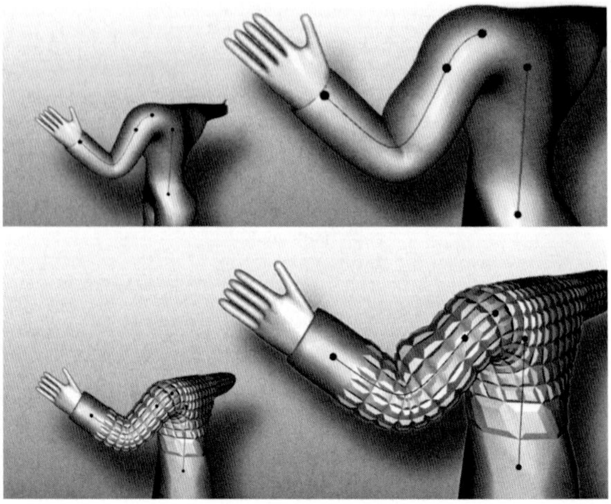

Figure 12: *Muscles: Created muscles can easily be applied to different characters simultaneously.*

In Fig.12, we present the method's ability to design transferable muscle bulges. The left side shows two characters using conventional spline-skinning, while the right side includes our deformation styles. As expected, the surface details of the character in the lower row do not interfere with the applied muscle-style. An example for modeling the deformation of a hollow material can be seen in Fig.13. We improved the realism by displacing the spline origin b_O along the binormal b_B while applying D_{rad} and D_{rect}. The successful prevention of self-intersections by using deformation styles can be seen in Fig.14. It is further an example for designed lateral bulges, whereas all curves are taken from Fig.8. The imitation of cloth is demonstrated by Fig.15, where we clearly can recognize the applied cloth style near the knee region. The textures that have been used in the results were painted using conventional imaging tools. However, for an improved workflow, interactive texture-painting in a WYSIWYG fashion might be advantageous.

For our implementation we used the OpenGL shading language GLSL and the render-to-vertexbuffer technique [Sch06], which can be realized in OpenGL by using the pixel-buffer-object (PBO) extension. The benchmark of our method is displayed in Fig.16, where we tested various algorithm configurations. In case that only basic spline skinning is used, our algorithm gets close to SSD and reaches the pleasing speed of 85 Million vertices per second. If our deformation methods are added step by step, the speed decreases to 30M vertices per second, which is still satisfactory for real-time applications. The speed is not equal for all objects, which might be caused by an implementation issue of our method. We switch the rendering context of the frame-buffer-object (FBO) for each object, which is a relatively expensive operation. However, there is no direct relation to computing the deformation.

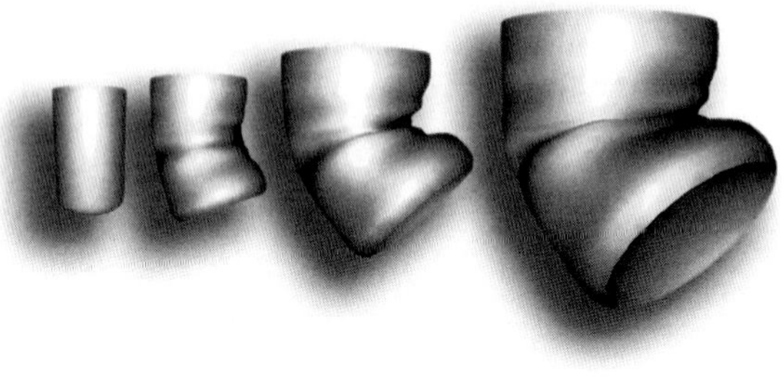

Figure 13: *Hollow materials: Here an animation of crunching an empty can.*

To measure our method's performance more detailed, we created a general timing-breakdown, shown in Table 1. We investigated the timing for two scenes—cuboid and cylinder. For each of the two objects, we also computed the skinning based on three spline-curves, each approximated by 32 samples. The scale texture resolution was 32x64 pixels. As for the timing breakdown, we can see that the major time consumption is caused by our two deformation methods (radial and rect deform) and followed by the spline-skinning (spline deform). Precalculating the spline matrices requires surprisingly less time. The step called *Copy FBO to VBO* is required by the OpenGL architecture and does a complete copy of all vertices from the FBO to the vertex-buffer-object. The final step for rendering the scene is relatively fast, as we did not include complex lighting evaluations. For benchmarking, we created character scenes consisting of about 1 Million vertices to get representative results. In Fig.16, the number in front of each character indicates the number of times it was duplicated to reach 1M vertices.

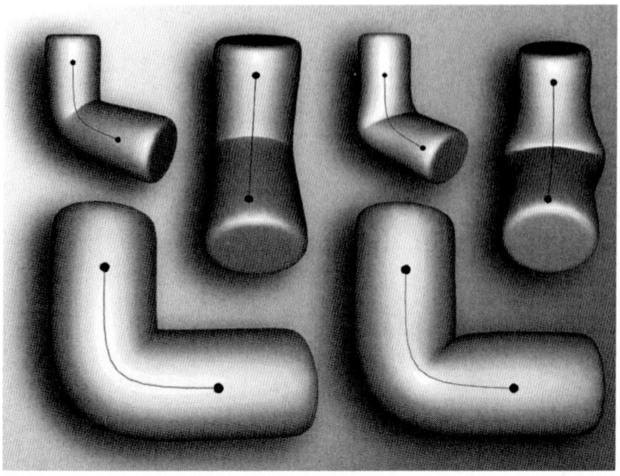

Figure 14: *Self intersections: Demonstrated is the efficient removal of self intersections (right) as well as modeled lateral bulges. The the non-style version is shown on the left.*

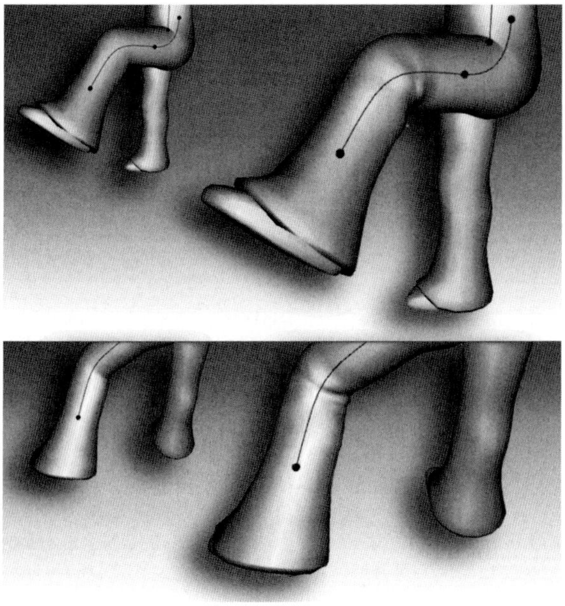

Figure 15: *Cloth: This example shows the algorithm's ability to imitate cloth-like wrinkles.*

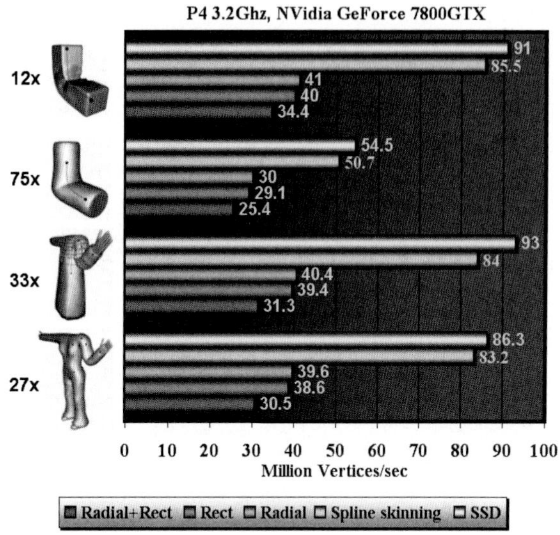

Figure 16: *Benchmark results: Spline skinning indicates basic spline aligned deformation, Radial adds D_{rad}, Rect adds D_{rect} and Rect+Radial adds both.*

Table 1: *Timing breakdown: The table shows the detailed timing of our GPU-based implementation. Cuboid and Cylinder refer to the first and second object in Fig.16.*

Scene	12x Cuboid	75x Cylinder
Vertices Object	12528	92526
Vertices Scene	12 x 12k = 0.94M	75 x 92k = 1.11M
Spline Samples	12 x 3 x 32 = 1152	75 x 3 x 32 = 7200
Timing (Scene)		
Spline Matrices	0.3 ms	0.3 ms
Deform (Radial)	7.8 ms	8.7 ms
Deform (Rect)	12.6 ms	9.7 ms
Deform (Spline)	5.5 ms	7.9 ms
Copy FBO to VBO	1.9 ms	4.9 ms
Render Scene	3.4 ms	4.5 ms
Total	31.7 ms	36.1 ms
Vertices/sec	34.4M	25.4M

11. Conclusion

In our initial research on deformation styles for character animation, we have presented an efficient implementation by utilizing sweep-based FFD, applied to spline skinning. Deformation styles have the advantage of allowing abstract design of a deformation which can be used over and over again for various animations and characters. In larger productions, this can be very useful, to save artist's time by creating individualized deformations which have to be applied to a multitude of different characters.

Our proposed method can further exhibit an excellent performance, as the final implementation is capable of rendering massive scenes with customized deformations in realtime. The implementation also contributes in the field of spline-based skinned skeletal animation, as our method significantly outperforms previous approaches. Since we apply the basic weight-based skinning method of SSD, integration in existing animation systems can be easily achieved. We believe that the idea of deformation styles can pave the way for further fruitful research and also can have many practical applications.

12. Future work

As our method only shows one way to achieve abstract pose dependent design, further research might come up with different or more general approaches. One idea might be for example the utilization of volumetric scale textures to achieve a more flexible deformation. Another one could be, to pass the deformation further detailed to the surface by utilizing bump- or displacement maps, which is in particular of interest for low-poly models.

References

[BMGK06] BOTSCH M., M.PAULY, GROSS M., KOBBELT L.: Primo: Coupled prisms for intuitive surface modeling. In *Eurographics Symposium in Geometry Processing* (2006), pp. 11–20.

[CGC*02] CAPELL S., GREEN S., CURLESS B., DUCHAMP T., POPOVIC Z.: Interactive skeleton-driven dynamic deformations. In *SIGGRAPH '02: ACM SIGGRAPH 2002 Papers* (2002), pp. 586–593.

[CSM05] CORNEA N., SILVER D., MIN P.: Curve-skeleton applications. In *Visualization, 2005. VIS 05. IEEE* (2005), pp. 95–102.

[DJW*06] DECAUDIN P., JULIUS D., WITHER J., BOISSIEUX L., SHEFFER A., CANI M.-P.: Virtual garments: A fully geometric approach for clothing design. *Computer Graphics Forum (EG'06 proc.) 25*, 3 (sep 2006), 625–634.

[FO06] FORSTMANN S., OHYA J.: Fast skeletal animation by skinned arc-spline based deformation. In *Eurogrpahics Short-Papers* (2006), pp. 1–4.

[HYC*05] HYUN D.-E., YOON S.-H., CHANG J.-W., SEONG J.-K., KIM M.-S., JÜTTLER B.: Sweep-based human deformation. *The Visual Computer 21*, 8-10 (2005), 542–550.

[JJT05] JING F., JONEJA A., TANG K.: Modeling wrinkles on smooth surfaces for footwear design. *Computer-Aided Design 37*, 8 (2005), 815–823.

[KCOZ06] KAVAN L., COLLINS S., O'SULLIVAN C., ZARA J.: Dual quaternions for rigid transformation blending. Technical report TCD-CS-2006-46, Trinity College Dublin, 2006.

[KZ05] KAVAN L., ZARA J.: Spherical blend skinning: a real-time deformation of articulated models. In *SI3D '05: Proceedings of the 2005 symposium on Interactive 3D graphics and games* (2005), pp. 9–16.

[LC04] LARBOULETTE C., CANI M.-P.: Real-time dynamic wrinkles. In *CGI '04: Proceedings of the Computer Graphics International (CGI'04)* (2004), pp. 522–525.

[LCF00] LEWIS J. P., CORDNER M., FONG N.: Pose space deformation: a unified approach to shape interpolation and skeleton-driven deformation. In *SIGGRAPH '00* (2000), pp. 165–172.

[MG04] MUELLER M., GROSS M.: Interactive virtual materials. In *GI '04: Proceedings of the 2004 conference on Graphics interface* (2004), pp. 239–246.

[MTLT88] MAGNENAT-THALMANN N., LAPERRIERE R., THALMANN D.: Joint-dependent local deformations for hand animation and object grasping. In *Proceedings of Graphics Interface '88* (1988), pp. 26–33.

[MTV05] MAGNENAT-THALMANN, VOLINO: From early draping to haute couture models: 20 years of research. *The Visual Computer 21*, 8–10 (2005), 506–519.

[PJS06] POPA T., JULIUS D., SHEFFER A.: Material-aware mesh deformations. In *SMI '06: Proceedings of the IEEE International Conference on Shape Modeling and Applications 2006 (SMI'06)* (2006), p. 22.

[SCFRC01] SLOAN P.-P. J., CHARLES F. ROSE I., COHEN M. F.: Shape by example. In *SI3D '01: Proceedings of the 2001 symposium on Interactive 3D graphics* (2001), pp. 135–143.

[Sch06] SCHEUERMANN T.: Render to vertex buffer with d3d9. Siggraph 2006 Course 3: GPU Shading and Rendering, 2006.

[SF98] SINGH K., FIUME E.: Wires: a geometric deformation technique. In *SIGGRAPH '98* (1998), pp. 405–414.

[SP86] SEDERBERG T. W., PARRY S. R.: Free-form deformation of solid geometric models. *j-COMP-GRAPHICS 20*, 4 (Aug. 1986), 151–160.

[SP04] SUMNER R. W., POPOVIC J.: Deformation transfer for triangle meshes. In *SIGGRAPH '04: ACM SIGGRAPH 2004 Papers* (2004), pp. 399–405.

[TRN06] TAEHYUN RHEE J. L., NEUMANN U.: Real-timeweighted pose-space deformation on the gpu. *Computer Graphics Forum (Eurographics'06 proc.) 25*, 3 (2006), 439–448.

[VMT99] VOLINO P., MAGNENAT-THALMANN: Fast geometrical wrinkles on animated surfaces. In *7th International Conference in Central Europe on Computer Graphics and Visualization* (1999), pp. 55–66.

[YK06] YOON S.-H., KIM M.-S.: Sweep-based freeform deformations. *Computer Graphics Forum (Eurographics'06 proc.) 25*, 3 (2006), 487–496.

[YSZ06] YANG X., SOMASEKHARAN A., ZHANG J. J.: Curve skeleton skinning for human and creature characters: Research articles. *Comput. Animat. Virtual Worlds 17*, 3/4 (2006), 281–292.

[ZHS*05] ZHOU K., HUANG J., SNYDER J., LIU X., BAO H., GUO B., SHUM H.-Y.: Large mesh deformation using the volumetric graph laplacian. In *SIGGRAPH '05: ACM SIGGRAPH 2005 Papers* (2005), pp. 496–503.

Eurographics/ ACM SIGGRAPH Symposium on Computer Animation (2007)
D. Metaxas and J. Popovic (Editors)

Harmonic Skeleton for Realistic Character Animation

Grégoire Aujay[1] Franck Hétroy[1] Francis Lazarus[2] Christine Depraz[1]

[1]EVASION - LJK (CNRS, INRIA and Univ. Grenoble)
[2]GIPSA-Lab (CNRS and Univ. Grenoble)

Abstract

Current approaches to skeleton generation are based on topological and geometrical information only; this can be insufficient for realistic character animation, since the location of the joints does not usually match the real bone structure of the model. This paper proposes the use of anatomical information to enhance the skeleton. Using a harmonic function, this information can be recovered from the skeleton itself, which is guaranteed not to have undesired endpoints. The skeleton is computed as a Reeb graph of such a function over the surface of the model. Starting from one point selected on the head of the character, the entire process is fast, automatic and robust; it generates skeletons whose joints can be associated with the character's anatomy. Results are provided, including a quantitative validation of the generated skeletons.

Categories and Subject Descriptors (according to ACM CCS): I.3.7 [Computer Graphics]: Three-Dimensional Graphics and Realism: Animation

1. Introduction

A common technique for animating a 3D model consists of creating a hierarchical articulated structure, named skeleton (or IK skeleton), whose deformation drives the deformation of the associated model. The location and displacement of the skeleton's joints dictate how the model moves (see Figure 1 for an example). A skeleton attached to a 3D model (usually represented as a mesh) can be either created by hand or computed. In the case of the *realistic* animation of a character (be it a human, an animal or a made-up monster), the first option is most often chosen by artists, although it is a time-consuming task which needs a skilled user. Indeed, professional artists may create an initial skeleton relatively quickly, but often need to make many adjustments during the rigging process because the skin is very sensitive to the exact location of the skeleton's joints: they often have to go back and forth several times between skeleton skinning and testing animation before getting it right. Automatic or semi-automatic methods have several drawbacks: they often allow little control over the result, they can produce noisy skeletons with unwanted joints, and most importantly they rely on the topology and the geometry of the model only, which is not sufficient for realistic animation where the anatomy of the model does not completely match its geometry. For instance, in most cases the spine of a character is close to its back, while the corresponding axis in computer-generated skeletons is usually centered within the body (see Figure 12). Moreover, animation skeletons may have some joints which do not match any anatomical part of the model but are useful for animation purpose (e.g., on the head, see Figure 2).

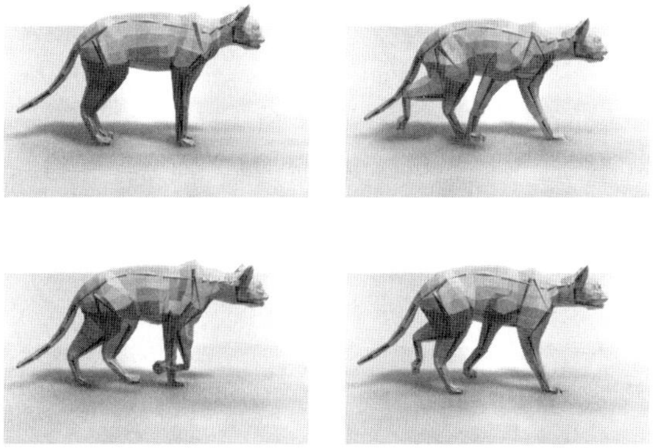

Figure 1: *Walking cat. These images are taken from an animation created using our harmonic skeleton (see the video): joints deformation drives the mesh deformation.*

This paper explains how to automatically, robustly and efficiently compute skeletons adapted to realistic character an-

Symposium on Computer Animation 2007, San Diego, CA, August 03-04, 2007.
© 2007 ACM 978-1-59593-624-4/07/0008 $5.00

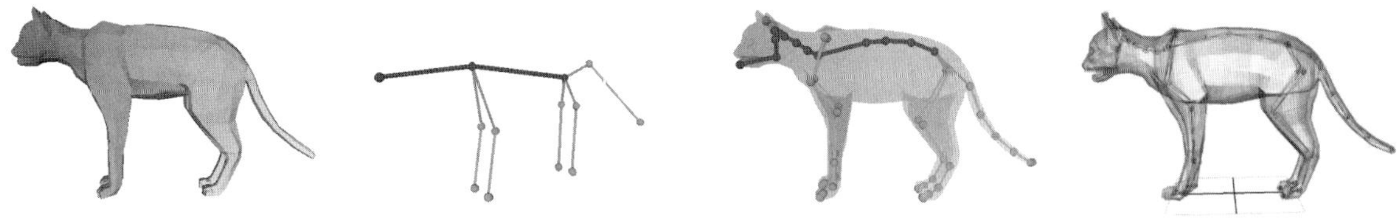

Figure 2: *From left to right: a cat model, the computed harmonic graph with its symmetry axis, the computed harmonic skeleton compared to a previously handmade animation skeleton.*

imation, starting from a single point selected by the user on the model. Generated skeletons match the ones that are created by hand by professionals in most biped and quadruped cases. Moreover, they carry anatomical information (that is to say, we know which joint corresponds to which part of the model), allowing a semantic decomposition of the input meshes.

1.1. Related work

Numerous algorithms have been proposed to compute skeletons of 3D shapes from their geometry. Bloomenthal and Lim [BL99] were among the first ones to point out that these geometric skeletons can be converted to IK skeletons and then used for animation purposes. However, to be useful for animation, skeletons should be structured as graphs, whose nodes correspond to the joints and whose edges correspond to their hierarchy. This discards two-dimensional skeletons such as the Medial Axis [Blu67].

Graph-like skeleton generation algorithms start either from the boundary surface [KT03, LWM*03, DS06, LKA06, TVD06] of the input model, or from its inner volume [GS01, WP02, CSYB05]. Methods working on a volumetric representation of a model have a major drawback: only features with a size greater than the voxel size can be taken into account. This often leads to computationally expensive algorithms.

Katz and Tal [KT03] extract a skeleton from a meshed model using a hierarchical decomposition of this mesh into meaningful parts. Generated skeletons are star-shaped (they contain a root joint, located in the center of mass of the model, from which all other joints derive) and thus are not suited for realistic animation. Lien et al. [LKA06] generate shape decomposition and skeleton simultaneously; the skeleton is computed using centroids and principal axes of the shape's components, which gives a skeleton with geometrically but not necessarily anatomically meaningful positions. The same problem appears with Dey and Sun's robust skeleton computation from the Medial Axis [DS06]. Liu et al. [LWM*03] propose to use a repulsive force field to position the joints. This method is quite slow (as reported in the paper, it takes several minutes to compute the skeleton for a model containing about 10,000 triangles), and does not guarantee that the result will capture all desired features.

Following Shinagawa et al. [SKK91], several authors have proposed to use a mathematical tool called the *Reeb graph* to capture the model's topology, before possible refinements to capture its geometry. A Reeb graph is defined with respect to a mathematical function, and the result highly depends on the choice of this function. In the next section, we precisely define the Reeb graph and then list some existing methods using this mathematical notion.

The algorithm we propose takes as input a triangle mesh. It first computes a Reeb graph of this mesh, in a fast and robust way (that is to say, the graph's leaves are only the desired ones). This abstract graph is then refined and embedded in the 3D space in order to be useful for realistic character animation; this is made possible thanks to a semantic decomposition of the model, given by the graph. Our algorithm computes the skeleton of a model with several hundred of thousand faces in no longer than a few seconds on a low-end computer.

1.2. Mathematical background

Let $f : M \to \mathbb{R}$ be a function defined over a 2-manifold M with or without boundary (that is to say, a surface for which each point has a neighboorhood homeomorphic to a disk or half-disk). Level sets of f are the sets $f^{-1}(u) = \{x \in M, f(x) = u\}$. Each of these sets, if it exists, can be connected or not. For instance, on Figure 3, where f is a height function, $f^{-1}(u)$ is connected for low and high values of u, but is made of several connected components for values around -0.7, 0 and 0.7. For some special values, the number of connected components of the level set changes: these values are called *critical values*, and the corresponding points x on the surface are called *critical points*. The *Reeb graph* of f [Ree46] is a graph whose nodes correspond to these critical points, and which encodes the connectivity between them (see Figure 3). In particular, notice that the leaves of the Reeb graph exactly match the local maxima and minima of f. Mathematically speaking, the Reeb graph of f is defined as the quotient space $M/\sim$, with $\sim$ the following equivalence relation on M:

$$x_1 \sim x_2 \iff \begin{cases} f(x_1) = f(x_2) \\ \text{and } x_1 \text{ and } x_2 \text{ belong to the same} \\ \text{connected component of } f^{-1}(f(x_1)) \end{cases}$$

More details about these notions can be found in e.g. [FK97].

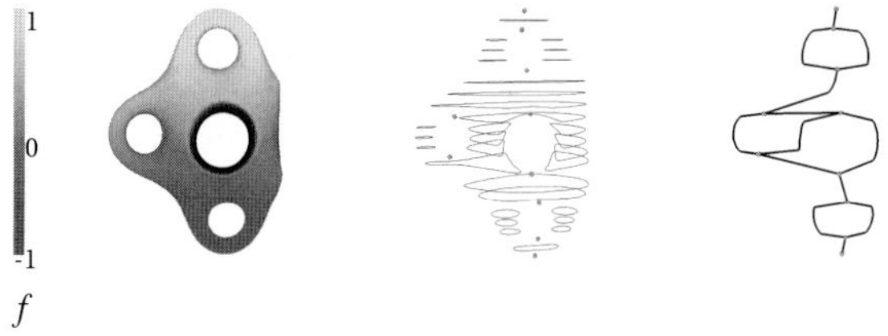

Figure 3: *From left to right: a surface, some level sets of f, the Reeb graph of f.*

A Reeb graph *w.r.t.* a triangulated surface with n edges can be computed in $O(n \log n)$ time [CMEH*03]. However, the choice of the function f is a key issue in revealing information about the surface, and several proposals have been made in order to obtain a relevant graph: the distance on the mesh to a source point [LV99], the integral over the mesh to such a distance (in order to avoid the choice of the source point) [HSKK01], a mapping function that highlights the relevant features [TVD06], etc. Following an idea proposed by Ni et al. [NGH04], we choose to find a "fair" function f, whose extrema will be anatomically significant, by solving Laplace's equation $\triangle f = 0$. Steiner and Fischer did the same [SF01], but their Reeb graph captured neither geometrical nor anatomical features, only the topology of the model.

The main property of such functions f, called *harmonic functions*, is their lack of extrema except at boundary points [NGH04]. They also have the following property: let M be a compact surface, B_M its boundary and $g : M \longrightarrow \mathbb{R}$ a function; there exists a unique solution $f : M \longrightarrow \mathbb{R}$ to the following system, called Laplace's equation with non-homogeneous Dirichlet boundary conditions:

$$\begin{cases} \triangle f(x) = 0 & \forall x \in M \\ f(x) = g(x) & \forall x \in B_M \end{cases} \tag{1}$$

In our case, B_M will be a (disjoint) set of vertices of the mesh, corresponding to anatomically significant parts of the model. We will compute the Reeb graph of the solution $f_{B_M,g}$ to the previous system (1), for some function g which will be described in section 2.1.1; thanks to the property of harmonic functions, the leaves of this graph will exactly match the chosen vertices: in other words, the graph is guaranteed not to be noisy.

1.3. Algorithm overview

The Reeb graph of a function *w.r.t.* a surface is a pair (V, E) with V a set of nodes and $E \subset V \times V$ a set of edges between these nodes. It is minimal in the sense that there is no regular node: each node has either one or at least 3 incident edges. Moreover, nodes do not have 3D coordinates. Thus, in order to construct a skeleton which is suitable for animation from such a graph, we must *embed* it in $\mathbb{R}^3$, that is to say link each node with 3D coordinates. Thus, our method first computes a Reeb graph, then embeds it in $\mathbb{R}^3$. In the following, *node* will refer to the graph while *joint* will refer to the skeleton and *vertex* to the mesh.

Our algorithm runs in seven successive stages:

1. the endpoints of the desired skeleton are chosen by the user or computed (however at least one of them, called the *source node/joint*, must be manually chosen on the head of the character);
2. the harmonic function f solving Laplace's equation with non-homogeneous Dirichlet boundary conditions is computed;
3. the Reeb graph of f is computed with the algorithm described in [CMEH*03];
4. this graph, which we call a *harmonic graph* since f is a harmonic function, is subsequently filtered to recover the symmetry of the character's morphology (i.e., overall structure);
5. starting from the source node, the symmetry axis of the graph is detected;
6. the harmonic graph is refined by inserting regular nodes and embedded in $\mathbb{R}^3$: this gives us the *harmonic skeleton*, which carries anatomical information about the input model (such as "this joint corresponds to the tail");
7. additional heuristics are used in case the model is detected to be a biped or quadruped with sagittally oriented legs (this excludes amphibians, but includes most mammals), in order to fit the IK skeleton that would be manually created by an expert. Although not presented in this paper, equivalent heuristics can be defined for other kinds of characters, such as birds or insects.

The contributions of this paper are the following:

- the computed skeleton is robust: endpoints are exactly the ones that have been chosen, and two meshes representing the same model under two different postures generate equivalent skeletons;
- our algorithm is fast and does not need user intervention, except for the selection of the source joint at the very beginning. However, controlling the skeleton generation is possible, by manually choosing its endpoints or tuning some parameters;
- our method gives a semantic decomposition of the shape (which is used for the embedding process): we know which part of the mesh corresponds to the head, the legs, the trunk and the tail of the character;
- we propose standard skeletons (graphs and their embeddings) for bipeds and quadrupeds with sagittally oriented limbs.

Moreover, in the case of quadrupeds, we have validated our results not only visually but also by comparing parameters with handmade animation skeletons. To our knowledge, this is the first time a quantitative validation is proposed.

The organization of this paper is as follows: section 2 describes stages 1 to 4 of our algorithm, that is to say the computation of the harmonic graph; section 3 explains the construction of the harmonic skeleton from the harmonic graph, that is to say stages 5 and 6; in section 4, we detail the proposed skeletons for bipeds and quadrupeds; we give results and discuss them in section 5; finally, we conclude in section 6.

2. Harmonic graph

2.1. Graph computation

2.1.1. Finding extrema

The first stage of our algorithm is to choose the endpoints of the skeleton; they will correspond to extremal joints. The user must select one source vertex x_{source} on the head of the character, which will give the source node of the graph. We set $f(x_{source}) = 0$. Other endpoints should match relevant anatomical features of the character that the user wants to animate: hands, feet and possibly tail, ears, etc. These endpoints can be either selected manually, or computed. In the latter case, we try to find vertices x such that the distance $d(x_{source}, x)$ on the mesh is locally maximum. Several methods have been proposed to solve this problem: for instance, Dong et al. [DKG05] choose to solve the Poisson equation $\triangle f = -\|\triangle x\|$; the algorithm proposed by Tierny et al. [TVD06] can also be applied, but it does not use the source vertex, which should be selected afterwards among the detected feature vertices, hence it does not ensure this vertex will be on the head of the character. The same problem arises when computing the average geodesic distance function over the mesh, as did Zhang et al. [ZMT05]. In our implementation, we use a fast and more straightforward solution: g is defined as a geodesic distance to x_{source}; we use Dijkstra's algorithm to compute shortest paths on the mesh from the source vertex to all other vertices, as proposed by Lazarus and Verroust [LV99]. This method, as Dong's, has one drawback: multiple neighboring local extrema can be found in almost flat regions. We propose a solution to cluster these extrema, which will be discussed in section 2.2. For each extremum vertex x (be it manually or automatically chosen), the value $f(x)$ is set to the length of the shortest path from the source vertex, as computed by Dijkstra's algorithm (it could also be set to the value given by Dong's method when using this algorithm). Doing so, the harmonic function f can be seen as a smooth approximated distance to the source vertex over the mesh.

2.1.2. Solving Laplace's equation

Once the boundary conditions to Laplace's equation are set, the system (1) is solved using a classical finite elements method of $P1$ type (the function f, defined for each vertex, is linearly interpolated inside each triangle). Since the assembled matrix is very sparse, computation can be done very efficiently (e.g. using the SuperLU solver [DEG*99]).

2.1.3. Generating the graph

The Reeb graph of f is then computed using Cole-McLaughlin's algorithm [CMEH*03]. This algorithm requires f to be a Morse function: this basically means that two neighboring critical points should have two different values for f. To ensure this property, we check if all vertices on the mesh have different values. If several vertices $x_1, \ldots, x_k$ have the same value $f(x_1) = \ldots = f(x_k)$, we order them and change their values slightly.

2.2. Graph filtering

2.2.1. Recovering the shape's symmetries

Even if the model is symmetric, Cole-McLaughlin's algorithm may generate a non-symmetric graph, because the source vertex may not be located exactly on the symmetry plane or axis. We propose here a simple way to recover these symmetries.

Each node n of the graph G is assigned with the value $f(x)$, where x is the critical vertex on the surface corresponding to n. Now, let us give weights to the edges of G. Let (n_1, n_2) be an edge of G. (n_1, n_2) is balanced by the following weight:

$$w(n_1, n_2) = \frac{|f(n_1) - f(n_2)|}{|\max_{n \in G} f(n) - \min_{n \in G} f(n)|} \quad (2)$$

Considering f as an approximated distance to the source vertex over the mesh (see section 2.1.1), $w(n_1, n_2)$ represents the normalized difference between the distance to the source vertex of two "topologically close" vertices. If $w(n_1, n_2)$ is small, this means that the corresponding vertices x_1 and x_2 are approximately at the same distance to the source vertex, and are also located in the same topological area (they are not necessarily geometrically close to each other). Thus, in order to recover the shape's symmetries, we propose to filter the graph by collapsing every *internal* edge with a weight lower than a given threshold t_1. We do not collapse edges containing a leaf node, since this could remove small features.

Notice that we can recover not only *geometrical* symmetries of the model, but also *morphological* ones: for instance, the octopus model of Figure 4 is not symmetric, geometrically speaking, because its tentacles are not in the same position; it can however be regarded as morphologically symmetric, because these tentacles have the same size and are regularly placed around a symmetry axis. As shown on the same model, we can recover not only symmetries *w.r.t.* a plane but also symmetries *w.r.t.* an axis.

2.2.2. Removing irrelevant extrema

As explained in section 2.1.1, it may happen that too many extremum vertices are computed. In order to remove irrelevant extrema, since extrema correspond exactly to the leaf nodes of the graph, we propose to remove the *external* edges (that is to say edges containing a leaf node) with a weight lower than a given threshold t_2, *together with their nodes*. However, these edges should be removed carefully (see Figure 5): in order to avoid extra deletion of edges, they should first be ordered by increasing weight.

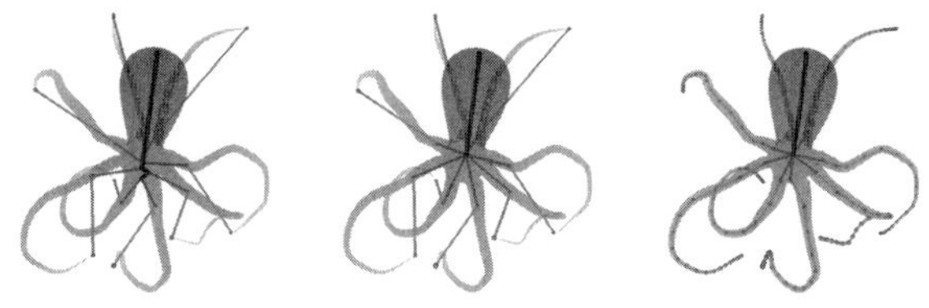

Figure 4: *Left: non-symmetric graph obtained from a model containing a symmetry. Middle: the same graph after filtering ($t_1 = 0.007$). Right: refined harmonic skeleton.*

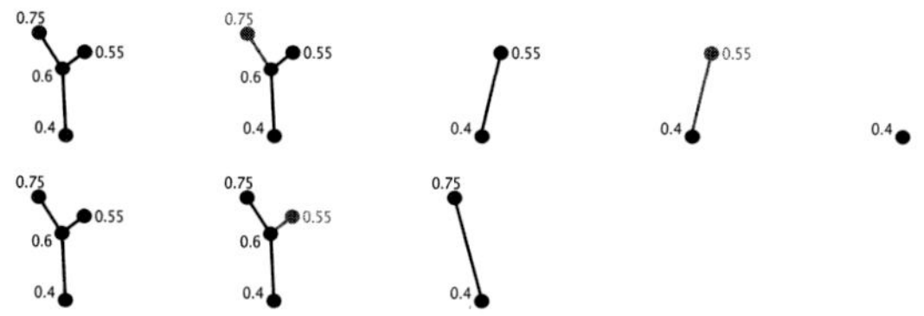

Figure 5: *Deletion of edges whose weight is lower than or equal to $t_2 = 0.15$. Top: without weight ordering. Bottom: with weight ordering.*

Both thresholds t_1 and t_2 can be set by the user, but they can also be computed. Indeed, unwanted edges usually have very small weights compared to the others', since they can be seen as noise while the others are associated with feature sizes. Thus, a statistical analysis upon all the edge's weights can help to set these parameters.

3. Harmonic skeleton

The harmonic graph gives the topological structure of the model. This is not enough to get an animation skeleton: we need to add 3D coordinates to its nodes, which will represent the joints of the skeleton; we may also need to refine the graph. Previous methods constructed the skeleton from a Reeb graph using only topological and geometrical information from the model, which is often not sufficient for realistic animation. We propose to take benefit from anatomical information to design the skeleton; this information will be recovered from the harmonic graph, knowing that the source vertex was chosen on the head of the character. In this section, we explain how to detect symmetries of the model's morphology on the graph and propose a skeleton in general case. In the next section, we show how to improve this general skeleton in the case of biped and quadruped characters.

3.1. Symmetry axis detection

We suppose here that the character's morphology is symmetric. This is often the case: typically, the model has two or four legs, two ears, and the head and the tail (if it exists) are centered with respect to the legs. Thus, the harmonic graph should also be symmetric with respect to an axis (or a node, but a node can be considered as a degenerate case of an axis). We propose here a heuristic to recover this symmetry axis starting from the source node, which is located on this axis since its corresponding vertex is supposed to be on the head of the character.

Finding symmetries on a graph is a NP-complete problem; that is why we must make some hypotheses about the graph to get an efficient algorithm. Several restrictions have been proposed in the graph theory community [DeF99]; we describe here a simple iterative algorithm based on the 3 following assumptions:

1. the source node is located on the symmetry axis;
2. the harmonic graph is actually a tree, i.e. it does not contain any cycle;
3. two subtrees are isomorphic if they have the same depth and if their root nodes have the same degree (that is to say, the same number of child nodes).

The two last hypotheses are relevant for our application, since harmonic graphs are usually simple: they are made of one node for the head, one node for each leg, possibly one extremal node for the tail, for each ear and/or each wing and/or each finger, and that is usually all.

We use n_0 to denote the source node of the harmonic graph, and $(n_0, n_1) = e_0$ as its incident edge: e_0 is on the symmetry axis. n and n' denote nodes of the harmonic graph, whereas e denotes an edge. Our algorithm proceeds as follows:

- $e = (n, n') \leftarrow e_0 = (n_0, n_1)$
- **while** $e \neq NULL$ **loop**
  - add e to the symmetry axis;
  - let $e_1 = (n', n'_1), e_2 = (n', n'_2), \ldots, e_k = (n', n'_k)$ be the incident edges to n', excepting e;
  - for each node n'_j, let T_j be the subtree of G whose root node is n'_j and which does not contain n';
  - store the T_j into sets $\mathcal{S}_1, \ldots, \mathcal{S}_l$ of isomorphic trees, according to assumption number 3;
  - **if** $\exists! \mathcal{S}_i$ which contains only one tree T_i **then** $e \leftarrow e_i = (n', n'_i)$
  - **else** $e \leftarrow NULL$
  - **end if**
- **end loop**

Figure 6 shows the successive steps of the algorithm on an example. It adds edges to the symmetry axis iteratively, discarding subtrees of the harmonic graph that are symmetric *w.r.t.* the computed part of the axis. Note that if several sets $\mathcal{S}_i$ containing one tree exist at the same time the algorithm stops, because it cannot tell which tree has its root on the axis. This algorithm can be applied not only to the harmonic graph G, but also to subtrees of G, in order to find non-principal symmetries. We can thereby obtain a hierarchy of symmetries, like [SKS06].

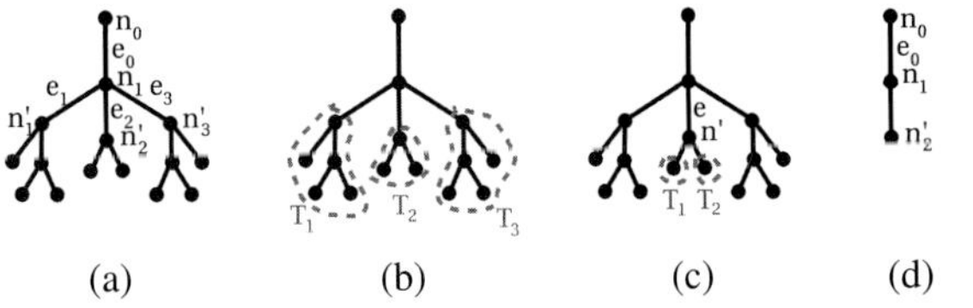

Figure 6: *Symmetry axis detection. (a) Initialization (b) First step: T_1 and T_3 are isomorphic trees, and T_2 is not isomorphic to any other known tree: $e_2 = (n_1, n_2')$ is on the symmetry axis. (c) Second step: T_1 and T_2 are isomorphic, there is no candidate tree to process further on, so the algorithm stops. (d) Detected symmetry axis.*

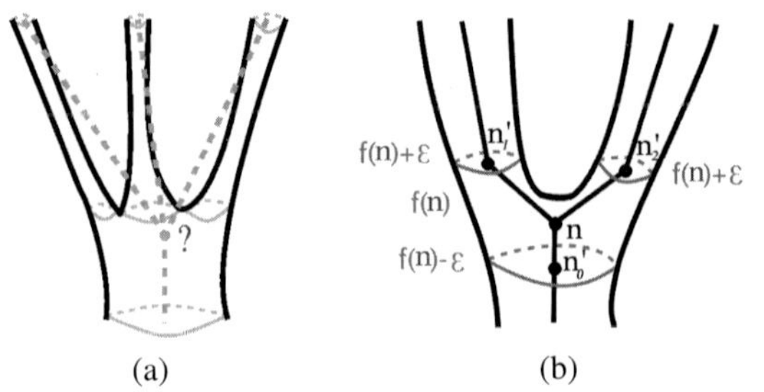

Figure 7: *(a) Some nodes may have more than one corresponding vertex on the mesh. (b) Added regular nodes and possible embedding for internal nodes with 3 incident edges.*

3.2. Simple embedding

Finding an appropriate embedding for each node of the harmonic graph is not a trivial task: even if each extremal node can be embedded onto the corresponding vertex on the mesh, this is not always possible for internal nodes, since they may have more than one corresponding vertex (Figure 7 (a)). Moreover, it is often more relevant to embed an internal node *inside* the model than *on* the surface. Before giving details about how internal nodes will be embedded in $\mathbb{R}^3$, we should explain how regular nodes (nodes with exactly two incident edges) that will be inserted to the graph will be embedded.

Let u be a regular value of f (that is to say a non-critical value), let $f^{-1}(u)$ be its level set, and let C be a connected component of $f^{-1}(u)$. C is a simple closed curve made of segments whose endpoints $p_1, p_2, \ldots, p_k, p_{k+1} = p_1$ intersect the edges of the mesh. We define the *center of C* as the center of mass of these segments [LV99]:

$$center(C) = \frac{\sum_{i=1}^{k} \|p_i p_{i+1}\| \frac{p_i + p_{i+1}}{2}}{\sum_{i=1}^{k} \|p_i p_{i+1}\|} \quad (3)$$

We embed a regular node with value $f(u)$ onto the center of its associated connected component C. This choice is more relevant that the center of mass of the points p_i, since the result is less dependent on the surface's discretization level.

Now, here is the algorithm we propose in order to embed an internal node n:

1. split each incident edge (n, n_i) to n in two, by inserting a new node n_i';
2. assign the value $f(n) + \varepsilon$ or $f(n) - \varepsilon$ to each n_i', depending whether $f(n) < f(n_i)$ or $f(n) > f(n_i)$ (ε should be a small scalar value, lower than the lowest weight among the graph's edges);
3. since each node n_i' is a regular node, embed it as explained before;
4. determine which nodes among these are on the symmetry axis:
   - if there is none, embed n onto the center of mass of the n_i''s embeddings;
   - if there is one, embed n onto the embedding of this node n_k';
   - if there are two (three or more is not possible), choose one of them, embed n onto its embedding and remove the other node from the graph;
5. finally, freeze the new edges (n, n_i'): this means that if one node's embedding is subsequently modified, the other should be modified the same way.

Figure 7 (b) shows the possible embeddings for internal nodes with 3 incident edges. Freezing edges has an important meaning: some degrees of freedom are removed for some joints of our animation skeleton, and freezing allows us to mirror the effect of bones such as the clavicle or the pelvis.

3.3. Joint hierarchy

Embedding the graph's nodes in $\mathbb{R}^3$ is not sufficient to get an applicable animation skeleton: we should also define a joint hierarchy. This can easily be done using the detected symmetry axis on the harmonic graph: the base joint can correspond to any node on this axis, then other joints recursively come from it. Common base joint choices include the head, that is to say the source joint, a node on the symmetry axis with a mean value for f, or the pelvis, which is the last node on the symmetry axis with at least three incident edges.

Once we have set up this hierarchy, we can use our embedded and augmented harmonic graph, which we call *harmonic skeleton*, as animation skeleton: nodes will be used as joints. The direction of the symmetry axis (or more precisely, of its embedding) can be used to set up the initial orientation of each joint. Moreover, additional joints can be added in a very simple way as regular nodes on the graph, with the embedding described in section 3.2. The value for f corresponding to a new joint, and hence its exact location, can be either set up by the user, or computed as the mean value between the two values of the edge's nodes (this is our default choice), or even computed so that the joint fits some geometrical feature (e.g. local minimum of the gaussian curvature, as proposed by [TVD06]).

4. Adapted embedding for bipeds and quadrupeds

In this section, we explain how the previously computed skeleton can be modified in order to better fit biped or quadruped mammals. Equivalent heuristics can be developed for other kinds of characters. These heuristics rely on semantic information about the model's anatomy associated to each joint of the skeleton, which can be recovered since the source joint corresponds to the head of the character and all skeleton extrema are known (see Figure 8 (a)). First, we propose a heuristic to check if the skeleton corresponds to a biped or a quadruped model.

4.1. Biped/quadruped discrimination

In the case of a biped or quadruped character, the computed harmonic graph should be as described in Figure 8 (a): the symmetry axis should have at least 2 nodes with at least 3 incident edges. The last of these nodes P matches the pelvis, and the previous one S matches the shoulders (we can have others, matching for example the ears). Since P and S have 3 or 4 incident edges, we know from section 3.2 that the ones not on the symmetry axis have been frozen: let P_1, P_2, S_1 and S_2 be their other endpoints; these nodes correspond to the beginning of the leg bones (when the subtree corresponding to the tail is isomorphic to the back legs, P_1 and P_2 are chosen among the three children of P so that $|SP.(PP_1 \times PP_2)|$ is maximum). We can now define 3 unit vectors: the spine direction $Spine = \frac{SP}{||SP||}$, a unit vector N_P normal to the triangle PP_1P_2 and a unit vector N_S normal to the triangle SS_1S_2. Since edges PP_1, PP_2, SS_1 and SS_2 are frozen with $f(P_1) \approx f(P_2) \approx f(P)$ and $f(S_1) \approx f(S_2) \approx f(S)$, we say that the model is a quadruped if $|Spine.N_P| \approx 1$ and $|Spine.N_S| \approx 1$, and a biped if $|Spine.N_P| \approx 0$ and $|Spine.N_S| \approx 0$ (see Figure 8 (b) and (c)). In the other cases, we cannot conclude.

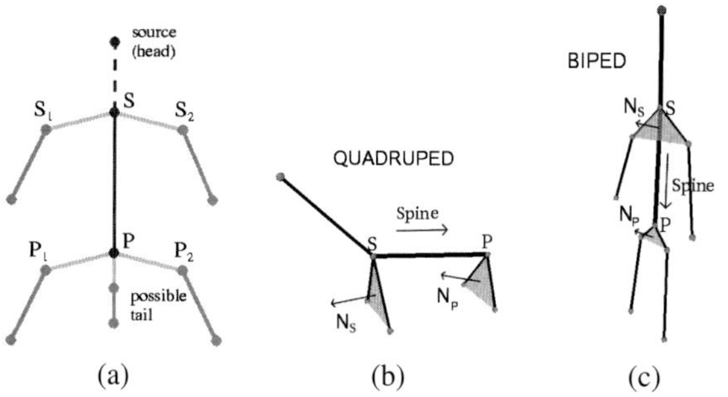

Figure 8: *(a) Minimal harmonic skeleton for a biped or a quadruped model. The symmetry axis is colored in purple and frozen edges are colored in orange. (b,c) Spine, N_P and N_S vectors for quadrupeds and bipeds.*

Actually, this heuristic is well-adapted for most quadrupeds, but not all. Indeed, vertebrate terrestrial quadrupeds can be classified into two groups, according to the orientation of their leg bones (see Figure 9): in the case of amphibians these bones approximately lie in a transversal plane (plane with constant altitude), while in the case of most mammals they lie in a sagittal plane (orthogonal to S_1S_2 and P_1P_2). While our test is adequate for "sagitally oriented" quadrupeds, it can fail for amphibians, for which the result can be the same than for bipeds: $|Spine.N_P| \approx 0$ and $|Spine.N_S| \approx 0$.

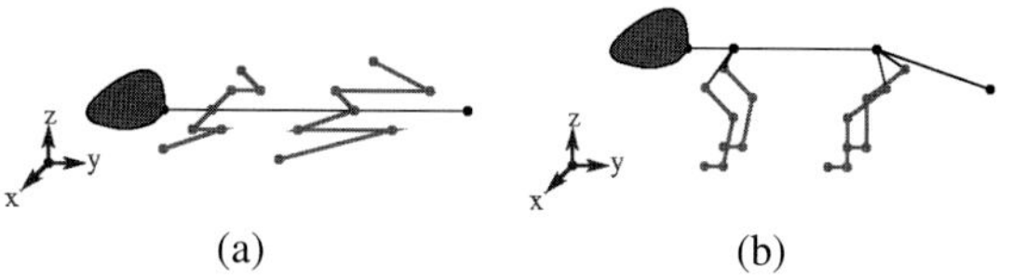

Figure 9: *(a) Schematic skeleton of an amphibian: the leg bones are in a tranversal plane ($z = cst$). (b) Mammal case: they are in a sagittal plane ($x = cst$).*

4.2. Biped embedding

If the character has been detected as a biped, we propose a special refinement of the harmonic skeleton. This refinement starts with the addition of several nodes to the graph:

- the spine, that is to say the edge SP, is subdivided into 4;
- a new node N is inserted on the symmetry axis before S;
- a new node J is inserted before N, and a new edge JM is added from J (M is a new extremum of the graph);
- each arm and each leg is subdivided into 3 edges;
- if there is a tail, it is subdivided into 4 edges.

The goal of this refinement is to match what would have created an artist. The nodes added to each arm will match elbows and wrists, while the nodes added to each leg will match knees and ankles; N will match the base of the neck, J the jaw and M the mouth. Notice that the source node and M do not match any real joint: these are in fact useful to better control the movement of the head and its size. We choose not to add edges for the rib cage, as it is not usually modeled for IK skeletons.

In order to shift some node embeddings and to embed the newly inserted nodes, we first give a reference frame to the model. This reference frame is defined by the previously introduced unit vector $Spine$, the unit vector $\frac{P_1P_2}{||P_1P_2||}$ and the unit vector $Spine \times \frac{P_1P_2}{||P_1P_2||}$, which gives the front-to-back (or back-to-front) direction. We can then embed newly inserted nodes, such as the nodes of the spine which can be slightly moved backward. To mimick what an artist would do, we have also chosen to unfreeze the SS_1 and SS_2 edges,and to embed S_1 and S_2 ahead of the embedding of S, in order to match clavicles. Regular nodes can be embedded either using a mean Euclidean position or a mean value for f *w.r.t.* the embeddings of their edge's endpoints, or fitting some geometric criterion, such as proposed by [TVD06]. The last solution can be particularly adapted for neck and wrists, which match constrictions of the shape.

4.3. Quadruped embedding

Automatic animation skeleton generation is much less developed for four-footed animals than for bipeds. In order to refine the harmonic skeleton for parasagittally oriented quadrupeds, we based our work on the reference animation skeletons proposed by [RFDC05]. These IK skeletons were constructed by hand, from anatomical references [Cal75]. We add the same nodes to the harmonic graph as for bipeds, except that each front leg is subdivided into 5 edges, each back leg into 4 edges, and instead of having 2 edges between J and S (JN and NS), we have 5: the 4 added nodes will match the first, the second, the fourth and the seventh (which is the last) cervical vertebrae. We also subdivide the edge starting from the source node in 3; the first inserted node J' will match the jaw, while this time J will match the cranium. As for bipeds, M does not match any real joint and is useful to control the head's size and its movement. It will be put on top of the head of the character. We use the same reference frame as for biped embedding; here is how some of the joints are embedded: P is lifted up along the $Spine \times \frac{P_1P_2}{\|P_1P_2\|}$ direction from the simple embedding position (the center of its connected component for $f^{-1}(f(P))$) in order to be close to the back; nodes on SP are also lifted up, and so are S_1, S_2, P_1 and P_2; S is lifted up in order to match the pelvis' height; the first inserted nodes on each leg are moved along the $-Spine$ direction. We found that the best choice to embed the node J was near the neck constriction (actually a bit closer to the source joint); its value for f and exact location depends on the neck length. Finally, a simple solution for J' is along the $-Spine \times \frac{P_1P_2}{\|P_1P_2\|}$ direction from J, close to the chin.

5. Results and validation

Figures 2 and 10 to 12 show harmonic skeletons computed with our method. In these cases extrema have been selected by hand, because automatic computation of the extremal features can be quite slow. Thus, the threshold t_2 has not been used (it has been set to zero). No fine tuning of t_1 has been necessary: for almost all models, setting t_1 between 0.001 and 0.150 is sufficient. Except the selection of the extrema and t_1, the entire process is automatic; no post-processing has been applied.

5.1. Biped and quadruped embeddings

Figure 11 shows the harmonic skeleton computed from a biped model, compared with a standard handmade skeleton (from Autodesk's Maya software). We have not modeled the rib cage, as explained before. As for the other models, the symmetry axis is colored in purple and frozen edges are colored in orange. Even though the graph is more complex than the minimal harmonic graph for a biped (Figure 8 (a)) because we decided to model the fingers, the symmetry axis has been correctly detected. Another biped skeleton is shown on the right of the figure. We have chosen to embed extremal nodes onto corresponding vertices on the mesh, but we could have easily embedded them inside the model instead, using a close but regular value for f and the definition (3) of the center of a connected component.

Results on two quadruped models are shown on figures 2 and 12. The cat's tail is not considered as part of the symmetry axis, since its corresponding subtree on the harmonic graph is isomorphic to the back legs. Our algorithm provides animation skeletons close to the model's anatomy and to traditional IK skeletons. Nevertheless, some joints may need to be slightly displaced for better animation, particularly in the head. It is also noticeable that the very beginning of the tail is actually included in a frozen edge; this is correct since it corresponds to the first coccygeal vertebrae which are indeed attached to the sacrum [Cal75].

Our harmonic skeletons have been used for animation, as can be seen on Figure 1 and on the accompanying video.

5.2. Robustness

Figure 10 shows the robustness of the skeleton generation *w.r.t* the pose, mesh deformation and source vertex location.

Two different poses of the same character generate the same graph, with approximately the same values for f on each node, as long as the model is not stretched from one to the other. The reason is twofold: we are guaranteed that the extremal nodes correspond to the selected or computed extremal vertices, and f can be approximated as a distance *over the mesh* to the source vertex. Then, the embedding is most often the same since it does not depend on the leg orientation, for instance: it depends mostly on the computed reference frame, which is the same except if the back has been bended. It can also depends on the surface's local geometry, if we use constrictions to fix some joints such as the neck and wrists.

If the pose deformation is not isometric, we cannot be sure to get the same harmonic graph, from a theoretical point of view. However, stretching or shortening one leg in a homogeneous way does not change neither the graph nor its embedding, since for instance the ratio forearm length over arm length is not modified.

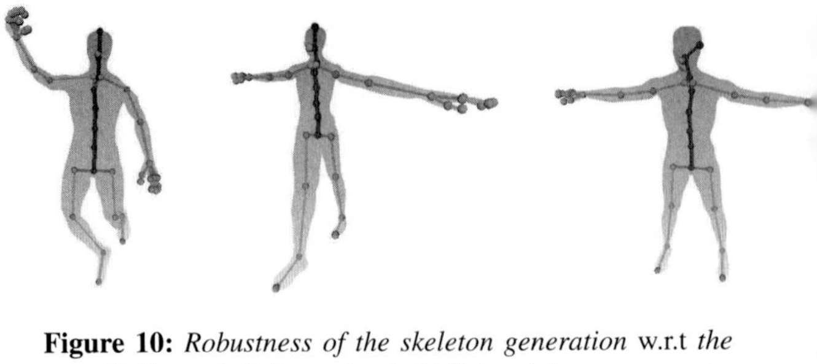

Figure 10: *Robustness of the skeleton generation* w.r.t *the pose (left), mesh deformation (middle) and the source vertex location (right). Compare to Figure 11.*

Our skeleton computation is also very robust *w.r.t* the

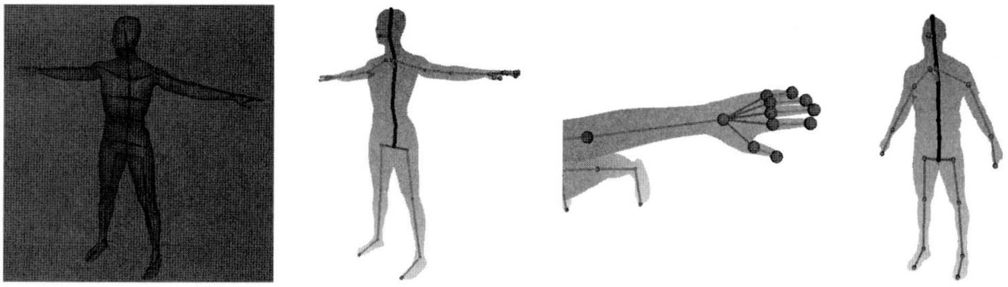

Figure 11: *Comparison on a standard biped model,* `MayaHuman`*, between a standard IK skeleton (left) and our harmonic skeleton (middle left). Middle right: hand close-up; right: harmonic skeleton for another biped model,* `MaleWB`*.*

[Liu et al. 2003] [Lien et al. 2006] [Tierny et al. 2006] Our method Horse anatomy

Figure 12: *Comparison on a horse model between several methods. Images are taken from the papers; the right image is taken from Wikipedia.*

source vertex location, as long as it is chosen on the head: even if it is not on the character's symmetry plane, the symmetry axis of the harmonic graph is recovered; then, since the embedding we propose does not depend on the source vertex location, it does not change.

5.3. Quantitative validation

To prove that our approach is useful, we have carried out a quantitative validation of our results: since [RFDC05] introduced parameters to define quadruped's skeletons (back and front leg height – or similarly spine tilt – and neck length, normalized by the spine length), we compared their values between our skeletons and IK skeletons, handmade from anatomical reference. Results for 6 models are provided in Table 1; in most cases our embedding of nodes S and J is correct, resulting in similar values between harmonic skeletons and IK skeletons for front leg height and neck length. The location of the pelvis is sometimes low in our harmonic skeletons, which explains the greater difference for back leg height.

5.4. Computation time

The Table 2 gives computation times for 5 models on a standard PC with a 2.4 GHz Pentium 4 processor. Even for a dense mesh, our algorithm generates the skeleton in less than 1 minute. The memory requirement is also low: at most 350 MB for a model made of 300,000 faces, 1.5 MB for a model with 15,000 faces (including the storage of the mesh). Most of the time is spent on the harmonic function computation; graph computation is then done in $O(n \log n)$ time for a mesh with n faces [CMEH*03], and embedding is done in nearly linear time because we only compute ray/mesh intersections for some joints in order to get their distance to the mesh, and the number of joints does not depend on the mesh's complexity.

Mesh	Back leg		Front leg		Neck	
	Harmo.	**IK**	**Harmo.**	**IK**	**Harmo.**	**IK**
Cat	1.2	1.3	1.2	1.2	0.4	0.4
Cow	1.0	1.1	0.9	0.9	0.3	0.4
Dog	1.3	1.3	1.1	1.2	0.5	0.4
Elephant	1.4	1.6	1.4	1.4	0.3	0.3
Horse	1.3	1.7	1.4	1.6	0.7	1.0
Panther	1.0	1.1	0.9	1.0	0.4	0.5

Table 1: *Parameter comparison between our harmonic skeletons and hand-built IK skeletons.*

Mesh	Nb. faces	Graph	Embedding	Total
Cat	2,566	0.085	0.108	0.193
`MayaHuman`	14,118	0.634	0.139	0.773
Octopus	33,058	1.393	0.061	1.454
Horse	96,966	6.268	3.525	9.793
`MaleWB`	296,272	30.816	5.230	36.046

Table 2: *Computation time (in seconds) for some meshes.*

6. Conclusion

In this paper we have presented a fully automatic method to compute an animation skeleton from a 3D meshed model in a few seconds after the selection of an initial point. In the case of most bipeds or quadrupeds, this skeleton fits the animation skeleton that would be hand-built by an expert starting from anatomical boards, and is thus adapted for realistic animation. The main idea is to construct the Reeb graph of a harmonic function, which gives the overall morphological structure of the model (especially its symmetry axis), then to refine and embed it using anatomical information. There are two main restrictions on the input mesh: it should be a triangulated 2-manifold (with or without boundary), and, in order to recover the symmetry axis of the shape's morphology, it should not have handles (otherwise the Reeb graph contains cycles). Although the method is fully automatic, the user can control the skeleton generation by tuning a few optional parameters. This tool has been designed both to help artists and to allow non-experts to quickly generate skeletons which can be used for realistic character animation. Computed skeletons can be edited and refined, for instance to add joints that correspond to wings or to the trunk of an elephant.

Given this skeleton generation process, we see three promising research directions. First, each vertex of the mesh is related to the joints of the skeleton, since we have given values for the harmonic function to the graph's nodes, and hence the skeleton's joints; these relations may be used to enhance skinning weights. Second, our semantic decomposition of the graph may also be used to define heuristics that give adapted skinning weights: weights may vary according to the meaning of neighboring joints. It may also help for automatic mesh segmentation into anatomically meaningful regions. Finally, even if not embedded to match the model's anatomy, the harmonic graph may be useful for other applications (e.g. shape matching), since its construction is robust and does not create unnecessary nodes.

Acknowledgments

The authors would like to thank Lionel Revéret for interesting discussions at the beginning of this work. The horse and `MaleWB` models are courtesy of Cyberware. The `MayaHuman` model is courtesy of Autodesk.

References

[BL99] BLOOMENTHAL J., LIM C.: Skeletal methods of shape manipulation. In *Shape Modeling International* (1999).

[Blu67] BLUM H.: A transformation for extracting new descriptors of shape. In *Symposium on Models for the Perception of Speech and Visual Form* (1967), pp. 362–380.

[Cal75] CALDERON W.: *Animal Painting and Anatomy*. Dover, 1975.

[CMEH*03] COLE-MCLAUGHLIN K., EDELSBRUNNER H., HARER J., NATARAJAN V., PASCUCCI V.: Loops in reeb graphs of 2-manifolds. In *Symposium on Computational Geometry* (2003), pp. 344–350.

[CSYB05] CORNEA N., SILVER D., YUAN X., BALASUBRAMANIAN R.: Computing hierarchical curve-skeletons of 3d objects. *The Visual Computer 21*, 11 (2005), 945–955.

[DeF99] DEFRAYSSEIX H.: An heuristic for graph symmetry detection. In *Symposium on Graph Drawing* (1999), pp. 276–285.

[DEG*99] DEMMEL J., EISENSTAT S., GILBERT J., LI X., LIU J.: A supernodal approach to sparse partial pivoting. *SIAM Journal on Matrix Analysis and Applications 20*, 3 (1999), 720–755.

[DKG05] DONG S., KIRCHNER S., GARLAND M.: Harmonic functions for quadrilateral remeshing of arbitrary manifolds. *Computer Aided Geometric Design, Special issue on Geometry Processing 22*, 5 (2005), 392–423.

[DS06] DEY T., SUN J.: Defining and computing curve-skeletons with medial geodesic function. In *Symposium on Geometry Processing* (2006), pp. 143–152.

[FK97] FOMENKO A., KUNII T.: *Topological Modeling for Visualization*. Springer-Verlag, 1997.

[GS01] GAGVANI N., SILVER D.: Animating volumetric models. *Graphical Models 63*, 6 (2001), 443–458.

[HSKK01] HILAGA M., SHINAGAWA Y., KOMURA T., KUNII T.: Topology matching for fully automatic similarity estimation of 3d shapes. In *SIGGRAPH* (2001), pp. 203–212.

[KT03] KATZ S., TAL A.: Hierarchical mesh decomposition using fuzzy clustering and cuts. In *SIGGRAPH* (2003).

[LKA06] LIEN J., KEYSER J., , AMATO N.: Simultaneous shape decomposition and skeletonization. In *ACM Symposium on Solid and Physical Modeling* (2006), pp. 219–228.

[LV99] LAZARUS F., VERROUST A.: Level set diagrams of polyhedral objects. In *ACM Symposium on Solid Modeling* (1999).

[LWM*03] LIU P., WU F., MA W., LIANG R., OUHYOUNG M.: Automatic animation skeleton construction using repulsive force field. In *Pacific Graphics* (2003), pp. 409–413.

[NGH04] NI X., GARLAND M., HART J.: Fair morse functions for extracting the topological structure of a surface mesh. In *SIGGRAPH* (2004), pp. 613–622.

[Ree46] REEB G.: Sur les points singuliers d'une forme de pfaff complètement intégrable ou d'une fonction numérique. *Comptes-Rendus de l'Académie des Sciences 222* (1946), 847–849.

[RFDC05] REVÉRET L., FAVREAU L., DEPRAZ C., CANI M.: Morphable model of quadruped skeletons for animating 3d animals. In *Symposium on Computer Animation* (2005).

[SF01] STEINER D., FISCHER A.: Topology recognition of 3d closed freeform objects based on topological graphs. In *Pacific Graphics* (2001), pp. 82–88.

[SKK91] SHINAGAWA Y., KUNII T., KERGOSIEN Y.: Surface coding based on morse theory. *IEEE Computer Graphics and Applications 11*, 5 (1991), 66–78.

[SKS06] SIMARI P., KALOGERAKIS E., SINGH K.: Folding meshes: Hierarchical mesh segmentation based on planar symmetry. In *Symposium on Geometry Processing* (2006).

[TVD06] TIERNY J., VANDEBORRE J., DAOUDI M.: 3d mesh skeleton extraction using topological and geometrical analyses. In *Pacific Graphics* (2006), pp. 409–413.

[WP02] WADE L., PARENT R.: Automated generation of control skeletons for use in animation. *The Visual Computer 18* (2002).

[ZMT05] ZHANG E., MISCHAIKOW K., TURK G.: Feature-based surface parameterization and texture mapping. *ACM Transactions on Graphics 24*, 1 (2005), 1–27.

Eurographics/ ACM SIGGRAPH Symposium on Computer Animation (2007)
D. Metaxas and J. Popovic (Editors)

Face Poser: Interactive Modeling of 3D Facial Expressions Using Model Priors

Manfred Lau[1,3] Jinxiang Chai[2] Ying-Qing Xu[3] Heung-Yeung Shum[3]

[1]Carnegie Mellon University [2]Texas A&M University [3]Microsoft Research Asia

Abstract

In this paper, we present an intuitive interface for interactively posing 3D facial expressions. The user can create and edit facial expressions by drawing freeform strokes, or by directly dragging facial points in 2D screen space. Designing such an interface for face modeling and editing is challenging because many unnatural facial expressions might be consistent with the ambiguous user input. The system automatically learns a model prior from a prerecorded facial expression database and uses it to remove the ambiguity. We formulate the problem in a maximum a posteriori (MAP) framework by combining the prior with user-defined constraints. Maximizing the posterior allows us to generate an optimal and natural facial expression that satisfies the user-defined constraints. Our system is interactive; it is also simple and easy to use. A first-time user can learn to use the system and start creating a variety of natural face models within minutes. We evaluate the performance of our approach with cross validation tests, and by comparing with alternative techniques.

Categories and Subject Descriptors (according to ACM CCS): I.3.5 [Computer Graphics]: Computational Geometry and Object Modeling-Modeling packages; I.3.6 [Computer Graphics]: Methodology and Techniques-Interaction techniques

1. Introduction

A long-standing challenge in computer graphics is to build an interactive system that allows users to model realistic facial expressions quickly and easily. Applications of such a system include synthesizing natural facial expressions for characters in films, games, or other virtual environments, and for facial avatars in instant communication programs. Such a system is also useful as a rapid prototyping tool: the user can efficiently create 3D face expressions for reviewing, discussions, or educational purposes.

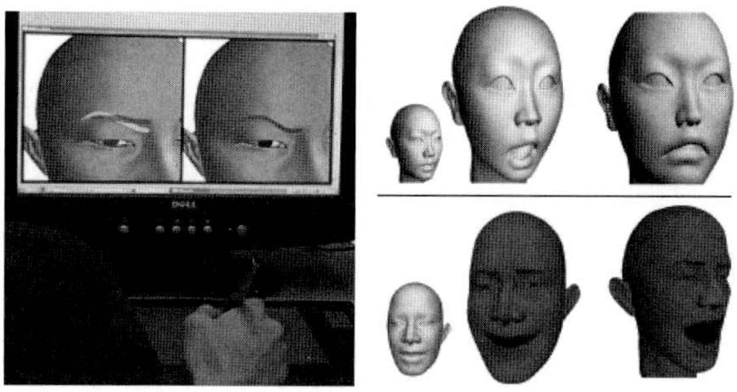

Figure 1: *(left) The Face Poser system in use with a graphics tablet. (right) A variety of face expressions created using the system. The lower left corner shows the neutral expression for each subject.*

In this paper, we present an intuitive and efficient interface for modeling 3D facial expressions (Figure 1). Our system starts with a 3D mesh model in a neutral expression. For the sketch-based interface, the user first selects a reference freeform stroke on the 2D screen space; the user then draws a target freeform stroke to indicate a desired deformation for the reference stroke. Both strokes can be drawn anywhere on the 2D screen space from any camera view. The system deforms the facial model based on these inputs. The user can continue to refine the model until a desired expression is achieved.

Building such an interface for 3D facial modeling is difficult because the information from the user is often ambiguous. In our system, the inputs are a small set of user-defined freeform strokes or control points. This information is quite low-dimensional as compared to a typical facial model, which is commonly represented by at least thousands of DOFs [PW96]. The user's inputs, therefore, cannot be used to fully determine a natural facial configuration

Symposium on Computer Animation 2007, San Diego, CA, August 03-04, 2007.
© 2007 ACM 978-1-59593-624-4/07/0008 $5.00

because they will be consistent with many disparate solutions. Some solutions might correspond to unnatural face expressions and not be what the user intends to model. We eliminate the ambiguity by imposing a prior embedded in a large database of pre-recorded face expressions. The prior describes the "likelihood" function over facial expressions and measures how natural a face expression is.

We formulate the face expression modeling problem in a probabilistic framework by combining user-defined constraints with a prior from the database. We model the prior as a mixture of factor analyzers [GH97] and learn it automatically from a pre-recorded facial expression database. Maximizing the posterior (likelihood of facial expressions give user-specified constraints) generates a natural and most desirable facial expression that achieves the goal specified by the user.

We demonstrate the power and flexibility of this approach by interactive modeling of 3D facial expressions with point constraints and stroke constraints. The constraints are specified on the 2D screen space. We thereby avoid the need for complex 3D interactions which are common in mesh editing software, and can be cumbersome for a naive user. We have found that a first-time user can learn to use the system in a few minutes, and be able to create desired facial expressions within tens of seconds. Figure 1 shows some examples of facial expressions generated by our system.

We evaluate the quality of synthesized facial expressions by comparison against ground truth data. We also compare alternative data-driven techniques for generating facial expressions from user-defined constraints. We compare our method against blendshape interpolation, optimization in the PCA subspace, and optimization with blendshapes.

2. Background

In the next section, we discuss related work in sketch-based interfaces for object modeling. Because we use prerecorded facial data in our system, we then review research utilizing examples for modeling.

2.1. Sketch-based interfaces

Our work is inspired by sketch-based systems that interpret the user's strokes for constructing and editing 3D models [ZHH96, IMT99]. Zeleznik and his colleagues [ZHH96] introduced a sketch-based interface to create and edit rectilinear objects. Igarashi and his colleagues [IMT99] developed the first sketch interface to interactively model and edit free-form objects. Recently, a number of researchers have explored sketch-based interfaces to edit mesh deformations [NSACO05, KG05]. Nealen and his colleagues [NSACO05] presented a sketch-based interface for laplacian mesh editing where a user draws reference and target curves on the mesh to specify the mesh deformation. Kho and Garland [KG05] demonstrated a similar interface for posing the bodies and limbs of 3D characters. Furthermore, Yang and his colleagues [YSvdP05] presented a 3D modeling system to construct 3D models of particular object classes by matching the points and curves of a set of given 2D templates to 2D sketches. Our goal is to develop an interface for interactively modeling and editing 3D facial expressions.

Chang and Jenkins [CJ06] presented a similar interface to edit a facial model. Their interface is different in that it works only for strokes drawn as lines on the screen. Our stroke interface allows for drawing any line, curve, shape, or region on the screen, and in any camera view. More importantly, our approach learns model priors from a prerecorded database and uses them to remove the modeling ambiguity.

2.2. Example-based modeling

Our work builds upon previous example-based modeling systems. Many example-based modeling systems are based on estimating weights to linearly combine example models [Par72, LCF00, SRC01] or eigen-models [BV99, BBPV03]. These weights can be computed from either user-specified constraints or images.

Zhang and his colleagues [ZSCS04] developed an example-based FaceIK system to edit a facial model by interactively dragging points on the face. Their face model is represented as a linear combination of pre-acquired 3D face scans. Researchers [JTDP03, ZLGS03] have also proposed to segment a model into multiple regions and represent each subregion as a convex linear combination of blend shapes. Besides facial modeling, example-based approach has also been applied to edit a skeleton structure. Sumner and Popovic [SZGP05] and Der and his colleagues [DSP06] learned a reduced deformable space from a small set of example shapes, and used an inverse kinematics approach to optimize the mesh in a reduced deformable space. Their system allows the user to interactively deform a skeletal model by posing just a few vertices.

An alternative way to estimate the weights of examples is to reconstruct them directly from images or video [BV99, PSS99, BBPV03]. Blanz and his colleagues [BV99, BBPV03] built a morphable model from 3D scans via Principal Component Analysis (PCA) [Bis96] and applied the morphable model to reconstruct a 3D model from a single image. Pighin and his colleagues [PSS99] demonstrated that they can estimate the weights of a small set of 3D morphed face models directly from images or video. Chai and his colleagues presented a real-time vision-based performance animation system which transforms a small set of automatically tracked facial features into facial animation by interpolating closest examples in a database at runtime [CXH03].

The main difference between our work and previous example-based modeling systems is that we learn a probabilistic model to represent the prior from example data and formulate the problem in a probabilistic framework by combining user-defined constraints with the prior. The system automatically learns a mixture of factor analyzers [GH97]

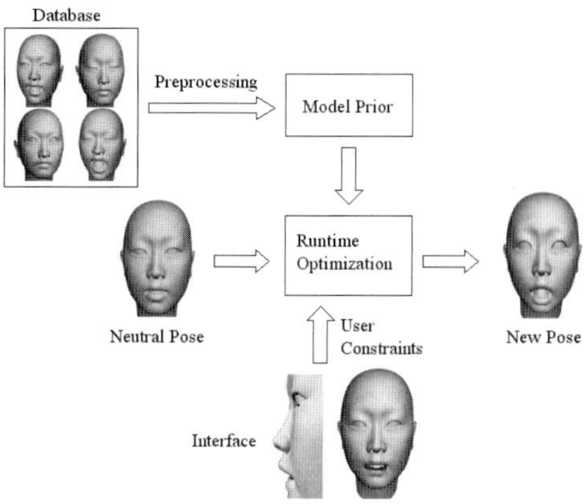

Figure 2: *System overview.*

from a facial database. With a collection of locally linear sub-models, our mixture of factor analyzers can model a nonlinear structure which cannot be modeled by existing linear models such as blendshapes or eigen-shapes.

A number of researchers have also developed statistical models for human poses and used them to estimate poses from kinematic constraints to solve the inverse kinematics problem. For example, Grochow and his colleagues [GMHP04] applied a global nonlinear dimensionality reduction technique, a Gaussian Process Latent Variable Model [Law04], to human motion data and then used the learned statistical pose model to compute poses from a small set of user-defined constraints. GPLVM works well for a small set of example data. However, it might not be appropriate for our application because the performance of the GPLVM deteriorates as the size and heterogeneity of the database increases.

Local statistical models are sufficient if the user provides continuous control signals (the performance animation problem). Chai and his colleagues used a series of local statistical pose models constructed at runtime to reconstruct full body motion from continuous, low-dimensional control signals obtained from video cameras [CH05]. Online local models are more appropriate for creating animations (a sequence of poses) from continuous temporal constraints. They are not appropriate for our application because user-defined constraints are usually not continuous.

3. Overview

The main idea of our approach is that model priors learned from pre-recorded facial expression data can be used to create natural facial expressions that match constraints specified by the user. The combination of the model priors and the user-defined constraints provide sufficient information to produce 3D facial expression models with a natural appearance. Figure 2 shows an overview of our system.

3.1. Data Preprocessing

We set up a Vicon motion capture system to record facial movement by attaching 55 reflective markers onto the face of the motion capture subject. We captured the subject performing various sets of facial actions. The data contains basic facial expressions such as anger, fear, surprise, sadness, joy, and disgust, and other common facial actions such as speaking and singing. We scanned the 3D model of the subject and then converted the recorded marker motions into a set of deforming mesh models [CXH03]. We translated and rotated each frame of the data to a default position and orientation because facial expression models should be irrelevant of head poses. We collected data for two subjects.

We denote a captured example in the database as $\mathbf{x} \in R^d$, where $\mathbf{x}$ is the stacked 3D positions of all vertices in the face model and d is three times the number of vertices in a facial model. Let M be the total number of samples for each subject. We use Principal Component Analysis (PCA) [Bis96] to preprocess the captured data; we then obtain a reduced subspace representation for $\mathbf{x}$:

$$\mathbf{x} = B \cdot \mathbf{p} + \bar{\mathbf{x}} \tag{1}$$

where the vector $\mathbf{p} \in R^r$ is a low-dimensional representation of a facial model $\mathbf{x} \in R^d$. The matrix B is constructed from the eigenvectors corresponding to the largest eigenvalues of the covariance matrix of the data, and $\bar{\mathbf{x}}$ is the mean of all the examples. Due to the large dimensions of $\mathbf{x}$, we perform PCA by an Incremental SVD method described by Brand [Bra02].

3.2. Problem Statement

We formulate our facial modeling problem in a maximum a posteriori (MAP) framework. From Bayes' theorem, the goal of MAP is to infer the most likely model $\mathbf{p}$ given the user-defined constraints $\mathbf{c}$:

$$\begin{aligned} \arg\max_{\mathbf{p}}\ pr(\mathbf{p}|\mathbf{c}) &= \arg\max_{\mathbf{p}} \frac{pr(\mathbf{c}|\mathbf{p})pr(\mathbf{p})}{pr(\mathbf{c})} \\ &\propto \arg\max_{\mathbf{p}}\ pr(\mathbf{c}|\mathbf{p})pr(\mathbf{p}) \end{aligned} \tag{2}$$

where $pr(\mathbf{c})$ is the normalizing constant that ensures that the posterior distribution on the left-hand side is a valid probability density and integrates to one.

In our implementation, we minimize the negative log of $pr(\mathbf{p}|\mathbf{c})$, yielding the following energy optimization problem for model $\hat{\mathbf{p}}$:

$$\hat{\mathbf{p}} = \arg\min_{\mathbf{p}} \quad -\ln pr(\mathbf{c}|\mathbf{p}) - \ln pr(\mathbf{p}) \tag{3}$$

where the first term measures how well a face model matches the user-specified constraints and the second term measures the *a priori* likelihood of the face model using the knowledge embedded in the example data.

3.3. System Components

The system contains three major components (see figure 2):

User Constraints. The system starts with a default facial model. The user interactively edits the facial model using two kinds of constraints: point constraints and stroke constraints. These constraints are specified on the 2D screen space. The interface allows the user to iteratively apply these constraints until a desired solution is obtained.

Model Priors. The system automatically learns a statistical model from the captured data in the reduced PCA subspace. This model is used to constrain the generated facial expression to lie in the space of natural facial expressions.

Runtime Optimization. The system uses nonlinear optimization to automatically find a facial model that best satisfies the user-specified constraints while matching the statistical properties of the captured data.

The model priors are learned off-line, while the other two stages are performed online based on input from the user. We describe these components in detail in the next three sections.

4. User Constraints

Our system starts with a default 3D facial model. In our implementation, we start with the mean pose $\bar{\mathbf{x}}$. The user can specify point constraints and stroke constraints to interactively edit facial expressions. For point constraints, the user can select any facial points and specify their desired positions on the screen space. For stroke constraints, the user selects a reference freeform stroke and then draws a target freeform stroke to specify a desired deformation for the reference stroke. This section focuses on deriving objective functions and their derivatives for both constraints.

We first derive the relationship between a facial model in the PCA subspace ($\mathbf{p}$) and the projection of a chosen vertex on the 2D screen space ($\mathbf{y}_i$). Let $\mathbf{x}_i$ denote the 3D coordinate of the ith vertex. Let $\mathbf{y}_i$ denote the 2D projection of the ith vertex on the screen space under the current camera viewpoint. We have

$$\begin{pmatrix} u_i \\ v_i \\ \omega_i \end{pmatrix} = \begin{pmatrix} f & 0 & 0 & 0 \\ 0 & f & 0 & 0 \\ 0 & 0 & 1 & 0 \end{pmatrix} \cdot \begin{pmatrix} \mathbf{r}_1^T & t_1 \\ \mathbf{r}_2^T & t_2 \\ \mathbf{r}_3^T & t_3 \\ \mathbf{0} & 1 \end{pmatrix} \cdot \begin{pmatrix} \mathbf{x}_i \\ 1 \end{pmatrix} \tag{4}$$

where f is the focal length of the camera, $\mathbf{r}_i^T$ is the ith row vector of the camera rotation matrix, and t_i is the corresponding camera translation component.

Let s_w and s_h denote the current width and height of the 2D screen respectively. We further have

$$\mathbf{y}_i = \begin{pmatrix} (\frac{u_i}{\omega_i}+1)\cdot\frac{s_w}{2} \\ (1-\frac{v_i}{\omega_i})\cdot\frac{s_h}{2} \end{pmatrix} = \begin{pmatrix} (\frac{f\mathbf{r}_1^T\mathbf{x}_i+ft_1}{\mathbf{r}_3^T\mathbf{x}_i+t_3}+1)\cdot\frac{s_w}{2} \\ (1-\frac{f\mathbf{r}_2^T\mathbf{x}_i+ft_2}{\mathbf{r}_3^T\mathbf{x}_i+t_3})\cdot\frac{s_h}{2} \end{pmatrix} \tag{5}$$

We can "select" the ith vertex of $\mathbf{x}$ with:

$$\mathbf{x}_i = W_i \cdot \mathbf{x} \tag{6}$$

where W_i is a $3\times 3N$ matrix, whose elements are zero except:

$$W_i(1:3, 3*i-2:3*i) = \begin{pmatrix} 1 & 0 & 0 \\ 0 & 1 & 0 \\ 0 & 0 & 1 \end{pmatrix} \tag{7}$$

Combining equations 1, 5, and 6 together, the 2D projection $\mathbf{y}_i$ of a 3D facial vertex can be represented as a nonlinear function of weights $\mathbf{p}$:

$$\begin{aligned} \mathbf{y}_i &= \mathbf{g}_i(\mathbf{p}) \\ &= \begin{pmatrix} (\frac{f\mathbf{r}_1^T W_i(B\mathbf{p}+\bar{\mathbf{x}})+ft_1}{\mathbf{r}_3^T W_i(B\mathbf{p}+\bar{\mathbf{x}})+t_3}+1)\cdot\frac{s_w}{2} \\ (1-\frac{f\mathbf{r}_2^T W_i(B\mathbf{p}+\bar{\mathbf{x}})+ft_2}{\mathbf{r}_3^T W_i(B\mathbf{p}+\bar{\mathbf{x}})+t_3})\cdot\frac{s_h}{2} \end{pmatrix} \end{aligned} \tag{8}$$

The Jacobian matrix can be computed as follows:

$$\begin{aligned} J_i(\mathbf{p}) &= \frac{\partial \mathbf{y}_i}{\partial \mathbf{p}} \\ &= \frac{\partial \mathbf{y}_i}{\partial \mathbf{x}_i}\cdot\frac{\partial \mathbf{x}_i}{\partial \mathbf{p}} \end{aligned} \tag{9}$$

The first Jacobian term can be computed as follows:

$$\frac{\partial \mathbf{y}_i}{\partial \mathbf{x}_i} = \begin{pmatrix} \frac{s_w}{2}\cdot\frac{f\mathbf{r}_1^T\cdot(\mathbf{r}_3^T\mathbf{x}_i+t_3)-\mathbf{r}_3^T\cdot(f\mathbf{r}_1^T\mathbf{x}_i+ft_1)}{(\mathbf{r}_3^T\mathbf{x}_i+t_3)^2} \\ -\frac{s_h}{2}\cdot\frac{f\mathbf{r}_2^T\cdot(\mathbf{r}_3^T\mathbf{x}_i+t_3)-\mathbf{r}_3^T\cdot(f\mathbf{r}_2^T\mathbf{x}_i+ft_2)}{(\mathbf{r}_3^T\mathbf{x}_i+t_3)^2} \end{pmatrix} \tag{10}$$

The second Jacobian term is

$$\frac{\partial \mathbf{x}_i}{\partial \mathbf{p}} = W_i \cdot B \tag{11}$$

4.1. Point Constraints

The first type of user-defined constraint allows the user to change the position of individual vertices on the mesh. This allows the user to have detailed control over the final result. The user first selects a set of 3D source vertices $\{\mathbf{x}_i | i = 1,...,N\}$ and then specifies a corresponding set of 2D target pixels $\{\mathbf{z}_i | i = 1,...,N\}$ of where the vertices should map to on the screen space. The user selects each 3D point by selecting a 2D screen pixel. We perform ray tracing with this pixel to choose the point on the mesh. Given these inputs, the problem is to find a face model so that each selected 3D vertex ($\mathbf{x}_i$) projects onto the corresponding 2D screen position ($\mathbf{z}_i$) in the current camera view. The optimization term for point constraints can be described as follows:

$$E_{point} = \frac{1}{N}\cdot\sum_i \|\mathbf{g}_i(\mathbf{p}) - \mathbf{z}_i\|^2 \tag{12}$$

The Jacobian matrix is

$$\begin{aligned} \frac{\partial E_{point}}{\partial \mathbf{p}} &= \frac{1}{N}\cdot\frac{\partial(\sum_i \|\mathbf{g}_i(\mathbf{p})-\mathbf{z}_i\|^2)}{\partial \mathbf{p}} \\ &= \frac{1}{N}\cdot\frac{\partial\sum_i\|\mathbf{y}_i-\mathbf{z}_i\|^2}{\partial \mathbf{y}_i}\cdot\frac{\partial \mathbf{y}_i}{\partial \mathbf{x}_i}\cdot\frac{\partial \mathbf{x}_i}{\partial \mathbf{p}} \\ &= \frac{1}{N}\cdot\sum_i[2(\mathbf{y}_i-\mathbf{z}_i)^T\cdot\frac{\partial \mathbf{y}_i}{\partial \mathbf{x}_i}\cdot\frac{\partial \mathbf{x}_i}{\partial \mathbf{p}}] \end{aligned} \tag{13}$$

The final Jacobian matrix is computed by combining the above equation with Equations 10 and 11.

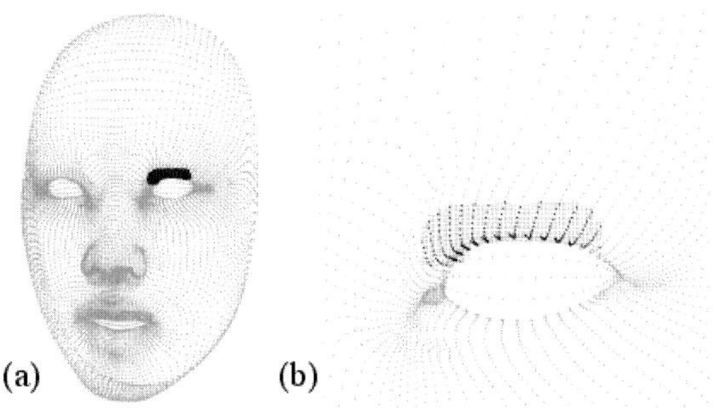

Figure 3: *(a) The dark gray points are 3D points on the mesh surface. They are selected by the source stroke for Stroke Constraints. (b) Closeup view. We see the individual dark gray points. They do not have to be the original vertices that make up the mesh. The black ones are also selected, and these are the original vertices in the mesh.*

4.2. Stroke Constraints

This constraint allows the user to select a group of 3D points and specify where these points should collectively project to on the screen. This is designed to allow the user to make large-scale changes to the mesh with minimal input. More specifically, the user first draws a source stroke to select a set of 3D points ($\mathbf{x}_s$'s) on the mesh (figure 3). Then the user draws a target stroke to provide a region of pixels ($\mathbf{z}_j$'s) where the 3D points should project to. These strokes can be in the form of a line, curve, or any freeform region. Unlike point constraints, the stroke constraints do not provide corresponding information between the source and target strokes.

Given a source stroke in the 2D screen space, we need to find the corresponding 3D points on the mesh efficiently. We ray traced the pixels of the source stroke in a hierarchical manner. We first consider the selected pixel region as blocks of 15 by 15 pixels, and find the triangles that intersect with each block. We then consider these blocks as 3 by 3 pixels, and find the triangles that intersect with each block. For each 3 by 3 block, we only test the triangles that intersected with the corresponding 15 by 15 block. Finally, we ray traced each pixel by testing only the triangles in the corresponding 3 by 3 block. This process selects the $\mathbf{x}_s$'s on the mesh (figure 3). We store the barycentric coordinates of each $\mathbf{x}_s$. The position of each $\mathbf{x}_s$ depends on the positions of the three vertices of the triangle ($\mathbf{x}_u$, $\mathbf{x}_v$, $\mathbf{x}_w$) that it belongs to. When the face mesh deforms, the position of each $\mathbf{x}_s$ is recomputed as:

$$\mathbf{x}_s = u \cdot \mathbf{x}_u + v \cdot \mathbf{x}_v + w \cdot \mathbf{x}_w \tag{14}$$

where u, v, and w are the barycentric coordinates. For a given $\mathbf{x}_s$, these barycentric coordinates are fixed, while the vertices ($\mathbf{x}_u$, $\mathbf{x}_v$, $\mathbf{x}_w$) may deform.

This set of 3D points on the mesh, $\mathbf{x}_s$'s, are projected back onto the 2D screen for comparison with the target stroke, $\mathbf{z}_j$'s. Let the projected region of pixels be $\mathbf{y}_i$'s. Let R be a constant region that contains both $\mathbf{y}_i$'s and $\mathbf{z}_j$'s. For efficiency, we choose the region R to be a joint region of $\mathbf{y}_i$'s and $\mathbf{z}_j$'s in our experiment. Let I_y be a binary image over the region R whose pixel values are zeros except the projected region of pixels, $\mathbf{y}_i$'s. I_y, therefore, depends on $\mathbf{x}_s$'s. We further define I_z to be a binary image over the region R whose pixel values are zero except the target stroke, $\mathbf{z}_j$'s. We measure the distance between the two strokes by computing the intensity difference between them. The optimization term for stroke constraints is

$$E_{stroke} = \sum_{r \in R}(I_y(\mathbf{y}_i) - I_z(r))^2 \tag{15}$$

We can compute its Jacobian matrix as follows:

$$\frac{\partial E_{stroke}}{\partial \mathbf{p}} = 2 \cdot \sum_{r \in R}[(I_y(\mathbf{y}_i) - I_z(r)) \cdot (\frac{\partial I_y(\mathbf{y}_i)}{\partial \mathbf{y}_i} \cdot \frac{\partial \mathbf{y}_i}{\partial \mathbf{x}_s} \cdot \frac{\partial \mathbf{x}_s}{\partial \mathbf{p}})] \tag{16}$$

The projected region of pixels, $\mathbf{y}_i$'s, are determined by forward projection of the current 3D points, $\mathbf{x}_s$'s. There might be multiple points projected to the same pixel. We choose to render the pixel using the 3D point that is closest to the camera. The partial derivative $\frac{\partial I_y(\mathbf{y}_i)}{\partial \mathbf{y}_i}$ is the image gradient computed by the Sobel operator [DH73]. We use Equation 10 to compute the partial derivative $\frac{\partial \mathbf{y}_i}{\partial \mathbf{x}_s}$. Finally based on Equation 14, $\frac{\partial \mathbf{x}_s}{\partial \mathbf{p}}$ can be computed as follows:

$$\frac{\partial \mathbf{x}_s}{\partial \mathbf{p}} = u \cdot \frac{\partial \mathbf{x}_u}{\partial \mathbf{p}} + v \cdot \frac{\partial \mathbf{x}_v}{\partial \mathbf{p}} + w \cdot \frac{\partial \mathbf{x}_w}{\partial \mathbf{p}} \tag{17}$$

where the partial derivatives on the right side of this equation can be substituted with Equation 11.

Our method of measuring the distance between the two strokes by computing the intensity difference is efficient. However, if the two strokes are far away from each other, the objective function in Equation 15 does not require the strokes to "move toward" each other. The energy value in Equation 15 will reach a local minimum without "moving" the strokes. There are many ways to solve this problem. We can use a more sophisticated function to represent I_y and I_z. For example, a signed distance function would allow the strokes to "move toward" each other. But computing this function at every iteration of the optimization would be time-consuming. Instead we choose to add an additional term to minimize the distance between the center of the pixels in the source stroke and the center of the pixels in the target stroke:

$$E_{extra} = \|\frac{\sum \mathbf{y}_i}{N_s} - \bar{\mathbf{z}}\|^2 \tag{18}$$

where N_s is the number of pixels in the source stroke, $\bar{\mathbf{z}}$ is the center of the pixels in the target stroke, and the summation is for all source pixels y_i. The Jacobian matrix is

$$\begin{aligned} \frac{\partial E_{extra}}{\partial \mathbf{p}} &= 2 \cdot (\frac{\sum \mathbf{y}_i}{N_s} - \bar{\mathbf{z}})^T \cdot \frac{\partial(\frac{\sum \mathbf{y}_i}{N_s})}{\partial \mathbf{p}} \\ &= \frac{2}{N_s} \cdot (\frac{\sum \mathbf{y}_i}{N_s} - \bar{\mathbf{z}})^T \cdot \sum(\frac{\partial \mathbf{y}_i}{\partial \mathbf{x}_s} \cdot \frac{\partial \mathbf{x}_s}{\partial \mathbf{p}}) \end{aligned} \tag{19}$$

The weight for this additional term in the optimization

changes depending on the objective value (Equation 18). As the distance between the centers of the two strokes decreases, this weight decreases. Intuitively, as the two strokes get closer to each other, we decrease the effect of this additional term.

5. Model Priors

There might be many facial models that satisfy the user-defined constraints. For example, when the user selects one facial vertex to edit the whole model, there might be many results that are consistent with this constraint. To remove ambiguities, we can constrain the generated model to lie in the space of real models by imposing a prior on the generated model.

We model the prior as a mixture of factor analyzers [GH97] and learn it automatically from a pre-recorded facial expression database. The MFA model learns a probability density function (P.D.F) in the PCA subspace that provides a model prior to measure the naturalness of facial expressions. The MFA model has also been successfully applied to model the prior for many high-dimensional nonlinear data such as handwritten digits [HDR97] and images [BW00].

A single factor analyzer (FA) assumes that an observed r-dimensional variable $\mathbf{p}$ is generated as a linear transformation of some lower q-dimensional latent variable $\tau \sim \mathcal{N}(0,I)$ plus additive Gaussian noise $\omega \sim \mathcal{N}(0,\Psi)$. Ψ is a diagonal matrix. The generative model can be described as:

$$\mathbf{p} = A\tau + \omega + \mu \tag{20}$$

Here, $A \in R^{r \times q}$ is a factor loading matrix. μ is a mean vector. The P.D.F. of the observed data in an FA model can be obtained by:

$$pr(\mathbf{p};\Theta) = \mathcal{N}(\mu, AA^T + \Psi) \tag{21}$$

A mixture of factor analyzers (MFA) is defined by a linear combination of K factor analyzers and can be thought of as a reduced dimension mixture of Gaussians. The MFA model extracts q-dimensional locally linear manifolds underlying the given high dimensional data. The P.D.F. of the observed data by a mixture of K FAs is given by:

$$pr(\mathbf{p};\Theta) \quad = \quad \textstyle\sum_{k=1}^{K} \pi_k \mathcal{N}(\mu_k, A_k A_k^T + \Psi_k) \tag{22}$$

where π_k is a mixing proportion ($\pi_k > 0$ and $\sum_{k=1}^{K} \pi_k = 1$). The system automatically learns the model parameters of the MFA model, $\Theta = \{\pi_k, \mu_k, A_k, \Psi_k | k = 1, ..., K\}$, from example data via expectation maximization techniques [GH97].

We minimize the negative log of $pr(\mathbf{p})$, yielding the energy formulation:

$$E_{prior}(\mathbf{p}) \quad = \quad -\ln \textstyle\sum_{k=1}^{K} \pi_i \mathcal{N}(\mu_k, A_k A_k^T + \Psi_k) \tag{23}$$

A smaller E_{prior} value means that $\mathbf{p}$ is closer to the samples in the motion data and therefore more natural. The inverse

	First subject	Second subject
M	7,790	10,036
d	51,333	49,503
r	20	15
K	30	20
q	10	6

Table 1: *Details of the data we used. M is the number of samples, d is the number of original dimensions (d equals 3 times the number of vertices), r is the number of reduced dimensions in the PCA step, K is the number of factors, and q is the number of dimensions for the latent variable τ_k in each factor of the MFA model.*

and determinant of the covariance matrices are precomputed for each factor to achieve a faster runtime.

The Jacobian matrix can be computed as follows:

$$\frac{\partial E_{prior}}{\partial \mathbf{p}} = \sum_k \frac{\pi_k \mathcal{N}(\mu_k, A_k A_k^T + \Psi_k)(\mathbf{p} - \mu_k)^T (A_k A_k^T + \Psi_k)^{-1}}{\sum_{k=1}^{K} \pi_k \mathcal{N}(\mu_k, A_k A_k^T + \Psi_k)} \tag{24}$$

6. Runtime Optimization

During runtime, the system optimizes in the reduced PCA subspace and find the 3D face model ($\mathbf{p}$) that best satisfies the user constraints ($\mathbf{c}$).

The overall objective function is a weighted combination of the user-defined constraint terms (equations 12, 15, 18) and the model prior term (equation 23):

$$\arg\min_{\mathbf{p} \in R^r} E_{point} + \lambda_1 E_{stroke} + \lambda_2 E_{extra} + \lambda_3 E_{prior} \tag{25}$$

In our experiments, λ_1 is set to 1; we choose an adaptive weight for λ_2 as discussed in section 4.2; λ_3 is selected dynamically by the user (in our experiments, we used a value between 2 and 5). Similarly, the overall jacobian term is a weighted combination of the individual jacobian terms.

Each factor in the MFA model has a mean face mesh. We initialize the optimization with the "best" mean among all factors, by explicitly computing the "best" $\mathbf{p}$:

$$\arg\min_{\mathbf{p} \in \{\mu_1, ..., \mu_K\}} E_{point} + \lambda_1 E_{stroke} + \lambda_2 E_{extra} + \lambda_3 E_{prior} \tag{26}$$

We use the Broyden-Fletcher-Goldfarb-Shanno (BFGS) optimization algorithm in the GSL library [GDT*03]. The solution converges rapidly due to a good starting point, a low-dimensional optimization space, and the symbolic evaluation of the jacobian terms.

7. Results

Table 1 shows the details of the two data sets. For the first subject, the 3D face model has 17,111 vertices and 34,168

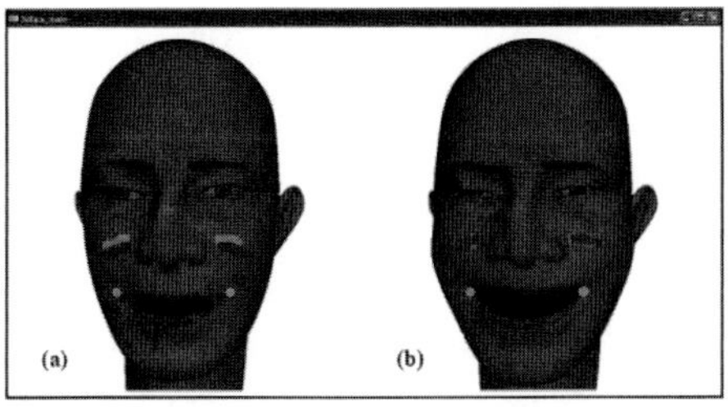

Figure 4: *(a) Original mesh: The user draws point and stroke constraints directly on the screen. The source point/stroke is in blue and target point/stroke is in green. (b) Result: The face model is deformed to satisfy the constraints.*

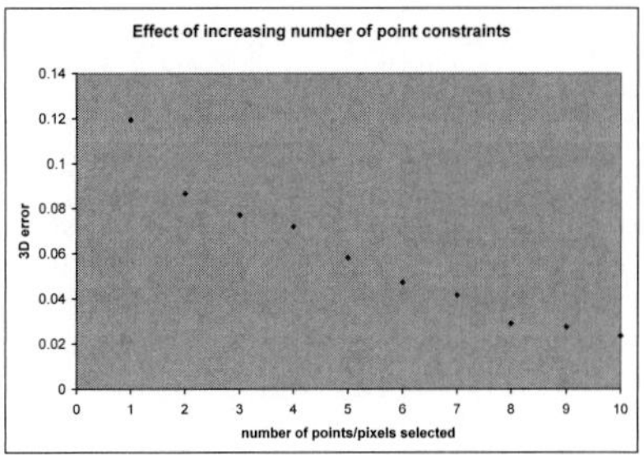

Figure 6: *Cross validation (section 7.3) results averaged over 5 trials.*

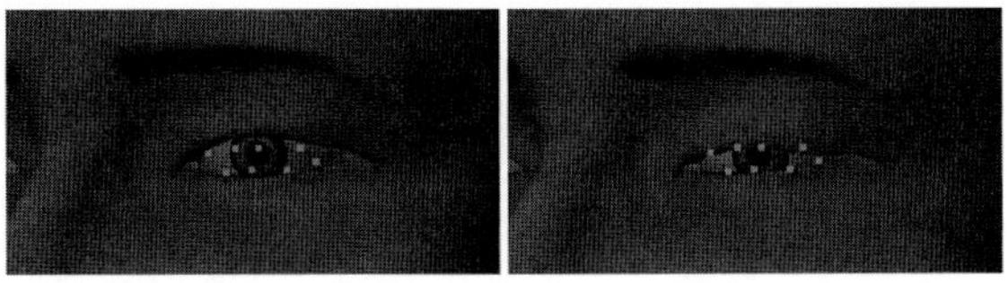

Figure 5: *The user iteratively adds as many constraints as desired. Starting from a neutral pose (left), the user creates a detailed eye geometry (right).*

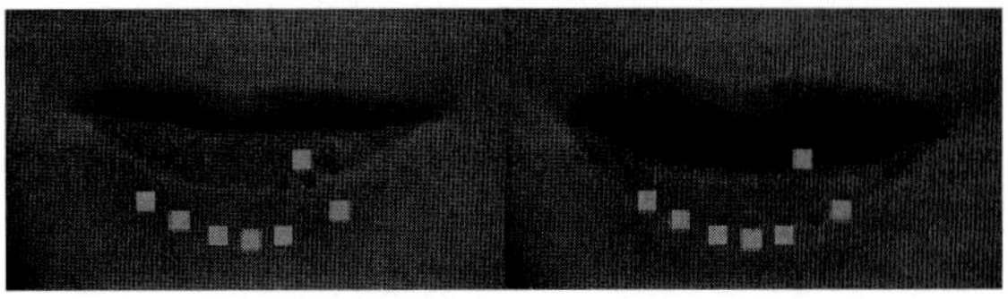

Figure 7: *If there are many constraints, some of them may conflict or "fight" with each other, since the system also tries to generate natural results. The inputs are shown on the left, and the synthesized result is on the right.*

faces. For the second subject, the 3D model has 16,501 vertices and 32,944 faces. The number of reduced dimensions for the first subject and second subject are 20 and 15 respectively by keeping 99 percent of the energy in the eigenvalues.

The Face Poser system can generate a variety of facial expressions. A first-time user learns to use the system within minutes, and is able to create realistic expressions within seconds. Our users have reported that the interface is intuitive and easy to use. The accompanying video shows live screenshots of the results.

7.1. User-Defined Constraints

Point Constraints Figure 4 shows an example with point constraints, where the user poses the shape of the mouth in the smiling expression with two points. In general, this constraint is particularly useful for detailed control of individual points. We can select a facial point and interactively drag it into a desired position in 2D screen space (see video for example). Even though the facial points are in 3D, this "dragging" in 2D screen space is still natural and generates good results. In figure 5, the user iteratively adds more constraints to achieve the desired result of a more detailed eye geometry. As the number of point constraints increase, the results are more accurate (figure 6). However, if there are constraints that do not match *any* natural facial expressions represented by our statistical model, not all the constraints will be satisfied (figure 7).

Stroke Constraints This constraint can be used to efficiently make large-scale changes to the face model. In figure 4, we draw strokes to "raise" the cheek regions to create a smiling expression. The point constraints are used in this example to fine-tune the corners of the mouth. Our users have reported that the sketch interface allows us to draw certain features of the face such as an eyebrow (figure 1 left) more easily. Although some results might also be achieved with point constraints, such a sketch interface is much more intuitive. Some interesting results are shown in figure 8. We can see the effect of having the additional distance term for stroke constraints in figure 9. By adding this term to the optimization, the source stroke will "move towards" the target stroke, even if they are originally far away from each other.

The computational time of the system depends on the number of user-specified constraints. As the number of constraints increases, the computational time increases linearly. This is expected as the computation time for the image intensities increases proportionally with the number of pixels. For example, the computational time for stroke constraints with 900 pixels (about the size of a curve drawn on the eyebrow) is about 0.4 seconds. The time for point constraints also increases linearly with the number of points. It takes about 0.18 seconds for 10 points. The computational time of the system does not depend on the number of example data in the database because the MFA model is learned off-line.

7.2. The Importance of Model Prior

The model prior term allows the generated faces to be natural. Changing the weight of the term in the optimization provides a tradeoff between satisfying user constraints and creating natural faces. We can change this weight dynami-

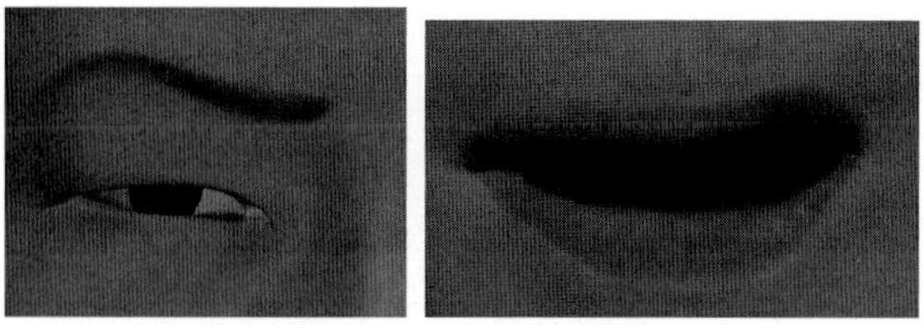

Figure 8: *We can create a raised eyebrow or a curled lip with stroke constraints.*

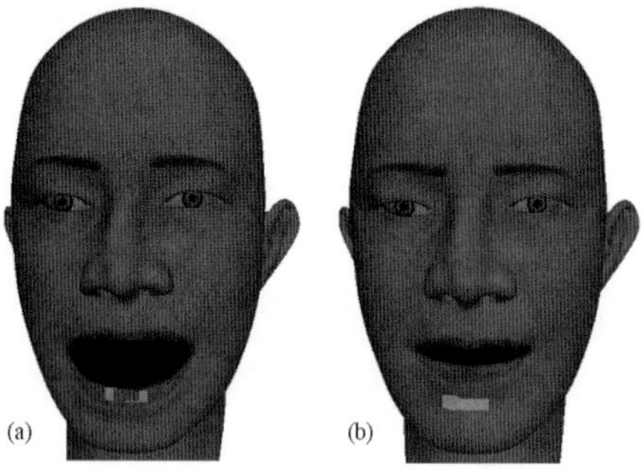

Figure 9: *With and without the additional distance term for stroke constraints. (a) With this term, the blue source stroke will match the green target stroke even if the two strokes are originally far away. (b) Without this term, the optimization gets stuck in a local minima.*

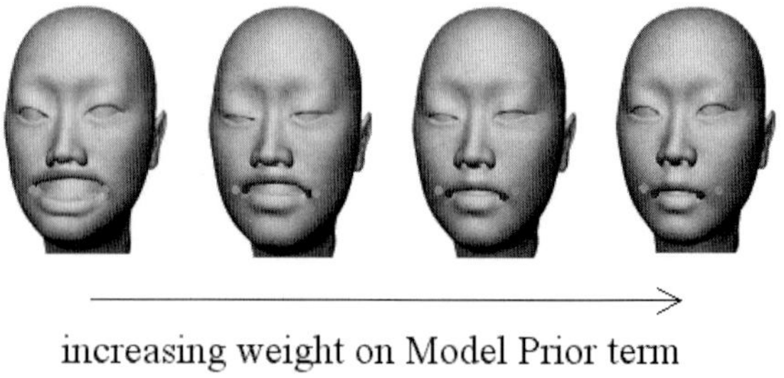

Figure 10: *As the weight increases, the expression becomes more natural. However, the constraints become less satisfied, and the 2D and 3D cross validation errors increase. The leftmost figure has a zero weight, and the rightmost figure has a high weight.*

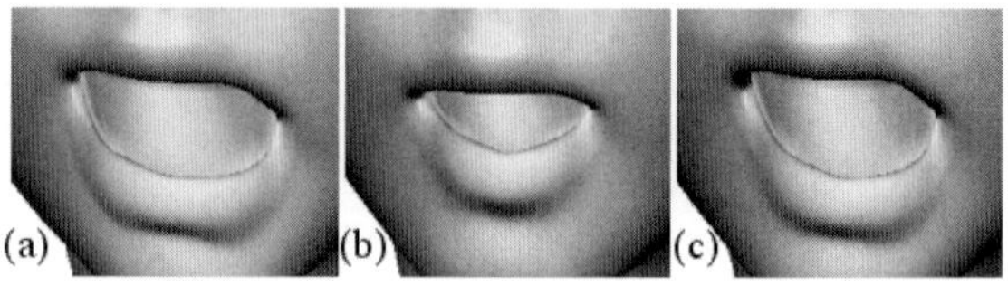

Figure 11: *Cross validation results. Optimization produces visually better results than interpolation. (a) Ground truth. (b) Interpolation, 2D error = 161.8, 3D error = 0.1921. (c) Optimization, 2D error = 10.5, 3D error = 0.0998.*

cally, thus providing an interesting spectrum of possibilities (figure 10) for the user to choose from.

7.3. Comparison Tests

We use new face models as testing data for cross validation tests. We start from a neutral pose and select the source constraints (any kind of constraints) as before. The corresponding target constraints are automatically generated based on the testing data. We then create the face models, and compare them against the original test data. In the results below, the 2D error is the value from equation 12. The 3D error is the average of the sum of the Euclidean distances between each vertex of the ground truth and synthesized 3D model.

	Point Cons	
	interp	opt
2D error	18.15	2.28
3D error	0.06704	0.03642

Table 2: *Cross validation results. Optimization produces more accurate results than interpolation. Each value is an average over 10 trials. We have similar results for other constraints.*

Table 2 shows a comparison of cross validation tests between the blend-shape interpolation and optimization methods. For interpolation, we compute a distance for each sample based on the objective functions in the optimization, and then use each distance to weigh (as in [AMS7a]) that sample accordingly. Figure 11 shows a visual comparison of the results.

We compare the MFA model used in this work against other methods (table 3). "Interp-all" takes all the samples, computes a weight on each sample based on equation 12, and blends the samples to find the solution [Par72, LCF00, SRC01]. "Opt-blend" represents the solution as a sum of weighted blendshapes and optimizes these weights [ZSCS04]. PCA performs the optimization in the PCA space [BV99, BBPV03]. LWR first finds k examples in the database that best matches the user constraints; it then performs a locally weighted regression [AMS7a, CXH03] where each sample is weighted based on equation 12. All optimization methods start with the same initial pose. Figure 12 shows a visual side-by-side comparison of one result.

	Interp-all	Opt-blend	PCA	LWR	MFA
1 point	0.197	0.160	0.157	0.155	0.060
4 points	0.191	0.156	0.154	0.149	0.047
time (ms)	53753	26954	103	52133	183

Table 3: *A comparison of our MFA method with other techniques, for different numbers of point constraints. The values are the 3D errors described above; each one is an average over 3 trials.*

In table 3, "Interp-all" and "Opt-blend" do not produce

Figure 12: *A visual comparison of cross validation results. (a) Ground truth. (b) Optimization with PCA. (c) Optimization with MFA.*

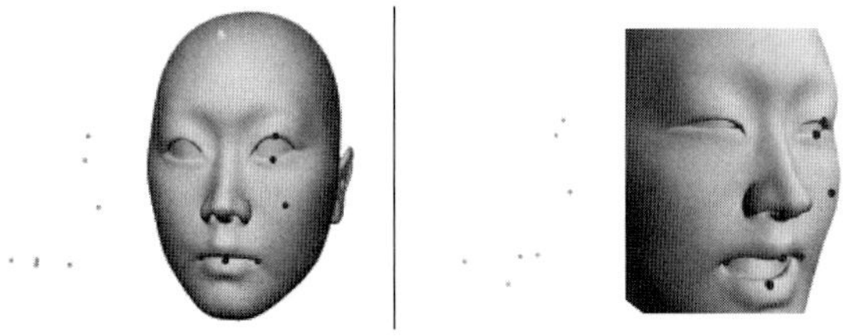

Figure 13: *Trajectory keyframing: We use seven 2D target points (green) to generate the 3D model (blue points are corresponding 3D source points). Two examples with different viewpoints are shown here. See the video for an animation.*

good results because the solution depends on all the samples. PCA also produces a large error because the number of constraints in our system is usually small and they are not sufficient to fully determine the weights of **p**. For LWR, the model provided by the closest samples might not be efficient because they do not provide any temporal coherence. "Interp-all" and LWR are slow since these methods have to iterate through every sample in the database. "Opt-blend" is also slow because there are many parameters in the optimization problem due to the large number of samples. PCA and MFA optimizes in a low-dimensional space and is therefore most efficient. Their models of the dataset are learned off-line. These results show that our technique produces a smaller error and is more efficient than previous methods.

7.4. Application: Trajectory Keyframing

Our optimization framework can be applied for trajectory keyframing. Given the trajectories of a few points, we can re-create the 3D face models using point constraints. Some examples are shown in figure 13. When we generate many frames for an animation, we add a smoothness term to minimize the change in velocity of the vertices between consecutive frames.

8. Discussion

We have presented an approach for generating facial models from two kinds of user constraints (point and stroke constraints) while matching the statistical properties of a database of example models. The system first automatically learns a statistical model from example data and then enforces this as a prior to generate/edit the model. The model prior, together with user-defined constraints, comprise a problem of maximum a posteriori estimation. Solving the MAP problem in a reduced subspace yields an optimal, natural face model that achieves the goals specified by the user.

The quality of the generated model depends on both model priors and user-defined constraints. Without the use of the model priors, the system would not generate natural models unless the user accurately specifies a very detailed set of constraints. One limitation of the approach, therefore, is that an appropriate database must be available. If a model database does not include highly detailed facial geometry such as wrinkles, our system will not generate wrinkles on the face model. We might re-use our database to pose facial expressions for different facial models by re-targeting the original data with expression cloning methods [NN01].

The quality of the generated model also depends on the naturalness of the constraints. Constraints are "natural" when there exists at least one natural facial model consistent with them. The user might not create natural facial expression if the constraints do not match any natural expression in the database or if the constraints are not consistent with each other.

The appearance of the final model is also influenced by the weight of the model prior term, which provides a tradeoff between the prior and the user-defined constraints. Instead of choosing a fixed weight, we allow the user to choose this weight dynamically; we can provide this capability because of the speed of the system.

The system allows for a "click done" mode and a "dragging" mode to create and edit a facial model. The user can choose the desired constraints and then click a button to generate the solution with the current constraints. This allows for placing multiple points and/or strokes in one optimization step. This can lead to large scale changes, but all the constraints may not be satisfied if they come in conflict with allowing for natural poses. The "dragging" mode provides a manipulation interface where the user can see the changes continuously. It allows for more detailed changes over the local region of the dragged point.

Our system allows the user to generate facial models from various types of user-defined constraints. Any kinematic constraints can be integrated into our statistical optimization framework as long as the constraints can be expressed as a function of 3D positions of vertices.

We tested our system with a keyboard/mouse interface and an electronic pen/tablet interface. The system is simple and intuitive, and appeals to both beginning and professional users. Our system greatly reduces the time needed for creating natural face models compared to existing 3D mesh editing software. The system could work with other types of input devices. For example, the user can specify desired facial deformation by dragging multiple facial points on a large touch screen or track a small set of facial points using a vision based interface.

A possible future extension is to model the face as separate regions, generate each region separately, and blend the regions back together. This might allow for fine-grained control over local geometry and improve the generalization ability of our model.

References

[AMS7a] ATKESON C. G., MOORE A. W., SCHAAL S.: Locally weighted learning. In *Artificial Intelligence Review*. 1997a. 11:11–73.

[BBPV03] BLANZ V., BASSO C., POGGIO T., VETTER T.: Reanimating faces in images and video. In *Computer Graphics Forum* (2003). 22(3):641–650.

[Bis96] BISHOP C.: *Neural Network for Pattern Recognition*. Cambridge University Press, 1996.

[Bra02] BRAND M.: Incremental singular value decomposition of uncertain data with missing values. In *Proceedings of ECCV* (2002). 707–720.

[BV99] BLANZ V., VETTER T.: A morphable model for the synthesis of 3d faces. In *Proceedings of ACM SIGGRAPH* (1999). 187–194.

[BW00] BISHOP C. M., WINN J. M.: Non-linear bayesian image modelling. In *Proceedings of ECCV*. 2000. 3–17.

[CH05] CHAI J., HODGINS J.: Performance animation from low-dimensional control signals. In *ACM Transactions on Graphics* (2005). 24(3):686–696.

[CJ06] CHANG E., JENKINS O. C.: Sketching articulation and pose for facial animation. In *Proceedings of ACM SIGGRAPH/Eurographics Symposium on Computer Animation* (2006). 271-280.

[CXH03] CHAI J., XIAO J., HODGINS J.: Vision-based control of 3d facial animation. In *Proceedings of ACM SIGGRAPH/Eurographics Symposium on Computer Animation* (2003). 193–206.

[DH73] DUDA R., HART P.: *Pattern Classification and Scene Analysis*. John Wiley and Sons, 1973.

[DSP06] DER K. G., SUMNE R. W., POPOVIĆ J.: Inverse kinematics for reduced deformable models. In *ACM Transactions on Graphics* (2006). 25(3):1174–1179.

[GDT*03] GALASSI M., DAVIES J., THEILER J., GOUGH B., JUNGMAN G., BOOTH M., ROSSI F.: *GNU Scientific Library Reference Manual - Revised Second Edition*. Network Theory Ltd., 2003. ISBN 0954161734.

[GH97] GHAHRAMANI Z., HINTON G. E.: The EM algorithm for mixtures of factor analyzers, 1997.

[GMHP04] GROCHOW K., MARTIN S. L., HERTZMANN A., POPOVIĆ Z.: Style-based inverse kinematics. In *ACM Transactions on Graphics* (2004). 23(3):522–531.

[HDR97] HINTON G. E., DAYAN P., REVOW M.: Modeling the manifolds of images of handwritten digits. In *IEEE Transactions on Neural Networks*. 1997. 8(1):65–74.

[IMT99] IGARASHI T., MATSUOKA S., TANAKA H.: Teddy: a sketching interface for 3d freeform design. In *Proceedings of ACM SIGGRAPH* (1999). 409–416.

[JTDP03] JOSHI P., TIEN W. C., DESBRUN M., PIGHIN F.: Learning controls for blendshape based realistic facial animation. In *Proceedings of ACM SIGGRAPH/Eurographics Symposium on Computer Aimation* (2003). 187–192.

[KG05] KHO Y., GARLAND M.: Sketching mesh deformations. In *Proceedings of ACM Symposium on Interactive 3D Graphics and Games* (2005). 147–154.

[Law04] LAWRENCE N. D.: Gaussian process latent variable models for visualization of high dimensional data. In *Advances in Neural Information Processing Systems 16* (2004). 329–336.

[LCF00] LEWIS J. P., CORDNER M., FONG N.: Pose space deformation: A unified approach to shape interpolation and skeleton-driven deformation. In *Proceedings of ACM SIGGRAPH*. 2000. 165–172.

[NN01] NOH J., NEUMANN U.: Expression cloning. In *Proceedings of ACM SIGGRAPH* (2001). 277–288.

[NSACO05] NEALEN A., SORKINE O., ALEXA M., COHEN-OR D.: A sketch-based interface for detail-preserving mesh editing. In *ACM Transactions on Graphics* (2005). 24(3):1142–1147.

[Par72] PARKE F. I.: Computer generated animation of faces. In *Proc. ACM National Conference* (1972). 1:451–457.

[PSS99] PIGHIN F., SZELISKI R., SALESIN D.: Resynthesizing facial animation through 3d model-based tracking. In *International Conference on Computer Vision*. 1999. 143–150.

[PW96] PARKE F. I., WATERS K.: Computer facial animation. A.K. Peter, Wellesley, 1996.

[SRC01] SLOAN P.-P., ROSE C., COHEN M. F.: Shape by example. In *ACM Symposium on Interactive 3D Graphics* (2001). 135-143.

[SZGP05] SUMNER R. W., ZWICKER M., GOTSMAN C., POPOVIĆ J.: Mesh-based inverse kinematics. In *ACM Transactions on Graphics* (2005). 24(3):488–495.

[YSvdP05] YANG C., SHARON D., VAN DE PANNE M.: Sketch-based modeling of parameterized objects. In *2nd Eurographics Workshop on Sketch-Based Interfaces and Modeling* (2005).

[ZHH96] ZELEZNIK R. C., HERNDON K. P., HUGHES J. F.: Sketch: an interface for sketching 3d scenes. In *Proceedings of ACM SIGGRAPH* (1996). 163–170.

[ZLGS03] ZHANG Q., LIU Z., GUO B., SHUM H.: Geometry-driven photorealistic facial expression synthesis. In *Proceedings of ACM SIGGRAPH/Eurographics Symposium on Computer Animation* (2003). 177-186.

[ZSCS04] ZHANG L., SNAVELY N., CURLESS B., SEITZ S. M.: Spacetime faces: high resolution capture for modeling and animation. In *ACM Transactions on Graphics* (2004). 23(3):548–558.

Eurographics/ ACM SIGGRAPH Symposium on Computer Animation (2007)
D. Metaxas and J. Popovic (Editors)

Time-critical distributed contact for 6-DoF haptic rendering of adaptively sampled reduced deformable models

Jernej Barbič[1] and Doug James[2]

[1]Carnegie Mellon University, Pittsburgh, PA, USA, [2]Cornell University, Ithaca, NY, USA

Abstract

Real-time evaluation of distributed contact forces for rigid or deformable 3D objects is important for providing multi-sensory feedback in emerging real-time applications, such as 6-DoF haptic force-feedback rendering. Unfortunately, at very high temporal rates (1 kHz for haptics), there is often insufficient time to resolve distributed contact between geometrically complex objects.
In this paper, we present a spatially and temporally adaptive sample-based approach to approximate contact forces under hard real-time constraints. The approach is CPU based, and supports contact between a rigid and a reduced deformable model with complex geometry. Penalty-based contact forces are efficiently resolved using a multi-resolution point-based representation for one object, and a signed-distance field for the other. Hard real-time approximation of distributed contact forces uses multi-level progressive point-contact sampling, and exploits temporal coherence, graceful degradation and other optimizations. We present several examples of 6-DoF haptic rendering of geometrically complex rigid and deformable objects in distributed contact at real-time kilohertz rates.

Categories and Subject Descriptors (according to ACM CCS): I.6.8 [Simulation and Modeling]: Types of Simulation: Animation, I.3.5 [Computer Graphics]: Computational Geometry and Object Modeling: Physically based modeling, I.3.7 [Computer Graphics]: Three-Dimensional Graphics and Realism: Virtual Reality

1. Introduction

In this paper, we address *distributed* contact between geometrically complex 3D objects, i.e., contact with potentially several simultaneous contact sites each distributed over a non-zero surface area (also called multi-point contact; see Figure 1). Distributed contact represents an important component of interactive physically based virtual environments. It is challenging to simulate due to competing demands of having interesting geometrically complex rigid and (more notoriously) deformable objects, as well as high real-time contact force calculations rates, e.g., 1 kHz to support haptic force-feedback rendering. We propose an efficient CPU-based algorithm suitable for hard real-time evaluation of distributed contact forces between geometrically complex models. These real-time forces can be used in a variety of applications, however, we focus on the challenging application of 6-DoF haptic rendering of rigid and deformable models.

Our approach is most closely related to the Voxmap-PointShell method (VPS) [MPT99], a 6-DoF haptic rendering algorithm capable of simulating distributed geometrically detailed contact between a *rigid* environment and a *rigid* point-sampled object (*pointshell*). The pointshell is a collection of points (with normals) positioned near-regularly at the surface of the object. The VPS environment is modeled as a *voxmap* datastructure: a voxelization of the polygonal environment geometry where each voxel contains a fixed-width (e.g., 2-bit) value (e.g., interior, surface, next to surface, free space). In every VPS haptic cycle, pointshell points are queried against the voxmap to determine contact.

Unfortunately, objects modeled by VPS and most notable recent works on 6-DoF haptic rendering are entirely rigid, and for good reason: nonlinear deformable objects are computationally expensive since (a) detailed finite element simulations can not easily achieve haptic rates (1000 Hz) for geometrically interesting models, and (b) deformable collision detection is expensive especially for close-proximity scenarios typical of contact. These fundamental difficulties have seriously hampered the progress of a variety of emerg-

Symposium on Computer Animation 2007, San Diego, CA, August 03-04, 2007.
© 2007 ACM 978-1-59593-624-4/07/0008 $5.00

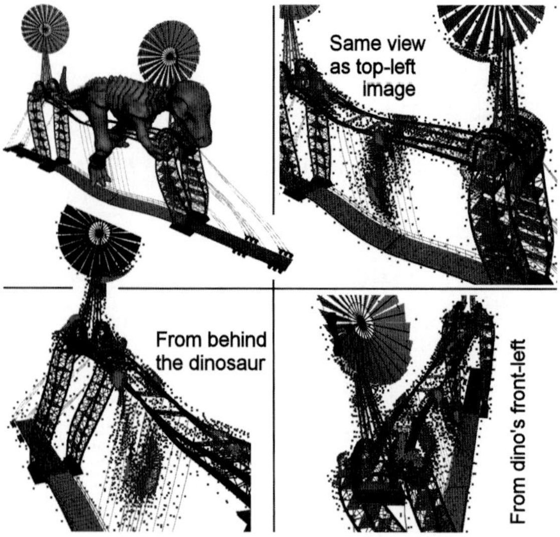

Figure 1: ***Distributed deformable contact:*** ***(Top Left)*** *contact configuration between a nonlinear reduced deformable bridge and a rigid dinosaur, with 12 separate contact sites;* ***(Other images)*** *contact sites viewed from three different camera angles. A total of 5200 points (in blue) were traversed, resulting in 426 points (in red) in contact. Note: temporal coherence was disabled for this figure.*

ing haptic rendering applications, such as haptic gaming. One other application of haptic rendering is virtual prototyping: haptics can allow airplane designers to check if a certain mechanical part can be positioned into (or removed from) designated locations, thereby avoiding critical design flaws before manufacturing the structure, e.g., fire detector removal from an aircraft engine assembly during routine servicing [WM03]. Supporting deformable geometry is important since airplanes include numerous deformable parts such as hoses, wires, plastic parts, sheet metal, etc. Part-removal analysis using only rigid simulations can lead to false reports that a part cannot be (dis)assembled when in reality it can. For example, wires and hoses may be deformed to let an object through a narrow passage (see Figure 2).

1.1. Overview

Our approach is designed to work with a variety of reduced deformable models that support a basic two-step simulation process: (1) a fast timestep of reduced deformable dynamics; (2) fast evaluation of individual deformed surface point positions and normals to adaptively resolve contact. Suitable reduced models include classic linear modal vibration models, reduced nonlinear models, simple low-resolution deformable models with embedded geometry, adaptive multiresolution models, articulated flexible multibodies, etc. The only requirement is that the model's reduced state can be time-stepped at high rates, and its deformed geometry sampled adaptively for time-critical contact force estimation. In our implementation we employ prior dimensional model reduction and Newmark subspace integration techniques for reduced geometrically nonlinear models [BJ05], which are suitable for large deformations with large rotations but small local strain. Such reduced models are based on formal reductions of large-deformation FEM models. They can simulate reduced dynamics of large deformations of geometrically detailed objects at haptic rates, e.g., much less than one hundred microseconds per timestep in our examples. We make extensive use of the low-dimensional shape parameterization for time-critical collision and force processing. Regardless of the particular reduced deformation model used, our approach addresses stable haptic display of distributed contact between two objects *each* with non-trivial geometry.

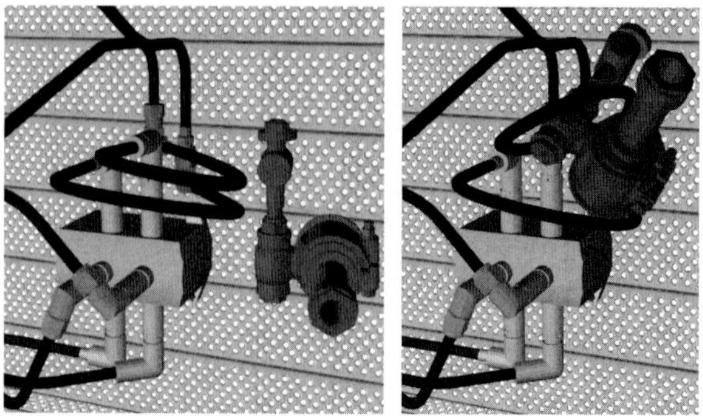

Figure 2: ***Real-time 6-DoF haptic rendering*** *of rigid and deformable objects in contact. The operator is navigating the green rigid part in between two deformable hoses.*

Instead of a VPS voxmap, we use a floating-point signed-distance field to (a) make the contact force continuous (improving stability), (b) support time-critical contact estimation, and (c) exploit temporal coherence. We support contact between a rigid and a reduced deformable model using a rigid distance field and a deformable pointshell (see Figure 3). Output-sensitive signed-distance field oracles for reduced deformable models can be used to support defo-defo contact [Bar07], but are beyond the scope of this paper. Our approach scales with increasing geometric detail, and is (to the best of our knowledge) the first approach that can support haptic rendering of deformable contact between such geometrically complex models.

To support haptic display of geometrically detailed models, e.g., involving a million pointshell points, we organize the pointshell into a *nested* multi-resolution hierarchy, by sampling points (and normals) from an appropriately defined *smooth manifold surface*. Our sampling is near-uniform which provides economic pointshells and improves haptic stability. We use a precomputed sphere-tree hierarchy to bound the pointshell points, *with sphere centers located at (non-leaf) pointshell points*. For deformable models, this gives a point-based modification of the Bounded Deformation Tree (BD-Tree) [JP04]. Such a hierarchy permits large pointshells, bigger than what could be examined point by point during one haptic cycle: if a point on some coarse

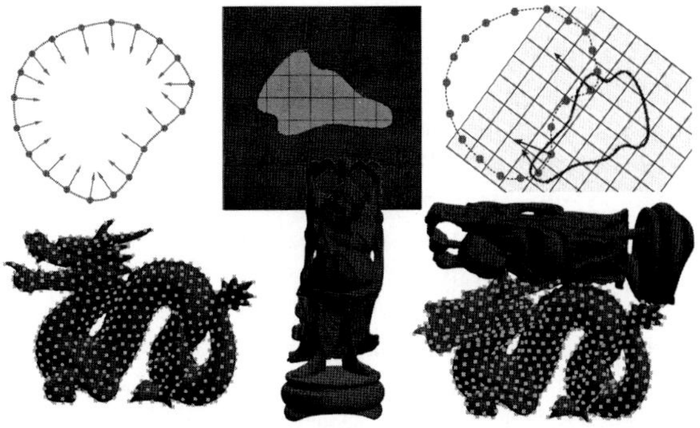

Figure 3: ***Point-contact model:*** *(**Left**) Reduced deformable pointshell with inward normals; (**Middle**) the distance field; (**Right**) deformable contact and contact forces.*

hierarchical level is sufficiently far from contact, none of the points in the subtree can be in contact, and then those points need not be checked. In contrast, if a large part of the pointshell is in contact or close to contact, few subtrees will be culled and a large part of the pointshell will need to be examined point by point. We address this problem by providing *graceful degradation of contact*: if there is not enough computation time to fully complete the tree traversal, the algorithm still returns a reasonable answer, with accuracy dependent on contact-configuration difficulty and available processing power. Graceful degradation is achieved by traversing the nested hierarchy in a breadth-first order, rendering deeper and deeper tree levels until out of computation time. We use two separate activation thresholds to avoid abrupt changes in the rendered depth during consecutive haptic cycles. The simulation also uses temporal coherence to time-sample the individual points at rates depending on distance to contact (temporal adaptivity).

We haptically display distributed contact using a novel first-order quasi-dynamic virtual coupling method. In haptics, higher update rates generally enable stable rendering of stiffer forces and torques; but reaching such high rates is challenging for models with detailed geometry. In our system, the deformations, collision detection and contact force computations run together in one loop at haptic rates (1000 Hz). We do not need to extrapolate from lower-rate signals. A multi-rate simulation using the contact gradients of Section 6 could exploit user's limited sensing bandwidth to further increase example complexity [OL06, OG07].

1.2. Other Related Work

Haptic rendering has received increasing attention over the last decade [LD07], and significant challenges remain especially for rendering deformable systems. Early methods were developed for tissue simulations during virtual surgery [KcM00], and mostly used mass-spring deformable objects. Space-time adaptive and multi-rate methods have been successful for real-time deformable object simulation [AH98, DDCB01], but time-critical distributed contact algorithms have received less attention (c.f. [MO06]). A variety of preprocessing techniques, such as precomputed Green's functions, exist for accelerating linear elastostatic models to support haptic force-feedback rendering of point-like contact, or modest multi-point contacts via low-rank updates [BNC96, CDA99, JP01, JP03, JCC06]. Unfortunately, most such haptic rendering papers assume interactions based on pulling on (or constraining) certain vertices, not performing real-time deformable-rigid object collision detection and distributed contact force and torque computations with complex geometry.

As mentioned, the Voxmap-PointShell (VPS) method was introduced by [MPT99] to support rigid-rigid contact rendering. Pointshell accuracy and virtual coupling stability were improved in [RPP*01]. In [WM03], they replaced the original VPS mass-spring-damper with a quasi-static spring. The recent paper of [MPT06] introduces wider voxmaps (4-bit), which now have more room to store distance-to-nearest-contact information for free-space voxels. Since the haptic device is user controlled, there exists an upper bound on the maximum possible velocity of a point shell point, and therefore points located in a voxel sufficiently far from contact need not be checked for several haptic cycles (temporal coherence). Also, the pointshell is traversed on two levels: a coarse level shell is tested against a coarse level voxmap, followed by finer tests if necessary. The hierarchy only consists of two levels, the simulation is rigid, and graceful degradation of contact was not addressed.

Our progressive interruptible point-based contact-sampling approach is analogous to the QSplat point-based rendering algorithm [RL00] which represented the point cloud hierarchically to enable level-of-detail control for *graphical* rendering. Our oriented pointshell can be seen as a surfel point cloud. A single-resolution contact algorithm for two mesh-free deformable point-sampled objects has been presented in [KMH*04]. The method computes the contact surface using the point-based surface projection operator, reaching interactive (but not haptic) rates: timesteps of 130-200 milliseconds were reported for two models of about 10,000 surfels each. Hierarchical point-contact handling was explored in [PPG04], where they demonstrate near-interactive (a few frames per second without precomputation) contact of point-based quasi-rigid (quasi-static and linear) deformable objects. In this paper, we present a hierarchical contact rendering method designed for high-rate (haptic rendering) applications. We demonstrate how to maintain upper bounds on the amount of computation per haptic cycle, and how to minimize contact force artifacts when run-time constraints force a transition to a different contact resolution level.

Bounding volume hierarchies can be used for *interruptible* collision detection for rigid [Hub95] and embedded deformable models [MO06] by traversing the hierarchy in a breadth-first manner. Time-critical contact can be approximated by applying contact forces between contacting (sphere) primitives at the deepest level traversed in a particular frame. Unfortunately, such approaches can have trouble resolving close-proximity and conforming contact configurations in high-rate scenarios (as in haptic rendering): finer bounding volumes more closely approximate the object, and as such the effective contact surface (and therefore forces) depend on the level of detail rendered at any instant. In our work, the points at different resolution levels progressively sample the same well-defined contact surface, thereby making contact at different levels of detail more consistent.

Six-DoF haptic rendering of complex *rigid* objects can be achieved using a number of techniques, in addition to VPS, such as multi-resolution collision detection on convex decompositions, followed by a clustering of contacts [KOLM03]. Multi-resolution contact haptics has been demonstrated for polygonal geometry by appropriately simplifying the objects at different hierarchical levels, to preserve the user haptic *sensation* [OL03, OL06]. The authors suggest that for contact sites of large area, resolving the contact at a coarser resolution will not result in significant sensation degradation; this has motivated our graceful degradation algorithm. These approaches, however, do not directly apply to point-sampled objects or deformable objects.

Linear complementary problem (LCP) solvers can be used to solve the Signorini contact problem between a rigid object and a linear deformable object [DDKA06]. LCP solvers are computationally demanding which limits the approach to models of modest geometric complexity. A deformable pointshell haptic rendering example has been demonstrated in [BJ05]; however, one of the two contacting objects (a small rigid ball) had trivial geometry. In this paper, *both* contacting objects have non-trivial geometry, resulting in a much more difficult collision detection problem; also the contact model of analytical gradients (as used with the ball) gives discontinuities if naively extended to non-trivial distance field geometry.

2. Penalty-based Point-contact Model

The point-contact model employed for rigid-rigid, or rigid-defo (or even defo-defo) contact are conceptually identical: the contact penalty forces are determined by querying the points of the pointshell object against the signed distance field of the other object (see Figure 3). The user interactively manipulates one of the two objects (the *haptic object*); in our implementation, the distance-field object is manipulated.

Both pointshell and the distance field are computed in a pre-processing stage. For completeness, our particular distance field preprocess is described in Appendix A. During every haptic cycle, pointshell points are queried against the signed-distance field, as illustrated in Figure 3. By convention, negative distance field values denote the interior of the distance field object, and therefore points in contact. Penalty forces are computed for points in contact. We choose the direction of the force to equal the inward normal of the pointshell point in contact (and as such the force acts to resolve contact; see also Section 4). The magnitude is determined from the amount of penetration: $F = -k_C \cdot d \cdot N$, where k_C is the contact penalty force stiffness, $d < 0$ is the signed distance field value, and N is the point's inward normal in the world coordinate system. The point world-coordinate position and normal computation are discussed in later sections. Note that the total force and torque can be computed easily using this model, and the trilinearly interpolated distance field.

We note that this contact model is not standard, but it has useful approximation properties for haptics. It avoids using the distance field gradients which are discontinuous across the object's interior medial axes. In fact, we first tried using distance field gradients to determine the direction of the penalty force, but the resulting force direction discontinuities gave poor haptic signals. In our contact model, the force on a point is a continuous function of objects' position and deformation. Only the normal of one of the two contacting objects (that of the pointshell object) determines force direction, and this is both an approximation used for speed, and robustness; also note that for smooth surfaces in non-penetrating contact, the normals of the two opposing surfaces at the contact point are colinear.

Comparison: We also implemented the standard VPS voxmap [MPT99] and found distance fields to provide more stable haptic feedback, especially at higher stiffness settings. We attribute this difference to discontinuities in voxmap contact force when crossing voxel boundaries. To reduce distance-field memory, a hybrid data structure would be possible, using a wide-bit voxmap in free space, and a distance field accessed via a hash table in the shallow contact force layer surrounding the object.

3. Sampling reduced deformable models

Without loss of generality (among reduced models) we assume the reduced deformation kinematics $u(t) = U \cdot q(t)$, where $u \in \mathbb{R}^{3n}$ is the displacement vector (e.g., for a FEM simulation mesh with n vertices), $U \in \mathbb{R}^{3n \times r}$ is a certain time-independent low-rank deformation basis matrix, and $q = q(t) \in \mathbb{R}^r$ is the vector of reduced coordinates. The key algorithmic idea is that once the reduced state, q and $\dot{q}$, has been updated by the reduced integrator, co-state quantities such as individual deformable point positions and normals can be sampled adaptively as needed by the tree traversal.

Point samples: Given the current reduced coordinates q of any haptic cycle, any of the deforming pointshell's S points can be reconstructed in $3r$-flops by summing up the r per-vertex displacement modes:

$$p_s = P_s + U_s\, q, \quad s = 1 \ldots S, \qquad (1)$$

where P_s is the undeformed pointshell position, and $U_s \in \mathbb{R}^{3\times r}$ is the precomputed modal displacement matrix (interpolated at P_s from U using the FEM shape functions). If the point is in contact ($d(p_s) < 0$), the normal will be computed, and the penalty contact force evaluated; this force $f_s \in \mathbb{R}^3$ is then applied as an external reduced force $U_s^T f_s \in \mathbb{R}^r$ to the reduced deformable object integrator to excite deformations. This integration timestep is performed at the end of the haptic cycle, producing q and $\dot{q}$ for the next haptic cycle.

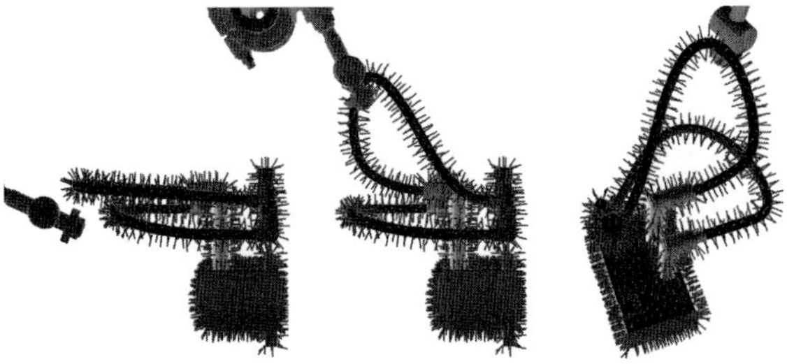

Figure 4: ***Our dynamic normals: (Left)*** *undeformed;* ***(Middle, Right)*** *deformed, viewed from two camera angles. In practice, normals need only be computed for pointshell points in contact. Maximum deviation from the correct surface normal is 5.2 degrees in this example; and less than 3.6 degrees for all but five points.*

Fast normal approximation: Normals must be computed for sparse pointshell points *in contact* for rapid evaluation of penalty forces. Rigid pointshells have static body-frame normals that can be precomputed. Deforming pointshell normals can be approximated in a variety of ways. In our implementation, we exploit the fact that our geometrically nonlinear deformable models involve large rotations but small strain. This enables us to well approximate the deformed normals simply by transforming the undeformed normal by the local deformation gradient, followed by normalization (see Figure 4). The deformation gradient at P_s ($\frac{\partial}{\partial P_s}$ of (1)), interpolated from the FEM model, is a linear function of q,

$$F_s(q) = I + \sum_{j=1..r} F_{s,j}\, q_j, \qquad (2)$$

where s is the index of the pointshell point, and $F_{s,j} \in \mathbb{R}^{3,3}$ can be computed from the deformation basis matrix U and the FEM shape functions. This allows us to construct a fast $3r$-flop pointshell normal approximation,

$$n_s = \frac{n_s'}{\|n_s'\|}, \quad n_s' \approx F_s(q) \cdot N_s = N_s + \Delta N_s\, q, \quad s = 1 \ldots S, \qquad (3)$$

where N_s is the undeformed normal, and $\Delta N_s \in \mathbb{R}^{3\times r}$ is a precomputed normal-correction matrix (whose j-th column equals $F_{s,j} \cdot N_s$) that accounts for large rotations–unlike the linearized approximation in [JP02]. Finally, at double the cost, true normals could be sampled by instead transforming the tangent space.

4. Nested Pointshell Hierarchy

Only small pointshells (~4000 points on our hardware) can be traversed linearly (point by point) in a haptic cycle. To some extent, larger pointshells are possible by using temporal coherence and wider voxels [MPT06]. To be able to simulate much larger pointshells (rigid or deformable), we organize the pointshell into a *nested tree hierarchy* (see Figure 5). This (deformable) pointshell hierarchy also serves as a (BD-Tree) bounding sphere hierarchy.

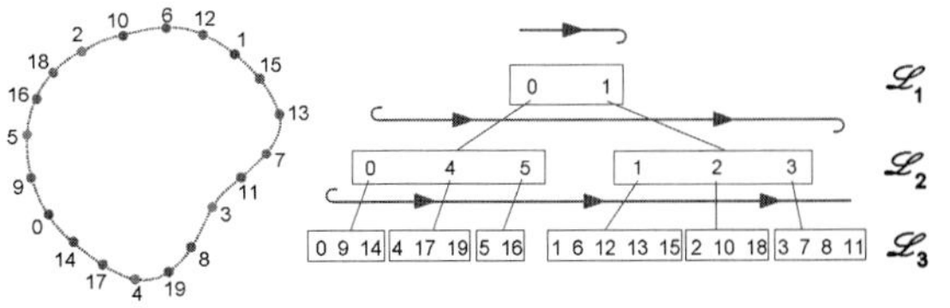

Figure 5: ***Nested point-tree: (Left)*** *The pointshell;* ***(Right)*** *the hierarchy, the traversal order and tree levels $\mathcal{L}_i$. Particle-repulsion levels are 0-1, 2-5, and 6-19 in this case.*

Uniform pointshell sampling and meaningful pointshell normals are important for providing reliable contact-force estimates and stable haptic rendering. At first, we considered pointshells sampling polygon soup geometry, but stable haptic rendering cannot be guaranteed due to unpredictable normals and the non-closed and non-oriented nature of the surface sampling. Consequently, we designed our pointshells to sample a *closed manifold oriented surface*. When combined with virtual coupling saturation (§ 6), this restricts the distance field object to outside of the pointshell object (or at most a shallow penetration). Another problem happens if points are too far apart, allowing a small feature in the distance field object to slip undetected in between two points; we address this by keeping the pointshell resolution equal or finer than the distance field resolution. In general, we found that pointshells sampling such surfaces tend to be stable; high frequency components, either in point locations or point normals tend to cause instabilities. Sharp corners can still be rendered, albeit not aggressively.

Multi-resolution pointshell via particle repulsion: We generate our pointshells by fitting a set of *particles* (points) onto a smooth manifold surface, using the ideas of particle repulsion [Tur92, WH94]. Similar to [Tur01], we construct a nested point hierarchy by progressively fitting increasing finer samplings of points (4× branching factor), while freezing coarser level points; we, however, fit points on a level set of a distance field as opposed to a triangle mesh (see Figure 6). Details are given in Appendix B.

Nested pointshell sphere-tree construction: After particle repulsion, each point is positioned, and assigned to one of the disjoint *particle-repulsion* levels. We proceed by organizing the points into a sphere-tree hierarchy. In the deformable case, this results in a point-based Bounded Deformation Tree (BD-Tree). We first generate *tree levels* $\mathcal{L}_i$:

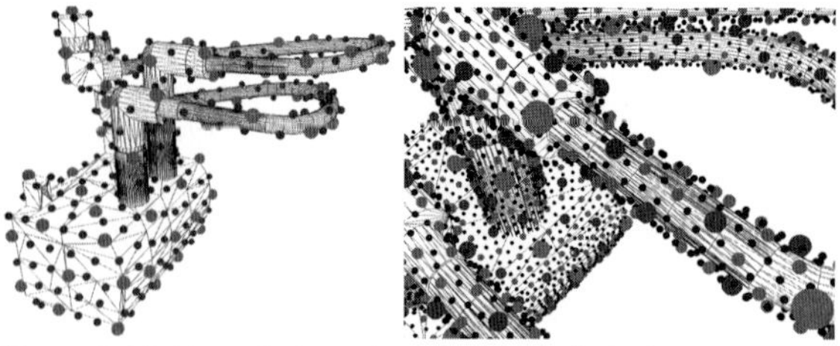

Figure 6: ***Multi-resolution oriented pointshell:*** *(**Left**) The first two levels of a part of the hose scene; (**Right**) detail with four levels shown. Points are fitted on a small-distance offset oriented manifold surface to support "polygon soup" input geometry, and provide oriented surface normals for contact.*

the set $\mathcal{L}_i$ consists of an instance of every point of particle-repulsion levels 1 through i (see Figure 5). Therefore, if a point first appears on particle-repulsion level i, an instance of this point will appear in all tree levels $\mathcal{L}_j$, for $j \geq i$. Instances can share common memory data. The deepest tree level consists of a single instance of all the points in the pointshell. The elements of $\mathcal{L}_i$ are our tree *nodes* on tree level i. This construction was chosen so that all nodes at all levels lie on the actual contact surface $\mathcal{T}$, and that each $\mathcal{L}_i$ samples $\mathcal{T}$ about uniformly (without gaps), with progressively finer resolution with level index i. We establish the tree parent-child relationships by traversing nodes at every level $\mathcal{L}_{i+1}$, and assigning each node to the nearest node from level $\mathcal{L}_i$. A bounding sphere radius is computed for each non-leaf tree node, centered at the location of the node, and covering all nodes in the subtree, in the undeformed configuration. The radius of the bounding sphere gets progressively smaller for instances of the same point at different levels. For deformable pointshells, the sphere radius is updated at runtime using appropriate precomputed BD-Tree datastructures (update cost is r flops per traversed node). The sphere center always coincides with the current node location.

5. Time-critical Progressive Contact Forces

We now describe the core approach for time-critical evaluation of contact forces when one object is represented as a rigid or deformable pointshell, and the other object provides a signed-distance oracle, $d(p)$.

Runtime tree traversal: At every haptic cycle, the algorithm traverses the pointshell hierarchy in breadth-first order. For every tree node, the algorithm looks up the value of the signed distance field at the node's location. Next, to support deformations, the BD-Tree method is used to update the radius of the bounding sphere covering points in the subtree rooted at the node. If the distance field value is greater than the radius, no point in the subtree can collide, and the subtree is not traversed further (see Figure 7 (Middle, e.g., node 2)). Otherwise, all children of the node are added to a list for future traversal (see Figure 7 (Middle, e.g., nodes 0, 3)). If the distance field value is negative (contact), a penalty force is assigned to the node, just like in the single-resolution case. If child copies of the node are visited during later traversal, no additional force is accumulated (but the copy is not skipped from traversal since its proper children may be in contact).

The subtle but algorithmically key point is that our point-based BD-Tree uses nested pointshell points as deformed sphere centers. This seemingly trivial choice enables time-critical testing of the point-based BD-Tree against a distance field: updating a BD-Tree sphere also updates a deformed pointshell point, p, which can in turn be immediately evaluated against the distance field, and if in contact ($d(p) < 0$) will contribute to the progressive accumulation of contact forces in a multi-resolution manner. Therefore, even in the expected case where there is insufficient time to completely test the BD-Tree against the distance field, approximate contact forces can still be accumulated in a time-critical fashion.

Temporal coherence: When a tree node is processed, an estimate of the earliest possible haptic cycle when the bounding ball at this node can enter contact is determined (and cached with the node), based on node's current distance to contact, sphere radius, and maximum point velocity that can occur in the simulation. This can be the immediate next cycle if the node is close to contact (or in contact), or it can be hundreds of cycles for points far from contact. Next time a node is about to be processed, we can safely skip it if the current haptic cycle is younger that what stored in the node. Temporal coherence reduced our simulation times 20%-45%.

Graceful degradation: If the contact scenario is not very involved, much of the tree will be quickly culled and only a small fraction of the pointshell will be traversed. In contrast, if there are many different contact sites, such as when the pointshell object is positioned close to the distance field object, a large fraction of the pointshell will need to be traversed, preventing a complete tree traversal within one haptic cycle. To support graceful degradation in such cases, we traverse the tree progressively level by level (see Figure 7). While traversing the list of nodes that need to be visited on level i (as determined by level $i-1$), we build the traversal list for level $i+1$. At the end of level i, we compare the size of this list to a measure of the remaining computation time for the haptic cycle. Only if enough time remains, we render the next level. The algorithm always either completes a level or does not start it. The resulting contact forces are identical to those obtained under an exhaustive tree-less traversal of points up to a given level. Note that such a scheme is of course approximate: only geometric features resolved by points on the deepest traversed level will be rendered. The benefit of our construction is that rendered surface resolution and contact force accuracy both increase with available computing power.

LOD control: The amount of work required to process a node is predictable and it is not necessary to time the execution explicitly. Instead, we count the total number of tree

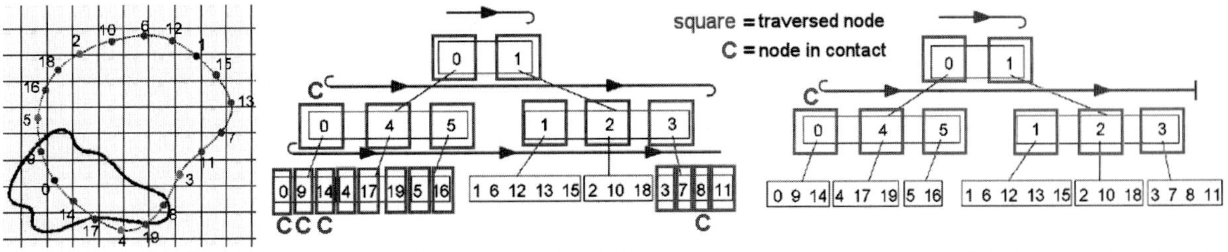

Figure 7: ***Graceful degradation:*** *With involved contact scenarios (**Left**), many tree nodes need to be traversed during a complete hierarchy traversal (**Middle**). Under graceful degradation (**Right**), tree is traversed only up to a shallow depth, as permitted by available CPU power.*

nodes visited, V, during the current haptic cycle. We use two thresholds to determine whether to render the next tree level. All the levels up to and including the deepest level rendered in the previous haptic cycle use the *warm threshold* V_W, whereas all deeper levels use the *cold threshold* $V_C < V_W$. A level is rendered if the total number of tree nodes visited before entering this level is below the level's threshold. Cold threshold is stricter to prevent popping back and forth among two levels during consecutive haptic cycles; we set $V_C = 0.8V_W$. In practice, we have seen LOD changes at most about 2-3$\times$ per second, and did not feel any popping haptic rendering artifacts. LOD changes can be made fewer by reducing V_C. We selected V_W manually by running the simulation and observing computation times per haptic cycle. The selection was not difficult and could be automated, as the cost to process each node is $O(r)$, establishing a high correlation between the number of traversed nodes and the total haptic cycle computation time.

6. Haptic Display of Distributed Contact

Until now we have abstracted 6-DoF haptic rendering as simply a matter of computing contact forces and torques at high rates. However, penalty forces and torques cannot simply be sent to the haptic device: each point in contact adds to the overall stiffness of the system and if enough points are added, maximum renderable stiffness of the haptic device is easily exceeded. Instead, it is customary to separate the *simulation* position of the haptic object from the position imposed by the haptic manipulandum, and connect the two with a generalized spring(*virtual coupling* [CGSS93]). This penalty spring of stiffness k_{VC} tries to align the simulation position and orientation of the haptic object to the manipulandum. We adopt *static* virtual coupling of [WM03] since it needs a relatively small number of parameters (unlike [MPT99]), and does not need device velocity estimates. We extend static coupling by introducing quasi-static damping. We also include large rotation terms in the static equilibrium equations (details in [Bar07]).

In every haptic cycle, we first read the position and orientation of the haptic device manipulandum. We then compute contact penalty forces and torques (by traversing the nested point-tree), virtual coupling forces and torques, *and their gradients* with respect to the *simulation* position of the haptic object (see Figure 3). The net force and torque on the simulation object, under a (small) incremental displacement Δx and (small) incremental rotation $\Delta\omega \in \mathbb{R}^3$, are then

$$F_{\text{net}} = F_{\text{VC}} + F_{\text{C}} + \Big(\frac{\partial F_{\text{VC}}}{\partial x} + \frac{\partial F_{\text{C}}}{\partial x}\Big)\Delta x + \Big(\frac{\partial F_{\text{VC}}}{\partial \omega} + \frac{\partial F_{\text{C}}}{\partial \omega}\Big)\Delta\omega \quad (4)$$

$$T_{\text{net}} = T_{\text{VC}} + T_{\text{C}} + \Big(\frac{\partial T_{\text{VC}}}{\partial x} + \frac{\partial T_{\text{C}}}{\partial x}\Big)\Delta x + \Big(\frac{\partial T_{\text{VC}}}{\partial \omega} + \frac{\partial T_{\text{C}}}{\partial \omega}\Big)\Delta\omega \quad (5)$$

where $F_{\text{VC}}, T_{\text{VC}}$ denote current virtual coupling force and torque [WM03], and $F_{\text{C}}, T_{\text{C}}$ denote the sum of all contact forces and torques. We displace the virtual object such that the net force and torque on the object vanish under this first-order model, by solving the non-symmetric 6x6 linear system of Equations 4,5 for $(\Delta x, \Delta\omega)$ using LU decomposition (fast, $\sim 5\mu s$ per solve). Finally, we compute the virtual coupling force and torque with respect to the new simulation position, and render them to the user. Virtual coupling gradients are determined through analytical differentiation of the virtual coupling forces and torques. Gradients of contact forces and torques are computed by treating each contact point as undergoing contact with an infinite halfspace (wall), oriented according to the contact normal (details in [Bar07]).

A simple calculation shows that the maximum stiffness felt by the user if m points are in contact is $1/(1/(m \cdot k_{\text{C}}) + (1/k_{\text{VC}}))$; therefore k_{VC} presents an upper bound on the stiffness ever rendered to the haptic device, regardless of m. Since time is sampled discretely, simulation stability is improved if k_{C} is scaled down when there are multiple points in contact; as in VPS, we replace k_{C} with $10k_{\text{C}}/m$ if $m \geq 10$ points are in contact. The displacement-force relationship of virtual coupling is designed to be linear only up to a certain displacement, after which it saturates to some maximum force value (c.f. virtual proxy [ZS95, RKK97]).

Quasi-static damping: The lack of dissipation in the static virtual coupling model can lead to slight instabilities, such as during fast sliding contact. We augmented the static virtual coupling model by introducing a quasi-static damping, or a damped state update: after $\Delta x, \Delta\omega$ are computed, we only change the simulation position and rotation by $(1-\alpha)\Delta x, (1-\alpha)\Delta\omega$, where $\alpha \in [0,1)$ controls the amount of static damping. Such damping exponentially restores the simulation position to the manipulandum position, similar to critical damping in mass-spring-damper dynamic virtual

Contact case; pointshell+distance field	Contact depicted at:	Pointshell		Dist. field resolution	Traversed nodes		Points in contact	LOD	Timings [μs]				
		levels	points		with TC	TC off			VC	StVK	TT	total	TL
knight(r) + axe(r)	Results	6	1.02 M	256	2050	3400	820	6	90	0	780	870	80,000
bridge(d) + dinosaur(r)	Figure 1	4	85K	256	1989	5200	426	4	90	45	710	845	12,200
CAD scene(d) + metallic part(r)	Figure 2	4	80K	128	530	1520	50	4	90	45	125	260	6,600
dragon(d) + Buddha(r)	Figure 3	5	256K	256	1750	2900	650	5	90	45	615	750	29,800
dragon(r) + dragon hole(r)	Figure 9	5	256K	256	1701	2642	843	2	90	0	722	812	45,000

Table 1: ***Model statistics*** *for representative contact configurations. Timings generated using an Intel Core 2 Duo 2.66 GHz processor with 2 Gb RAM. All deformable models use $r = 15$ deformation modes for comparative purposes. LEGEND: r=rigid, d=deformable, VC=virtual coupling and manipulandum transformations, StVK=deformable FEM dynamics, TT=tree traversal, TC=temporal coherence, LOD=level of detail rendered (in the particular configuration), TL=time under a tree-less pointshell traversal.*

coupling models [MPT99]. We set $\alpha = 0.5$ in all our simulations; high values of α are avoided since they introduce a surface stickiness effect.

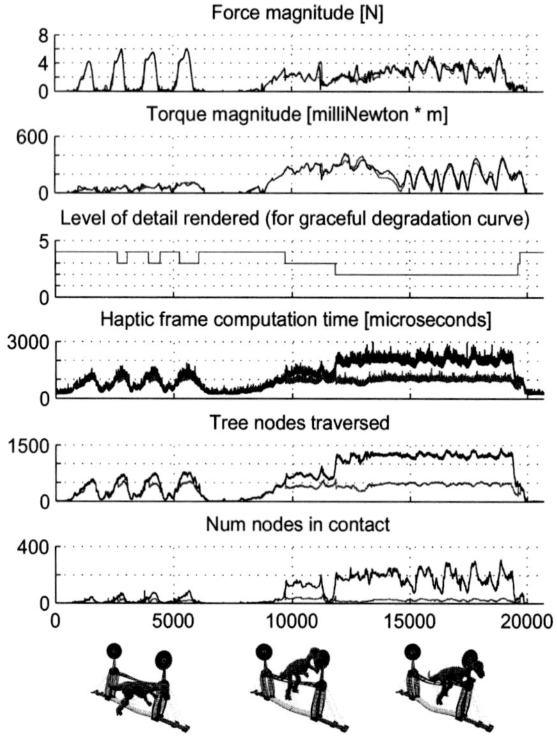

Figure 8: ***Illustration of graceful degradation (GD):*** *Simulation data for a pre-recorded manipulandum trajectory is rendered in two ways: using GD (in red) with warm threshold at 600 nodes; without GD (in black) with all four tree levels. The pointshell has* 85,018 *points total. The common x-axis corresponds to haptic frames. This data was recorded on a three-year-old 3.0 GHz dual Intel Xeon processor with 2.75 Gb of memory, illustrating algorithm's adaptivity to different computer speeds. On the (faster) machine of Table 1, the black timing curve reaches a maximum of ~800 μs.*

7. Results

Statistics on all haptic rendering examples are provided in Table 1. In our first 6-DoF haptic rendering example, we simulate a detailed deformable bridge in contact with a detailed rigid dinosaur (see Figure 1). We recorded a characteristic manipulandum trajectory, and report simulation data under this trajectory computed offline under different force approximations (see Figure 8). We also present a detailed deformable dragon in contact with a rigid Buddha mesh. Figure 9 demonstrates the benefits of graceful degradation to simulate very large contact areas. Interactive (dis)assembly and path planning are illustrated in Figure 2 by example where the user can manipulate a metallic rigid component in contact with deformable hose geometry typical of modern airplanes. Large hose deformations allow the operator to interactively navigate the component in between the hoses.

Interactive haptic gaming is an emerging application area. In this example, the user can swing a detailed rigid axe to "interact" with an armored rigid knight. This example demonstrates crisp contact with detailed million-point pointshells possible when our method is used for rigid-only simulations.

8. Conclusion

We have demonstrated that real-time haptic rendering of distributed contact between geometrically complex models is possible for both rigid and reduced deformable models. A key ingredient has been the exploitation of low-dimensional parameterizations of deformable models for fast dynamics, point-based deformation bounds, and output-sensitive evaluation of pointshell points and contact normals for time-critical evaluation of contact forces.

Discussion: First, our deformations are not fully general; in the future, fully general complex FEM deformable objects might run at haptics rates on commodity workstations, but this is not the case today. Our deformable model is adaptive: more basis vectors can be added to the basis as processor speeds will increase. While our current demonstrations run on standard Windows or Linux platforms, simulation on operating systems and parallel architectures that can guarantee hard real-time scheduling is a natural area of exploration.

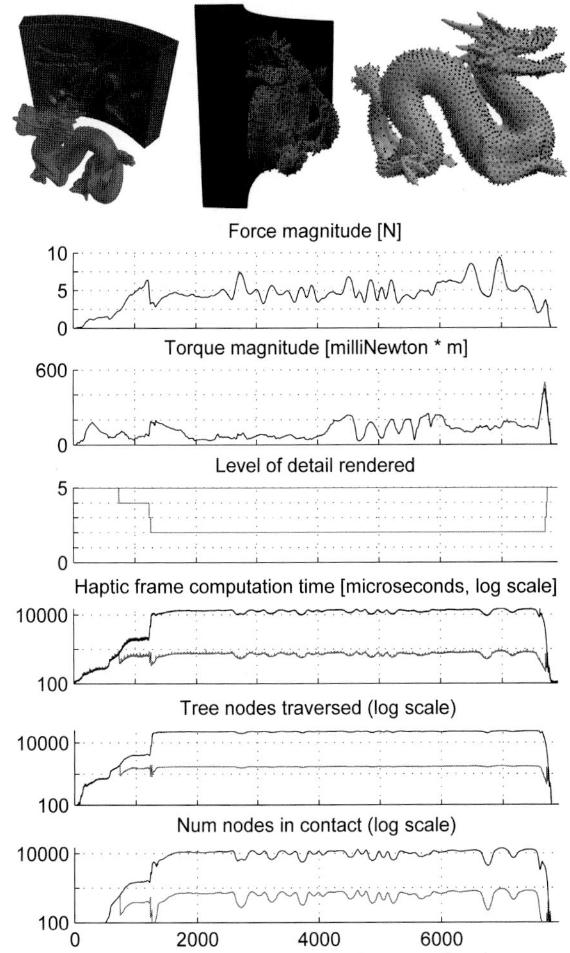

Figure 9: ***Graceful degradation supports large conforming contacts*** *to allow time-critical approximation of very difficult contact configurations (here under 1 millisecond). (**Top Left**) A dragon "peg" inserting into a matching dragon "hole" obtained via CSG difference. (**Top Middle**) dragon manipulated haptically into the hole. (**Top Right**) Large contact area with traversed points in blue (43% of all L2 points), and contacting points in red (21% of all L2 points). (**Bottom Graphs**) Simulation data for a pre-recorded manipulandum trajectory is rendered in two ways: using GD (in red) with warm threshold at 2000 nodes; without GD (in black) with all five tree levels. Same machine as in Table 1. The common x-axis corresponds to haptic frames.*

The simulation can be simplified if the signed distance field is replaced by a simpler implicit function with an analytical formula. Our offset surfaces are not reaching down to the exact geometry in case of polygon "soup" input geometry, when the contact surface is not well-defined. Quality of the offset surface degrades under offsets too small compared to distance field resolution. Large deformations can potentially introduce undersampled pointshell surface regions; however this was not problematic in our case of deformations mostly consisting of large rotations and small strain. Other reduced deformable models should be investigated, including low-resolution models that deform embedded meshes, and multi-resolution models. Much higher rank StVK models are being investigated. Although our implementation is not highly optimized, we did implement some time-critical routines (Uq and ΔNq mtx-vec multiplies) in assembly (SSE2 multimedia instructions), and carefully laid out data in memory to optimize cache performance. A system speedup of about $2\times$ was obtained. Perceptual studies may be useful in determining speed-accuracy trade-offs, such as maximum necessary contact resolution or perception of deformation complexity, similar to other studies done in rigid-rigid contact rendering [OL03]. Another interesting area of future work is simulating friction, which can play an important role in applications such as analysis of mechanical part removability and accessibility. Some applications may be limited by the fact that modification or cutting of the models is prohibited by the preprocessing employed for performance. Although unaddressed in our implementation, large deformations can necessitate self-collision processing, and this remains a significant computational challenge for hard real-time *haptic* rendering applications (c.f. [GKJ*05]).

Acknowledgements: This research was sponsored by the Boeing Company, the National Science Foundation (CAREER-0430528), the Link Foundation, Pixar, Nvidia, Intel, and donation of Maya licenses from Autodesk.

Appendix A: Distance Field Construction

Computing a *signed* distance field is straightforward for closed manifold meshes. In the common case of "polygon soups" we first compute an *unsigned* distance field, then extract an isosurface for some small distance value using marching cubes to obtain a closed manifold mesh [LLVT03] (see also [SOS04]). Next we remove any mesh components completely contained inside another component, and then compute a *signed* distance field with respect to the remaining closed manifold mesh(es). At runtime, we interpolate the distance field grid values to the query location when inside the distance field box. If outside the box, we conservatively estimate $d(p) \geq d_{\text{box}} + d_{\text{boundary}}$, where d_{box} is the shortest distance from the query to the distance field box, and d_{boundary} is the query-independent minimum distance field value on the surface of the distance field box; proof of this inequality follows by connecting the query to its closest point on the surface.

Appendix B: Nested Pointshell Construction

We fit the particles onto a level set of a distance field. If point shell object is given as a closed manifold triangle mesh, we compute a signed distance field and use the zero-distance level set. If it is given as a triangle "soup", we compute an unsigned distance field, and use the level set of some small positive distance value. In either case, call the resulting level set surface $\mathcal{T}$. We also construct a smooth level set *triangulated* surface $\mathcal{S}$ using marching cubes. For unsigned distance fields, we also remove any connected surface components lying completely inside another component.

Our nested hierarchy construction is similar to [Tur01]. We first "inject" n_1 points of level 1 (coarsest level), by using stratified area-weighted random sampling of $\mathcal{S}$ [Tur92]. We then let the particles repel each other, constrained to $\mathcal{T}$. We do so by alternating particle repulsion and constraint stabilization to $\mathcal{T}$. Our repulsion potential among two particles is radial. Its gradient equals $2(d/R)^3 - 3(d/R)^2 + 1$, where R is the finite influence radius, and d is the Euclidean distance among two particles. Gradient is set to zero for $d \geq R$. At every iteration step, we assemble the repulsion gradients, then move each particle a distance of $-\eta$ in the direction of the net gradient, where $\eta > 0$ is the descent parameter. This step will move the particle (slightly) off the level set surface $\mathcal{T}$. We restore it back to $\mathcal{T}$ by performing a Newton solve using the distance field and its gradients. This two stage process is repeated until particles have sufficiently converged. Then, we permanently fix the position of the particles, and inject n_2 new particles that will form level 2. Again, the level 2 particles are iterated until convergence, when we fix then, and insert level 3 particles. This procedure is repeated until a desired number of levels, or a desired sampling accuracy, has been reached. We use $n_{i+1} = 4n_i$ so that surface sampling resolution about doubles with every level. We also decrease the particle repulsion radius R by a factor of two for each new level. The resulting multi-resolution pointshell has the property that for every level k, the set of points up to level k samples the level set surface $\mathcal{T}$ about uniformly (see Figure 6). Note that the triangle surface $\mathcal{S}$ is only necessary to efficiently draw initial random positions of particles.

Pointshell points need to be assigned (inward-pointing by convention) normals. We do so by locating the closest triangle of $\mathcal{S}$, assigning the normal to be the pseudonormal [BA05] of the closest feature (face, edge, or vertex). Other variations include using barycentrically-weighted pseudonormals, the normalized gradient of the distance field, or, if original geometry is a closed manifold mesh, the pseudonormal of the closest feature on that mesh, which better preserves sharp corners.

References

[AH98] Astley O., Hayward V.: Multirate Haptic Simulation Achieved by Coupling Finite Element Meshes Through Norton Equivalents. In *Proc. of the IEEE Int. Conf. on Robotics and Automation* (1998).

[BA05] Bærentzen J., Aanæs H.: Signed distance computation using the angle weighted pseudo-normal. *IEEE Transactions on Visualization and Computer Graphics 11*, 3 (2005), 243–253.

[Bar07] Barbič J.: *Real-time Reduced Nonlinear Deformable Objects for Computer Graphics and Haptics*. PhD thesis, Computer Science Department, Carnegie Mellon University, 2007.

[BJ05] Barbič J., James D. L.: Real-Time Subspace Integration for St. Venant-Kirchhoff Deformable Models. *ACM Transactions on Graphics (SIGGRAPH 2005) 24*, 3 (Aug. 2005).

[BNC96] Bro-Nielsen M., Cotin S.: Real-time Volumetric Deformable Models for Surgery Simulation using Finite Elements and Condensation. *Comp. Graphics Forum 15*, 3 (1996), 57–66.

[CDA99] Cotin S., Delingette H., Ayache N.: Realtime Elastic Deformations of Soft Tissues for Surgery Simulation. *IEEE Trans. on Vis. and Comp. Graphics 5*, 1 (1999), 62–73.

[CGSS93] Colgate J., Grafing P., Stanley M., Schenkel G.: Implementation of Stiff Virtual Walls in Force-Reflecting Interfaces. In *Proc. of IEEE Virtual Reality Annual Int. Symp.* (1993), IEEE, pp. 202–208.

[DDCB01] Debunne G., Desbrun M., Cani M.-P., Barr A. H.: Dynamic Real-Time Deformations Using Space & Time Adaptive Sampling. In *Proc. of ACM SIGGRAPH 2001* (August 2001), pp. 31–36.

[DDKA06] Duriez C., Dubois F., Kheddar A., Andriot C.: Realistic Haptic Rendering of Interacting Deformable Objects in Virtual Environments. *IEEE Trans. on Vis. and Comp. Graphics 12*, 1 (2006), 36–47.

[GKJ*05] Govindaraju N. K., Knott D., Jain N., Kabul I., Tamstorf R., Gayle R., Lin M. C., Manocha D.: Interactive collision detection between deformable models using chromatic decomposition. *ACM Transactions on Graphics 24*, 3 (Aug. 2005), 991–999.

[Hub95] Hubbard P. M.: *Collision Detection for Interactive Graphics Applications*. PhD thesis, Department of Comp. Science, Brown University, 1995.

[JCC06] Jun S., Choi J., Cho M.: Physics-based s-adaptive haptic simulation for deformable object. In *Proc. of the Symp. on Haptic Interfaces For Virtual Environment and Teleoperator Systems* (2006), pp. 72–78.

[JP01] James D. L., Pai D. K.: A Unified Treatment of Elastostatic Contact Simulation for Real Time Haptics. *Haptics-e, The Electronic J. of Haptics Research (www.haptics-e.org) 2*, 1 (September 2001).

[JP02] James D. L., Pai D. K.: DyRT: Dynamic Response Textures for Real Time Deformation Simulation With Graphics Hardware. *ACM Trans. on Graphics 21*, 3 (July 2002), 582–585.

[JP03] James D. L., Pai D. K.: Multiresolution Green's Function Methods for Interactive Simulation of Large-scale Elastostatic Objects. *ACM Trans. on Graphics 22*, 1 (2003), 47–82.

[JP04] James D. L., Pai D. K.: BD-Tree: Output-Sensitive Collision Detection for Reduced Deformable Models. *ACM Trans. on Graphics 23*, 3 (2004), 393–398.

[KcM00] Kühnapfel U., Çakmak H., MaassH.: Endoscopic surgery training using virtual reality and deformable tissue simulation. *Computers & Graphics 24* (2000), 671–682.

[KMH*04] Keiser R., Müller M., Heidelberger B., Teschner M., Gross M.: Contact Handling for Deformable Point-Based Objects. In *Proc. of Vision, Modeling, Visualization 2004* (2004), pp. 339–346.

[KOLM03] Kim Y. J., Otaduy M. A., Lin M. C., Manocha D.: Six degree-of-freedom haptic display using incremental and localized computations. *Presence-Teleoperators and Virtual Environments 12*, 3 (2003), 277–295.

[LD07] Laycock S., Day A.: A Survey of Haptic Rendering Techniques. *Computer Graphics Forum 26* (2007), 50–65.

[LLVT03] Lewiner T., Lopes H., Vieira A. W., Tavares G.: Efficient implementation of Marching Cubes' cases with topological guarantees. *Journal of Graphics Tools 8*, 2 (2003), 1–15.

[MO06] Mendoza C., O'Sullivan C.: Interruptible collision detection for deformable objects. *Computer & Graphics 30*, 2 (2006).

[MPT99] McNeely W. A., Puterbaugh K. D., Troy J. J.: Six degree-of-freedom haptic rendering using voxel sampling. In *Proc. of ACM SIGGRAPH 99* (1999), ACM, pp. 401–408.

[MPT06] McNeely W., Puterbaugh K., Troy J.: Voxel-Based 6-DOF Haptic Rendering Improvements. *Haptics-e 3*, 7 (2006).

[OG07] Otaduy M. A., Gross M.: Transparent Rendering of Tool Contact with Compliant Environments. In *Proc. of the World Haptics Conference* (2007), pp. 225–230.

[OL03] Otaduy M. A., Lin M. C.: Sensation Preserving Simplification for Haptic Rendering. In *Proc. of ACM SIGGRAPH 2003* (2003), ACM, pp. 543–553.

[OL06] Otaduy M. A., Lin M. C.: A Modular Haptic Rendering Algorithm for Stable and Transparent 6-DoF Manipulation. *IEEE Trans. on Robotics 22*, 4 (2006), 751–762.

[PPG04] Pauly M., Pai D. K., Guibas L.: Quasi-Rigid Objects in Contact. In *Proc. of the Symp. on Comp. Animation 2004* (2004).

[RKK97] Ruspini D. C., Kolarov K., Khatib O.: The Haptic Display of Complex Graphical Environments. In *Proc. of ACM SIGGRAPH 97* (Aug. 1997), Whitted T., (Ed.), Addison Wesley, pp. 345–352.

[RL00] Rusinkiewicz S., Levoy M.: Qsplat: A multiresolution point rendering system for large meshes. In *Proceedings of ACM SIGGRAPH 2000* (July 2000), Computer Graphics Proceedings, Annual Conference Series, pp. 343–352.

[RPP*01] Renz M., Preusche C., Pötke M., Kriegel H.-P., Hirzinger G.: Stable haptic interaction with virtual environments using an adapted voxmap-pointshell algorithm. In *Proc. of Eurohaptics* (2001), pp. 149–154.

[SOS04] Shen C., O'Brien J. F., Shewchuk J. R.: Interpolating and approximating implicit surfaces from polygon soup. In *Proceedings of ACM SIGGRAPH 2004* (Aug. 2004), ACM Press, pp. 896–904.

[Tur92] Turk G.: Re-Tiling Polygonal Surfaces. *Computer Graphics (Proc. of ACM SIGGRAPH 92) 26*, 2 (1992), 55–64.

[Tur01] Turk G.: Texture Synthesis on Surfaces. In *Proceedings of ACM SIGGRAPH 2001* (Aug. 2001), Computer Graphics Proceedings, Annual Conference Series, pp. 347–354.

[WH94] Witkin A. P., Heckbert P. S.: Using particles to sample and control implicit surfaces. In *Proceedings of SIGGRAPH 94* (July 1994), Computer Graphics Proceedings, Annual Conference Series, pp. 269–278.

[WM03] Wan M., McNeely W. A.: Quasi-Static Approximation for 6 Degrees-of-Freedom Haptic Rendering. In *Proc. of IEEE Visualization 2003* (2003), pp. 257–262.

[ZS95] Zilles C., Salisbury J.: A Constraint-based God-object Method for Haptics Display. In *Proc. of IEEE/RSJ Int. Conf. on Intelligent Robots and Systems* (1995), IEEE, pp. 146–151.

Eurographics/ ACM SIGGRAPH Symposium on Computer Animation (2007)
D. Metaxas and J. Popovic (Editors)

Adaptive Deformations with Fast Tight Bounds

Miguel A. Otaduy[1], Daniel Germann[1], Stephane Redon[2] and Markus Gross[1]

[1]Computer Graphics Laboratory, ETH Zurich, Switzerland
[2]i3D - INRIA Rhone-Alpes, Grenoble, France

Abstract

Simulation of deformations and collision detection are two highly intertwined problems that are often treated separately. This is especially true in existing elegant adaptive simulation techniques, where standard collision detection algorithms cannot leverage the adaptively selected degrees of freedom. We propose a seamless integration of multigrid algorithms and collision detection that identifies boundary conditions while inherently exploiting adaptivity. We realize this integration through multiscale bounding hierarchies, *a novel unified hierarchical representation, together with an adaptive multigrid algorithm for irregular meshes and an adaptivity-aware hierarchical collision detection algorithm. Our solution produces detailed deformations with adapted computational cost, but it also enables robust interactive simulation of self-colliding deformable objects with high-resolution surfaces.*

Categories and Subject Descriptors (according to ACM CCS): I.3.5 [Computer Graphics]: Physic. based modeling

1. Introduction

Simulation of deformable bodies has long attracted the attention of computer graphics, and today we can find sophisticated methods for highly-realistic simulation of e.g., human biomechanics [ITF04], cloth [BFA02], or fracture effects [OBH02] among others. In later years, deformable bodies have also seen application in videogames or virtual surgery, through the development of plausible interactive simulation techniques [JP03, BJ05, MHTG05].

Contact exacerbates the complexity of simulating deformable bodies, by exciting arbitrarily many deformation modes and inducing rich and diverse deformations. To attack the complexity of the problem, adaptive simulation methods [DDCB01, GKS02, CGC*02] employ fewer degrees of freedom (DoFs) on regions that allow for lower resolution. However, in computer graphics, the boundary of the simulation domain (i.e., the surface) plays a central role, and handling of boundary conditions for producing accurate surface deformations requires the use of high-resolution surfaces. Collision detection becomes then a central component of the simulation, as part of the process for setting boundary conditions. To the best of our knowledge, there is no prior technique that bridges the simulation of deformations and collision detection, and that exploits adaptivity for setting (i.e., detecting) boundary conditions. The BD-Tree [JP04] and reduced deformable models have been combined to produce an elegant solution for cases where deformations are described by a few constant DoFs, but can hardly handle some of the rich effects produced by contact deformation dynamics.

Figure 1: ***Interactive Deformation with Self-Collisions.*** *A dragon with* 13480 *triangles deforms interactively (almost* 10 *fps on average), with accurate handling of self-collisions.*

In this paper, we propose a seamless integration of multigrid methods [Bra77, BHM00] and hierarchical collision detection [GLM96] for exploiting adaptivity when setting boundary conditions in the context of contact and deformation simulations. This integration relies on three main contributions:

- **Multiscale bounding hierarchy (MBH):** A unified representation that combines a hierarchy of irregular non-nested tetrahedral meshes and a bounding volume hierarchy (BVH), and maps tetrahedra at multiple scales to the BVs.

Symposium on Computer Animation 2007, San Diego, CA, August 03-04, 2007.
© 2007 ACM 978-1-59593-624-4/07/0008 $5.00

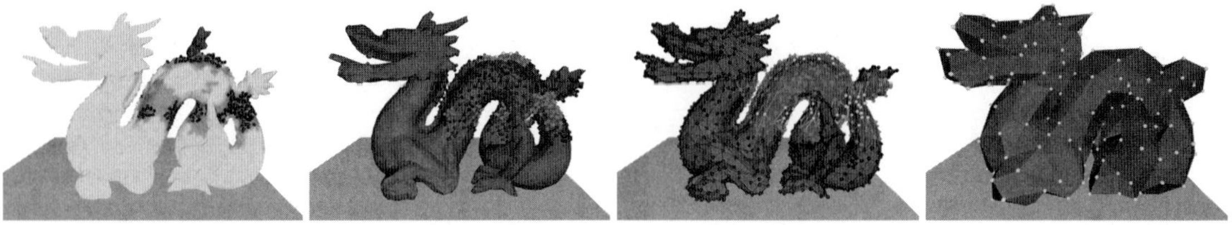

Figure 2: ***Adaptive Refinement of a Mesh Hierarchy.*** *Left: surface of the fine mesh M_1 of the dragon model, color-coded by the local active resolution ('yellow' is coarse, 'red' is fine). Rest: boundary of tetrahedral meshes M_2, M_3, and M_5 with interior (orange), front (green), and interface nodes (blue). Notice the change of genus in the hierarchy.*

- **Adaptive multigrid on irregular meshes:** Through careful augmentation of mesh data structures and refinement/coarsening strategies, the algorithm is as simple as adaptive multigrid for regular nested meshes [Bra77], but conforms well to rich object boundaries using non-nested irregular meshes. We have applied it to corotational linear elasticity with implicit integration [MG04].
- **Adaptivity-aware (self-)collision detection:** Exploiting the MBH to perform efficient on-demand refitting of bounding volumes, the cost for collision (and self-collision) detection depends on the active DoFs and the number of (potential) contacts, not surface complexity.

We demonstrate our approach on collision-intensive multi-object scenes (See Fig. 4), and accurate computation of contact manifolds in self-collions (See Fig. 5). But, most importantly, and as shown in Fig. 1, the seamless connection between simulation of deformations and collision detection allows for efficient and robust handling of (self-)collisions with high-resolution surfaces at interactive rates.

In §2 we discuss related work, and in §3 we formulate the dynamic deformation problem at hand, and we discuss its solution with adaptive multigrid on regular nested meshes. In §4 we describe our adaptive solution for irregular meshes, based on an elegant augmentation of the data structures and refinement/coarsening strategies that permits the use of the very same algorithm as for regular nested meshes. In §5 we describe the MBH in detail, and we present our collision detection algorithm, exploiting adaptively selected DoFs. We also present an extremely fast method for computing tight bounds for sets of points interpolated inside a simplex. We finally discuss the results of our experiments, as well as possible directions of future work.

2. Related Work

We focus here on methods for adaptive simulation of deformable objects and collision detection. As our paper introduces no novel deformation model, we refer the reader to comprehensive surveys for details [GM97, NMK*05].

Grinspun et al. [GKS02] developed a general method for adaptive simulation with the finite element method (FEM) in computer graphics, with the advantage that adaptivity is achieved through refinement of basis functions, not decomposition of mesh elements. Their method requires subdivision connectivity of the meshes. Capell et al. [CGC*02] proposed another technique built on subdivision, but they embedded the surface of the object to be deformed. Their technique allows, for example, the application of constraints on the embedded mesh. Debunne et al. [DDCB01], instead, designed a method for adaptive simulation of deformations using non-nested irregular meshes, which conform more accurately to the boundary with fewer elements. A fundamental difference of our multigrid approach is a hierarchical definition of the deformation problem, which naturally enables a link between the data structures for adaptive simulation and collision detection. Moreover, in Debunne's approach, interpolation at the interface between different mesh resolutions is not symmetric, therefore making the method not well suited for full implicit simulation with fast iterative solvers. Similar to adaptive methods, reduced models provide very fast simulations with a few DoFs that drive complex surfaces [BJ05]. However, their strength is in global deformations, not accurate surface deformations during contact.

Multigrid algorithms were initially intended (and show optimal linear convergence) for solving elliptic boundary value PDE problems. Nonetheless, they see application on a much larger range of problems, and under multiple variants. We refer to books on the topic [BHM00, TOS01] for a comprehensive treatment. The common feature of multigrid algorithms is to solve the problem by smoothing the error through iterative relaxation on different scales. The typical implementation of multigrid is based on a correction scheme that filters the fine-scale residual and corrects it on a coarser scale. Brandt [Bra77] introduced the full approximation storage (FAS) scheme, which filters both the residual and the fine-scale estimate of the solution, thus correcting the full solution on the coarser scale. FAS allowed Brandt to implement multilevel adaptive technique (MLAT) solutions on nested regular meshes. The fast adaptive composite (FAC) grid method [MT86] constitutes another popular adaptive multigrid technique, but it relies strongly on the use of regular meshes. Little work exists in the application of adaptive multigrid to irregular meshes in 3D, due to the difficulty in maintaining interface regions of locally refined meshes, and smoothly interpolating values across meshes.

In the context of computer graphics, multigrid has been used for simulating thin shells [GTS02], enhancing the stability

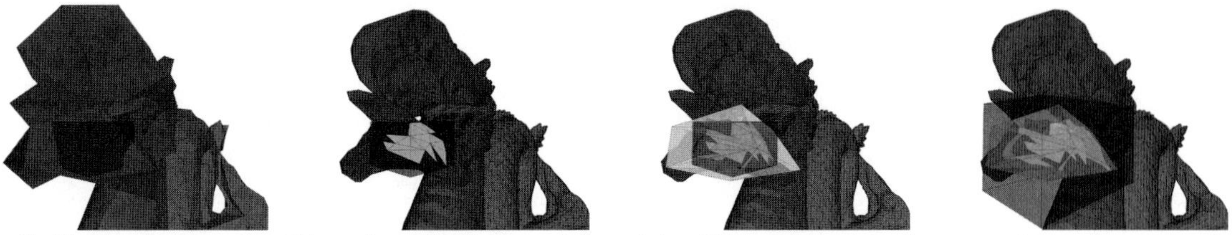

Figure 3: ***Multiscale Bounding Hierarchy (MBH).*** *From left to right: (i) Mesh M_4 of the dragon model, and one bounding volume B (in blue) at the corresponding level L_4 of the BVH. (ii) Finest mesh M_1, and the surface patch (in white) bounded by B. (iii) When M_4 is the locally finest active mesh, B can be updated directly from its effective governor tetrahedra $G^*(B) \in M_4$ (superimposed in yellow), without accessing or evaluating the finest surface ∂M_1. (iv) Notice the loose AABB computed from the tetrahedra, as opposed to the tight AABB computed with our method based on simplex interpolation (in the other images).*

of explicit integrators [WT04], accelerating the simulation of deformable models in a non-adaptive manner [GW05], or recently for fast mesh deformations in geometric modeling [SYBF06]. Aksoylu et al. [AKS05] have designed general multigrid solvers on unstructured meshes.

Collision detection of deformable objects has been addressed using techniques such as: BVHs [dB97], spatial hashing [THM*03], visibility-based culling [GRLM03], or second-order Voronoi diagrams [SGG*06] (See [TKH*05] for a recent survey). Self-collision further complicates the problem [VMT94, VMT06], as primitive adjacency is difficult to distinguish from actual collisions. For a surface with n primitives, most techniques have a best-case $O(n)$ cost. The BD-tree [JP04] for linear parametric models constitutes a notable exception. It may prune non-colliding objects by testing only the root of the tree, which can be updated with a cost linear in the number of deformation modes, not the size of the surface. Our multiscale bounding hierarchy (MBH) is also optimal in the sense that its best-case update cost (i.e., for a non-colliding object) is linear in the number of DoFs of the simulation. As opposed to hybrid approaches for updating BVHs [LAM01], it presents a $O(1)$ cost for tightly updating bounding volumes on demand. Moreover, by combining features of BVHs and spatial hashing, it also allows for fast hierarchical pruning in self-collision detection. Last, visual or haptic perceptual metrics [ODGK03, OL03] can be incorporated for implementing interruptible or adaptive collision detection.

3. Adaptive Multigrid Deformations

In this section we describe the discretized dynamic deformation problem, its multigrid solution with the FAS scheme, and the addition of adaptivity with the MLAT algorithm for regular nested meshes, This algorithm sets the foundations for our extension to irregular non-nested meshes, which we will describe in §4.

3.1. Discretized Deformation Dynamics

Linear FEM discretization of linear-elastic deformation dynamics leads to motion equations $\mathbf{M}\ddot{\mathbf{x}} + \mathbf{D}\dot{\mathbf{x}} + \mathbf{K}\mathbf{x} = \mathbf{F}_{ext}$, where $\mathbf{M}$, $\mathbf{D}$, and $\mathbf{K}$ are, respectively, mass, damping, and stiffness matrices, and $\mathbf{F}_{ext}$ is a vector of external forces (See [NMK*05] for more details). We apply lumping to yield diagonal $\mathbf{M}$ and $\mathbf{D}$ matrices, and per-tetrahedron stiffness warping [MG04] to improve the behavior of linear elasticity under large deformations. Backward Euler implicit integration with a first order approximation of forces [BW98] yields the following linear system for computing node positions:

$$\mathbf{A}\mathbf{x}_i = \mathbf{b}, \tag{1}$$

$$\mathbf{A} = \mathbf{M} + \Delta t \mathbf{D} + \Delta t^2 \mathbf{K}, \tag{2}$$

$$\mathbf{b} = \mathbf{A}\mathbf{x}_{i-1} + \Delta t\,(\mathbf{M} + \Delta t \mathbf{D})\,\mathbf{v}_{i-1} + \Delta t^2 \mathbf{F}_{i-1}. \tag{3}$$

3.2. FAS Multigrid

The first component of our novel multiscale bounding hierarchy (MBH) is a sequence of non-nested irregular tetrahedral meshes $\mathcal{M} = \{M_1, M_2, \ldots M_m\}$ (See an example in Figure 2). Unlike the common numbering convention in the literature, we denote by M_1 the highest resolution mesh, to establish a clear correspondence between levels of $\mathcal{M}$ and the BVH. In this section, and w.l.o.g., we will consider $\mathcal{M}$ as a sequence of nested regular meshes. We assume that the deformation field animates a high-resolution surface S, and, for simplicity, throughout the paper we assume $S = \partial M_1$.

We have implemented a V-cycle of FAS multigrid [BHM00, TOS01] on the hierarchy $\mathcal{M}$ of meshes to solve the discretized linear problem (1). FAS computes an approximation to the full position $\mathbf{x}$ on every mesh (i.e., approximations with different frequency components), and this property is important for computing bounds of $\mathbf{x}$ based on coarse mesh information, and thus designing the BVH. On the top-down pass (from fine to coarse), the algorithm successively relaxes the error on each level using Gauss-Seidel (G-S) iteration, and *restricts* (R) the residual $\mathbf{b} - \mathbf{A}\mathbf{x}$ to the next coarser level. On the bottom-up pass (from coarse to fine), the algorithm *prolongs* (P) the coarse corrected solution to the next finer level and performs further error relaxation. On the coarsest level, we use a Conjugate Gradient (CG) iterative solver.

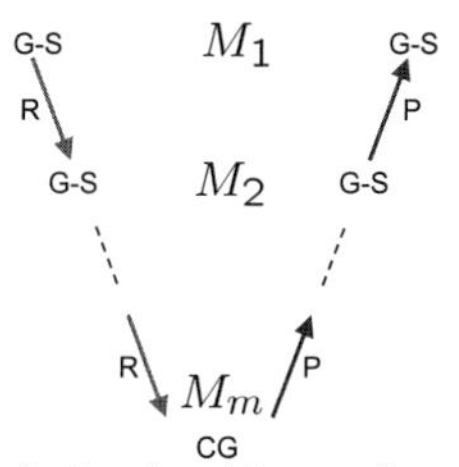

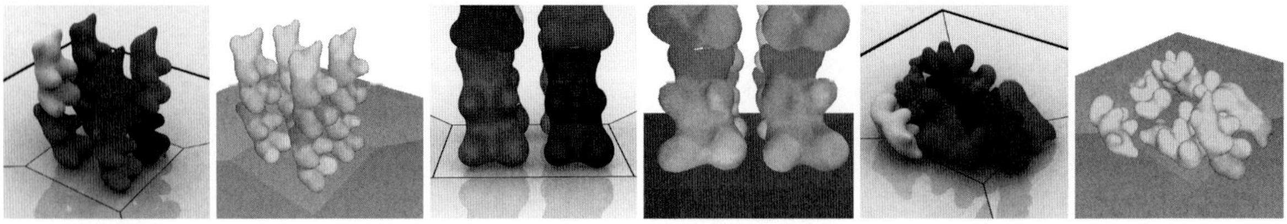

Figure 4: ***Adaptively Deformed Gummy Bears.*** *Each bear has a 6-mesh hierarchy (from 85 to 6418 tetrahedra). Notice the refinement (red) when collisions induce high stress, and the coarsening (yellow) when the bears come to rest. Our adaptive algorithm offers about 10x speed-up over full-resolution conjugate gradient or non-adaptive multigrid. See details in Table 1.*

In FAS, the right-hand side on a coarse mesh M_{j+1} is formulated using a *residual restriction operator* $\mathbf{R}$, and a *solution restriction operator* $\tilde{\mathbf{R}}$ as:

$$\mathbf{b}^{j+1} = \mathbf{R}^{j+1}\left(\mathbf{b}^j - \mathbf{A}^j\mathbf{x}^j\right) + \mathbf{A}^{j+1}\tilde{\mathbf{R}}^{j+1}\mathbf{x}^j. \qquad (4)$$

The corrected solution is prolonged to M_j by a *prolongation operator* $\mathbf{P}$ as:

$$\mathbf{x}^j \leftarrow \mathbf{x}^j + \mathbf{P}^j(\mathbf{x}^{j+1} - \tilde{\mathbf{R}}^{j+1}\mathbf{x}^j). \qquad (5)$$

On the finest mesh, we use as initial estimate

$$\mathbf{x}_i^1 \leftarrow \mathbf{x}_{i-1}^1 + \Delta t \mathbf{v}_{i-1}^1. \qquad (6)$$

On coarser meshes M_{j+1}, we use as initial estimate the restricted solution, $\tilde{\mathbf{x}}^{j+1} = \tilde{\mathbf{R}}^{j+1}\mathbf{x}^j$.

We define $\mathbf{A}^j$ by discretizing the dynamic deformation problem on every mesh, which provides a formulation independent of the level of refinement in the adaptive setting. We leave the description of the interpolation operators $\mathbf{P}$, $\mathbf{R}$, and $\tilde{\mathbf{R}}$ to the specific case of irregular tetrahedral meshes in §4.1.

3.3. MLAT Algorithm

In MLAT, each mesh M_j is active on a domain Ω_j, and may be refined locally to yield an active domain $\Omega_{j-1} \subseteq \Omega_j$ on the finer mesh M_{j-1}. We define as active nodes those that belong to an active domain Ω. Error relaxation should be executed on the active domains Ω_j, which requires the evaluation of values on inactive nodes on the *interface* $\partial\Omega_j$. We further divide active and inactive nodes into four subclasses:

- *Interior*: active nodes on regions that are refined.
- *Front*: active nodes on regions that are not further refined.
- *Interface*: inactive nodes where the function $\mathbf{x}$ needs to be evaluated in the context of the multigrid algorithm.
- *Idle*: all other (inactive) nodes.

Values on interface nodes should be interpolated from the coarser active regions in which they lie. On regular nested meshes, coarse nodes are simply a subset of fine nodes, and interpolation of interface nodes is straightforward [Bra77, TOS01], because the nodes on a coarse mesh M_{j+1} that define the value $\mathbf{x}$ on an interface node of the next finer mesh M_j are by construction active or interface themselves. The FAS algorithm can be modified to account for active subdomains and adaptivity, leading to the MLAT algorithm:

Algorithm 1 ***V-Cycle of MLAT.***

//Top-Down Pass
for meshes $M_j, j = 1 \rightarrow m-1$,
  Initialize $\mathbf{x}^j$ on front nodes based on (6).
  Set $\mathbf{b}^j$ on front nodes based on (3).
  Perform G-S pre-relaxation on $\mathbf{x}^j$ on active nodes.
  Restrict $\tilde{\mathbf{x}}^{j+1} \leftarrow \tilde{\mathbf{R}}^{j+1}\mathbf{x}^j$ to interior nodes.
  Restrict $\mathbf{b}^{j+1}$ to interior nodes as in (4).
//Coarse Mesh Solution
Solve $\mathbf{A}^m\mathbf{x}^m = \mathbf{b}^m$ with Conjugate Gradient.
//Bottom-Up Pass
for meshes $M_j, j = m-1 \rightarrow 1$,
  Interpolate $\mathbf{x}^j$ on interface nodes based on $\mathbf{P}$.
  Correct $\mathbf{x}^j$ by prolongation (5) on active nodes.
  Perform G-S post-relaxation on $\mathbf{x}^j$ on active nodes.

4. MLAT on Irregular Meshes

In this section we describe our extension of MLAT to irregular meshes, through appropriate interpolation operators, an augmentation of node neighborhoods, and simple refinement and coarsening strategies. We also describe our error criterion, the interpolation of the deformation to the animated surface, and constraint-based collision response.

4.1. Irregular Meshes and Interpolation Operators

We construct the meshes $\{M_j\}$ in a way such that their boundaries approximate the animated surface S, and all vertices of S are contained in every mesh M_j in the rest configuration. Note, however, that we do not enforce topological equivalence across meshes (e.g., the meshes may have different genus) (See Figure 2 for an example). To construct each mesh M_j, we start from the triangle mesh S, create an offset surface, apply triangle mesh decimation, and mesh the interior with an off-the-shelf tetrahedral mesh generator.

Prolongation $\mathbf{P}$ can be regarded as upsampling, and is typically implemented as interpolation. Specifically, for every node $N \in M_j$, we identify the tetrahedron $T \in M_{j+1}$ that is closest to or encloses N. W.l.o.g., we refer to it as the *coarse enclosing* tetrahedron T^+ of N, $T = T^+(N)$. We define the corresponding row of $\mathbf{P}^j$ by the barycentric coordinates of N in $T^+(N)$ in the rest configuration. For the residual restriction operator $\mathbf{R}$, we follow the common choice of

$\mathbf{R}^{j+1} = \left(\mathbf{P}^j\right)^T$ [BHM00]. For the solution restriction operator $\tilde{\mathbf{R}}$, however, we choose barycentric interpolation of each coarse node $N \in M_j$ in the closest or enclosing tetrahedron $T \in M_{j-1}$. W.l.o.g., we refer to it as the *fine enclosing* tetrahedron T^- of N, $T = T^-(N)$.

On irregular meshes, we identify the following sources of potential inconsistencies in the cross-mesh interpolations of Algorithm 1, which we avoid through the augmentation of mesh data structures and careful refinement and coarsening strategies presented in the next subsection:

- Prolongation to an active node $N \in M_j$ according to (5) in the bottom-up pass of Algorithm 1 may use inactive nodes in M_{j+1} in a straightforward application to irregular meshes. In order to satisfy appropriate convergence of the multigrid algorithm, the algorithm must use only active nodes in M_{j+1}. Moreover, the correction $\mathbf{x} - \tilde{\mathbf{x}}$ is conceptually a correction to the residual only for interior coarse nodes in M_{j+1}. For front coarse nodes, we consider $\tilde{\mathbf{x}}$ simply as the initial value in the top-down pass of the V-cycle.
- Interpolation to an interface node may use idle nodes without a proper solution estimate, and correct interpolation must use only active or interface nodes.
- Similarly, restriction to an interior node may use idle nodes, but must use only active or interface nodes. In the residual restriction to a node $N \in M_j$ according to (4), we set a value 0 for the residual of interface nodes in M_{j-1}.

4.2. Refinement and Coarsening

To guide the refinement and coarsening, we construct a *node forest* $\mathscr{N}$ similar to the one of Debunne et al. [DDCB01]. For each node $N \in M_j$, we set as its parent in $\mathscr{N}$ the closest node from $T^+(N) \in M_{j+1}$. Note that Debunne's forest definition would not avoid the interpolation inconsistencies.

Furthermore, we define a set of *cascade neighbors* $C(N)$ on each node N, which conceptually augments the 1-ring neighborhood of N, and can be precomputed without additional run-time bookkeeping. Specifically, N_j belongs to $C(N)$ if at least one of the following conditions holds: (a) N_j belongs to the 1-ring neighborhood of N; (b) given a 1-ring neighbor N_k of a child of N, N_j is one of the nodes in $T^+(N_k)$; (c) N_j is the parent in $\mathscr{N}$ of a node in $T^-(N)$; and/or (d) N is a cascade neighbor of N_j (to ensure symmetry of the definition). We can now introduce the following simple refinement and coarsening strategies for irregular meshes:

Refinement: If a front node N does not satisfy the error criterion (See §4.3), we refine it by converting it into an interior node, and activating all its children in $\mathscr{N}$. At the same time, we enforce that all nodes in $C(N)$ must be active, which may induce cascading refinements.

Coarsening: If all children of an interior node N are front, none of their cascade neighbors is an interior node, and N satisfies the error criterion, we coarsen N by converting it into a front node, and deactivating all its children in $\mathscr{N}$.

Our definition of node forest, cascade neighbors, and simple refinement and coarsening strategies enable the use of the very same MLAT Algorithm 1 on irregular meshes. Refinement is executed after a complete execution of Algorithm 1, and starts on the coarsest mesh M_m. Coarsening is executed after refinement, and starts on the finest mesh M_1. After refinement and coarsening are completed, we initialize the interface for the next time step, by setting inactive neighbors and children of front nodes as interface, and initializing $\mathbf{x}$ on them in a bottom-up pass (from coarse to fine).

4.3. Error Criterion

We determine the locally required resolution of the multigrid hierarchy $\mathscr{M}$ by comparing the solution on the two finest active levels. Specifically, and as common in adaptive finite element simulations [Ran99], we compute on a front node $N \in M_j$ a local residual that weights by the local linear system $\mathbf{A}$ the difference between the local solution and the one prolonged from the next coarser level:

$$e(N) = \|\mathbf{A}^j(\mathbf{x}^j - \mathbf{P}^j\mathbf{x}^{j+1})\|. \tag{7}$$

Our error criterion measures the local quality of the linear approximation on M_{j+1}, and maintains M_j as a conservative level for error computations. By weighting the solution difference by $\mathbf{A}$, the error criterion depends on the local stiffness of the equations, thus reducing possible popping due to dynamic refinement and coarsening. We compare $e(N)$ to predefined error thresholds, but they could also be weighted by distance to the camera, amount of occlusion, or size of the contact area, to account for visual or haptic perception [ODGK03, OL03]. Note that the error threshold may not be too high, or popping will be inevitable.

4.4. Surface Evaluation and Collision Response

Application of boundary conditions in the dynamic simulation requires the definition of positions $\mathbf{x}$ on the animated surface S. Note that, for collision detection, we compute bounds of regions of S, and $\mathbf{x}$ is explicitly evaluated only on colliding points. We define a tetrahedron T as *front* if at least one of its nodes is a front node. Then, we define the position $\mathbf{x}$ of a vertex $V \in S$ as a barycentric combination of the nodes of its finest enclosing front tetrahedron (in rest configuration), denoted by $T^F(V)$. Due to the containment of S on all multigrid meshes, $\mathbf{x}$ is strictly defined as a *convex* combination of nodes, and this is crucial for designing the BVH (See §5).

Our adaptive multigrid solution to dynamic deformations allows the use of diverse contact handling methods, such as penalty-based or constraint-based. In our simulations, we have followed the approach of solving a linear complementarity problem (LCP) using the projected Gauss-Seidel method [CPS92]. We first solve a collision-free version of the discretized forward dynamics problem (1), then we execute continuous collision detection [RKC02] to detect and formulate (inequality) contact constraints, and finally solve

Figure 5: ***Self-Collisions in a Knot.*** *A knot with* 42254 *triangles and a* 7*-mesh hierarchy* (119399 *tets in* M_1) *is dropped and suffers large self collisions. The middle image shows the resolution near the surface ('yellow' is coarse, 'red' is fine), achieving smooth deformations and accurate handling of contact boundary conditions. Table 2 evaluates collision detection performance.*

the LCP. Figure 5 shows smooth and robust contact surfaces that can be achieved by combining an LCP formulation with our simulation and collision detection approach. Constraint-based collision response is costly when applied to high-resolution objects undergoing a large number of contacts, but our multigrid hierarchy accelerates response computations, as each contact force is applied directly on the nodes of $T^F(V)$ for each colliding vertex V, and the effect propagates quickly through the object on the coarse meshes.

5. Adaptivity-Aware Collision Detection

We now complete the definition of the MBH, as we describe the multiscale connections between BVs and tetrahedra, the fast fitting of tight bounds for sets of points interpolated in a simplex, and our novel adaptivity-aware self-collision detection. We first introduce the concepts for a non-adaptive simulation with a high-resolution surface S embedded in a coarse simulation mesh M_f, and later extend them to the adaptive setting. Our algorithms are independent of the type of BV, but here we discuss an AABB-based implementation.

5.1. Multiscale Bounding Volumes

Our novel MBH consists of the sequence of non-nested irregular tetrahedral meshes $\mathcal{M} = \{M_1, M_2, \ldots M_m\}$ introduced in §3.2, and the levels of a BVH $\mathcal{B} = \{L_1, L_2, \ldots L_l\}$ (with M_1 and L_1 the finest mesh and level). For bounding the motion of the animated surface S, we enforce that all meshes M_j and BVH levels L_j bound S.

The BVH $\mathcal{B}$ is a tree of *multiscale bounding volumes* (MBVs) that bound S in a hierarchical manner. Conceptually, we set a bidirectional correspondence between the lower m levels of $\mathcal{B}$ and the meshes in $\mathcal{M}$. Classical BVH refitting first computes the leaf BVs and then updates the rest of the hierarchy in a bottom-up manner. The intuitive idea behind our adaptivity-aware collision detection algorithm is to exploit the correspondences between levels of $\mathcal{B}$ and meshes of $\mathcal{M}$, to refit coarse MBVs directly and in a fast manner (i.e., with cost $O(1)$) using active tetrahedra.

We define the tree connectivity of $\mathcal{B}$ as a preprocessing operation, by successive splitting of the triangles of S at the median of the longest axis defined by the covariance matrix [GLM96]. Let us assume, w.l.o.g., that this procedure yields a perfectly binary tree with l levels. In this way, a MBV B at level L_j must bound a set of 2^{j-1} triangles in S.

5.1.1. Governors for Efficient Dynamic Refitting

Let us start with the assumption that the front of $\mathcal{M}$ is fixed at a coarse mesh M_f (i.e., only M_f and coarser levels are active) and later relax this assumption in §5.4. Given M_f, we similarly define its corresponding BVH level L_f as the front of $\mathcal{B}$. For each MBV $B \in L_j, j \le f$, we define the *effective governor* tetrahedra $G^*(B) \in M_f$ as those that bound (in the rest configuration) the set of vertices $V(B) \in S$ that must be bounded by B. Figure 3 shows one BV $B \in L_4$, its governors $G^*(B) \in M_4$, and the patch it bounds in $S = \partial M_1$. When the locally finest active mesh is $M_f = M_4$, we can detect collisions using only DoFs from M_4, without ever evaluating M_1.

5.1.2. Refitting Algorithm

We exploit the knowledge about the front of $\mathcal{M}$ to refit $\mathcal{B}$ with an adaptivity-aware cost in the following manner. Before a collision detection query, we bound MBVs in L_f using effective governors. Then, we bound all other MBVs in the subtree $\mathcal{B}_f = \{L_j, j \ge f\}$ in a bottom-up manner.

During a collision detection query, we compute bounds on demand for each visited MBV B below the front L_f, using its effective governors $G^*(B) \in M_f$. In simulations with temporal coherence, we cache the front of the subtree $\mathcal{B}^*$ of $\mathcal{B}$ visited during the previous collision query. Then, before the next query, we apply the adaptivity-aware refitting to the front of the subtree $\mathcal{B}^* \cup \mathcal{B}_f$ instead.

Our refitting algorithm is optimal if the contribution of each governor to the bounds can be computed in $O(1)$ time and every MBV $B \in L_f$ has $O(1)$ governors. In the next subsection we present an efficient $O(1)$ computation of tight bounds. The number of governors can be controlled during the meshing process, by ensuring low enough sampling at each mesh M_j. As a reference, the required mesh size ratio is $\frac{\|M_j\|}{\|M_{j+1}\|} \ge \sqrt{8}$ for a cube with uniform sampling.

5.2. Tight Bounds in Simplex Interpolation

We now present a novel and fast method for computing tight bounds along a direction x of a set of points V interpolated inside a simplex T (in our case, a tetrahedron). It is more efficient than evaluating the points even for very small sets, and often yields much tighter bounds than simply bounding the simplex. We use it for computing tight AABBs in the dynamic refitting of MBVs on or below the front of $\mathcal{B}$.

Using planes of minimum and maximum barycentric coordinates in rest configuration, we define a convex polyhedron that bounds V and is entirely contained in T. This polyhedron constitutes an 8-DOP for a tetrahedron, and the same concept has been used before for bounding skinned surfaces [KZ05]. Given vertices $\{V_A, V_B, V_C, V_D\}$, the 8-DOP is defined by barycentric intervals $\{[a_A, b_A], [a_B, b_B], [a_C, b_C], [a_D, b_D]\}$ (See Figure 6 (left) for a 2D example). At runtime computation of the AABB, we conservatively bound V by bounding the 8-DOP instead.

Instead of evaluating the corners of the 8-DOP, we propose a novel method that sorts the vertices of T and computes bounds in close-form. Note that every front tetrahedron constitutes typically an effective governor for many MBVs, but it only needs to be sorted once per time step. For a direction x, we sort the vertices of T, resulting in $x_0 \leq x_1 \leq x_2 \leq x_3$ for a tetrahedron (Figure 6 (right) shows a 2D example). Then, we efficiently compute AABB bounds $[a_x, b_x]$ by indexing the barycentric intervals according to the sorted vertices as:

$$\begin{aligned} a_x &= b_0 x_0 + a_3 x_3 + a_2 x_2 + (1 - b_0 - a_3 - a_2) x_1, \\ b_x &= b_3 x_3 + a_0 x_0 + a_1 x_1 + (1 - b_3 - a_0 - a_1) x_2. \end{aligned} \quad (8)$$

This procedure is not guaranteed to optimally bound the 8-DOP, as it may make a wrong, but conservative, assumption on the intersection of barycentric planes that define the 8-DOP corners. However, in practice it provides very tight bounds, as demonstrated in Figure 3. The method is extensible to simplex interpolation in higher (or lower) dimensions. It is important to note that the 8-DOP may not be replaced by an AABB or an OBB in rest configuration, because their corners may not be defined by convex combination in T, therefore they may not bound V during deformation.

5.3. Self-Collision Handling

We also exploit knowledge about the multigrid hierarchy $\mathscr{M}$ to devise an adaptivity-aware test for self-collision detection. We combine features of spatial hashing [THM*03] and BVHs to design a self-collision detection algorithm with a best-case (i.e., no collision) cost linear in the number of front tetrahedra near the surface. If the front mesh M_f is notably coarser than the surface S, our algorithm largely outperforms those linear in the size of S. Moreover, performance degrades gracefully under actual self-collisions, and many areas are pruned with a minor cost as shown in Figure 8.

5.3.1. Potentially Self-Colliding Patches

Given a front mesh M_f that contains S and does not self-intersect in the rest configuration, let us first define a patch $S_a \subset S$ as *potentially self-colliding* if one (or more) of its effective governors $G^*(S_a) \in M_f$ intersects some other tetrahedron in M_f. Then, our algorithm builds on the following lemma: Given two patches $S_a, S_b \subset S$ that do not intersect in the rest configuration, S_a and S_b do not collide if at least one of them is not potentially self-colliding. The same lemma is

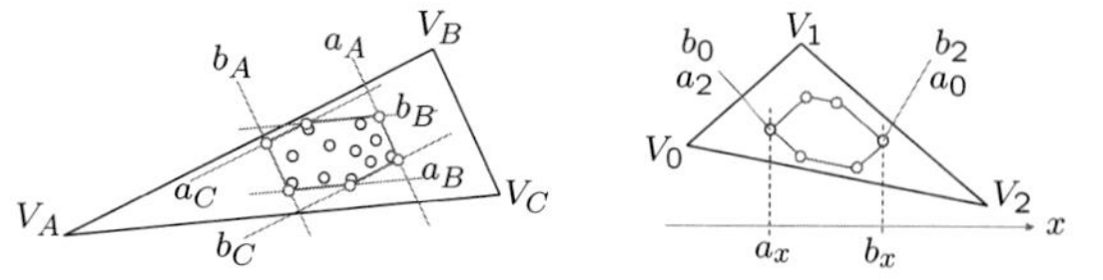

Figure 6: ***Tight Fitting k-DOP.*** *Left: 2D example showing a set of vertices (in blue) enclosed in a triangle, and the 6-DOP (in red) defined by barycentric coordinate bounds. Right: To compute the bounds $[a_x, b_x]$ of the 6-DOP along x, it suffices to sort the vertices of the triangle and evaluate a close-form definition of the extreme corner of the 6-DOP.*

valid for a self-collision (S_a, S_a). We do not consider tetrahedra that share only a vertex, an edge, or a face, as intersecting, thus pruning potential self-collisions due to adjacency.

5.3.2. Hierarchical Self-Collision Query

Before a self-collision query, we perform a CCD intersection test (using spatial hashing) between front tetrahedra of M_f that are effective governors of some MBV (They are the tetrahedra enclosing S). Then, we flag a front MBV $B \in L_f$ as potentially self-colliding if at least one of its effective governors $G^*(B)$ intersects some other front tetrahedron. We propagate the information up in $\mathscr{B}$ by flagging a MBV as potentially self-colliding if at least one of its children is flagged. If a collision query descends below the front L_f, we flag MBVs using information from the effective governors directly.

Hierarchical self-collision pruning can then be easily implemented as follows. A self-collision test (B_a, B_a) can be pruned if B_a is not potentially self-colliding. Otherwise, one must split B_a and test its children. Notice that, in most hierarchical algorithms, a test (B_a, B_a) can never be pruned ([VMT94] is an exception, but its cost is linear in the size of S), but in our case a self-collision query may be pruned right at the root of the BVH! A self-collision test (B_a, B_b) can be pruned if at least one MBV is not potentially self-colliding, or if the AABBs do not collide (as in a regular query).

5.4. Extension to Adaptive Meshes

With adaptive meshes, the front of $\mathscr{M}$ may combine multiple meshes M_j, therefore effective governors cannot be known a priori. We extend the basic BVH refitting algorithm described in §5.1 by including governors at multiple levels, a definition of BVH front for the adaptive setting, and an algorithm for efficiently determining effective governors.

We extend the self-collision algorithm by flagging a MBV as potentially self-colliding if some effective governor intersects other tetrahedra, or the effective governors lie on different mesh levels. The spatial-hashing test between front tetrahedra must be carried out at each level independently.

5.4.1. Multiscale Governors

As a preprocessing, and for every MBV $B \in L_j, j \leq m$, we identify the *governor* tetrahedra $G(B)$ at coarser levels,

$G(B) \in \{M_k\}, m \geq k \geq j$, that may contribute to the dynamic definition of the bounds of B, and we store them in a directed graph, as shown in Figure 7 for a 2D example. We set an edge from a governor tetrahedron $T_a \in M_j$ to a coarser governor tetrahedron $T_b \in M_{j+1}$, if both T_a and T_b bound at least one common vertex in the set $V(B)$ to be bounded by B.

5.4.2. Definition of the BVH Front

A MBV $B \in L_j$ is a *potential front* MBV if at least one of its governors at the corresponding level, $T \in G(B) \cap M_j$, is a front tetrahedron. Then, B is a front MBV if it is a potential front MBV and it has no potential front descendants. With this definition, the front of $\mathscr{B}$ is formed by roughly as-coarse-as-possible MBVs that can be conservatively refit with $O(1)$ cost each, and with an adaptivity-aware cost altogether, i.e., linear in the number of front tetrahedra in $\mathscr{M}$.

To find the front of $\mathscr{B}$ at runtime, we first mark the MBVs governed by each front tetrahedron at its corresponding level. Then we perform a bottom-up flooding toward the root of $\mathscr{B}$, marking other visited MBVs, and finally we perform a top-down pass to detect the boundary of the marked region.

5.4.3. Effective Governor Tetrahedra

In order to compute the bounds of a front MBV B, we seek to identify those governors that effectively define the position $\mathbf{x}$ of some surface vertex V bounded by B. We refer to them as *effective governors* $G^*(B)$, and they are, according to §4.4, the finest active enclosing tetrahedra $\{T^F\}$ of all vertices bounded by B. Given a front MBV $B \in L_j$, we find $G^*(B)$ by performing a bottom-up search on $G(B)$, seeded at governors from the corresponding mesh, $\{T\} \in G(B) \cap M_j$.

Finding effective governors varies slightly for MBVs updated on-demand during a collision detection query. In the traversal of $\mathscr{B}$ during the query, every MBV B passes to its children the level j of its finest effective governor. Then, the children seed the search for finding their effective governors at level j in the governor graph. The rest of the fitting algorithm is identical as for front nodes.

6. Results

We have performed all our simulations on a dual 3.2 GHz. processor PC with 2 GB of memory. They include a scene with multiple gummy bears suffering impacts and deformations (See Figure 4), a knot falling on the ground and experiencing self-collisions (See Figure 5), and the interactive deformation of a dragon model also undergoing self-collisions (See Figures 1 and 8).

The bears experience drastic yet smooth and stable changes in the refinement of the multigrid hierarchy, due to impact-induced deformations, as can be clearly seen in the accompanying video. Each bear is described by a 6-mesh hierarchy, from 85 tetrahedra in M_6 to 6418 in M_1. We have compared our adaptive algorithm to full resolution conjugate gradient and a non-adaptive FAS multigrid solver, as shown in

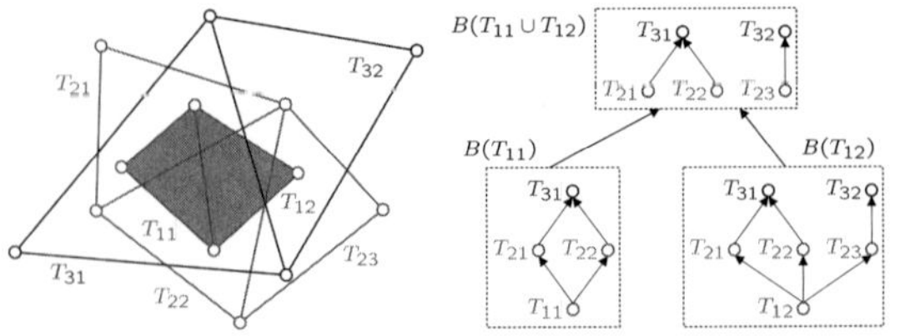

Figure 7: ***MBV Governors in 2D.*** *Left: Two triangles, $T_{11} \in M_1$ and $T_{12} \in M_1$ (in red), and their bounding triangles in M_2 (in green) and M_3 (in blue); Right: Graphs of governors for the MBVs $B(T_{11})$, $B(T_{12})$, and $B(T_{11} \cup T_{12})$.*

Table 1, in scenarios with 1 and 8 bears. The first conclusion is that FAS multigrid imposes no overhead on the solution. Second, our adaptive algorithm offers about 10x average speed-up both in the dynamics update as in the complete simulation, even though the bears reach full resolution (locally) at times. Constraint-based collision response becomes the bottleneck, and our integrated algorithm for adaptive simulation and collision detection shows its power at best when the bears come close to rest in a large contact group, reaching a frame rate of 12 fps in this situation.

The falling knot in Figure 5 shows the ability to robustly handle smooth contact areas, even for self-collisions. We have also evaluated the performance of collision detection, as outlined in Table 2, using a surface mesh $S = \partial M_1$ with 42 254 triangles and a non-adaptive simulation mesh $M_f = M_4$ with 558 tetrahedra. Our algorithm shows an average performance of 23.6 fps. Even though this benchmark is a worst-case scenario, as large regions of the BVH are visited due to the large contact areas, we obtain 7x average speed-up over full refitting of the BVH, and 3x speed-up over spatial hashing applied to the surface S (Not to be confused with our use of spatial hashing for tetrahedra). Speedups would grow with a denser surface S, thanks to the sublinear cost of our algorithm, as well as with smaller contact regions.

A compelling application of our unified treatment of adaptive simulation and collision detection is the interactive deformation of the self-colliding dragon. The model suffers global deformations as well as detailed localized deformations due to contact with the bear. However, note that potential colliding areas are inherently large as we solve a self-collision detection problem. We used a surface mesh $S = \partial M_1$ with 13 480 triangles, and a simulation mesh $M_f = M_4$ with 2 552 tetrahedra. We disabled adaptive refinements to ensure that constraint-based collision response remained tractable at interactive rates. The frame rate varied from 8 to 15 fps when playing a pre-recorded bear trajectory (Performance halves when the haptic device is connected at runtime). The time per frame can be approximately decomposed into: 50 ms for the forward dynamics update, 15 ms for the intersection query of front tetrahedra through spatial hashing, 20 ms for the update of the BVH, 5 to 25 ms for the BVH self-collision query (notice the fast query due to hier-

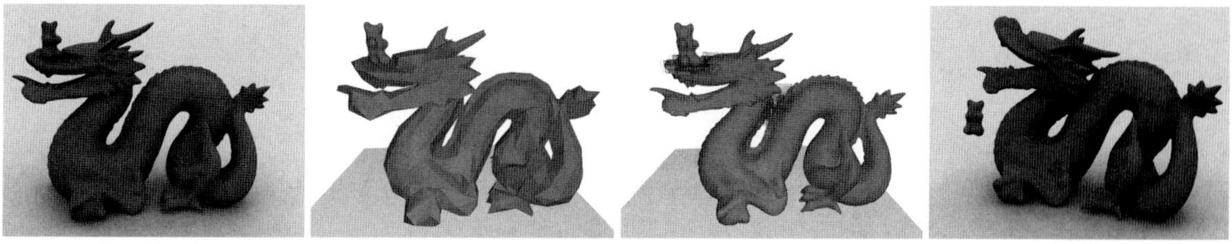

Figure 8: ***Hierarchical Pruning of Self-Collisions.*** *(i) A dragon with a surface* $S = \partial M_1$ *with* 13480 *triangles is simulated using (ii) a mesh* M_4 *(with* 2552 *tetrahedra). (iii) In the level* L_3 *of the BVH, only the MBVs depicted in blue need to be updated, as our hierarchical self-collision detection algorithm can prune regions governed by non-intersecting tetrahedra at high levels of the BVH. (iv) The self-collision between back and neck is handled accurately and effiicently.*

Num.	Fw. Update (fps)			Total (fps)		
Bears	CG	MG	Ours	CG	MG	Ours
1	15.3	17.8	383.2	3.07	3.37	58.2
8	1.89	2.15	26.7	0.40	0.36	2.98

Table 1: ***Comparison of Solvers.*** *The benchmark of Figure 4 is executed with* 1 *and* 8 *bears: (i) at full res. with conjugate gradient (CG); (ii) at full res. with a multigrid solver (MG); (iii) with our adaptive multigrid solver. Average total performance and for forward dynamics update are shown.*

Full	Hash	W/o	W/o	Ours		
BVH	Grid	k-DOP	Sort	(1)	(2)	(3)
282.5	111.9	314.8	62.4	21.6	2.8	18.0

Table 2: ***Self-Collision Detection Timings (in ms.).*** *Our algorithm (1: MBH refit, 2: tet hashing, 3: query) Vs. (i) a full BVH-based query, (ii) spatial hashing on the full surface, (iii) no k-DOPs, and (iv) no tet sorting, on a* 42254*-triangle knot simulated with* 558 *tetrahedra (See Figure 5).*

archical pruning), and up to 250 ms for collision response (10 ms per constraint anticipation, and 40 ms for the final response computation).

Our algorithm exploits simulation adaptivity to produce considerable speed-ups in collision detection even for moderately-sized surface meshes (tens of thousands of triangles), and speed-ups would be higher with denser surfaces. Although not shown here, our framework can also incorporate interruptible collision detection and/or perceptual error metrics. Examples like the dragon show the ability to simulate in real-time challenging self-collisions, but our framework is also applicable to offline simulations, for example for fast preview of simulations of complex embedded surfaces. One can compute a coarse simulation (and render a coarse preview surface) while conforming to the boundary conditions of the full resolution surface, therefore guaranteeing that the final rendering will be collision-free.

7. Summary and Future Work

Motivated by the observation that setting boundary conditions in previous adaptive deformable simulation methods required handling the boundary in a non-adaptive manner, we have designed data structures and algorithms for seamless integration of adaptive simulation and collision detection. In particular, our novel multiscale bounding hierarchies link mesh hierarchies employed in adaptive simulation with BVHs for collision detection. Coupled with novel adaptive multigrid simulation and collision detection methods, they enable robust and accurate handling of contact boundary conditions with a cost independent on the boundary's complexity. As an example, self-collision of complex surfaces with tens of thousands of triangles, governed by a few thousand DoFs, can be simulated interactively.

As with other hierarchical and/or adaptive techniques, performance comes with the price of memory consumption ($O(n \lg n)$ for our multiscale bounding hierarchies) and the algorithms require slightly more elaborate implementation. This was not a major issue in our case, because the collision detection builds on well-known algorithms, and our contributions in the adaptive simulation enable the use of the very same algorithms as in the past (but now on irregular meshes).

Although we have not suffered lack of convergence problems in the simulations, it is recommendable to analyze the influence of our interpolation and relaxation strategies for irregular meshes. From a performance point of view, collision response becomes the bottleneck in our simulations in situations with large contact areas. We plan to explore solutions for contact clustering that exploit adaptivity as well. And, in the future, we would also like to extend our method to handle the simulation of 2D manifolds embedded in 3D.

Acknowledgements

We would like to thank the anonymous reviewers, Sabine Coquillart, Kaspar Schüpbach, Gilles Debunne, Nico Galoppo, Remo Ziegler, Denis Steinemann, Mario Botsch, Nico Pietroni, Martin Wicke, and others at the CGL at ETH Zurich. This project was supported in part by the NCCR Co-Me of the Swiss National Science Foundation.

References

[AKS05] Aksoylu B., Khodakovsky A., Schröder P.: Multilevel solvers for unstructured surface meshes. *SIAM Journal on Scientific Computing 26*, 4 (2005), 1146–1165.

[BFA02] BRIDSON R., FEDKIW R., ANDERSON J.: Robust treatment of collisions, contact and friction for cloth animation. *Proc. of ACM SIGGRAPH* (2002).

[BHM00] BRIGGS W. L., HENSON V. E., MCCORMICK S. F.: *A Multigrid Tutorial, 2nd Edition.* SIAM, 2000.

[BJ05] BARBIČ J., JAMES D. L.: Real-time subspace integration for St. Venant-Kirchhoff deformable models. *Proc. of ACM SIGGRAPH* (2005).

[Bra77] BRANDT A.: Multi-level adaptive solutions to boundary-value problems. *Mathematics of Computation 31*, 138 (1977).

[BW98] BARAFF D., WITKIN A.: Large steps in cloth simulation. *Proc. of ACM SIGGRAPH* (1998).

[CGC*02] CAPELL S., GREEN S., CURLESS B., DUCHAMP T., POPOVIC Z.: A multiresolution framework for dynamic deformations. *Proc. of ACM SIGGRAPH SCA* (2002).

[CPS92] COTTLE R., PANG J., STONE R.: *The Linear Complementarity Problem.* Academic Press, 1992.

[dB97] DEN BERGEN G. V.: Efficient collision detection of complex deformable models using aabb trees. *J. Graphics Tools 2*, 4 (1997), 1–14.

[DDCB01] DEBUNNE G., DESBRUN M., CANI M. P., BARR A. H.: Dynamic real-time deformations using space and time adaptive sampling. *Proc. of ACM SIGGRAPH* (2001).

[GKS02] GRINSPUN E., KRYSL P., SCHRÖDER P.: CHARMS: A simple framework for adaptive simulation. *Proc. of ACM SIGGRAPH* (2002).

[GLM96] GOTTSCHALK S., LIN M., MANOCHA D.: OBB-Tree: A hierarchical structure for rapid interference detection. *Proc. of ACM SIGGRAPH* (1996), 171–180.

[GM97] GIBSON S. F., MIRTICH B. V.: *A Survey of Deformable Modeling in Computer Graphics.* Tech. rep., Mitsubishi Electric Research Laboratory, 1997.

[GRLM03] GOVINDARAJU N., REDON S., LIN M., MANOCHA D.: CULLIDE: Interactive collision detection between complex models in large environments using graphics hardware. *Proc. of ACM SIGGRAPH/Eurographics Workshop on Graphics Hardware* (2003), 25–32.

[GTS02] GREEN S., TURKIYYAH G., STORTI D.: Subdivision-based multilevel methods for large scale engineering simulation of thin shells. *Proc. of ACM Symposium on Solid Modeling and Applications* (2002), 265–272.

[GW05] GEORGII J., WESTERMANN R.: A multigrid framework for real-time simulation of deformable volumes. *Proc. of VRIPHYS* (2005).

[ITF04] IRVING G., TERAN J., FEDKIW R.: Invertible finite elements for robust simulation of large deformation. *Proc. of ACM SIGGRAPH/Eurographics SCA* (2004), 131–140.

[JP03] JAMES D. L., PAI D. K.: Multiresolution Green's function methods for interactive simulation of large-scale elastostatic objects. *ACM TOG 22*, 1 (2003).

[JP04] JAMES D. L., PAI D. K.: BD-Tree: Output-sensitive collision detection for reduced deformable models. *Proc. of ACM SIGGRAPH* (2004).

[KZ05] KAVAN L., ZARA J.: Fast collision detection for skeletally deformable models. *Proc. of Eurographics* (2005).

[LAM01] LARSSON T., AKENINE-MÖLLER T.: Collision detection for continuously deforming bodies. *Eurographics* (2001).

[MG04] MÜLLER M., GROSS M.: Interactive virtual materials. *Proc. of Graphics Interface* (2004).

[MHTG05] MÜLLER M., HEIDELBERGER B., TESCHNER M., GROSS M.: Meshless deformations based on shape matching. *Proc. of ACM SIGGRAPH* (2005), 471–478.

[MT86] MCCORMICK S. F., THOMAS J.: The fast adaptive composite grid (FAC) method for elliptic equations. *Mathematics of Computation 46*, 174 (1986), 439–456.

[NMK*05] NEALEN A., MÜLLER M., KEISER R., BOXERMANN E., CARLSON M.: Physically based deformable models in computer graphics. *Eurographics STAR* (2005).

[OBH02] O'BRIEN J. F., BARGTEIL A. W., HODGINS J. K.: Graphical modeling and animation of ductile fracture. *Proc. of ACM SIGGRAPH* (2002), 291–294.

[ODGK03] O'SULLIVAN C., DINGLIANA J., GIANG T., KAISER M. K.: Evaluating the visual fidelity of physically based animations. *Proc. of ACM SIGGRAPH* (2003), 527–536.

[OL03] OTADUY M. A., LIN M. C.: Sensation preserving simplification for haptic rendering. *Proc. of ACM SIGGRAPH* (2003).

[Ran99] RANNACHER R.: Error control in finite element computations. *NATO Science Series, Series C: Mathematics and Physical Sciences 536* (1999), 247–278.

[RKC02] REDON S., KHEDDAR A., COQUILLART S.: Fast continuous collision detection between rigid bodies. *Proc. of Eurographics* (2002).

[SGG*06] SUD A., GOVINDARAJU N. K., GAYLE R., KABUL I., MANOCHA D.: Fast proximity computation among multiple deformable models using discrete voronoi diagrams. *Proc. of ACM SIGGRAPH* (2006).

[SYBF06] SHI L., YU Y., BELL N., FENG W.-W.: A fast multigrid algorithm for mesh deformation. *Proc. of ACM SIGGRAPH* (2006).

[THM*03] TESCHNER M., HEIDELBERGER B., MÜELLER M., POMERANETS D., GROSS M.: Optimized spatial hashing for collision detection of deformable objects. *Proc. of Vision, Modeling and Visualization* (2003).

[TKH*05] TESCHNER M., KIMMERLE S., HEIDELBERGER B., ZACHMANN G., RAGHUPATHI L., FURHMANN A., CANI M.-P., FAURE F., MAGNENAT-THALMANN N., STRASSER W., VOLINO P.: Collision detection for deformable objects. *Computer Graphics Forum 24*, 1 (2005).

[TOS01] TROTTENBERG U., OOSTERLEE C., SCHÜLLER A.: *Multigrid.* Academic Press, 2001.

[VMT94] VOLINO P., MAGNENAT-THALMANN N.: Efficient self-collision detection on smoothly discretized surface animations using geometrical shape regularity. *Eurographics* (1994).

[VMT06] VOLINO P., MAGNENAT-THALMANN N.: Resolving surface collisions through intersection contour minimization. *Proc. of ACM SIGGRAPH* (2006).

[WT04] WU X., TENDICK F.: Multigrid integration for interactive deformable body simulation. *International Symposium on Medical Simulation* (2004).

Eurographics/ ACM SIGGRAPH Symposium on Computer Animation (2007)
D. Metaxas and J. Popovic (Editors)

Real-time Simulations of Bubbles and Foam within a Shallow Water Framework

N. Thürey[2], F. Sadlo[2], S. Schirm[1], M. Müller-Fischer[1] and M. Gross[2]

[1]AGEIA
[2]ETH Zurich, Switzerland

Abstract

Bubbles and foam are important fluid phenomena on scales that we encounter in our lives every day. While different techniques to handle these effects were developed in the past years, they require a full 3D fluid solver with free surfaces and surface tension. We present a shallow water based particle model that is coupled with a smoothed particle hydrodynamics simulation to demonstrate that real-time simulations of bubble and foam effects are possible with high frame rates. A shallow water simulation is used to represent the overall water volume. It is coupled to a particle-based bubble simulation with a flow field of spherical vortices. This bubble simulation is interacting with a smoothed particle hydrodynamics simulation including surface tension to handle foam on the fluid surface. The realism and performance of our approach is demonstrated with several test cases that run with high frame rates on a standard PC.

Categories and Subject Descriptors (according to ACM CCS): I.3.7 [Three-Dimensional Graphics and Realism]: Animation

1. Introduction

Secondary fluid effects such as bubbles are prominent in every day situations such as cooking or filling a cup of coffee. They are, however, more difficult to capture than the overall fluid motion itself, as they obey complex laws governed by surface tension, the behavior of the gas phase, and the properties of very thin fluid sheets. The goal of this paper is to capture these three-dimensional effects within the framework of an essentially two-dimensional shallow water (SW) simulation. We will demonstrate that the complexity of the mechanisms that lead to bubble dynamics and foam formation can be reduced significantly to make interactive simulations with high frame rates possible. As physically based simulations are an important part of modern computer games, our approach makes it possible to include fluids with bubbles and foam into this area. Moreover, we will demonstrate that the algorithm can be used to efficiently simulate these effects for off-line renderings as well.

Figure 1: *Two images from a bubble and foam simulation generated with our approach.*

The contributions of this paper are:

- a shallow water based bubble simulation model that introduces spherical vortices to efficiently generate a three-dimensional flow field,
- and a foam simulation based on smoothed particle hydrodynamics (SPH) with surface tension to capture the formation and clustering of foam bubbles.

2. Related Work

The topic of fluid simulations was first brought up in [KM90], where the wave equation was solved to gen-

Symposium on Computer Animation 2007, San Diego, CA, August 03-04, 2007.
© 2007 ACM 978-1-59593-624-4/07/0008 $5.00

erate a height field fluid simulation. Since then, two-dimensional methods have been used, e.g., for generating splashes [OH95] or coupled to terrains and rigid bodies [CdVLHM97]. A different class of methods for wave generation are the spectral approaches, e.g., as described in [HNC02], [Lov03], or in [Tes04]. These approaches are especially suitable for deep water waves with dispersive effects. In the following, we will use a shallow water discretization, as it can be computed efficiently and the equations are conservative. Moreover, wave dispersion is not crucial for the scale of effects we are targeting.

Solving the full three-dimensional equations for fluid flow, the Navier-Stokes (NS) equations, was made popular by Stam [Sta99] together with Foster and Fedkiw [FF01]. As these simulations often require huge amounts of computation, they have recently been combined with two-dimensional techniques to reduce the required computational cost [IGLF06, TRS06]. However, these approaches are not targeted towards real-time applications, but allow the simulation of more detailed fluid effects. In [GH04] the authors generate bubbles in the flow field of such a solver for enhanced realism, while Mihalef et. al present a full two-phase simulation for bubbly flows in [MUM*06]. The handling of thin fluid sheets for foam like structures was addressed in [ZYP06]. Another approach that dealt with rendering and a physically based model for foam simulation was presented in [KVG02]. Moreover, the behavior of bubbles is an important topic in mechanical engineering [CGW78], e.g., to better understand and optimize bubble flow reactors [BDR05]. In the following, we will use a SW simulation for the main fluid volume, as it can efficiently handle the wave propagation on the fluid surface and guarantees the overall conservation of fluid mass. The bubble dynamics will be simplified and reduced to the vortices induced in the flow, a buoyancy force, and effects such as merging.

The vortex filament methods, e.g., as presented in [AN05] and [ANSN06], are based on the vorticity formulation of the NS equations. They have the advantage of defining a vorticity preserving flow field around a set of vortex primitives. We will present a similar method, that, however, directly evaluates an analytical and Navier-Stokes conforming flow field around spherical vortices. It can be evaluated efficiently and has the advantage of yielding a flow field around the spherical vortex region that also correctly captures the fluid dynamics around it.

An alternative approach for solving the NS equations that does not require a computational grid are smoothed particle hydrodynamics (SPH) [Mon92]. As was demonstrated in [MCG03] and [MSRG05] they can be used to capture a variety of fluid effects, and are interesting for real time environments due to their particle based nature. In [MSRG05] the authors also perform a boiling simulation, but in contrast to our approach, SPH is used to fully simulate both the gas and the liquid phase. This would require huge amounts of particles for scenes such as Figure 1. Furthermore, our approach is aimed at fluids with lower viscosities. We make use of SPH to model the foam structures on the SW surface. In addition, surface tension is used to cause a clustering of the foam bubbles.

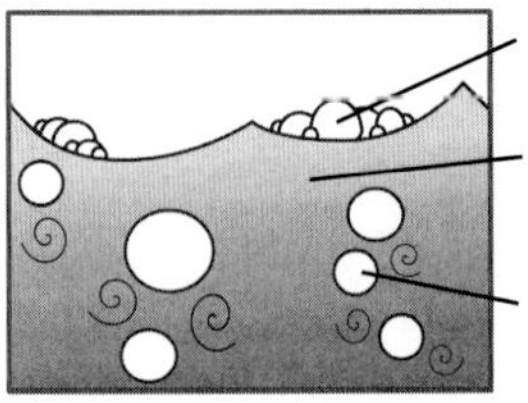

Figure 2: *An overview of the three different coupled simulation techniques.*

3. The Shallow Water Equations

Shallow water (SW) simulations reduce the complexity of the full Navier-Stokes equations to the simplified two-dimensional representation of a height field. Note that, in the following, it will be assumed that the gravity force is acting along the z axis. Thus, the plane for the 2D simulation corresponds to the x-y plane. One simplifying assumption of the SW equations is that the velocity does not vary significantly along the z axis, and that there is a constant pressure gradient from the water surface to the bottom. The only two forces driving the flow are pressure and gravity. It is furthermore assumed that the liquid under consideration has a very low viscosity. Thus, the viscosity term of the NS equations can be neglected.

In the following, $H(\mathbf{x},t)$ is the height of the water above ground, while $\mathbf{v}$ is the horizontal velocity of the fluid, and $\mathbf{g} = (0,0,g)^T$ is the gravitational force perpendicular to the 2D simulation plane. The simulation region consists of N_x grid nodes with size Δx, and N_y grid nodes with size Δy in x and y direction, respectively. The simplified shallow water equations can now be written as

$$\frac{\partial H}{\partial t} = -\mathbf{v}\cdot\nabla H - H\left(\frac{\partial v_x}{\partial x} + \frac{\partial v_y}{\partial y}\right) \tag{1}$$

$$\frac{\partial v_x}{\partial t} = -\mathbf{v}\cdot\nabla v_x - g\frac{\partial H}{\partial x}\text{ , and} \tag{2}$$

$$\frac{\partial v_y}{\partial t} = -\mathbf{v}\cdot\nabla v_y - g\frac{\partial H}{\partial y}\ . \tag{3}$$

We use a staggered grid together with a semi-Lagrangian advection step to solve these equations [Sta99]. A good overview of such a SW solver can be found, e.g., in [Bri05]. To simplify the equations, we do not take a changing ground topology into account. Our approach, however, also works for variable ground heights.

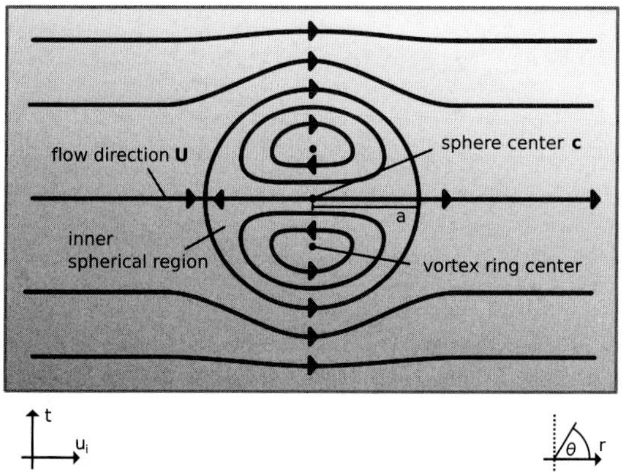

Figure 3: *Streamlines for a spherical Hill vortex.*

4. Simulating Bubbles

The actual flow around bubbles in a liquid with a very low viscosity, such as water, is usually very turbulent and hard to compute. We make a number of simplifications to capture this phenomenon within a real-time simulation. As described above, the main volume of the liquid is simulated with the SW equations of Section 3. The bubbles are simulated as particles that interact with the shallow water surface, and among each other. Here we assume a flow and shape regime (according to [CGW78]) of relatively low bubble velocities, and strong surface tension, as present in water. Therefore, each bubble is treated as a spherical particle, and has the following properties: a position in space $\mathbf{p}_i = (p_{i_x}, p_{i_y}, p_{i_z})$, a velocity $\mathbf{u}_i$, a radius r_i and a volume (or mass) m_i. While the bubble is rising, we update the position with Euler steps. The simulation of foam on the water surface is handled by an SPH simulation, as will be described in Section 5. An overview of the combination of these simulation techniques is shown in Figure 2.

4.1. Spherical vortices

For the flow of the fluid around the bubbles, we make use of the concept of Hill's spherical vortex [Hil94]. Such a vortex consists of a flow field that describes the irrotational flow past a sphere, and a closed-streamline vortex inside of this sphere [Ach90]. In contrast to a toroidal vortex with a small core cross section, such as a smoke ring, this vortex is distinguished by the confined vorticity within its spherical region, and the absence of a hole in its middle. The streamlines of a Hill's vortex are shown in Figure 3. Such vortices were experimentally detected around bubbles, an example can be found in, e.g., [Bat67]. This is only an approximation of the flow around a bubble in general, but we will in the following use it to model the flow around the bubbles in our simulation.

Hill's spherical vortex is usually given as a stream function in polar coordinates (r, θ). This stream function Ψ_i is given by:

$$\Psi_i(r,\theta,a) = \begin{cases} \frac{1}{2}\left(r^2 - \frac{a^3}{r}\right) sin^2\theta & \text{for } r \geq a \\ -\frac{3}{4} r^2 \left(1 - \frac{r^2}{a^2}\right) sin^2\theta & \text{for } r < a\,, \end{cases} \tag{4}$$

where a is the radius of the spherical vortex. The velocity field along the isolines of this function could be computed directly with spatial derivatives, but in the following we will use the analytical solution, which is, according to [Saf94]

$$\mathbf{u}_h(\mathbf{x}, d) = \begin{cases} \begin{pmatrix} xz \\ yz \\ z^2 + 1 - 2d^2 \end{pmatrix} & \text{for } d < 1, \\ \begin{pmatrix} xz r^{-5} \\ yz r^{-5} \\ z^2 r^{-5} - 1/3 r^{-3} - 3/2 \end{pmatrix} & \text{for } d \geq 1\,. \end{cases} \tag{5}$$

This equation yields a divergence-free velocity field that, together with an appropriate pressure field, solves the NS equations, and has a zero vorticity outside the spherical region. This analytical solution of the flow field allows an efficient computation of bubble interactions.

The center $\mathbf{c}_i$ of the spherical vortex is computed with the bubble center $\mathbf{p}_i$ as $\mathbf{c}_i = \mathbf{p}_i - (a_i - r_i/2)\mathbf{u}_i/|\mathbf{u}_i|$, where a_i is again radius of the spherical region. Thus, the bubble is placed at the front of the inner spherical region of the vortex. In the following, we choose $a_i = 3r_i$. This parameter can be used to control the extent of the vortices. For $a_i = r_i$, only the flow around the bubble will remain, while larger values will result in trailing vortices behind the bubbles. An example of the flow around a bubble due to a spherical vortex can be found in the accompanying animation.

In the following, $\mathbf{d}_{ij} = \mathbf{p}_j - \mathbf{c}_i$ will denote the distance between the position of bubble j and the center of the spherical vortex around bubble i. $\mathbf{d}_{ij}$ is transformed into the local coordinate system of the spherical vortex (of bubble i), so that the z axis aligns with the bubble velocity $\mathbf{u}_i$. The velocity influence for a bubble j is given by the sum of vorticity forces from all other bubbles i, multiplied by a fall off function f_v, and the velocity of the shallow water simulation $\mathbf{v}$ as:

$$\mathbf{f}_j^v = \left[\mathbf{v}(\mathbf{p}_j) + \sum_i \mathbf{u}_h\left(\frac{\mathbf{d}_{ij}}{a_i}, \frac{|\mathbf{d}_{ij}|}{a_i}\right) f_v(|\mathbf{d}_{ij}|, a_i)\right] \frac{\Delta t}{m_j}\,. \tag{6}$$

The SW velocity in the x-y plane is directly given by the simulation, while the z component can be computed from the heights of the last two time steps as $\mathbf{v}_z = h(t) - h(t - \Delta t)$. For velocity values inside of the fluid volume, we exponentially scale down the velocity values [Ger04]. Once a bubble breaks through the surface and is removed from the simulation, the vortex behind it would dissipate in the fluid over time. This effect is accounted for by letting the vortex sphere of a deleted bubble fade out at its last position, which gives the impression of fluid inertia.

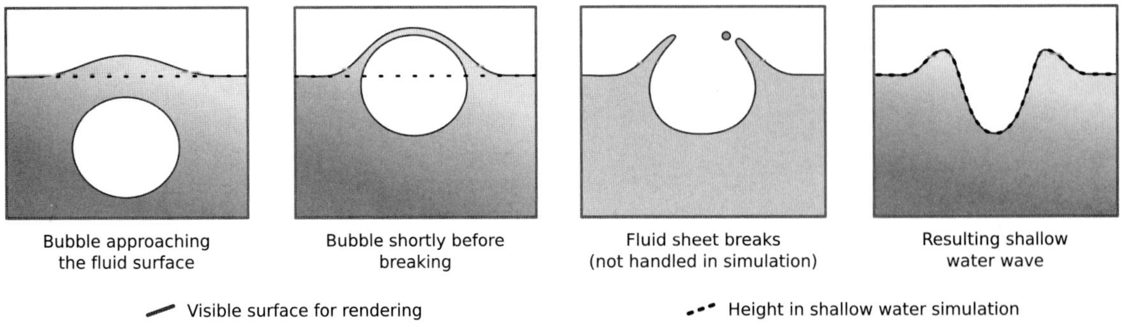

Figure 4: *A bubble approaching the fluid surface and breaking. To the right, the wave initialized for the shallow water simulation is shown.*

For f_v, we use a simple linear fall off function and restrict the force to act within a finite radius of $3a$:

$$f_v(r,a) = \begin{cases} 1 & \text{for } r < 2a \\ 3 - r/a & \text{for } 2a \leq r < 3a \\ 0 & \text{for } r \geq 3a\,. \end{cases} \quad (7)$$

Hence, the correct Navier-Stokes solution of Equation (5) is retained within a radius of $2a$. Further away, we blend the already small values of $\mathbf{u}_h$ to zero.

4.2. Shallow Water Coupling

The coupling of the bubbles and the shallow water simulation has no effect on the latter before the bubbles break through the water surface. While a bubble is fully submerged, the flow around it is smooth enough to only lead to a displacement of the fluid surface, due to our assumptions of the flow properties. This displacement is computed using the normalized spline kernel $W(h,d)$, with width h that is evaluated at distance d. According to [MKN*04], it is computed as:

$$W(h,d) = \begin{cases} \frac{315(h-d)^3}{64\pi h^9} & \text{for } d \leq h \\ 0 & \text{otherwise}\,. \end{cases} \quad (8)$$

The displacement itself $d_i(\mathbf{x})$, which depends on the distance of the bubble to the fluid surface is then computed with

$$\begin{aligned} d_i(\mathbf{x}) &= \frac{m_i}{1 + (H(\mathbf{x}) - p_{i_z})} W(h, |\mathbf{p}_i - \mathbf{x}|)\,,\ \text{with} \quad (9) \\ h &= 2r_i\Big(1 + H(\mathbf{x}) - p_{i_z}\Big)\,. \end{aligned}$$

Note that d_i is only used as an offset for the rendering of the water surface, but does not influence the SW simulation itself. However, the integral of d_i is equal to the volume of the bubble (for $H(\mathbf{x}) = p_{i_z}$), hence it correctly represents the volume of the gas inside of it.

Once the bubble breaks through the surface, meaning that $(H(\mathbf{x}) + d_i(\mathbf{x}) - p_{i_z}) < 0$, we modify the shallow water surface to represent a circular wave around the bubble. We thus add

$$d_i(\mathbf{x})' = W(h, |\mathbf{p}_i - \mathbf{x}|) - W(h/2, |\mathbf{p}_i - \mathbf{x}|) \quad (10)$$

to the fluid heights $H(\mathbf{x})$ of the SW simulation, as shown in Figure 4. This results in a surface wave within the shallow water simulation according to the size of bubble. Note that Equation (10) preserves the mass of the SW simulation. Thus, it corresponds to a case where the gas of the bubbles is, e.g., streamed into the fluid with a nozzle below it. To account for a loss of fluid mass due to a phase change, e.g., when heating the liquid, the mass of the SW simulation could be explicitly and uniformly reduced whenever a bubble is created. However, we will in the following keep the overall fluid mass constant.

For the integration of the bubble velocities, we compute the forces acting upon the bubble in the fluid. In our model, we only incorporate buoyancy and velocity forces:

$$\mathbf{u}_i(t + \Delta t) = \mathbf{u}_i(t) + \Delta t(\mathbf{f}_i^b + \mathbf{f}_i^v)/m_i\,. \quad (11)$$

The buoyancy force is given by the volume of the fluid displaced by the bubble and the gravity $\mathbf{g}$ as $\mathbf{f}_i^b = -\mathbf{g}\gamma_b m_i$. Here γ_b is a parameter to set the density difference between the gas and the fluid, for simplicity, we use $\gamma_b = 1$. For more viscous fluids, a drag force counteracting the current bubble velocity could also be added at this point.

4.3. Coalescence and Surface Animation

The algorithm described so far can already produce realistic motions of interacting bubbles. However, another important effect is the coalescence of bubbles. If the distance between two bubbles i and j is less than the sum of their radii, they are removed from the simulation, and a new bubble with a volume m_n that is equal to the sum of the two touching bubbles $(m_i + m_j)$ is introduced. The other properties of the bubble are now interpolated according to this volume. The velocity, for example, is initialized as

$$\mathbf{u}_m = \frac{\mathbf{u}_i m_i}{m_n} + \frac{\mathbf{u}_i m_j}{m_n} \; . \tag{12}$$

The radius of the new bubble on the other hand is computed from its volume with $r_n = 3/4\, m_n^{1/3}$. This also leads to a corresponding change of the radius of the bubble's spherical vortex.

Although a spherical bubble shape is assumed for the simulation, the bubble surfaces are animated for rendering. As a bubble also represents a free surface, it likewise exhibits wave propagation once the surface is perturbed. This is important, e.g., when two bubbles merge. To achieve this effect, a sinusoidal offset is added along the direction of the bubble movement, with a frequency given by the bubble velocity and size. We make the assumption that larger and faster bubbles experience stronger perturbations from the surrounding fluid. When two bubbles merge, the frequency and amplitude of this displacement is also temporarily increased.

4.4. Limitations

As will be shown in Section 6, the approach described so far yields realistic simulations of bubbly flows, yet, it has some inherent limitations. Obviously, due to the coupling between velocity forces and bubble positions, inertia effects of the fluid cannot be really handled. Hence, interesting flow structures will only be visible around bubbles, and as long as bubbles are in the fluid. Without bubbles, only the SW simulation is left for the fluid volume, which cannot capture any three-dimensional flow effects. Moreover, the resulting velocity field is not divergence free. However, this should not be a problem for targeted applications such as computer games, as the overall mass conservation of the fluid volume is still guaranteed by our approach.

5. Simulating Foam

Foam structures on a fluid surface are caused by bubbles that exhibit delayed breaking due to surface tension effects. The surface tension also leads to the typical clustering of the foam bubbles among each other, and to hydrophilic walls. For the simulation of such a foam we use an SPH simulation with a surface tension algorithm and forces applied from the shallow water simulation.

5.1. Smoothed Particle Hydrodynamics

SPH algorithms numerically solve the Navier-Stokes equations with a Lagrangian approach. The volume of the fluid is represented by particles, and a spherical kernel function is used to evaluate macroscopic fluid quantities such as pressure and velocity. In the following, we use the SPH algorithm as described in [MKN*04]. Thus, a fluid property A is

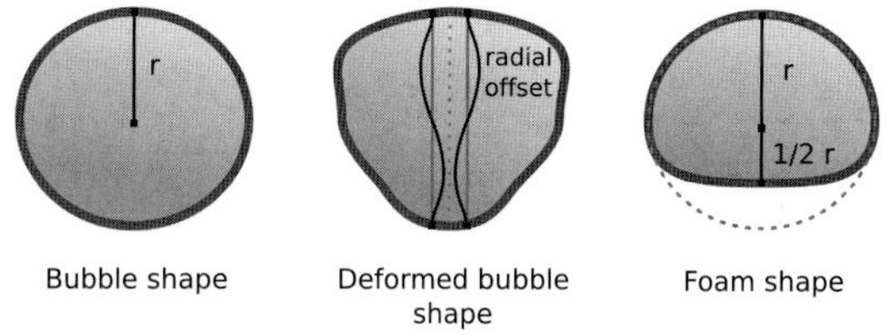

Figure 5: *The shape of a bubble beneath the surface to the left, and a foam bubble to the right.*

evaluated at a point $\mathbf{x}$ in space from the per particle properties A_i with

$$A(x) = \sum_i A_i v_i W(\mathbf{x} - \mathbf{x}_i, h) \; , \tag{13}$$

where the particle volume v_i is given by the initial sampling. These interpolations are used to compute pressure and viscosity forces acting upon the particles.

5.2. Foam Model

For the foam simulation, we do not represent the actual fluid in the thin sheets of a foam with the SPH simulation, but the overall volume of the foam. Each bubble in the foam is represented with an SPH particle. The surface tension in the SPH simulation, which acts on the scale of the SPH particles, is used to model the agglomeration of bubbles in a foam.

The particle size s_i of the SPH simulation is initialized with the average size of the bubbles that are generated within the bubble simulation of Section 4. We generate foam particles with a user defined probability p_f from bubbles. Instead of performing the wave initialization with Equation (10) for a bubble deletion, we initialize a foam particle at the position of the deleted bubble. Although the size of the SPH particles is fixed to s_i, each particles stores a virtual size r_i that is inherited from the original bubble. This size value is used for rendering of the foam, and generating the surface forces. For a typical water based foam, the foam bubbles on the surface are not spherical, but have a more hemispherical shape, as shown in Figure 5. Once a foam bubble is deleted (after a randomized life time), a surface wave is initialized as for a breaking bubble with Equation (10).

The typical clustering of foam bubbles is achieved by adding surface tension to the SPH simulation. The surface tension within SPH is computed by evaluating a color field function c_s on the particles to generate normals, as described in [MKN*04]. The divergence of these normals is used to compute the curvature and the resulting strength of the surface tension force:

$$\mathbf{f}_t = -\gamma_{st} \nabla^2 c_s \frac{\mathbf{n}}{|\mathbf{n}|} \; . \tag{14}$$

Here γ_{st} is the parameter to control the strength of the applied force. A detailed description of this approach for com-

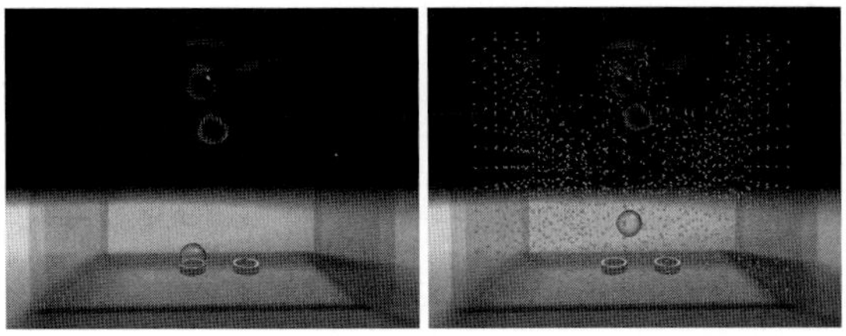

Figure 6: *Vortex interactions between two bubbles. The picture to the right shows the flow movement around the bubbles with marker particles.*

Table 1: *Simulation settings (SW simulation resolution, maximal number of bubble particles, maximal number of foam SPH particles) and performance measurements (lowest frame rate) for the different test cases.*

	SWS	Bubbles	Foam	FPS
Figure 7	40*x*66	81	133	161.2
Figure 8	50*x*50	142	131	144.1
Figure 11	50*x*80	501	466	34.3
Figure 12	50*x*80	654	1129	18.9

puting surface tension forces within an SPH simulation can be found in [MKN*04].

To make the foam float and spread out on the SW surface, we add forces along the gravity direction to each particle during the SPH update step. The force $\mathbf{f}_s$ for a SPH particle at position $\mathbf{x}_i$ is calculated to move the particle to the z-position of the SW height field during the next SPH update step:

$$\mathbf{f}_s = \frac{\mathbf{g}}{|\mathbf{g}|}\Big(H(\mathbf{x}) - (\mathbf{x}_z + \frac{r_i}{2})\Big)/\Delta t \qquad (15)$$

Note that these forces are not a hard constraint, but together with the SPH forces allow the particles to move into an equilibrium state between SW surface, SPH and surface tension forces.

6. Results

The following simulations were run on a standard PC with a Core 2 Duo CPU (2.4 GHz) and a Geforce 7900 GPU (with a single thread). Details of the different resolutions and settings can be found in Table 1. The frame rate measurements, which are minimum over the course of the simulation, include the rendering, which took on average 1/3 of the overall computation time.

A simple test case to demonstrate the interactions of two bubbles due to the spherical vortices can be seen in Figure 6. Varying the flow rate of the nozzles at the bottom can lead to very different flow behavior - from orderly rising bubbles, to chaotic interactions. A larger test case, with more than one hundred bubbles and more than thousand foam particles can be seen in Figure 7. Such a simulation runs with more than 18.9 frames per second, and exhibits a high amount of detail and interesting flow effects. In this case the computations are clearly dominated by the SPH simulation due to the high number of foam particles.

A different test case is shown in Figure 8, where a user controlled heated source is moved at the bottom of a basin of fluid, with a minimal frame rate of 144. Depending on the speed of the movement, the bubbles either quickly merge to larger ones, or rise as clusters of many small ones. Several other examples and variations of these test cases can be found in the accompanying animation.

7. Conclusions

We have presented an algorithm to perform simulations of bubbles and foam in real-time. The high performance of our approach is achieved by coupling a shallow water simulation to particle based bubble and foam simulations. A flow field with vortices is efficiently generated around the bubbles by the use of spherical vortices. Per particle forces from the SW simulation lead to the formation and clustering of foam within the SPH simulation. This makes complex scenes with several hundred bubble and foam particles possible, which still run with high frame rates on a standard PC.

As future work, we would like to enhance the shaders for rendering the foam. These could also compute the intersections of the foam bubbles, and generate fluid sheets between them, as suggested in [KVG02]. Another extension would be to handle thick layers of foam, by applying the forces from Equation (15) only to a layer of particles near the SW surface. Moreover, it would be possible to create a force field around hydrophilic objects in the fluid, to make the foam particles cluster around it.

The animation of the bubbles could be enhanced by allowing for stronger deformations of the spherical shapes to animate large or merging bubbles. Moreover, this could be used to select different shape regimes from [CGW78] for the simulation, e.g., leading to cap-shaped instead of spherical bubbles.

8. Acknowledgements

Thanks to AGEIA for funding this research. Moreover, thanks to Anders Stenberg, Hermes Lanker and Philipp Hatt for help with the implementation, as well as to Ronny Peikert and Mark Pauly for helpful comments.

References

[Ach90] ACHESON D. J.: *Elementary Fluid Dynamics*. Oxford University Press, 1990.

[AN05] ANGELIDIS A., NEYRET F.: Simulation of smoke based on vortex filament primitives. *SCA '05: Proceedings of the 2005 ACM SIGGRAPH/Eurographics symposium on Computer animation* (2005), 87–96.

Figure 7: *Several images from a larger bubble simulation.*

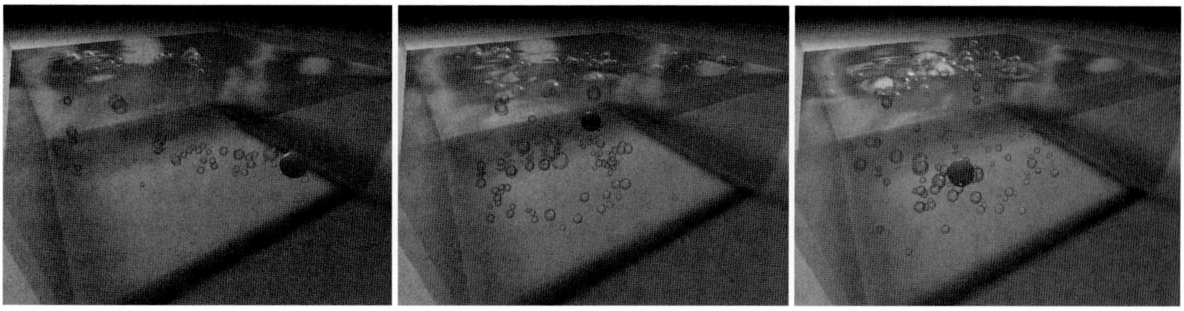

Figure 8: *A user interactively controls the heated source at the bottom of the basin to generate bubbles.*

[ANSN06] ANGELIDIS A., NEYRET F., SINGH K., NOWROUZEZAHRAI D.: A controllable, fast and stable basis for vortex based smoke simulation. *SCA '06: Proceedings of the 2006 ACM SIGGRAPH/Eurographics symposium on Computer animation* (2006), 25–32.

[Bat67] BATCHELOR G. K.: *An Introduction to Fluid Dynamics*. Cambridge Mathematical Library, 1967.

[BDR05] BUWA V. V., DEO D. S., RANADE V. V.: Eulerian-Lagrangian Simulations of Unsteady Gas-Liquid Flows in Bubble Columns. *Int. J. Multiphase Flow* (2005).

[Bri05] BRIDSON R.: Shallow water discretization, Lecture notes Animation Physics, 2005.

[CdVLHM97] CHEN J. X., DA VITORIA LOBO N., HUGHES C. E., MOSHELL J. M.: Real-time fluid simulation in a dynamic virtual environment. *IEEE Comput. Graph. Appl.* (1997).

[CGW78] CLIFT R., GRACE J. R., WEBER M. E.: *Bubbles, Drops and Particles*. Academic Press, London, 1978.

[FF01] FOSTER N., FEDKIW R.: Practical animation of liquids. In *Proc. of ACM SIGGRPAH* (2001), pp. 23–30.

[Ger04] GERSTNER F. V.: *Theory of waves*. Abhandlungen der Königlichen böhmischen Gesellschaft der Wissenschaften zu Prag, 1804.

[GH04] GREENWOOD S. T., HOUSE D. H.: Better with bubbles: enhancing the visual realism of simulated fluid. *SCA '04: Proceedings of the 2004 ACM SIGGRAPH/Eurographics symposium on Computer animation* (2004), 287–296.

[Hil94] HILL M. J. M.: On a spherical vortex. *Philos. Trans. Roy. Soc. London A 185* (1894), 213–245.

[HNC02] HINSINGER D., NEYRET F., CANI M.-P.: Interactive Animation of Ocean Waves. *Proc. of the 2002 ACM SIGGRAPH/Eurographics Symposium on Computer animation* (July 2002).

[IGLF06] IRVING G., GUENDELMAN E., LOSASSO F., FEDKIW R.: Efficient Simulation of Large Bodies of Water by Coupling Two and Three Dimensional Techniques. *ACM Trans. Graph. 25* (2006).

[KM90] KASS M., MILLER G.: Rapid, Stable Fluid Dynamics for Computer Graphics. *ACM Trans. Graph. 24*, 4 (1990), 49–55.

[KTH*05] KÖRNER C., THIES M., HOFMANN T., THÜREY N., RÜDE U.: Lattice Boltzmann Model for Free Surface Flow for Modeling Foaming. *Journal of Statistical Physics 121 [1-2]* (October 2005), 179–196.

[KVG02] KÜCK H., VOGELGSANG C., GREINER G.: Simulation and rendering of liquid foams. *Proc. Graphics Interface '02* (2002), 81–88.

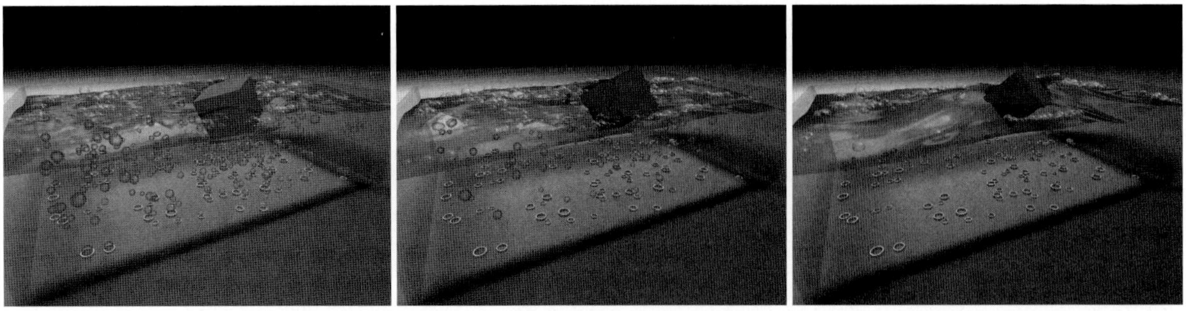

Figure 9: *A user interactively moves the obstacle, pushing away the foam and bubbles.*

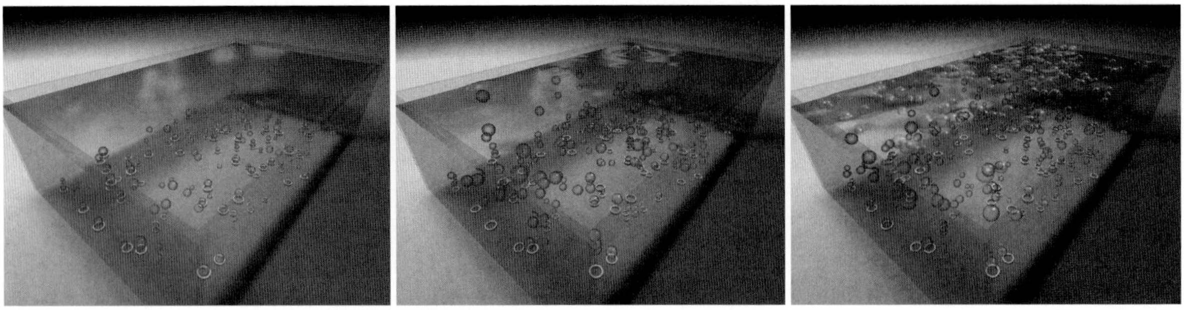

Figure 10: *Two images from a bubble and foam simulation generated with our approach. This simulation makes use of more than 650 interacting bubble particles, and more than 1100 foam SPH particles.*

[Lov03] LOVISCACH J.: Complex Water Effects at Interactive Frame Rates. *Journal of WSCG 11* (2003), 298–305.

[MCG03] MÜLLER M., CHARYPAR D., GROSS M.: Particle-based fluid simulation for interactive applications. *Proc. of the 2003 ACM SIGGRAPH/Eurographics Symposium on Computer animation* (2003), 154–159.

[MKN*04] MÜLLER M., KEISER R., NEALEN A., PAULY M., GROSS M., ALEXA M.: Point based animation of elastic, plastic and melting objects. In *Proc. of the 2004 ACM SIGGRAPH/EUROGRAPHICS Symposium on Computer Animation* (Aug 2004).

[Mon92] MONAGHAN J.: Smoothed particle hydrodynamics. *Annu. Rev. Astron. Phys. 30* (1992), 543–574.

[MSRG05] MÜLLER M., SOLENTHALER B., RICHARD, GROSS M.: Particle-based fluid-fluid interaction. *Proc. of the 2005 ACM Siggraph/Eurographics Symposium on Computer Animation* (2005).

[MUM*06] MIHALEF V., UNLUSU B., METAXAS D., SUSSMAN M., HUSSAINI M. Y.: Physics based boiling simulation. *Proceedings of the 2006 ACM SIGGRAPH/Eurographics Symposium on Computer animation* (2006), 317–324.

[OH95] O'BRIEN J. F., HODGINS J. K.: Dynamic simulation of splashing fluids. p. 198.

[Saf94] SAFFMAN P. G.: *Vortex Dynamics*. Cambridge Monographs on Mechanics, 1994.

[Sta99] STAM J.: Stable Fluids. *Proc. of ACM SIGGRAPH* (1999), 121–128.

[Tes04] TESSENDORF J.: Simulating Ocean Surfaces. *SIGGRAPH 2004 Course Notes 31* (2004).

[TRS06] THÜREY N., RÜDE U., STAMMINGER M.: Animation of Open Water Phenomena with coupled Shallow Water and Free Surface Simulations. *Proc. of the 2006 ACM SIGGRAPH/Eurographics Symposium on Computer Animation* (2006).

[ZYP06] ZHENG W., YONG J.-H., PAUL J.-C.: Simulation of bubbles. *SCA '06: Proceedings of the 2006 ACM SIGGRAPH/Eurographics symposium on Computer animation* (2006), 325–333.

Eurographics/ ACM SIGGRAPH Symposium on Computer Animation (2007)
D. Metaxas and J. Popovic (Editors)

Animation of Chemically Reactive Fluids Using a Hybrid Simulation Method

Byungkwon Kang Yoojin Jang Insung Ihm

Department of Computer Science, Sogang University, Korea

Abstract

Chemical phenomena abound in the real world, and often comprise indispensable elements of visual effects that are routinely created in the film industry. In this paper, we present a hybrid technique for simulating chemically reactive fluids, based on the theory of chemical kinetics. Our method makes synergistic use of both Eulerian grid-based methods and Lagrangian particle methods to simulate real and hypothetical chemical mechanisms effectively and efficiently. We demonstrate that by modeling chemical reactions using a particle system, an established, physically based fluid system can be extended easily to generate a wide range of chemical phenomena, ranging from catalysis and erosion to fire and explosions, with only a small additional cost.

Categories and Subject Descriptors (according to ACM CCS): I.3.7 [Computer Graphics]: Three-Dimensional Graphics and Realism – Animation; I.6.8 [Simulation and Modeling]: Type of Simulation – Animation

1. Introduction

1.1. Background and Our Contribution

Chemical phenomena are abundant in the real world, and often comprise important elements of various visual effects that are routinely created in the film industry. Catalysis, erosion, weathering, fire and flame, and explosion are only a few examples of chemical reactions.

When such natural phenomena are to be animated, chemically reactive fluids are one of the most easily applicable ways to depict a wide range of interesting chemical effects. In computational fluid dynamics, reacting fluids have generally been simulated by extending the Navier–Stokes equations to handle the relevant reaction mechanism [Chu02]. However, these general simulation models are often too complicated to be used directly in the generation of animation effects, although a few effective numerical methods have been studied using appropriate assumptions. For example, refer to [Fed97].

In the computer animation community, a simplified computational model was proposed for use in simulating reactive fluids [Gat02], where the behavior of the chemical species in the reaction process was modeled using a transport-reaction system coupled with a simple equation for the energy conservation. More recently, the theory of chemical kinetics was exploited in a simulation process to handle gases containing multiple reacting species [IKC04]. This method, extending the well-accepted fluid simulation model [FSJ01], has been shown to be very effective in generating various reaction phenomena by adopting real or hypothetical chemical mechanisms.

A problem with this simulation scheme [IKC04] is that its entire simulation pipeline is carried out purely on a grid base. In particular, an additional grid buffer must be allocated for each chemical species participating in the reaction mechanism to contain its molar concentration. This often entails an enormous demand for memory space if a complicated reaction mechanism involving many species is to be simulated, or a high resolution grid needs to be adopted for a detailed animation. In addition to the requirement for a large memory space, the additional computation time required for simulating chemical reactions increases cubically with respect to the grid resolution.

In this paper, we present a more effective numerical simulation method for animating chemically reactive fluids. In contrast to previous methods, we exploit a Lagrangian particle system to complement the Eulerian grid-based fluid simulation model. In particular, the computational efficiency is markedly enhanced by computing the chemical reaction step using a simple particle-based computation procedure. It is shown that only a moderate number of particles is required to numerically simulate a chemical reaction process without having to allocate a series of grid buffers holding the molar concentrations of all species.

Our hybrid method is simple to implement, and is flexible

Symposium on Computer Animation 2007, San Diego, CA, August 03-04, 2007.
© 2007 ACM 978-1-59593-624-4/07/0008 $5.00

enough to enable an animator to create a wide range of visual effects concerning chemical phenomena, ranging from catalysis and erosion to fire and explosions. We demonstrate the effectiveness of our hybrid method by generating several animation examples and analyze their computational performance.

1.2. Related Work

In the graphics community, little effort has been expended toward the general modeling of chemically reactive fluids, except for the results described in Ref. [Gat02, IKC04]. On the other hand, many computer graphics techniques can simulate natural phenomena that are directly or indirectly related to chemical processes. Several researchers have applied the concept of chemical reactions to the generation of natural phenomena, such as stone weathering effects [DEJ*99] and seashell patterns [FMP92]. It has also been shown that chemical mechanisms are effective in the synthesis of textures on arbitrary manifolds [Tur91, WK91].

While not involving the direct application of chemical kinetics, special effects in regard to reactive flows have been simulated frequently in computer animations. Ad hoc or physically motivated methods have been explored to simulate fire and flame in numerous studies [CMTM94, SF95, BPP01, NFJ02, LF02, WLMK02, LSF06]. Animating realistic explosions has also been a big challenge in computer animation, and diverse practical simulation schemes have been presented [NF99, MMA99, YOH00, BY01, FOA03, RNGF03, SRF05]. Recently, surface reactions between multiple interacting liquids were considered in a multiphase level set framework [LSSF06].

While grid-based methods prevail in physically based fluid animation, particle-based methods have also been explored. A set of particles were used to solve diffusion type equations that modeled gaseous phenomena, overcoming the memory overhead caused by grid-based schemes [SF95]. Since it was applied to the animation of viscous fluids [DG96], the Smoothed Particle Hydrodynamics method and other hybridized variants have been exploited in liquid animation [MCG03, MSKG05, PTB*03, ZB05, CBP05].

Lagrangian particles have often been explored as a means of complementing the Eulerian grid-based schemes. As well as being utilized to enhance the front-tracking process [FF01, EMF02, LSSF06], particles have been directly applied to the creation of fine details of liquids, such as droplets, splashes, and bubbles that are difficult to create with the purely grid-based solutions [Sim90, OH95, FF01, TFK*03, GH04, GSLF05, KCC*06].

In addition to liquids, particles have also been used in simulations of gaseous phenomena. A particle system was combined with a grid-based simulation method to provide a stable and effective animation of explosions, where suspended particles advected in the grid space were used to model the motion of particulate fuel and combustion products [FOA03]. Particles were also proven to be effective in generating large-scale explosions [RNGF03], while a purely particle-based method that employs flame and air particles was presented for the simulation of explosive flames [TOT*03]. Vorticity-carrying particles have also been utilized to create the turbulent appearance of fluids in both Eulerian and Lagrangian simulation schemes [AN05, PK05, SRF05].

2. Particles and Grids in Simulations

Our hybrid simulation scheme couples Lagrangian particle-based methods with Eulerian grid-based methods to effectively exploit the advantages of both schemes.

2.1. Grids

In our method, Eulerian grids were used to model fluids that carried chemical species, while Lagrangian particles were employed primarily to simulate reaction mechanisms. On these grids, only attributes such as the velocity, the density, the temperature, and the external force were defined. This contrasts with previous simulation methods [IKC04] that need to allocate as many grid buffers as the number of participating species. As will be shown later, separating the reaction computation from the entire simulation pipeline avoids an impractical demand on the memory required, which is often needed when dealing with a complicated reaction mechanism, or when a high-resolution simulation grid is desired. In addition, it speeds up the simulation process.

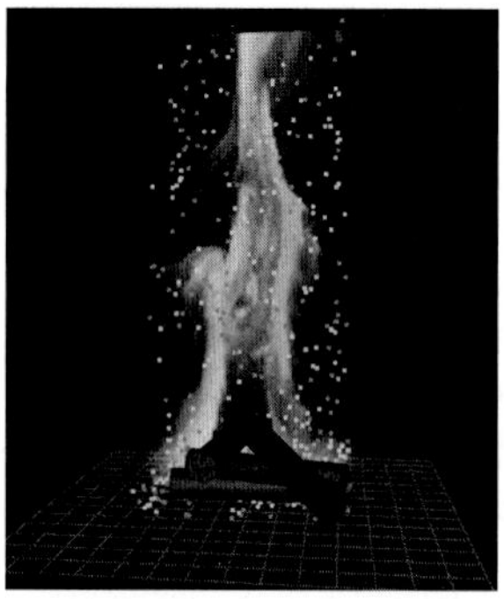

Figure 1: *Hybrid representation of a reaction mechanism, $S_1 + S_2 \xrightarrow{r_1} 2S_3$. This usually produces a very effective result when the species in the reaction mechanism are assigned different duties. In this example hypothetical reaction, applied for the purpose of generating the campfire scene shown in Figure 5(a), the reactants, S_1 and S_2, denoted by the green and yellow particles, respectively, have the role of triggering the reaction process. On the other hand, the resulting product, S_3, in volumetric density aims to represent the fluid to be visualized in the rendering stage.*

Our simulation scheme is different from another related method [FOA03] in that a hybrid representation of fluids (and chemical species) was possible. In the previous method, the fluid itself was modeled using particles, and basically rendered using a particle-rendering method. Our

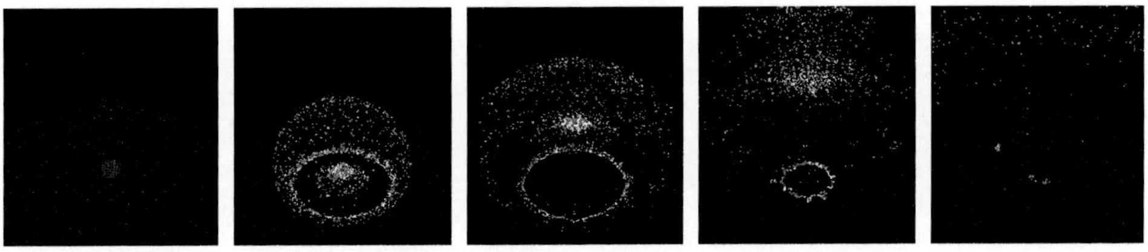

(a) Material and vortex particles

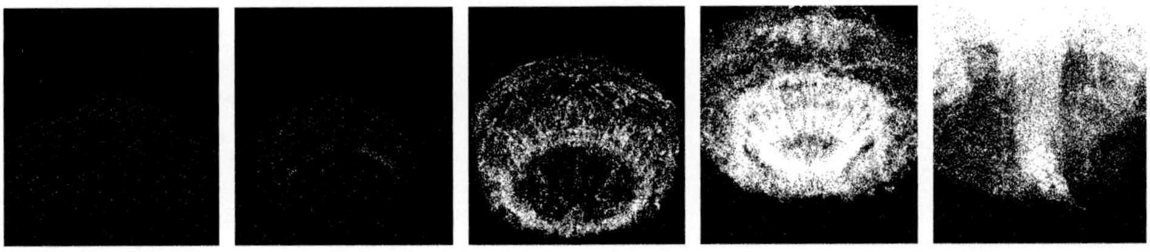

(b) Soot particles

Figure 2: *Particles used in the simulation. These images demonstrate how the three types of particles move around the space when the example scene shown in Figure 5(b) was simulated. In (a), the colored dots (i.e., the larger dots) represent material particles, while the white dots (i.e., the smaller dots) model vortex particles. On the other hand, soot particles are illustrated in (b). The material particles led the simulation process as the reaction mechanism, computed numerically using them, basically determined the overall behavior of the reactive fluids.*

method also allowed us to model the fluid to be rendered using particles, and provided another option where the chemical species could be partitioned into two classes, depending on their roles in the simulation. The *Lagrangian species* were those that were represented by particles throughout the simulation. Their function was to bring about a chemical reaction that affected the overall flow of the fluid. On the other hand, the *Eulerian species* were those species whose role was to model the fluid to be visualized in the rendering stage. Unlike the Lagrangian species, these are represented using a volumetric density field in the grid space. When chemical species of this class were produced as a consequence of the reaction, the increase in their molar concentration was converted to the equivalent amount in density, and was reflected in the density field. By adopting this hybrid scheme, we could exploit state-of-the-art volume-rendering techniques, creating fine-scale detail of simulated fluids while limiting the number of particles used in the simulation to a moderate size. See Figure 1.

2.2. Material, Soot and Vortex Particles

During a simulation, up to three types of particle can be involved (refer to Figure 2). First, *material particles*, which are mandatory, model the chemical species participating in the chemical reaction system. Each of these represents a single species, and is associated with a descriptor that consists of its position (3), velocity (3), and radius of influence (1), as well as its species indicator, S_i (1), and molar concentration, $[S_i]$ (1). The figure in parentheses indicates the number of data fields necessary for representing the corresponding attribute, where a one-byte unsigned character is adequate for S_i, while floating-point numbers must be used for the others.

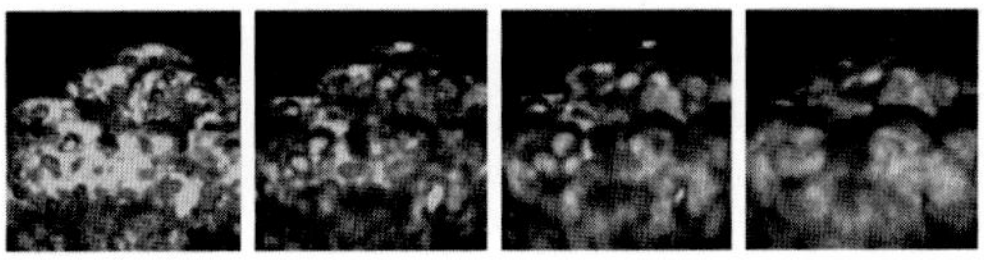

Figure 3: *Soot particles in rendering. In the rendering stage, the soot particles, if used, are converted to volumetric density data using a Gaussian smoothing kernel, which is then used to depict solid combustion products. Depending on their radii of influence, a wide range of appearances can be created in rendering.*

When the initial locations and molar concentrations of all the chemical species are described by an animator, the number of material particles to be placed in the reaction system is determined per chemical species, proportional to the given concentration. Then, these new particles are distributed in the specified areas in a jittered fashion. Once added, they react with the other reactants already in the reaction system. To ease the computational burden in handling the particle set, material particles whose concentrations fall below a threshold level during the reaction process are treated as being insignificant, and are eliminated immediately from the particle system.

The second class of particles, *soot particles*, have been shown to improve the rendering quality by depicting solid combustion products in a realistic manner [FOA03]. These are created, if needed, in each cell in the grid space whose temperature falls below a threshold temperature level (see Subsection 3.4.4 for details on how the soot particles are generated). Initially, each soot particle is assigned a short life span that decreases with increasing time. The soot particles diminish from the reaction system when their span expires. These are massless, and do not affect the reaction process. Each soot particle has a description that includes its position (3), remaining life span (1), and radius (1) that is used to decide its extent in the rendering stage. Notice that the soot particles are optional and ignored when an applied chemical reaction does not create any soot.

We also adopted optional *vortex particles* to create the detailed turbulent appearance of a fluid. As utilized successfully in previous methods, for example, [SRF05], these particles are intended to reintroduce small-scale details lost when the fluid is simulated using a semi-Lagrangian scheme. In our method, they are generated in each cell of the grid proportional to the intensity of the chemical reaction that occurred in the cell. The vortex particles can then affect the velocity field via the vorticity confinement force, as will be explained later. The description of a vortex particle consists of its position (3), direction (3), and radius (1).

3. Simulation Methods

For a consistent explanation of our method, we adopted the following hypothetical chain mechanism that involved six chemical species.

$$\left.\begin{array}{l} S_1 \xrightarrow{r_1} 2S_4, \;\; S_2 \xrightarrow{r_2} 2S_5, \;\; S_4+S_2 \xrightarrow{r_3} S_6+S_5 \\ S_5+S_1 \xrightarrow{r_4} S_6+S_4, \;\; S_1+S_2+S_6 \xrightarrow{r_5} S_6+5S_3 \end{array}\right\} \quad (1)$$

This artificial chain reaction mechanism, similar to a gas-phase hydrogen–oxygen explosion, is well suited to the modeling of very rapid reactions, such as explosions. Here, it is assumed that two highly combustible materials, S_1 and S_2, react instantaneously with each other with the help of intermediate materials, S_4, S_5, and S_6, to produce the remnant of reaction S_3, where the exponentially growing radicals, S_4 and S_5 trigger a very fast reaction (refer to Ref. [Lev02] for more detail). In this example mechanism, S_3 works as a Eulerian species, while the others are regarded as Lagrangian species.

3.1. Update of Fluid Velocity (Step 1)

The velocity, $\mathbf{u}$, of the fluid is updated in the grid space using the Euler equation. $\frac{\partial \mathbf{u}}{\partial t} = -(\mathbf{u}\cdot\nabla)\mathbf{u} - \frac{1}{\rho}\nabla p + \frac{\mathbf{f}}{\rho}$, where p, ρ and $\mathbf{f}$ denote the fluid pressure, the density, and the external force acting on the fluid, respectively. When an explosive fluid is to be simulated, it is important to be able to properly control the abrupt expansion or contraction of reacting fluids. As introduced in previous work [FOA03], and used later by an ensuing method [IKC04], we applied the modified divergence equation, $\nabla\cdot\mathbf{u} = \phi$, where the constraint, ϕ, controls the expansion or contraction of the fluid due to the chemical reaction. In our method, this is adjusted at each voxel in the final step of the simulation, reflecting the reaction that takes place in the corresponding cell region.

3.2. Advection of Fluid Density and Temperature (Step 2)

Once the velocity field is computed, the density, d, and the temperature, T, of the fluid are evolved through the updated velocity field using the advection–diffusion equations, $\frac{\partial d}{\partial t} = -(\mathbf{u}\cdot\nabla)d + \kappa_d\nabla^2 d$ and $\frac{\partial T}{\partial t} = -(\mathbf{u}\cdot\nabla)T + \kappa_T\nabla^2 T + H_T$, with diffusion coefficients, κ_d and κ_T. In the second equation, H_T denotes a heat source term that represents the increase or decrease in heat energy induced by the chemical reaction.

3.3. Advection of Particles (Step 3)

Once the first two Eulerian steps are complete, the particles in the reaction system are moved through the fluid. First, the massless soot and vortex particles are advected through the velocity field, $\mathbf{u}$, using a simple rule, $\mathbf{x}_P^{t+\Delta t} = \mathbf{x}_P^t + \mathbf{u}_{\mathbf{x}_P}^t\cdot\Delta t$, where the position, $\mathbf{x}_P$, of a particle, P, is modified using the trilinearly interpolated velocity, $\mathbf{u}_{\mathbf{x}_P}$.

The material particles, on the other hand, are treated differently, as they convey mass as well as their own velocity, $\mathbf{v}_P$. Once they are moved using $\mathbf{v}_P$, as $\mathbf{x}_P^{t+\Delta t} = \mathbf{x}_P^t + \mathbf{v}_P^t\cdot\Delta t$, their velocity is updated using the equation $\mathbf{v}_P^{t+\Delta t} = \mathbf{v}_P^t + \frac{\mathbf{f}_{\mathbf{x}_P}}{m_P}\cdot\Delta t$. Here, m_P denotes the mass of the particle, P, that can be expressed as the product of its molar concentration, $[S_i]$, and molar mass, M_{S_i}. The term, $\mathbf{f}_{\mathbf{x}_P}$, is another physical quantity that must be set properly as a driving force. The first choice for this parameter is the external force $\mathbf{f}$ that is trilinearly interpolated at $\mathbf{x}_P$. An alternative would be to use a function of the fluid's velocity that allows for easier control to introduce some interesting physical phenomena, for example, a drag force. In our implementation, we used a heuristic linear combination of the trilinearly interpolated fluid's velocity and external force for this driving force.

3.4. Application of Chemical Kinetics (Step 4)

The chemical reaction is now ready to take place. The key to an effective simulation of chemical kinetics is to discretize the reaction mechanism numerically. Unlike the method in Ref. [IKC04] that simulates a reaction at each voxel in the grid space, our method utilizes material particles to approximate the kinetics process.

3.4.1. A Quick Review on Chemical Kinetics

Chemical kinetics is a branch of kinetics that studies the mechanisms of chemical reactions, and describes the nonequilibrium states of fluid systems containing several reactive substances. Given the chemical reaction, $aA + bB \longrightarrow eE + fF$, where A, B, E, and F denote the chemical species, and a, b, e, and f are their stoichiometric coefficients, respectively, the reaction is described by the following differential equations:

$$r = -\frac{1}{a}\frac{d[A]}{dt} = -\frac{1}{b}\frac{d[B]}{dt} = \frac{1}{e}\frac{d[E]}{dt} = \frac{1}{f}\frac{d[F]}{dt},$$

where the rate of reaction, r, determines the change in molar concentration, $[\cdot]$ (in mol/L) of the reactants A and B, and the products E and F.

The rate of reaction is a time-dependent function, $r = f_r([A],[B],[E],[F],t)$ of the concentration of species present at a time, t. For a large class of chemical reactions, it is found experimentally to be proportional to the concentration of each reactant and/or product raised to a given power. For example, if only a forward reaction occurs, then it can be expressed in the form, $r = f_r([A],[B],t) = k[A]^{\alpha}[B]^{\beta}$, for orders α and β, where the rate constant, k, is a function of temperature and pressure. Usually, the constant depends strongly on the temperature, while the pressure dependence is usually ignored. From the viewpoint of fluid animation, the rate function may be treated as a control parameter that is determined by an animator. For more details on the theory of chemical kinetics, refer to a textbook on physical chemistry, for example, in Ref. [Lev02].

Recall the multistep mechanism given in Eq. (1), in which r_e $(e = 1,2,\cdots,5)$ denotes the rate of the eth reaction. Assuming that only a forward reaction takes place, then this chemical process is simulated by updating the molar concentrations of the six species in each time frame through a system of ordinary differential equations

$$\begin{aligned}
\frac{d[S_1]}{dt} &= -k_1[S_1]^{\sigma_1} - k_4[S_1]^{\sigma_1}[S_5]^{\sigma_5} \\
&\quad - k_5[S_1]^{\sigma_1}[S_2]^{\sigma_2}[S_6]^{\sigma_6} \\
\frac{d[S_2]}{dt} &= -k_2[S_2]^{\sigma_2} - k_3[S_2]^{\sigma_2}[S_4]^{\sigma_4} \\
&\quad - k_5[S_1]^{\sigma_1}[S_2]^{\sigma_2}[S_6]^{\sigma_6} \\
\frac{d[S_3]}{dt} &= 5k_5[S_1]^{\sigma_1}[S_2]^{\sigma_2}[S_6]^{\sigma_6} \\
\frac{d[S_4]}{dt} &= 2k_1[S_1]^{\sigma_1} - k_3[S_2]^{\sigma_2}[S_4]^{\sigma_4} + k_4[S_1]^{\sigma_1}[S_5]^{\sigma_5} \\
\frac{d[S_5]}{dt} &= 2k_2[S_2]^{\sigma_2} + k_3[S_2]^{\sigma_2}[S_4]^{\sigma_4} - k_4[S_1]^{\sigma_1}[S_5]^{\sigma_5} \\
\frac{d[S_6]}{dt} &= k_3[S_2]^{\sigma_2}[S_4]^{\sigma_4} + k_4[S_1]^{\sigma_1}[S_5]^{\sigma_5}.
\end{aligned}$$

3.4.2. Update of Molar Concentration

The first step to be taken in the chemical reaction step is to update the molar concentrations of the reacting species according to the applied reaction mechanism. This process proceeds by solving the corresponding system of ordinary differential equations numerically. The second-order (or third-order) Runge–Kutta method is usually sufficient for the time discretization. Spatially, on the other hand, a different numerical method must be applied, as the continuous molar concentration field has been discretized by material particles where particulate species of different types are intermingled.

To simulate the chemical process, we traversed the material particles in a random order while integrating the differential equations in the particle space. When a particle, P, at $\mathbf{x}_P$ is visited, then the particle system, organized in a dynamic kd-tree, is searched to locate neighboring material particles that exist in the spherical region defined by the center, $\mathbf{x}_P$, and radius, r_{sp}.

Suppose that n_P particles are found in the neighborhood. They can be viewed as locally approximate the molar concentration field around $\mathbf{x}_P$. To model the local reaction process, we first estimate the concentrations of all the reacting species at $\mathbf{x}_P$. An effective way of doing this is to collect the molar concentration from the neighboring material particles on a species-by-species basis

$$[S_s]_{\mathbf{x}_P} = \sum_{i=1}^{n_P} \delta_{s<P_i>} \cdot w_i(\mathbf{x}_P) \cdot [S_{<P_i>}]_{\mathbf{x}_{P_i}},\ 1 \le s \le 6,$$

where $< P_i >$ denotes the index of the species of the ith-found particle, P_i, and $\delta_{s<P_i>} = 1$ if $s = < P_i >$, or otherwise, zero. In this process, we applied a normalized Gaussian kernel, $w_i(\mathbf{x}) = \frac{1}{(2\pi)^{\frac{3}{2}} r_{sp}^3} e^{-\|\mathbf{x}-\mathbf{x}_i\|^2/2r_{sp}^2}$, to adjust the contribution from each local particle appropriately.

Once collected for all species, these are used to integrate the differential equation system for the time interval, Δt. As a result, we obtain the rate of reactions at $\mathbf{x}_P$ and more importantly the increment, $\Delta[S_s]_{\mathbf{x}_P}$, that indicates the changes in the reactive species resulting from their local chemical reaction. To reflect the reaction phenomena to the particle system, we return the changes to the local material particles by evaluating the following equation for all local particles, $1 \le i \le n_P$, and all species, $1 \le s \le 6$,

$$\begin{aligned}
[S_{<P_i>}]^{t+\Delta t} &= [S_{<P_i>}]^t \\
&\quad + \frac{\delta_{s<P_i>} \cdot w_i(\mathbf{x}_P)}{\sum_{j=1}^{n_P} \delta_{s<P_j>} \cdot w_j(\mathbf{x}_P)} \cdot \Delta[S_s]_{\mathbf{x}_P}.
\end{aligned}$$

During this return process, it may be possible that there are no, or very few, particles of a specific type in the local region that can increase in concentration. In this case, more particles are randomly created in the region so that they can carry a moderate amount of material, which avoids the creation of over-heavy material particles.

Our proposed method solves the system of differential equations on a particle basis through a sequential traversal of the material particles. We must make sure that this sequential visit does not add a serious bias to the solutions, because the reacting particles are interrelated, requiring the system to be integrated simultaneously. A simple and efficient method to prevent a possible bias is to subdivide the time interval, Δt, into n_s segments, and repeat the traversal process for the time interval, $\frac{\Delta t}{n_s}$, each time with a different random order.

Figure 4 shows simulation results generated using n_s = 1 and 5, for the explosion scene shown in Figure 5(b). The scene was designed to create a symmetrical shaped flame, although the randomized placement of material particles caused some asymmetry. Compared to the cases when a multistep integration was carried out (for instance, see figure (b)), a small bias was observed when no subdivision of the time intervals was carried out (figure (a)). However, the difference was very small, and was usually difficult to find even when a ten-step integration method was tested. Considering

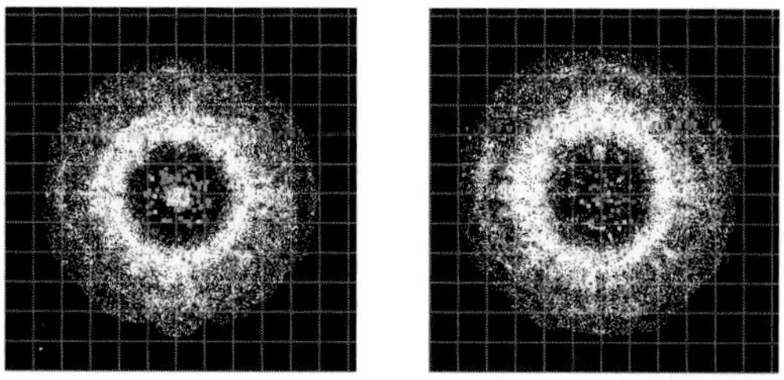

(a) 1-step integration (b) 5-step integration

Figure 4: *Particle-based simulation of a chemical reaction. The randomized traversal method offers a reliable space discretization scheme for particle-based integration of the differential equation system. The images contrast the particles produced when a five-step integration technique was applied (seen from the above, just after the explosion (the 10th frame) in the scene shown in Figure 5(b)). Even using a one-step integration, as illustrated in (a), the result shows only a slight bias for such a stiff reaction mechanism. In fact, the difference is quite small, and is usually difficult to find in animation results.*

that the tested scene involved a very stiff reaction mechanism, that is, an explosion, the bias introduced by the proposed sequential visit was small, even when no subdivision was applied, and was often unnoticeable in the rendering images.

Note that, when the scene was simulated using a one-step integration process, the chemical kinetics step (Step 4) took 0.52 seconds per frame on average, as shown in Table 1 in Section 4. Hence, the extra time for the multistep computation, if needed, had only a slight effect on the entire simulation time. In conclusion, the randomized traversal method, coupled with the Gaussian smoothing kernel, provides a reliable integration scheme for the simulation of chemical reactions.

3.4.3. Adjustment of Density and Temperature

In addition to the molar concentration, the chemical reaction process may affect other physical attributes of the reacting fluid. For example, when a Eulerian species is adopted in the simulation, its density must be updated too. In the example reaction mechanism where S_3 is the Eulerian species, $\Delta[S_3]_{\mathbf{x}_P}$, in molar concentration indicates how much has been created as a result of the reaction. In our method, we convert the added material with mass $M_{S_3} \cdot \Delta[S_3]_{\mathbf{x}_P}$ to the equivalent density, and distribute it to the nearby cells contained in the local spherical region. Considering the fact that density is mass divided by volume, we can update the density values at the neighboring voxel, (i, j, k), as:

$$d_{ijk}^{t+\Delta t} = d_{ijk}^{t} + \frac{\frac{w_{ijk}(\mathbf{x}_P)}{w_{total}} \cdot M_{S_3} \cdot \Delta[S_3]_{\mathbf{x}_P}}{V},$$

where V is the volume of cell in the grid space. As before, the distribution of material is weighted by the Gaussian kernel, in which $w_{ijk}(\mathbf{x}_P)$ represents the weight to voxel (i, j, k) with respect to the center of the sphere, and w_{total} is the total sum of all the weights involved. This update process is repeated for all Eulerian species if there are more than one present.

Furthermore, the voxel temperature, T_{ijk}, was also updated, if necessary, through the heat source term H_T in the temperature equation, as explained in the second step. In the all presented animations, we employed a linear control function, $H_T = f_r(r_1, r_2, \cdots, r_5)$ with respect to the reaction rates to define heat generated at the reacting particles, while a different type of control function may be used. The amount of heat produced at each material particle was then distributed to the surrounding voxels as $T_{ijk}^{t+\Delta t} = T_{ijk}^{t} + w_{ijk}(\mathbf{x}_P) \cdot (H_T)_{\mathbf{x}_P}$. By allowing such a user-defined function, the animator can control the flow of reacting fluid through the temperature-buoyancy force-velocity chain.

3.4.4. Generation of Soot and Vortex Particles

For a chemical reaction that generates soot, our simulation scheme enables us to handle soot particles. In previous research [FOA03], these were created when the soot mass had accumulated from sufficient fuel particles. In our method, they are produced when the temperature at a voxel falls below a threshold value after the temperature update process has been carried out. For this, the amount of density to be transformed into soot is first determined proportional to the magnitude of the decrease in temperature. Then, a proper number of soot particles is created and scattered randomly in the corresponding cell region. In addition to its position, each soot particle is assigned two attributes: a lifespan and a radius that decrease slowly with increasing time. These attributes are exploited in the rendering stage to represent soot that naturally fades away.

As well as the soot particles, vortex particles are also generated at this stage, with the aim of creating highly turbulent flows in the region of an intense reaction. In particular, to reflect a chemical reaction that actually takes place, we utilized the rates of reaction obtained at the material particles to control the magnitude of the vorticity. To create a vortex particle, the number of new particles, n_{vp}, was determined using a user-controllable function, $n_{vp} = f_{vort}(r_1, r_2, \cdots, r_5)$, again, linear to the reaction rates in our examples, for each material particle with a high rate of reaction. Then, this number of vortex particles was scattered in the spherical region around the material particles with an initial vorticity vector, ω_{vp}, that was based on the gradient field of the rates of reaction. In the case of our example mechanism, we used r_5 as the rate of reaction that produces the Eulerian species, S_3, so that $\omega_{vp} = c_{vort} \cdot \frac{\nabla r_5}{||\nabla r_5||}$, where c_{vort} is a parameter that controls the overall strength of vorticity. After generated, the soot and vortex particles move through the velocity field as massless particles.

Once all these computations were complete, the molar concentration and lifespan attributes of the material and soot particles, respectively, were examined, deleting those that showed insignificant differences from the particle system.

3.5. Update of External Force and Divergence Constraint (Step 5)

A chemical reaction occurring in the simulation domain altered the flow of a fluid. In our model, the reaction process at a material particle modified the external force and the divergence constraint through the rate of reaction that, in turn, affected the computation of the velocity field in the ensuing time frame. The external force, $\mathbf{f} = \mathbf{f}_{buoy} + \mathbf{f}_{vort}$, was defined as the sum of the buoyancy force, $\mathbf{f}_{buoy}$, and the vorticity force, $\mathbf{f}_{vort}$, possibly using another user-controlled force term [FM97, FSJ01, IKC04]. The new density, d, and temperature, T, updated in the previous stages, were reflected in the calculation of $\mathbf{f}_{buoy}$, as $\mathbf{f}_{buoy} = -\alpha d\mathbf{z} + \beta(T - T_{amb})\mathbf{z}$, where $\mathbf{z}$ and T_{amb} are the direction opposite to the force of gravity and the ambient temperature, respectively.

The vorticity force, $\mathbf{f}_{vort}$, was also updated at each voxel from the set of vortex particles. For each vortex particle, the Gaussian kernel was applied in a similar manner as before to accumulate the smoothed vorticity force onto its surrounding voxels. Finally, the divergence constraint, ϕ, was set to adjust the method of expansion or contraction of the reacting gaseous fluid using yet another linear control function, $\phi = f_\phi(r_1, r_2, \cdots, r_5)$, of the rates of reaction.

4. Experimental Results

To show its effectiveness, we implemented our method and tested it using several example scenarios. Figure 5 shows some animations generated using the presented hybrid method and visualized by a photon-mapping based ray tracer, capable of rendering both density and particle data.

Table 1 summarizes the statistics collected on a desktop PC with a 3.2 GHz Intel Pentium 4 CPU and 2 GB RAM for the three test scenes illustrated in Figure 5(a) to (c). The first scene shows a campfire scene generated using very simple chemical kinetics, $S_1 + S_2 \xrightarrow{r_1} 2S_3$, where the fuel was continuously fed through two Lagrangian species, S_1 and S_2, and the flame was represented by a Eulerian species, S_3. On the other hand, the other two explosion scenes were created using the chain reaction mechanism given in Eq. (1), in which the Lagrangian chemical explosives, S_1 and S_2, reacted with each other to explode instantly, producing the Eulerian smoke, S_3.

As can be seen in the step-by-step dissection of the simulation times, the additional cost ('Step3' and 'Step4'), required to extend the established fluid simulation model [FSJ01] to include the chemical kinetics, was very low. Mostly, the first two grid-based steps ('Step1' and 'Step2') for solving the Navier–Stokes equations and advecting the density and temperature dominated the computation time (refer to Table 2 to see how the timings for these two steps depended on the grid resolution). This table also shows that chemical reaction phenomena may be simulated effectively using a moderate number of particles. Only a couple of thousand material particles were needed to trigger the hypothetical chemical reaction to create a natural flame in the campfire scene (Table 1(a)). For the two explosion scenes, the average number of material particles was much less than the maximum number, because most of these burnt out in an instant in the first few frames after ignition (Table 1(b) and (c)).

As implied by the test data, when soot particles were used they usually dominated the particle use. Our method was able to adjust the size of the soot particle set. In the first explosion scene (Table 1(b)), we intended to produce a large enough number of soot particles to depict a detailed and somewhat grainy soot appearance. On the other hand, we controlled the soot parameter to limit the generation of soot particles in the next scene (Table 1(c)) in an attempt to obtain a different rendering appearance. Although we may not be able to directly compare the simulation statistics from previous methods, for example, [FOA03], it is clear that our method utilizes particles quite efficiently in the simulation of chemically reacting fluids.

Table 2 compares our hybrid technique with a previous grid-based method [IKC04]. The scenario used to produce the explosion scene in Figure 5(b), was tested using four different grid resolutions. As revealed in the first table (Table 2(a)), the previous method ('Grid-only method') consumed about twice the memory of our method ('Hybrid method') for the example chain mechanism that employed six chemical species. This is because the former method needs to allocate six additional copies of the grid buffer to hold the respective molar concentrations. On the other hand, our hybrid technique replaces this memory burden by a moderate number of particles (refer to the table in Table 2(b) to see how the numbers of employed particles vary as the resolution increases).

From a temporal aspect, our method also markedly outperformed the previous method that relies on grids only, as revealed in Table 2(c). Recall that the chemical reaction was applied in the grid-based third step ('Step3') in the previous method, while the same task was carried out in the particle-based third and fourth steps ('Step3' and 'Step4') in our method, as explained in Subsection 3.3 and 3.4. Obviously, the differences in timing mainly arose from the chemical reaction steps. As indicated by the table, the particle-based simulation was less dependent on the grid resolution, which allows for easier simulations on higher-resolution grids.

Finally, Figure 5(d) to (g) illustrate an extra set of animation scenes created using the presented method. Scene (d) used seven chemical species in total in such a way that the three different types of gases exploded only when the blue gas met the other gases. On the other hand, scene (e) demonstrates an example where 11 species were intermingled. The last two scenes in figure (f) and (g) show examples where catalytic agents scattered on the surfaces reacted with other reactants to create the interesting animations.

5. Conclusion

In summary, we have presented a hybrid simulation method that is suitable for modeling chemically reactive fluids based on the theory of chemical kinetics. It was built to take advantage of both Eulerian and Lagrangian frameworks. By

(a) Campfire scene (grid resolution: $160 \times 160 \times 180$)

	Simulation time per frame (seconds)					Number of particles per frame		
	Step1	Step2	**Step3**	**Step4**	Step5	Material	Soot	Vortex
Mean	145.01	136.26	0.03	1.35	1.93	2,026	0	55
Max	145.86	137.20	0.05	1.58	2.06	2,378	0	94

(b) Explosion scene 1 (grid resolution: $160 \times 160 \times 200$)

	Simulation time per frame (seconds)					Number of particles per frame		
	Step1	Step2	**Step3**	**Step4**	Step5	Material	Soot	Vortex
Mean	163.66	151.64	4.45	0.52	3.31	119	176,594	584
Max	164.27	152.23	10.08	13.02	4.00	3,999	400,162	886

(c) Explosion scene 2 (grid resolution: $220 \times 200 \times 160$)

	Simulation time per frame (seconds)					Number of particles per frame		
	Step1	Step2	**Step3**	**Step4**	Step5	Material	Soot	Vortex
Mean	224.29	207.17	0.22	0.44	10.96	116	7,487	636
Max	225.75	208.48	0.50	6.31	14.84	2,998	17,887	717

Table 1: *Simulation Statistics. The running times and particles used in our method were measured for three scenarios illustrated in the first three images of Figure 5. The statistics, given as both average and worst case numbers, reveals that the third and fourth steps ('Step3' and 'Step4'), added to extend the established fluid simulation method [FSJ01] for handling reactive fluids, comprised only a small portion of the entire simulation time. Furthermore, the test results also imply that only a moderate number of particles, in particular, material particles, is enough to simulate the chemical reaction mechanism in a natural manner.*

adding a particle-based simulator to a well-accepted grid-based Navier–Stokes equation solver, we effectively animated a wide range of chemical phenomena, including catalysis, erosion, fire and flame, and explosions. From tests on various example scenarios, we found that real or hypothetical chemical reaction mechanisms allowed us to generate natural and interesting animation effects easily employing user-defined control parameters.

Acknowledgements. This research was supported by the Ministry of Information and Communication of Korea under the IT Research Center support program.

References

[AN05] ANGELIDIS A., NEYRET F.: Simulation of smoke based on vortex filament primitives. In *Proc. of ACM SIGGRAPH/Eurographics Symposium on Computer Animation* (2005), pp. 87–96.

[BPP01] BEAUDOIN P., PAQUET S., POULIN P.: Realistic and controllable fire simulation. In *Proc. of Graphics Interface 2001* (2001), pp. 159–166.

[BY01] BASHFORTH B., YANG Y.-H.: Physics-based explosion modeling. *Graphical Models 63*, 1 (2001), 21–44.

[CBP05] CLAVET S., BEAUDOIN P., POULIN P.: Particle-based viscoelastic fluid simulation. In *Proc. of ACM SIGGRAPH/Eurographics on Computer Animation 2005* (2005), pp. 219–228.

[Chu02] CHUNG T.: *Computational Fluid Dynamics*. Cambridge University Press, ISBN 0-521-59416-2, 2002.

[CMTM94] CHIBA N., MURAOKA K., TAKAHASHI H., MIURA M.: Two dimensional visual simulation of flames, smoke and the spread of fire. *Journal of Visualization and Computer Animation 5*, 1 (1994), 37–53.

[DEJ*99] DORSEY J., EDELMAN A., JENSEN H., LEGAKIS J., PEDERSEN H.: Modeling and rendering of weathered stone. In *Proc. of ACM SIGGRAPH 1999* (1999), pp. 225–234.

[DG96] DESBRUN M., GASCUEL M.-P.: Smoothed particles: a new paradigm for animating highly deformable bodies. In *Proc. of the Eurographics Workshop on Computer Animation and Simulation 1996* (1996), pp. 61–76.

[EMF02] ENRIGHT D., MARSCHNER S., FEDKIW R.: Animation and rendering of complex water surfaces. *ACM Transactions on Graphics (ACM SIGGRAPH 2002) 21*, 3 (2002), 736–744.

[Fed97] FEDKIW R.: *A Survey of Chemically Reacting, Compressible Flows*. PhD thesis, Dept. of Mathematics, Univ. of California, Los Angeles, 1997.

[FF01] FOSTER N., FEDKIW R.: Practical animation of liquids. In *Proc. of ACM SIGGRAPH 2001* (2001), pp. 23–30.

[FM97] FOSTER N., METAXAS D.: Modeling the motion of a hot, turbulent gas. In *Proc. of ACM SIGGRAPH 1997* (1997), pp. 181–188.

[FMP92] FOWLER D., MEINHARDT H., PRUSINKIEWICZ P.: Modeling seashells. In *Proc. of ACM SIGGRAPH 1992* (1992), pp. 379–387.

[FOA03] FELDMAN B., O'BRIEN J., ARIKAN O.: Animating suspended particle explosions. *ACM Transactions on Graphics (ACM SIGGRAPH 2003) 22*, 3 (2003), 708–715.

[FSJ01] FEDKIW R., STAM J., JENSEN H.: Visual simulation of smoke. In *Proc. of ACM SIGGRAPH 2001* (2001), pp. 23–30.

[Gat02] GATES W.: *Animation of Reactive Fluids*. PhD thesis, Dept. of Computer Science, The Univ. of British Columbia, 2002.

[GH04] GREENWOOD S. T., HOUSE D. H.: Better with bubbles: enhancing the visual realism of simulated fluid. In *Proc. of ACM SIGGRAPH/Eurographics on Computer Animation 2004* (2004), pp. 287–296.

[GSLF05] GUENDELMAN E., SELLE A., LOSASSO F., FEDKIW R.: Coupling water and smoke to thin deformable and rigid shells. *ACM Transactions on Graphics (ACM SIGGRAPH 2005) 24*, 3 (2005), 973–981.

[IKC04] IHM I., KANG B., CHA D.: Animation of reactive gaseous fluids through chemical kinetics. In *Proc. of ACM SIGGRAPH/Eurographics Symposium on Computer Animation 2004* (2004), pp. 203–212.

[KCC*06] KIM K., CHA D., CHANG B., KOO B., IHM I.: Practical animation of turbulent splashing water. In *Proc. of ACM SIGGRAPH/Eurographics Symposium on Computer Animation 2006* (2006), pp. 335–344.

[Lev02] LEVINE I.: *Physical Chemistry*, 5th ed. McGraw-Hill, ISBN 0-07-253495-8, 2002.

[LF02] LAMORLETTE A., FOSTER N.: Structural modeling of flames for a production environment. *ACM Transactions on Graphics (ACM SIGGRAPH 2002) 21*, 3 (2002), 729–735.

[LSF06] LOSASSO F., SELLE T., FEDKIW R.: Multiple interacting liquids. *ACM Transactions on Graphics (ACM SIGGRAPH 2006) 25*, 3 (2006), 812–819.

[LSSF06] LOSASSO F., SHINAR T., SELLE A., FEDKIW R.: Multiple interacting liquids. *ACM Transactions on Graphics (ACM SIGGRAPH 2006) 25*, 3 (2006), 812–819.

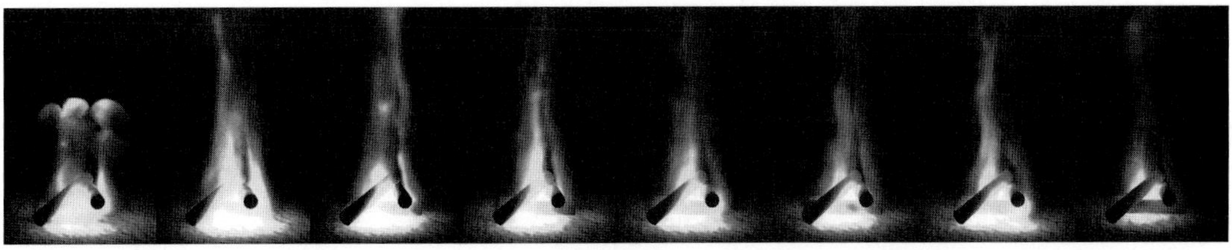

(a) Campfire scene

(b) Explosion scene 1

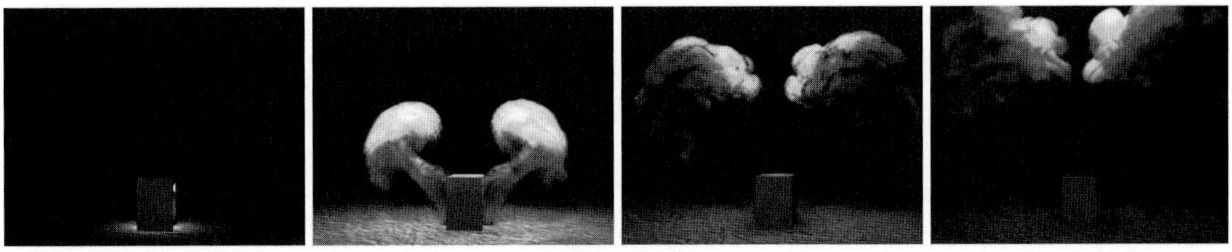

(c) Explosion scene 2

(d) Explosion scene 3

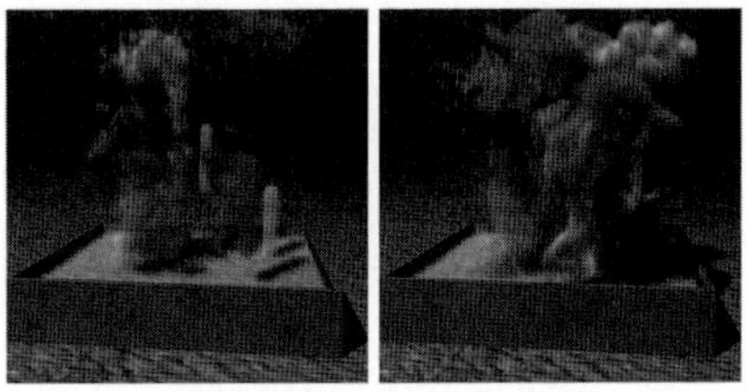

(e) Eleven species scene

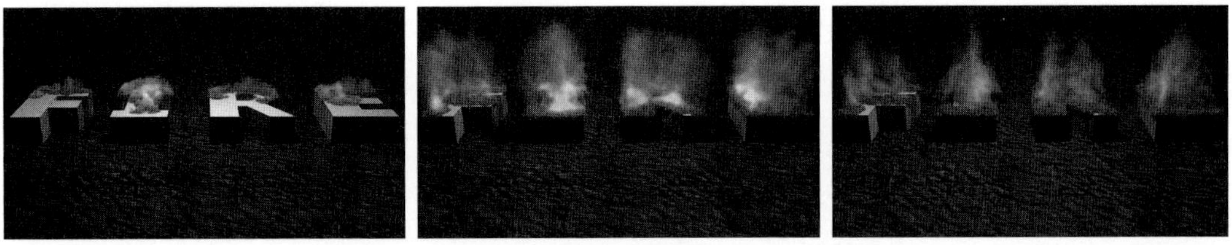

(f) Catalysis scene 1

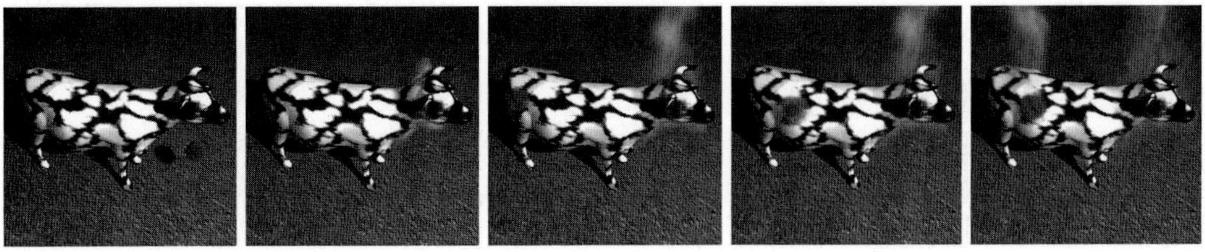

(g) Catalysis scene 2

Figure 5: *Example animation scenes.*

(a) Memory use per frame (MBytes)

	Grid resolution							
	80 × 80 × 80		120 × 120 × 120		160 × 160 × 160		240 × 240 × 240	
	Mean	Max	Mean	Max	Mean	Max	Mean	Max
Grid-only method	78.16	78.16	263.67	263.67	625.00	625.00	(2,109.37)	(2,109.37)
Hybrid method	39.14	40.25	131.89	135.02	312.57	318.94	1,054.83	1,056.08

(b) Number of used particles per frame

	Grid resolution							
	80 × 80 × 80		120 × 120 × 120		160 × 160 × 160		240 × 240 × 240	
	Mean	Max	Mean	Max	Mean	Max	Mean	Max
Material	415	3,999	413	3,997	412	3,998	418	3,998
Vortex	942	1,047	1,055	1,172	1,082	1,206	1,024	1,601
Soot	71,554	191,015	81,652	214,923	109,202	309,046	131,638	373,537

(c) Simulation time per frame (seconds)

		Grid-only method					Hybrid method					
		Step1	Step2	**Step3**	Step4	Total	Step1	Step2	**Step3**	**Step4**	Step5	Total
80^3	Mean	13.61	13.65	23.91	0.17	51.34	13.40	13.00	0.27	0.08	0.74	27.49
	Max	13.80	13.81	32.59	0.20	60.40	13.59	13.31	0.58	5.64	0.78	32.89
120^3	Mean	49.61	48.70	127.36	0.56	226.23	50.42	46.85	0.81	1.10	2.06	101.24
	Max	49.88	48.83	160.55	0.64	259.90	50.78	47.34	2.09	9.42	2.27	108.42
160^3	Mean	121.33	119.86	213.22	1.27	455.68	119.73	114.78	1.59	1.89	4.96	242.95
	Max	121.92	120.42	324.16	1.41	567.91	121.09	116.48	4.42	15.94	5.42	254.89
240^3	Mean	–	–	–	–	–	283.24	234.32	2.60	3.18	18.22	541.56
	Max	–	–	–	–	–	287.44	237.89	7.58	26.16	20.17	561.95

Table 2: *Performance comparison with a previous method. For the example scenario shown in Figure 5(b), our method ('Hybrid method') is compared to the previous method ('Grid-only method') [IKC04] with respect to various grid resolutions. In the grid-only method, the chemical reaction was applied in the grid-based third stage ('Step3'), while in the hybrid method, the corresponding task was carried out in the particle-based third and fourth stages ('Step3' and 'Step4'). In both spatial and temporal respects, our hybrid technique markedly outperformed the previous method that carried out all computations on the Eulerian grids. Omitted timings were unavailable because our PC with 2 GB of RAM was unable to allocate enough memory space (the estimated memory requirement is given in the first table).*

[MCG03] MÜLLER M., CHARYPAR D., GROSS M.: Particle-based fluid simulation for interactive applications. In *Proc. of ACM SIGGRAPH/Eurographics Symposium on Computer Animation 2003* (2003), pp. 154–372.

[MMA99] MAZARAK O., MARTINS C., AMANATIDES J.: Animating exploding objects. In *Proc. of Graphics Interface 1999* (1999), pp. 211–218.

[MSKG05] MÜLLER M., SOLENTHALER B., KEISER R., GROSS M.: Particle-based fluid-fluid interaction. In *Proc. of ACM SIGGRAPH/Eurographics on Computer Animation 2005* (2005), pp. 237–244.

[NF99] NEFF M., FIUME E.: A visual model for blast waves and fracture. In *Proc. of Graphics Interface 1999* (1999), pp. 193–202.

[NFJ02] NGUYEN D., FEDKIW R., JENSEN H.: Physically based modeling and animation of fire. *ACM Transactions on Graphics (ACM SIGGRAPH 2002) 21*, 3 (2002), 721–728.

[OH95] O'BRIEN J., HODGINS J.: Dynamic simulation of splashing fluids. In *Proc. of Computer Animation 1995* (1995), pp. 198–206.

[PK05] PARK S., KIM M.: Vortex fluid for gaseous phenomena. In *Proc. of ACM SIGGRAPH/Eurographics Symposium on Computer Animation* (2005), pp. 261–270.

[PTB*03] PREMOŽE S., TASDIZEN T., BIGLER J., LEFOHN A., WHITAKER R. T.: Particle-based simulation of fluids. *Computer Graphics Forum (Eurographics 2003) 22*, 3 (2003), 401–410.

[RNGF03] RASMUSSEN N., NGUYEN D., GEIGER W., FEDKIW R.: Smoke simulation for large scale phenomena. *ACM Transactions on Graphics (ACM SIGGRAPH 2003) 22*, 3 (2003), 703–707.

[SF95] STAM J., FIUME E.: Depicting fire and other gaseous phenomena using diffusion processes. In *Proc. of ACM SIGGRAPH 1995* (1995), pp. 129–136.

[Sim90] SIMS K.: Particle animation and rendering using data parallel computation. In *Proc. of ACM SIGGRAPH 1990* (1990), pp. 405–413.

[SRF05] SELLE A., RASMUSSEN N., FEDKIW R.: A vortex particle method for smoke, water and explosions. *ACM Transactions on Graphics (ACM SIGGRAPH 2005) 24*, 3 (2005), 910–914.

[TFK*03] TAKAHASHI T., FUJII H., KUNIMATSU A., HIWADA K., SAITO T., TANAKA K., UEKI H.: Realistic animation of fluid with splash and foam. *Computer Graphics Forum (Eurographics 2003) 22*, 3 (2003), 391–400.

[TOT*03] TAKESHITA D., OTA S., TAMURA M., FUJIMOTO T., MURAOKA K., CHIBA N.: Particle-based visual simulation of explosive flames. In *Proc. of the 11th Pacific Conference on Computer Graphics and Applications* (2003), pp. 482–486.

[Tur91] TURK G.: Generating textures on arbitrary surfaces using reaction-diffusion. In *Proc. of ACM SIGGRAPH 1991* (1991), pp. 289–298.

[WK91] WITKIN A., KASS M.: Reaction-diffusion textures. In *Proc. of ACM SIGGRAPH 1991* (1991), pp. 299–308.

[WLMK02] WEI X., LI W., MUELLER K., KAUFMAN A.: Simulating fire with texture splats. In *Proc. of IEEE Visualization 2002* (2002), pp. 227–234.

[YOH00] YNGVE G., O'BRIEN J., HODGINS J.: Animating explosions. In *Proc. of ACM SIGGRAPH 2000* (2000), pp. 29–36.

[ZB05] ZHU Y., BRIDSON R.: Animating sand as a fluid. *ACM Transactions on Graphics (ACM SIGGRAPH 2005) 24*, 3 (2005), 965–972.

Eurographics/ ACM SIGGRAPH Symposium on Computer Animation (2007)
D. Metaxas and J. Popovic (Editors)

Weakly compressible SPH for free surface flows

Markus Becker Matthias Teschner

University of Freiburg

Abstract

We present a weakly compressible form of the Smoothed Particle Hydrodynamics method (SPH) for fluid flow based on the Tait equation. In contrast to commonly employed projection approaches that strictly enforce incompressibility, time-consuming solvers for the Poisson equation are avoided by allowing for small, user-defined density fluctuations. We also discuss an improved surface tension model that is particularly appropriate for single-phase free-surface flows. The proposed model is compared to existing models and experiments illustrate the accuracy of the approach for free surface flows. Combining the proposed methods, volume-preserving low-viscosity liquids can be efficiently simulated using SPH. The approach is appropriate for medium-scale and small-scale phenomena. Effects such as splashing and breaking waves are naturally handled.

Categories and Subject Descriptors (according to ACM CCS): I.3.3 [Computer Graphics]: Three-Dimensional Graphics and Realism: Animation

Keywords: Physically-based simulation, Fluid dynamics, Smoothed Particle Hydrodynamics, Tait equation, volume preservation, surface tension

1. Introduction

Simulating turbulent liquids with breaking waves and splashes is among the most desired features in fluid animation. Lagrangian methods such as SPH are a promising way to capture such properties.

Particle-based approaches have been introduced by Miller and Pearcy [MP89]. While this early method is based on simple particle-particle forces, Stam and Fiume [SF95] have been the first to apply SPH in the simulation of gas and fire phenomena. Similarly, Takeshita et al. [TOT*03] have used particle methods for explosive flames. In addition to these compressible phenomena, SPH has also been used for the simulation of liquids [MCG03, KAG*05].

These approaches employ the ideal gas equation to relate pressure and density. This results in high compressibility and oscillations which is – in contrast to gases – undesired and visually displeasing. Enforcing incompressibility for particle methods is a challenging problem. Cummins and Rudman [CR99] propose a projection method for Lagrangian methods that is also used in Eulerian approaches. Similarly, Premoze et al. [PTB*03] have realized incompressibility for the Moving Particles Semi-implicit method (MPS). In this approach, a velocity estimate is projected onto a divergence free sub space based on a pressure correction. Therefore, the Poisson equation has to be solved. Although large time steps can be handled, the conjugate gradient solver used to solve the Poisson equation is time-consuming for large systems. Premoze notes 3 min for 100k particles, while compressible SPH implementations can process similar complexities in 5-10 s per time step.

In our SPH simulation, we propose to use the Tait equation with a high speed of sound, which results in a weakly compressible formulation with very low density fluctuations [Mon94]. The method avoids implausible simulation results due to compressibility as previously reported for SPH [KAG*05, BFMF06]. Although the approach requires smaller time steps compared to the Poisson method, the computation per time step is significantly faster and the implementation easily fits into the SPH framework. The computation time of the weakly compressible form corresponds to the time that is required for the compressible form based on the ideal gas equation.

In addition to volume preservation, surface tension plays an important role in realistic fluid animations. Since the handling of small details is mainly governed by surface tension, it is commonly considered in Lagrangian approaches

Symposium on Computer Animation 2007, San Diego, CA, August 03-04, 2007.
© 2007 ACM 978-1-59593-624-4/07/0008 $5.00

for free surface fluids, e. g. [KAG*05, MCG03]. However, these methods have been originally designed for multi phase flows [Mor99, HA06]. While not assessable in highly dynamic settings, they cannot handle large curvatures correctly. This is due to the fact, that particles have too few neighbors in those regions. Further, [Mor99] requires to calculate the second derivative of a color field which is very sensitive to particle disorder and thus not adequate for turbulent settings.

We propose a surface tension model based on cohesion forces. The model is particularly appropriate for single-phase flows, but can also handle multiple phases. The computation of derivatives is avoided which improves the efficiency and the stability of the approach.

2. Related work

Inspired by early procedural approaches of Max [Max81] and Peachy [Pea86], fluid simulation in computer graphics is mainly comprised of Eulerian and Lagrangian approaches. In general, Eulerian approaches exhibit a number of useful features. To name just a few, computations are performed on a stationary grid and the time-consuming search for neighbors – as required in Lagrangian approaches – is avoided. Further, inflow and outflow can easily be handled by setting the appropriate boundary conditions.

In [KM90], Kass and Miller present a height-field model based on a linearization of the shallow water equation. In [FM96], Foster and Metaxas introduce a finite-difference solution for the full set of Navier-Stokes equations in three dimensions. A 2D height field and surface marker particles are used to track the free surface and a one-way coupling of the fluid and rigid objects is realized. In [FM97], the 2D marker particle method is extended to 3D and a locally adaptive damping method is presented to improve the stability. An unconditionally stable solver for the incompressible Navier-Stokes equations in 3D is presented by Stam [Sta99]. Foster and Fedkiw augment the method for liquids [FF01] using an improved surface tracking by combining level sets and surface marker particles to alleviate mass dissipation. This is known as the particle level set method [EFFM02]. Elcott et al. [ETK*07] provide a thorough overview of further extensions of [Sta99]. They use the same semi-Langragian advection strategy, but present a circulation-preserving integration scheme.

Other authors have introduced extensions to handle multi phase flow involving two or more fluids [LSSF06], two-way coupling with moving rigid solids [CMT04], deformable solids [CGFO06], and local refinement [LGF04]. O'Brien and Hodgins [OH95] enhance grid-based approaches by using a particle system to model droplets and Mihalef et al. [MMS04] address breaking waves for Eulerian fluid simulation. Recently, the Lattice Boltzmann method has been presented in fluid simulation [TIR06,ZQFK07]. In this alternative grid-based approach, particle distributions are evolved on a finite grid using collision and propagation rules.

The investigation of Lagrangian approaches in computer graphics is – at least to some extend – motivated by interactive applications. Lagrangian approaches are comparatively efficient in terms of memory and computation time. They are flexible for time-varying simulation domains and they are easy to implement. Based on the above-mentioned fundamental SPH approaches [SF95, MCG03, KAG*05], various extensions have been presented. SPH applications for fluids range from the simulation of rivers [KW06], multi phase fluid simulations [MSKG05] and high-viscous fluids [CBP05, SAC*99] to fluid control [TKPR06]. Desbrun and Cani [DG96] present an elastic SPH approach for deformable solids. Hadap and Magnenat-Thalmann [HMT01] use SPH for hair dynamics. In [MST*04], two-way coupling of SPH-based fluids and deformable solids is realized. Solenthaler et al. [SSP07] present a unified SPH approach for liquids, elastic and rigid objects. SPH has also been applied in virtual surgery, e. g. [Mül04].

Bell et al. [BYM05] present a particle method for granular materials based on Molecular Dynamics. Zhu and Bridson [ZB05] extend the Particle-In-Cell method to simulate water and granular materials.

For a good introduction into various fluid simulation techniques in graphics we refer to the excellent SIGGRAPH course notes of Bridson, Fedkiw and Müller-Fischer [BFMF06]. A thorough and comprehensive introduction of SPH is given in [Mon05].

3. SPH fluid model

In SPH, particles are used to interpolate a continuous function $A(\mathbf{x})$ at a position $\mathbf{x}$. The contributing particles, relevant for a position, are determined by a kernel function W of finite support associated with each particle. For a fluid, the interpolation is given as

$$A(\mathbf{x}) = \sum_j m_j \frac{A_j}{\rho_j} W(\mathbf{x} - \mathbf{x}_j, h). \tag{1}$$

The value m_j denotes the mass of a particle, ρ_j denotes the density at the position of the particle and h the particle radius. In our SPH implementation, we use a B-cubic spline interpolation kernel W with a support of length $4h$. For a detailed discussion of kernel functions we refer to [GM82] and [MCG03].

3.1. The governing equations and their SPH formulation

In our approach, we solve the Euler equations, a simplification of the Navier-Stokes equations for inviscid flow. Momentum-conserving artificial viscosity is explicitly added to the model in order to improve the numerical stability of the method. In non-conservation form, the Euler equations are given as

$$\frac{d\rho}{dt} = -\rho\nabla\cdot\mathbf{v} \quad \text{(continuity equation)} \tag{2}$$

$$\frac{d\mathbf{v}}{dt} = -\frac{1}{\rho}\nabla P+\mathbf{g} \quad \text{(momentum equation)} \tag{3}$$

with $\mathbf{v}$ denoting the velocity, P the pressure and $\mathbf{g}$ external forces.

Continuity equation. The original SPH approach uses a summation formula to calculate the density:

$$\rho_a = \sum_b m_b W_{ab} \tag{4}$$

with $W_{ab} = W(\mathbf{x}_a - \mathbf{x}_b)$. Since the mass is carried by the particles, this form conserves mass exactly. However, due to the fact that surface particles in free surface scenarios have less neighbors, (4) computes an erroneous (lower) density near the surface for equally spaced particles.

Several approaches address this problem. For instance, [SDD06] uses an adaptive kernel length h to enforce constant density at the surface and to model small scale effects at the surface. An alternative approach is introduced by Monaghan [Mon94] and used in [SAC*99] by solving the continuity equation, which results in the SPH form

$$\frac{d\rho_a}{dt} = \sum_b m_b \mathbf{v}_{ab}\nabla_a W_{ab} \tag{5}$$

with $\mathbf{v}_{ab} = \mathbf{v}_a - \mathbf{v}_b$. Each particle is initialized with a density ρ_0 and density changes are only due to relative motion of particles. The differential update (5) guarantees a correct density at free surfaces. Although initialization is easier using (5), the summation approach (4) is more stable and has been used in our experiments. We discuss an initialization procedure in Sec. 5.

Momentum equation. In SPH form, the momentum equation is written as

$$\frac{d\mathbf{v}_a}{dt} = -\sum_b m_b\left(\frac{P_a}{\rho_a^2}+\frac{P_b}{\rho_b^2}\right)\nabla_a W_{ab}+\mathbf{g} \tag{6}$$

This symmetrized version conserves linear and angular momentum.

Equation of state. There exist various forms to relate pressure and density. If incompressibility is required, the Poisson equation $\nabla^2 P = \rho\frac{\nabla\mathbf{v}}{\Delta t}$ is commonly solved in Eulerian approaches, e. g. [FF01], and Lagrangian approaches [PTB*03]. However, solving the Poisson equation is time-consuming. In contrast, [MCG03] uses the ideal gas equation $P = k_p\rho$ or $P = k_p(\rho-\rho_0)$ with pressure constant k_p for SPH which results in a rather high compressibility.

In contrast to both approaches, we use the Tait equation [Mon94, Bat67] that enforces very low density variations and is efficient to compute. Neglecting atmospheric pressure that can simply be added as a constant pressure term, Tait's equation has the form

$$P = B\left(\left(\frac{\rho}{\rho_0}\right)^\gamma - 1\right) \tag{7}$$

with $\gamma = 7$. The pressure constant B governs the relative density fluctuation $\frac{|\Delta\rho|}{\rho_0}$ with $\Delta\rho = \rho-\rho_0$. To determine values for B, we consider that compressibility effects scale with $O(M^2)$ with M denoting the Mach number of the flow. This results in the following relation

$$\frac{|\Delta\rho|}{\rho_0} \sim \frac{|\mathbf{v}_f|^2}{c_s^2} \tag{8}$$

with $\mathbf{v}_f$ denoting the speed of flow and c_s denoting the speed of sound in the fluid. Thus, we can ensure that $\frac{|\Delta\rho|}{\rho_0} \sim \eta$ if the speed of sound is assumed to be large enough such that $\frac{\mathbf{v}_f}{c_s} < \sqrt{\eta}$. Typically, η is set to 0.01, i. e. allowing density variations of the order of 1%. To enforce this condition, B is chosen as

$$B = \frac{\rho_0 c_s^2}{\gamma} \tag{9}$$

Example. We have a collapsing column of water with initial density $\rho_0 = 1000\frac{kg}{m^3}$, $\eta = 0.01$, height $H = 4m$, gravity $9.81\frac{m}{s^2}$, and particle radius $h = 0.1m$. Using the estimation $\mathbf{v}_f \sim \sqrt{2gH}$ for the maximum velocity, we get $c_s \approx 88.5\frac{m}{s}$ and $B \approx 1119kPa$.

Assuming a high speed of sound to keep density fluctuations low, Tait's equation requires smaller time steps compared to incompressible particle approaches [PTB*03]. In the above-mentioned example, we have used a time step of $\Delta t = 4.52\cdot 10^{-4}$s. However, each time step needs considerably less computation time since we avoid to solve the Poisson equation. For 100k particles, one time step can be computed twenty times faster compared to MPS. Experiments indicate that the Tait equation can be used to efficiently enforce volume preservation (see Sec. 5).

3.2. Viscosity

In order to improve the numerical stability and to allow for shock phenomena, artificial viscosity is employed [Mon05]. It is given as

$$\frac{d\mathbf{v}_a}{dt} = \begin{cases} -\sum_b m_b \Pi_{ab}\nabla_a W_{ab} & \mathbf{v}_{ab}^T\mathbf{x}_{ab} < 0 \\ 0 & \mathbf{v}_{ab}^T\mathbf{x}_{ab} \geq 0 \end{cases} \tag{10}$$

with $\mathbf{v}_{ab}^T\mathbf{x}_{ab} > 0$ being equivalent to $\nabla\cdot\mathbf{v} > 0$. Π_{ab} is given as

$$\Pi_{ab} = -\nu\left(\frac{\mathbf{v}_{ab}^T\mathbf{x}_{ab}}{|\mathbf{x}_{ab}|^2+\varepsilon h^2}\right) \tag{11}$$

with the viscous term $\nu = \frac{2\alpha h c_s}{\rho_a+\rho_b}$ and the viscosity constant α. α is in between 0.08 and 0.5 for our experiments. The term εh^2 is introduced to avoid singularities for $|\mathbf{x}_{ab}| = 0$, with $\varepsilon = 0.01$. Linear and angular momentum are conserved in (11). Π_{ab} is Galilean invariant and vanishes for rigid body rotations [Mon05].

3.3. Surface Tension

In this section, we briefly introduce existing surface tension models followed by the presentation of our new approach.

Current surface tension models are commonly based on a color value c_a assigned to a particle a [Mor99, MCG03, KAG*05]. All particles of a phase have the same color value and color values are interpolated according to

$$c = \sum_b \frac{m_b c_b}{\rho_b} W_{ab} \tag{12}$$

The surface normal is calculated as $\mathbf{n} = \nabla c$ and tension forces corresponding to a surface tension κ are calculated as

$$\mathbf{f}^{tension} = -\kappa \nabla^2 c \frac{\mathbf{n}}{|\mathbf{n}|} \tag{13}$$

Due to the normalization, normals are only considered if their length exceed a certain threshold [MCG03]. This model has several drawbacks. Calculating the curvature $-\nabla^2 c$ is error-prone close to the surface where particles have only a few neighbors. Further, calculating the second derivative is sensitive to particle disorder.

Hu and Adams [HA06] propose a modified version of [Mor99]. The express the surface tension as the divergence of the stress tensor Π which is uniquely defined by the color field c:

$$\Pi = \kappa \frac{1}{|\nabla c|}\left(\frac{1}{3}\mathbf{I}|\nabla c|^2 - \nabla c \nabla c^T\right) \tag{14}$$

This expression results in the acceleration equation

$$\frac{d\mathbf{v}_a}{dt} = \frac{1}{m_a}\sum_b \nabla W_{ab}\left(\frac{\Pi_a}{\sigma_a^2} + \frac{\Pi_b}{\sigma_b^2}\right) \tag{15}$$

with $\sigma_a = \sum_b W(r_a - r_b)$. Hu and Adams solve the above-mentioned issues of [Mor99], since they do not calculate the curvature explicitly and the tensor naturally tends to zero for $|\nabla c| \to 0$.

Although [Mor99] and [HA06] have been applied in free-surface problems, both approaches have originally been intended for multi-phase scenarios. Therefore, they do not compute correct surface tension forces in absence of a second phase. They lack an appropriate number of adjacent particles, particularly in surface areas with high curvature.

We propose a new surface tension model that relies on cohesion forces. As previous methods have adopted a macroscopic view of the model, our approach is inspired by a microscopic view since - on a molecular level - surface tension arises due to attractive forces between molecules. The approach is closely related to the model of [TM05]. In contrast to [TM05], we scale the attractive forces using the smoothing kernel W as a weighting function:

$$\frac{d\mathbf{v}_a}{dt} = -\frac{\kappa}{m_a}\sum_b m_b W(\mathbf{x}_a - \mathbf{x}_b) \tag{16}$$

Our method does not rely on a second phase and is well-suited for free-surface problems with high curvatures. The attractive forces can be computed efficiently. The proposed method can easily be generalized to multi-phase problems by applying attractive forces only to particles of the same phase. In Sec. 5, we compare our approach with [HA06].

4. Visualization

Some visualization techniques for particle methods are based on an explicit surface reconstruction, e. g. [MCG03]. Using Marching Cubes [LC87], an iso-surface is reconstructed from a characteristic function. However, capturing small details requires a very fine or an adaptive discretization of the underlying space.

Particle level sets do not only use an iso-surface, but additionally introduce tracer particles which are advected with the velocity field [FF01, EFFM02]. They can handle small drops using the tracer particles. However, these drops do not necessarily capture the resolution of the simulation. For large deformations, tracer particles must be re-seeded. In [KCC*06], tracer particles are advected with a Lagrangian approach.

We employ a ray tracing approach that is inspired by the surface splatting algorithms of Zwicker et al. [ZPvBG01] and Adams et al. [ALD06]. The visualization of small splashes and single drops is inspired by [KCC*06] and [TRS06]. The method guarantees that features down to the size of a single particle are captured appropriately. The normal of each pixel is calculated similar to [Mor99] as

$$\mathbf{n}_a = \sum_b \frac{m_b}{\rho_b} \nabla W(\mathbf{x}_a - \mathbf{x}_b) \tag{17}$$

where we sum over all particles hit by a ray. Visualizing 130k particles takes about 1-2 seconds on a Pentium 4 with 3.4 GHz.

5. Results

In this section, we illustrate some properties of our SPH implementation. We start with discussing the simulation time step, the boundary conditions, and the initialization of the approach. Afterwards, we illustrate the effect of using the Tait equation compared to the ideal gas equation and we discuss the properties of our surface tension model. Finally, we present an exemplary scenario with breaking waves.

If not stated otherwise, performance is measured using an Intel Pentium 4 with 3.4 GHz and 2 GB RAM. Neighborhood search is realized with uniform spatial subdivision.

Integration is performed with a Leap-frog scheme. All experiments are performed using the density of water $\rho_0 = 1000\frac{kg}{m^3}$.

Time step. The appropriate choice of the time step is crucial for stability **and** convergence. In our case, the time step is derived from the Courant-Friedrichs-Lewy(CFL) condition, the viscous term, and the force terms [Mon92]:

$$\Delta t = \min\left(0.25 \cdot \min_a\left(\frac{h}{|\mathbf{f}_a|}\right), 0.4 \cdot \frac{h}{c_s \cdot (1+0.6\alpha)}\right) \quad (18)$$

with $\mathbf{f}_a$ denoting external forces. Although the time step could be larger with respect to numerical stability, we use the proposed time step to ensure convergence.

Boundary conditions. Boundary particles are inserted where fluid particles collide with a boundary. Following [Mon05], the force $\mathbf{f}_{ak}$ applied to a fluid particle a that collides with a boundary particle k is computed as:

$$\mathbf{f}_{ak} = \frac{m_k}{m_a + m_k}\Gamma(\mathbf{x}_a, \mathbf{x}_b)\frac{\mathbf{x}_a - \mathbf{x}_k}{|\mathbf{x}_a - \mathbf{x}_k|} \quad (19)$$

The function Γ is defined as

$$\Gamma(\mathbf{x}_a, \mathbf{x}_b) = 0.02\frac{c_s^2}{|\mathbf{x}_a - \mathbf{x}_b|}\begin{cases} \frac{2}{3} & 0 < q < \frac{2}{3} \\ (2q - \frac{3}{2}q^2) & \frac{2}{3} < q < 1 \\ \frac{1}{2}(2-q)^2 & 1 < q < 2 \\ 0 & \text{otherwise} \end{cases} \quad (20)$$

with $q = \frac{|\mathbf{x}_a - \mathbf{x}_b|}{h}$.

Initialization. In order to obtain a valid state of nearly constant density using the summation approach (4), we evolve the particles for one hundred steps with a heavily damped version of (6). In case of a simple initial geometry, this initialization can lead to small visual artifacts as can be seen in the accompanying video.

5.1. Volume preservation

We have performed two experiments in order to compare our implementation based on the Tait equation with the ideal gas equation. In both experiments, we measure the ratio of the maximum density and the initial density in order to assess the volume preservation.

In the first experiment, we simulate a corner-breaking dam scenario with 130k particles. The height of the dam is $H = 5$. For the Tait equation, the density fluctuation η is set to 0.01. For the gas equation, the pressure constant k_p is set to 300. The density fluctuation and pressure constant are minimized and maximized, respectively, in order to use the same time step in both approaches. In both versions, the particle radius and the initial spacing are 0.1, the viscous term α is 0.1, and the computation time is about 4.5 s per time step. The measured density ratio for the gas equation is 4.06, the density ratio for the Tait equation 1.01, which is illustrated in Fig. 1.

In the second experiment, we simulate two breaking dams

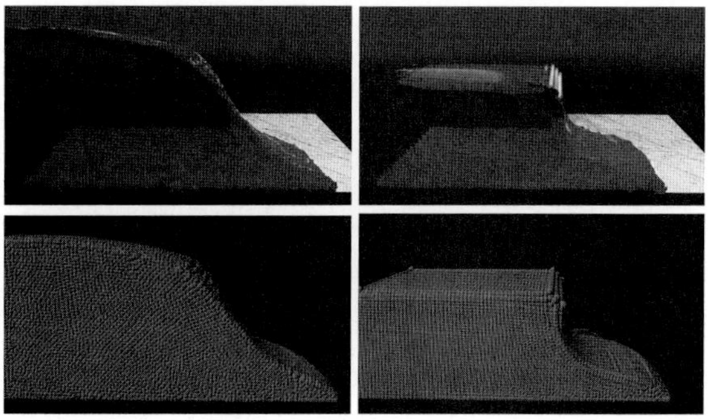

Figure 1: *Corner-breaking dam using the Tait equation (left) and the ideal gas equation (right). The gas equation leads to high compressibility.*

of height $H = 2$ with an overall number of 16k particles and viscosity $\alpha = 0.5$ colliding with each other in a rectangular basin. The pressure constant k_p for the gas equation is set to 200, the density fluctuation parameter η is set to 0.01. The maximum measured density ratio using the gas equation is 1.2. As determined by the parameters, the measured density ratio is 1.01 for the Tait equation.

Both experiments have been initialized with the same density and the same mass per particle. Experiments indicate that for constant initial density and particle radius the density ratio for the gas equation increases with the volume of the simulated fluid and thereby with the number of particles. In contrast to the weakly compressible approach, considerable volume changes are observed for the gas equation. This is especially perceivable when the dams collapse. Using our weakly compressible approach, the density fluctuation can be kept constant for an increasing number of particles. In terms of volume preservation, the Tait equation is therefore appropriate for handling large particle systems.

5.2. Surface tension

In order to compare our surface tension approach with [HA06], we use a fluid cube with 27k particles that is supposed to deform to a drop in a zero-gravity scenario. For comparable results, surface tension is 0.8 for our approach and 30.6 for [HA06]. Alternative parameter settings mostly influence the rate of convergence to an equilibrium state. The qualitative result is not affected as long as the parameters stay within a reasonable range. Results can be seen in Fig. 2.

Since [HA06] has originally been intended for multi phase scenarios, it is less appropriate for high curvatures in free surface scenarios. In contrast to our approach, high curvatures of the initial state are basically preserved.

In another experiment, we investigate parameter settings for our surface tension model. Therefore, we simulate a corner-breaking dam with two different surface tensions.

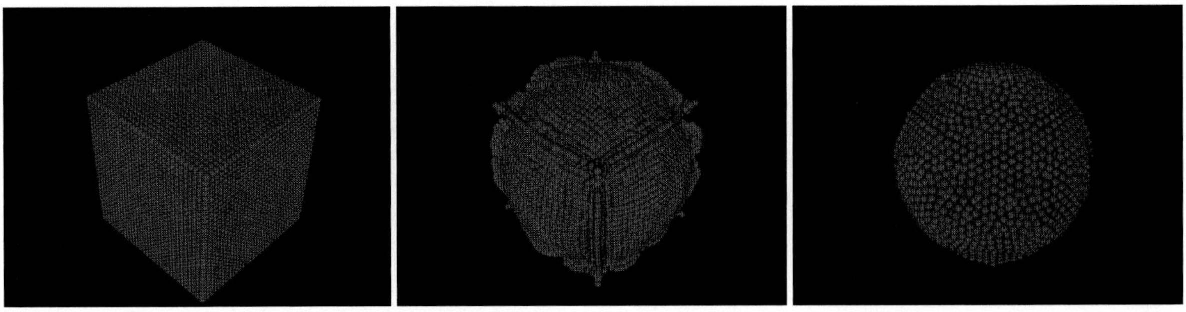

Figure 2: *The effect of surface tension. Initial state (left), resulting equilibrium using [HA06] (middle) and our surface tension approach (right).*

The surface tension 0.01 is close to water, the value 3.4 is the maximum stable value in this setting. As can be seen in Fig 3, choosing a larger surface tension value results in larger splashes of the fluid.

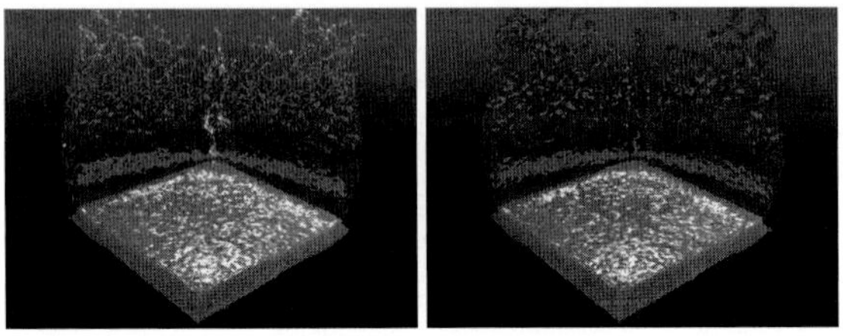

Figure 3: *Two corner-breaking dams using a surface tension of 0.01 (left) and 3.4 (right).*

5.3. Breaking waves

We have designed a scenario to illustrate the handling of breaking waves. We use 200k particles in a 26 x 5 basin with a ground plane of slope 12°. Radius and initial spacing are set to 0.1. The density fluctuation is set to 0.01. The viscosity term is $\alpha = 0.08$. To generate the waves, we use a planar wave generator. The computation time is 7.5 s per time step. As can be seen in Fig. 4, splashing and breaking waves can be modeled using our approach.

6. Conclusion

We have presented a weakly compressible SPH approach for free surface flows. By allowing for small user-defined density fluctuations, the Tait equation is an efficient alternative compared to approaches that strictly enforce incompressibility. In contrast to the gas equation, density fluctuations remain small even for a large number of particles. The volume preservation has been illustrated in various scenarios. Natural phenomena such as breaking waves in low viscous fluids with splashing drops can be simulated using our methods.

Additionally, we have proposed a modified surface tension algorithm based on cohesion forces. In contrast to previous approaches, high curvatures in single-phase free-surface flows can be handled by our model.

Ongoing work focuses on surface tension for multiple phases and adaptive viscosity schemes, as e. g. proposed in [MM97].

7. Acknowledgments

We would like to thank Hendrik Tessendorf for his help with creating the videos.

References

[ALD06] Adams B., Lenaerts T., Dutre P.: *Particle Splatting: Interactive Rendering of Particle-Based Simulation Data.* Tech. Rep. CW 453, Katholieke Universiteit Leuven, 2006.

[Bat67] Batchelor G.: *An Introduction to Fluid Dynamics.* Cambridge University Press, 1967.

[BFMF06] Bridson R., Fedkiw R., Müller-Fischer M.: Fluid simulation: Siggraph 2006 course notes. In *SIGGRAPH '06: ACM SIGGRAPH 2006 Courses* (New York, NY, USA, 2006), ACM Press, pp. 1–87.

[BYM05] Bell N., Yu Y., Mucha P. J.: Particle-based simulation of granular materials. In *SCA '05: Proceedings of the 2005 ACM SIGGRAPH/Eurographics symposium on Computer animation* (New York, NY, USA, 2005), ACM Press, pp. 77–86.

[CBP05] Clavet S., Beaudoin P., Poulin P.: Particle-based viscoelastic fluid simulation. In *SCA '05: Proceedings of the 2005 ACM SIGGRAPH/Eurographics symposium on Computer animation* (New York, NY, USA, 2005), ACM Press, pp. 219–228.

[CGFO06] Chentanez N., Goktekin T., Feldman B., O'Brien J.: Simultaneous coupling of fluids and deformable bodies. In *SCA '06: Proceedings of the 2006 ACM SIGGRAPH/Eurographics symposium on Computer animation* (Aire-la-Ville, Switzerland, Switzerland, 2006), Eurographics Association, pp. 83–89.

[CMT04] CARLSON M., MUCHA P., TURK G.: Rigid fluid: animating the interplay between rigid bodies and fluid. In *SIGGRAPH '04: ACM SIGGRAPH 2004 Papers* (New York, NY, USA, 2004), ACM Press, pp. 377–384.

[CR99] CUMMINS S., RUDMAN M.: An SPH Projection Method. *Journal of Computational Physics 152*, 2 (1999), 584–607.

[DG96] DESBRUN M., GASCUEL M.: Smoothed particles: A new paradigm for animating highly deformable bodies. *6th Eurographics Workshop on Computer Animation and Simulation '96* (1996), 61–76.

[EFFM02] ENRIGHT D., FEDKIW R., FERZIGER J., MITCHELL I.: A hybrid particle level set method for improved interface capturing. *Journal of Computational Physics 183*, 1 (2002), 83–116.

[ETK*07] ELCOTT S., TONG Y., KANSO E., SCHROEDER P., DESBRUN M.: Stable, circulation-preserving, simplicial fluids. *ACM Trans. Graph. 26*, 1 (2007), 4.

[FF01] FOSTER N., FEDKIW R.: Practical animation of liquids. In *SIGGRAPH '01: Proceedings of the 28th annual conference on Computer graphics and interactive techniques* (New York, NY, USA, 2001), ACM Press, pp. 23–30.

[FM96] FOSTER N., METAXAS D.: Realistic animation of liquids. In *GI '96: Proceedings of the conference on Graphics interface '96* (Toronto, Ont., Canada, 1996), Canadian Information Processing Society, pp. 204–212.

[FM97] FOSTER N., METAXAS D.: Controlling fluid animation. In *CGI '97: Proceedings of the 1997 Conference on Computer Graphics International* (Washington, DC, USA, 1997), IEEE Computer Society, pp. 178–188.

[GM82] GINGOLD R., MONAGHAN J.: Kernel estimates as a basis for general particle methods in hydrodynamics. *Journal of Computational Physics 46* (1982), 429–453.

[HA06] HU X., ADAMS N.: A multi-phase SPH method for macroscopic and mesoscopic flows. *Journal of Computational Physics 213*, 2 (2006), 844–861.

[HMT01] HADAP S., MAGNENAT-THALMANN N.: Modeling Dynamic Hair as a Continuum. *Computer Graphics Forum 20*, 3 (2001), 329–338.

[KAG*05] KEISER R., ADAMS B., GASSER D., BAZZI P., DUTRÉ P., GROSS M.: A Unified Lagrangian Approach to Solid-Fluid Animation. *Eurographics Symposium on Point-Based Graphics* (2005), 125–133.

[KCC*06] KIM J., CHA D., CHANG B., KOO B., IHM I.: Practical Animation of Turbulent Splashing Water. *Proceedings of the 2006 ACM SIGGRAPH/Eurographics symposium on Computer animation* (2006), 335–344.

[KM90] KASS M., MILLER G.: Rapid, stable fluid dynamics for computer graphics. *Proceedings of the 17th annual conference on Computer graphics and interactive techniques* (1990), 49–57.

[KW06] KIPFER P., WESTERMANN R.: Realistic and interactive simulation of rivers. *Proceedings of the 2006 conference on Graphics interface* (2006), 41–48.

[LC87] LORENSEN W. E., CLINE H. E.: Marching cubes: A high resolution 3d surface construction algorithm. In *SIGGRAPH '87: Proceedings of the 14th annual conference on Computer graphics and interactive techniques* (New York, NY, USA, 1987), ACM Press, pp. 163–169.

[LGF04] LOSASSO F., GIBOU F., FEDKIW R.: Simulating water and smoke with an octree data structure. *International Conference on Computer Graphics and Interactive Techniques* (2004), 457–462.

[LSSF06] LOSASSO F., SHINAR T., SELLE A., FEDKIW R.: Multiple interacting liquids. In *SIGGRAPH '06: ACM SIGGRAPH 2006 Papers* (New York, NY, USA, 2006), ACM Press, pp. 812–819.

[Max81] MAX N.: Vectorized procedural models for natural terrain: Waves and islands in the sunset. In *SIGGRAPH '81: Proceedings of the 8th annual conference on Computer graphics and interactive techniques* (New York, NY, USA, 1981), ACM Press, pp. 317–324.

[MCG03] MÜLLER M., CHARYPAR D., GROSS M.: Particle-based fluid simulation for interactive applications. In *SCA '03: Proceedings of the 2003 ACM SIGGRAPH/Eurographics symposium on Computer animation* (Aire-la-Ville, Switzerland, Switzerland, 2003), Eurographics Association, pp. 154–159.

[MM97] MORRIS J., MONAGHAN J.: A Switch to Reduce SPH Viscosity. *Journal of Computational Physics 136*, 1 (1997), 41–50.

[MMS04] MIHALEF V., METAXAS D., SUSSMAN M.: Animation and control of breaking waves. In *SCA '04: Proceedings of the 2004 ACM SIGGRAPH/Eurographics symposium on Computer animation* (Aire-la-Ville, Switzerland, Switzerland, 2004), Eurographics Association, pp. 315–324.

[Mon92] MONAGHAN J.: Smoothed particle hydrodynamics. *Ann. Rev. Astron. Astrophys. 30* (1992), 543–574.

[Mon94] MONAGHAN J.: Simulating free surface flows with SPH. *Journal of Computational Physics 110*, 2 (1994), 399–406.

[Mon05] MONAGHAN J.: Smoothed particle hydrodynamics. *Reports on Progress in Physics 68*, 8 (2005), 1703–1759.

[Mor99] MORRIS J.: Simulating surface tension with smoothed particle hydrodynamics. *Int. J. Numer. Meth. Fluids 33* (1999), 333–353.

[MP89] MILLER G., PEARCE A.: Globular Dynamics: A Connected Particle System for Animating Viscous Fluids. *Computers and Graphics 13*, 3 (1989), 305–309.

[MSKG05] MÜLLER M., SOLENTHALER B., KEISER R., GROSS M.: Particle-based fluid-fluid interaction. *Proceedings of the 2005 ACM SIGGRAPH/Eurographics symposium on Computer animation* (2005), 237–244.

[MST*04] MÜLLER M., SCHIRM S., TESCHNER M., HEIDELBERGER B., GROSS M.: Interaction of fluids with deformable solids. *Computer Animation and Virtual Worlds 15*, 34 (2004), 159–171.

[Mül04] MÜLLER M.: Interactive blood simulation for virtual surgery based on smoothed particle hydrodynamics. *Technology and Health Care 12*, 1 (2004), 25–31.

[OH95] O'BRIEN J. F., HODGINS J. K.: Dynamic simulation of splashing fluids. In *CA '95: Proceedings of the Computer Animation* (Washington, DC, USA, 1995), IEEE Computer Society, p. 198.

[Pea86] PEACHEY D.: Modeling waves and surf. In *SIGGRAPH '86: Proceedings of the 13th annual conference on Computer graphics and interactive techniques* (New York, NY, USA, 1986), ACM Press, pp. 65–74.

[PTB*03] PREMOZE S., TASDIZEN T., BIGLER J., LEFOHN A., WHITAKER R.: Particle-based simulation of fluids. *Computer Graphics Forum (Proc. of Eurographics) 22* (2003), 401–410.

[SAC*99] STORA D., AGLIATI P., CANI M., NEYRET F., GASCUEL J.: Animating lava flows. *Graphics Interface 99* (1999), 203–210.

[SDD06] SIGALOTTI L., DAZA J., DONOSO A.: Modelling free surface flows with smoothed particle hydrodynamics. *Condensed Matter Physics 9*, 2(46) (2006), 359–366.

[SF95] STAM J., FIUME E.: Depicting fire and other gaseous phenomena using diffusion processes. In *SIGGRAPH '95: Proceedings of the 22nd annual conference on Computer graphics and interactive techniques* (New York, NY, USA, 1995), ACM Press, pp. 129–136.

[SSP07] SOLENTHALER B., SCHLÄFLI J., PAJAROLA R.: A unified particle model for fluid solid interactions: Research articles. *Comput. Animat. Virtual Worlds 18*, 1 (2007), 69–82.

[Sta99] STAM J.: Stable fluids. *Proceedings of the 26th annual conference on Computer graphics and interactive techniques* (1999), 121–128.

[TIR06] THÜREY N., IGLBERGER K., RÜDE U.: Free surface flows with moving and deforming objects with lbm. In *Vision, Modeling, Visualization VMV'06* (2006), pp. 193–200.

[TKPR06] THÜREY N., KEISER R., PAULY M., RÜDE U.: Detail-preserving fluid control. In *SCA '06: Proceedings of the 2006 ACM SIGGRAPH/Eurographics symposium on Computer animation* (Aire-la-Ville, Switzerland, Switzerland, 2006), Eurographics Association, pp. 7–12.

[TM05] TARTAKOVSKY A., MEAKIN P.: Modeling of surface tension and contact angles with smoothed particle hydrodynamics. *Physical Review E 72*, 2 (2005), 26301.

[TOT*03] TAKESHITA D., OTA S., TAMURA M., FUJIMOTO T., MURAOKA K., CHIBA N.: Particle-based visual simulation of explosive flames. *Computer Graphics and Applications, 2003. Proceedings. 11th Pacific Conference on* (2003), 482–486.

[TRS06] THUEREY N., RUEDE U., STAMMINGER M.: Animation of Open Water Phenomena with Coupled Shallow Water and Free Surface Simulations. *Proceedings of the 2006 ACM SIGGRAPH/Eurographics symposium on Computer animation* (2006), 157–164.

[ZB05] ZHU Y., BRIDSON R.: Animating sand as a fluid. In *SIGGRAPH '05: ACM SIGGRAPH 2005 Papers* (New York, NY, USA, 2005), ACM Press, pp. 965–972.

[ZPvBG01] ZWICKER M., PFISTER H., VAN BAAR J., GROSS M.: Surface splatting. In *SIGGRAPH '01: Proceedings of the 28th annual conference on Computer graphics and interactive techniques* (New York, NY, USA, 2001), ACM Press, pp. 371–378.

[ZQFK07] ZHAO Y., QIU F., FAN Z., KAUFMAN A.: Flow Simulation with Locally-Refined LBM. In *Proc. of ACM SIGGRAPH Symposium on Interactive 3D Graphics and Games* (2007). to appear.

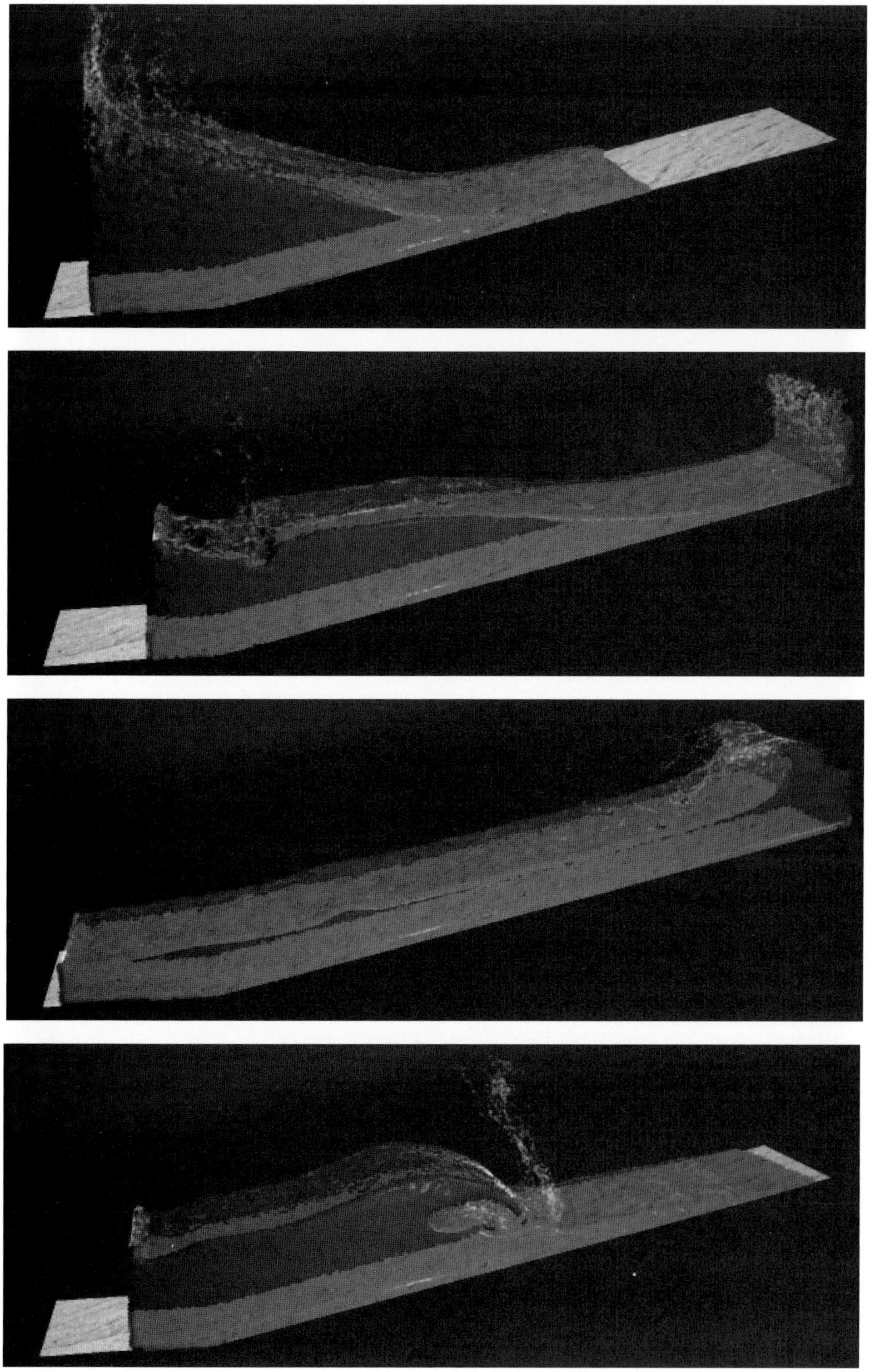

Figure 4: *A breaking wave is generated using a wave generator.*

Eurographics/ACM SIGGRAPH Symposium on Computer Animation (2007)
D. Metaxas and J. Popovic (Editors)

Liquid Simulation on Lattice-Based Tetrahedral Meshes

Nuttapong Chentanez, Bryan E. Feldman, François Labelle, James F. O'Brien, Jonathan R. Shewchuk

University of California, Berkeley

Abstract

We describe a method for animating incompressible liquids with detailed free surfaces. For each time step, semi-Lagrangian contouring computes a new fluid boundary (represented as a fine surface triangulation) from the previous time step's fluid boundary and velocity field. Then a mesh generation algorithm called isosurface stuffing *discretizes the region enclosed by the new fluid boundary, creating a tetrahedral mesh that grades from a fine resolution at the surface to a coarser resolution in the interior. The mesh has a structure, based on the body centered cubic lattice, that accommodates graded tetrahedron sizes but is regular enough to aid efficient point location and to save memory used to store geometric properties of identical tetrahedra. Although the mesh is warped to conform to the liquid boundary, it has a mathematical guarantee on tetrahedron quality, and is generated very rapidly. Each successive time step entails creating a new triangulated liquid surface and a new tetrahedral mesh. Semi-Lagrangian advection computes velocities at the current time step on the new mesh. We use a finite volume discretization to perform pressure projection required to enforce the fluid's incompressibility, and we solve the linear system with algebraic multigrid. A novel thickening scheme prevents thin sheets and droplets of liquid from vanishing when their thicknesses drop below the mesh resolution. Examples demonstrate that the method captures complex liquid motions and fine details on the free surfaces without suffering from excessive volume loss or artificial damping.*

Categories and Subject Descriptors (according to ACM CCS): I.3.5 [Computer Graphics]: Computational Geometry and Object Modeling, Physically Based Modeling; I.3.7 [Computer Graphics]: Three-Dimensional Graphics and Realism, Animation; I.6.8 [Simulation and Modeling]: Types of Simulation, Animation

Keywords: natural phenomena, physically based animation, computational fluid dynamics, tetrahedral mesh

1. Introduction

Convincingly animating the complex motion of a liquid's surface has proven challenging for both hand and computer-based methods. Currently, the most successful methods use computer simulation of the physical laws that govern real-world liquids. However, real liquids exhibit characteristics, such as fine surface detail and thin structures, that stress the capabilities of even the most sophisticated simulation methods.

The most commonly used methods for simulating incompressible liquids employ regular hexahedral grids or meshless collections of points, but some recent methods use unstructured tetrahedral meshes [FOK05, KFCO06, ETK*07]. Tetrahedral meshes offer advantages over regular grids: they more easily conform to complex boundaries, and tetrahedron sizes can be graded to focus computational effort where it is most beneficial. Tetrahedral meshes have been successful in simulations with no free surfaces—for instance, where a gas flows through a static simulation domain. But simulating free surfaces is substantially harder because the meshes must track the movement of those surfaces, and substantially more tetrahedra are usually necessary to faithfully track the surface detail and discretize the thin features that arise.

Moreover, dynamic liquids often form droplets, filaments, or thin sheets, which can disappear because of the finite resolution of the mesh. These artifacts are often called *volume loss*. In real life, surface tension prevents liquids such as water from forming arbitrarily small structures, but faithful simulation of surface tension effects on thin sheets exacts a prohibitive computational cost for the amount of water typically used in animations. For thin features, surface tension acts at a scale that is well below the finest feasible resolution in a simulation used for animation.

We address these problems with several techniques that are, to our knowledge, novel in fluid animation: a fast algorithm for generating semi-regular, graded, guaranteed-quality tetrahedral meshes that conform to a liquid's boundary; a novel thickening strategy for reducing volume loss

Symposium on Computer Animation 2007, San Diego, CA, August 03-04, 2007.
© 2007 ACM 978-1-59593-624-4/07/0008 $5.00

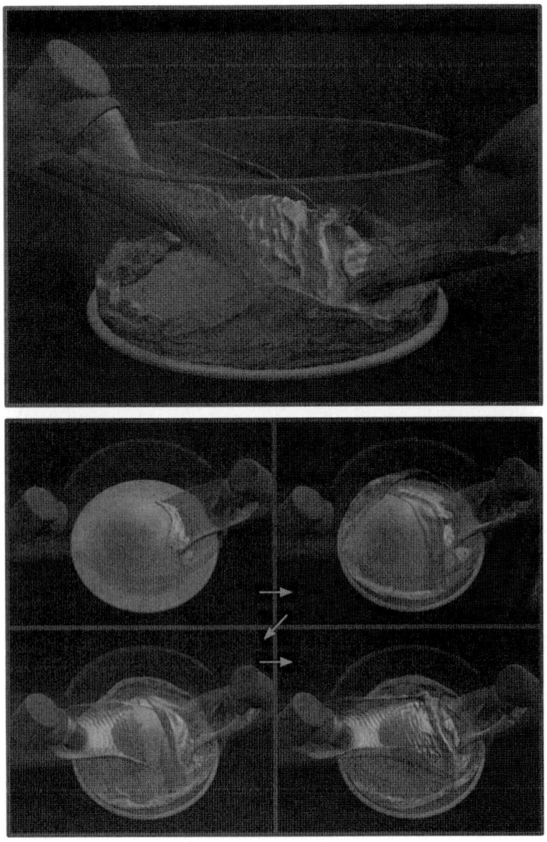

Figure 1: *Two views of a liquid pouring down a pair of chutes into a transparent container.*

and preventing the artifact of disappearing droplets or sheets of fluid; and the use of algebraic multigrid to speed up the pressure projection step commonly used to enforce the divergence-free velocity property of incompressible fluids. These techniques make it feasible to use large tetrahedral meshes.

The mesh generation algorithm we use, called *isosurface stuffing* [LS07], creates a tetrahedral mesh that conforms accurately to smooth liquid boundaries. It tiles space using the vertices and the octant centers of a balanced octree that encloses the fluid region. If the octree were refined so that all its leaf octants had the same size, the vertices in the interior of the tetrahedral mesh would lie on a body centered cubic lattice. Instead, the octree is refined so that the liquid surface (where high resolution is needed) is covered with fine leaf octants (all of the same size), but coarser leaf octants appear in the liquid interior, keeping the number of elements (and thus the computational cost) from exploding. The mesh vertices near the surface are warped, and some tetrahedra are subdivided, so that the mesh boundary conforms to the fluid surface. Isosurface stuffing is fast, and it guarantees that all the tetrahedra have good quality, with their dihedral angles bounded between 10.7° and 164.8°. We exploit the semi-regular structure of the mesh to obtain significant savings in memory and computation by reusing geometric information for identical tetrahedra and by using the octree for point location (needed for semi-Lagrangian advection).

To track the moving fluid surface we use *semi-Lagrangian contouring* (SLC), first developed by Strain [Str99, Str01] and then extended to three dimensions by Bargteil *et al.* [BGOS06]. At the beginning of a time step, SLC computes a new fluid boundary, in the form of a high-resolution surface triangulation, from the previous time step's fluid boundary and velocity field. From the new fluid boundary, isosurface stuffing creates a new tetrahedral mesh. The surface triangulation is used for rendering and as part of SLC, and the tetrahedral mesh is used for computing the fluid velocities in the current time step.

Although semi-Lagrangian contouring tracks a fluid's free surface well, sheets, filaments, and droplets of fluid that become thinner than the grid's finest resolution are lost, as with any grid-based level set tracking method. This behavior leads to noticeable volume loss and ugly artifacts of disappearing liquid. To combat this problem, we propose a simple particle-based method that mimics some of the effects of surface tension, albeit at a much coarser scale, without the excessive cost of simulating surface tension in a physically accurate way.

Our particle-based method thickens regions where the fluid is dangerously thin by redistributing mass from nearby thin regions (which causes tendrils of liquid to break up rather than become thinner) and adding some thickness artificially. A few parameters allow the user to control the effects of the thickening algorithm.

Finally, we show how an algebraic multigrid solver can be used to efficiently perform the pressure projection required to ensure that the fluid behaves incompressibly. Our algebraic multigrid solver proved to be easy to implement, despite the complex free surfaces. It significantly outperforms the commonly used alternative of preconditioned conjugate gradients.

Our results, like the example shown in Figure 1, show that tetrahedral meshes can be used to animate liquids that feature substantial surface detail and thin sheets of liquid. The graded tetrahedron sizes and the use of a triangular surface mesh even finer than the boundary of the tetrahedral mesh make it possible to capture fine simulation detail at the surface, while using a computationally feasible number of tetrahedra.

2. Related Work

Fluid simulation by numerical methods has been widely adopted by the visual effects industry. Early computer graphics techniques for simulating smoke and water [FM96, Sta99, FF01] are still commonly used. These methods have been extended to more exotic materials and phenomena, including fire [NFJ02], explosions [FOA03], viscoelastic materials [GBO04], and bubbles [ZYP06]. Techniques are available to model the interaction of fluids with rigid bodies [CMT04], deformable bodies [CGFO06], thin membranes [GSLF05], and other fluids [LSSF06]. Treuille *et al.* [TLP06] use model reduction techniques to make fluid simulations run in real time.

It is difficult to realistically simulate free liquid surfaces with good detail, stability, and speed. Methods to enhance detail without losing too much speed include vorticity confinement [FSJ01] and vortex particles [SRF05]. Thürey *et al.* [TKPR06] propose methods for maintaining detail when applying control forces to guide a simulation toward keyframes.

Although most papers discuss regular hexahedral grids and Eulerian discretization, some focus on more flexible geometric structures. Losasso *et al.* [LGF04] use an octree to simulate gases and liquids. Klingner *et al.* [KFCO06] use an unstructured tetrahedral mesh for gases and smoke. Some authors eschew grids entirely in favor of meshless collections of Lagrangian particles [CD97, DC96, MKN*04, PTB*03, TPF89].

We choose semi-structured tetrahedral grids. Mesh generation is a huge field, too large to summarize here; see Bern and Eppstein [BE92] and Owen [Owe98] for surveys. We use isosurface stuffing [LS07] because no other boundary-conforming meshing algorithm offers the same combination of speed, numerical robustness, and guaranteed quality.

Surface tracking is crucial both for simulation (determining where the liquid is) and for generating a surface to render. Methods based on grids and isosurfaces, such as the particle level set method (PLS) [EMF02] and semi-Lagrangian contouring (SLC) [BGOS06] are largely successful at creating high-quality surfaces. Their main difficulty is the disappearance of features smaller than the resolution of the grid. Proposals for coping with this volume loss include replacing the thin sheets with particles [GSLF05, KCC*06]. Our approach is to combine SLC with a variation of the particle-based surface tracking method of Zhu and Bridson [ZB05].

3. Simulation Methods

Our simulation steps are illustrated in Figure 2. At the beginning of time step t, we have a triangulation S_t of the liquid surface and a tetrahedral mesh M_t that approximates the volume bounded by S_t. A time step consists of the following operations.

1. Create a new surface mesh S_{t+1} for the next time step by a combination of semi-Lagrangian contouring and our thickening method.
2. Generate a tetrahedral mesh M_{t+1} that approximates the volume bounded by the liquid surface S_{t+1}, with some additional thickening.
3. Advect the fluid velocity field from M_t to M_{t+1} using generalized semi-Lagrangian advection [FOKG05]. Update the velocities on M_{t+1} by explicit time integration of the external forces, and apply pressure correction to make the velocities divergence-free.

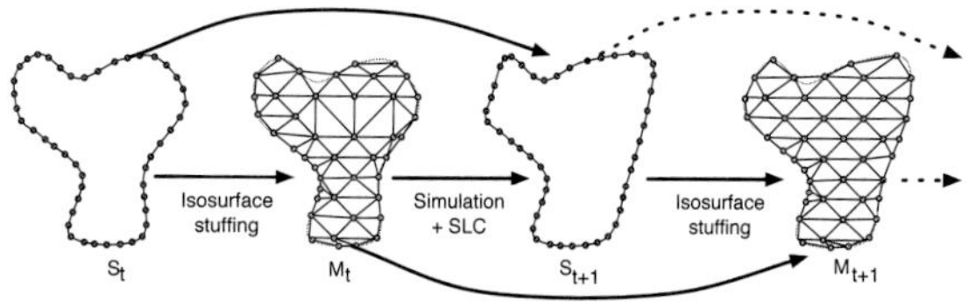

Figure 2: *Each time step uses one surface triangulation and one tetrahedral mesh. A new time step's surface S_{t+1} is created by semi-Lagrangian advection: tracing paths backward in time through the velocity field on M_t to locate a point relative to S_t. The isosurface stuffing algorithm generates a tetrahedral mesh M_{t+1} (with coarser surface resolution) from S_{t+1}. Velocities are interpolated/extrapolated from M_t.*

The following sections discuss these steps in detail. Many of the components we use are taken from prior work, and we focus on how to integrate and change the components so they work together.

3.1. Governing Equations and Discretization

Inviscid, incompressible liquids are governed by the Euler equations,

$$\frac{\partial \mathbf{u}}{\partial t} = -(\mathbf{u}\cdot\nabla)\mathbf{u} + \frac{\mathbf{f}}{\rho} - \frac{\nabla p}{\rho}, \qquad (1)$$

subject to the volume conservation constraint

$$\nabla \cdot \mathbf{u} = 0, \qquad (2)$$

where $\mathbf{u}$ is the fluid velocity field, p is the pressure field, t is time, ρ is density (which we will assume constant everywhere), $\mathbf{f}$ is a field of external forces, and $\nabla = [\partial/\partial x, \partial/\partial y, \partial/\partial z]^\mathsf{T}$.

We integrate Equation (1) forward in time using operator splitting; itegrating each term of Equation (1) separately as follows.

$$\mathbf{u}^* = \text{Advect}(\mathbf{u}_t), \qquad (3)$$

$$\mathbf{u}^{**} = \mathbf{u}^* + \frac{h}{\rho}\mathbf{f}, \qquad (4)$$

$$\nabla^2 p = \frac{\rho}{h}\nabla\cdot\mathbf{u}^{**}, \text{and} \qquad (5)$$

$$\mathbf{u}_{t+1} = \mathbf{u}^{**} - \frac{h}{\rho}\nabla p, \qquad (6)$$

where h is the length of a time step, $\mathbf{u}_t$ and $\mathbf{u}_{t+1}$ are velocity fields at two successive time steps whose domains are two successive tetrahedral meshes M_t and M_{t+1}, and $\mathbf{u}^*$ and $\mathbf{u}^{**}$ are intermediate velocity fields over M_{t+1}.

To implement Equation (3), velocities are advected by the method of Feldman *et al.* [FOKG05], a generalization of the semi-Lagrangian advection method of Stam [Sta99]. Specifically, we assign velocities to the new mesh M_{t+1}, where velocities are stored at face barycenters, by tracing the path of each barycenter backward in time through the piecewise linear velocity field defined over M_t. When we reach the end of a path, we determine the velocity at the endpoint by interpolation on M_t, and assign it to the barycenter in M_{t+1}. (To

Figure 3: *Top: A wave of liquid flowing over a hemispherical obstacle. Center: Cutaway view of the tetrahedra enclosed by the green box in the top image. Bottom: Portions of the surface triangulation and tetrahedral mesh, respectively, enclosed by the yellow box in the top image.*

be precise, we only assign the scalar component of velocity normal to the face.)

Equations (5) and (6) together perform *pressure correction*, which ensures that $\mathbf{u}_{t+1}$ satisfies the volume conservation (divergence-free velocity) condition, Equation (2). Observe that Equation (5) entails the solution of a Poisson equation. We discretize it with a finite volume method, yielding a system of linear equations.

We take our methods for discretizing the derivative operators and interpolating the velocities from Klingner *et al.* [KFCO06]. We summarize them briefly here; see the original work for details. We store one pressure value at the center of each tetrahedron. At the center of each triangular face, we store one scalar value representing the normal component of the velocity.

The gradient of the pressure normal to a face f is denoted

$$\nabla p \cdot \mathbf{n}_f = \frac{p_2 - p_1}{d_f}, \tag{7}$$

where p_1 and p_2 are the pressures at the centers of the two tetrahedra adjoining f, and d_f is the perpendicular distance between those centers. The average divergence within a tetrahedron is denoted

$$(\nabla \cdot \mathbf{u})_{\text{avg}} = \frac{1}{V} \sum_{i=1}^{4} z_i A_i s_i, \tag{8}$$

where V is the volume of the tetrahedron, and for each tetrahedron face indexed $i \in \{1,2,3,4\}$, A_i is the area of face i, z_i is the velocity component normal to face i, and s_i is a sign ($+1$ or -1) that orients face i's normal outward.

To interpolate velocities within a tetrahedral mesh, we first compute a velocity vector at each tetrahedron center from its four face normal velocities, following Elcott *et al.* [ETK*07]. As the authors point out, this step does not cause artificial smoothing. To interpolate at an arbitrary point, we use generalized barycentric interpolation [WSHD04] over dual cells of the mesh.

When we trace paths backward through time for semi-Lagrangian advection (to advect both the free surface and the velocities), we find that using a smoothed version of the velocity field for integrating the path does not produce objectionable artifacts. We take advantage of this observation to speed up advection substantially: we compute velocity vectors at the primal mesh vertices by generalized barycentric interpolation; then based on these vectors, we use standard barycentric interpolation (which is appreciably faster) over the tetrahedra to perform backward tracing.

However, once we have traced a path back to its endpoint one time step earlier, we use the more expensive generalized barycentric interpolation to evaluate the velocity at the endpoint. If we were to use standard barycentric interpolation for this evaluation, successive errors would accumulate over time, manifesting as artificial damping of the velocity field, as Klingner *et al.* [KFCO06] report.

We differ from Klingner *et al.* by storing pressures and velocities at the barycenters of the tetrahedra and triangular faces, instead of at the circumcenters. The gradient and interpolation operators were designed with the geometric properties of circumcenters in mind, but we find that storing quantities at the barycenters works well in practice.

3.2. Surface Tracking by Semi-Lagrangian Contouring

Surface tracking is the act of computing an updated liquid boundary S_{t+1} from the previous time step's boundary S_t and the velocity field $\mathbf{u}_t$ defined over the mesh M_t. We use semi-Lagrangian contouring (SLC), devised for two dimensions by Strain [Str01] then extended to three dimensions by

Bargteil *et al.* [BGOS06] (who also provide an open-source implementation). We briefly review the method here.

SLC begins by defining a *signed distance function* $f(\mathbf{p})$ over $\mathbb{R}^3$ that is positive inside S_t, negative outside, and zero on the boundary. See Bargteil *et al.* for details on how to use an octree to approximate the signed distance function. (The function is exact near the surface, but at a distance we approximate by interpolating over the octree.) Note that $f(\mathbf{p})$ is the function used as an input to isosurface stuffing (described in Section 3.3) to construct the graded tetrahedral mesh M_t, which approximately fills the surface $S_t = \{\mathbf{p} : f(\mathbf{p}) = 0\}$. (The resolution of M_t is chosen so its boundary edges generally have twice the length of the edges of S_t.)

The next step is to implicitly construct a second signed distance function $f^+(\mathbf{p})$ that represents the liquid surface after it moves for the duration of a time step. The final step is to use Marching Cubes to construct a high-resolution triangulated approximation S_{t+1} of the surface $\{\mathbf{p} : f^+(\mathbf{p}) = 0\}$.

To calculate the function $f^+(\mathbf{p})$ at a given point $\mathbf{p}$, we use the same semi-Lagrangian advection method, described in Section 3.1, that we use to advect the velocity field: trace a path from $\mathbf{p}$ backward in time through the velocity field $\mathbf{u}_t$ defined over M_t. We also modify the function $f^+(\mathbf{p})$ to prevent penetration of obstacles, as described in Section 3.3.1, and to thicken the liquid where necessary, as described in Section 3.4.

3.3. Mesh Generation

The tetrahedral meshes we use for simulation conform to the volume occupied by the fluid, as Figure 3 shows. This approach has several merits. First, it simplifies the handling of boundary conditions during pressure correction, as the mesh boundary is the fluid boundary. Second, computation is only expended on the region occupied by fluid. Lastly, because the mesh is recreated each frame, we can grade the mesh so that it is fine near the surface, where we want detail, but coarse in the interior, speeding up every part of our simulation method.

Our mesh generation algorithm, called isosurface stuffing [LS07], takes a signed distance field as its input, and produces a mesh whose boundary approximates the field's zero-surface, so the algorithm enjoys a natural marriage with a level-set surface tracking method, in our case semi-Lagrangian contouring. It builds a balanced octree that covers the liquid surface with leaf octants, all the same size. This octree serves as a skeleton for a tetrahedral *background grid* inspired by the Delaunay triangulation of the body centered cubic lattice. (Producing the background grid is not quite as simple as subdividing each octant into tetrahedra; some tetrahedra span two octants.) Vertices of the background grid that are too close to the liquid surface are warped so that they lie on the surface. New vertices are added where edges of the background grid cut the surface. Finally, some background tetrahedra are subdivided into smaller tetrahedra to accommodate the new vertices, using stencils of precomputed tetrahedra in the same fashion that Marching Cubes uses stencils of precomputed triangles. All the vertices on the boundary of the final mesh lie on the surface of the liquid.

Isosurface stuffing is extremely fast and numerically robust because it does little geometric computation (compared to most meshing algorithms). The tetrahedra it produces are mathematically guaranteed to have high quality. (See the original paper [LS07] for details.) It is these features that collectively make it feasible to generate a new, large mesh for every time step.

3.3.1. Modifications for Obstacles

Our simulations include interactions with solid obstacles such as walls and containers. Semi-Lagrangian contouring generally produces a signed distance function that does not perfectly conform to obstacles, because of numerical errors and the discretization of time and the velocity field. To prevent liquid from penetrating a rigid obstacle, we build a signed distance function for the obstacle. The input to our mesher is a function that is the minimum of two signed distance functions—one that is positive inside the liquid, and one that is negative inside the obstacle.

The opposite problem can occur too: persistent thin gaps between a liquid and an obstacle. We fix these problems after the mesh is built. Vertices that are within one eighth of the edge length of the leaf octants from an obstacle are "snapped" onto the obstacle boundary by orthogonal projection. We have found that snapping vertices this way does not introduce badly shaped tetrahedra.

We classify a face of the mesh as a liquid-obstacle interface if all of its vertices lie on the obstacle. All other boundary faces are liquid-air interfaces. When we build the linear system for the discretization of Equation (5), we treat liquid-obstacle faces with closed, non-slip boundary conditions, and we treat liquid-air faces with open boundary conditions, following Klingner *et al.* [KFCO06].

3.3.2. Exploiting Properties of the Mesh

Isosurface stuffing makes it feasible to use a large number of tetrahedra (in our examples, about 1–3 million). Besides its speed and numerical robustness, a more subtle benefit is that its meshes are semi-structured: in the interior, they use only four shapes of tetrahedra (in graded sizes). In our simulations, roughly two thirds of the tetrahedra have one of these four shapes. Therefore, many tetrahedra have the same volume, face areas, and face normals (possibly scaled by a power of two), which are needed for our finite volume discretization (Section 3.1). We save a substantial amount of memory by not storing these quantities for tetrahedra having standard shapes. Thus we realize some of the storage savings usually associated with structured grids, without sacrificing grading or boundary conformity.

Another way we exploit the structure of our meshes is by using the octree for point location. When we perform semi-Lagrangian advection of the velocities, we need to trace each

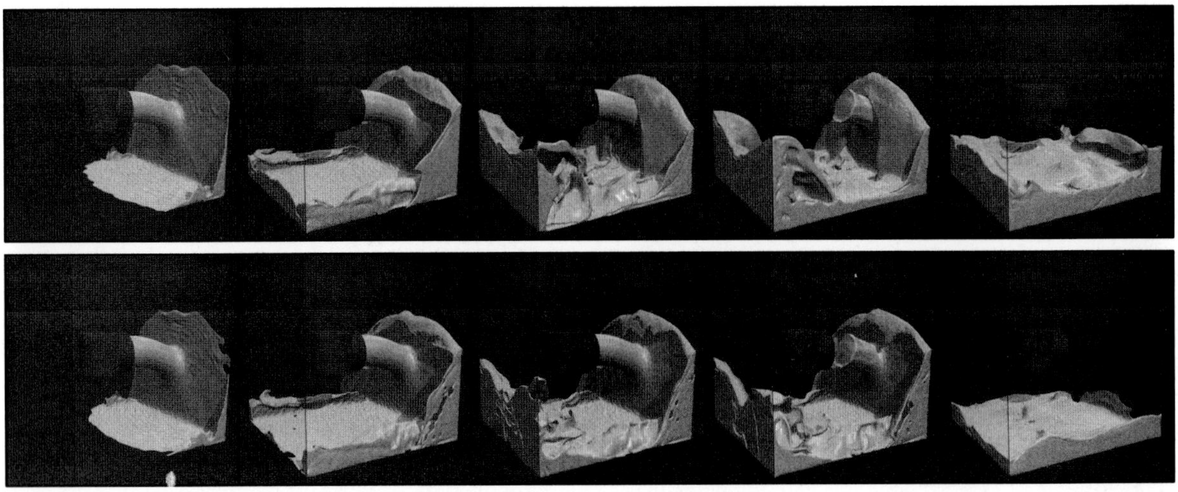

Figure 4: *A comparison of images taken from animations generated with our thickening scheme (top) and without (bottom). The example with no thickening suffers from visible holes and artifacts where thin structures vanish. Observe the difference in liquid volume between the last frames of the two sequences: without thickening, the simulation has lost appreciable volume.*

face barycenter of the new mesh M_{t+1} backward in time through the velocity field defined over the old mesh M_t. Likewise, advection of the surface also entails tracing a path through M_t. The first step in doing so is to find the tetrahedron in M_t that contains the starting point. We walk down the octree until we reach the finest octant containing the point, then we use standard walking point location to home in on the right tetrahedron.

Occasionally, a path is traced right outside the mesh M_t, so we need to extrapolate velocities. For this task, we use the efficient octree extrapolation technique of Losasso *et al.* [LGF04] on our mesh generator's octree.

3.4. Thickening

Like other grid level-set surface tracking methods, semi-Lagrangian contouring cannot resolve sheets or tendrils of fluid that become thinner than the leaf octants of the octree used store the signed distance function. The visual results can include small droplets spontaneously vanishing, large holes opening up in thin sheets of liquid, and rapid loss of total fluid volume, as shown in the bottom row of Figure 4. Moreover, the resolution of the tetrahedral mesh M_t is typically a factor of two coarser than the resolution of the surface S_t. Although this sampling strategy allows us to maintain finely detailed surfaces, it can create circumstances where M_t has no tetrahedra near a thin part of the fluid volume bounded by S_t, so the fluid cannot be simulated.

To solve both problems, we have developed a thickening technique that modifies the signed distance function $f(\mathbf{p})$ in regions where the fluid is thin. We heuristically detect these regions and place particles approximately on their medial axes. The radii of the particles are proportional to the distance from the medial axis to the surface (Section 3.4.1). These particles thicken the liquid by modifying the signed distance function $f(\mathbf{p})$ (Sections 3.4.2 and 3.4.3). A second-order Runge-Kutta method advects the particles forward through the velocity field $\mathbf{u}$.

We use different thickening approaches for surface tracking and mesh generation, because we desire different behavior from each. For surface tracking, we prefer a smooth surface to a bumpy one, even at the cost of some volume loss. For meshing, we do not want to leave any of the surface S_t hanging outside the simulation mesh M_t, but bumps in the mesh surface are harmless and do not affect the appearance of the rendered liquid surface.

Given that we use particles in thin regions, why do we not use them everywhere as a replacement for semi-Lagrangian contouring? In our experience, particle level set methods tend to create bumpy surfaces. These can be fixed by smoothing, albeit with a concomitant loss of detail. We turned to SLC because it gives us better detail for a fixed resolution grid.

3.4.1. Medial Axis Estimation

The medial axis of a surface is the set of centers of spheres that touch the surface at more than one point, but are entirely enclosed by the surface [Blu67]. Three-dimensional medial axes are unstable and difficult to compute. Several researchers, such as Foskey *et al.* [FLM03], propose simplified approximations of the medial axis, but even these are computationally expensive. We do not need much accuracy, and we need the approximation only in thin regions, so we have found the following simple strategy to be adequate.

For each vertex $\mathbf{x}_i$ of S_t, shoot a ray from $\mathbf{x}_i$ in the negative normal direction $-\mathbf{n}_i$ as illustrated in Figure 5, and check if the ray hits S_t again within a "thinness" threshold γ. If so, compute the midpoint $\mathbf{m}_i$ between $\mathbf{x}_i$ and the first point where the ray intersects S_t. The point $\mathbf{m}_i$ is a candidate that may be near the medial axis of the thin region. We estimate the minimum distance d_i from $\mathbf{m}_i$ to S_t, using the

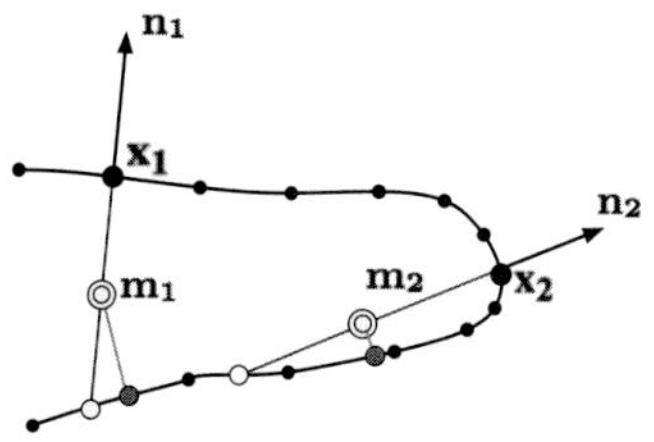

Figure 5: *Finding points that lie approximately on the medial axis. In this example,* $\mathbf{m}_1$ *is used but* $\mathbf{m}_2$ *is rejected.*

signed distance function for S_t, and throw away $\mathbf{m}_i$ if d_i is substantially shorter than the distance from $\mathbf{x}_i$ to $\mathbf{m}_i$ (see Figure 5). For surface thickening, we choose γ to be 1.2 times the edge length of the smallest leaf octant of the octree that represents S_t (and the signed distance function). For mesh thickening, we choose γ to be 1.2 times the edge length of the mesh generator's smallest leaf octants.

3.4.2. Mesh Thickening

Given the surface S_t, we define its signed distance function $f(\mathbf{p})$. From $f(\mathbf{p})$ and the particles sampled near the medial axis of S_t, we create a "thickened" function $f^*(\mathbf{p})$, which isosurface stuffing takes as input to generate the mesh M_t.

The thickened function f^* is the sum of the original function f and an *offset function* that thickens $f^*(\mathbf{p})$ enough so that M_t encloses the entire liquid surface S_t. The offset is

$$\text{offset}(\mathbf{p}) = \frac{\sum_i W(\mathbf{p}-\mathbf{m}_i,h)(\gamma_{\text{mesh}}-d_i)}{\sum_i W(\mathbf{p}-\mathbf{m}_i,h)},$$

where γ_{mesh} and h are respectively 0.6 times and 4 times the edge length of the mesh generator's smallest leaf octant. Following Müller *et al.* [MCG03], W is the kernel

$$W_{\text{poly6}}(\mathbf{z},h) = \frac{315}{64\pi h^9}\begin{cases}(h^2-|\mathbf{z}|^2)^3 & 0 \le \mathbf{z} \le h,\\ 0 & \text{otherwise.}\end{cases}$$

3.4.3. Surface Thickening

We compute the next surface S_{t+1} by thickening the signed distance function $f(\mathbf{p})$ for S_t. Thickening of $f(\mathbf{p})$ for S_t is done differently then the thickening method used for input to the meshing algorithm (Section 3.4.2) because our goal for the surface is to prevent liquid disappearance while maintaining a smooth surface and avoiding creating too much extra volume. We prevent excessive volume gain by redistributing the volume in medial axis particles from one location to another, in a way that tends to make thin regions break apart.

After the medial axis particles have been advected, we divide them into two groups, Q_{small} and Q_{big}. Q_{small} contains particles with $d_i \le \beta_{\text{slc}}$ and Q_{big} contains those with $d_i > \beta_{\text{slc}}$, where d_i is the thickness defined in Section 3.4.1, and β_{slc} depends on the size of the background contouring grid (see below). For each particle $q_s \in Q_{\text{small}}$, we look for the subset Q_{near} of particles in Q_{big} that are within a distance of r_{redis} from q_s. We then redistribute the radius of q_s to the particles in Q_{near} by uniformly incrementing the radius of particles in Q_{near} by $d_s/|Q_{\text{near}}|$. Although it might seem more sensible to distribute volume instead of radius, or to non-uniformly distribute based on distance from q_s, our strategy is fast and works well in practice.

After the redistribution step, we increment the radius of the particles in Q_{big} by r_{ib} (see below). We delete from Q_{small} the particles that found nearby Q_{big} particles in the step above, and increase the radius of the remaining particles in Q_{small} by r_{is}, thereby thickening the liquid slightly in the thin regions.

In the animations we present in Section 4, β_{slc} is 0.5γ, r_{ib} is 0.25 times the smallest grid size, and r_{is} is 0.15 times the smallest grid size. By choosing r_{redis} to be between 0 and 3 times the smallest grid size, we control how difficult it is to break thin sheets of liquid apart.

After we update the radius of the particles, we construct an implicit function L_{par} defined by the particles' positions and radii, as described by Zhu and Bridson [ZB05]. We unite L_{par} with the signed distance function f generated by the original SLC method by defining a new signed distance function

$$f^{**}(\mathbf{p}) = \max(f(\mathbf{p}), L_{\text{par}}(\mathbf{p})),$$

whose zero-surface is triangulated by Marching Cubes to yield the new surface S_{t+1}.

3.5. Algebraic Multigrid for Incompressibility

We enforce the incompressibility of the fluid by solving Poisson's equation (5), yielding a pressure field p such that the final velocity field $\mathbf{u}_{t+1}$, computed by Equation (6), is divergence-free. Discretizing Equation (5) yields a large, sparse, symmetric linear system, which we solve efficiently using algebraic multigrid.

Multigrid speeds up a standard iterative method by using it to compute a quick, inaccurate solution, then correcting the error in the approximate solution with help from an approximate solution to a coarser version of the problem, which can be solved more quickly. The coarser version is recursively solved by using an even coarser version of the problem. The base case is a linear system small enough to solve quickly with a direct method. See McCormick [McC87] or Trottenberg *et al.* [TOS01] for a detailed description of multigrid.

Suppose the system we wish to solve is $A_q\mathbf{x}_q = \mathbf{b}_q$, where $\mathbf{x}_q$ is unknown. The hierarchy of linear systems is $A_k\mathbf{x}_k = \mathbf{b}_k$, with k ranging from 1, the coarsest system, to q, the finest. Each A_k in some sense approximates the finest matrix A_q.

Multigrid uses a sequence of linear *prolongation operators* $P_{k,k-1}$ that expand a coarse solution (with few unknowns) to a finer one (with more), and a sequence of linear *restriction operators* $R_{k-1,k}$ that reduce a fine solution to a coarser one (with some loss of information). In the original, geometric formulation of multigrid, the fine and coarse solutions are nodal values on regular grids of two different resolutions, prolongation is done (exactly) by interpolating, and restriction is done (approximately) by projection. The matrices for the coarser levels, A_k are formed by applying the discretization stencils on the coarsened meshes.

V-cycle multigrid begins by applying a *relaxation operator* $\mathbf{S}(A_k, \mathbf{x}_k, \mathbf{b}_k)$, which returns an approximation solution (usually with poor accuracy) to the system $A_k\mathbf{x}_k = \mathbf{b}_k$. We use two Gauss-Seidel iterations. Next, it computes the residual of the system, restricts it to the next coarser grid, and recursively solves the coarse problem on the restricted residual. It prolongs the coarse solution and adds it, as a corrective term, to the fine solution. Finally, the relaxation operator is applied again. We use full-cycle multigrid, which uses V-cycle multigrid as a subroutine as follows.

VCYCLEMULTIGRID($\mathbf{x}_k, \mathbf{b}_k, k$)
  if $k = 1$
    $\mathbf{x}_k \leftarrow A_1^{-1}\mathbf{b}_k$
  else
    $\mathbf{x}_k \leftarrow \mathbf{S}(A_k, \mathbf{x}_k, \mathbf{b}_k)$
    $\mathbf{r}_{k-1} \leftarrow R_{k-1,k}(\mathbf{b}_k - A_k\mathbf{x}_k)$
    $\mathbf{w}_{k-1} \leftarrow \mathbf{0}$
    VCYCLEMULTIGRID($\mathbf{w}_{k-1}, \mathbf{r}_{k-1}, k-1$)
    $\mathbf{x}_k \leftarrow \mathbf{x}_k + P_{k,k-1}\mathbf{w}_{k-1}$
    $\mathbf{x}_k \leftarrow \mathbf{S}(A_k, \mathbf{x}_k, \mathbf{b}_k)$

FULLCYCLEMULTIGRID($\mathbf{x}, \mathbf{b}$)
  $\mathbf{r}_q \leftarrow \mathbf{b} - A\mathbf{x}$
  for $k \leftarrow q$ **to** 2
    $\mathbf{r}_{k-1} \leftarrow R_{k-1,k}\mathbf{r}_k$
  $\mathbf{z}_1 \leftarrow A_1^{-1}\mathbf{r}_1$
  for $k \leftarrow 2$ **to** q
    $\mathbf{z}_k \leftarrow P_{k,k-1}\mathbf{z}_{k-1}$
    VCYCLEMULTIGRID($\mathbf{z}_k, \mathbf{r}_k, k$)
  $\mathbf{x} \leftarrow \mathbf{x} + \mathbf{z}_q$

Simulation domains with sinuous shapes make it difficult to geometrically coarsen a mesh in a way suitable for multigrid—clustering unstructured tetrahedra does not create larger tetrahedra. This problem can occur even for regular hexahedral grids on irregularly shaped domains. We circumvent this problem with algebraic multigrid, which uses only the finite volume matrices, and not the geometry, to construct the prolongation and restriction operators. From the prolongation and restriction operators the system matrices can be defined by $A_{k-1} = R_{k-1,k}A_kP_{k,k-1}$.

To form the restriction and prolongation operators, we partition the level k variables into *coarse* and *fine* variables. Coarse variables survive into the coarser level $k-1$; fine variables do not. $P_{k,k-1}$ is a matrix that prolongs a level $k-1$ solution by assigning each fine level k variable the average of the values of its coarse neighbors from the level $k-1$ solution. (Variables i and j are *neighbors* if A_{ij} is non-zero.) Some researchers advocate using weighted averages based on matrix coefficients [McC87], but we find that simple averages converge faster. They also save memory and time by obviating the need to compute weights. For restriction, we use the popular Galerkin projection method [TOS01], in which $R_{k-1,k} = P_{k,k-1}^{\mathrm{T}}$.

	Sim	Mesh	SLC	Tets (M)	Tris (M)
Chutes	61	59	350	1.0	2.1
Spray (T)	37	53	169	0.8	1.4
Spray (NT)	40	54	176	0.8	1.4
Angel	30	24	276	1.0	1.4
Dam Break	49	42	196	1.3	1.2

Table 1: *Simulation times for our examples, in seconds per frame of animation.* Sim *denotes the time used for velocity advection and pressure correction.* Mesh *is the time for mesh generation.* SLC *is the time used by the surface tracker. The last two columns show the average numbers, in millions, of tetrahedra in the simulation mesh and triangles in the surface triangulation. (T) and (NT) indicate thickening and no thickening.*

Each level k variable must have at least one neighbor labeled *coarse* (possibly itself). A good partition has *coarse* variables that support good interpolation of values from the coarser to the finer level, but also keep the number of *coarse* variables modest, so that the coarser linear system is as small as possible. The following greedy algorithm for labeling variables, though not optimal, strikes a good balance between simplicity and effectiveness in practice.

1. Assign each variable a counter storing its number of neighbors.
2. Select a variable at random; label it *coarse*.
3. Label the neighbors of the new *coarse* variable *fine*.
4. For each unlabeled neighbor of each new *fine* variable, decrement the count of its number of unlabeled neighbors.
5. Select the unlabeled variable that neighbors a *fine* variable and has the most unlabeled neighbors. Label it *coarse*.
6. Repeat steps 3 to 5 until every variable is labeled.

Our algebraic multigrid scheme is not novel, but we are not aware of its prior use in graphics for fluid animation. Our simulations use between 0.8 million and 1.3 million tetrahedra. For these systems, our algebraic multigrid solver is between 1.8 and 2.1 times faster than a preconditioned conjugate gradient solver. In a test with a five million tetrahedron mesh, our solver was three times faster than preconditioned conjugate gradients. We believe that the solver would work similarly well for fluid simulations with other discretizations, and that the performance benefit would grow for larger systems.

4. Results and Discussion

We have a prototype implementation, written in C++, which we used to animate several scenarios, depicted in Figures 1, 4, 6, and 7 (also seen in Figure 3). We ran the simulations single-threaded on 2.8 or 3.2 GHz Intel processors with 3 or 4 GB of memory. All figures were rendered by PIXIE.

Table 1 shows the running times. The cost of velocity advection and pressure projection is roughly equal to the cost

Figure 6: *A sequence beginning with a fluid configuration in the shape of an angel. Once the simulation begins, the structure falls, creating a complex splash pattern.*

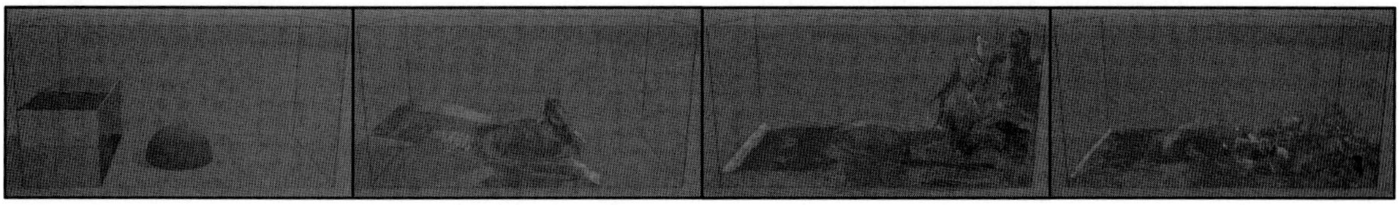

Figure 7: *A sequence wherein a block of liquid is released at one side of a closed container. The wave of water flows over an obstacle and crashes against the far side of the container.*

of mesh generation. The running times of the spray examples with and without thickening show that the cost of thickening is negligible. In all our simulations, surface tracking dominates the overall cost. More than a third of the surface tracking time is in a fast marching method that approximates the signed distance function. Most of the remaining time is spent tracing the velocity field backward. We believe there is substantial room for speed improvement through faster algorithms for signed distance approximation and path tracing. For example, it might be possible to exploit temporal coherence to avoid recomputing the signed distance field from scratch at every time step, and our point location and path tracing does not take advantage of spatial locality.

Our methods are not without flaws. Some of our examples exhibit a small amount of volume loss. However, we are not aware of a liquid simulation method that preserves volume perfectly. Our thickening scheme has adjustable parameters that allow a user to reduce this effect, although excessive use of the thickening scheme can result in volume *gain* artifacts. Another imperfection is that our discretization of the Poisson operator is not linearly consistent, so our free surfaces move even when gravity is the only force applied to a pool of water. This artifact is not apparent in dynamic scenes, but it is visible in scenes with very slow moving water. The octree method of Losasso *et al.* [LGF04] exhibits similar artifacts when the octree grades from coarse to fine along a direction orthogonal to the direction of gravity.

Future work includes adding viscoelasticity to a simulation. This goal requires additional differential operators, defined in a consistent and stable manner. It is probably straightforward to extend our methods to multiple-phase liquids, as the meshing algorithm can create high-quality tetrahedra on both sides of an interface. We could also couple our liquids to moving rigid bodies using the methods of Klingner *et al.* [KFCO06] and Chentanez *et al.* [CGFO06], who also use tetrahedral meshes.

Acknowledgments

We thank the Berkeley graphics group for helpful criticism and comments, and Adam Bargteil for comments and help with the SLC code. This work was supported in part by California MICRO 03-067 and 04-066, by the National Science Foundation under Awards CCF-0430065 and CCF-0635381, by generous support from Apple Computer, Pixar Animation Studios, Intel Corporation, Sony Computer Entertainment America, the Hellman Family Fund, and by two Alfred P. Sloan Research Fellowships.

References

[BE92] BERN M., EPPSTEIN D.: Mesh generation and optimal triangulation. In *Computing in Euclidean Geometry*, Du D.-Z., Hwang F., (Eds.), vol. 1 of *Lecture Notes Series on Computing*. World Scientific, Singapore, 1992, pp. 23–90.

[BGOS06] BARGTEIL A. W., GOKTEKIN T. G., O'BRIEN J. F., STRAIN J. A.: A semi-Lagrangian contouring method for fluid simulation. *ACM Transactions on Graphics 25*, 1 (Jan. 2006), 19–38.

[Blu67] BLUM H.: A transformation for extracting new descriptors of shape. *Models for the Perception of Speech and Visual Form* (1967), 362–380.

[CD97] CANI M.-P., DESBRUN M.: Animation of deformable models using implicit surfaces. *IEEE Transactions on Visualization and Computer Graphics 3*, 1 (Jan. 1997), 39–50.

[CGFO06] CHENTANEZ N., GOKTEKIN T. G., FELDMAN B. E., O'BRIEN J. F.: Simultaneous coupling of fluids and deformable bodies. In *2006 Symposium on Computer Animation* (Sept. 2006), pp. 83–89.

[CMT04] CARLSON M., MUCHA P. J., TURK G.: Rigid fluid: Animating the interplay between rigid bodies and fluid. *ACM Transactions on Graphics 23*, 3 (Aug. 2004), 377–384. Special issue on Proceedings of SIGGRAPH 2004.

[DC96] DESBRUN M., CANI M.-P.: Smoothed particles: A new paradigm for animating highly deformable bodies. In *Computer Animation and Simulation '96* (Aug. 1996), pp. 61–76.

[EMF02] ENRIGHT D. P., MARSCHNER S. R., FEDKIW R. P.: Animation and rendering of complex water surfaces. *ACM Transactions on Graphics 21*, 3 (July 2002), 736–744. Special issue on Proceedings of SIGGRAPH 2002.

[ETK*07] ELCOTT S., TONG Y., KANSO E., SCHRÖDER P., DESBRUN M.: Stable, circulation-preserving, simplicial fluids. *ACM Transactions on Graphics 26*, 1 (Jan. 2007).

[FF01] FOSTER N., FEDKIW R.: Practical animation of liquids. In *Computer Graphics (SIGGRAPH 2001 Proceedings)* (Aug. 2001), pp. 23–30.

[FLM03] FOSKEY M., LIN M., MANOCHA D.: Efficient computation of a simplified medial axis. In *8th Symposium on Solid Modeling and Applications* (June 2003), pp. 96–107.

[FM96] FOSTER N., METAXAS D.: Realistic animation of liquids. In *Graphics Interface 1996* (May 1996), pp. 204–212.

[FOA03] FELDMAN B. E., O'BRIEN J. F., ARIKAN O.: Animating suspended particle explosions. *ACM Transactions on Graphics 22*, 3 (July 2003), 708–715. Special issue on Proceedings of SIGGRAPH 2003.

[FOK05] FELDMAN B. E., O'BRIEN J. F., KLINGNER B. M.: Animating gases with hybrid meshes. *ACM Transactions on Graphics 24*, 3 (Aug. 2005), 904–909. Special issue on Proceedings of SIGGRAPH 2005.

[FOKG05] FELDMAN B. E., O'BRIEN J. F., KLINGNER B. M., GOKTEKIN T. G.: Fluids in deforming meshes. In *2005 Symposium on Computer Animation* (July 2005), pp. 255–259.

[FSJ01] FEDKIW R., STAM J., JENSEN H. W.: Visual simulation of smoke. In *Computer Graphics (SIGGRAPH 2001 Proceedings)* (Aug. 2001), pp. 15–22.

[GBO04] GOKTEKIN T. G., BARGTEIL A. W., O'BRIEN J. F.: A method for animating viscoelastic fluids. *ACM Transactions on Graphics 23*, 3 (Aug. 2004), 463–468. Special issue on Proceedings of SIGGRAPH 2004.

[GSLF05] GUENDELMAN E., SELLE A., LOSASSO F., FEDKIW R.: Coupling water and smoke to thin deformable and rigid shells. *ACM Transactions on Graphics 24*, 3 (Aug. 2005), 973–981. Special issue on Proceedings of SIGGRAPH 2005.

[KCC*06] KIM J., CHA D., CHANG B., KOO B., IHM I.: Practical animation of turbulent splashing water. In *2006 Symposium on Computer Animation* (Sept. 2006), pp. 335–344.

[KFCO06] KLINGNER B. M., FELDMAN B. E., CHENTANEZ N., O'BRIEN J. F.: Fluid animation with dynamic meshes. *ACM Transactions on Graphics 25*, 3 (Aug. 2006), 820–825. Special issue on Proceedings of SIGGRAPH 2006.

[LGF04] LOSASSO F., GIBOU F., FEDKIW R.: Simulating water and smoke with an octree data structure. *ACM Transactions on Graphics 23*, 3 (Aug. 2004), 457–462. Special issue on Proceedings of SIGGRAPH 2004.

[LS07] LABELLE F., SHEWCHUK J. R.: Isosurface stuffing: Fast tetrahedral meshes with good dihedral angles. *ACM Transactions on Graphics 26*, 3 (Aug. 2007). Special issue on Proceedings of SIGGRAPH 2007.

[LSSF06] LOSASSO F., SHINAR T., SELLE A., FEDKIW R.: Multiple interacting liquids. *ACM Transactions on Graphics 25*, 3 (Aug. 2006), 812–819. Special issue on Proceedings of SIGGRAPH 2006.

[McC87] MCCORMICK S. F.: *Multigrid Methods.* Society for Industrial and Applied Mathematics, Philidelphia, 1987.

[MCG03] MÜLLER M., CHARYPAR D., GROSS M.: Particle-based fluid simulation for interactive applications. In *2003 Symposium on Computer Animation* (Aug. 2003), pp. 154–159.

[MKN*04] MÜLLER M., KEISER R., NEALEN A., PAULY M., GROSS M., ALEXA M.: Point based animation of elastic, plastic and melting objects. In *2004 Symposium on Computer Animation* (July 2004), pp. 141–151.

[NFJ02] NGUYEN D., FEDKIW R., JENSEN H.: Physically based modeling and animation of fire. *ACM Transactions on Graphics 21*, 3 (Aug. 2002), 721–728. Special issue on Proceedings of SIGGRAPH 2002.

[Owe98] OWEN S. J.: A survey of unstructured mesh generation technology. In *7th International Meshing Roundtable* (July 1998), pp. 239–267.

[PTB*03] PREMOŽE S., TASDIZEN T., BIGLER J., LEFOHN A., WHITAKER R.: Particle-based simulation of fluids. *Computer Graphics Forum 22*, 3 (Sept. 2003), 401–410.

[SRF05] SELLE A., RASMUSSEN N., FEDKIW R.: A vortex particle method for smoke, water, and explosions. *ACM Transactions on Graphics 24*, 3 (July 2005), 910–914. Special issue on Proceedings of SIGGRAPH 2005.

[Sta99] STAM J.: Stable fluids. In *Computer Graphics (SIGGRAPH '99 Proceedings)* (Aug. 1999), pp. 121–128.

[Str99] STRAIN J. A.: Semi-Lagrangian methods for level set equations. *Journal of Computational Physics 151*, 2 (May 1999), 498–533.

[Str01] STRAIN J. A.: A fast semi-Lagrangian contouring method for moving interfaces. *Journal of Computational Physics 169*, 1 (May 2001), 1–22.

[TKPR06] THÜREY N., KEISER R., PAULY M., RÜDE U.: Detail-preserving fluid control. In *2006 Symposium on Computer Animation* (Sept. 2006), pp. 7–12.

[TLP06] TREUILLE A., LEWIS A., POPOVIĆ Z.: Model reduction for real-time fluids. *ACM Transactions on Graphics 25*, 3 (Aug. 2006), 826–834. Special issue on Proceedings of SIGGRAPH 2006.

[TOS01] TROTTENBERG U., OOSTERLEE C. W., SCHÜLLER A.: *Multigrid.* Academic Press, London, 2001.

[TPF89] TERZOPOULOS D., PLATT J., FLEISCHER K.: Heating and melting deformable models (from goop to glop). In *Graphics Interface 1989* (June 1989), pp. 219–226.

[WSHD04] WARREN J., SCHAEFER S., HIRANI A. N., DESBRUN M.: Barycentric coordinates for convex sets. Advances in Computational and Applied Mathematics, 2004.

[ZB05] ZHU Y., BRIDSON R.: Animating sand as a fluid. *ACM Transactions on Graphics 24*, 3 (Aug. 2005), 965–972. Special issue on Proceedings of SIGGRAPH 2005.

[ZYP06] ZHENG W., YONG J.-H., PAUL J.-C.: Simulation of bubbles. In *2006 Symposium on Computer Animation* (Sept. 2006), pp. 325–333.

Eurographics/ ACM SIGGRAPH Symposium on Computer Animation (2007)
D. Metaxas and J. Popovic (Editors)

Solving General Shallow Wave Equations on Surfaces

Huamin Wang[†] and Gavin Miller[‡] and Greg Turk[†]

[†]Georgia Institute of Technology
[‡]Adobe Systems Incorporated

Abstract

We propose a new framework for solving General Shallow Wave Equations (GSWE) in order to efficiently simulate water flows on solid surfaces under shallow wave assumptions. Within this framework, we develop implicit schemes for solving the external forces applied to water, including gravity and surface tension. We also present a two-way coupling method to model interactions between fluid and floating rigid objects. Water flows in this system can be simulated not only on planar surfaces by using regular grids, but also on curved surfaces directly without surface parametrization. The experiments show that our system is fast, stable, physically sound, and straightforward to implement on both CPUs and GPUs. It is capable of simulating a variety of water effects including: shallow waves, water drops, rivulets, capillary events and fluid/floating rigid body coupling. Because the system is fast, we can also achieve real-time water drop control and shape design.

Categories and Subject Descriptors (according to ACM CCS): I.3.5 [Computer Graphics]: Computational Geometry and Object Modeling–Physically based modeling;

1. Introduction

Water is crucial to human life. People see, use and drink water everyday, thus it is not surprising that water simulation plays an important role in computer graphics. Incompressible fluid dynamics in general can be described by the *Navier-Stokes* equations. Due to the complexity of the 3D Navier-Stokes equations, water behavior varies significantly under different circumstances. Researchers have invented and adopted many numerical methods to generate various realistic water effects by solving the Navier-Stokes equations. While most previous research has been focused on simulating the high-speed dynamics of large bodies of water, our main interest in this paper is to provide a fast and accurate technique for graphics applications to simulate small-scale fluid dynamics and its interaction with solid surfaces, such as toy boats floating in the bathtub and water drops streaming down a glass.

Compared with other representations such as particles, tetrahedral meshes or grid structures, we believe that a height field is more suitable to represent small-scale water in low-speed fluid animations. A height-field-based system is easier to implement and its computational space increases only quadratically with spatial resolution. Also, restricting the Navier-Stokes equations to 2D makes it possible to apply implicit numerical schemes, which usually means more stability and higher efficiency. However, previous height-field-based techniques only supported a limited range of effects. In particular, surface tension was neglected, which diminished the accuracy of small-scale liquid simulations.

In order to remove these limitations, our first contribution is a general height-field-based system (Section 3) that solves the new General Shallow Wave Equations (GSWE) that are extensions of the traditional shallow wave equations. Our system builds height columns along surface normals rather than in the absolute gravity direction, as the left picture in Fig. 1 shows. External forces in our system include gravity (Section 4) and surface tension (Section 5), and they are solved by implicit schemes which are significantly more stable and efficient than explicit schemes. We further incorporate a two-way liquid/rigid body coupling method in Section 6 for floating and drifting effects. Finally in Section 7, we demonstrate how our system can be optimized to run in

[†] Email: {whmin, turk} @ cc.gatech.edu
[‡] Email: gmiller @ adobe.com

Symposium on Computer Animation 2007, San Diego, CA, August 03-04, 2007.
© 2007 ACM 978-1-59593-624-4/07/0008 $5.00

real time on both CPUs and GPUs, which allows users to control and design fluid shapes interactively.

This system is most suitable for simulating low-speed fluid dynamics of small-scale 3D water flows on surfaces, which is expensive to generate with particle systems or grid systems. It provides an efficient way to predict the behavior of high speed dynamics before applying more accurate but time-consuming techniques. While each different system is capable of efficiently generating some specific effects, a comprehensive system that combines height fields with particles or grids as in [OH95, IGLF06] should be able to capture more aspects of water animations in the future. We believe that the work presented in this paper will be an important sub-component of such a system.

2. Related Work

Water animation is notoriously difficult and time-consuming to produce because solving the 3D Navier-Stokes equations requires a huge computational domain. The computational space increases cubically in 3D when water is represented either by particle systems [Mon92, MCG03] or 3D grid systems [FM96, Sta99, FF01, EMF02], not to mention the extra computational cost required by the CFL condition. As expected, a natural solution to improve simulation performance is to reduce the computational space. Instead of using completely uniform grids in 3D, Losasso et al [LGF04], Houston et al. [HNB*06] and Nielsen and Museth [NM06] proposed to use non-uniform grids such as octree structures or cells with various lengths. Feldman et al. [FOK05], Klingner et al. [KFCO06] and Elcott et al. [ETK*07] considered solving fluid dynamics on unstructured tetrahedral meshes rather than grid structures. Treuille et al. [TLP06] used Principal Component Analysis (PCA) to further reduce a static computational space. However, it is difficult to extend this method to free surface water animations.

Since the computational space of a height-field-based system increases only quadratically with the spatial resolution, height fields were introduced to the graphics community by the work of Kass and Miller [KM90] for rapid fluid simulations. This technique was later augmented with semi-Lagrangian velocity advection by Layton and van de Panne [LvdP02]. Instead of using shallow wave equations, Chen and da Vitoria Lobo [CdVLHM97] proposed to only solve pressure projection in 2D while keeping other simulation steps in 3D. Recently, Irving et al. [IGLF06] demonstrated how to combine a height field representation with a grid structure in order to simulate some non-height-field behaviors such as overturning and splashing.

In order to simulate 2D water flows on curved surfaces, Stam [Sta03] proposed the use of quadrilateral meshes from Catmull-Clark subdivision. Flow simulation directly on manifold triangle meshes was demonstrated by Shi and Yu [SY04] and Elcott et al. [ETK*07] using discrete differential geometry (DDG) operators. Kim et al. [KLLR07] further adopted the BFECC method to reduce numerical dissipation in surface flows. Our method also simulates water flows on meshes directly, and we allow surfaces with arbitrary topology.

Considerable research has been done recently on grid systems and particle systems to model coupling between water and other objects, including rigid bodies, cloth and thin shells and other fluids. For height-field-based systems, fluid/rigid body coupling methods were proposed by O'Brien and Hodgins [OH95] and Chen and da Vitoria Lobo [CdVLHM97] to simulate waves caused by moving objects.

Other topics related to our work include water drop simulation [FHP98, NHS02], water wave simulation [HNC02, MMS04], fluid surface tension [HK03, CM04, SSK05, WMT05], and fluid control [TMPS03, MTPS04, FL04, SY05].

3. General Shallow Wave Equations

Our goal in this section is to extend traditional Shallow Wave Equations (SWE) [KM90] to our new General Shallow Wave Equations (GSWE). As their names imply, SWE and GSWE are both based on the shallow wave assumptions: the wave velocity is low and the wave height variation is small. The original shallow water equations can be derived from the Navier-Stokes equations according to the method of Saint-Venant [UJ04]. However, the height field in SWE is built in the absolute gravity direction and the only external force is the gravity force in the horizontal direction. While a SWE system can be greatly simplified because of these, it suffers from the following limitations. Firstly, solid surfaces could not be too steep otherwise water drops will not be properly represented, as shown by the upper left picture in Fig. 1. Secondly, it is not clear how to incorporate arbitrary external forces, such as surface tension forces and user control forces, nor how to develop implicit schemes for arbitrary external forces. Interaction between height-field-based water and the environment is also difficult to model in a physically-based manner.

The height field in GSWE is constructed along surface normals rather than in the absolute gravity direction as Fig. 1 shows. In order to avoid self-intersection of water columns when the surface is fully detailed with small bumps, we use averaged surface normals from a low-resolution surface and represent the difference between the original surface and the low-resolution surface as a terrain height field $b(x)$ in the local background. The water height field is then defined as a function $h(x,t)$ of the surface position x and time t. Horizontal water velocity is $\vec{u}(x,t)$, and vertical velocity is implicitly given as $\partial h/\partial t$. Since our system allows arbitrary external forces, we first separate a 3D force $\vec{f}_{ext}$ into a 1D pressure component P_{ext} and a 2D acceleration component $\vec{a}_{ext}$ as the

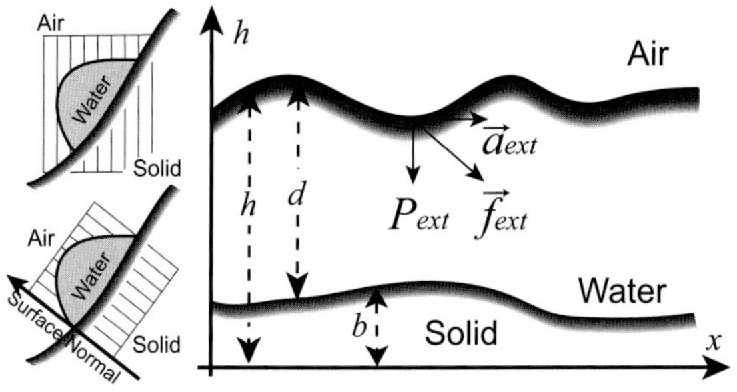

Figure 1: *Left: The height field is built along surface normals rather than in the absolute gravity direction. Right: External forces are separated into pressure and acceleration components.*

right picture in Fig. 1 shows. Although these two components act on the water based on different mechanisms, they both take effect by changing the water's horizontal velocity $\vec{u}$. The pressure component, including air pressure, surface tension pressure and vertical gravity pressure, squeezes water and causes horizontal movement due to pressure difference. On the other hand, the acceleration component, including user control force and horizontal gravity acceleration, acts on the horizontal velocity immediately. By restricting the 3D Navier-Stokes equations to 2D surfaces, we can formulate the non-viscid General Shallow Wave Equations as follows:

$$\vec{u}_t = -(\vec{u}\cdot\nabla)\vec{u} - \nabla P_{ext}/\rho + \vec{a}_{ext} \tag{1}$$

$$h_t + \nabla\cdot(h-b)\vec{u} = 0 \tag{2}$$

in which ρ is the water density. Eq. 1 updates the horizontal velocity due to both P_{ext} and $\vec{a}_{ext}$. Eq. 2 updates the height field and maintains the incompressibility implicitly. Eq. 2 can be reorganized into:

$$h_t + (h-b)\nabla\cdot\vec{u} + \vec{u}\cdot\nabla h = 0 \tag{3}$$

Since we are targeting at slow water, we ignore the velocity term $(\vec{u}\cdot\nabla)\vec{u}$ in Eq. 1. According to the method of characteristics, we first solve the height field advection due to the velocity using an explicit solver:

$$h_t + \vec{u}\cdot\nabla h = 0 \tag{4}$$

The rest of Eq. 1 and 3 are then simplified by differentiating Eq. 3 with respect to t and Eq. 1 with respect to the spatial dimensions, and then eliminating cross-derivatives:

$$\frac{\partial^2 h}{\partial t^2} = \frac{d\Delta P_{ext}}{\rho} - d\nabla\cdot(\vec{a}_{ext}) \tag{5}$$

When external forces vary slowly through time such as user control forces, we treat them as if they are temporally invariant so that Eq. 5 can be safely solved by explicit methods at each time step. However, two common natural forces, the gravity force and the surface tension force, are quite sensitive to height field changes as time evolves. If we still use explicit solvers in this case, the system would require significantly smaller time steps according to the CFL condition in order to avoid instability. Therefore, we develop implicit schemes for both of these forces in Sections 4 and 5 respectively. They are combined and solved together in a single matrix system:

$$(\mathbf{A_g} + \mathbf{A_s} + \mathbf{I} - \mathbf{I_c})h^t = b - b_c \tag{6}$$

in which h^t is the unknown height field at time t, and the previous height fields $h^{t-1}, h^{t-2}, \ldots$ at time $t-1, t-2, \ldots$ are already known. Matrices $\mathbf{A_g}$ and $\mathbf{A_s}$ are formulated from implicit schemes for gravity and surface tension respectively. $\mathbf{I_c}$ and b_c are the coupling matrix and vector, which will be discussed in Section 6. b is the prospective height field augmented with artificial viscosity effects by a factor τ:

$$b = h^{t-1} + (1-\tau)(h^{t-1} - h^{t-2}) \tag{7}$$

After the height field has been solved, we update the velocity field using Eq. 1 and apply the surface friction by a damping factor $\frac{h(x)}{h(x)+d}$. When d is zero, there is no friction and when d goes larger, the friction effect becomes more obvious.

3.1. Spatial Discretization

Because the height field is built along solid surface normals, spatial discretization in our system depends on solid surfaces rather than absolute 3D space. We discretize flat surfaces into regular grids and then use finite differencing schemes to formulate the GSWE matrix system.

For curved surfaces, we uniformly discretize them by a particle repulsion algorithm, instead of relying on parameterizing them into quadrilateral grids. We then build a height column at each particle as Fig. 2 shows. During each repulsion step, we search for the six closest particles and these particles become the neighborhood $\mathrm{U_i} = \{\mathrm{X}_{i_1}, \mathrm{X}_{i_2}, \ldots, \mathrm{X}_{i_6}\}$ of each particle X_i. We use six neighbors because this is the average number of neighbors once such a relaxation system converges. We find this approach produces similar results to other methods such as repulsion of all points within a fixed radius. Next, we sort the neighbors in counter-clockwise order. The repulsion force applied on X_i is then calculated as:

$$f(\mathrm{X_i}) = a\sum_j w_{i,j}(\mathrm{X_j} - \mathrm{X_i}) \qquad w_{i,j} = \cot\alpha_{i,j} + \cot\beta_{i,j} \tag{8}$$

The force magnitude factor a is usually between 0.01 and 0.2 in our experiments. $w_{i,j}$ is a non-zero weight factor only when $\mathrm{X_j} \in \mathrm{U_i}$ as in [GSD05], and $\alpha_{i,j}$ and $\beta_{i,j}$ are two angles facing toward the same edge $(\mathrm{X}_i, \mathrm{X}_j)$ as Fig. 2 shows. The advantage of calculating repulsion forces using Eq. 8 instead of polynomials in [Tur91] or Gaussian falloffs in [Hec97] is to facilitate the surface tension scheme, as will be discussed later in Section 5. In order to make $w_{i,j}$ symmetric,

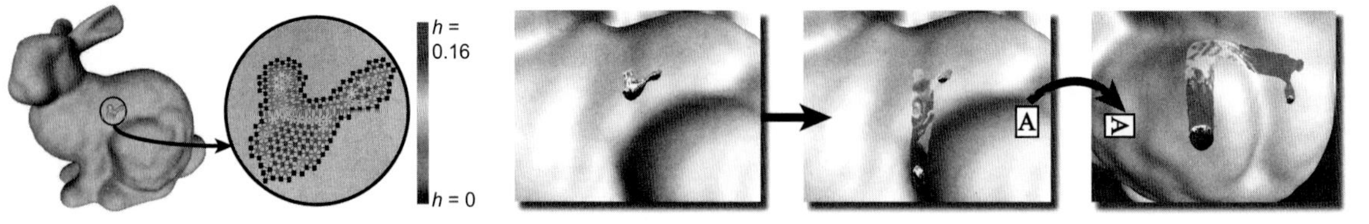

Figure 3: *BUNNY: The left picture illustrates spatial discretization and the cell connectivity on the bunny model. Colored cells are water cells and black cells are boundary cells. The right picture shows a water drop changes its path after the bunny model was rotated* 90°.

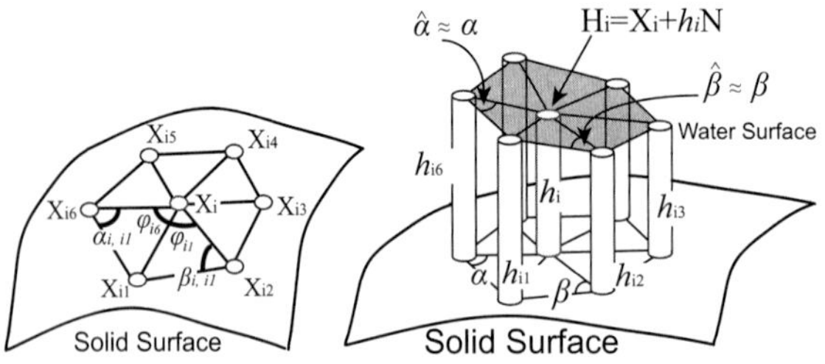

Figure 2: *Particles and their height columns are constructed on a solid surface.*

we add X_i into X_j's neighborhood once we know $X_j \in U_i$, even though X_i may not be necessarily in U_j. After the repulsion process has converged, we construct the particle connectivity from the nearest neighbors and then we calculate the differential geometry operators directly from the neighborhood according to [GSD05]. In this way, we do not need to reconstruct manifold triangle meshes as required in [SY04, ETK*07].

3.2. Boundary Conditions

When simulating large bodies of water with no dry areas, we use either Dirichlet boundary conditions or Neumann boundary conditions for different wave reflection effects on the boundary.

When simulating water drops that are sparsely distributed on surfaces, we do not define the height field in dry regions in order to save memory and computational cost. But unlike undefined regions for large bodies of water, these dry regions are dynamic and need to be updated as long as the water flows. Naively, we can recognize dry regions as cells with non-positive heights. However, in order to avoid grid artifacts, we also define boundary cells with negative heights immediately next to water cells so that a more accurate boundary can be estimated through interpolation. The left picture in Fig. 3 illustrates boundary cells in black on the bunny model. Boundary cells only exchange water with neighboring water cells when we solve GSWE in defined regions, including both boundary cells and water cells. We apply the boundary conditions between boundary cells and water cells, where the actual boundary is specified: Neumann conditions prevent water from entering that boundary, while Dirichlet conditions allow water to move freely.

After the height field has been updated, we remove boundary cells from defined regions if they are no longer next to water cells. When a boundary cell becomes a water cell, its neighborhood may contain new boundary cells as well. Boundary oscillation may be caused by a surface discontinuity if new boundary cells are not initialized with proper height values. Similar to the fast marching algorithm [Set99, OF02], our method initializes new boundary cells with C^1 continuity, which is sufficient in most cases.

4. Implicit Gravity Scheme

Since the height field is built along surface normals rather than in the gravity direction, we separate the gravity into two components (vertical and horizontal) as in Section 3:

$$\begin{aligned} P_g(X_i) &= \rho g_i h_i \\ \vec{a}_g(X_i) &= \vec{g} - g_i N_i \end{aligned} \tag{9}$$

in which g_i is the vertical gravity acceleration at X_i: $g_i = -\vec{g} \cdot N_i$. We can calculate $\vec{a}_g$ directly after mesh resampling because each g_i at X_i is a temporal invariant. On the other hand, P_g depends on the height field and requires an implicit scheme for greater stability.

Our implicit gravity scheme is extended from [KM90] by applying a different gravity acceleration g_i at each position X_i. Given a 1D height field $h = \{h_1, h_2, ..., h_n\}$ from X_1 to X_n, by treating P_g as P_{ext} in Eq. 5 and differentiating h_i^t using finite differencing in the spatial domain, we obtain the implicit matrix $\mathbf{A_g}$ as the coefficients for h^t in the system Eq. 6:

$$\begin{aligned} a_{i,i} &= \tfrac{1}{4\Delta x^2}[(d_i + d_{i+1})(g_i + g_{i+1}) + (d_i + d_{i-1})(g_i + g_{i-1})] \\ a_{i,i+1} &= a_{i+1,i} = -\tfrac{1}{4\Delta x^2}(d_i + d_{i+1})(g_i + g_{i+1}) \end{aligned} \tag{10}$$

Similarly, the matrix for curved surfaces by the differential geometry scheme is:

$$\begin{aligned} a_{i,i} &= \tfrac{1}{8A}\sum_j w_{i,j}(d_i + d_j)(g_i + g_j) \\ a_{i,j} &= a_{j,i} = -\tfrac{1}{8A} w_{i,j}(d_i + d_j)(g_i + g_j) \end{aligned} \tag{11}$$

The particle surface area A is assumed to be uniform for all particles, after the solid surface has been uniformly sampled by the particle repulsion algorithm.

5. Implicit Surface Tension Scheme

According to Laplace's law, surface tension pressure P_{surf} is related to surface mean curvature K, which can be estimated using the Laplace-Beltrami operator in [GSD05]:

$$\begin{aligned} P_{surf}(\mathrm{H_i}) &= \gamma \cdot K_i \\ K_i &= \frac{1}{2A}\left|\sum_j \hat{w}_{i,j}(\mathrm{H_j}-\mathrm{H_i})\right| \\ \mathrm{H_i} &= \mathrm{X_i} + h_i \mathrm{N_i} \end{aligned} \quad (12)$$

in which γ is the surface tension coefficient, and $\mathrm{H_i}$ is the water surface extended along surface normal $\mathrm{N_i}$ at $\mathrm{X_i}$ as in Fig. 2. We assume that $\mathrm{N_i}$ is locally constant after the solid surface has been densely sampled. We also assume that the weight factor $\hat{w}_{i,j}$ on water surfaces is close to the weight factor $w_{i,j}$ on solid surfaces under the shallow wave assumptions. Since the repulsion force in Eq. 8 diminishes to zero after sampling, Eq. 12 is simplified to:

$$\begin{aligned} K_i &= \frac{1}{2A}\left|\left(\sum_j w_{i,j}(\mathrm{X_j}-\mathrm{X_i}) + \sum_j w_{i,j}(h_j\mathrm{N_j}-h_i\mathrm{N_i})\right|\right. \\ &= \frac{|\mathrm{N_i}|}{2A}\sum_j w_{i,j}(h_j-h_i) = \frac{1}{2A}\sum_j w_{i,j}(h_j-h_i) \end{aligned} \quad (13)$$

The Laplace-Beltrami operator on a curved surface is a generalized version of the Laplacian on a flat surface. This operator is naturally normalized since the sum of all coefficients for a particular node $\mathrm{X_i}$ is zero from Eq.13.

One way to formulate an implicit scheme for surface tension from Eq. 12 and 13 is to treat all h_i and h_j as unknowns completely at the next time step. Let us just consider the flat surface as an example. The Laplacian of the height field gives surface tension pressure, which needs to be processed by the Laplacian again according to Eq. 5. By central differencing, the matrix $\mathbf{A_s}$ for flat surfaces will have cell kernels that take the form:

$$\begin{pmatrix} & & 1 & & \\ & 2 & -8 & 2 & \\ 1 & -8 & 20 & -8 & 1 \\ & 2 & -8 & 2 & \\ & & 1 & & \end{pmatrix} \quad (14)$$

as coefficients. We omit the more complicated matrix formula for curved surfaces here. Although this complete implicit scheme is numerically stable, its matrix is not straightforward, symmetric or sparse like that of the gravity scheme, because the kernel spans more than the 1-ring neighborhood. Fortunately we notice from Eq. 14 that cells beyond the 1-ring neighborhood have much less influence than those in the 1-ring neighborhood. Therefore, we propose another incomplete implicit scheme by only treating height columns within the 1-ring neighborhood as unknowns after applying P_{surf} in Eq. 12 into the system Eq. 5. This gives us a symmetric and sparse matrix $\mathbf{A_s}$ as:

$$\begin{aligned} a_{i,i} &= \frac{\gamma}{4\rho A^2}\sum_j w_{i,j}^2(d_i+d_j) \\ a_{i,j} &= -\frac{\gamma}{4\rho A^2} w_{i,j}^2(d_i+d_j) \end{aligned} \quad (15)$$

Height columns beyond the 1-ring neighborhood will be considered as knowns by taking values from the current time step. They formulate a vector b_s, which is added to vector b:

$$\begin{aligned} b_s(i) &= -\frac{\gamma}{8\rho A^2}\left\{B_i^{t-1} + 2\sum_j w_{i,j}^2(d_i+d_j)(h_j^{t-1}-h_i^{t-1})\right\} \\ B_i^{t-1} &= \sum_j w_{i,j}(d_i+d_j)(K_j^{t-1}-K_i^{t-1}) \\ K_i^{t-1} &= \sum_j w_{i,j}(h_j^{t-1}-h_i^{t-1}) \end{aligned} \quad (16)$$

We implemented and tested both implicit schemes, and we did not notice any significant benefits from using the complete scheme. Since the incomplete scheme is more efficient, we choose the incomplete surface tension scheme for all of the following experiments if we do not explicitly say otherwise.

5.1. Drops: Surface Tension and Contact Angles

There are two important factors that contribute to the shape and motion of water drops: surface tension forces at the air/water interface, and the effect of the hydrophilicity of the surface on which drops are forming. To account for surface tension forces at the air/water interface, we apply surface tension pressures to both the water cells and the boundary cells as discussed in Section 3.2. To account for hydrophilicity, we use the virtual surface method proposed in [WMT05] to produce water drops with various contact conditions. Such contact conditions allow us to simulate hydrophobic surfaces on which drops will bead up, and hydrophilic surfaces on which drops are flattened. Although the actual boundary (also called the contact front) is between boundary cells and water cells, our experiments showed that it is safe to simply assume boundary cells as exact contact fronts and apply boundary surface tension pressures only to them. The 1D case is shown in Fig. 4a. Since surface tension is estimated as weighted difference as in Eq.13, the virtual surface is interpreted as height difference between boundary cell h_b and virtual surface cell h_v:

$$\Delta h_v = h_b - h_v = \Delta x \tan\theta_c \quad (17)$$

in which θ_c is the contact angle. For the 2D regular grid, we incorporate an angular factor α to count for the fact that the boundary normal is not aligned with the grid axis:

$$\begin{aligned} \Delta h_v &= \alpha \Delta x \tan\theta_c \\ \alpha &= \begin{cases} N_{bx}+N_{by}, & w_l+w_r+w_u+w_d = 1 \\ (w_l+w_r)N_{bx}+(w_u+w_d)N_{by}, & otherwise \end{cases} \end{aligned} \quad (18)$$

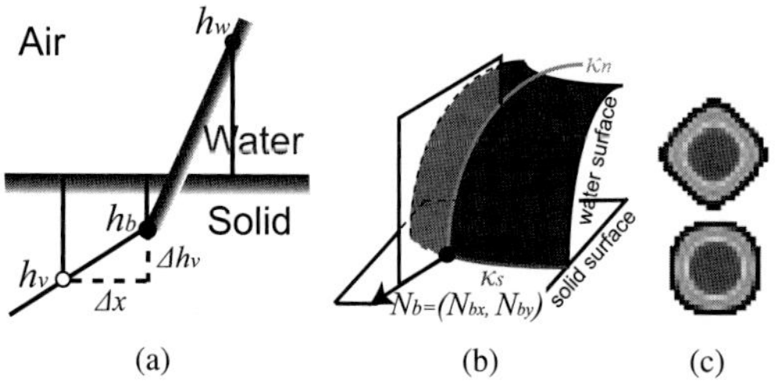

Figure 4: *Illustrations of the virtual surface method. Part (a) gives the virtual surface in the 1D case. Part (b) shows the contact line normal N_b and two assumed principal components κ_n and κ_s. Part (c) shows water drop shapes without (top) and with (bottom) the angular factor α.*

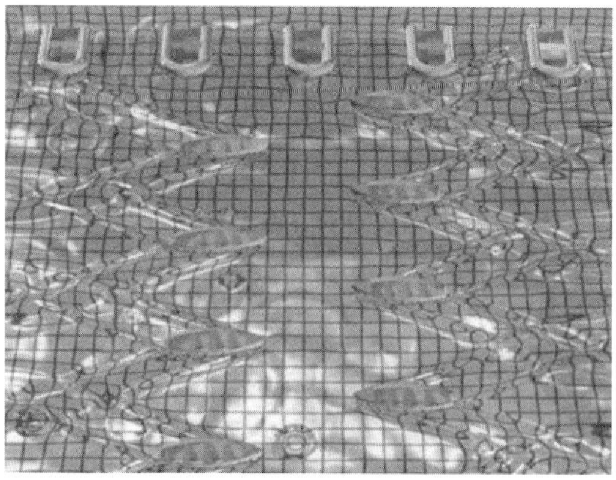

Figure 5: *BOATS: Floating boats interact with water waves.*

in which w_l, w_r, w_u and w_d are 1 if left, right, up or down neighbor cells are in defined regions, otherwise 0. N_{bx} and N_{by} are the boundary's surface normal coordinates as shown in Fig. 4b. Fig. 4c shows that a water drop can correctly bead up into a circle by using the angular factor, otherwise it might become a diamond shape. On curved surfaces, since the connectivity between height columns could be arbitrary, instead of finding a proper angular factor, we sum the boundary mean curvature from two assumed principal components κ_n and κ_s as Fig. 4b shows. The depth component κ_n in the normal plane modulates how steep the surface is, which can be estimated similarly to the 1D case. The angular component κ_s in the horizontal plane measures the contact line curvature as:

$$\kappa_s = \sigma \sum_i \begin{cases} \varphi_i, & h_i - h_b > 0 \text{ and } h_{i+1} - h_b > 0 \\ \frac{(h_i - h_b)\varphi_i}{h_i - h_{i+1}}, & h_i - h_b > 0 \text{ and } h_{i+1} - h_b < 0 \\ \frac{(h_{i+1} - h_b)\varphi_i}{h_{i+1} - h_i}, & h_i - h_b < 0 \text{ and } h_{i+1} - h_b > 0 \end{cases} \tag{19}$$

in which σ is a scalar factor to modulate κ_s's magnitude, and φ_i is the angle between two neighboring edges as in Fig.2. We maintain a wetness map from water paths and choose the contact angle based on the surface wetness.

6. Two-Way Fluid/Rigid Body Coupling

In order to make our system complete for wave effects, we also incorporate a simple two-way fluid/rigid body coupling algorithm based on the method proposed by O'Brien and Hodgins [OH95]. This algorithm is separated into three steps. In Step 1, we recognize those height columns in which solid objects contact with water. For planar cases, this can be accelerated by using the depth buffer in graphics hardware. In Step 2, we solve the dynamics system (Eq. 5) as before except for those constrained columns recognized in Step 1. They are supplied with the coupling matrix $\mathbf{I_c}$ and vector $\mathbf{b_c}$ as in [OH95]:

$$\begin{aligned} \mathbf{I_c}(i,i) &= 1 \\ b_c(i) &= s_i^t \end{aligned} \tag{20}$$

to count for the impact effects of the rigid object. Finally, in Step 3, the state of the rigid object is updated according to standard rigid body dynamics. The water pressure to the rigid object is calculated when calculating the rigid object impact during Step 2.

This coupling approach assumes the rigid object to be small and floating on the water, so it cannot handle completely immersed objects so far. We also assume that the contact region between the rigid object and water is nearly convex due to the height field representation limit.

7. Interactive Fluid Control

Since our system has little restriction on external forces, we can interactively control fluid shapes by specifying various external control forces. We provide two techniques to implement such external control forces $\vec{f_{ext}}$.

The first method uses external pressures calculated from distance maps to a target fluid shape. For example, the pressure field in the SCA example (Fig. 10) uses the Euclidean distance. To put it another way, if we express the control pressure field as a terrain height field, control shapes are terrain valleys and the water flows from peaks to valleys as expected. Because distance maps are C^1 continuous in most places, those control forces are smooth and continuous in most places as well. As expected, this method is comparatively stable and robust. It is faster when the target shape is static, since reconstructing the distance map (by a fast marching algorithm in our practice) can be expensive.

Instead of constructing a pressure field, the second method modifies the fluid velocity directly by external accelerations. We create these accelerations from cursor motions, similar to some digital painting tools. We also clamp the magnitude of these synthetic accelerations in order to prevent instability caused by arbitrary user inputs. Fig. 6 is a screenshot captured from our interactive shape design system. This method is straightforward and efficient.

Name	Type	Resolution	Gravity $g\ (m/s^2)$	Surface Tension $\gamma\ (N/m)$	Viscosity τ	Simulation Speed (frames per sec)
BUNNY	Curved Surface	160,000	9.8	0.073	0.5	CPU: 11.0
GLASS	Curved Surface	160,000	9.8	0.073	0.5	CPU: 4.1
POOL	Regular Grid	400×400	9.8	0.073	0.3	CPU: 4.3
WINDOW	Regular Grid	400×400	9.8	0.073	0.3	GPU: 9.2, CPU: 11.0
SPHERES	Coupling	400×400	9.8	0	0	GPU: 1.2, CPU: 0.4
DRIFT	Coupling	$1,200 \times 250$	9.8	0	0	GPU: 2.0, CPU: 0.8
BOATS	Coupling	400×400	9.8	0	0	GPU: 3.3, CPU: 1.3
INTERACTIVE	Accel. Control	400×400	0	0.073	0.3	CPU: 20
SCA	Pressure Control	400×400	9.8	0.073	0.3	GPU: 4.2, CPU: 3.0

Table 1: *Simulation statistics. When available, we list simulation speeds for both CPU and GPU solvers (rightmost column).*

Figure 6: *INTERACTIVE: Fluid control by external accelerations due to the motion of a user's cursor.*

8. Matrix Solver and Data Structures

We take advantage of the surface mesh connectivity to store the sparse GSWE matrices. Diagonal elements are stored at vertices, and off-diagonal elements are stored at mesh edges between each vertex and its 1-ring neighbors. We use directional edges when the matrix is not symmetric. We also create *hyper* edges that form connections between vertices and their 2-ring neighborhoods in order to store the matrix required by the complete surface tension scheme.

To solve the symmetric positive definite matrix system defined by the implicit gravity scheme and the incomplete surface tension scheme, we use the preconditioned conjugate gradient method with either a Jacobi preconditioner or a modified incomplete Cholesky decomposition preconditioner. We also implemented the preconditioned Bi-Conjugate Gradient Stabilized method (Bi-CGSTAB) with modified incomplete LU decomposition to test the complete surface tension scheme.

The 2D regular grid matrix solver is implemented on both CPUs and GPUs (with a Jacobi preconditioner), in order to improve the performance as Table 1 shows. Details about GPU implementation can be found in [BFGS03]. The extension to a GPU matrix solver for curved surfaces should be straightforward, but remains as future work.

9. Results and Discussion

(Please check the accompanying video for more results.) Our system was implemented using all the techniques described in the previous sections. We tested a variety of applications using this system on a Dell^{TM} XPS 700 PC with Intel Core2Extreme 2.92Ghz CPU and Dual Geforce 7950 graphics card. Test statistics are listed in Table 1. We use real-world units and parameters, including the water density ρ, which is $1.0 \times 10^3 kg/m^3$ at $3.98°C$. The frame rate for each example is measured in the worst case with maximum simulation burden. Table 1 shows that the GPU matrix solver runs faster on large bodies of water, such as the coupling examples. On the other hand, the CPU solver can better take advantage of sparse water, like the examples with water drops.

Compared with particle systems or grid systems that usually require several minutes to generate a single frame under similar resolution, most of our applications run at interactive rates and some of them run in real time. Compared with previous height field systems, the general system has a slightly higher computational cost for several reasons. Firstly, the overhead to handle a general system is small but not negligible. Secondly, more iterations are needed to solve the matrix system with a surface tension matrix $\mathbf{A_s}$, especially when the surface tension coefficient γ is large. The two-way coupling algorithm introduces more iterations too, since constrained cells cause the whole matrix to be less diagonally dominant. This is clearly shown in Table 1 from the SPHERES example and the DRIFT example. Although SPHERES uses lower resolution, the DRIFT example runs twice as fast since it involves less constrained cells than SPHERES.

Interestingly, when gravity is in the same direction as the surface normal, the gravity pressure component g_i in Eq. 9

becomes negative, which causes a less diagonally dominant matrix. Eventually with sufficiently strong gravity, the matrix is failed to be positive definite and its solution becomes unpredictable. Since the influence of $\mathbf{A_g}$ on the matrix system depends on the water depth, ideally we can remove redundant water from the height field in order to keep the system solvable. This scenario corresponds to water drops dripping from the bottom of a solid surface, after the amount of accumulated water goes above some threshold.

The WAVE example shown in Fig. 10 illustrates water waves due to a raised column of water. Our result matches with dispersion relations in that waves under both gravity and surface tension will disperse faster than waver under gravity only. It should be noted that shallow wave assumption implies that the wave length should be much larger than the water depth, which means the system theoretically cannot exactly represent Kelvin waves in deep ocean or capillary waves with wave lengths $< 1.7cm$. Fortunately, we noticed from our examples that when the water depth is close to the wave length, shallow waves still provides a reasonable and fast approximation to gravity-capillary waves for graphics applications, like ripples on a small pool.

One limitation of our GSWE approach is that water columns may intersect if the surface is concave. We eliminate high - frequency curved regions by using averaged normals and the background height field $b(x)$, but this cannot entirely remove all concavities. We have not come across problems from concavities in our examples, but this issue will arise for some geometric configurations.

We provided GPU rendering with single reflection and refraction during online simulation for all of our applications. Some examples were supported by offline GPU rendering with multi-sampling to remove aliasing artifacts. We also used an offline photorealistic ray tracer to produce high-quality videos for some examples.

10. Conclusion and Future Work

We have presented a new physically based framework to efficiently simulate small-scale 3D water flows on solid surfaces under shallow wave assumptions. This framework is governed by the General Shallow Wave Equations (GSWE) and it is based on a height field representation. We have developed several techniques within this framework including an implicit gravity scheme, an implicit surface tension scheme and two-way fluid/rigid body coupling. Our experiments show that our system is fast, stable, straightforward to implement on both CPUs and GPUs. The approach is flexible enough to produce multiple effects such as water waves, rivulets, water drop effects, fluid/rigid body coupling and interactive control and shape modeling.

Looking into the future, our short-term plan includes developing a GPU matrix solver for curved surfaces and incorporating our algorithm into an interactive media painting system. In the long term, we would like to study how to combine height field techniques with particle systems and grid systems so that non-height-field effects can be efficiently produced as well. Motion reduction of the height field provides another possibility to explore in the future.

Acknowledgments

This research was funded by Adobe Systems Inc., an NVIDIA fellowship, and by NSF grant CCF-0625264.

References

[BFGS03] BOLZ J., FARMER I., GRINSPUN E., SCHRÖDER P.: Sparse matrix solvers on the *GPU*: conjugate gradients and multigrid. *ACM Trans. Graph. 22*, 3 (2003), 917–924.

[CdVLHM97] CHEN J. X., DA VITORIA LOBO N., HUGHES C. E., MOSHELL J. M.: Real-time fluid simulation in a dynamic virtual environment. *IEEE Comput. Graph. Appl. 17*, 3 (1997), 52–61.

[CM04] COHEN J. M., MOLEMAKER M. J.: Practical simulation of surface tension flows. In *SIGGRAPH Sketches* (2004), p. 70.

[EMF02] ENRIGHT D., MARSCHNER S., FEDKIW R.: Animation and rendering of complex water surfaces. In *Proc. of ACM SIGGRAPH '02* (2002), pp. 736–744.

[ETK*07] ELCOTT S., TONG Y., KANSO E., SCHRÖDER P., DESBRUN M.: Stable, circulation-preserving, simplicial fluids. *ACM Trans. Graph.* (2007).

[FF01] FOSTER N., FEDKIW R.: Practical animation of liquids. In *Proc. of SIGGRAPH '01* (2001), pp. 23–30.

[FHP98] FOURNIER P., HABIBI A., POULIN P.: Simulating the flow of liquid droplets. In *Graphics Interface* (1998), pp. 133–142.

[FL04] FATTAL R., LISCHINSKI D.: Target-driven smoke animation. In *Proc. of SIGGRAPH '04* (2004), p. 441.

[FM96] FOSTER N., METAXAS D.: Realistic animation of liquids. *Graph. Models Image Process. 58*, 5 (1996).

[FOK05] FELDMAN B. E., OĄŔBRIEN J. F., KLINGNER B. M.: Animating gases with hybrid meshes. In *Proc. of ACM SIGGRAPH '05* (2005).

[GSD05] GRINSPUN E., SCHRÖDER P., DESBRUN M.: Discrete differential geometry: An applied introduction. SIGGRAPH Course #14, 2005.

[Hec97] HECKBERT P.: Fast surface particle repulsion. SIGGRAPH '97: New Frontiers in Modeling and Texturing Course, pages 95–114, 1997.

[HK03] HONG J.-M., KIM C.-H.: Animation of bubbles in liquid. *Comp. Graph. Forum (Eurographics Proc.) 22*, 3 (2003), 253–262.

[HNB*06] HOUSTON B., NIELSEN M. B., BATTY C., NILSSON O., MUSETH K.: Hierarchical *RLE* level set: A compact and versatile deformable surface representation. *ACM Trans. Graph. 25*, 1 (2006), 151–175.

[HNC02] HINSINGER D., NEYRET F., CANI M.-P.: Interactive animation of ocean waves. In *Proc. of SCA '02* (2002), pp. 161–166.

[IGLF06] IRVING G., GUENDELMAN E., LOSASSO F., FEDKIW R.: Efficient simulation of large bodies of water by coupling two and three dimensional techniques. In *Proc. of ACM SIGGRAPH '06* (2006), p. 38.

[KFCO06] KLINGNER B. M., FELDMAN B. E., CHENTANEZ N., O'BRIEN J. F.: Fluid animation with dynamic meshes. In *Proc. of ACM SIGGRAPH 2006* (2006).

[KLLR07] KIM B., LIU Y., LLAMAS I., ROSSIGNAC J.: Advections with significantly reduced dissipation and diffusion. *IEEE TVCG* (2007).

[KM90] KASS M., MILLER G.: Rapid, stable fluid dynamics for computer graphics. In *Proc. of ACM SIGGRAPH '90* (1990), pp. 49–57.

[LGF04] LOSASSO F., GIBOU F., FEDKIW R.: Simulating water and smoke with an octree data structure. In *Proc. of SIGGRAPH '04* (2004), no. 3, pp. 457–462.

[LvdP02] LAYTON A. T., VAN DE PANNE M.: A numerically efficient and stable algorithm for animating water waves. *The Visual Computer 18*, 1 (2002), 41–53.

[MCG03] MÜLLER M., CHARYPAR D., GROSS M.: Particle-based fluid simulation for interactive applications. In *Proc. of SCA '03* (2003), pp. 154–159.

[MMS04] MIHALEF V., METAXAS D., SUSSMAN M.: Animation and control of breaking waves. In *Proc. of SCA '04* (2004), pp. 315–324.

[Mon92] MONAGHAN J. J.: Smoothed particle hydrodynamics. *Annual Review of Astronomy and Astrophysics 30* (1992), 543–574.

[MTPS04] MCNAMARA A., TREUILLE A., POPOVIĆ Z., STAM J.: Fluid control using the adjoint method. In *Proc. of SIGGRAPH '04* (2004), pp. 449–456.

[NHS02] NEYRET F., HEISS R., SENEGAS F.: Realistic rendering of an organ surface in real-time for laparoscopic surgery simulation. *the Visual Computer 18*, 3 (may 2002), 135–149.

[NM06] NIELSEN M. B., MUSETH K.: Dynamic tubular grid: An efficient data structure and algorithms for high resolution. *Journal of Scientific Computing 26*, 3 (2006).

[OF02] OSHER S., FEDKIW R.: *Level Set Methods and Dynamic Implicit Surfaces*. Springer-Verlag, 2002.

[OH95] O'BRIEN J. F., HODGINS J. K.: Dynamic simulation of splashing fluids. In *Computer Animation '95* (1995), pp. 198–205.

[Set99] SETHIAN J.: *Level Set Methods and Fast Marching Methods*. Cambridge University Press, 1999.

[SSK05] SONG O.-Y., SHIN H., KO H.-S.: Stable but nondissipative water. *ACM Trans. Graph. 24*, 1 (2005).

[Sta99] STAM J.: Stable fluids. In *Proc. of ACM SIGGRAPH '99* (1999), pp. 121–128.

[Sta03] STAM J.: Flows on surfaces of arbitrary topology. In *Proc. of SIGGRAPH '02* (2003), vol. 22, pp. 724–731.

[SY04] SHI L., YU Y.: Inviscid and incompressible fluid simulation on triangle meshes. *Comput. Animat. Virtual Worlds 15*, 3-4 (2004), 173–181.

[SY05] SHI L., YU Y.: Controllable smoke animation with guiding objects. *ACM Trans. Graph. 24*, 1 (2005).

[TLP06] TREUILLE A., LEWIS A., POPOVIĆ Z.: Model reduction for real-time fluids. *Proc. of ACM SIGGRAPH '06 25*, 3 (2006), 826–834.

[TMPS03] TREUILLE A., MCNAMARA A., POPOVIĆ Z., STAM J.: Keyframe control of smoke simulations. In *Proc. of SIGGRAPH '03* (2003), vol. 22, pp. 716–723.

[Tur91] TURK G.: Generating textures on arbitrary surfaces using reaction-diffusion. In *Proceedings of ACM SIGGRAPH '91* (1991), pp. 289–298.

[UJ04] UIJTTEWAAL W. S., JIRKA G. H.: *Shallow Flows: Research Presented at the International Symposium on Shallow Flows, Delft, Netherlands*. A.A. Balkema, 2004.

[WMT05] WANG H., MUCHA P. J., TURK G.: Water drops on surfaces. In *Proc. of ACM SIGGRAPH '05* (2005), pp. 921–929.

Figure 7: *WINDOW: Water drops are flowing on the window panel with a white waterproof boundary "water".*

Figure 8: *SPHERES: Spheres cause waves and splashes in the height field. They have different volumes but identical mass.*

Figure 9: *Several effects generated by our system. Examples are: WAVE, POOL, SCA and DRIFT, which demonstrate wave dispersion, water drops on a glass, user-controlled fluid shapes, and fluid/rigid body interaction.*

Eurographics/ ACM SIGGRAPH Symposium on Computer Animation (2007)
D. Metaxas and J. Popovic (Editors)

On the Beat! Timing and Tension for Dynamic Characters

Brian Allen, Derek Chu, Ari Shapiro and Petros Faloutsos

Department of Computer Science
University of California, Los Angeles

Abstract

Dynamic simulation is a promising complement to kinematic motion synthesis, particularly in cases where simulated characters need to respond to unpredictable interactions. Moving beyond simple rag-doll effects, though, requires dynamic control. The main issue with dynamic control is that there are no standardized techniques that allow an animator to precisely specify the timing of the motion while still providing natural response to external disturbances. The few proposed techniques that address this problem are based on heuristically or manually tuning proportional-derivative (PD) control parameters and do not generalize easily.

We propose an approach to dynamic character control that is able to honor timing constraints, to provide natural-looking motion and to allow for realistic response to perturbations. Our approach uses traditional PD control to interpolate between key-frames. The key innovation is that the parameters of the PD controllers are computed for each joint analytically. By continuously updating these parameters over time, the controller is able to respond naturally to both external perturbations and changes in the state of the character.

Categories and Subject Descriptors (according to ACM CCS): I.3.7 [Computer Graphics]: Three-Dimensional Graphics and Realism

1. Introduction

The acceptance of physical simulation as a standard component in interactive entertainment and "serious" games brings great possibilities to character animation. Although recent work has made significant progress in the simulation of dynamic characters, current control methods are difficult to use and require significant tuning for proper behavior. In this paper, we provide a practical solution to two troubling facets of physical characters: natural response to perturbations and precise timing control.

Small physical disturbances are a ubiquitous part of everyday life, from being bumped while queuing at the store to a shooting foul while playing basketball. Animation with natural responses to such perturbation "sells" the physicality of a character. Overly stiff or loose reactions break the viewer's suspension of disbelief.

Despite their promise, dynamic characters have seen limited use in interactive simulations outside of simple rag-doll behavior. A key impediment is that developers and animators have been asked to sacrifice a significant amount of control compared to kinematic animation. The advantage of physicality– natural response to perturbation– becomes a weakness when precisely timed motion is needed. Of course, traditional kinematic animation has no such limitation, but neither such a capacity. Control over the timing of motion is often critical for interactive applications– catching a ball, for example, is problematic if you cannot guarantee the hand's location when the ball arrives. To solve these issues, we present a method to drive a dynamic character by *physical interpolation* of key-frames.

Redefining the dynamics control problem as one of physical interpolation proves to be quite flexible. We describe three applications built on physical interpolation: pose control, key-frame animation, and tracking motion capture.

2. Overview

Our approach to dynamic character control is able to provide natural-looking motion while honoring timing constraints and providing realistic response to perturbation. We use traditional proportional-derivative (PD) feedback controllers to interpolate between key-frames in a manner analogous to classic key-frame animation. In general, PD controllers compute the magnitude of the control torque τ around a joint for

Symposium on Computer Animation 2007, San Diego, CA, August 03-04, 2007.
© 2007 ACM 978-1-59593-624-4/07/0008 $5.00

each time-step as

$$\tau = k_s(\hat{\theta} - \theta) + k_d(\hat{\omega} - \omega), \qquad (1)$$

where $\hat{\theta}$ and $\hat{\omega}$ are the desired position and angular velocity, θ and ω the current position and angular velocity, and k_s and k_d the parameters that specify the trajectory of the joint's motion.

The key innovation of our approach is that the parameters of the PD equation, k_s and k_d, are updated in a principled manner for each joint axis and for each control time-step. By continuously altering the PD parameters, the controller is able to respond both to changes in the state of the character and to external perturbations, all while maintaining timing constraints.

Many prior dynamic control systems in computer graphics have used PD control, and each has needed some method for choosing the parameters. The most common approach in computer graphics has been to carefully "tune" the parameters until the desired motion trajectory is obtained.

A key draw-back to this common approach is that it simply cannot support more than one motion with timing requirements. To illustrate, suppose an animator wishes a character's arm to swing from position A to B in one second (Figure 1, upper). In typical usage, the user would need trial-and-error to find appropriate (k_s, k_d) parameters for this motion timing. If the next step of the animation required the arm to swing from B to C, the (k_s, k_d) tuned for the previous swing now also define the timing of the *second* swing as well. The user has no control over timing without breaking the previous (hard won) timing from A to B. It is important to realize that, even in this extremely simple example, there is simply no single (k_s, k_d) that will satisfy this animator's modest needs.

Indeed, the difficulty of manually choosing PD parameters does not end there. If the character wishes to perform the same arm-swing with the same timing as before, but now with a bent elbow (Figure 1, lower), the previous hand-tuned (k_s, k_d) parameters will no longer suffice. This is because the *composite inertia* of the arm has changed– the bent arm needs less torque to swing than the straightened arm.

In addition to the timing, the animator is also likely to wish to control shape of the trajectory for the arm-swing. With a PD controller, the character of the motion trajectory is determined by the ratio of $k_d : k_s$. An under-damped controller, with too low a ratio, will cause the arm to oscillate unnaturally. But increasing the ratio too much yields an over-damped controller, which moves too slowly and gives the impression of a character moving underwater. The compromise ratio produces an arm-swing that is fast, smooth and does not oscillate. This motion is said to be *critically damped*. However, the critically damped ratio between k_s and k_d depends on the moment of inertia at the joint, which in-turn depends on the limb's composite inertia. With so many varying dependencies, hand-tuning PD controllers can be a daunting task.

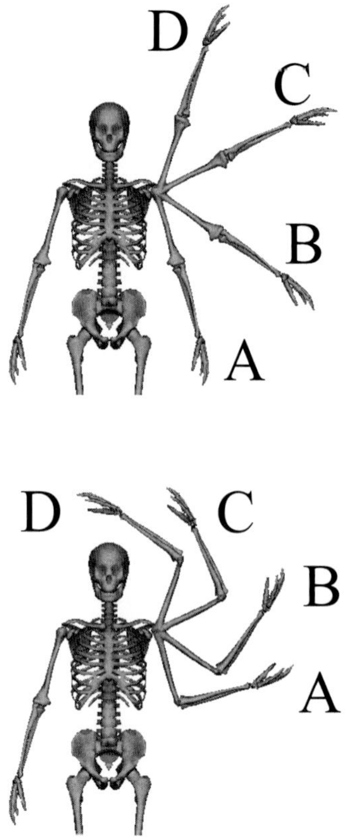

Figure 1: *The character demonstrates a simple, single-axis rotation with two arm positions. The moment of inertia at the shoulder joint changes dramatically with the bent elbow.*

Our approach is to eliminate hand-tuning and heuristic methods to determine the PD parameters, and instead compute them analytically. As was demonstrated with the simple example of a character swinging a bent arm, any method to automatically compute the PD parameters must first determine the composite inertia of all controlled links. In our approach, we descend the character's articulated hierarchy and recursively calculate and store each link's composite inertia. The implementation, described in Section 4.2, is efficient and absolutely critical to PD control with timing.

An additional complication to PD control is that the control torque is computed (1) for each joint in isolation. This introduces error, since the torque from each joint has a direct effect on every other joint in the hierarchy. To account for this effect, we use *parent-torque compensation*– that is, each joint is computed with the knowledge of the net torque of its parent joints. This approach is an efficient approximation that provides more precise control and is described in Section 4.4.

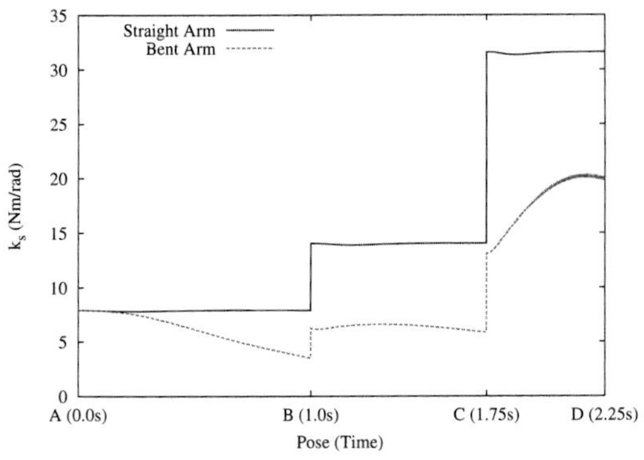

Figure 2: *The proportional parameters (k_s) used to drive the examples shown in Figure 1.*

Arbitrary trajectories, such as motion capture data, can also be tracked using this low-level controller. By sampling the motion data, a target key-frame is created and given as input to the low-level controller. Setting a key-frame based on the motion data in the near-future provides a principled means of determining muscle tension, similar to the torque-based model proposed in [YCP03].

Our approach to control provides several advantages: timing support, dynamic interpolation, and natural response with principled tension control.

A key feature of our approach is that timing control remains possible even when the character is subject to unknown perturbations. Thus our approach offers dynamic animation the reliability and specifiability familiar to kinematic animation. This combination of control and support for interaction is of critical importance to real-time games. Secondly, our method yields natural dynamic responses to perturbations. The user specifies the tension of the response by designating the time allowed before the character returns to the target trajectory. By providing tension control in human-readable units (seconds), tension control becomes intuitive and complements the general focus on precise timing.

3. Background

Currently, the dominant approaches to dynamic control for real-time animation are robotics-derived controllers [Woo98, FvdPT01a] and tracking of motion capture [ZH99]. While robotics-derived controllers have been shown to perform a surprising variety of motions [HWBO95], they also require a surprising amount of work for each new behavior. To ameliorate this burden, much effort has gone into re-using kinematic animation approaches, especially motion capture, for the control of physically simulated characters. [RGBC96] describes an approach to generate physically plausible transitions that stitch together disparate motion data. Transitions are found that minimize the applied torque, which is computed using an inverse dynamics algorithm [BP92] that determines composite inertia in a recursive manner similar to ours. [MZW99, WJM06] report that world-space error, instead of joint-space error, provides more stable tracking with a wider range of control parameters. Weinstein et al [WGF06] provides a feedback-based trajectory tracking scheme that uses a similar analytical formulation to ours to guarantee single time-step error elimination. The focus is exclusively tracking, however, and perturbation response is not considered. [ZH99, ZH02, ZMCF05] use stiff feedback controllers to track the motion capture trajectory in joint-local space. [ZMCF05, SPF03] consider circumstances where the original motion was no longer reachable due to an obstruction or large perturbation; although we detect such cases, our approach does not attempt to handle failure circumstances. [ZH02] handles reaction to perturbation by switching to heuristically determined control parameters that require human "tuning."

To provide control after a perturbation, [ZH02, ZMCF05] use an *inertia-scaled* proportional-derivative controller. This formulation scales the calculated torque by the mass of the joint's out-board link. We follow a similar approach, but compute the *composite inertia* of all links distal to the joint being controlled. Much more accurate control torque is possible if the correct composite inertia is used. Note that prior works, such as [ZH99], have suggested using composite inertia in control, but, to our knowledge, the details required to compute the composite inertia have not been provided in the computer graphics literature.

Lee and Terzopoulos [LT06] describe a biomechanical approach to tension control based on modeling multiple antagonistic muscles. Their approach produces high-quality motion with controllable levels of tension, and even demonstrates tracking of motion capture data. However, it is unclear how or even if such detailed modeling could be scaled to control entire characters in real-time.

Neff and Fiume [NF02] provide an approach to automatically computing the PD control parameters, which is the basis of our physical interpolation approach. However, their approach is limited to pose-to-pose transitions by design, and it remains unclear how it might be used to interpolate between general key-frames (with non-zero end velocities) or track motion capture.

Tension control has also been examined specifically in the context of tracking motion capture data. Zordan and Hodgins [ZH02] provide a heuristic rule for determining the proportional-derivative parameters for perturbation response. Yin et al [YCP03] suggest obtaining the tension level from an estimation of muscle activation, where activation is derived from joint torque computed using inverse dynamics. This is directly analogous to our handling of tension during motion tracking, and is a direct result of high-torques being derived from high-stiffness control parameters.

Both inverse dynamics [YCP03] and very stiff feedback controllers [ZH02] provide excellent solutions to the problem of tracking motion, but such tracking suffers from being *too* precise– natural responses to perturbations are lost. In fact, both of these approaches resort to PD control for perturbation response.

4. Physical Interpolation of Key-Frames

Our control approach is based on the ability to drive a character's joint to a specified key-frame. For our purposes, a key-frame, or "physical key-frame," is a tuple of desired joint-position $\hat{\theta}$, desired joint-velocity $\hat{\omega}$ and target time $\hat{t}$: $\gamma = (\hat{\theta}, \hat{\omega}, \hat{t})$. The control approach described in this section allows an animator to specify a set of key-frames directly analogous to traditional spline-based kinematic interpolation. Additionally, this low-level approach can be used to track existing motion trajectories, as described in Section 5.3.

The torque of the ith joint τ_i targeting the kth key-frame $\gamma_k = (\hat{\theta}_k, \hat{\omega}_k, \hat{t}_k)$ is computed using the proportional-derivative controller (1). During the controller update cycle, the PD control parameters, k_s and k_d, are calculated to match the timing of the next key-frame. The function $\psi(\cdot)$ is used to compute these parameters and is defined as

$$(k_s, k_d) = \psi(\mathbf{D}(\mathbf{q}), \gamma_k) = \psi(\mathbf{D}(\mathbf{q}), (\hat{\theta}_k, \hat{\omega}_k, \hat{t}_k)), \qquad (2)$$

where $\mathbf{D}(\mathbf{q})$ is the combined inertia tensor of the out-board body segments, and depends on the current state of the character $\mathbf{q}$. Calculating ψ requires determining the composite moment of inertia (Section 4.2), the scalar moment (Section 4.3), and compensating for the effect of parent joint's torque (Section 4.4). An example of the output of $\psi(\cdot)$ for a simple key-frame animation is provided in Figure 3.

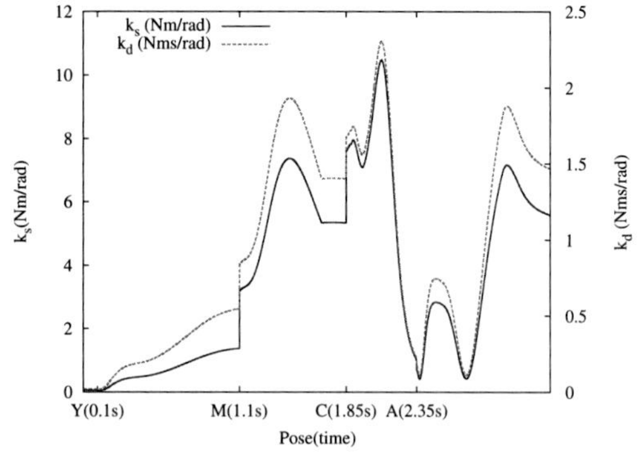

Figure 3: *The character moves through a series of poses in time to a popular song. The poses targeted are arm positions for the letters YMCA (see supplemental video). Throughout the animation, each controller update calculates $\psi(\cdot) \rightarrow (k_s, k_d)$. The calculated values for the character's shoulder joint change with each time-step to ensure correct timing throughout the animation. Manually determining these values, even for a single joint, would be difficult.*

4.1. Proportional-Derivative Parameters

The method of automatic calculation of the proportional-derivative parameters using ψ, defined in (2), is a major element of this paper's contribution. ψ provides the parameters that allow a particular joint to reach its target state in time $\hat{t}$, using the PD controller from (1). This can be written as a second-order ordinary differential equation in θ, with $\dot{\theta} = \omega$ and m as the moment of inertia about the joint axis,

$$m\ddot{\theta} - k_s(\hat{\theta} - \theta) - k_d(\hat{\omega} - \omega) = 0. \qquad (3)$$

The analytical solution provides the basis for determining ψ. In particular, the difference between the desired θ and ω and the system's actual state is reduced in the shortest time when the system is *critically damped*. This requires the parameters to satisfy $k_s^2 \; - \; 4 \; m \; k_d = 0$, where m is the moment of inertia around the axis of applied torque [Bar98]. With this constraint, a simpler parameterization can be derived using the desired time $\hat{t}$ to eliminate a given fraction of the error f. A reasonable value for f is 0.9, which reduces the error to 10% in time t_d [Bar98].

Since the decay rate of the error is exponential when critically damped, the number n of time constants needed to eliminate the fraction f of the error is $n = -1/\ln(f)$ [BD91]. This determines the time constant, λ, needed to reduce the error adequately in time $\hat{t}$: $\lambda = \hat{t}/n$.

$$\tau = \frac{m}{\lambda^2}(\hat{\theta} - \theta) + 2\frac{m}{\lambda}(\hat{\omega} - \omega). \qquad (4)$$

This approach is directly analogous to the second-order differential equation describing the decay of constraint error in Barzel and Barr [BB88], but rather than attempting to eliminate the error in one time-step, our method reaches the target state in $\hat{t}$ seconds and provides support for a non-zero target first-derivative.

4.2. Composite Inertia Tensor

To determine the moment m in (4) the composite inertia tensor of out-board links is needed. Inertia tensors sum naturally, so $\mathbf{D}^{i..n} = \sum_{j=i}^{n} \mathbf{D}_j$ is the composite inertia tensor for joints i through n. However, this expression holds only for inertia tensors in the same coordinate system. Dynamics simulators typically store each link's inertia tensor in link-local coordinates for efficiency and convenience, so conversion to a consistent frame is required.

The recursive Newton-Euler formulation, proposed by [LWP80], is efficient [Lil93] and easy to implement. For each connecting joint in the articulated object, transform the child's inertia tensor into the parent's coordinate frame, and replace the parent's inertia tensor with the sum of parent and child. By starting the recursion at each end-effector and ensuring to accumulate over each joint once, the composite inertia for each link is compute in $O(n)$ time.

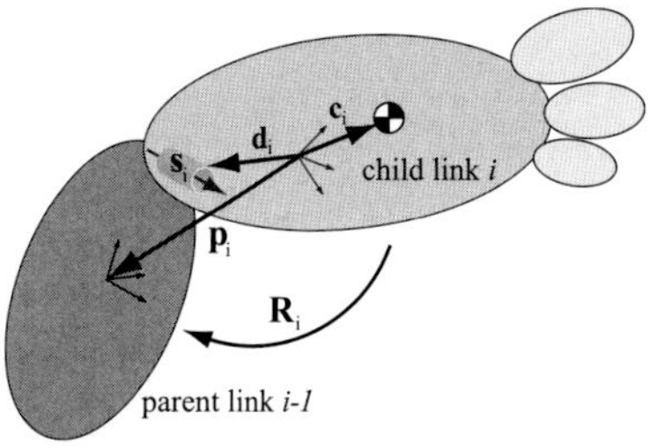

Figure 4: *This schematic shows the geometrical elements used by (5) to transform the inertia tensor of the ith child link into the parent link's $(i-1)$th coordinate frame, and by (7) to calculate the moment around joint axis $\mathbf{s}_i$. The transformation from child to parent is a translation $\mathbf{p}_i$ and rotation $\mathbf{R}_i$. In the child's link-local origin, the position vector of the center-of-mass is $\mathbf{c}_i$ and the position vector of the joint is $\mathbf{d}_i$.*

To perform the transformation from child to parent, the coordinate system transform is decomposed into a rotation matrix, $\mathbf{R}$, and the linear distance from the child's to the parent's coordinate frame $\mathbf{p}$. The position vector of the center of mass in the child's coordinate frame is $\mathbf{c}$. The child's inertia tensor $\mathbf{D}$ is transformed to its parent's coordinate frame $\mathbf{D}'$ by

$$\mathbf{D}' = \mathbf{RDR}^T - M([\mathbf{p}][\mathbf{Rc}] + [\mathbf{Rc}][\mathbf{p}] + [\mathbf{p}][\mathbf{p}]), \qquad (5)$$

where M is the scalar mass of the child link and $[\cdot]$ is the notation for the skew-symmetric matrix defined by $\mathbf{u} \times \mathbf{v} = [\mathbf{u}]\mathbf{v}$, or equivalently,

$$[\mathbf{u}] = \begin{pmatrix} 0 & -u_z & u_y \\ u_z & 0 & -u_x \\ -u_y & u_x & 0 \end{pmatrix}. \qquad (6)$$

Using this expression, a composite inertia tensor $\mathbf{D}_i^{i..n}$ for link i can be computed recursively, from distal to proximal. The composite tensor is expressed in the ith link's coordinate frame, and combines its own and all of its out-board links' inertia, from i to the distal-end link n.

4.3. Moment of Inertia about the Joint Axis

With the composite inertia tensor of the ith joint in link-local coordinates $\mathbf{D}_i^{i..n}$ available, we can compute the moment of inertia about the ith joint's axis of torque $\mathbf{s}_i$ using the parallel-axis theorem as

$$m_i = \mathbf{s}_i \cdot \mathbf{D}_i^{i..n}\mathbf{s}_i + M_{i..n}\left\|(\mathbf{c}_i^{i..n} - \mathbf{d}_i) \times \mathbf{s}_i\right\|^2, \qquad (7)$$

where $\mathbf{c}_i^{i..n}$ is the vector from the combined center of mass and $M_{i..n}$ the combined scalar mass of the ith link and all child links, $\mathbf{d}_i$ is the vector from the link's coordinate frame to the joint, and $\mathbf{s}_i$ is a unit vector. Both $\mathbf{c}_i^{i..n}$ and $M_{n..i}$ can be computed during the same recursive traversal from end-effectors to the root that is used to compute $\mathbf{D}_i^{i..n}$ (see Section 4.2), keeping the time-complexity at $O(n)$.

4.4. Parent-Torque Compensation

The computation of ψ in each controller update provides a precise estimate of the torque needed to reach the target key-frame at the appropriate time. To improve its accuracy, each joint estimates how the combined torque of all inboard (parent) joints will affect it. The joint then is able to compensate for the induced acceleration on its axis of rotation, $\mathbf{s}_i$. The total angular acceleration applied to joint i in world coordinates is

$$\mathbf{a}_i = \sum_{j=0}^{i-1} \frac{\tau_j}{m_j}\mathbf{G}_j^w\mathbf{s}_j, \qquad (8)$$

where $\mathbf{G}_j^w$ is the transformation matrix from the jth link-local coordinates to world coordinates, m_j is the moment of composite inertia (7), and τ_j is the computed scalar torque around the jth joint from (4).

The required torque to compensate for the applied angular acceleration $\mathbf{a}_i$ is that acceleration projected onto the joint-axis in world coordinates,

$$\mathbf{u}_i = \mathbf{a}_i \cdot (\mathbf{G}_j^w\mathbf{s}_i). \qquad (9)$$

With the addition of this term, we obtain the final expression for the control torque of the ith joint, so (4) becomes,

$$\tau_i = \frac{m_i}{\lambda^2}(\hat{\theta}_i - \theta_i) + 2\frac{m_i}{\lambda}(\hat{\omega}_i - \omega_i) + \mathbf{a}_i \cdot (\mathbf{G}_j^w\mathbf{s}_i). \qquad (10)$$

This final torque is applied to the joint as long as $\tau_i < \tau_{max}$, i.e., as long as the computed torque is below the maximum allowed torque for the joint. If the torque exceeds τ_{max}, then the character is not strong enough to match the desired motion. A failure message can be communicated to the controlling application, and [ZMCF05, SPF03] suggest approaches to handling such conditions.

4.5. Efficiency of Control

The full process of calculating the control torque consists of two passes through articulated link hierarchy and is summarized in Algorithm 1. First, the composite inertia pass, described in Section 4.2, recursively descends from each end-effector toward the root, visiting each link once to accumulate the composite inertia for the current state, $\mathbf{D}(\mathbf{q})$. Second, the torque is computed once for each joint in (10) is computed once for each joint, accumulating the link's angular acceleration $\mathbf{a}_i$ following the hierarchy from root to end-effector.

5. Applications

5.1. Key-Frame Animation

We have described a method to physically interpolate key-frames. It is simple to integrate this low-level controller into

Algorithm 1 $ComputeControlTorque(\mathbf{q},\gamma) \rightarrow \tau$

for all links l, descending **do**
  if $parent(l)$ exists **then**
    $\mathbf{D}_l \leftarrow \mathbf{D}_l + transformInertia(\mathbf{D}_{parent(l)}, l)$ {see (5)}
  end if
  $j = outboardJointOfLink(l)$
  $\mathbf{a}_j \leftarrow 0$
end for
for all joints i, ascending **do**
  $l \leftarrow outboardLinkOfJoint(i)$
  $(k_{si}, k_{di}) \leftarrow \psi(\mathbf{D}_l, \gamma_i)$
  $m_i \leftarrow moment(\mathbf{D}_l, i)$ {see (7)}
  $\mathbf{u}_i \leftarrow parentTorque(i, \mathbf{a}_i)$ {see (9)}
  $\tau_i \leftarrow PD(\mathbf{q}_l, m_i, k_{si}, k_{di}, \gamma_i, \mathbf{u}_i)$ {see (10)}
  $\tau_i \leftarrow \min(\tau_i, \tau_{max})$
  for all joints c in $children(l)$ **do**
    $\mathbf{a}_c \leftarrow \mathbf{a}_c + transform(\tau_i/m_i, c)$ {see (8)}
  end for
end for
return τ

a traditional key-frame animation system. As detailed in Algorithm 1, the required input to the system is the current state vector $\mathbf{q}$ and a vector of the target key-frames $(\gamma_1, \gamma_2, \ldots)$. The motion between key-frames is specified by the first derivatives $\hat{\omega}$, analogous to Hermite spline interpolation, and determined by the dynamics of PD control.

5.2. Pose Control

If a set of target key-frames specifies all the controllable degrees-of-freedom for a particular time, then that set of key-frames is said to define a *pose*. Dynamic controllers of surprising complexity [FvdPT01b, HWBO95, vKF94, YLv07] have been built by creating a finite-state machine (FSM) that controls the target pose. Our physical interpolation system supports this approach directly through a simple scripting system.

As an example of simple control, the supplementary video includes an animation of a skeleton conducting Beethoven's Fifth Symphony. The controlling script demonstrates the power of the approach– only target (pose, time) tuples are specified. It should be noted that no other parameters are provided to the system and no "hand-tuning" has taken place. Below is an excerpt of the script.

```
...
skeleton.setTargetPose( "ArmsFront", 0.3 )
skeleton.setTargetPose( "ArmsUp", 0.3 )
skeleton.setTargetPose( "Out", 0.3 )
skeleton.setTargetPose( "UpBeat", 0.4 )
skeleton.setTargetPose( "DownBeat", 0.545 )
skeleton.setTargetPose( "UpBeat", 0.545 )
...
```

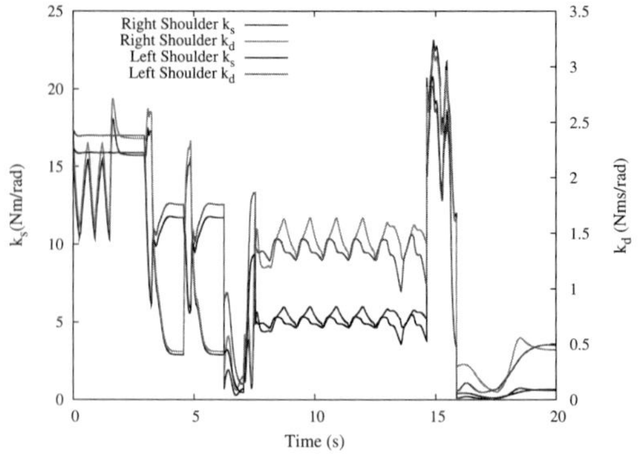

Figure 5: *The output of $\psi(\cdot)$ for the X-axis of the left and right shoulders during the conducting motion shown in the supplementary video.*

The parameters for the character's shoulder joints generated by this script are shown in Figure 5.

5.3. Tracking Motion Capture

A variety of approaches to tracking motion capture has been proposed in animation literature, with the most common being stiff PD control [ZH02, ZMCF05], and inverse dynamics [YCP03]. Our approach also uses PD control, building directly on the physical key-frame interpolation control described (Section 4).

At each control time-step, a desired key-frame γ is created by sampling the motion capture data. This key-frame contains joint velocity, which be obtained from the motion capture data by using the finite difference between frames.

5.3.1. Perturbation Response

When a perturbation to the character is detected (such as an unexpected collision), a parameter δ controls the stiffness of the response by specifying the time, in seconds, to resolve the perturbation and return the character's motion to the motion capture trajectory.

On disturbance, a new key-frame vector $\gamma_{t+\delta}$ is created by sampling the motion capture data at time $(t+\delta)$. Targeting $\gamma_{t+\delta}$ guarantees that the perturbation response will be completed by time $t+\delta$. During this δ second window, the motion capture is no longer tracked and only the new key-frame at $t+\delta$ is used.

The δ parameter allows a principled, known-units (seconds) parameter for controlling the response stiffness.

6. Results

With our method, the animator need only specify a set of key-frames containing desired position, velocity and timing information. In Figure 6 (top row), a character catches a moving ball based on a single key-frame with timing information. In the bottom row, the character's arm responds to an external disturbance and still catches the ball at the correct time, without requiring any additional effort or information from the animator.

In Figure 7, we compare our method to a manually tuned PD controller. The two characters go through four key-frames following the popular "YMCA" dance. The manually tuned system has been adjusted to reach the "Y" key-frame at the appropriate time. As expected, the timing of the subsequent key-frames is off. It is worth noting that in the case of the manually tuned system, it took a fairly experienced student several minutes to get the timing of the "Y" key-frame correct. Using our approach, the user has only to specify the desired time of the key-frame.

In Figure 8, we compare our method to a "locally" critically damped PD controller that does not account for the composite inertia of the articulated chain. This method has been widely used, such as in [ZH02, ZMCF05]. The two characters conduct the opening movement of Beethoven's Fifth Symphony by interpolating between twelve poses. Our approach provides natural looking motion with correct timing.

6.1. Implementation

The results provided used a character model with 39 degrees-of-freedom and human-like limb-lengths, masses, and moments of inertia. We used the DANCE animation environment [SFNTH05] with the Open Dynamics Engine [Smi07] for forward-dynamics simulation and collision detection.

7. Discussion and Limitations

The described approach to dynamic character control emphasizes practical utility and natural-looking motion. Since PD control is equivalent to a spring force, using a PD controller to resolve error from perturbation is equivalent to the parallel-elastic element of the Hill-type muscle model [ZW90], providing a representation of passive neuromotor feedback [YCP03]. This approximation may not be sufficiently accurate for demanding applications. In particular, muscle stiffness is known to be a non-linear function of a variety of factors, most importantly extension length [WC00]. In addition, PD control is well-known to exhibit steady-state error in the presence of external forces (such as gravity). As our approach is based on PD control, it also suffers from such errors and key-frame targets may not be reached precisely.

Our approach for compensating for parent torque, in Section 4.4, uses only a single pass from the root to end-effectors. Although efficient, the algorithm does not take into account subsequent effects of child torques on parent joints. An $O(n^3)$ algorithm that simultaneously solves for the torque at all joints is described as Method 3 in [WO82].

An additional complication to our recursive formulation is that it assumes the character has a fixed base serving as root. This assumption suffices for upper-body motion, since the torso dominates the mass of the system and provides an approximately fixed platform. The fixed-root assumption is particularly well-suited for systems using balance-assisting root springs to stabilize the character [vL95, WJM06, SCAF07]. However, the proposed method is not appropriate for determining control parameters for support limbs.

Perturbations that are sufficiently strong and close to a target key-frame will require unnaturally large joint torques to meet the timing constraint. In these cases, we apply a per-joint limit on torque (see τ_{max} in Section 4.4). A single, time-invariant, per-joint limit does not accurately model maximum muscle exertion, since a variety of additional factors are known [WC00], such as fatigue.

8. Conclusion

We have presented an approach to controlling the timing and apparent stiffness of motion using PD control for dynamic characters. An animator specifies a set of key-frames and the associated timing information. Our system automatically computes the proportional and derivative parameters of the PD controller. The resulting parameters yield control torques that honor the timing of the provided key-frames even when the character is disturbed by external forces. The resulting character motion exhibits natural stiffness. The proposed approach is efficient, straight-forward to implement, and entirely automatic.

Acknowledgments

The authors thank the anonymous reviewers for their suggestions and comments, and Demetri Terzopoulos and Sung-Hee Lee for many helpful discussions and suggestions. BBC Radio and the Internet Archive graciously provided to the public domain the performance of Beethoven's Fifth Symphony used in the supplemental video. The work in this paper was partially supported by NSF grant No. CCF-0429983. We thank Intel Corp., Microsoft Corp., ATI Corp., and AGEIA Corp. for their generous support through equipment and software grants.

References

[Bar98] BARUH H.: *Analytical Dynamics*. McGraw-Hill, 1998.

[BB88] BARZEL R., BARR A. H.: A modeling system based on dynamic constraints. *Computer Graphics 22*, 4 (August 1988), 179–188.

[BD91] BOYCE W. E., DIPRIMA R. C.: *Dynamic Analysis of Robot Manipulators: A Cartesian Tensor Approach*, 1st ed. Springer, 1991.

[BP92] BALAFOUTIS C., PATEL R.: *Elementary Differential Equations and Boundary Value Problems*, 5th ed. Wiley and Sons, 1992.

[FvdPT01a] FALOUTSOS P., VAN DE PANNE M., TERZOPOULOS D.: Composable controllers for physics-based character animation. In *Proceedings of ACM SIGGRAPH 2001* (Aug. 2001), Computer Graphics Proceedings, Annual Conference Series, pp. 251–260.

[FvdPT01b] FALOUTSOS P., VAN DE PANNE M., TERZOPOULOS D.: The virtual stuntman: Dynamic characters with a repertoire of autonomous motor skills. *Computers & Graphics 25*, 6 (2001), 933–953.

[HWBO95] HODGINS J. K., WOOTEN W. L., BROGAN D. C., O'BRIEN J. F.: Animating human athletics. In *SIGGRAPH '95: Proceedings of the 22nd annual conference on Computer graphics and interactive techniques* (1995), ACM Press, pp. 71–78.

[Lil93] LILLY K. W.: *Efficient Dynamic Simulation of Robotic Mechanisms*, 1st ed. Kluwer Academic Publishers, 1993.

[LT06] LEE S.-H., TERZOPOULOS D.: Heads up! Biomechanical modeling and neuromuscular control of the neck. *ACM Trans. Graph. 25*, 3 (2006), 1188–1198.

[LWP80] LUH J. Y. S., WALKER M. W., PAUL R. P. C.: Online computational scheme for mechanical manipulators. *Trans. ASME, J. Dynamic Systems, Measurement and Control 102*, 2 (1980), 69–76.

[MZW99] MATARIĆ M. J., ZORDAN V. B., WILLIAMSON M. M.: Making complex articulated agents dance. *Autonomous Agents and Multi-Agent Systems 2*, 1 (1999), 23–43.

[NF02] NEFF M., FIUME E.: Modeling tension and relaxation for computer animation. In *SCA '02: Proceedings of the 2002 ACM SIGGRAPH/Eurographics Symposium on Computer Animation* (2002), ACM Press, pp. 81–88.

[RGBC96] ROSE C., GUENTER B., BODENHEIMER B., COHEN M. F.: Efficient generation of motion transitions using spacetime constraints. In *SIGGRAPH '96: Proceedings of the 23rd annual conference on Computer graphics and interactive techniques* (New York, NY, USA, 1996), ACM Press, pp. 147–154.

[SCAF07] SHAPIRO A., CHU D., ALLEN B., FALOUTSOS P.: A dynamic controller toolkit. In *The 2nd Annual ACM SIGGRAPH Sandbox Symposium on Videogames* (2007).

[SFNTH05] SHAPIRO A., FALOUTSOS P., NG-THOW-HING V.: Dynamic animation and control environment. In *GI '05: Proceedings of the 2005 conference on Graphics interface* (2005), pp. 61–70.

[Smi07] SMITH R.: Open dynamics engine. http://www.ode.org/, 2007.

[SPF03] SHAPIRO A., PIGHIN F. H., FALOUTSOS P.: Hybrid control for interactive character animation. In *11th Pacific Conference on Computer Graphics and Applications* (2003), pp. 455–461.

[vKF94] VAN DE PANNE M., KIM R., FIUME E.: Virtual windup toys for animation. In *Proceedings of Graphics Interface '94* (1994), pp. 208–215.

[vL95] VAN DE PANNE M., LAMOURET A.: Guided optimization for balanced locomotion. In *Eurographics Workshop on Computer Animation and Simulation '95* (1995), Terzopoulos D., Thalmann D., (Eds.), Springer-Verlag, pp. 165–177.

[WC00] WINTERS J., CRAGO P.: *Biomechanics and Neural Control of Posture and Movement.* Springer New York, 2000.

[WGF06] WEINSTEIN R., GUENDELMAN E., FEDKIW R.: Impulse-based pd control for joints and muscles. In *Sketches, Proceedings of ACM SIGGRAPH* (2006).

[WJM06] WROTEK P., JENKINS O. C., MCGUIRE M.: Dynamo: Dynamic data-driven character control with adjustable balance. In *Sandbox 06: Proceedings of the 2006 ACM SIGGRAPH Video Games Symposium* (2006).

[WO82] WALKER M. W., ORIN D. E.: Efficient dynamic computer simulation of robotic mechanisms. *Journal of Dynamic Systems, Measurement, and Control 104* (1982), 205–211.

[Woo98] WOOTEN W.: *Simulation of Leaping, Tumbling, Landing and Balancing Humans.* PhD thesis, Georgia Institute of Technology, 1998.

[YCP03] YIN K., CLINE M. B., PAI D. K.: Motion perturbation based on simple neuromotor control models. In *PG '03: Proceedings of the 11th Pacific Conference on Computer Graphics and Applications* (2003), IEEE Computer Society, p. 445.

[YLv07] YIN K., LOKEN K., VAN DE PANNE M.: SIMBICON: Simple biped locomotion control. *ACM Trans. Graph.* (2007).

[ZH99] ZORDAN V. B., HODGINS J. K.: Tracking and modifying upper-body human motion data with dynamic simulation. In *In Proceedings of Computer Animation and Simulation '99* (September 1999).

[ZH02] ZORDAN V. B., HODGINS J. K.: Motion capture-driven simulations that hit and react. In *In Proceedings of the 2002 ACM SIGGRAPH/Eurographics symposium on Computer animation* (2002), ACM Press, pp. 89 – 96.

[ZMCF05] ZORDAN V. B., MAJKOWSKA A., CHIU B., FAST M.: Dynamic response for motion capture animation. *ACM Trans. Graph. 24*, 3 (2005), 697–701.

[ZW90] ZAJAC F., WINTERS J.: Modeling musculoskeletal movement systems: Joint and body segmental dynamics, musculoskeletal actuation, and neuromuscular control. *Multiple Muscle systems, JM Winters and SL-Y Woo editors. Springer Verlag, New York* (1990), 121–148.

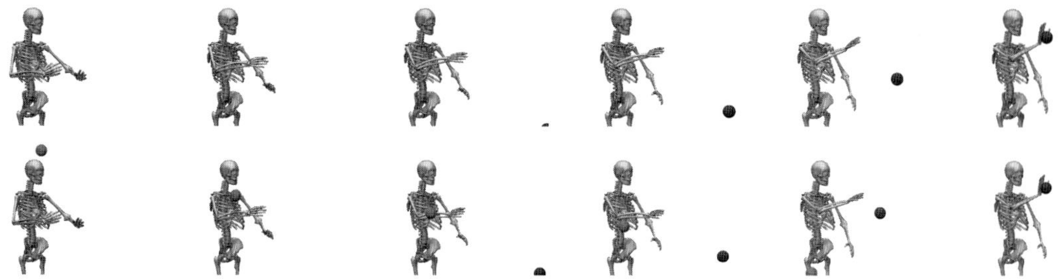

Figure 6: *A character catches a red ball at the specified time both undisturbed (top) and when disturbed by a dynamic object (bottom).*

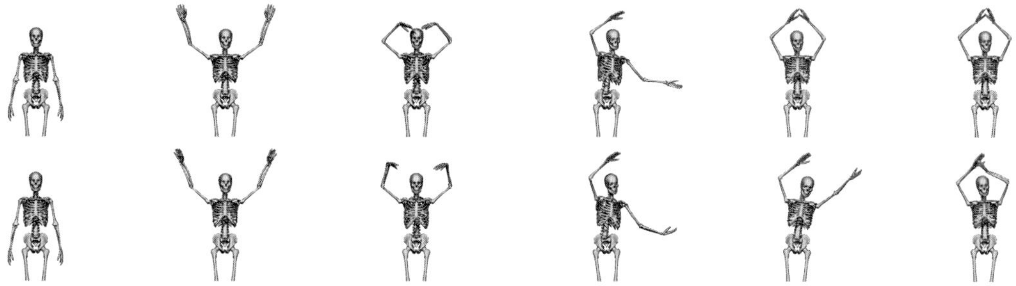

Figure 7: *Snapshots from characters performing the YMCA "dance." Our method (top) vs. PD controllers using constant, manually tuned parameters (bottom).*

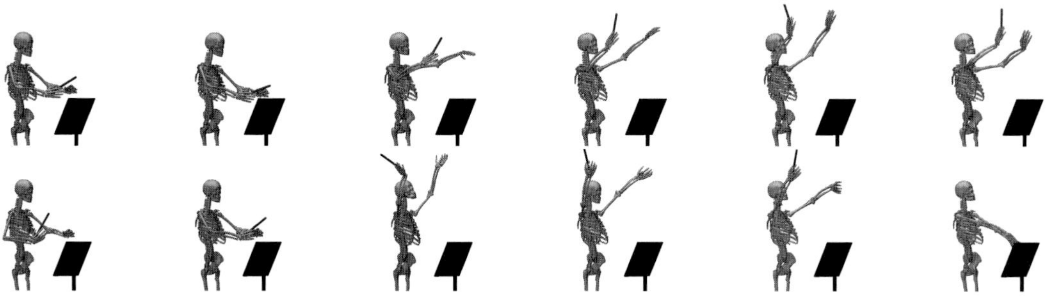

Figure 8: *Snapshots from characters conducting Beethoven's 5th. Our method (top) vs. critically damped PD controllers calculated using only single-link inertia (bottom).*

Eurographics/ ACM SIGGRAPH Symposium on Computer Animation (2007)
D. Metaxas and J. Popovic (Editors)

Multiobjective Control with Frictional Contacts

Yeuhi Abe   Marco da Silva   Jovan Popović

Computer Science and Artificial Intelligence Laboratory
Massachusetts Institute of Technology

Abstract

Standing is a fundamental skill mastered by humans and animals alike. Although easy for adults, it requires careful and deliberate manipulation of contact forces. The variation in contact configuration (e.g., standing on one foot, on uneven ground, or while holding on for support) presents a difficult challenge for interactive simulation of humans and animals, especially while performing tasks in the presence of external disturbances. We describe an analytic approach for control of standing in three-dimensional simulations based upon local optimization. At any point in time, the control system solves a quadratic program to compute actuation by maximizing the performance of multiple motion objectives subject to constraints imposed by actuation limits and contact configuration. This formulation is suitable for interactive animation and it adapts to the proportions of any character model in any non-planar, frictional contact configuration.

Categories and Subject Descriptors (according to ACM CCS): I.3.7 [Computer Graphics]: Three Dimensional Graphics and Realism, Animation

1. Introduction

Dynamic simulation of passive phenomena, such as cloth, fluids, and articulated bodies, is used in many animation systems and has enabled the creation of increasingly complex virtual environments, while reducing demands on talented human animators. This is particularly the case of games and simulations where truly interactive bodies are rapidly replacing static, precomputed motions.

The simulation of active bodies such as humans, robots, and animals has lagged behind, preventing automated animation of characters that act in concert with their dynamic surroundings. Despite previous demonstrations of simulated characters performing impressive actions, including walking, running, diving and swimming [HWBO95, WH96, YLS04], many animation systems still rely on recorded motions or passive ragdoll physics.

The widespread adoption of simulated active bodies is hindered by over-specialization. Most controllers operate correctly only for specific body postures, geometries, or physical properties of the environment. For example, a controller designed to balance a standing character on flat ground many not work on uneven or slippery ground or while leaning against a wall for support. The objective of balancing is conceptually similar in each case, but adapting a controller from one setting to another can be as difficult as developing a new one. Hence, a key advantage of general purpose simulation—automatic motion synthesis under all circumstances—disappears with current control techniques.

We describe an analytic control formulation that solves a local, online optimization to reduce over-specialization in controllers for active bodies. The optimization automatically adapts the control to the frictional properties of the simulation, the mass properties of the character, the posture of the character, and the changing task-specific goals of actions being performed. It also accounts for the constraints imposed by frictional contacts with the environment. Hence the same controller applies to simulation of active bodies in many different situations.

We explore this approach for an important class of actions involving sustained frictional contact with the environment (Figure 1). Such contact occur whenever a character pushes against the environment and uses the resulting force to control its motion. We call this fundamental behavior standing, noting that it is a precursor to locomotion and other complex behaviors. Our approach simplifies the design of standing controllers by decoupling the description of motion from the computation of forces required to accomplish them. A multi-

Symposium on Computer Animation 2007, San Diego, CA, August 03-04, 2007.
© 2007 ACM 978-1-59593-624-4/07/0008 $5.00

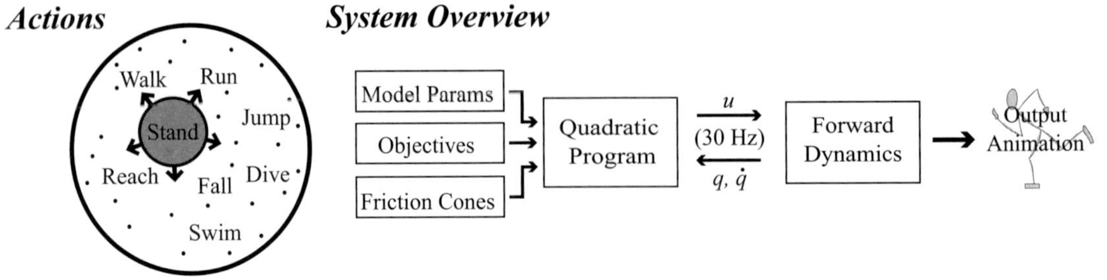

Figure 1: *Previous control systems demonstrate that many human actions can be simulated. Fundamentally, these actions require careful exploitation of external contact forces during periods of sustained contact. We informally refer to these periods as "standing." Multiobjective control ensures robust execution of actions while standing. Given a control strategy and physical properties of the body and environment, our control system uses the current state of the active body* $(\mathbf{q}, \dot{\mathbf{q}})$ *to solve a quadratic program that computes the necessary control torques* $\mathbf{u}$*. This allows us to take a fundamental behavior such as standing and expand its range of application in simulations with different bodies, poses, geometries, and frictional properties.*

objective formulation allows for a compromise between several conflicting motion goals, such as balancing and tracking.

A key component of our approach is a quadratic program (QP) that maximizes instantaneous performance objectives subject to limits on actuation and contact forces. Related formulations have also been proposed in robotic manipulation [CHS88, FOK98, WC06], but current animation techniques still rely on simpler, spring-damper mechanisms. Our experiments reveal that a QP solution improves on the traditional spring-damper techniques by adapting to changing properties of the body, the environment, and the contact. We describe its construction for frictional and non-planar contacts, its use in simulations with large disturbances, and the specifics of accomplishing multiple objectives.

We begin by reviewing the dynamics of active bodies in frictional contact with the environment and highlight the difficulties of controlling such underactuated systems (§2). Next we define multiobjective control with frictional contacts in terms of a local optimization that maximizes instantaneous performance metrics subject to limits on actuation and contact forces (§3). Then we discuss practical strategies needed to accomplish common control objectives in spite of contact variations caused by significant disturbances (§4) and we present lifelike, animations of standing characters in challenging physical environments (§5), all of which were simulated at interactive rates using a standard rigid-body simulator. The results suggest that multiobjective control may be combined with previously proposed control policies for locomotion and other complex behaviors (§6) and used in the design of a new generation of adaptive control systems (§7).

2. Contact Dynamics

Motion of a body in contact with the environment is more complex than unencumbered motion in free space. This is due to the presence of reaction forces that push on the body at each contact point. For the common case of sustained contact, however, control can exploit the linear relationship between joint torques, reaction forces, and joint accelerations. This relationship can be computed at interactive rates and used to control active bodies. In this section we establish our notation by reviewing contact mechanics and the equations of motion for active articulated bodies [CHS88, Wie02].

2.1. Contact Mechanics

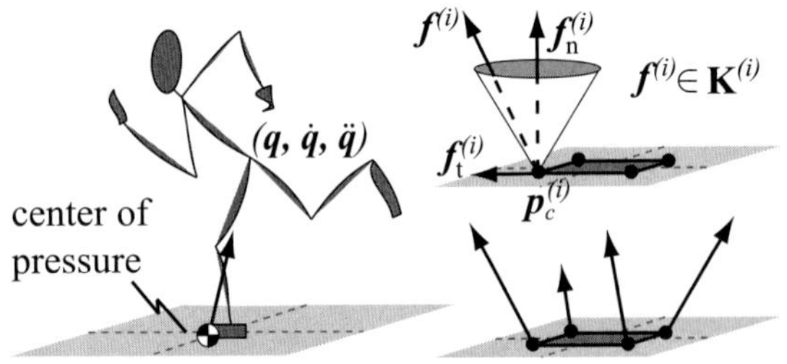

Figure 2: *Contact dynamics expresses the relationship between the motion* $(\mathbf{q}, \dot{\mathbf{q}}, \ddot{\mathbf{q}})$ *of an articulated body, its internal torques, and external forces. We model the contact between two surfaces with a set of point contacts* $\mathbf{p}_c^{(1)} \ldots \mathbf{p}_c^{(m)}$ *and the matching contact forces* $\mathbf{f}^{(1)} \ldots \mathbf{f}^{(m)}$*. Each contact force is restricted by a convex cone* $\mathrm{K}^{(i)}$ *according to the standard Coulomb's model of friction.*

Contacts with environment, as shown in Figure 2, restrict the relative velocity of each contact point $\boldsymbol{p}_c^{(i)} \in \mathbb{R}^3$, for $i = 1 \ldots m$. In the case of a non-slipping contact, the relative velocity is zero: $\dot{\boldsymbol{p}}_c^{(i)} = \mathbf{0}$. This condition can also be expressed in terms of joint velocities $\dot{\boldsymbol{q}} \in \mathbb{R}^n$ by using the Jacobian matrix $\boldsymbol{G}^{(i)} \in \mathbb{R}^{3\times n}$ to compute the body velocity at the point of contact:

$$G^{(i)}\dot{q} = \dot{p}_c^{(i)} = 0. \tag{1}$$

A point contact yields a frictional contact force $f^{(i)} \in \mathbb{R}^3$ that prevents geometric overlap by pushing back on the body. Unlike the forces in a joint linkage (bilateral contact), a contact force does not pull the body in case of separation (unilateral contact) implying that its normal component must be positive: $f_n^{(i)} \geq 0$. Coulomb's model of friction limits the tangential component of the contact force: $\|f_t^{(i)}\| \leq \mu f_n^{(i)}$, where $\mu > 0$ is a coefficient of friction at the contact point. We collect these limits into a friction cone $\mathrm{K}^{(i)}$ that restricts the direction and magnitude of the contact force:

$$f^{(i)} \in \mathrm{K}^{(i)} = \left\{\mathbf{x} \mid \|\mathbf{x}_t\| \leq \mu \mathbf{x}_n\right\}. \tag{2}$$

By the principle of virtual work, a linear map $G^\top f$ determines the total joint torque by aggregating all contact forces and all Jacobian matrices into one vector $f \in \mathbb{R}^{3m}$ and matrix $G \in \mathbb{R}^{3m\times n}$.

2.2. Active Body Dynamics

Conservation of momentum dictates that the total sum of contact forces equals the total change in linear and angular momentum. In the absence of contact forces, it is impossible for an active body to control the location of its center of mass (COM). An active body propels itself using joint torques $u \in \mathbb{R}^{n-6}$. These torques affect only internal joints $q_1 \in \mathbb{R}^{n-6}$ leaving the global position and orientation of the body $q_2 \in \mathbb{R}^6$ as unactuated degrees of freedom. Using this same separation on equations of motion produces two sets of equations, with and without actuation:

$$M_1(q)\ddot{q} + n_1(q,\dot{q}) + G_1^\top(q) f = u \tag{3}$$

$$M_2(q)\ddot{q} + n_2(q,\dot{q}) + G_2^\top(q) f = 0. \tag{4}$$

The first two terms in both equations combine the inertial and gravitational forces on the body. The two equations summarize the main challenge of active body control with frictional contacts: the dimension of the quantity we need to control q exceeds the dimension of torques u at our disposal. Careful manipulation of contact forces f is the only way to accomplish a specific objective, and yet they are restricted by the friction cone: $f \in \mathrm{K} = \mathrm{K}^{(1)} \times \cdots \times \mathrm{K}^{(m)}$.

3. Multiobjective Control

Our multiobjective control computes the joint torques that drive the motion of an active body in simulation. These joint torques are chosen to try and satisfy several objectives at once. Each objective describes a different facet of the desired motion: one objective may track motion data, another may command the location of the center of mass, and yet a third may force the hands to a specific destination. At each instance in time, the conflicts and trade-offs between different objectives are managed by a fast optimization that respects the dynamics of the current contacts and automatically accounts for the physical properties of the active body. Since speed is a primary requirement of online control, we express all constraints and objectives in a quadratic program that can be solved quickly.

3.1. Optimization

Given the current pose q and velocity $\dot{q}$ for the body, the optimization computes joint torques u, joint accelerations $a \in \mathbb{R}^n$, and contact forces f that maximize performance of several objectives $g^{(1)} \ldots g^{(\ell)}$:

$$\min_{a,f,u} \quad \{g^{(1)},\ldots,g^{(\ell)}\}$$

$$\text{subject to} \quad Ma + n + G^\top f = \begin{bmatrix} \mathbf{I} \\ \mathbf{0} \end{bmatrix} u \tag{5a}$$

$$f \in \mathrm{K}, \quad u \in \mathrm{L} \tag{5b}$$

$$Ga + \dot{G}\dot{q} = 0 \tag{5c}$$

In the above, Equation (5a) restricts the solution to be consistent with the instantaneous contact dynamics of active articulated bodies. This is a linear constraint on the vector unknowns because the remaining quantities M, n, and G are constant for the current pose and velocity. Equation (5b) limits the contact forces and control torques according to current friction cones Kand constant-bound torque limits L. Lastly, Equation (5c) ensures that accelerations remain compatible with the no-slip contact condition [Bar89] in Equation (1).

3.2. Quadratic Program

Our implementation approximates the general multiobjective formulation with quadratic programming. This requires choosing quadratic objectives whose trade-offs are weighed either by strict prioritization or through a combined weighted-sum objective. We also approximate the nonlinear friction cone constraint with a conservative polygonal approximation, noting that, if needed, interior point methods could also manage the conical convex constraint in its original form [BV04].

3.2.1. Quadratic Objectives

Control strategies include one or more quadratic objectives. For example, objectives can be used to simultaneously track a desired posture while commanding the position of hands and feet. Quadratic objectives regulate the values of such kinematic quantities $x(q)$ by choosing their accelerations $\ddot{x}(q)$ at each time step.

The value of each objective $g^{(i)}$ measures the difference between the current $\ddot{x}^{(i)}$ and desired $d^{(i)}$ acceleration:

$$g^{(i)} = \|\ddot{x}^{(i)} - d^{(i)}\| = \|J^{(i)}a + \dot{J}^{(i)}\dot{q} - d^{(i)}\|, \tag{6}$$

where the Jacobian matrix $\boldsymbol{J}^{(i)}$ describes the linear relationship between joint velocities and the velocities of regulated kinematic quantities: $\dot{\boldsymbol{x}}^{(i)} = \boldsymbol{J}^{(i)}\dot{\boldsymbol{q}}$.

For example, we can incorporate recorded motion trajectories $\boldsymbol{m}(t)$ by computing the desired accelerations to encourage critically damped tracking:

$$\boldsymbol{d} = k_s\big(\boldsymbol{m}(t) - \boldsymbol{x}\big) + 2\sqrt{k_s}\big(\dot{\boldsymbol{m}}(t) - \dot{\boldsymbol{x}}\big) + \ddot{\boldsymbol{m}}(t), \qquad (7)$$

where t is the current simulation time and k_s is the tracking stiffness. We use the same equation to track a single posture by choosing a constant value for $\boldsymbol{m}(t)$, setting $\dot{\boldsymbol{m}}(t)$ and $\ddot{\boldsymbol{m}}(t)$ to zero.

Stiffness values will depend on desired motion. High stiffness will produces animations that follow motion data despite external disturbances. Low stiffness will produces more realistic animations that react to external disturbances. Note that low-stiffness tracking was more difficult to achieve with previous techniques [ZH02, YCP03, YN03].

3.2.2. Control Trade-Offs

Multiobjective control seeks a compromise among various, often conflicting, objectives. One approach to conflict resolution is to identify strict priority levels. A sequence of quadratic programs can then recursively optimize each objective. First, we optimize the most important objective. Next, we constrain its value to the computed optimum in the optimization of the second most important objective. Strict priorities ensure that some objectives (e.g., reaching) are minimized before others (e.g., posture) are even considered. However, our experiments show that strict priorities should not be used for control of standing because balance tasks usually interfere with other tasks such as tracking recorded motions, which leads to less realistic motions.

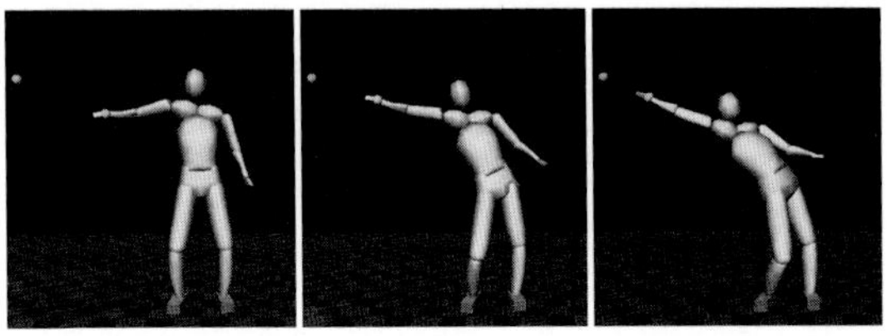

Figure 3: *The weight of a reaching objective is gradually increased, pushing the character to a more precarious stance. In the accompanying video, the reach objective weight is increased to the point where it outweighs the balance objective, and the character falls over. Objective weights from left to right are: 0.01, 0.05, and 0.15.*

We attain a more flexible scheme by using a weighted-sum objective g to strike a compromise between different control objectives:

$$g = w_1 g^{(1)} + w_2 g^{(2)} + \cdots + w_n g^{(n)}. \qquad (8)$$

The weights w_i determine the relative importance of each objective $g^{(i)}$ and account for scaling differences in the units of measure. We show the effect of different weights in Figure 3. At first, the reaching objective is given zero weight and the arm does not move. As the importance of the reach increases, the body progressively departs from its balanced stance until the importance of balance is outweighed by the emphasis on reach and the body falls over. This example illustrates that choosing weights is not a burden, but a vital aspect of any control strategy. Balance, for example, may be a top priority for athletes until they have the opportunity to dive for a ball. The weighting in the objective function determines the precise manner in which such motions are accomplished.

4. Practical Standing Control

In simulation, contact between two objects is neither perfectly detected nor perfectly maintained. Numerical errors due to integration can create variations in detected contact points at almost every time step. External disturbances are even more disruptive. Applying multiobjective control in such an environment requires addressing two major challenges. First, we must complement our general theoretical treatment with practical strategies that account for frequent contact variation. Second, we must devise strategies that guide the body to positions from which it is capable of accomplishing control objectives such as standing upright to avoid falling.

4.1. Stabilizing Contacts

Our theoretical model of contact forces assumes that contacts are maintained. However, numerical errors in the dynamics and the kinematics will often create unintentional contact changes even before external disturbances are introduced. When contacts break, the control must adapt or it will fail.

To prevent contacts from breaking in the first place, we ensure that contact forces computed by the control are strictly positive. The friction cone $\mathrm{K}^{(i)}$ is modified so that the magnitude of contact forces $\boldsymbol{f}^{(i)}$ are above a conservative, threshold (> 50 N in our experiments, for a 70 kg character). This directs the QP solution to compute torques that push on each contact point and hence discourage incidental changes, or, in the case of small separation, re-establish the contacts in just a few simulation steps. Higher values yield better contact stabilization, but extremely large thresholds may generate unrealistic motion or infeasible QP problems. The best practice is to scale the threshold with the weight of the character.

We also use conservative estimates of the location of each contact point, $\boldsymbol{p}_c^{(i)}$. First, we define a contact region to be the closed, polygonal surface defined by a set of contact points (e.g., one contact region exist for each foot or hand used for support). The conservative estimate assumes a modified version of the contact region, shrunken to the strict interior of the actual region. This increases the likelihood that an aggregate contact force (i.e., the sum of all contact forces at the contact points surrounding a contact region) originates within the strict interior of the actual contact region. The QP is modified by relocating each contact point, $\boldsymbol{p}_c^{(i)}$, (used in the construction of K) to be closer to the center of the associated contact region. A larger reduction will produce a more conservative solution, but also restrict the possible movement of the character. In our experiments we found that reducing the size of the contact region by 30 percent was a nice compromise, though many different reductions from 0 percent to 90 percent also worked.

Despite these modifications, external disturbances will inevitably cause contacts to break. We measure the scale of a contact disturbance by how far a contact point is from the surface it should contact. For small disturbances ($< 1e-4$ m, for a normal human sized character) we ignore the break, reasoning that the strictly positive contact forces will re-establish contact soon. If the disturbance becomes medium sized ($< 2e-2$ m) we collapse the friction cone $\mathrm{K}^{(i)}$ (setting the coefficient of friction to zero) to disallow tangential contact force and encourage immediate recovery without tangential slipping. However, if the disturbance becomes large ($> 2e-2$ m), we remove the contact point from the QP formulation. In that case, we add a new motion objective that guides the former contact point toward its projection on the external contact surface as a last-ditch attempt to re-establish the contact.

In our experiments, control outcomes were not overly sensitive to precise values of threshold parameters. We chose the reported values to increase the stability of our control for larger disturbances. Most other settings worked well with smaller disturbances.

4.2. Maintaining Balance

Everybody falls on occasion and Equation (4) shows us why: the global position and orientation of a body is not directly controlled by joint torques. Humans adapt to this limitation with both anticipatory and reactive movements. Anticipatory movements, such as bracing for the motion of a bus by leaning in the direction of its motion, generally require sophisticated motion planning. Our low-level control does not handle anticipatory aspects of balance, but it does provide a reactive mechanism to maintain an upright posture while accomplishing motion objectives that are nearly balanced. This is done by regulating the horizontal position of the center of mass.

Once the COM is too far from a desired, upright position, it may become impossible to return to that position due to underactuation. Contact dynamics gives us a precise condition for knowing when a given return trajectory is feasible (§2). The motion of a body $\boldsymbol{q}(t)$ is feasible if and only if there are contact forces $\boldsymbol{f} \in \mathrm{K}$ that satisfy Equation (4):

$$\boldsymbol{M}_2(\boldsymbol{q})\ddot{\boldsymbol{q}} + \boldsymbol{n}_2(\boldsymbol{q},\dot{\boldsymbol{q}}) + \boldsymbol{G}_2^\top(\boldsymbol{q})\boldsymbol{f} = \boldsymbol{0}. \tag{9}$$

This a strict generalization of the often used criteria that the zero-moment point (ZMP) should remain within the support polygon [Wie02]. Whereas the ZMP criteria assumes an infinite coefficient of friction and planar contact with the ground, the above condition accounts for the friction cone and applies to any three-dimensional contact configuration. As with the ZMP criteria, direct application of this condition to plan an optimal recovery from a given dynamic disturbance is beyond the computational budget of online control systems. (The equations are no longer linear because the state of the body changes over time.) For example, efficient implementations of optimal control [SP05] require several seconds of computation time, at least an order of magnitude too slow for online control.

Instead of computing an optimal recovery strategy, our control implements a simple heuristic strategy based on guiding the center of mass toward a more stable configuration for most disturbances. The COM for a human standing on flat ground, for example, is usually above the mid-point between the two footprints. In general, this is a stable configuration for many disturbances because, for small deviations, the COM is fully controllable in the horizontal direction and can be brought back to the desired position.

Since the COM is a kinematic quantity $\boldsymbol{x}(\boldsymbol{q})$, we can use multiobjective control to direct its motion by providing a desired acceleration, $\boldsymbol{d}$, in Equation (6). We found in our experiments that a simple first order damped approach works well for many motions:

$$\boldsymbol{d} = k_s(\boldsymbol{x}_d - \boldsymbol{x}) - k_d\dot{\boldsymbol{x}}, \tag{10}$$

where $\boldsymbol{x}_d$ is the desired horizontal position of the COM and k_s and k_d are manually tuned constants. However, to recover from larger deviations from the desired position we found that this simple strategy was not sufficient. For high values of k_s the strategy tended to be overly forceful, resulting in instability. For lower values of k_s the strategy would fail to reach the goal. Instead, we found that we could achieve better results by varying k_s with the distance from the desired COM position. In our experiments we scaled k_s with the inverse square-root distance: $1/\sqrt{||\boldsymbol{x}_d - \boldsymbol{x}||}$.

When standing on uneven ground with one foot on the pedestal or with one hand on the wall, we still control the COM in the plane perpendicular to the force of gravity. The desired location of the COM is placed near the mid-point of the horizontal projection of all contact points. This ensures that for small deviations from the desired position, the COM is still controllable in the horizontal direction and can be returned to the desired position. The exact location is not important, but different choices will affect the ability to recover from different types of disturbances. For example, a character that places more weight on a forward foot, will be able to recover from larger unexpected forces coming from the front.

The key to understanding our strategy is to observe that it does not prevent falling on its own: the COM can fall to the ground and still be above the horizontal position. Instead, falls are prevented with a combination of this objective and others that prescribe *standing* motions or postures. When the COM wanders significantly outside the support polygon the character falls because it can no longer accomplish the objective of standing. However, we found that our simple strategies worked well even for many significant disturbances.

5. Results

We demonstrate the capabilities of multiobjective control by discussing a few simulations we have created of active characters balancing, tracking motion, and responding to a dynamic disturbances.

5.1. Experiments

The supplementary video includes a few typical runs from the following experiments:

Sobriety. A human-like character balances on a moving platform while reaching for its nose with its hands. Both balancing and reaching are accomplished despite the significant motion of the platform and other disturbances introduced by a human, interactively, during the simulation.

Pelted. A human-like character tracks motion data closely while balancing in response to many collisions with objects. As with all of these simulations, the character balances under its own power and there are no artificial aids preventing the character from falling over.

Platform. A human-like character balances on a moving platform. Varying the coefficient of friction between the feet and the platform cause changes in the balancing motion.

Alien. The human character in the "Pelted" and "Platform" simulations is replaced with a lighter and smaller character. Although the geometry, weight, and proportions differ from those of the human character, the same control works without modification. Since the character has a larger head, however, the posture stiffness of the waist joint was decreased to encourage more waist motion.

Wall. A human character places its hand on a nearby wall for additional support while balancing on a moving platform. The control automatically adapts the strategy of using the hand to provide additional leverage to maintain balance despite severe tipping of the platform. The control adapts easily to the non-planar contact configurations, involving both feet and hands, through the use of friction cone constraints.

Mishap. The character stands with one leg perched on a flimsy table. Friction cone constraints prevent the character from immediately toppling the table. When the table suddenly collapses, the character regains its balance on one foot. The balancing maneuver occurs automatically, though we do direct the free foot to a desired location using an end-effector objective.

We manually modeled the geometry of both characters in our simulations. Their inertial properties were computed automatically using the volume of each limb and standard mass distributions [Win90]. The motions tracked by our control system were recorded with an optical motion capture system. Forward dynamics with frictional contacts were computed with the Open Dynamics Engine (*www.ode.org*), a general purpose rigid body simulator. The QP problems were solved by the MOSEK software system (*www.mosek.com*), which employs the interior point method to solve convex optimization problems [BV04].

The QP control problem is solved 30 times per second of simulation, while we use many more simulation steps in the same interval, between 1000 and 5000. Each solution required around 15 iterations to converge for an average running time of 17 milliseconds. The "Wall" simulation took slightly longer than the others (see Table 1) because of the additional hand contact. All simulations were fast enough to allow the entire system (simulation and control) to run at 30 frames per second, or better, on a 2.8 GHz Intel Pentium 4.

5.2. Direction

Our experiments demonstrate that multiobjective control enables artistic direction of active bodies with two familiar animation mechanisms: control of poses and end effector positions.

In most of our experiments, we track a single recorded posture, but tracking motions is just as easy. Tracking fast motions, such as dodging incoming objects, is accomplished accurately, but "loosely" enough to respond interestingly to collisions with other objects (Pelted).

End-effector objectives are used to control individual limbs: arms, hands, feet, and so on. Our experiments include two simple examples. One directs hands to touch the nose (Sobriety) and the other controls the swing leg to direct the look of a balancing maneuver (Mishap). (§4.2). In both cases, the accelerations of the end-effectors where simply chosen to converge toward a desired goal position. Though tracking of more complex trajectories is possible.

5.3. Friction Cones

Many control systems assume planar contact with flat ground, which limits possible applications. Multiobjective control manages this special case (Pelted, Alien) but it also handles more general contact configurations by using friction cone constraints. Examples of this include uneven footing (Sobriety, Mishap) and hand contact with the wall (Wall).

Since friction cones prevent feet from slipping, the control need not insist on a perfect match between the body and recorded postures. A shorter character, for example, can easily track the recorded trajectory of a full-size human (Alien) without slipping causing a fall.

Friction cones can also be manipulated to create interesting animation. By restricting the allowable friction cones, different balancing motion that respect those limitations emerge automatically(Platform). Friction cones were also instrumental in the Mishap simulation where a very narrow friction cone was used initially on the front foot to instruct the character to apply only vertical forces on the precarious table.

5.4. Balance Objective

Many of our experiments feature a character on a moving platform. Under such conditions, our control system maintains balance by coaxing the COM back toward a conservatively chosen position. We emphasize that treating the control of the COM as a strict priority, above all other objectives, has not produced satisfactory results in our experience. Instead, the corrective motion is weighted against other active objectives, contributing to the quality of the motion. Although our simple balance strategy can be improved with further work, multiobjective control can easily accommodate new strategies once they are available.

5.5. Adaptation

Multiobjective control adapts automatically to external disturbances and physical properties of the character and the environment.

The allure of physically based animation is clearly demonstrated by a rich diversity of interactions characters can have with their environment. However, this is only possible if characters can adapt naturally to physical disturbances. We present a couple of examples (Pelted, Mishap) that suggest definite progress in this direction. Complex motions, including natural but counter-intuitive balance recoveries, such as lunging in the direction of the fall (Mishap), emerge without explicit modeling.

Multiobjective control also adapt to bodies with different inertial parameters (Alien). Our shorter character is capable of withstanding significant disturbances by using a general control strategy initially tested on a taller and heavier character. This highlights a key advantage of our control system: it decouples the description of control strategies from the computation of required torques. Hence, the objectives are independent of mass distribution, model geometry, and contact dynamics.

Simulation	Vars.	Avg. QP Time	Avg. Iterations
Platform	140	13ms	14.5
Pelted	140	13ms	14.5
Sobriety	146	16ms	13.8
Mishap	143	14ms	15.8
Wall	172	29ms	17.7

Table 1: *The number of variables, average optimization time, and average number of iterations for the multiobjective QP per simulation.*

6. Related Work

Active body control has a long history in graphics and robotics. We review some of this work in the context of our main design decisions: the choice of local optimization for control, the form of the quadratic objective function, and the choice of constraints for modeling general frictional contacts.

6.1. Active Body Control

Multiobjective optimizations complement strengths of previous approaches in computer animation but reduces the need for manual adjustment of control parameters. Raibert and Hodgins [RH91] relied on spring-damper mechanisms to compute torques for online control, leading to some of the most dramatic simulations of active bodies [HWBO95, Woo98, FvdPT01]. Similar control strategies now appear in commercial software systems for computer animation (*www.naturalmotion.com*). The specifics of these commercial systems are unknown, but they likely require tuning of individual rest lengths and spring constants for most characters, tasks, and simulation environments, similar to the predecessors [HP97, FvdPT01].

Manual tuning can be reduced to some extent with dynamic scaling laws and automated search, but it reaches its limits when adapting to new environments, mass distributions, and other variations [HP97]. Our control system enables modular specification of general control policies for the case of sustained frictional contact. Instead of designing and tuning spring-based dampers for each joint, we divorce the specification of control policies from the computation of required control torques. Hence, our control system adjusts more easily to new situations and different environments.

Limit-cycle control tracks periodic motions by computing control perturbations needed to return the present motion back to the desired limit cycle (i.e. limit-cycle control strategy or periodic motion data) [LvdPF96]. Instead of relying on explicit models of contact dynamics, it approximates the Poincaré return map. The advantage of such an approach is that it also incorporates the effect of collisions into execution of control policies: a difficult problem that we do not address in this paper. A potential liability is that approximated return maps might be valid only for small perturbations from limit-cycle trajectories.

Other tracking alternatives have also been proposed to create dynamically responsive motions from kinematic or preplanned trajectories [ZH02, YCP03, ZMCF05]. These approaches scale spring constants by inertial parameters or feed-forward torques magnitudes to reduce the difficulty of tuning parameters, but none explicitly account for contact dynamics. Some techniques have pursued a hybrid alternative instead, accounting for some dynamic parameters with the goal of generating dynamically feasible *motions* instead of controls [GM85, SC89, Pai90, SC92, YN03, KP06]. Our multiobjective control was designed to integrate with any general purpose simulator of rigid bodies. As a result, we can easily animate complex interactions with many moving objects using any rigid-body simulator.

6.2. Quadratic Objective

Our multiobjective approach was inspired by prioritized control of articulated bodies [KSPW04]. The principal advantage of such an approach is automatic coordination of multiple objectives, which makes it easy to combine task-specific objectives with the less specific postural objectives gleaned from motion data [AP06]. Our experimentations, however, showed that prioritization of balance control interferes with posture tracking, which makes it difficult to combine the two in a life-like manner. Instead, we rely on the quadratic weighted-sum objective in all of our experiments to attain necessary tradeoffs between tracking, balance, and other tasks.

Earlier applications of local optimization proposed similar quadratic objectives without incorporating a general model of contact dynamics [SC89, SC92]. Inaccurate modeling of contact dynamics is also a potential drawback of most prioritized control systems: they often assume the existence of bilateral contact constraints, as if the bodies were pinned at contact points. As illustrated in Figure 4, bilateral contacts lead to unrealistic control strategies. Recent developments in prioritized control suggest an iterative active-set solution [SK06], but this approach is less robust and harder to implement than our QP-based method.

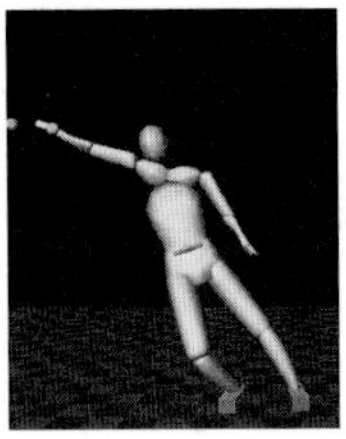

Figure 4: *This illustration underscores the importance of incorporating ground contact constraints into any control formulation. Ignoring contact dynamics, a character can reach for the object as if his feet were pinned to the ground. With proper contact dynamics and multiobjective control, the character strikes a compromise between reaching and not falling as seen in Figure 3.*

6.3. Friction Cones

Friction-cone constraints generalize the zero-moment point (ZMP) constraint, which is often used in local optimizations as an alternative to bilateral contact constraints [HMPH04, KKI02]. The ZMP is a criterion of physical feasibility for bodies in contact with the ground plane [VB04]. For example, its position outside the contact polygon indicates a physically infeasible motion. The ZMP criterion is sometimes incorrectly defined as a measure of dynamic stability in both graphics and robotics literature. Instead, the ZMP criterion enables successful tracking of controllable trajectories by ensuring physically realizable control policies [SKG03, HHHT98]. Hofmann and colleagues, for example, use quadratic programming to restrict the ZMP to remain within the contact polygon [HMPH04]. This approach assumes planar contact configurations (e.g., standing on flat ground) with infinite friction. For example, control systems based on ZMP constraints may lead to slipping and falling in simulations with realistic frictional properties. In contrast, we use friction-cone constraints that are more accurate and valid for general three-dimensional (e.g., standing on uneven ground) contacts with friction [Wie02].

According to a survey by Srinivasa [Sri05], the first control system with an explicit model of contact dynamics appeared in the robotics literature as a solution to multifingered manipulation of two-dimensional objects [CHS88]. The control systems proposed in graphics literature, however, did not employ explicit formulations of contact dynamics until Fang and Pollard [FP03] demonstrated their value in *offline* optimal control. We demonstrate the feasibility and importance of this model for *online* control in interactive animations of active bodies.

Two methods in robotics literature have relied on a similar QP formulations to ours for the control of walking bipeds [FOK98, WC06], but without addressing contact variations and significant disturbances. Our work also defines the concept of multiobjective control with frictional contacts and examines its role in animations of standing active bodies. We emphasize the resilient treatment of disturbances, reasoning that locomotion and more complex behaviors can be robust only after standing is more robust.

7. Conclusion

We have presented a multiobjective control formulation based upon local optimization that models and respects frictional contact dynamics. We arrive at three important conclusions about such systems. First, friction-cone constraints, which generalize ZMP constraints, improve control of active bodies in simulation with arbitrary frictional contacts. Second, the compromise between multiple conflicting motion objectives should be accomplished with soft trade-offs rather than strict priorities, especially when actively regulating the center of mass. And third, special care must be taken to stabilize frictional contacts in simulations with large dynamic disturbances.

Our multiobjective control is restricted in scope: it assumes the existence of a proper high-level control policy instead of searching for one. The more difficult problem has been tackled *offline* with many approaches including continuous optimization [WK88], dynamic programming [vdPFV90], genetic algorithms [Sim94, NM93], neural networks [GTH98], and simulated annealing [vdPF93, GT95]. In the future we plan to apply similar ideas to online control by solving appropriate approximations of the offline problem. Another possible direction would be to complements multiobjective control with kinematic methods that ignore physics but learn from data and other studies of natural motion [KKKL94, RSC01, GMHP04, YKH04]. These would be the next steps toward designing adaptive control strategies for walking, running, jumping, and other complex behaviors.

8. Acknowledgments

We are grateful to Eugene Hsu and Daniel Vlasic for motion-capture assistance and acting; Tom Buehler for video production; and Russ Tedrake for comments throughout the project. This work was supported in part by the Singapore-MIT GAMBIT Game Lab.

References

[AP06] ABE Y., POPOVIĆ J.: Interactive animation of dynamic manipulation. In *Symposium on Computer Animation (SCA)* (2006), pp. 195–203. 8

[Bar89] BARAFF D.: Analytical methods for dynamic simulation of non-penetrating rigid bodies. In *Computer Graphics (Proceedings of SIGGRAPH 89)* (July 1989), Annual Conference Series, ACM SIGGRAPH, pp. 223–232. 3

[BV04] BOYD S., VANDENBERGHE L.: *Convex Optimization*. Cambridge University Press, 2004. 3, 6

[CHS88] COLE A., HAUSER J., SASTRY S.: Kinematics and control of multifingered hands with rolling contact. In *International Conference on Robotics and Automation (ICRA)* (1988), vol. 1, IEEE, pp. 228–233. 2, 8

[FOK98] FUJIMOTO Y., OBATA S., KAWAMURA A.: Robust biped walking with active interaction control between foot and ground. In *International Conference on Robotics and Automation (ICRA)* (1998), IEEE, pp. 2030–2035. 2, 8

[FP03] FANG A. C., POLLARD N. S.: Efficient synthesis of physically valid human motion. *ACM Transactions on Graphics 22*, 3 (July 2003), 417–426. 8

[FvdPT01] FALOUTSOS P., VAN DE PANNE M., TERZOPOULOS D.: Composable controllers for physics-based character animation. In *Proceedings of ACM SIGGRAPH 2001* (Aug. 2001), Annual Conference Series, pp. 251–260. 7

[GM85] GIRARD M., MACIEJEWSKI A. A.: Computational modeling for the computer animation of legged figures. In *Computer Graphics (Proceedings of SIGGRAPH 85)* (July 1985), vol. 19, pp. 263–270. 8

[GMHP04] GROCHOW K., MARTIN S. L., HERTZMANN A., POPOVIĆ Z.: Style-based inverse kinematics. *ACM Transactions on Graphics 23*, 3 (Aug. 2004), 522–531. 9

[GT95] GRZESZCZUK R., TERZOPOULOS D.: Automated learning of muscle-actuated locomotion through control abstraction. In *Proceedings of SIGGRAPH 95* (Aug. 1995), Annual Conference Series, pp. 63–70. 9

[GTH98] GRZESZCZUK R., TERZOPOULOS D., HINTON G.: NeuroAnimator: Fast neural network emulation and control of physics-based models. In *Proceedings of SIGGRAPH 98* (July 1998), Annual Conference Series, pp. 9–20. 9

[HHHT98] HIRAI K., HIROSE M., HAIKAWA Y., TAKENAKA T.: The development of honda humanoid robot. In *International Conference on Robotics and Automation (ICRA)* (1998), IEEE, pp. 1321–1326. 8

[HMPH04] HOFMANN A., MASSAQUOI S., POPOVIC M., HERR H.: A sliding controller for bipedal balancing using integrated movement of contact and non-contact limbs. In *International Conference on Intelligent Robots and Systems (IROS)* (2004), vol. 2, IEEE/RSJ, pp. 1952–1959. 8

[HP97] HODGINS J. K., POLLARD N. S.: Adapting simulated behaviors for new characters. In *Proceedings of SIGGRAPH 97* (Aug. 1997), Computer Graphics Proceedings, Annual Conference Series, pp. 153–162. 7

[HWBO95] HODGINS J. K., WOOTEN W. L., BROGAN D. C., O'BRIEN J. F.: Animating human athletics. In *Proceedings of ACM SIGGRAPH 95* (Aug. 1995), Annual Conference Series, pp. 71–78. 1, 7

[KKI02] KUDOH S., KOMURA T., IKEUCHI K.: The dynamic postural adjustment with the quadratic programming method. In *International Conference on Intelligent Robots and Systems (IROS)* (2002), pp. 2563–2568. 8

[KKKL94] KOGA Y., KONDO K., KUFFNER J., LATOMBE J.-C.: Planning motions with intentions. In *Proceedings of SIGGRAPH 94* (July 1994), Computer Graphics Proceedings, Annual Conference Series, pp. 395–408. 9

[KP06] KRY P. G., PAI D. K.: Interaction capture and synthesis. *ACM Transactions on Graphics 25*, 3 (July 2006), 872–880. 8

[KSPW04] KHATIB O., SENTIS L., PARK J.-H., WARREN J.: Whole body dynamic behavior and control of human-like robots. *International Journal of Humanoid Robotics 1*, 1 (2004), 29–43. 8

[LvdPF96] LASZLO J. F., VAN DE PANNE M., FIUME E. L.: Limit cycle control and its application to the animation of balancing and walking. In *Proceedings of SIGGRAPH 96* (Aug. 1996), Annual Conference Series, pp. 155–162. 7

[NM93] NGO J. T., MARKS J.: Spacetime constraints revisited. In *Proceedings of ACM SIGGRAPH 2000* (Aug. 1993), Annual Conference Series, pp. 343–350. 9

[Pai90] PAI D. K.: *Programming Anthropoid Walking: Control and Simulation*. Tech. Rep. TR–90–1178, Cornell University, 1990. 8

[RH91] RAIBERT M. H., HODGINS J. K.: Animation of dynamic legged locomotion. In *Computer Graphics (Proceedings of SIGGRAPH 91)* (July 1991), Annual Conference Series, ACM SIGGRAPH, pp. 349–358. 7

[RSC01] ROSE C. F., SLOAN P.-P. J., COHEN M. F.: Artist-directed inverse-kinematics using radial basis function interpolation. *Computer Graphics Forum 20*, 3 (2001), 239–250. 9

[SC89] STEWART A. J., CREMER J. F.: Algorithmic control of walking. In *International Conference on Robotics and Automation (ICRA)* (1989), IEEE, pp. 1598–1603. 8

[SC92] STEWART A. J., CREMER J. F.: Beyond keyframing: an algorithmic approach to animation. In *Graphics Interface* (1992), pp. 273–281. 8

[Sim94] SIMS K.: Evolving virtual creatures. In *Proceedings of SIGGRAPH 94* (July 1994), Computer Graphics Proceedings, Annual Conference Series, pp. 15–22. 9

[SK06] SENTIS L., KHATIB O.: A whole-body control framework for humanoids operating in human environments. In *International Conference on Robotics and Automation (ICRA)* (2006), IEEE, pp. 2641–2648. 8

[SKG03] SHIN H. J., KOVAR L., GLEICHER M.: Physical touchup of human motions. In *Proceedings 11th Pacific Conference on Computer Graphics and Applications* (2003), pp. 194–203. 8

[SP05] SULEJMANPASIĆ A., POPOVIĆ J.: Adaptation of performed ballistic motion. *ACM Transactions on Graphics 24*, 1 (Jan. 2005), 165–179. 5

[Sri05] SRINIVASA S.: *Control synthesis for dynamic contact manipulation*. PhD thesis, Carnegie Mellon University, 2005. 8

[VB04] VUKOBRATOVIC M., BOROVAC B.: Zero-moment point – thirty five years of its life. *International Journal of Human Robotics 11*, 1 (2004), 157–173. 8

[vdPF93] VAN DE PANNE M., FIUME E.: Sensor-actuator networks. In *Computer Graphics (Proceedings of SIGGRAPH 93)* (Aug. 1993), Annual Conference Series, ACM SIGGRAPH, pp. 335–342. 9

[vdPFV90] VAN DE PANNE M., FIUME E., VRANESIC Z.: Reusable motion synthesis using state-space controllers. In *Computer Graphics (Proceedings of SIGGRAPH 90)* (Aug. 1990), Annual Conference Series, ACM SIGGRAPH, pp. 225–234. 9

[WC06] WIEBER P.-B., CHEVALLEREAU C.: Online adaptation of reference trajectories for the control of walking systems. *Robotics and Autonomous Systems 54*, 7 (July 2006), 559–566. 2, 8

[WH96] WOOTEN W. L., HODGINS J. K.: Animation of human diving. *Comput. Graph. Forum 15*, 1 (1996), 3–13. 1

[Wie02] WIEBER P. B.: On the stability of walking systems. In *International Workshop on Humanoid and Human Friendly Robotics* (2002). 2, 5, 8

[Win90] WINTER D. A.: *Biomechanics and Motor Control of Human Movement*, 2nd ed. John Wiley and Sons, Inc., New York, 1990. 6

[WK88] WITKIN A., KASS M.: Spacetime constraints. In *Computer Graphics (Proceedings of SIGGRAPH 88)* (Aug. 1988), vol. 22, pp. 159–168. 9

[Woo98] WOOTEN W.: *Simulation of Leaping, Tumbling, Landing, and Balancing Humans*. PhD thesis, Georgia Institute of Technology, 1998. 7

[YCP03] YIN K., CLINE M., PAI D. K.: Motion perturbation based on simple neuromotor control models. In *Pacific Conference on Computer Graphics and Applications (PG)* (2003), pp. 445–449. 4, 8

[YKH04] YAMANE K., KUFFNER J. J., HODGINS J. K.: Synthesizing animations of human manipulation tasks. *ACM Transactions on Graphics 23*, 3 (Aug. 2004), 532–539. 9

[YLS04] YANG P.-F., LASZLO J., SINGH K.: Layered dynamic control for interactive character swimming. In *Symposium on Computer Animation (SCA)* (2004), ACM SIGGRAPH/Eurographics, pp. 39–47. 1

[YN03] YAMANE K., NAKAMURA Y.: Dynamics filter—concept and implementation of online motion generator for human figures. *IEEE Transactions of Robotics and Automation 19*, 3 (2003), 421–432. 4, 8

[ZH02] ZORDAN V. B., HODGINS J. K.: Motion capture-driven simulations that hit and react. In *Symposium on Computer Animation (SCA)* (July 2002), pp. 89–96. 4, 8

[ZMCF05] ZORDAN V. B., MAJKOWSKA A., CHIU B., FAST M.: Dynamic response for motion capture animation. *ACM Transactions on Graphics 24*, 3 (Aug. 2005), 697–701. 8

Eurographics/ ACM SIGGRAPH Symposium on Computer Animation (2007)
D. Metaxas and J. Popovic (Editors)

Smooth Movers: Perceptually Guided Human Motion Simulation

Rachel McDonnell,[†1] Fiona Newell,[2] and Carol O'Sullivan[1]

[1]Graphics, Vision and Visualisation Group, [2]Institute of Neuroscience,
Trinity College Dublin, Ireland

Abstract

To animate a character, a number of poses are displayed in quick succession in order to create the illusion of motion. For most real-time applications, such as games, the pose update rate is largely constrained by the available hardware and overall simulation complexity. To date, no analysis of the factors that affect the perceived smoothness of animated virtual characters has been presented. In the first perceptual studies aimed at identifying such factors and their interactions, we have determined some thresholds that could be used to produce acceptably smooth human animations in a variety of conditions. Some interesting results were found, e.g., that character type, clothing, scene complexity or motion synchronicity had no effect on smoothness perception in our experiments, but cycle rate, linear velocity, motion complexity and group size all had a significant effect, with slower or lower intensity movements generally requiring fewer updates. Our results should be of real practical use to character animators in various application areas, but in particular to developers of real-time applications where Simulation Levels Of Detail (SLOD) need to be employed.

Categories and Subject Descriptors (according to ACM CCS): I.3.7 [Computer Graphics]: Three Dimensional Graphics and Realism

1. Introduction

Pose update rate, expressed in poses per second (pps), can be defined as the frequency of individual simulation steps displayed when animating a character (see Figure 1). Depending on the application domain, this rate can be as low as 10 or 12 pps (e.g., for simple game characters or "claymation" figures such as Aardman's Wallace and Gromit), between 30 and 60pps for most 3D games, and sometimes even higher for production-level motion. In stop motion animation and traditional cartoons, creating double frames (i.e., simulating at 12pps while filming at 24fps), reduces the level of working hours required in these already labor-intensive processes. For most real-time applications, such as games, the pose update rate is largely constrained by the available hardware and overall scene complexity. Simulation Level of detail (SLOD) methods are often employed to optimize resource allocation, perhaps by updating the motions of unimportant characters less frequently, thus reducing computational costs. Furthermore, individual mesh or image-based (impostor) keyframes can be "pre-baked" for background characters, which reduces rendering and simulation costs but increases memory consumption (thus the pps must remain low).

While significant advances have been made in terms of the technical aspects of creating animations of characters, the perceptual significance of certain design or engineering choices is still not fully understood. For example, what impact does a particular pose update rate have on the visual fidelity of an animation - what is the threshold below which it becomes unacceptable, or the upper limit above which we are simply wasting valuable resources on imperceptible detail? Are these thresholds always the same, regardless of the motion or scene properties being depicted, or are there factors that lower or raise them? Our answers to these questions could be used as metrics for perceptually guided human motion simulation.

In this paper, we identify some factors and thresholds for the perceived smoothness of animated virtual characters. In a Baseline Experiment (Section 3), we first determined whether different pose update rates are in fact needed for

† Rachel.McDonnell@cs.tcd.ie

Symposium on Computer Animation 2007, San Diego, CA, August 03-04, 2007.
© 2007 ACM 978-1-59593-624-4/07/0008 $5.00

human motions with different character and motion properties - we found that the type of character and clothing have no effect, whereas different motion types do. Our detailed Movement Experiment (Section 4) examined the impact and interactions of various motion properties - we found, for example, that motions with lower cycle rate, complexity and linear velocity needed significantly fewer pose updates. Finally, several experiments were carried out to determine the effects of having different Simulation Levels of Detail (Section 5) in a scene, where we found that lower pose update rates were acceptable for background characters, and that neither synchronicity of their motions nor the complexity of the scene had any effect on the perceived smoothness of the animations.

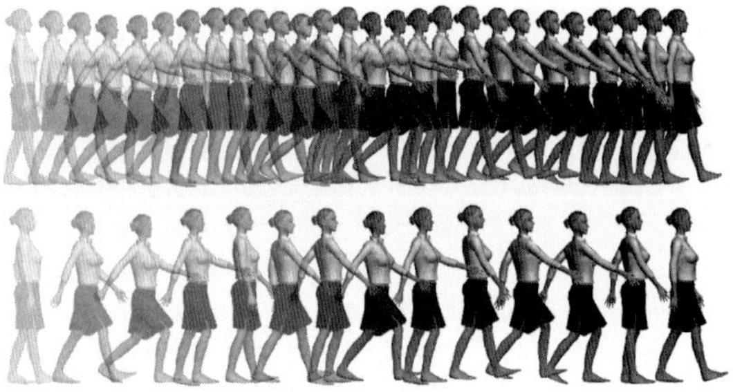

Figure 1: *The update rate or poses per second (pps) used to update characters typically varies based on the application domain. In this figure, the animation on the top is being updated at 30pps, whereas the one on the bottom is only updated at 15pps.*

2. Background

The issue of appropriate pose update rates for animation is related to the study of frame rates for movies and refresh rates for monitors and televisions. Much research has been conducted into the factors that affect the *critical fusion frequency*, which is the refresh rate of a display device above which a picture stops flickering and fuses into a steady image (e.g., [Rog83,Lan54]). More closely related to our work, Watson et al. [WAF86] looked for the critical sample rate necessary for observers to consider sampled images indistinguishable from continuous moving images (i.e., when they appeared smooth). They found, for the simple moving lines tested, that this rate depended on the spatial and temporal acuity of the observer and on the velocity and spatial-frequency content of the image. While these results could form a good theoretical basis for a motion metric, it is difficult to see how we could directly derive them from the typically complex parameters that animators of virtual characters manipulate.

Research from the fields of psychology and neuroscience has shown that different sources of information, such as color and form, can contribute to the perception of motion. Johansson [Joh73] showed that 12 moving light points, affixed to the main joints of the body, suffice to create a rich perception of a moving human figure, within a very short onset time (200msec). This stimulus was designed to separate biological motion information from other sources of information that are normally intermingled with the motion of a human, such as form or outline. These "point-light walkers" have since been used extensively to examine the sophisticated pattern analysis processes that the brain uses for biological motion perception. Dittrich [Dit93] found that better and faster human motion recognition occurred when the lights on the walker were displayed in the normal (upright) orientation, than when upside-down, indicating that higher level (or top-down) cognitive processes are being used for the familiar motion, whereas the unfamiliar (inverted) motion is more likely to be seen as a collection of randomly moving dots. Despite people's relative insensitivity to missing or inaccurate *spatial* data for walking stimuli, they are not so forgiving of missing or distorted *temporal* data. For example, Mather et al. [MRW92] found that inserting blank frames for >=48msec between displayed frames of a walking human (i.e., a pose update rate of about 20pps in our terminology) significantly reduced people's ability to recognize the direction of motion.

Computer Animation researchers have also investigated the limits of user sensitivity to animated human motion and have developed perceptual metrics for improving human animation quality [HOT98, OHJ00, RP03, HRvdP04, WB04, MSCO06]. Despite these promising results, automatic measurement of the visual fidelity of human motion is still not possible for most practical applications such as motion compression or optimization. Arikan [Ari06] recently reported the inadequacy of existing measures of visual fidelity for compressed human motion, RMS error proving particularly unsuitable. While trying to reduce the dimensionality of the search space of human motions for optimization purposes, Safonova et al. [SHP04] used the average squared error between the angles of a full-dimensional motion and its k-dimensional representation as a measure of motion quality. They computed this metric for a number of varying human behaviors (e.g., walking, running, jumping, boxing, etc.) and plotted the error values for increasing motion dimensions (one curve for each behavior). They manually annotated each curve by indicating the dimensions at which the motion a) exhibited visual artifacts, b) looked similar to, or c) was indistinguishable from the full-dimensional motion. While these measures were approximate and not based on psychophysical evaluation, they did indicate that the type of behavior depicted did have an effect on the average error *and* on the level at which the motion started to look acceptable.

In real-time applications such as games, characters are often simulated at different levels of detail in order to balance the need for visual quality and high frame-rates (e.g., [CH97]). When simulating large-scale crowds, simpler representations such as image-based impostors or pre-baked meshes are often used. In order to reduce the memory consumption,

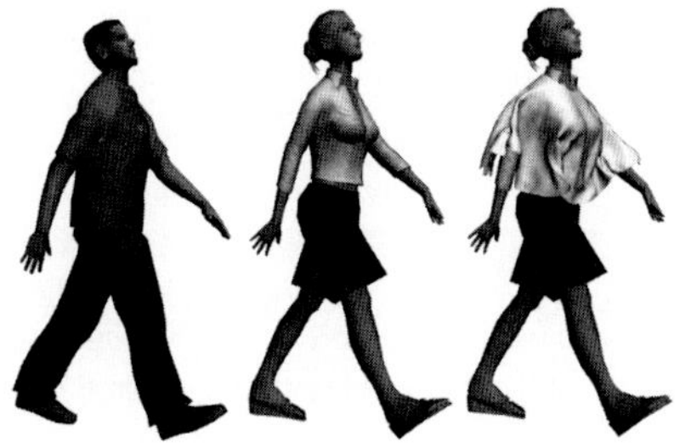

Figure 2: *Character 1, character 2 and character 2 with deformable clothing.*

a low number of poses (typically 10pps) are stored and displayed, which can result in perceptibly jerky motion of the crowd members. Dobbyn et al. [DHOO05] use a hybrid approach with impostors in the background and geometry in the foreground - popping artifacts based on rendering differences have been eliminated, but no evaluation of the effects of switching between different SLODs has been carried out. Pettre et al. [PdHCM*06] employ multiple SLODs, from 4pps for faraway characters to 25pps for characters at the front of a crowd. While this does improve the smoothness of many of the motions, the motion simplifications can sometimes be quite noticeable.

3. Baseline Experiment

Our first experiment was designed to identify baseline factors that affected the perceived smoothness of animated human motion. We hypothesized: that *character type* would not affect smoothness perception, as we had observed that the motion of characters with different colors and shapes appeared to be equally smooth; that the *type of character clothing* would have an effect, i.e., that those wearing deformable clothing would need more pose updates than linear blend skinned characters, as the subtle deformations would otherwise not be seen clearly; that *motion type* would make a difference, where more "energetic" or "active" motions would need more updates (partially motivated by the observations of Safonova et al. mentioned above).

As predicted, we found that character type did not affect update rate in our experiments. Surprisingly, deformable clothing did not have an effect. However, motion type did have a significant effect, with motions moving further across the screen needing more updates than other motions. The experimental method and analysis are described in the following sections.

Method

Fourteen participants (11M, 3F) aged between 18 and 40 took part in the experiment and received a book voucher as a reward. The experiment trials were run on a high specification workstation (Dell precision PWS670 with 3.5GHz Xeon CPU, 3GB of RAM, and an X850 Radeon graphics card) with a Dell UltraSharp 2405FPW 24-inch widescreen Liquid Crystal Display (LCD) monitor, with 16ms black to white response time. This monitor was reported to be good at displaying games, even fast moving games such as Microsoft's Freelancer.[†‡]

Alternatively, we could have used a Cathode Ray Tube (CRT) monitor, but because CRT's are becoming obsolete in desktop computer systems and televisions, we felt that our results would be of more relevance when carried out on a typical high-end gamer's monitor instead. Input was provided using an adjacent laptop keyboard.

As a test to ensure that the monitor was consistently producing the correct pose per second rates, we captured a video while displaying the experiment stimuli using a high speed camera[§] that could capture 60 frames per second. We were then able to playback the screen capture per frame and check that the poses were being updated at the correct rate (in our movies, pps was always equal to fps). We were able to test this accurately for all pose update rates up to 60pps, and found that the monitor was in fact displaying the movies correctly.

We used the method of constant stimuli to determine thresholds, where the stimulus level was the *pose update rate*, displayed at 15 different levels, ranging from 4pps to the highest possible rate achievable on our monitor, which was 63pps (having a response rate of 16ms) . The experiment was divided into two randomized blocks, each with a two-way design, in order to avoid confusing participants with too many different conditions. The goal in both blocks was to find the threshold among the 15 update rates at which the participants found the different animations smooth, for each of the conditions.

In Block 1 the conditions were *character type* (a male 'character 1' and a female 'character 2' shown in Figure 2) and *motion type* (motion captured kungfu kick, jumping jack, walking and jogging). Movies, each two seconds long, were generated in 3D Studio Max for each character type (2) performing their assigned motions (4) at each of the different stimulus levels (15), each with 3 repetitions of each condition, resulting in a total of 360 stimuli. In Block 2 the first condition was *character cloth type* (i.e., character 2 as depicted in Block 1 with simple skinned clothing, and character 2 with physically simulated deformable clothing), and the second condition was again *motion type* (kungfu kick, jumping jack and walk - jogging was omitted). Two hundred and seventy movies were created as above: 2 x 3 x 15 x 3.

Before the experiment began, participants were shown an animation at 4pps and one at 63pps of a different male character performing a boxing animation and were told that these were examples of jerky and smooth animations. To avoid learning and ordering effects, we randomly chose the order in which each participant did Block 1 or Block 2 and presented each of them with a different randomized playlist.

† see http://www.extremetech.com/article2/0,1697,1764462,00.asp
‡ see http://www.pcmag.com/article2/0,1895,1774272,00.asp
§ see http://www.ptgrey.com/products/flea/index.asp

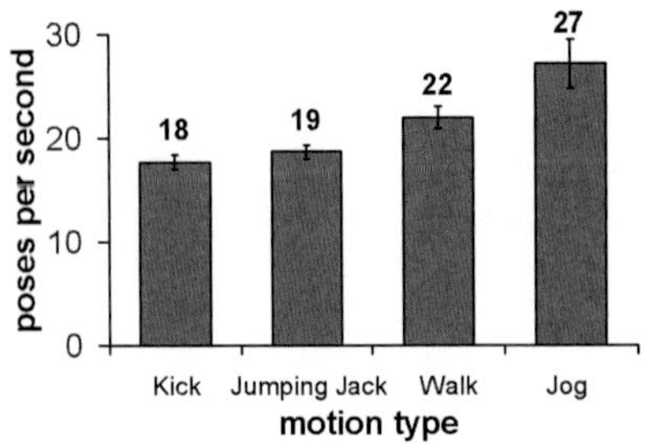

Figure 3: *Mean 50% threshold values for different animation types. Error bars show the standard error of the mean.*

The participant pressed the left or right mouse button on the laptop to indicate "smooth" or "jerky" for each movie and we randomly interchanged their meanings per participant to avoid left-right bias.

We chose this design over a discrimination/matching task since we wanted to avoid the situation where participants might attend to a single feature and base judgements on that. Also, we were more interested in how participants categorize smooth and jerky animations rather than their ability to discriminate - we did not want to provide a reference for the "ideally smooth" case, rather we wanted participants to use their own reference. Later, in our SLOD experiment we explore the situation where 2 different pose update rates could be displayed alongside one another.

Analysis

For each condition, we wished to find the thresholds within the 15 update rates at which participants found the different motions smooth. The 50% threshold is a typical value reported in psychophysics. In this experiment, this would correspond to the update rate at which participants were equally likely to rate a motion as 'smooth' or 'jerky'. The mean number of 'smooth' responses at each pose update rate was calculated for each participant for each condition. These values were then plotted, and psychometric curves were fitted to them.

A two factor ANalysis Of VAriance (ANOVA) showed that there was no main effect of character type or character clothing type. However, there was a main effect of motion type in both blocks. This shows that the number of updates needed for smooth animations was the same regardless of whether the character was male or female, or whether the character was wearing deformable clothing or not. However, there was a significant effect of motion type ($F_{3,96} = 8.7, P \approx 0$), indicating that the different motion types needed different pose update rates to produce smooth animations. In Figure 3 it can be seen that the jog motion had the highest mean 50% threshold value, indicating that it needed the most number of updates in order for participants to find the animation smooth. The walk motion had the second highest mean 50% threshold value, while the jumping jack and kick motions had the lowest. This indicates that participants found the jumping jack and kung fu kick motion smoother with fewer updates than the walk or jog.

We felt that the distance that the character moved across the screen must have been a factor, as the walk and jog motion moved much more across the screen than the other two motions. Furthermore, the amount of activity in the motion clip seemed to have an effect. Therefore we designed our next set of experiments to focus on these two factors in particular.

4. Movement Experiment

The second experiment examined more formally the effect of different motion types and their interactions. We hypothesized: that there would be a main effect of *linear velocity*; i.e., that a character moving faster across the screen would need more updates; that increased *motion complexity* (i.e., more energetic bodily movements) would necessitate more poses to look smooth; and that motions with a high *cycle rate* (i.e., cyclical speed of limbs) would also require more updates. We found that all of our hypotheses were accepted with statistical significance (>95%). Furthermore, we found an interaction effect between linear velocity and cycle rate, where for animations with high cycle rates, linear velocity had no effect, whereas for animations with low and medium cycle rates, fewer updates were needed for lower linear velocities.

Method

Thirty one participants took part in this experiment (13F, 18M), aged between 12 and 38. All participants were familiar with computer games or had a background in computer science and had normal or corrected to normal vision. As before, participants viewed the experiments on a 24-inch monitor and user input was provided by an adjacent laptop (Figure 4). Participants received a book voucher for their efforts.

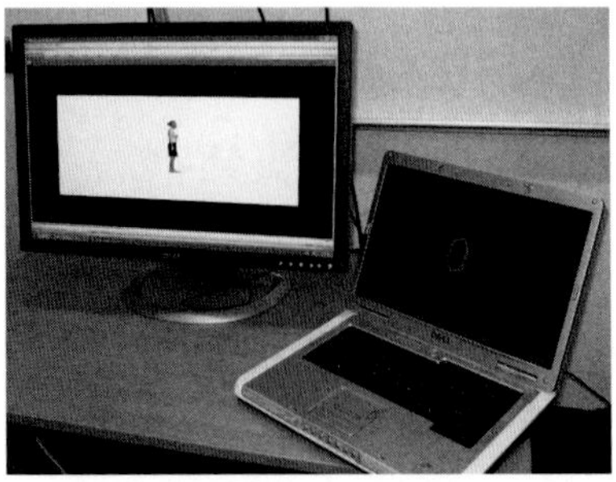

Figure 4: *System Setup for Movement Experiment.*

Again, we used the method of constant stimuli to determine thresholds and the stimulus level was the *pose update rate*, displayed this time at 10 different levels, ranging from 5 to 60pps (by observing the trends of the pose updates in the baseline study, we were able to eliminate some redundancy in the update rates). The experiment was a three-way design, divided into four randomized blocks. Again, the goal was to find the threshold among the 10 update rates at which the participants found the different animations smooth, for each of the conditions.

Two motion complexities were chosen: *Normal walk* with arms by the side, and *Complex walk*, the same walk motion with added activity in the arms, torso and head, each moving in time with the legs of the walk cycle.

Three different cycle rates were chosen: *Lo* (1.5 cycles/sec), *Med* (2.72 cycles/sec) and *Hi* (3.75 cycles/sec). These were generated in 3D Studio Max using the *footstep* modifier, which allows the distance between steps to be altered, creating walk motions of different cycle lengths - any arm, torso and head movements were also altered to match the cycle of the legs.

Four different linear velocities were chosen: *V0* (walking on the spot), *V1* (walking 1/3rd of the distance across the screen, i.e., 7.75screen centimetres/sec), *V2* (walking 4/6ths of the distance across the screen, 15.5cm/sec) and *V3* (walking the full distance across the screen, 23cm/sec). We calculated the distance travelled across the screen per second, for each of the linear velocities, and converted this into km/hr, by comparing the length of the character on screen to an average human height. It was found that V1 was approximately the typical speed of a normal walker, 4km/hr, V2 was higher 9km/hr and V3 was 13km/hr which was similar to the speed of an olympic race walker. Such linear velocities of characters across the screen are achieved, for example, if walking characters are viewed from a camera moving rapidly through a scene.

We split the 4 linear velocities into four separate experiment blocks, as we felt that viewing all linear velocities together would result in a long and tiring experiment with no break, and might confuse the participant as the character would begin the animation at different areas on the screen. In order to generate movies of the same length (2 seconds), using the normal and complex walks at the three different cycle rates, at the four different linear velocities, we chose to animate the character on the spot, but to move the camera viewing the character by 3 different amounts, resulting in the character moving at velocities V1, V2 and V3 across the screen. Two-second movies were generated for each of the walks, at each cycle rate, at each linear velocity, for the 10 different update rates, each with 3 repetitions. A white background was used in order to provide good contrast and we did not use a ground plane (and therefore did not project shadows) as we did not need perspective, and did not want any distracting factors that could distort our results.

In Block 1 we tested the effect of the normal and complex walk at each of the cycle rates, with the character walking on the spot (V0). The goal was to find 50% threshold values from the range of 10 update rates, for each of the conditions. One hundred and eighty movies were viewed in this experiment: 2 walk animations (normal and complex)* 3 cycle rates (Lo, Med, Hi) * 10 update rates * 3 repetitions. The movies were randomly placed in a playlist, with a two-

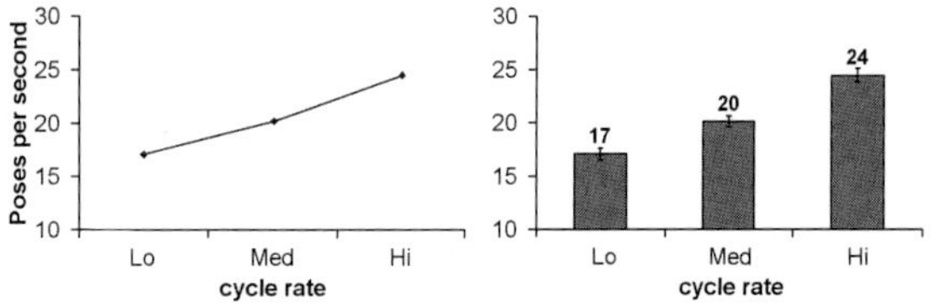

Figure 5: *(l) Cycle rate main effect. (r) Mean 50% threshold values for cycle rate. Error bars show the standard error of the mean.*

second blank video in between. Blocks 2, 3 and 4 were the same as Block 1, except that the distance travelled across the screen by the character was V1, V2 and V3 respectively throughout the block.

Before the experiment, participants were shown examples of 'smooth' and 'jerky' animations of a different character, on the spot and travelling at V3, and were told to focus on the smoothness of the character's animation itself when making their judgements.

Participants viewed all four blocks (each 12 minutes), with a one minute break in between each block. We randomly ordered Blocks 1 to 4 for each participant, to avoid any fatigue or learning effects, and presented them with a randomly ordered playlist. As before, they were asked to indicate whether the animation looked "smooth" or "jerky" at each trial, and we randomly chose the left or right buttons on the laptop mouse as input per participant.

Analysis

As in the baseline experiment, we fitted psychometric curves to participants' data for each of the conditions, and were thus able to calculate their 50% threshold values. We could not fit meaningful psychometric curves to the data for four of the participants, which indicated that they were inconsistent in their decisions on smoothness throughout the entire study. Four further participants had large amounts of inconsistent data which was evident from the large standard deviation values of their psychometric curves. Therefore, we removed the data for all 8 participants (4M, 4F) in order to be able to perform a full 3-way ANOVA on the data.

There were three different factors (motion complexity, cycle rate and linear velocity), therefore a three factor ANOVA with repeated measures was performed on all of the data. We found a main effect of motion complexity ($F_{1,22} = 28, P < 0.00003$), where the average 50% threshold value for the normal walk was 19pps and the average for the complex walk was 22pps, indicating that the walk with added bodily movement needed more updates than the normal walk. As there were only two variables, no post-hoc analysis was necessary.

We also found a main effect of cycle rate ($F_{2,44} = 30, P \approx 0$), indicating that the different cycle rates needed different pose update rates in order for participants to perceive them as smooth (Figure 5). Post-hoc analysis was then performed using a standard Newman-Keuls test for pairwise comparisons

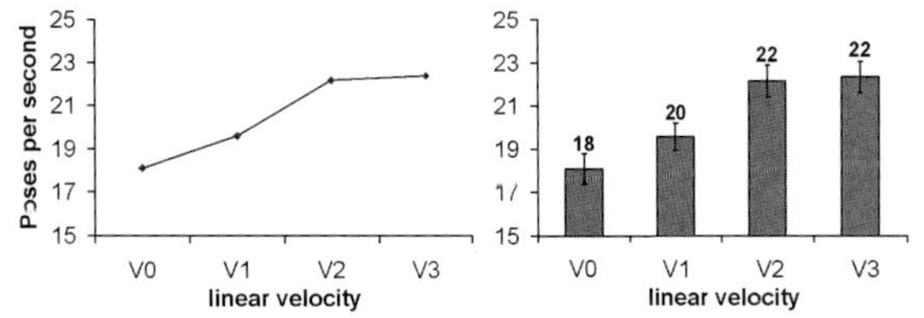

Figure 6: *(l) Linear Velocity main effect. (r) Mean 50% threshold values for Linear Velocity. Error bars show the standard error of the mean.*

among means. We found that 50% threshold values for all three velocities were statistically significant from each other, (with P $<$ 0.003 in all cases).

Finally, there was a main effect of linear velocity ($F_{3,66} = 7, P < 0.0004$), indicating that different update rates were needed for the four velocities - V0 to V3 (Figure 6). A post-hoc analysis showed us that there was no statistically significant difference between V0 and V1 or V2 and V3. However, there was statistical difference between V0 and V2 and V3 and between V1 and V2 and V3, which indicated that it was not the level of cycle rate that seemed to have an effect, but rather the presence of high linear velocity or low linear velocity.

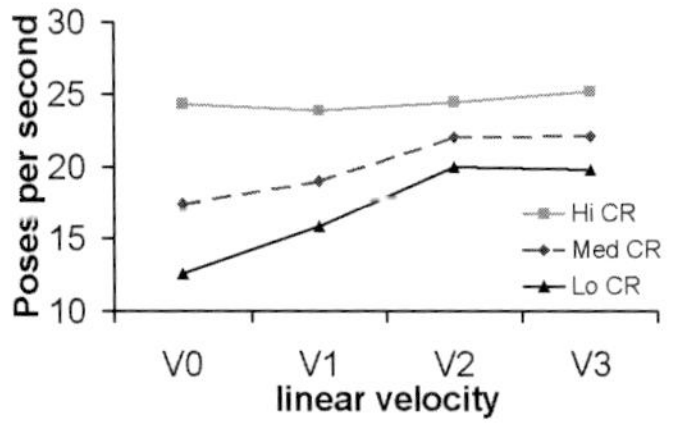

Figure 7: *Interaction effect between Linear Velocity and Cycle Rate (CR).*

Interestingly, we also found an interaction effect between linear velocity and cycle rate (Figure 7). It can be seen that for the high cycle rate, the linear velocity had almost no effect, whereas it had an effect for low and medium cycle rate. This implies that for animations with high cycle rates, a high update rate is needed regardless of the linear velocity, whereas for animations with low and medium cycle rates, it is possible to get away with fewer updates for lower linear velocities. There were no other interaction effects.

In Figure 8 *(l)* and *(r)* we have plotted mean 50% threshold values. It can clearly be seen from these graphs that there is a difference between the thresholds for each cycle rate, and that the effect of camera decreases with increasing cycle rate.

Another interesting result was the main effect of motion complexity. As there was also a main effect of cycle rate, it was clear that the walk with added motion complexity needed more updates than the normal walk, but not more than either of the motions at the next cycle rate up, (e.g., the walk with added motion complexity at low cycle rate needed

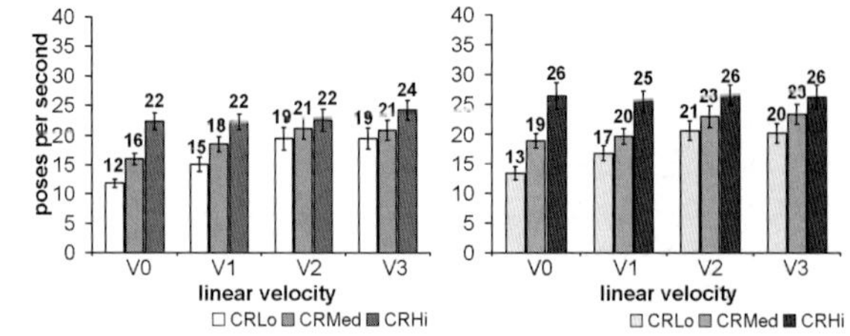

Figure 8: *(l) 50% threshold values for normal walk. (r) 50% threshold values for complex walk. Error bars show the standard error of the mean. CR=Cycle Rate.*

fewer updates than the normal walk at medium cycle rate). In order to explain this effect, we thought that perhaps the angular velocity of the main moving joints at the different cycle rates could have been a factor. For this to have been the case, the angular velocity of the arms at the low cycle rate should have been lower than the angular velocity of the legs in the medium cycle rate, but in fact it was actually twice that of the legs (and higher than the medium cycle legs), so we rejected this explanation. We then hypothesized that the effect of complex motion may have had something to do with extra motion being displayed on the screen, or the familiarity of the motion, as the complex motion was an unfamiliar motion.

In order to address this issue, we repeated Block 1 (with linear velocity at V0 for the entire experiment) on eleven participants (2F, 9M), but with the screen rotated by 180° (inspired by similar experiments on point-light walkers, as discussed in Section 2 and in Dittrich [Dit93]). Surprisingly, we observed that the 50% threshold values were similar to those for the right side up character. We found that, as before, there was a main effect of cycle rate (P $\approx$ 0). However, this time there was no effect of motion complexity. This might indicate that when displayed the right way up, participants used their basic perception of motion when determining the smoothness at different cycle rates, but used a higher cognitive level with knowledge of walkers to separate out familiar from unfamiliar motions. This resulted in added sensitivity to unfamiliar motions. When placed upside-down, all motions were unfamiliar and so we resorted to our basic perception of smoothness for both cycle rate and complexity of motion, which resulted in no added sensitivity to complex motions.

5. Simulation Level of Detail (SLOD)

We wished to further examine the factors, identified above, that affected the perceived smoothness of character motion in different settings. We first considered situations where the number of poses stored or generated is a limiting factor and aimed to simulate such typical scenarios in a controlled experiment. We then reflected upon situations where the number of poses is not a limiting factor and asked the question whether or not super smoothness can be achieved with increasingly high pose update rates, or whether this is simply wasted detail.

5.1. SLOD Experiments

For memory critical systems such as real-time crowds using impostors, the fewer poses required to make an animation appear smooth the better. We have provided thresholds of acceptability for different characters, depending on their cycle rate, complexity and the amount of camera motion in the scene. However, we have not yet established whether different pose updates would be acceptable if displayed together in one scene as our previous experiments showed one image at a time. Therefore, in this experiment, we consider simulation level of detail by examining the effect of its implementation on perceived motion smoothness. We give participants a discrimination task, in which they can view two pose update rates simultaneously and make their decisions based on a comparison of the two.

SLOD Experiment 1

Seventeen participants (3F, 14M) took part, all with normal or corrected to normal vision. All were either computer science or engineering students or had an interest in computer games. The experimental setup was the same as in the previous experiments. This time participants were asked at every trial "are all of the characters moving smoothly?" and used the laptop mouse to input the answer 'yes' or 'no'.

We used the same character as in the previous experiments (character 2), animated with the normal walk at the medium cycle rate and travelling at V1. This time, the character walked at V1 across the screen and the camera remained stationary, in order to produce a more natural looking scenario. Each movie displayed one character in the front and a group of characters in the back (all characters used the same model). The characters in the background were updated at 5 different rates, ranging from 5 to 30pps, and this was the stimulus level - again, using the method of constant stimuli, we wished to determine the thresholds among the 5 update rates at which all characters appeared smooth, for each set of conditions. A ground plane, white with far spaced black vertical lines, was shown in this experiment in order for participants to be able to judge the relative distance between the background and foreground characters. This provided distance and perspective cues without causing too much distraction (see color plate Figure 1).

This experiment had a 3-way design. The first condition was walk type: *in step* (i.e., all characters started at the same pose, and moved like an army) or *out of step* (i.e., all characters started at different poses which represented a more natural setting for a crowd of pedestrians.); the second condition was background group size: *small* (1 character), *medium* (6 characters) or *large* (12 characters); and the third condition was foreground character update rate: *update1* (30pps, which from our previous experiment we know to be the threshold at which 99% of participants perceived the motion presented in this experiment to be smooth) or *update2* (20pps, the threshold with a 75% probability of being perceived smooth). There were 90 two-second movies generated in total: 3 crowd sizes * 2 walk conditions * 5 background update rates * 3 repetitions. Random playlists were generated from these movies for each participant.

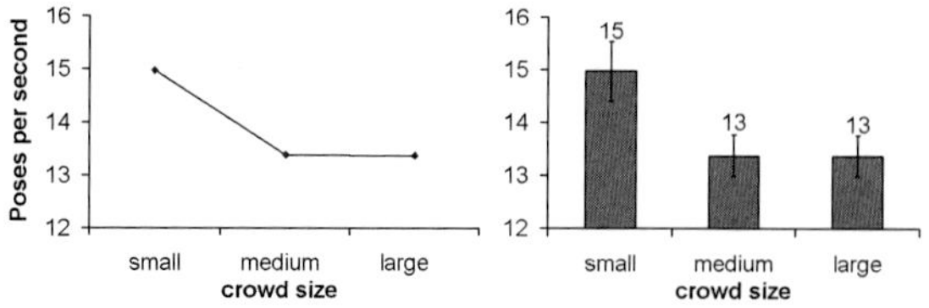

Figure 9: *(l) Crowd size main effect. (r) Mean 50% threshold values for Crowd Size.*

SLOD Experiment 2

We also wished to examine how a more natural scenario, such as that found in games, would affect our results. Therefore, we compared the 'out of step' large group from SLOD Experiment 1 to a new 'out of step' large crowd where all characters were different and appeared in a more complex background scene (see color plate Figure 2), depicting a blue sky and two cars parked on a pavement behind the characters. The ground plane in this experiment was a tiled gravel plane, which still provided distance cues, but in a more real-world setting. We hypothesized that the more natural crowd would mask the differences between the update rates more than the controlled crowd, due to the distracting factors. Fourteen participants (11M, 3F) took part in this experiment, and the method was the same as in SLOD Experiment 1.

Analysis

As before, we found 50% threshold values for each participant, for each condition. A 3-factor ANOVA was then performed on all of the data in SLOD Experiment 1 in order to determine the main effects and interactions.

There was a main effect of group size ($F_{2,32} = 4, P < 0.03$). As before, we used Newman-Keuls tests to perform post-hoc analysis and found that the small crowd was significantly different from the medium and large crowds, but there was no statistical difference between the medium and large crowd. This implies that it is the presence or absence of multiple background characters that has the effect and not the actual crowd size (Figure 9).

Surprisingly, there was no main effect of foreground character update rate, i.e., participants were equally likely to perceive all characters to be smooth at a particular update rate, irrespective of whether the front character was updated at 30 or 20pps. There was also no main effect of walk type, which shows that participants were equally likely to find all characters smooth for a given update rate, regardless of the synchronicity of their motions (Figure 10). There was one interaction effect between crowd size and walk type ($F_{2,32} = 4, P < 0.03$). On further investigation we found that the main effect found for group size only held for in step characters, but not for out of step characters.

In order to analyze SLOD Experiment 2, a two-way ANOVA

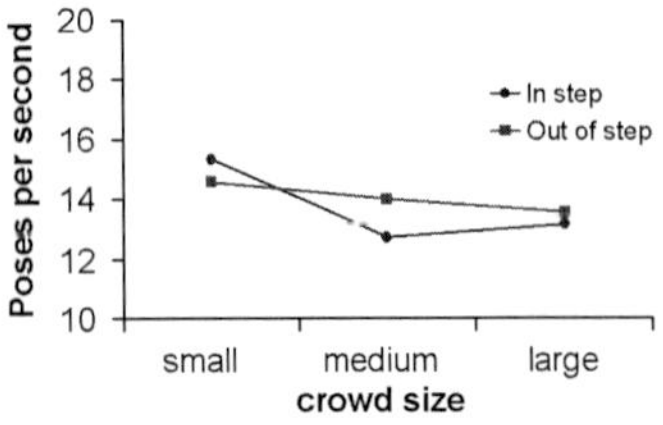

Figure 10: *Interaction effect between crowd size and walk type.*

was performed on the data as we had two different conditions - update rate of foreground character (20 and 30pps) and crowd setting (natural and experiment setting). We found that there was no significant effect of foreground character update rate as before, but also found that surprisingly there was no significant effect of scene complexity.

5.2. Sorting Experiment

We found in our movement experiment that for participants to find a motion smooth 80% of the time, no more than 35pps were needed (Figure 12), even for the most complex motion that we depicted in our study. However, while 35pps may be sufficient for smooth animations, it may not be the upper limit for highly realistic animations. Therefore, in this short experiment, we attempted to determine whether 35pps is the smoothest possible (at least for the scenarios we are depicting) or whether people would find higher pose rates even smoother. Therefore, we tested people's ability to directly compare a number of different pose update rates and correctly sort them from most jerky to most smooth. We used a similar approach to [MSCO06], where we placed 8 different movies on the screen and asked participants to move them around until they were in the correct order of increasing smoothness. Twelve participants (3F, 9M) took part in this experiment, all with normal or corrected to normal vision.

We placed 8 movies of one of the motions randomly on the screen, each playing in a loop and using one of 8 different update rates ranging from 5 to 63pps. In order to ensure that the monitor was actually displaying these rates correctly on the screen, we again recorded the screen using a 60fps high speed camera. On playing back the recording frame by frame, we could see that all of the movies up to 60pps were displaying correctly, and there were no frames dropped.

The experiment was divided into two blocks, where the first block showed all of the 8 different update rates on the screen using the normal walk from the Movement Experiment at a medium cycle rate. The second block was similar except that the complex walk with a high cycle rate was used. The normal walk was typical of the speed of a pedestrian, whereas the complex walk was considered our worst case scenario.

We recorded the sequence in which the twelve participants ordered the different movies and compared them to the correct sequence. To analyze these results we assigned a penalty of x for each of the movies that were not placed in the correct order, with x corresponding to the number of places that the movie deviated from its correct placing in our perceived stiffness scale. A two-factor ANOVA was then performed over the full dataset. It was found that there was no significant effect of walk type, with participants finding the complex walk just as difficult to sort as the normal walk. There was a significant main effect of pose update rate ($F_{1,7} = 6.11, P \approx 0$). Post hoc analysis showed that participants found rates 5-20 equally easy to sort, whereas they found rates 40-63 equally difficult to sort, and the ordering errors of rates 5-20 were statistically significantly different to rates 40-63 (all statistical differences with $P < 0.04$). Pose update rate 30 was somewhere in-between, being neither significantly different from the 5-20 nor 40, 50 and 63. It was found to be statistically significantly different from 60pps however ($P < 0.04$), implying that participants found it easier to place 30pps in the correct position than 60pps. The fact that participants found rates 40-63 equally difficult to sort suggests that they had trouble in seeing the differences between them, and therefore found all four to be equally smooth. There was also a significant interaction effect ($F_{1,7} = 2.8, P < 0.02$) (Figure 11). This implies that participants' errors in sorting differed for normal and complex walks at certain pose update rates.

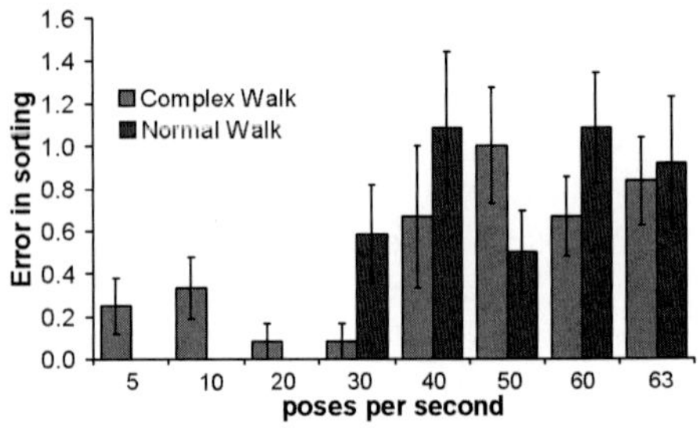

Figure 11: *Interaction effect between walk type and pose update rate.*

In order to test if a CRT monitor would have produced similar results, we repeated the second block on 12 naive participants using a 21-inch CRT monitor instead of the LCD, but using the same workstation. We found that participants found the top rates (40pps and above) just as difficult to sort on the CRT as the LCD. When we compared the results statistically we found that monitor type did not have an significant effect.

6. Conclusions and Future Work

We have presented the first perceptual analysis of the factors that affect the choice of pose update rate for smooth animation of virtual characters. We have discovered interesting results that can provide helpful guidance to developers in order to choose optimal update rates for the characters in their applications.

To summarize our findings for the Movement experiment, in Figure 12 we show a chart of the 80% acceptance thresholds (i.e., the level at which observers will say 'smooth' 80% of

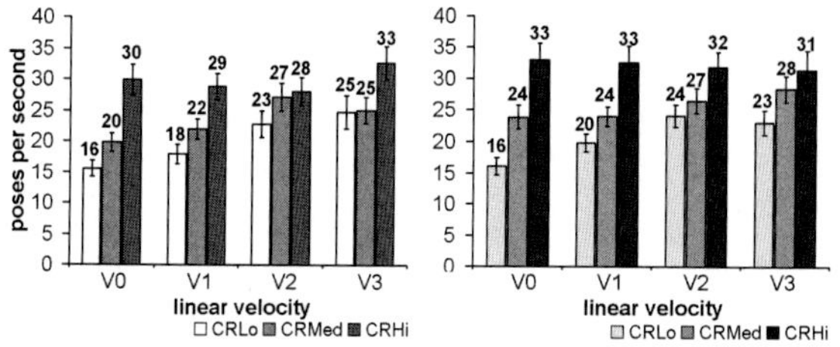

Figure 12: *(l) Thresholds for 80% probability of acceptance for normal walk. (r) Thresholds for 80% probability of acceptance for complex walk. Error bars show the standard error of the mean. CR=Cycle Rate.*

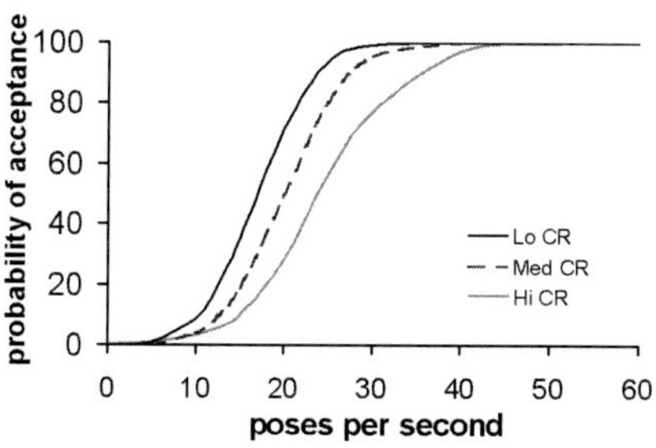

Figure 13: *Average probability of acceptance curves for Cycle Rate.*

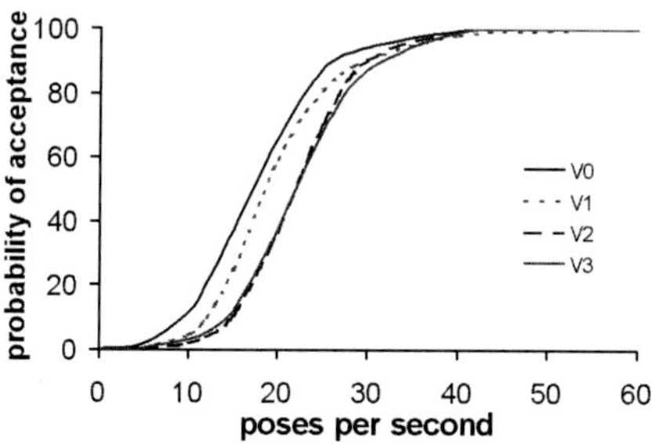

Figure 14: *Average probability of acceptance curves for Linear Velocity.*

the time). We felt that these values could be of practical use to developers since the thresholds at this level were reasonable for real-time performance. Color plate Figure 3 depicts these values in a more useful way for developers to choose the correct update rates for their particular animations.

In order to better view the behavior of the participants, we plotted average psychometric probability curves (Figures 13 and 14) derived from all of the data, using the average of all participants' 50% threshold values (μ) and standard deviations (σ) in Equation 1:

$$f(\theta;\mu,\sigma) = \frac{1}{2\pi\mu} e^{-(\frac{(\theta-\mu)^2}{2\sigma^2})} \qquad (1)$$

Where θ is a parameter that ranges from 0 to 100% probability of acceptance. These graphs show the different pose update rates necessary for participants to judge a motion as smooth for a range of different acceptability levels (i.e., from 0 to 100%). It can be seen that the curves become linear at 40pps, which implies that 40pps is the rate at which participants judged all of the motions used in the movement experiments to be smooth 100% of the time. Our sorting experiment validated that a threshold of approximately 40pps was considered to be the point at which animations began looking really smooth, since participants found it difficult to see the difference in smoothness for levels above 40pps.

These results will perhaps be of most use (and immediately applicable) for real-time character simulation, particularly when the characters have cyclical motions. In a preprocessing step, each motion could be labeled with an optimal update rate, based on the cyclical update rate and complexity of the motion. At run-time, this rate for all characters could change priority when the camera is moving fast, to account for the added jerkiness which occurs with fast camera motion.

In order for our SLOD experiment results to be of use to developers, we analyzed the 80% probability of acceptance values, estimated from participants' psychometric curves. We found that 16pps was considered sufficient for all background characters that we tested (at 80% probability of acceptance there was no significant main effect of crowd size, walk type, or foreground character update rate). This result could be of great benefit to LOD crowd systems in particular. At present, in hybrid geometry/impostor crowds (e.g., [DHOO05]), 10pps are used for both foreground and background characters due to the memory consumption of impostors. However, this rate results in jerky looking animation. Using 30pps for the geometry and 10pps for the impostors resulted in noticeable differences, and using 30pps for the impostors is too costly in terms of memory. If, as our results suggest, it is possible to display geometry at 30pps and impostors at 16pps without observers noticing the difference, this will result in the ability to store double the number of characters in memory than would be possible if the impostors were being displayed at 30pps.

We plugged this value of 16pps for background characters into a simple geometry/impostor crowd scenario and found the differences in SLOD to be imperceptible (as shown in the supplemental video). Although the differences were imperceptible in the example we tested, all of the characters were walking on the spot and so switching between update rates as the characters moved from foreground to background was not present. In the future, we would like to extend our study to include an analysis of the effect of the switch. Also, it would be interesting to extend the SLOD experiments in order to test if lower pose update rates could be used for characters in the distance, and to investigate if an extremely low pose update rate (e.g., 2 poses per second) would ever be sufficient.

Limitations

One limitation of these results is that it might be difficult to annotate non-cyclical motion clips (e.g., in a pre-processing step for mocap databases). However, the baseline experiment motions were not cyclical, but we can see that the threshold levels that they produced were in the same range as for the cyclical motions. It would be interesting to find an appropriate alternative to the cycle rate factor for non-cyclical motions. A promising direction for future work would be to implement a pre-processing step for automatic annotation of motions in a motion capture database with optimal update rates.

Although we picked an LCD monitor that was recognized as good for gaming, we still saw some minor ghosting when we played back the frames of animation after being captured on our 60fps video camera. This ghosting could have added a slight motion blur effect to the animations which would mean that the thresholds might differ on this monitor to a CRT monitor or DLP projector. When we tested our sorting experiment on a CRT we found no effect of monitor type, which indicates that our results should hold for CRTs. However, a more thorough investigation of the effect of monitor type would be of benefit.

For the majority of the experiments, characters were viewed from the side profile. This view was chosen as we wanted to change the maximum number of pixels per pose (i.e., a 'worst case' scenario). The effect of view angle is something that we would like to investigate further.

Motion blur is also a factor that we did not consider in these experiments. It would be interesting to analyze the effect of motion blur on our perception of smoothness, and whether the thresholds could be significantly reduced when motion blur is added.

Acknowledgements

We would like to thank the reviewers for their helpful comments. This work was supported by Science Foundation Ireland.

References

[Ari06] ARIKAN O.: Compression of motion capture databases. *ACM Transactions on Graphics 25*, 3 (2006), 890–897.

[CH97] CARLSON D. A., HODGINS J. K.: Simulation levels of detail for real-time animation. In *Proceedings of the conference on Graphics interface '97* (1997), pp. 1–8.

[DHOO05] DOBBYN S., HAMILL J., O'CONOR K., O'SULLIVAN C.: Geopostors: a real-time geometry / impostor crowd rendering system. In *SI3D '05: Proceedings of the 2005 symposium on Interactive 3D graphics and games* (2005), pp. 95–102.

[Dit93] DITTRICH W.: Action categories and the perception of biological motion. *Perception 22*, 1 (1993), 15–22.

[HOT98] HODGINS J., O'BRIEN J., TUMBLIN J.: Perception of human motion with different geometric models. *IEEE Transactions on Visualization and Computer Graphics 4*, 4 (1998), 307–316.

[HRvdP04] HARRISON J., RENSINK R. A., VAN DE PANNE M.: Obscuring length changes during animated motion. *ACM Transactions on Graphics 23*, 3 (2004), 569–573.

[Joh73] JOHANSSON G.: Visual perception of biological motion and a model for its analysis. *Perception and Psychophysics 14*, 2 (1973), 201–211.

[Lan54] LANDIS C.: Determinants of the critical flicker-fusion threshold. *Physiological Reviews 34* (1954), 259–286.

[MRW92] MATHER G., RADFORD K., WEST S.: Low-level visual processing of biological motion. In *Proceedings of the Royal Society of London, Series B* (1992), vol. 249, pp. 149–155.

[MSCO06] MCDONNELL R., S.DOBBYN, COLLINS S., O'SULLIVAN C.: Perceptual evaluation of LOD clothing for virtual humans. In *Proceedings of the 2006 ACM SIGGRAPH/Eurographics Symposium on Computer Animation* (2006), pp. 117–126.

[OHJ00] OESKER M., HECHT H., JUNG B.: Psychological evidence for unconscious processing of detail in real-time animation of multiple characters. *Journal of Visualization and Computer Animation 11*, 2 (2000), 105–112.

[PdHCM*06] PETTRE J., DE HERAS CIECHOMSKI P., MAÏM J., YERSIN B., LAUMOND J.-P., THALMANN D.: Real time navigating crowds: Scalable simulation and rendering. *Computer Animation and Virtual World (CAVW) Journal - CASA 2006 special issue 17* (2006), 445–455.

[Rog83] ROGOWITZ B. E.: The human visual system: A guide for the display technologist. In *Society for Information Display* (1983), vol. 24/3, pp. 235–252.

[RP03] REITSMA P., POLLARD N.: Perceptual metrics for character animation: Sensitivity to errors in ballistic motion. *ACM Transactions on Graphics 22*, 3 (2003), 537–542.

[SHP04] SAFONOVA A., HODGINS J. K., POLLARD N. S.: Synthesizing physically realistic human motion in low-dimensional, behavior-specific spaces. *ACM Transactions on Graphics 23*, 3 (2004), 514–521.

[WAF86] WATSON A., AHUMADA A., FARRELL J.: Window of visibility: a psychophysical theory of fidelity in time-sampled visual motion displays. *Journal of the Optical Society of America A 3*, 3 (1986), 300–307.

[WB04] WANG J., BODENHEIMER B.: Computing the duration of motion transitions: an empirical approach. In *Proceedings of the 2004 ACM SIGGRAPH/Eurographics Symposium on Computer Animation* (2004), pp. 335–344.

Figure 1: *Crowd in experiment setup.*

Figure 2: *Crowd in game setting used in SLOD experiment 2. Characters have different form and color from one another and background is not white.*

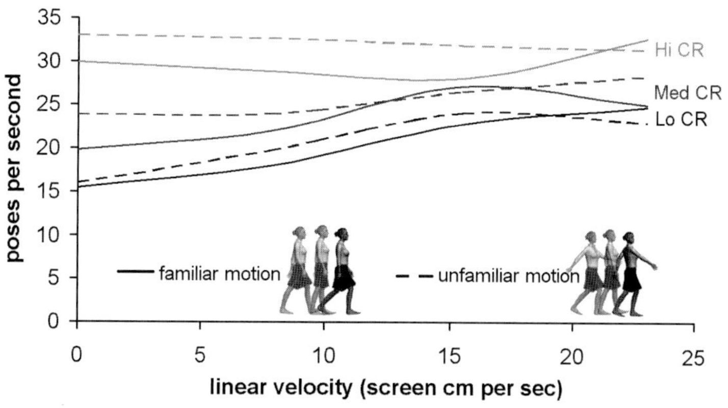

Figure 3: *Summary of Movement Experiment results. For the familiar motion, the legs were the fastest moving body parts. We calculated that the fastest pixel was moving at 7 screen cm/sec (Lo CR), 12cm/sec (Med CR), and 15cm/sec (Hi CR). For the unfamiliar motion, the arms were the fastest and we calculated that the fastest moving pixel was moving at 13cm/sec, 23cm/sec and 32cm/sec for Lo, Med and Hi CR.*

Eurographics/ ACM SIGGRAPH Symposium on Computer Animation (2007)
D. Metaxas and J. Popovic (Editors)

Animation Collage

Christian Theobalt [1], Christian Rössl [2], Edilson de Aguiar [3], and Hans-Peter Seidel [3]

[1]Stanford University
[2]INRIA Sophia-Antipolis, France
[3]MPI Informatik, Germany

Abstract

We propose a method to automatically transform mesh animations into animation collages, i.e. moving assemblies of shape primitives from a database given by an artist. An animation collage is a complete reassembly of the original animation in a new abstract visual style that imitates the spatio-temporal shape and deformation of the input. Our algorithm automatically decomposes input animations into plausible approximately rigid segments and fits to each segment one shape from the database by means of a spatio-temporal matching procedure. The collage is then animated in compliance with the original's shape and motion. Apart from proposing solutions to a number of spatio-temporal alignment problems, this work is an interesting add-on to the graphics artist's toolbox with many applications in arts, non-photorealistic rendering, and animated movie productions. We exemplify the beauty of animation collages by showing results created with our software prototype.

Categories and Subject Descriptors (according to ACM CCS): J.5 [Arts and Humanities]: Fine arts I.3.7 [3D Graphics and Realism]: Animation I.3.5 [Computational Geometry and Object Modeling]: Geometric algorithms

1. Introduction

The collage is an abstract and expressive visual style that has found its way into many forms of visual arts, including painting, photography and sculpturing. When creating a collage (from the French word coller=glueing), the artist intends to build a new whole by assembling different primitive forms in a special way.

Many researchers in computer graphics have been inspired by the idea to develop algorithms that enable the computer and even unexperienced users to reproduce the look of certain styles of visual arts. This is also true for collages. Kim et al. [KP02] have developed a system that can automatically turn arbitrary photographs into collage mosaics that comprise of an arrangement of elementary image tiles. Rother et al. [RBHB06] automatically arrange and blend photographs from a database into a perceptually pleasing way. Gal et al. [GSP*07] present a recent method to approximate static 3D shapes with other meshes, but they do not handle the case of mesh animations.

In this paper, we introduce a new method that brings together the traditional art form of a collage with the most prominent art form in computer graphics, namely 3D animation. Our algorithm allows the computer artist to automatically convert her favorite mesh animation into a moving assembly of 3D shape primitives in a database. This *animation collage* is glued together in such a way that it approximates the sequence of shapes of the original mesh animation, while deforming in the same spatio-temporally consistent way as the original. While the method can fully-automatically build moving collages, our algorithm purposefully gives the artist the possibility to postprocess and fine-tune the results according to her imagination. To our knowledge, the proposed method is the first of its kind in the literature.

Since to most people the term collage is synonymical with a static piece of art, we had to firstly define what ought to be the visual style of an animation collage. This particular style eventually determines the new algorithmic contributions of our approach which are detailed in the remainder of this paper. First, we decided to process mesh animations since this makes our algorithm independent of the specific way that was used to create the input in the first place. Second, our method ought to not only approximate the shape of meshes at single time steps individually. It rather decomposes and reassembles the mesh animations in such a way that the time-varying shape and the spatio-temporal deformation of the assembly is plausible. We concluded that the most appropriate way to achieve this goal is to automatically decompose the mesh animations into moving approx-

Symposium on Computer Animation 2007, San Diego, CA, August 03-04, 2007.
© 2007 ACM 978-1-59593-624-4/07/0008 $5.00

Figure 1: *Our method automatically generates moving 3D collages out of mesh animations by rebuilding them as moving assemblies of shape primitives. In the example above the galloping horse has been transformed into two galloping sets of fruits.*

imately rigid volume segments, henceforth called *animation cells*. This decomposition is learned from the moving input meshes by means of a spectral clustering approach. Our algorithm employs a spatio-temporal matching criterion that analyzes the motion and deformation of each animation cell and finds a shape primitive in the database that best approximates its time-varying geometry. Shape primitives and cells are spatio-temporally aligned and the fitted shapes are moved and deformed according to the deformation of the cells. The deformations are driven via spatio-temporally consistent offset shapes that are automatically built from the animation cells and whose tightness controls the deformation's stiffness. Since it was our aim to develop new algorithmic recipes for a novel artistic tool, we took care that the animator can influence the final result at all stages of the processing pipeline.

2. Related Work

While our idea was inspired by the work of visual artists, our algorithmic approach was inspired by previous research on mesh and animation decomposition, image mosaicing, as well as shape matching and approximation.

Recently, researchers proposed to exploit temporal coherence in mesh animation for compression [Len99]. Sattler et al. [SSK05] propose to use Lloyd relaxation and clustered principal component analysis to group vertices based on their trajectories. Günther et al. [GFW*06] also apply a Lloyd relaxation to motion-decompose mesh animations for fast ray-tracing. However, in contrast to our segmentation approach, their method does not consider spatial coherence of the clustered surface areas, their optimization may run into local minima, and automatic determination of the number of clusters is difficult. James and Twigg [JT05] proposed an algorithm to cluster triangles in mesh animations based on their rotations using a mean shift approach. While their segmentation yields statistically meaningful near rigid areas, they neither correspond to underlying kinematic hierarchies nor are they guaranteed to be spatially connected.

In contrast to prior work, our approach generates more meaningful spatially and temporally consistent segmentations of mesh animations. In other words, they closely correspond to the true kinematic skeleton hierarchy if the input can be assumed to have one, as in the case of our moving animals. Our decomposition approach is based on spectral clustering, it is robust and produces plausible results even for challenging motions. As an additional benefit, it can produce segmentations at different user-controlled levels of detail, and it can also automatically detect the optimal number of clusters [NJW02].

Our segmentation approach is related to recent methods from optical motion capture that automatically reconstruct kinematic skeletons from marker trajectories [KOF05, HSDK05, YP06, dATS06]. They are based on the idea that the segmentation of these marker-trajectories into rigid bodies corresponds to finding an optimal clustering into mutually intersecting motion spaces, each of them corresponding to one rigid body. To perform this segmentation, they typically cluster marker trajectories based on distance invariants between points on the same segments. We capitalize on these ideas, and exploit similar distance invariants, a spatial coherence criterion, and a volumetric decomposition approach to subdivide mesh animations into plausible approximately rigid segments using a robust spectral clustering approach.

Animation collages has also been inspired by the work on automatic image mosaicing [KP02, Hau01]. In a similar line of thinking, we developed a way to decompose mesh animations into spatio-temporally meaningful volume cells. By this means, we can efficiently find approximating shapes for each cell individually. Furthermore, the explicit cell decomposition enables us to rebuild animations with a minimum of overlap between shapes while only having to solve local matching problems.

The approximation aspect of our pipeline is also related to previous work on fitting of static shapes with ellipsoids or general quadrics. Such fitting methods have been used in geometry processing, e.g., for efficient data transmission [BK02], medical visualization [BJMR01], or segmentation and piecewise shape approximation [WK05] in reverse engineering. In our application, we don't have the freedom to construct best approximating shapes, but are bound to work with given primitives from a database.

Therefore, we can also capitalize on previous work on 3D shape matching. Global shape matching approaches compare different shapes based on numerical descriptors, such as shape distributions [OFCD01], Fourier descriptors [VSR01], moment invariants [ETA02, NK03], or spherical harmonics [KFR03]. Local shape matchers can also identify correspondences between subparts of shapes using artificial surface features [GCO06] or topology graph-based alignment [HSKK01]. Since we are attacking a time-dependent matching problem, we have developed a novel spatio-temporal matching approach based on spherical harmonic descriptors [KFR03].

Also related to our approach is the idea presented by Gal et al. [GSP*07]. They intend to rebuild static triangle meshes from individual shapes in a database. Static shape approximation is a very challenging research problem in itself. In building collages of animated scenes, we have to take on challenges very different from the static setting.

We have combined a variety of algorithmic recipes to rebuild mesh animations as sequences of approximating shapes. To our best knowledge, this is the first paper in the literature that takes on this problem. While we propose a solution to an interesting spatio-temporal matching problem, we also produced a tool that is fun to use. It enables easy creation of an artistic visual style that has many applications in non-photorealistic rendering, cartoon production and the visual arts in general.

3. Overview

The input to our algorithm comprises of two elements. The first is a triangle mesh animation of N time-steps, i.e. a mesh structure $\mathscr{M} = (\mathscr{V}, \mathscr{T})$ with constant graph structure — here denoted by vertices $\mathscr{V}$ and their triangulation $\mathscr{T}$ — and time-dependent data: associated to every vertex $v_j \in \mathscr{V}$ is a sequence of 3D positions $p_t(v_j) = (x_j, y_j, z_j)_t$, $1 \leq j \leq \#\mathscr{V}$, $0 \leq t < N$. Then coordinate sets $P_t = \{p_t(v_j)\}$ together with $\mathscr{M}$ describe a time-varying surface. The second input element is a database of K static shapes, each being represented as a textured triangle mesh.

The first step in our pipeline is the motion-decomposition of the mesh. To this end, we employ a segmentation based on spectral clustering that analyzes the motion of the mesh and delivers contingent triangle patches of $\mathscr{M}$'s surface that represent approximately rigid elements, Sect. 4 and Fig. 2(a). To enable the fitting of shape primitives, we transform the rigid surface elements into approximately rigid volume cells, so-called animation cells. To this end, a sequence of medial axis meshes is computed from the animation which, in conjunction with the previously identified rigid surface segments, is used to create these closed volume cells, Sect. 5 and Figs. 2(b),(c). Once the animation cells have been identified, we automatically fit to each of them a shape primitive from the database. For each animation cell, an optimal shape for fitting is selected based on spherical harmonic shape descriptors and a spatio-temporal matching procedure, Sect. 6. The final moving collages are generated by deforming the fitted shapes according to the transformation of their respective animation cells, Fig. 2(d). To achieve this, we generate spatio-temporally consistent offset meshes from the animation cells that drive the shape primitives' deformations, Sect. 7.

4. Rigid Body Segmentation

The first step in our pipeline segments the input animation given by $\mathscr{M}$ and P_t into spatially coherent patches of triangles that undergo approximately the same rigid transformations over time-steps $0 \leq t < N$. Our surface segmentation examines the motion trajectories of the mesh's vertices and their mutual distance variation over time. Our motivation for decomposing the mesh into approximately rigid patches is that this seems intuitive and plausible to the viewer. Many characters in cartoons and animation films, for instance the main actors in 20-th century Fox's "Robots" [Rob05], were rendered in this particular style.

The deformations of general mesh animations can not be described by rigid transformations alone. Animators often purposefully combine rigid transformations with non-rigid ones in order to create a lifelike look. In contrast to motion segmentation approaches that generate merely a statistically plausible segmentation, we intend to isolate the underlying rigid deformations from the non-rigid ones in a kinematically plausible way. By this we mean that in case there exists a true kinematic segment hierarchy, our method approximates it as good as possible. For us it is also important that regions on the surface are spatially connected, a requirement that is also not fulfilled by many related methods such as [JT05, GFW*06]. Only if this is assured, a faithful decomposition into volume cells becomes feasible, Sect. 5.

We apply the spectral clustering method of Ng et al. [NJW02] to a subset of sample vertices. Similar to [dATS06] in the context of optical motion capture, we use an affinity criterion to obtain clusters of similarly moving vertices, which we then transform into rigidly moving coherent triangle patches, Fig. 3.

Given is a mesh $\mathscr{M} = (\mathscr{V}, \mathscr{T})$. To initialize our segmentation approach, we select a subset $\mathscr{V}_s \subset \mathscr{V}$ of ℓ sample vertices that are required to be distributed evenly on the mesh. For sample selection we only consider a reference pose P_{t_r} (typically the first time step $t_r = 0$ of the animation), and employ the curvature-based segmentation method of Yamauchi et al. [YGZS05] to decompose $\mathscr{M}$ into ℓ surface patches. The sample vertices are chosen as the vertices closest to the patch centers. This subsampling enables reasonably fast de-

(a) (b) (c) (d)

Figure 2: *Important steps in our pipeline: the mesh is decomposed into rigidly moving surface patches (a), skeletons are extracted (b), and animation cells assembled (c), here only some cells are shown. Shapes are spatio-temporally fitted to the cells and deformed over time to build the animation collage (d).*

composition of even large meshes. We typically choose ℓ to be in the range of $1000-2000$.

The motion trajectories of the sample vertices throughout the whole animation form the input to our spectral clustering approach which groups them into k approximately rigidly moving groups. It exploits the invariant that mutual distances between points on the same rigid patch should only exhibit a small variance while the mesh is moving.

Spectral clustering commences by building a spatial affinity matrix $\mathbf{A}$. For our purpose, we define $\mathbf{A}$ with entries

$$a_{i,j} = \exp\left(-\frac{\sigma_{i,j}}{\rho^2}\right), \quad (1)$$

where $\sigma_{i,j}$ is the standard deviation of the Euclidean distance $\delta(i,j,t)$ between sample vertex i and sample vertex j over time and $\rho = \frac{1}{N^2}\sum_t \delta(i,j,t)$ is a scaling term controlling convergence behavior (where N is again the number of frames in the sequence). The scaling term reduces the affinity values of vertex pairs with large average mutual distance. Thereby, we try to force spectral clustering to put spatially far apart groups of vertices with similar motion into separate clusters. Intuitively, the symmetric matrix $\mathbf{A}$ encodes the likelihood that two samples lie on the same rigid body.

The clustering approach proceeds by rearranging the ℓ input samples in k well-separated clusters on the surface of a k-dimensional hypersphere. It achieves this by building a diagonal matrix $\mathbf{D}$ whose (i,i)-element is the sum of $\mathbf{A}$'s i-th row. Now the Laplacian matrix $\mathbf{L} = \mathbf{D}^{-1/2}\mathbf{A}\,\mathbf{D}^{-1/2}$ is built, its k largest eigenvalues $e_1,\dots,e_k$ are computed and stacked into columns to form the matrix $\mathbf{X} \in \mathbb{R}^{\ell\times k}$. The rows of $\mathbf{X}$ are normalized and considered as points in $\mathbb{R}^k$. Then the ℓ row vectors are split into k clusters using standard k-means clustering. Every original sample vertex $v_i \in \mathcal{V}_S$ is assigned to a cluster j if and only if row i of $\mathbf{X}$ was assigned to cluster j. We remind that k-means clustering is effective because in the transformed data $\mathbf{X}$ clusters are well-separated.

The above procedure separates the sample vertices into k distinct approximately rigidly moving clusters of vertices. From this, we associate triangle clusters $T_0 \cup \ldots \cup T_{k-1} = \mathcal{T}$ by assigning each triangle $\Delta = (w_0, w_1, w_2) \in \mathcal{T}$ to the marker vertex v_j whose average geodesic distance to w_0, w_1, and w_2 is minimal. Δ is added to that triangle cluster for which the sample v_j is part of the associated vertex cluster. The resulting clusters partition the mesh. Note that (a discrete approximation to) geodesic distance is used here to provide contiguous surface patches.

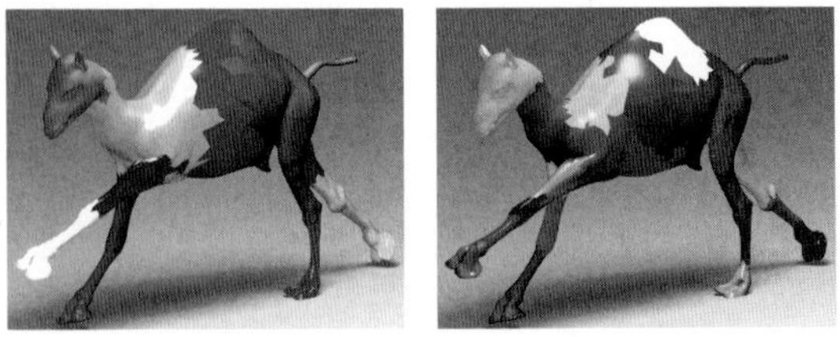

Figure 3: *Segmentation into approximately rigid surface patches – While with $k = 13$ patches (left) merely the larger rigid segments are identified, but the feet are merged with the lower legs, at $k = 31$ the full kinematic detail has been discovered (each color used several times, adjacent segments colored differently).*

Spectral clustering has a number of intriguing advantages over other clustering approaches. Conveniently, the optimal number of clusters may be inferred from the eigen-gap of $\mathbf{X}$ [NJW02]. However, the optimal segmentation is not always the one favored by the artist. Thus she also has the opportunity to specify the number of rigid surface patches that she would like to find. In Fig. 3, the segmentation of the camel's mesh is shown for two different values of k. At a smaller k-value, the lower legs and the hoofs form one cluster since the relative motion between these two was less significant than the relative motion between other segments. For a larger k-value, they have been split in two, which shows that with increasing level k of detail, our segmentation intuitively produces plausible and more detailed segmentations. Furthermore, spectral clustering is robust against outliers, performs well on segmentation problems with a challenging cluster structure on which other approaches, like standard k-means, perform significantly worse [NJW02].

Generally, our affinity metric (1) in combination with the triangle clustering procedure generates coherent surface patches in all our test cases which is important for later steps of our overall pipeline. In the rare case that we obtain disconnected patches nonetheless, we split them.

5. Building Animation Cells

Approximately rigid surface patches are not yet the appropriate shape representation for building animation collages. Although each patch is the outer boundary of a volumetric subsegment that moves approximately rigidly, it does not describe the spatial extent of this subsegment in the interior of the original mesh. To approximate these volumetric subsegments, we extend each surface patch into a so-called *animation cell*, i.e. a closed watertight triangle mesh that bounds an approximately rigidly moving slice of the original mesh's volume. Fig. 2(c) shows some animation cells computed from the horse animation. This volumetric decomposition of input animations has a couple of advantages. First, volumetric animation cells define 3D placeholders to which approximating shapes are to be fitted in order to generate visually pleasing collages with decent shape and deformation approximation. Thus, volumetric decomposition is a clever way to break down the fitting problem for the whole mesh into a set of fitting problems for individual cells. If we make sure that a fitting shape approximates the outline of an animation cell at each time step of the video, we implicitly take care that mutual shape intersections remain in the range that is anyway needed to prevent big holes in the collage. Furthermore, by deforming approximating shapes like their encompassing rigid cells, the deformation of the shapes remains in visually pleasing bounds.

The input for building animation cells is the set of rigid surface patches $T_0,\ldots,T_{k-1}$ that was computed in the previous section. It is our goal to extend each surface patch into a closed and watertight animation cell mesh. Looking only at the graph structure of each patch, this is easily achieved by inserting a new vertex for every boundary loop, triangulating the arising fan, and thereby removing the boundary loop. Although the principal idea is fairly easy, a proper way to insert the additional vertex for the boundary loop is crucial. In the remainder of this section, we discuss how we compute closing vertices based on skeleton meshes and describe how we generate spatio-temporally consistent cells.

We firstly compute a sequence of medial axis meshes $\mathcal{S}_0,\ldots,\mathcal{S}_{N-1}$ from the input animation, Fig. 2(b). We take care that the number of vertices and the connectivity of each $\mathcal{S}_i$ match the properties of the respective $\mathcal{M}_i$ that it was computed from: for computing the skeletal mesh $\mathcal{S}_i$, we employ the Voronoi-based two-sided approximation of the medial axis that has originally been proposed in [HBK02]. Every vertex of $\mathcal{M}_i$ is associated with a Voronoi cell. One-to-one correspondences between the vertices of $\mathcal{M}_i$ and the vertices of $\mathcal{S}_i$ are established by using the Voronoi poles as skeletal mesh vertices [ABK98]. The connectivity of $\mathcal{S}_i$ is copied from $\mathcal{M}_i$. In consequence, we have established one-to-one correspondences between both vertices and triangles of the outer and the skeleton mesh. In order to remove undesired spikes in the skeletal mesh, we employ tangential Laplacian smoothing.

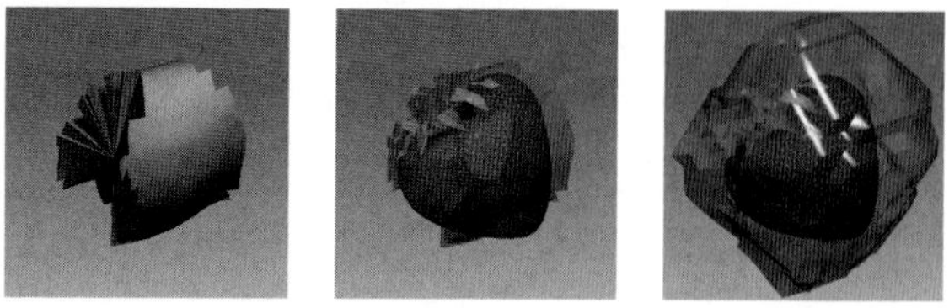

Figure 4: *An animation cell at a certain time-step for the center segment of the horse (left), the strawberry fitted to it (center), and the offset cell for the center segment (right).*

As the skeletons share the graph structure of the animation meshes they can be partitioned into the same patches. In the following, we describe how to build animation cells for all patches at a single time step t. By applying the same procedure to all time steps, we generate the appropriately deformed versions of each cell. Consider a patch T_k and its associated vertex positions taken from P_t. For all boundary loops of T_k at time-step t, we compute the center of gravity of associated vertex positions in the skeleton $\mathcal{S}_t$. The new vertex for fan-triangulation of the boundary loop is positioned at this center. Fig. 4 (left) illustrates this using a center segment of the horse animation as an example.

Note that a simple strategy like choosing the center of gravity of the boundary loop's vertices for fan-triangulation would not have fulfilled our requirements. Our experiments showed that in this case very flat animation cells may occur for extreme geometric configurations which would lead to inappropriate volumes for the subsequent steps of our method. Depending on the geometric setting, similar problems may occur if one tries to directly triangulate a hole without inserting a vertex. Although our cell decomposition does not strictly partition the volume, it generates volume slices that are tailored to our purpose.

6. Assembling the Collage

As already outlined in the previous section, the sequence of moving animation cells can be regarded as a sequence of volumetric placeholders to which approximating shapes from the database are fitted. In our opinion, it is the most reasonable and visually most appealing way to approximate each cell with a single shape. While by this means, it may not be possible to exactly reproduce the true shape of each cell, in particular its outer surface, the overall appearance of the mesh animation is still very faithfully approximated. We already argued that the decomposition of the animation into cells bears many further algorithmic advantages. The overall fitting problem simplifies to a fitting problem between individual shapes and segments. Furthermore, it becomes easier to assure that the shapes which we fit not only match the outlines of their respective animation cells at a single time step. Since the animation cells undergo mainly rigid deformations, the slight non-rigid deformations of the approximating shapes that may be necessary to assure good approximation over the whole sequence can be kept in reasonable bounds, Sect. 7.

To put this into practice, a shape similarity measure is needed, Sect. 6.1, that we apply in our spatio-temporal matching and alignment approach to fit a database shape to a deforming animation cell, Sect. 6.2.

6.1. Shape Similarity Measure

Due to the diversity of database shapes, and potential differences in orientation and uniform scaling, we require a similarity measure that is rotation-, pose- and scale-independent. Spherical harmonic descriptors fulfill all these requirements and have proven to be superior to many other global descriptors [KFR03]. Given a mesh $\mathcal{K}$ we compute its spherical harmonic descriptor as follows: First, the spatial occupancy function $O(x,y,z)$ is sampled on a regular grid within the mesh's bounding box by rasterizing the mesh into a voxel volume of dimension $\ell_1 \times \ell_2 \times \ell_3$ [NT03, Min03]. The voxel volume is intersected with q equidistant spheres $W_0, \ldots, W_{q-1}$ that are concentrically arranged around the center of gravity of the voxel set. The discretized occupancy function is resampled on the surface of each spherical shell, yielding q spherical functions $o_0(\theta,\phi), \ldots, o_{q-1}(\theta,\phi)$. Each of these q spherical functions is decomposed into its harmonic frequency components

$$f_\ell(\theta,\phi) = \sum_{m=-\ell}^{m=\ell} a_{\ell m} Y_\ell^m(\theta,\phi),$$

where ℓ is the frequency band, $a_{\ell m}$ is the m-th coefficient on band ℓ, and Y_ℓ^m is the m-th spherical harmonic basis function for band ℓ [Gre03]. For each spherical function, the norms of its frequency components are computed as

$$SH(o_h) = \{\|f_0(\theta,\phi)\|, \|f_1(\theta,\phi)\|, \ldots, \|f_{\ell-1}(\theta,\phi)\|\}.$$

The complete shape descriptor $D(\mathcal{K})$ is the two-dimensional $q \times h$-array that is indexed by the sphere radius and the frequency band. Four our purpose, we found that descriptors with $h = 20$ and $\ell = 10$ are sufficient. The difference $d(D_1, D_2)$ between two descriptors D_1 and D_2 is obtained by interpreting each of them as $(q \cdot h)$-dimensional vectors and computing the angle that they span.

6.2. Spatio-temporal Shape Fitting

Using the above shape descriptor and the associated distance measure, we find a shape from the database that best matches the time-varying shape of each animation cell throughout the whole sequence. To keep processing times and memory consumption in reasonable bounds while sampling the range of deformations sufficiently densely, we propose the following approach to fit a shape to one animation cell $\mathcal{Z}_j$:

At first, a set of representative time steps $0 \le t_1, \ldots, t_r < N$ is chosen in which the whole mesh undergoes a characteristic range of deformations. Let the vertex positions of $\mathcal{Z}_j$ at the r time steps be $P_{t_1}(\mathcal{Z}_j), \ldots, P_{t_r}(\mathcal{Z}_j)$. For each of the r cell poses, a descriptor is computed, yielding a set $U = \{D_{t_1}(\mathcal{Z}_j), \ldots, D_{t_r}(\mathcal{Z}_j)\}$. For each of the shapes in the database and their associated descriptors D_i, a global distance to all descriptors in U is computed as

Figure 5: *Effect of spatio-temporal fitting for the tail of the camel (left): One frame of the result animation is shown with a single (center) or three representative time steps (right) used during spatio-temporal fitting.*

$$d_{\text{glob}}(D_i, U) = \sum_{t \in t_1,\ldots,t_r} d(D_i, D_t(\mathcal{Z}_j)) \quad \text{for } 0 \le i < K\,.$$

The above distance assesses the spatio-temporal goodness-of-fit between a database shape and a cell over time. Accordingly, the index c of the database shape that matches the shape of $\mathcal{Z}_j$ at all representative time steps best is found as

$$c = \underset{i}{\text{argmin}}\; d_{\text{glob}}(D_i, U)$$

Database shape c is fitted to the single pose $P_{t_m}(\mathcal{Z}_j)$ of $\mathcal{Z}_j$ out of all the representative poses which best matches the shape of c, thus

$$t_m = \underset{t \in \{t_1,\ldots,t_r\}}{\text{argmin}}\; d_{\text{glob}}(D_c, P_t(\mathcal{Z}_j))$$

This way we guarantee that the shape is fitted to the optimally matching configuration of the cell, and thus the required transformation of c during the fitting itself is minimal. The effect of spatio-temporal fitting is compared against single-time step fitting in Fig. 5.

The fitting itself first coarsely registers shape c and $\mathcal{Z}_j$ in pose $P_{t_m}(\mathcal{Z}_j)$ by aligning their centers of gravities and principal components in orientation and scaling. Thereafter, the initial fitting is refined by running an ICP-like alignment [BM92].

Although shape matching and fitting are fully automatic processes, user interaction is possible to meet artistic preferences. On the one hand, the user can restrict matching to a subset of the database or even manually choose a collage shape which will be fitted into the cell. On the other hand, she can manually adjust the fitted shape's position, scale and orientation.

Finally, we note that while there are many applications for *partial* shape matching, the use of a *global* approach is essential to our method: our goal is to faithfully fill in the whole cell. This way, self-intersections and artifacts during the animation are minimized since the cell's have a near-rigid structure. Furthermore, bigger holes in the collage are prevented. Consequently, we decided to fit only one shape per cell to provide the most plausible results for the animation. Putting it another way, we first simplify the global filling problem to a local one using cell decomposition and cell matching, and only then individual collage shapes are matched globally to cells.

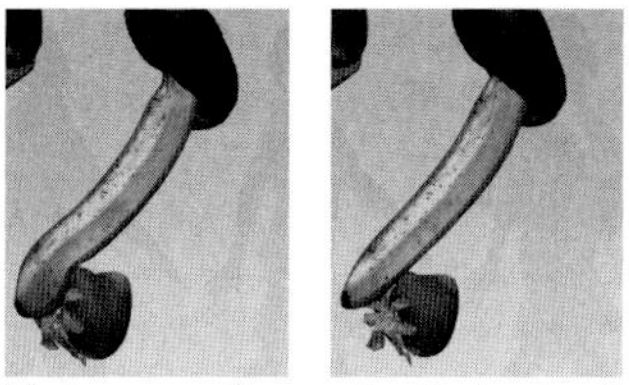

Figure 6: *With larger offsets, the fruits in the horse's leg deform more stiffly (right) than with tighter ones (left).*

7. Animating the 3D collage

In the final stage of our method we compute the animation collage from the set of animation cells and associated collage shapes. Remember that each of the collage shapes has potentially been fitted to a different reference time step t_m by the procedure described in the previous section.

Our approach proceeds again cell-wise: per-frame transformation of the animation cells is propagated to the fitted shapes. We consider this transformation as a general deformation of the cell, which is expected to be nearly rigid. Among the many surface deformation methods which are available in the literature we chose free-form deformation based on 3D mean-value coordinates [Flo03, FKR05, JSW05], because it can directly process our input data, produces good results and is moreover robust and simple in implementation. Using the standard approach, the triangulation of the animation cell would serve directly as control mesh for the deformation: the collage shape is rigidly fitted into the geometry of the animation cell $P_{t_m}(\mathscr{X})$ at a reference time step t_m, and then mean value coordinates are used to reconstruct shapes which deform like the geometry of cell $P_t(\mathscr{X})$ at any other time step $0 \leq t < N$. However, there are two requirements which render this immediate deformation impractical for our special animation collage setting: first, we want to provide the user some additional global control over the deformation, second we have to ensure numerical robustness. Both requirements are related, and we apply a two-step deformation with spatio-temporal offsets which is described in the following.

The key idea of our deformation is to use certain morphological offsets of the animation cells as control meshes, i.e., roughly speaking, the cells' geometry is extruded in direction of the surface normal (but avoiding self-intersections). This way, we can control the stiffness of the deformation by taking advantage the well-known behavior of the pseudo-harmonic fields induced by mean value coordinates for the new, enlarged boundary polyhedra, Fig. 6. One such offset cell for the torso segment of the horse is shown in Fig. 4(right) At the same time we avoid numerical instabilities resulting from evaluating the field in the vicinity of the control mesh, a situation which cannot be generally avoided when using the animation cells' geometry directly. Now the challenge is to efficiently compute *offset cells* which are not only geometrically consistent but provide also consistent control meshes for different time-steps similar to the original animation cells.

Our offsets can be easily constructed in a volumetric representation using level-sets. As accuracy is not crucial for us here, we use an even simpler approach and compute a discrete voxel model for each animation cell mesh (from [Min03]) which is then dilated and converted back into a triangle mesh using marching cubes. Here the voxel resolution and dilation radius define the offset radius. This way we compute an offset cell for each animation cell w.r.t. the reference time step. The computation is efficient and guarantees watertightness and no self-intersections, however, we lose control over the combinatorial structure of the offset mesh, i.e., it does not share the animation cell's connectivity. Therefore we require an alternative mapping to the animation cell which is provided by a second deformation step.

The final animation of a single collage shape proceeds as follows: first, the time-dependent geometry of the animation cell is used as control mesh to compute a deformed offset cell. Second, the offset cell is used as control mesh and its deformation is propagated to the collage shape. Note that by volumetric construction the genus of the offset cell might differ from that of the respective animation cell. However, using the free-form deformation approach influencing the the cell's volume this does not imply any problem.

The offset radius provides an additional parameter to control the effect of the deformation: the more distant the offset, the stiffer the deformation. Fig. 6 shows an example. While this parameter has no physically plausible meaning we find it intuitive to use without asking too much of the user.

8. Results and Discussion

We have generated a variety of animation collages from mesh sequences of a *galloping* and a *collapsing horse*, a galloping *camel*, as well as two scanned humans performing a motion captured *jump* and a *cartwheel* (video only). For none of the sequences, ground truth kinematics, e.g. in the form of animation skeletons, are available. Our shape database comprises of 20 collage shapes, ranging from fruits, over industrial shapes like screws, to barrels and bottles (see additional material). Even the authors as unexperienced artists were able to create a variety of animation collages with different appealing visual styles by restricting the database to subsets of shapes, Fig. 7 shows a selection. The collages do not only have very aesthetic looks at single-time steps, but nicely approximate the spatio-temporal appearance of the input animation, see Fig. 1 and, in particular, the accompanying video. On all our test sequences, our motion-based segmentation approach created plausible animation cells that closely correspond to the true kinematics of the moving subjects, a prerequisite for appealing animation collages, see Fig. 3.

The top row in Fig. 7 shows freeze-frames from the front and the back of an animation collage showing a *jumping human*. For the original sequence motion capture data was used to animate a laser-scan. With both fruits, as well as barrels,

Seq.	N	$\#\mathcal{T}$	k	Seg	Cell	Fit	Anim
jumping	216	26 312	25	416	401	46	171
gal. horse	48	16 843	35	297	190	64	134
camel	47	43 758	13	914	139	59	131
cartwheel	120	7 318	11	45	188	22	68

Table 1: *Typical animation data: Shown are time-steps N, number of triangles in mesh $\#\mathcal{T}$, and number of animation cells k. Furthermore, measured computation times (in seconds) are given for four parts of the pipeline (see Sect. 8).*

bottles and screws, the 25 computed animation cells are both faithfully and sometimes funnily approximated. We particularly liked the head being automatically approximated by a strawberry or a pear. Please refer to the video to also see that due to our offset-based deformation, the moving collages maintain the subtle motion details of the input which lends them a very human-like motion style.

The *galloping horse* is shown for fine and coarse segmentations with 35 and 17 animation cells, respectively. In comparison one sees clearly the non-rigid transformation for the coarse segmentations, for instance in the lower legs where the hoofs are not covered by additional cells. However, even these deformations appear rather natural due to stiffness provided by the offset cells. Of course the individual impression depends on the viewers particular expectations and preferences, and spending more animation cells usually leads to better approximations of rigid parts. Notably, many viewers to who we presented our work particularly liked the slight non-rigid deformations. Moreover, our choice of using a single collage shape per cell is justified by the fact that the animation looks plausible and there are hardly any holes and only few self-intersections.

The *galloping camel* is shown for fine (left block) and coarse segmentations (right block) with 31 and 13 animation cells, respectively. We would like to point out the nice approximation of the hunch, e.g., by pears (coarse) and by bananas (fine). Especially the arrangement of bananas in is non-trivial and the impression of a sophisticated design is given. Such arrangements are enabled by the partition in animation cells, and the example thus nicely confirms our algorithmic approach to break the fitting problem into cell-wise problems.

The majority of results in Fig. 7 was generated fully-automatically. Only in some cases, marked with a black dot in the upper right, we changed the position or the kind of at most two shapes to match personal preferences. Table 1 summarizes information on input animation complexity and run-times measured on a Pentium IV 3.0 GHz. Our approach is very efficient: run-times are dominated by rigid body segmentation (**Seg**) and cell generation (**Cell**), both of which need to be run just once per input sequence. In particular for large meshes most of the processing time for segmentation is due to the geodesic distance computation when assembling triangle patches. The most time-consuming part during cell computation is the mean-value-coordinate-based generation of offset segments. Shape fitting and alignment (**Fit**), as well as the animation of the collage (**Anim**) are performed once for each collage style created from an input sequence. Even for sequences with more than 200 frames, both steps can be finished in less than four minutes. Run-times could be further sped up by working with decimated input or cell meshes, however we always worked on the originals. In comparison to the rendering times of around 4 minutes per frame (with POVRAY at 1600x1200 resolution), the overall processing times are negligible. The same is true for any of the manual corrections which were performed in only a couple of seconds.

Our approach is subject to a couple of limitations. While our *clustering* algorithm provides excellent results for the shown input animations, its output generally depends on these inputs: a meaningful segmentation can only be expected if there is actual relative motion of all limbs in an animation. We conclude that this approach works best for animations with kinematic structure. For the *melting horse* animation shown in the video this is not given. Therefore, the galloping horse segmentation was used to generate it which yields good results.

For our *fitting* we remark that the following limitations apply: inherently, fitting is limited by the shapes available in the database. If no proper shape is available, unnatural deformations may be necessary. As the database also defines the visual style, we leave this as an artistic problem that has to be considered by the user. From a more technical point of view, our approach requires that segments span a volume. The approach is thus not able to fit collage shapes to, e.g., nearly planar segments. Note that the spatio-temporal segmentation (which provides the segments) is not at all affected. In addition, for fitting we assume that the animation cells are in motion and hence being transformed. This is different to considering a static fitting problem, where alternative approaches such as Gal et al. [GSP*07] may show better results, and where it may be advantageous to allow for more shapes per cell.

Despite these limitations we presented a compendium of spatio-temporal matching and segmentation techniques that enable us to build beautiful animation collages from mesh animations.

9. Conclusion

We defined the animation collage as a visual style which expresses a time-variant input shape in terms of an arrangement of shape primitives in space-time. While this is motivated from static scenes, the processing of animations turns out to be a setting of its own which reveals new and different problems. With our novel approach to fully-automatic creation of animation collages from animations we particularly provide new solutions to a couple of geometric problems: automatic and kinematically plausible segmentation of the animated mesh into near-rigid surface patches, spatio-temporal matching and fitting of shapes from a database, and spatio-temporally consistent transfer of rigid transformation and non-rigid deformation from the time-varying surface to collage shapes. A key ingredient of our method is the motion-based decomposition of the overall fitting problem into smaller local ones. Our software prototype is fun to use and allows also untrained people to produce high-quality results. For future work we see a variety of applications of our algorithmic components in animation compression, spatio-temporal matching and fitting. Furthermore, color and texture harmony could be incorporated as matching criteria.

Acknowledgements. This work is supported by EC within FP6 under Grant 511568 with the acronym 3DTV, the German Academic Exchange Service (DAAD), and the Max-Planck Center for Visual Computing and Communication. We would like to thank Torsten Langer, Hitoshi Yamauchi, and Shin Yoshizawa for letting us use their code.

References

[ABK98] AMENTA N., BERN M., KAMVYSSELIS M.: A new voronoi-based surface reconstruction algorithm. In *Proc. ACM SIGGRAPH* (1998), pp. 415–421.

[BJMR01] BANÉGAS F., JAEGER M., MICHELUCCI D., ROELENS M.: The ellipsoidal skeleton in medical applications. In *ACM Solid Modeling and Applications* (2001), pp. 30–38.

[BK02] BISCHOFF S., KOBBELT L.: Ellipsoid decomposition of 3D-model. In *IEEE 3DPVT* (2002), pp. 480–489.

[BM92] BESL P., MCKAY N.: A method for registration of 3-d shapes. *IEEE Trans. PAMI 14*, 2 (1992), 239–256.

[dATS06] DE AGUIAR E., THEOBALT C., SEIDEL H.-P.: Automatic learning of articulated skeletons from 3d marker trajectories. In *Proc. ISVC* (2006), pp. 485–494.

[ETA02] ELAD M., TAL A., AR S.: Content based retrieval of vrml objects: an iterative and interactive approach. In *Proc. Eurographics workshop on Multimedia 2001* (2002), pp. 107–118.

[FKR05] FLOATER M. S., KÓS G., REIMERS M.: Mean value coordinates in 3D. *CAGD 22*, 7 (2005), 623–631.

[Flo03] FLOATER M. S.: Mean value coordinates. *CAGD 20*, 1 (2003), 19–27.

[GCO06] GAL R., COHEN-OR D.: Salient geometric features for partial shape matching and similarity. *ACM Transaction on Graphics 25*, 1 (2006), 130–150.

[GFW*06] GÜNTHER J., FRIEDRICH H., WALD I., SEIDEL H.-P., SLUSALLEK P.: Ray tracing animated scenes using motion decomposition. *Computer Graphics Forum (Proc. Eurographics) 25*, 3 (2006), 517–525.

[Gre03] GREEN R.: Spherical harmonic lighting: The gritty details. In *Tutorial: Game Develpers Conference* (2003).

[GSP*07] GAL R., SORKINE O., POPA T., SHEFFER A., COHEN-OR D.: Non-realistic expressive modeling. In *NPAR* (to appear 2007).

[Hau01] HAUSNER A.: Simulating decorative mosaics. In *Proc. ACM SIGGRAPH* (2001), pp. 573–580.

[HBK02] HISADA M., BELYAEV A., KUNII T. L.: A skeleton-based approach for detection of perceptually salient features on polygonal surfaces. *Comp. Graphics Forum 21*, 4 (2002), 1–12.

[HSDK05] HORNUNG A., SAR-DESSAI S., KOBBELT L.: Self-calibrating optical motion tracking for articulated bodies. In *IEEE Virtual Reality 2005* (2005), pp. 75–82.

[HSKK01] HILAGA M., SHINAGAWA Y., KOHMURA T., KUNII T.: Topology matching for fully automatic similarity estimation of 3d shapes. In *Proc. ACM SIGGRAPH* (2001), pp. 203–212.

[JSW05] JU T., SCHAEFER S., WARREN J. D.: Mean value coordinates for closed triangular meshes. *ACM Transaction on Graphics (Proc. SIGGRAPH) 24*, 3 (2005), 561–566.

[JT05] JAMES D., TWIGG C.: Skinning mesh animations. *ACM Transactions on Graphics (Proc. SIGGRAPH) 24*, 3 (2005).

[KFR03] KAZHDAN M., FUNKHOUSER T., RUSINKIEWICZ S.: Rotation invariant spherical harmonic representation of 3d shape descriptors. In *Proc. Eurographics/ACM Symp. on Geometry Processing* (2003), pp. 156–164.

[KOF05] KIRK A., O'BRIEN J., FORSYTH D.: Skeletal parameter estimation from optical motion capture data. In *CVPR* (June 2005), pp. 782–788.

[KP02] KIM J., PELLACINI F.: Jigsaw image mosaics. In *Proc. ACM SIGGRAPH* (2002), pp. 657–664.

[Len99] LENGYEL J.: Compression of time-dependent geometry. In *Proc. I3D* (1999), pp. 89–95.

[Min03] MIN P.: binvox. http://www.google.com/search?q=binvox, 2003.

[NJW02] NG A. Y., JORDAN M., WEISS Y.: On spectral clustering: Analysis and an algorithm. In *Proc. NIPS 2002* (2002).

[NK03] NOVOTNI M., KLEIN R.: 3d zernike descriptors for content based shape retrieval. In *Proc. ACM Symp. on Solid Modeling* (2003), pp. 216–225.

[NT03] NOORUDDIN F. S., TURK G.: Simplification and repair of polygonal models using volumetric techniques. *IEEE TVCG 9*, 2 (2003), 191–205.

[OFCD01] OSADA R., FUNKHOUSER T., CHAZELLE B., DOBKIN D.: Matching 3d models with shape distributions. In *Proc. Shape Modeling International* (2001), pp. 154–166.

[RBHB06] ROTHER C., BORDEAUX L., HAMADI Y., BLAKE A.: Autocollage. *ACM Transactions on Graphics (Proc. SIGGRAPH) 25*, 3 (2006), 847–852.

[Rob05] ROBOTS:. www.robotsmovie.com, 2005.

[SSK05] SATTLER M., SARLETTE R., KLEIN R.: Simple and efficient compression of animation sequences. In *Proc. Symp. on Computer Animations* (2005), pp. 209–217.

[VSR01] VRANIC D., SAUPE D., RICHTER J.: Tools for 3d-object retrieval: Karhunen-loeve transform and spherical harmonics. In *IEEE MMSP* (2001), pp. 293–298.

[WK05] WU J., KOBBELT L.: Structure recovery via hybrid variational surface approximation. In *Comp. Graphics Forum (Proc. Eurographics)* (2005), vol. 24, pp. 277–284.

[YGZS05] YAMAUCHI H., GUMHOLD S., ZAYER R., SEIDEL H.-P.: Mesh segmentation driven by gaussian curvature. *The Visual Computer 21*, 8-10 (2005), 649–658.

[YP06] YAN J., POLLEFEYS M.: Automatic kinematic chain building from feature trajectories of articulated objects. In *Proc. CVPR* (2006), pp. 712–719.

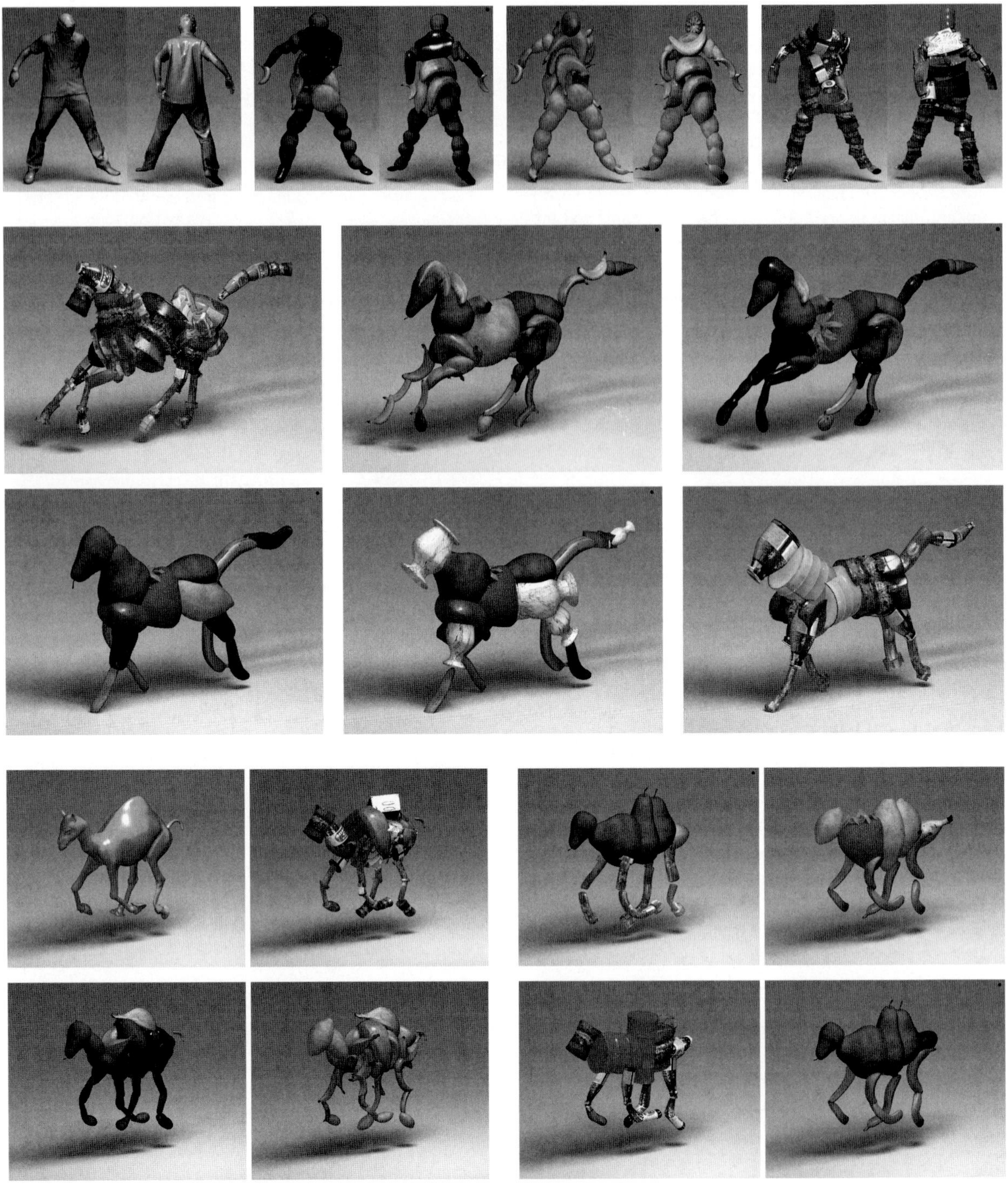

Figure 7: *Different visual styles for distinct frames of jumping human, galloping horse, and galloping camel sequences. Black dots in the upper right mark animations including manual changes of position or kind of at most two shape primitives.*

Program Committee and Reviewers

General Chairs

Michael Gleicher
University of Wisconsin - Madison

Daniel Thalmann
EPFL

Program Chairs

Dimitris Metaxas
Rutgers University

Jovan Popović
Massachusetts Institute of Technology

Posters Chair

Bill Baxter
OLM Digital

Local Chair

Matthias Zwicker
University of California San Diego

Assistant Local Chair

Heather Shrewsbury
MeniThings

Program Committee

Ken Anjyo
OLM Digital, Inc.

Okan Arikan
University of Texas

Bruno Arnaldi
INSA Rennes & IRISA

Norman Badler
University of Pennsylvania

Adam Bargteil
Berkeley University

William Baxter
OLM Digital, Inc.

Program Committee

Volker Blanz
Max-Planck-Institut Informatik

Bobby Bodenheimer
Vanderbilt University

Ronan Boulic
EPFL

David Breen
Drexel University

Chris Bregler
New York University

Robert Bridson
University of British Columbia

Armin Bruderlin
Picture Imageworks

Mark Carlson
DNA Productions, Inc

Matthieu Desbrun
Caltech

Yoshinori Dobashi
Hokkaido University

Stephane Donikian
IRISA / CNRS

Irfan Essa
Georgia Tech

Petros Faloutsos
University of California, Los Angeles

François Faure
University Grenoble 1

Eugene Fiume
University of Toronto

David Forsyth
Berkeley University

Program Committee

Eitan Grinspun
Columbia University

Markus Gross
ETH Zurich

Sunil Hadap
PDI/DreamWorks

James Hahn
George Washington University

Aaron Hertzmann
University of Toronto

Jessica Hodgins
Carnegie Mellon University

Donald House
Texas A&M University

Suejung Huh
Rutgers University

Doug James
Carnegie Mellon University

Hyeong-Seok Ko
Seoul National University

Taku Komura
The University of Edinburgh

James Kuffner
Carnegie Mellon University

Shigeru Kuriyama
Toyohashi University of Technology

Jean-Paul Laumond
LAAS Toulouse

Jehee Lee
Seoul National University

J.P. Lewis
Stanford University

Program Committee and Reviewers

Program Committee

Ming Lin
University of North Carolina at Chapel Hill

Karen Liu
University of Southern California

Nadia Magnenat-Thalmann
University of Geneva

Matthias Mueller
AGEIA

Ken Museth
Linkoping University

Victor Ng-Thow-Hing
Honda R&D Americas

James O'Brien
University of California at Berkeley

Carol O'Sullivan
Trinity College Dublin

Miguel Otaduy
ETH Zurich

Dinesh Pai
Rutgers University

Rick Parent
Ohio State University

Mark Pauly
ETH Zurich

Fred Pighin
Industrial Light & Magic

Nancy Pollard
Carnegie Mellon University

Hong Qin
State University New York

Stephane Redon
INRIA

Program Committee

Lionel Reveret
INRIA

Dimitris Samaras
State University New York

Hans-Peter Seidel
Max-Planck-Institut Informatik

Sung Yong Shin
KAIST

Karan Singh
University of Toronto

Jos Stam
Autodesk

Mark Sussman
Florida State University

Demetri Terzopoulos
University of California at Los Angeles

Matthias Teschner
Univ Freiburg

Jerry Tessendorf
Rhythm and Hues Studios

Nils Thuerey
ETH Zurich

Greg Turk
Georgia Tech

Michiel van de Panne
University of British Columbia

Luiz Velho
IMPA

Pascal Volino
University of Geneva

Markus Wacker
University of Dresden

Program Committee

Yizhou Yu
University of Illinois at Urbana-Champaign

Victor Zordan
University of California, Riverside

External Reviewers

Brian Allen
Ilya Baran
Markus Becker
Schubert Carvahlo
Patrick Coleman
Marco da Silva
Rebecca Flannery
David Harmon
Woosuck Hong
Eugene Hsu
Ge Jin
Danny M. Kaufman
Liliya Kharevych
Taesoo Kwon
Bongcheol Park
Julien Pettre
Kurt Phillips
Shawn Singh
Jonas Spillman
Shinjiro Sueda
Robert W. Sumner
Yiying Tong
Daniel Vlasic
Robert Wang
Cem Yuksel

Cover Image Credits

Front Cover (top to bottom)

Screen Space Meshes
Matthias Mueller, Simon Schirm, Stephan Duthaler
pp. 9–16.

Animation Collage
Christian Theobalt, Christian Rössl, Edilson de Aguiar, Hans-Peter Seidel
pp. 271–280.

Legendre Fluids: A Unified Framework for Analytic Reduced Space Modeling and Rendering of Participating Media
Mohit Gupta, Srinivasa G. Narasimhan
pp. 17–26.

Back Cover (top to bottom)

Animation of Chemically Reactive Fluids Using a Hybrid Simulation Method
Byungkwon Kang, Yoojin Jang, Insung Ihm
pp. 199–208.

Cubic Shells
Akash Garg, Eitan Grinspun, Max Wardetzky, Denis Zorin
pp. 91–98.

(middle and lower left)

A Simple Boiling Module
Theodore Kim, Mark Carlson
pp. 27–34.

(middle right)

Deformation Styles for Spline-based Skeletal Animation
Sven Forstmann, Jun Ohya, Artus Krohn-Grimberghe, Ryan McDougall
pp. 141–150.

Author Index

Notes

Notes

Notes

Notes